Volume **3**

FUNDAMENTAL
Accounting Principles

ELEVENTH CANADIAN EDITION

Kermit D. Larson
University of Texas—Austin

Suresh S. Kalagnanam
University of Saskatchewan

McGraw-Hill
Ryerson

Toronto   Montréal   Boston   Burr Ridge, IL   Dubuque, IA   Madison, WI
New York   San Francisco   St. Louis   Bangkok   Bogotá   Caracas
Kuala Lumpur   Lisbon   London   Madrid   Mexico City   Milan
New Delhi   Santiago   Seoul   Singapore   Sydney   Taipei

The McGraw-Hill Companies

McGraw-Hill
Ryerson

Fundamental Accounting Principles
Volume 3
Eleventh Canadian Edition

ISBN: 0-07-091653-5

1 2 3 4 5 6 7 8 9 10   TCP   0 9 8 7 6 5

Care has been taken to trace ownership of copyright material contained in this text; however, the publisher will welcome any information that enables them to rectify any reference or credit for subsequent editions.

Vice President and Editorial Director: *Pat Ferrier*
Executive Sponsoring Editor: *Nicole Lukach*
Developmental Editor: *Brook Nymark*
Director of Marketing: *Jeff MacLean*
Marketing Manager: *Kim Verhaeghe*
Manager, Editorial Services: *Kelly Dickson*
Supervising Editor: *Joanne Murray*
Copy Editor: *Gillian Scobie*
Production Coordinator: *Madeleine Harrington*
Composition: *Bookman Typesetting Co.*
Cover Design: *Dianna Little*
Cover Photos: *Oliver Strewe/Gettyimages*
Printer: *Transcontinental Printing Group*

National Library of Canada Cataloguing in Publication Data

Larson, Kermit D.
    Fundamental accounting principles / Kermit D. Larson, Tilly Jensen. —
11th Canadian ed.

Includes bibliographical references and index.
Contents: v. 1.   Chapters 1–11 — v. 2.   Chapters 12–20 —
    v. 3.   Chapters 21–28 / Kermit D. Larson, Suresh Kalagnanam.

ISBN 0-07-091649-7 (v. 1).—ISBN 0-07-091652-7 (v. 2).—
ISBN 0-07-091653-5 (v. 3)

1. Accounting.   2. Accounting—Problems, exercises, etc.
I. Jensen, Tilly   II. Kalagnanam, Suresh Subbarao   III. Title.

HF5635.L343 2003   657   C2003-906284-8

Kermit D. Larson, University of Texas – Austin

Kermit D. Larson is the Arthur Andersen & Co. Alumni Professor of Accounting Emeritus at the University of Texas at Austin. He served as chairman of the University of Texas, Department of Accounting and was visiting associate professor at Tulane University. His scholarly articles have been published in a variety of journals, including *The Accounting Review, Journal of Accountancy,* and *Abacus.* He is the author of several books, including *Financial Accounting* and *Fundamentals of Financial* and *Managerial Accounting,* both published by Irwin/McGraw-Hill.

Professor Larson is a member of the American Accounting Association, the Texas Society of CPAs, and the American Institute of CPAs. His positions with the AAA have included vice president, southwest regional service president, and chairperson of several committees, including the Committee of Concepts and Standards. He was a member of the committee that planned the first AAA doctoral consortium and served as its director.

Suresh S. Kalagnanam, University of Saskatchewan

Suresh Kalagnanam is an Associate Professor of Accounting at the University of Saskatchewan, where he currently teaches and researches management accounting. He is a graduate of the University of Madras in India where he obtained his bachelor of engineering. He subsequently obtained an MBA from Gujarat University in India, an MBA and a Master of Science in Accounting from the University of Saskatchewan, and a PhD from the University of Wisconsin-Madison in the United States. He is also a Certified Management Accountant (CMA). Professor Kalagnanam's scholarly work has been published in *Accounting Organizations and Society, International Journal of Business and Economics, Journal of Accounting Case Research, Journal of Cost Management, Management Accounting,* and other books. He is a member of the American Accounting Association, Canadian Academic Accounting Association, CMA Canada, and the Institute of Management Accountants, and serves on the editorial advisory board of *Accounting Horizons.*

Brief Contents

Contents

Chapter 24 Cost Allocation and Performance Measurement 1246

Chapter 25 Cost-Volume-Profit Analysis 1296

The Larson Advantage

We may have raised the bar for pedagogical excellence with the Tenth Canadian Edition, but we have achieved even higher standards this time out. The Eleventh Canadian Edition includes even more real-world examples, innovative pedagogical features, and thought-provoking examples.

Very well done … gives non-accounting students an intro into the benefits of accounting to businesses. I like it much better than other texts.

Real-World Emphasis

Instructors asked for more real-life examples, so we interviewed real business people and incorporated their perspectives on accounting into the text.

Social responsibility is important in the real world. Through the Did You Know? feature, FAP describes accounting's role in social responsibility by both reporting and assessing its impact.

Annual Reports

The features and assignments that highlight companies like WestJet and Leon's show accounting in a modern, global context. FAP challenges students to apply learned knowledge in practical and diverse ways with analytical problems, research requirements, and communication exercises.

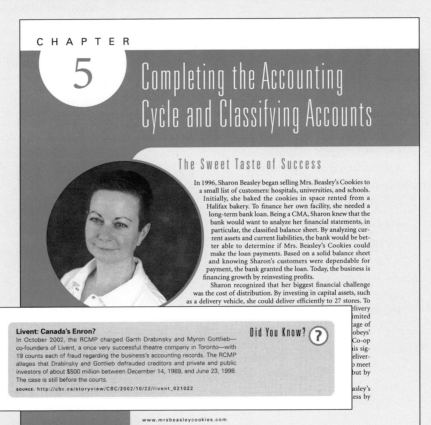

CHAPTER 5

Completing the Accounting Cycle and Classifying Accounts

The Sweet Taste of Success

In 1996, Sharon Beasley began selling Mrs. Beasley's Cookies to a small list of customers: hospitals, universities, and schools. Initially, she baked the cookies in space rented from a Halifax bakery. To finance her own facility, she needed a long-term bank loan. Being a CMA, Sharon knew that the bank would want to analyze her financial statements, in particular, the classified balance sheet. By analyzing current assets and current liabilities, the bank would be better able to determine if Mrs. Beasley's Cookies could make the loan payments. Based on a solid balance sheet and knowing Sharon's customers were dependable for payment, the bank granted the loan. Today, the business is financing growth by reinvesting profits.

Sharon recognized that her biggest financial challenge was the cost of distribution. By investing in capital assets, such as a delivery vehicle, she could deliver efficiently to 27 stores. To

Did You Know? ❓

Livent: Canada's Enron?
In October 2002, the RCMP charged Garth Drabinsky and Myron Gottlieb—co-founders of Livent, a once very successful theatre company in Toronto—with 19 counts each of fraud regarding the business's accounting records. The RCMP alleges that Drabinsky and Gottlieb defrauded creditors and private and public investors of about $500 million between December 14, 1989, and June 23, 1998. The case is still before the courts.
SOURCE: http://cbc.ca/storyview/CBC/2002/10/22/livent_021022

www.mrsbeasleycookies.com

Questions

1. In the chapter's opening article, what does Wynne Powell identify as the key to success in business?
2. Identify three businesses that offer services and three businesses that offer products.
3. Describe three forms of business organizations and their characteristics.
4. Identify the two organizations for which accounting information is available in Appendix I at the end of the book.
8. Describe the internal role of accounting for organizations.
9. What is the purpose of accounting in society?
10. What ethical issues might accounting professionals face in dealing with confidential information?
11. Technology is increasingly used to process accounting data. Why, then, should we study accounting?
12. What is the relation between accounting and technology?
13. Identify four managerial accounting tasks performed by both private and government accountants.

The advantage of the Larson text is the language used, which is easy for students to understand. They can relate to the material because they see businesses like these every day—in the news and at home.

In terms of problem material, Larson, Jensen, and Kalagnanam still set the standard for quantity and quality of end-of-chapter question material. Over 150 new questions have been added, and even more have been modified and updated.

> *There is an excellent variety of assignment material from which to choose and enough questions to assign supplemental extra questions to students who may need the extra practice.*

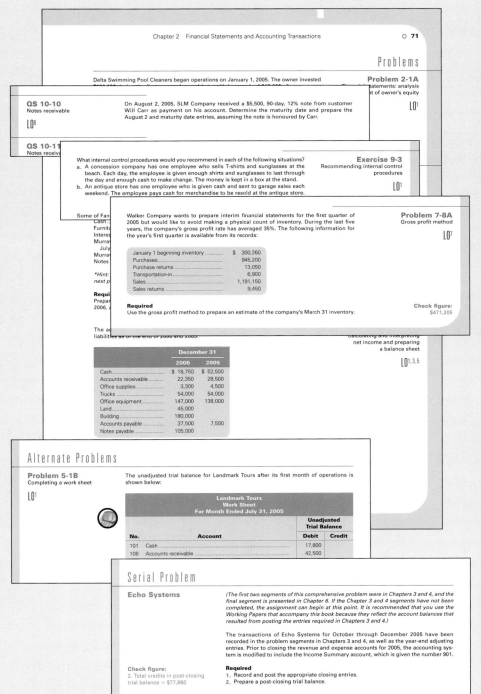

Confidence-Building Problem Material

Starting with the basic concepts, FAP moves students through Questions **and** Quick Study **material that covers definitions and concepts. Once these are completed,** Exercises **focuses on the practice of single concepts, thus preparing the way for the multi-concept** Problems. **Tied to the** Learning Objectives **and with** Check Figures **available, students have the resources they need to stay on track and stay motivated to finish assignments.**

In keeping with the growing exposure of technology in accounting and the classroom, we have updated and expanded the Excel® **templates. Questions with these templates are indicated with a marginal icon.**

Alongside the new end-of-chapter material are perennial favourites—updated or rewritten to reflect the changing scope of accounting as well as the changing needs of our learners.

THE ACCOUNTING STANDARD

The Accounting Standard

We listened! In addition to obtaining individual reviewer comments, we held focus groups in cities throughout Canada to hear the issues and concerns instructors like you have about the materials you use to teach introductory financial accounting. An author attended every session to listen and ask questions. We received excellent feedback, and have integrated your comments and experience into the Eleventh Canadian Edition for your benefit. We were the first textbook to go to these lengths for market research, and we do more every year. We think you'll like what you see.

Highlights of Chapter Changes in Volume 3

Chapter 21

Chapter material reorganized to improve flow and continuity.

Chapter material revised to improve clarity of concepts.

Lean business model introduced.

Exhibits revised to enhance illustration of concepts.

Service examples introduced.

Chapter 22

Opening vignette revised using a service example.

New "Did You Know" box has been added featuring a service example.

Material revised to improve flow and clarity.

End-of-chapter material revised to feature service companies.

Chapter 23

Learning objectives revised.

Exhibits revised to enhance illustration of concepts.

Weighted-average method of process cost accounting introduced.

Redundant material deleted.

New end-of-chapter material introduced.

Chapter 24

Learning objectives revised.

New sections introduced to enhance understanding of concepts.

New exhibits added to enhance illustration of concepts; some exhibits revised to introduce service examples.

End-of-chapter material revised to tie in better with the chapter material.

Chapter 25

Changes made throughout the chapter to improve clarity.

New exhibit added to enhance illustration of concepts.

New end-of-chapter material added.

Chapter 26

Chapter material revised to tighten the chapter and improve clarity.

New "Did You Know" box inserted.

Material moved from main chapter to an appendix.

End-of-chapter material revised.

Chapter 27

Material revised to eliminate duplication and improve clarity.

Non-business example introduced.

New "Did You Know" box featuring service functions and the service sector introduced.

Material from previous chapters integrated to illustrate relationships.

Chapter 28

Material revised to illustrate service organizations and to clarify that many investments may result in cost savings rather than generating revenues.

Judgment Call revised to reflect a non-manufacturing setting.

End-of-chapter material revised using a non-manufacturing setting.

Reviewers

The unprecedented review process and success of this revision of *Fundamental Accounting Principles* is the result of an ongoing process that has gone beyond the scope of a single edition. In the Tenth Canadian Edition, we went to instructors and students from across Canada, and their feedback launched the rigorous research and investigative process that have made this edition what it is. Accordingly, we would like to thank all those who reviewed both the Tenth and the Eleventh Editions for their hard work and frank honesty.

Eleventh Edition Reviewers

Cecile Ashman	*Algonquin College*	Geraldine Joosse	*Lethbridge Community College*
Les Barnhouse	*Athabasca University*	Barbara Jordan	*Cambrian College*
Keith Barrett	*Humber College*	Jane Kaake-Nemeth	*Durham College*
Maria Belanger	*Algonquin College*	Dave Kennedy	*Lethbridge Community College*
Gary Biggs	*Grant MacEwan College*	Val Kinnear	*Mount Royal College*
Mark Binder	*Red River College*	Laurette Korman	*Kwantlen University College*
Dave Bopara	*Toronto School of Business*	Rafik Kurji	*Mount Royal College*
Rick Boyack	*Southern Alberta Institute of Technology*	Douglas Leatherdale	*Georgian College*
		Michael Lee	*Humber College*
Walt Burton	*Okanagan University College*	Cynthia Lone	*Red River College*
Cheryl Christoff	*Toronto School of Business*	Marie Madill-Payne	*George Brown College*
Alice Cleveland	*Nova Scotia Community College*	Michael Malkoun	*St. Clair College*
Louise Connors	*Nova Scotia Community College*	Patricia Margeson	*New Brunswick Community College*
Joan Conrod	*Dalhousie University*		
Suzanne Coombs	*Kwantlen University College*	Bonnie Martel	*Niagara College*
William Cormier	*St Francis Xavier University*	Dani Moss	*Durham College*
John Currie	*Humber College*	Jan Nyholdt	*Southern Alberta Institute of Technology*
John Daye	*New Brunswick Community College*	Penny Parker	*Fanshawe College*
Randy Dickson	*Red Deer Community College*	Clifton Philpott	*Kwantlen University College*
Chaman Doma	*Centennial College*	Joe Pidutti	*Durham College*
Carolyn Doni	*Cambrian College*	Sharon Ramstad	*Grant MacEwan College*
Dave Eliason	*Southern Alberta Institute of Technology*	Traven Reed	*Canadore College*
		Clara Reid	*Lethbridge Community College*
Sheila Elworthy	*Camosun College*	Doug Ringrose	*Grant MacEwan College*
Albert Ferris	*University of Prince Edward Island*	David Sale	*Kwantlen University College*
		Giuseppina Salvaggio	*Dawson College*
David Fleming	*George Brown College*	Michael Sirtonski	*Assiniboine College*
Amanda Flint	*Trinity Western University*	Melbourne Sparks	*Lambton College*
Jeremy Frape	*Humber College*	Greg Streich	*DeVry Institute of Technology (Calgary)*
Henry Funk	*Red River College*		
Jack Halliday	*Northern Alberta Institute of Technology*	Selina Tang	*Douglas College*
		Marie Templeton	*Southern Alberta Institute of Technology*
Ern Harley	*Sheridan Institute of Technology and Advanced Learning*	John Varga	*George Brown College*
Elizabeth Hicks	*Douglas College*	John Vermeer	*Humber College*
Michael Hockenstein	*Vanier College*	Jeannine Wall	*Red River College*
Sue Hogan	*Capilano College*	Brenda Warner	*Conestoga College*
Pat Humphreys	*Medicine Hat College*	Dennis Wilson	*Centennial College*
Stephanie Ibach	*Northern Alberta Institute of Technology*	Richard Wright	*Fanshawe College*
		Brian Zwicker	*Grant MacEwan College*
Connie Johl	*Douglas College*		

THE ACCOUNTING STANDARD

Technology Solutions To Meet Your Every Need

Over 200,000 post-secondary educators in North America alone use the Internet in their courses. Some are just getting started, while others are eager to embrace the very latest advances in educational Content Delivery and Course Management.

That's why McGraw-Hill Ryerson supports instructors and students alike with the most complete range of digital solutions. Your students can use our complete Online Learning Centre (OLC), access Mobile Resources and Premium Content areas, or work with assessment solutions such as GradeSummit and Lyryx/LIFA.

In addition to an Instructor's CD-ROM, faculty have access to nearly every supplement online. These assets range from the Instructor's Resource Manual and Microsoft® PowerPoint® slides, to the powerful supplements integration guide and a range of course-management systems, including PageOut, McGraw-Hill's proprietary system.

McGraw-Hill has always set the standard as a leader in bringing helpful technology into the classroom. With Larson, Jensen, and Kalagnanam, your class gets all the benefits of the digital age without any set-up issues or confusion.

> *Larson has a very strong technological advantage in that it integrates several computer applications, such as Excel spreadsheets, LIFA software, etc. This is becoming an important issue as more courses are converted to online learning, hybrid format and laptop environments.*

Create a custom course Website with **PageOut**, free with every McGraw-Hill Ryerson textbook.

To learn more, contact your McGraw-Hill Ryerson publisher's representative or visit www.mhhe.com/solutions

LYRYX LEARNING INC
Online Learning and Assessment
lyryx.com

www.blackboard.com

Online Learning Centre

The *Fundamental Accounting Principles* Online Learning Centre holds a wealth of resources unmatched in educational publishing. With valuable study tools, fingertip availability of teaching aids, and a little fun to help the learning process, the Online Learning Centre has resources for every teaching and learning style.

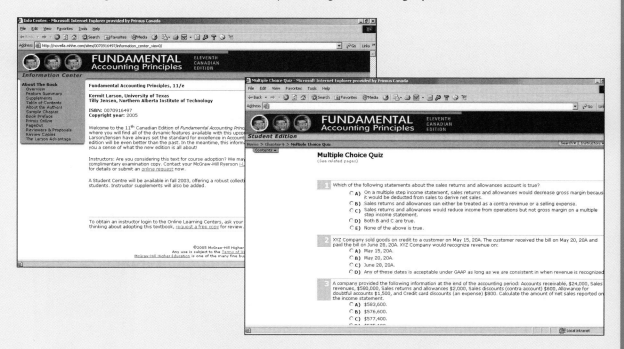

Students have more research and practice opportunities than ever before, with

- Extend Your Knowledge links for further study,
- practice quizzes,
- searchable glossary,
- and even a crossword puzzle to practise the key terms for each chapter.

As usual, instructors will have all supplements available online (with the exception of the test bank), as well as a digital repository of selected exhibits and tables.

New to the Eleventh Canadian Edition, Larson, Jensen, and Kalagnanam now offer the Online Learning Advantage: a fully integrated, premium Web site featuring

- mobile versions of almost all OLC content, sized to fit a laptop or PDA
- **TetrAccounting**, the accounting videogame
- interactive journal entries and trial balance tutorials
- animated conceptual objects that visually reinforce textbook material
- PowerWeb and PowerWeb-to-Go: the latest news and worldwide developments—right at your fingertips!

I think that the Online Learning Centre is a great study tool for reviewing the concepts presented in the textbook. Doing the true/false, multiple-choice, and fill-in-the-blank questions has helped me to grasp all the concepts from the text.

THE ACCOUNTING STANDARD

Mobile Learning

The businesses and companies of today want their new employees to be adept in all aspects of the changing business environment. They are quick to tell us they want graduates with the skills of tomorrow . . . today. From laptops to cell phones to PDAs, the new medium is mobility.

As a leader in technology and innovation, McGraw-Hill Ryerson has developed material providing students with optimum flexibility for use anytime, anywhere they need to study—whether with a laptop, PDA, or tablet. These innovations provide instructors with a number of exciting ways to integrate technology into the learning process.

We have integrated several wireless activities as part of our Online Learning Centre. Now, whether you are waiting in line, riding on transit, or just filling some spare time, homework and practice are just a click away. **Study to Go** allows you to access quizzes from your PDA, and **PowerWeb to Go** provides a link to our research library from anywhere!

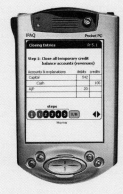

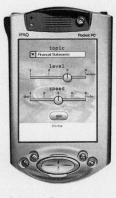

Interactive Journal Entries These problems can be assigned as homework on the go or just for practice.

TetrAccounting Practise your Debits and Credits, and your financial statements in an exciting, interactive videogame: you score points, gain levels, and improve your accounting knowledge. Who said accounting couldn't be fun?!

Streaming Video Download informative, educational interviews with experts from the field. Watch them in your spare time.

Using such innovations as wireless communication, Personal Digital Assistants (PDAs), digital content from textbooks, and more, we are providing a dynamic learning environment and laying the framework for more fusion of education and technology.

Superior Service

Service takes on a whole new meaning with McGraw-Hill Ryerson and Accounting. More than just bringing you the textbook, we have consistently raised the bar for innovation and educational research—both in accounting and in education in general. These investments in learning and the education community have helped us to understand the needs of students and educators across the country, and allowed us to foster the growth of truly innovative, integrated learning.

Integrated Learning

Your Integrated Learning Sales Specialist is a McGraw-Hill Ryerson representative who has the experience, product knowledge, training, and support to help you assess and integrate any of our products, technology, and services into your course for optimum teaching and learning performance. Whether it's using our test bank software, helping your students improve their grades, or putting your entire course online, your *i*-Learning Sales Specialist is there to help you do it. Contact your local *i*-Learning Sales Specialist today to learn how to maximize all of McGraw-Hill Ryerson's resources!

i-Learning Services Program

McGraw-Hill Ryerson offers a unique iServices package designed for Canadian faculty. Our mission is to equip providers of higher education with superior tools and resources required for excellence in teaching. For additional information, visit www.mcgrawhill.ca/highereducation/eservices.

Teaching, Technology & Learning Conference Series

The educational environment has changed tremendously in recent years, and McGraw-Hill Ryerson continues to be committed to helping you acquire the skills you need to succeed in this new milieu. Our innovative Teaching, Technology & Learning Conference Series brings faculty together from across Canada with 3M Teaching Excellence award winners to share teaching and learning best practices in a collaborative and stimulating environment. Pre-conference workshops on general topics, such as teaching large classes and technology integration, will also be offered.

We will also work with you at your own institution to customize workshops that best suit the needs of your faculty at your institution. These include our Teaching Excellence and Accounting Innovation symposium series.

Research Reports into Mobile Learning and Student Success

These landmark reports, undertaken in conjunction with academic and private-sector advisory boards, are the result of research studies into the challenges professors face in helping students succeed and the opportunities that new technology presents to impact teaching and learning.

INSTRUCTOR'S SUPPLEMENTS

For the Instructor

Instructor's Resource CD-ROM (ICD)

This CD-ROM contains materials for managing an active learning environment. In addition to the core supplements below, the ICD includes a Lecture Outline, a chart linking Learning Objectives to end-of-chapter material, and transparency masters. For instructors' convenience, student copies of these visuals are provided in the Study Guide. If students do not acquire the Study Guide, adopters are permitted to duplicate these visuals for distribution. Note: Not all supplements are available for Volume 3.

Solutions Manual

Larson, Jensen, and Kalagnanam set the standard in quality control: six different instructors technically checked the Solutions Manuals at three different stages of development. The manuals contain solutions for all text questions, exercises, and problems.

Test Bank and Computerized Testbank

The Test Bank has been revamped and expanded to reflect the changes in the text, and to improve the quality of this core supplement. A significant number of the questions are new to the Eleventh Canadian Edition. Volumes 1 and 2 are also available in hard copy, and a computerized version is available for all three volumes. Grouped according to Learning Objectives, the Test Bank contains a wide variety of questions—including true/false, multiple choice, matching, short essay, quantitative problems, and completion problems of varying levels of difficulty.

PowerPoint® Presentation Slides

The Microsoft® PowerPoint® Presentation slides have been re-developed in their entirety to better illustrate chapter concepts. This package is available on the Instructor CD or as a download from the OLC.

New Supplements Integrator

This pioneering instructional resource from McGraw-Hill Ryerson is your road map to all the other elements of your text's support package. Keyed to the chapters and topics of your McGraw-Hill Ryerson textbook, the Integrator ties together all of the elements in your resource package, guiding you to where you'll find corresponding coverage in each of the related support package components!

New Transition Guides

Moving to a new textbook or edition is that much easier with the Larson, Jensen, and Kalagnanam Advantage. New to the Eleventh Canadian Edition are Transition Guides that make it easy to adapt your notes and assignments to this new edition. These guides are available for Volumes 1 and 2.

New Exhibits Database

A number of the text exhibits have been saved in an easy to use JPG format so you can use them when creating classroom presentations and reference materials. These images are available on both the Instructor's CD-ROM and the Online Learning Centre.

Course Management

For faculty requiring online content, Larson, Jensen, and Kalagnanam is available in three of the most popular delivery platforms: WebCT, Blackboard, and Desire2Learn. These platforms are designed for instructors who want complete control over course content and how it is presented to students. This format provides instructors with more user-friendly and highly flexible teaching tools that enhance interaction between students and faculty. In addition, PageOut, McGraw-Hill's proprietary course-management system, is available free to all adopters.

For the Student

Working Papers

Updated for the Eleventh Canadian Edition, these volumes match end-of-chapter assignment material for Volumes 1 and 2. They include papers that can be used to solve all of the Quick Studies, Exercises, and Problems. Each chapter contains papers for both the A-Problems and the B-Problems.

Study Guide

An essential study aid for students, the Study Guide volumes review the Learning Objectives and the summaries, outline the chapter, and provide a variety of practice problems and solutions. Study Guides are available for Volumes 1 and 2.

Student Solutions Manual

This manual provides the solutions to the odd-numbered exercises and problems in the text for Volumes 1 and 2.

Excel® Templates (SPATS)

Selected end-of-chapter exercises and problems, marked in the text with an icon, can be solved using these Microsoft® Excel® templates, located on the Online Learning Centre.

GradeSummit

Take your grades to the next level. One of the premier academic practice and assessment tools available anywhere, GradeSummit provides you with thousands of practice questions and targeting assessments. You find out what you know and what you need to practice. Contact your bookstore for more details, or go directly to www.GradeSummit.com and try a sample chapter. GradeSummit is available for Volumes 1 and 2.

Lyryx: LIFA

New

Lyryx Interactive Financial Accounting (LIFA) is a Web-based teaching/learning tool that has captured the attention of post-secondary institutions across the country. Offering significant benefits not only to the student but *also* to the instructor, LIFA has instant appeal because it parallels the classroom environment. More than just questions and problems, LIFA mixes interactive tutorials with problems and labs that guide you through each step of the accounting process. Algorithmically generated and automatically graded, you get feedback tutoring on the spot. Plus, the problems and practice material are always new, so you can practise as much as you need to—without ever repeating the same question. Try it out at http://lifa.lyryx.com (guest username: **student1** guest password: **student1**).

PowerWeb and PowerWeb-to-Go

Bombardier, Enron, Nortel, or Air Canada—for both successes and scandals, PowerWeb keeps you on top of the ever-changing world of accounting and business news and events. Continuously updated, PowerWeb is a rich, dynamic source of what is happening right now, all over the world. Visit www.dushkin.com/powerweb for more details.

Practice Sets

Need something that brings the whole picture together? McGraw-Hill Ryerson publishes a number of dynamic and useful practice sets to help students practise any number of scenarios over the course of several weeks of study. For more information on these and other accounting resources, visit www.mcgrawhill.ca/college/accounting.

Managerial Accounting Concepts and Principles

Where Do I Start?

Halifax—Sharon West thought she'd made it. A graduate of Dalhousie University, four years accounting experience, and a new job as manager of special projects at MacKains. Yet here she was, asking her supervisor "Where do I start?"

West's new job was to assist managers with accounting analysis. In her first week, she met with managers in marketing, sales, purchasing, and manufacturing. Purchasing needed help in establishing criteria for selecting suppliers. Manufacturing needed help in planning equipment purchases. Marketing needed help measuring the financial effects of advertising strategies, and Sales needed help redesigning compensation plans.

West took notes, asked questions, and went back to her new office. She reviewed financial statements, internal monthly reports, and strategic plans. Nowhere did she find the information she needed.

Discouraged, she went to the controller. "I'll never forget how helpless I felt," recalls West. "I looked him straight in the eye, swallowed my pride, and said 'I don't know where to start.' I thought I knew where to look for answers. But the answers weren't in the usual accounting records."

West said the controller smiled and told her "Welcome to management accounting. The answers are in the future, not in past data." West's experience is common. Probably the most important skill of top managers is the ability to go beyond the numbers. Use it, yes. Depend on it, no.

Today West believes one must identify the question and only then gather relevant data. "But," stresses West, "You must go and learn about business operations." These days, West spends much of her time learning operating activities. Little time is spent in her office. And about that question—Where do I start? West smiles, "Management accounting is a great beginning, but understanding operations is crucial. And," adds West "don't let anyone tell you this is an office job!"

Learning Objectives

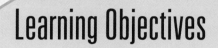

LO¹ Explain the purpose of managerial accounting.

LO² Describe the major characteristics of managerial and financial accounting.

LO³ Describe commonly used lean business practices.

LO⁴ Describe the different ways of classifying costs.

LO⁵ Define product and period costs and explain how they impact financial statements.

LO⁶ Explain manufacturing activities and the flow of manufacturing costs.

LO⁷ Explain differences in the balance sheets of manufacturing and merchandising companies.

LO⁸ Explain differences in the income statements of manufacturing and merchandising companies.

LO⁹ Compute cost of goods sold for a manufacturer.

LO¹⁰ Prepare a manufacturing statement and explain its purpose and links to financial statements.

Chapter Preview

Managerial accounting, like financial accounting, provides information to help users make better decisions. Yet there are important differences between managerial and financial accounting, which we explain. We first discuss the purpose of managerial accounting and compare it with financial accounting. We then introduce the changes taking place in the business environment. We then explain how costs can be classified in different ways, and conclude the chapter with a description of how manufacturing activities are reported.

Managerial Accounting

Broadly speaking, there are three types of businesses: service, merchandising, and manufacturing. A service company earns its revenues by providing services to customers (e.g., a law firm, medical clinic or an advertising agency). A merchandising firm, such as your local corner store, sells products without changing its condition. A small corner store may buy its stock from another merchandising company (large retailer such as Walmart Canada or a wholesaler such as Costco). A large retailer or wholesaler typically buys goods from a manufacturing company, which is engaged in producing goods by converting raw materials into finished products for sale to customers. One important difference between the three types of firms is that a service firm *does not* carry inventory whereas the other two types of firms do. Therefore, merchandising and manufacturing firms must carefully account for their inventory (this is discussed in greater detail later in the chapter).

Managerial accounting, also called **management accounting**, is an activity that provides financial and nonfinancial information to managers and other internal decision makers of a business. It is important to remember that although we will focus largely on "profit-seeking" businesses, other types of organizations also exist whose objectives do not include generating a profit. Examples include government departments, educational institutions, and charitable and other types of non-profit organizations. This section explains the purpose of managerial accounting and compares it with financial accounting.

Purpose of Managerial Accounting

LO¹ Explain the purpose of managerial accounting.

Both managerial accounting and financial accounting share the common purpose of providing useful information to decision makers. They do this by collecting, managing, and reporting information in a manner useful to users of accounting data. Both areas of accounting also share the common practice of reporting monetary information. They even report some of the same information.[1] For example, the financial statements of a company contain information useful for both the managers of a company (insiders) and other persons who are interested in the company (outsiders).

The remainder of this book takes a more careful look at managerial accounting information, how accounting professionals gather it, and how managers use it. The next two chapters describe two distinct cost accounting systems; later chapters cover management accounting topics relevant to planning, implementation, and evaluation.

Planning. Every business usually develops key objectives which then drive its planning process. For example, one of Bell Canada Enterprises' (BCE's) strate-

---

[1] Modern management accounting practices include the reporting of nonmonetary information in addition to monetary information.

gic objectives is to lead the telecommunications industry in revenue growth, operating efficiency and financial returns. Planning, in the context of BCE, would involve setting specific goals and making plans to achieve them. Generally, companies formulate long-term (strategic) plans that usually span a five- to ten-year horizon and then refine them using medium- and short-term plans. A common example of a short-term plan is the annual budget that most organizations prepare each year.

Implementation. Once the plans are in place, managers must ensure that they are actually carried out; this is the implementation stage and involves managers directing and motivating their employees. Implementation may include activities such as developing a new product/service, a new customer database or a new quality control process, producing goods (buying raw materials and turning them into finished goods), hiring new employees, etc. Implementing the plans results in outputs that will generate revenues for the company. Managers often use cost and other management accounting information to make implementation-related decisions.

Control. Developing plans and implementing them is not sufficient. Managers must also monitor plans regularly to ensure that the desired results are being achieved. The control function includes measuring and evaluating actions, processes and outcomes. Timely feedback to managers regarding their plans and actions—through regular performance reports—is essential for effective control. The planning-implementation-control cycle is illustrated in Exhibit 21.1.

Although Exhibit 21.1 appears to indicate that planning, implementation, and control take place in some sort of a sequence, it is important to understand that the feedback loop (as indicated by the dashed lines in the exhibit) suggests that the planning-implementation-control cycle represents a continuous process. During implementation, businesses may find that plans may need some "fine-tuning," which may result in tweaking some of the assumptions made or the numbers used in generating the plans. The control stage is also extremely important for knowing how well a business has achieved its objectives. Businesses generate control reports at regular intervals (daily, weekly, monthly, quarterly or annually) which are used to review plans and actions and refine them if needed. Therefore, planning, implementation, and control represent the three-stage cycle

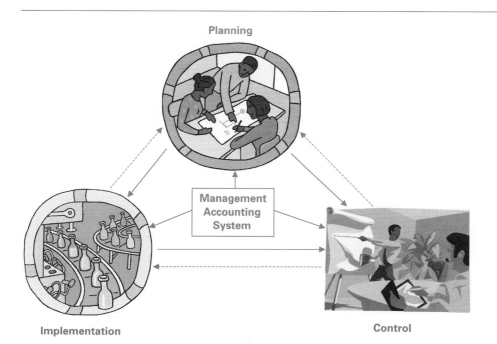

Planning

Management
Accounting
System

Implementation

Control

Exhibit 21.1

Planning, Implementation, and Control

of running a business. As explained in later chapters, management accounting information is useful in all three stages.

Nature of Managerial Accounting

Managerial accounting has its own special characteristics. To understand these characteristics we compare managerial accounting to financial accounting. There are at least seven important differences. These are summarized in Exhibit 21.2.

LO² Describe the major characteristics of managerial and financial accounting.

Exhibit 21.2

Differences Between Managerial Accounting and Financial Accounting

	Financial Accounting	Managerial Accounting
1. Users and decision makers	Investors, creditors, and other users external to the organization	Managers, employees, and decision makers internal to the organization
2. Purpose of information	Assist external users in making investment, credit, and other decisions	Assist managers in planning, implementation and control
3. Flexibility of practice	Structured and often controlled by GAAP	Relatively flexible (no GAAP)
4. Timeliness of information	Often available only after an audit is complete	Available quickly without the need to wait for an audit
5. Time dimension	Historical information with minimum predictions	Many projections and estimates; historical information also presented
6. Focus of information	Emphasis on whole organization	Emphasis on projects, processes, and subdivisions of an organization
7. Nature of information	Monetary information	Mostly monetary; some nonmonetary information

Users and Decision Makers

Companies accumulate, process, and report financial accounting and managerial accounting information for different groups of decision makers. Financial accounting information is provided primarily to external users. These include investors, creditors, and regulators, who rarely have a major role in managing the daily activities of a company. Managerial accounting information is primarily provided to internal users, who are responsible for making and implementing decisions about a company's business activities.

Purpose of Information

Investors, creditors and other external users of financial accounting information must often decide whether to invest in or lend to a company. They must choose the terms of investment or lending. If they have already invested in a company or loaned to it, they must decide whether to continue owning the company or carrying the loan. Internal decision makers must plan the future of a company. They seek to take advantage of opportunities or to overcome obstacles to implement their plans. They also try to control activities and ensure they are being carried out efficiently. Managerial accounting information helps these internal users make planning, implementation, and control decisions.

Flexibility of Practice

Because external users make comparisons between companies and because they need protection against false or misleading information, financial accounting relies on accepted practices. These principles are enforced through an extensive set of rules and guidelines (GAAP).

Internal users need managerial accounting information for planning, implementing, and controlling their company's activities rather than for external comparison. Different types of information are required depending on the activity. Because of this it is difficult to standardize managerial accounting systems across companies. Instead, managerial accounting systems are flexible. Also, since managers have access to most company data, they require less protection against false or misleading information compared to external users.

The design of a company's managerial accounting system depends largely on the nature of the business and the arrangement of the internal operations of the company. Managers can decide for themselves what information they want and how they want it reported. Even within a single company, different managers often design their own systems to meet their special needs. This flexibility allows managers to modify their systems quickly in response to changes in the environment.

Timeliness of Information

Formal financial statements that report past transactions and events are not immediately available to outside parties. Often, independent public accountants must audit the financial statements of a company before reporting to external users. Because audits can take one to three months to complete, annual financial reports to outsiders usually are not available to users until well after the end of the year.

Managerial accounting information can be forwarded to managers quickly. External auditors need not review it. Estimates and projections are acceptable. To get information quickly, managers often accept less precision in reports. As an example, an early internal report to management prepared right after the end of the year might say net income for the year is between $4.2 and $4.8 million. An audited income statement might later show net income for the year at $4.55 million. While the internal report is not precise, its information can be more useful because it is available earlier.

Although accounting reports to managers are available without waiting for completion of an audit, *internal auditing* plays an increasingly important role. Managers are responsible for preventing and detecting fraudulent activities in their companies. Most companies respond by strengthening internal audit functions. In a recent *Auditors' Report*, the external auditors for Infosys Technologies Limited, India's "most respected company" and 2002 recipient of the Golden Peacock Award for Excellence in Corporate Governance in the global category awarded by the World Council for Corporate Governance, London, reported as follows:

> In our opinion and according to the information and explanations given to us, … there are adequate internal control procedures, commensurate with the size of the Company and the nature of its business for the purchase of computer hardware and software, consumables, plant and machinery, equipment and other assets.

Internal auditors evaluate the flow of information not only inside the company but also outside the company. Internal audits often help avoid situations as depicted in the following Judgement Call.

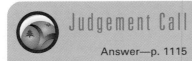

Answer—p. 1115

Judgement Call

Personal Banker
You accept a new job as a personal banker and invite three of your former class-mates for a celebration at a restaurant. When the dinner cheque arrives, David, a self-employed entrepreneur, picks it up saying, "Here, let me pay. I'll deduct it as a business expense on my tax return. It won't cost me as much." Denise, a sales-person for a medium-sized company, takes the cheque from David's hand and says, "I'll put this on my company's credit card. It won't cost us anything." Derek, a factory manager for a company, laughs and says, "Neither of you understand. I'll put this on my company's credit card and call it overhead on a cost-plus contract* my company has with the government." Adds Derek, "That way, my company pays for dinner and makes a profit on it too." Who should pay the bill?

*A cost-plus contract means the company receives its costs plus a percent of those costs.

Time Dimension

To protect external users from false expectations, financial reports deal primarily with results of both past activities and current conditions. While some predictions are necessary, such as service lives and salvage values of capital assets, financial accounting avoids predictions whenever possible. Managerial accounting regularly includes predictions of future conditions and events. As an example, one important managerial accounting report is a budget. A budget predicts sales, expenses, and other items. If managerial accounting reports were restricted to the past and present, managers would be less able to plan activities and less effective in managing current activities.

Focus of Information

While companies often organize into divisions and departments, investors rarely can buy shares in one division or department. Nor do creditors lend money to a single division or department of a company. Instead, investors own shares in or creditors make loans to the whole company. Since these external users need information about the whole company, financial accounting is focused primarily on a company as a whole.

The focus of managerial accounting is different. Managers need information dealing with specific activities, projects, and segments for which they are responsible. For example, division sales managers are *directly* responsible only for the results achieved by their divisions. While they often want to see results for all divisions, they usually do not need a company-wide sales report. Division sales managers need information about results achieved by their specific divisions to improve their personnel's performance. This information includes the level of success achieved by each salesperson in each division.

Nature of Information

Both financial and managerial accounting systems report monetary information. Yet within managerial accounting, there is an increasing emphasis on nonmonetary information. In the chapter's opening article we saw Sharon West helping with important decisions in purchasing, marketing, sales, and manufacturing departments. While monetary information is an important part of these decisions, nonmonetary information also plays a crucial role. This is especially true in cases where monetary effects are difficult to measure. One common example of important nonmonetary information is the quality and delivery criteria of purchasing decisions.

General Manager

You are the general manager of a growing financial consulting company. At a recent executive meeting, you are asked to explore the potential of establishing an in-house marketing team instead of contracting out the marketing function as is currently done. What information would you collect in evaluating the two options?

Judgement Call

Answer—p. 1115

Decision Making Focus

While we emphasize differences between financial and managerial accounting, they are not entirely separate. Similar information is useful to both external and internal users. For instance, information about the costs of products or services is useful to all users in their decisions.

We must also remember that both financial and managerial accounting can affect people's actions. In the chapter's opening article, West's job at MacKains demanded an understanding of accounting. West needed to quantify future costs and revenues associated with projects. But just as important were West's understanding of operations and the people making decisions using cost or revenue data.

Important managerial decisions often are related to each other and to people's behaviour. For example, management's design of a sales compensation plan affects the behaviour of its sales force. Management also must estimate the dual effects of promotion and sales compensation plans on buying patterns of customers. These estimates affect the equipment purchase decisions for manufacturing. They can also affect the supplier selection criteria established by purchasing. Financial and managerial accounting systems do more than measure; they affect people's decisions and actions.

1. Managerial accounting produces information: (a) to meet the needs of internal users, (b) to meet specific needs of a user, (c) often focused on the future, or (d) all of the above.

2. What is the difference between the intended users of financial and managerial accounting information?

3. Do generally accepted accounting principles control the practice of managerial accounting?

Flashback

Answers—p. 1116

Increased Relevance of Managerial Accounting

We have explained the importance of managerial accounting for planning, implementation and control. Although the analytical tools and techniques have always been useful, their relevance and importance have greatly increased in the past decade. This has happened because of changes in the business environment, as explained below.

Two important factors have encouraged companies to become more effective and efficient in running their operations. First, there is an increased recognition that the *customer* is the most important constituent of a business; customers expect to get *value* for the money they spend on buying products or services. Second, competition is truly *global* these days; many countries are opening their doors to foreign competition and investments. Given the fierce global competi-

 LO³ Describe commonly used lean business practices.

tion, companies must constantly search for new ideas to stay ahead in the race. This means looking for ways to enhance revenues and reduce costs.

Many companies have responded by adopting **lean business practices** to achieve continuous improvement by eliminating waste while satisfying the customer and also providing a positive return to the company. We now briefly describe some common lean business practices.

Total Quality Management

Total Quality Management (or TQM) achieves continuous improvement by relentlessly focusing on improving quality everywhere in the organization. Indeed, the word "Total" implies everyone, everywhere. The main principle underlying TQM is the reduction of defects/errors/mistakes down to the lowest level in an attempt to achieve the goal of "zero defects" through identifying the root causes of problems and eliminating them once and for all.

The principles underlying TQM are equally applicable to manufacturing and non-manufacturing settings although the notion of a defect may be different in each type of organization. At Homewood Health Centre (HHC), a Guelph, Ontario-based mental health and addiction facility, one measure of quality is low addiction relapse rates. Quality is so important to HHC that it implemented a top-notch quality system and was recognized as one of the recipients of the Canada Awards for Excellence instituted by the National Quality Institute (whose vision is to inspire excellence in Canada).

Just-In-Time

Just-in-Time (JIT) also embraces the philosophy of continuous improvement by ensuring that products or services are provided only when needed and in the right amount. In the case of manufacturing firms, this would translate into drastically reducing inventory levels so that materials are purchased only when needed and finished goods are produced only against orders (i.e., a *demand-pull* system). Implementing a demand-pull system requires companies to streamline their flow of operations by aligning processes and avoiding duplication and delays. This aspect of JIT applies equally to service functions and service companies; for example, a hospital would also be equally interested in streamlining its processes to reduce waste and increase efficiencies. Another important aspect of JIT is a company's relations with its customers and suppliers. One downside of JIT is that it is more susceptible to disruptions, compared with a traditional system with "excess fat" built into it.

Theory of Constraints

Theory of Constraints (TOC) is yet another method or technique to achieve continuous improvement by focusing on identifying the bottlenecks within a system. A bottleneck or a constraint chokes a system, creating delays. TOC is designed to identify bottleneck(s) and systematically eliminate them. One major emphasis of TOC is maximizing the **throughput** or output of a system—measured as sales revenue minus direct material costs—while minimizing investments and operating expenses.

Success with JIT

Toronto-based electronics manufacturer Celestica Inc. proved that JIT resulted in success. Aligning JIT with its work culture was one of its toughest obstacles but Celestica's proactive approach to dealing with change facilitated implementation. Overall, JIT's primary benefits included improved asset management throughout the entire materials pipeline, and improvements in manufacturing asset and capital utilization. Customer-related benefits included improvements in delivery, flexibility, quality and responsiveness, and increased customer satisfaction. Thanks to JIT, Celestica managed to find a solution for all its subsequent challenges.

SOURCE: Fretty, Peter. "Electronics Component Producer Celestica Implements JIT Company-Wide." http://www.advancedmanufacturing.com/September01/justintime.htm. September 2001.

Implications for Managerial Accounting

Adopting lean business practices can be challenging because all systems and procedures that a company follows must be realigned to foster their implementation. Managerial accounting has an important role to play by providing accurate and relevant cost and performance information. Companies must understand the nature and sources of cost and must develop systems that capture costs accurately.

4. Why are companies adopting lean business practices?
5. List the three lean business practices and identify their objectives.

Flashback

Answers—p. 1116

Cost Concepts

We can classify costs on the basis of their (1) behaviour, (2) traceability, (3) controllability, (4) relevance, and (5) function. This section explains each of these concepts in classifying costs to products and services.

LO⁴ Describe the different ways of classifying costs.

Classification by Behaviour

At a basic level, a cost can be classified as fixed or variable with respect to an activity. A **fixed cost** does not change with changes within a certain range of activity volume (known as the relevant range). Straight-line amortization on a machine is a fixed cost. A **variable cost** changes in proportion to changes in the volume of activity. Sales commissions based on a percent of revenue dollars is a variable cost. Additional examples of fixed and variable costs are provided in Exhibit 21.3. When cost items are combined, total cost can be fixed, variable, or mixed (a combination of fixed and variable costs). Utility costs often include a minimum fixed amount and a variable portion based on the amount of usage. Classification of costs by behaviour is helpful in cost-volume-profit analyses and short-term decision making. In particular, variable cost information is useful in computing **unit contribution margin** which is equal to a product's sale less its total variable costs per unit. We elaborate on these concepts in Chapters 25 and 28.

Exhibit 21.3

Fixed and Variable Costs

Fixed Cost: Rent for Kentucky Fried Chicken restaurant building is $2,000. It does not change with the number of customers served.

Variable Cost: Cost of take-out boxes varies with the number of customers served. This cost is $0.15 per box.

Exhibit 21.4

Direct and Indirect Costs

Direct Costs:
- Salaries of maintenance department employees
- Salary of maintenance department manager
- Equipment purchased by maintenance department
- Materials purchased by maintenance department
- Maintenance department equipment amortization

Indirect Costs:
- Factory accounting
- Factory administration
- Factory rent
- Factory managers' salary
- Factory light and heat

Classification by Traceability

Managers often find it useful to trace costs to different cost objects to get a better estimate of the total costs associated with the cost object. Examples of a **cost object** include such things as a product or service, process, department, division or a customer group. When a cost is traceable, it is classified as either a direct or indirect cost. **Direct costs** are those incurred for the benefit of one specific cost object. For example, if we use product as a cost object, material and labour costs are usually directly traceable. **Indirect costs** are incurred for the benefit of more than one cost object. Exhibit 21.4 shows both direct and indirect costs in a manufacturing plant that arise from the maintenance department (the desired cost object). Classification of costs by traceability is useful for cost allocation, and is discussed in Chapter 24.

Judgement Call

Answer—p. 1115

Budget Officer

You are the budget officer of a manufacturer. You are told by your boss to trace as many of the assembly department's direct costs as possible. You are able to trace 90% of the direct costs in an economical manner. To trace the other 10% you need a sophisticated and costly accounting software package. Do you purchase this package?

Exhibit 21.5

Controllability of Costs

Division Vice President

Controls costs of investment in equipment and buildings.

Sales Supervisor

Controls many daily expenses such as supplies, and overtime.

Classification by Controllability

A cost can be defined as **controllable** or **not controllable**. Whether a cost is controllable or not depends on the employee's responsibilities, as shown in Exhibit 21.5. This is often referred to as identifying the hierarchical levels in management, or the pecking order. For example, investments in machinery are controllable by upper-level managers but not lower-level managers. Many daily operating expenses such as overtime often are controllable by lower-level managers. Classification of costs by controllability is especially useful for evaluating the performance of managers.

Classification by Relevance

A cost can be classified based on its relevance to a particular decision. A **relevant cost** influences or affects the decision, whereas an irrelevant cost has no bearing on the decision. A **sunk cost** is one that has already incurred and cannot be avoided or changed. Sunk costs are irrelevant to future decisions. One example is the cost of complex computer software previously purchased by WestJet. An **out-of-pocket cost** requires a future outlay of cash and is relevant for future decision making. Future purchases of production equipment involve out-of-pocket costs.

A discussion of relevant costs must consider opportunity costs. An **opportunity cost** is the potential benefit lost by choosing a specific action out of two or more alternatives. One example is a student giving up wages from a job to attend summer school. Consideration of opportunity costs is important when, for example, a computer manufacturer must decide between internally manufacturing a chip versus buying it externally. This is discussed in Chapter 28.

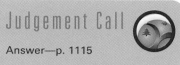

Purchase Manager

You are the purchase manager of a motorcycle manufacturer. You are evaluating two potential suppliers of seats for your motorcycles. One supplier (A) quotes a price of $145 per seat and assures 100% quality standards and on-time delivery schedules. The second supplier (B) quotes a price of $115 per seat and does not give any written assurances on quality or delivery. You decide to award the contract to the second supplier (B), saving $30 per seat. Are there any opportunity costs of this decision?

Answer—p. 1115

Classification by Function

Another classification of costs relevant to manufacturers is based on function (i.e. the purpose for which these expenses are incurred). Expenses that are necessary and integral to the production of finished goods are called **manufacturing costs**; these include direct materials, direct labour, and manufacturing overhead (these will be described later in this chapter). Manufacturing companies also incur operating expenses such as sales and marketing, and general administration; these are called **non-manufacturing costs**.

 LO⁵ Define product and period costs and explain how they impact financial statements.

In addition to the above, classification by function relevant both to merchandisers and manufacturers includes the notion of product versus period costs. **Product costs** refer to the expenses that are incurred for acquiring (purchasing) or manufacturing the goods to be sold. Merchandising companies acquire the goods they sell, whereas manufacturing companies produce the goods they sell. In the case of manufacturing companies, product costs are the same as the manufacturing costs explained above. Product costs are also known as *inventoriable costs* because they are carried forward to inventory; they represent a future value to the business.

Period costs pertain to expenditures on activities that are *non-inventoriable* or not part of the manufacturing or purchasing process. Instead, they are typically associated with activities such as selling and general administration. Period costs flow directly to the income statement as expenses for the period in which they are incurred, whereas product costs are carried forward as assets to the inventory account on the balance sheet to be expensed only when products are sold. Exhibit 21.6 shows the different effects of product and period costs incurred by a merchandiser such as Canadian Tire.

Exhibit 21.6

Period and Product Costs in
Financial Statements

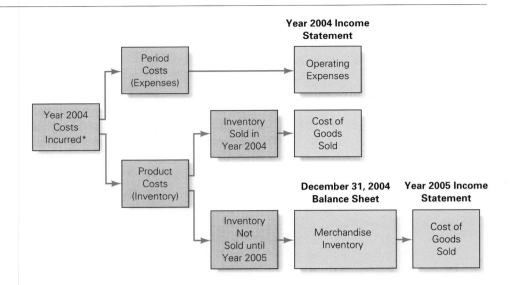

Product costs for Canadian Tire are first assigned to inventory. Final treatment of product costs depends on when inventory is disposed of or sold. Product costs assigned to inventory in year 2004 are reported on Canadian Tire's year 2004 income statement as part of cost of goods sold. Product costs assigned to unsold inventory are carried forward on Canadian Tire's balance sheet at the end of year 2004. If this inventory is sold in 2005, product costs assigned to it are reported in that year's income statement.

Identifying Cost Classification

It is important to understand that a cost item can be classified using any of the five different methods described above. To do this, we must understand costs and operations. Using our five classifications, we must be able to identify the: *activity* for behaviour, *cost object* for traceability, *management hierarchical level* for controllability, *decision* for relevance, and *benefit period* for functional. Factory rent, for instance, can be classified as a product cost, is fixed with respect to units produced, indirect with respect to products, and not controllable by a production operator. Potential multiple classifications are shown in Exhibit 21.7 using different cost items incurred in manufacturing mountain bikes. The finished bike is the cost object.

Exhibit 21.7

Examples of Multiple Cost
Classifications

Cost Item	By Behavior	By Traceability	By Function
Tires	variable	direct	Product
Wages of assembly worker	variable	direct	Product
Advertising	fixed	indirect	Period
Production manager's salary	fixed	indirect	Product
Office amortization	fixed	indirect	Period

Proper allocation of these costs, and decisions made using cost data, depend on our ability to correctly identify cost classifications.

Flashback

Answers—p. 1116

6. Which type of cost behaviour causes total costs to increase when volume of activity increases?

7. How might traceability of costs improve managerial decisions?

Mid-Chapter Demonstration Problem

This chapter described several new managerial and cost concepts and terms. It is important that we understand these and be able to properly classify terms. This problem assists in this process. Consider the following company, Chip Making Systems (CMS), which manufactures computer chips. CMS incurs various costs both in manufacturing these chips and in the operations of the company. These costs include:

1. Plastic board used to mount the chip, $3.50 each.
2. Assembly worker pay of $15 per hour to attach chips to plastic board.
3. Salary for factory maintenance and repair workers. These workers maintain and repair equipment throughout the factory.
4. Factory foreman pay of $55,000 per year to supervise employees.
5. Real estate taxes paid on the factory, $14,500.
6. Real estate taxes paid on the company office, $6,000.
7. Amortization costs on machinery used by workers, $30,000.
8. Salary paid to the chief financial officer, $95,000.
9. Advertising costs of $7,800 paid to promote products.
10. Salespersons are paid a commission of $0.50 for each assembled chip sold.
11. *Note*: Instead of producing and assembling chips, CMS could rent the manufacturing plant to store medical records for six local hospitals.

In the table below, classify each of these costs according to the terms labelled across the top of the chart. Refer to the chapter and glossary of terms to help classify these costs. A cost can be classified under more than one category. The plastic board used to mount chips, for instance, is classified as a direct material product cost and as a direct unit cost.

	Period Costs	Product Costs			Unit Cost Classification		Sunk Cost	Opportunity Cost
Cost	Selling and Administrative	Direct Material (prime cost)	Direct Labour (prime and conversion cost)	Factory Overhead (conversion cost)	Direct	Indirect		
1. Plastic board used to mount the chip, $3.50 each		✔			✔			

SOLUTION TO Mid-Chapter Demonstration Problem

Cost	Period Costs Selling and Administrative	Product Costs Direct Material (prime cost)	Direct Labour (prime and conversion cost)	Factory Overhead (conversion cost)	Unit Cost Classification Direct	Indirect	Sunk Cost	Opportunity Cost
1.		✔			✔			
2.			✔		✔			
3.				✔		✔		
4.				✔		✔		
5.				✔		✔		
6.	✔							
7.				✔		✔	✔	
8.	✔							
9.	✔							
10.	✔							
11.								✔

Reporting Manufacturing Activities

Much of our focus in this book has been on the business activities of merchandising and service companies. We described these activities and how to account for them. As explained earlier, manufacturing activities are different from both selling merchandise and providing services. Also, the financial statements of manufacturing companies have unique features. This section looks at some of these features and compares them to accounting for a merchandising company.

Flow of Manufacturing Activities

Exhibit 21.8 shows the flow of activities for Rocky Mountain Bikes. This exhibit has three important sections: *materials activity*, *production activity*, and *selling activity*. We explain each of these activities in this section.

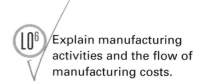

LO⁶ Explain manufacturing activities and the flow of manufacturing costs.

Exhibit 21.8

Flow of Activities and Costs in Manufacturing

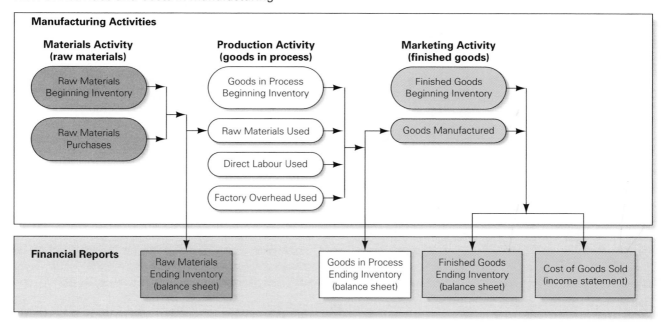

Materials Activity

The left column of Exhibit 21.8 shows the flow of raw materials. Rocky Mountain Bikes, like most manufacturers, usually starts a period with some beginning raw materials inventory. This is shown as carried over from the previous period. During the current year, the company acquires additional raw materials. When these purchases are added to beginning inventory, we get total raw materials available for use in production. These raw materials are then either used in production in the current period or remain on hand at the end of the period for use in future periods.

Production Activity

The middle column of Exhibit 21.8 describes production activity. Four factors come together in production. They are beginning goods in process inventory, direct materials, direct labour, and factory overhead (these terms are further described later in this chapter). Beginning goods in process inventory consists of partly assembled bikes from the previous period.

Production activity results in bikes that are either finished or remain unfinished at the end of a period. The cost of the finished bikes makes up the cost of goods manufactured for the current period. Unfinished bikes are identified as ending goods in process inventory. The cost of unfinished bikes consists of direct materials, direct labour, and factory overhead. This cost is reported on the current period's balance sheet. The costs of both finished goods manufactured and goods in process are *product costs*. Period costs (expenses) are not part of cost of goods manufactured.

Marketing Activity

The company's marketing activity is portrayed in the right column of Exhibit 21.8. Newly completed units are combined with beginning finished goods inventory to make up total finished goods available for sale in the current period. The cost of finished bikes sold is reported on the income statement as cost of goods sold. The cost of bikes not sold is reported on the current period's balance sheet as ending finished goods inventory.

We have discussed how some manufacturing costs are transferred to the balance sheet and others to the income statement. We have also introduced the term cost of goods manufactured, which is available from the Manufacturing Statement. Each of the three reports for a manufacturer is discussed below.

Balance Sheet of a Manufacturer

LO⁷ Explain differences in the balance sheets of manufacturing and merchandising companies.

Manufacturers carry several different kinds of assets that are unique to them. Manufacturers usually have three types of inventory instead of a single inventory type carried by merchandising companies. Exhibit 21.9 shows three different inventories in the current asset section of the balance sheet for Rocky Mountain Bikes. The three are: raw materials, goods in process, and finished goods.

Exhibit 21.9

Balance Sheet for a
Manufacturer

Rocky Mountain Bikes Balance Sheet December 31, 2004		
Assets:		
Current assets:		
Cash..		$ 11,000
Accounts receivable	$ 32,000	
Allowance for doubtful accounts	(1,850)	30,150
Raw materials inventory		9,000
Goods in process inventory...................		7,500
Finished goods inventory		10,300
Supplies		350
Prepaid insurance		300
Total current assets		$ 68,600
Capital assets:		
Small tools		1,100
Delivery equipment	9,000	
Accumulated amortization	(4,000)	5,000
Office equipment...................................	1,700	
Accumulated amortization	(400)	1,300
Factory machinery	72,000	
Accumulated amortization	(6,500)	65,500
Factory building	90,000	
Accumulated amortization	(3,300)	86,700
Land..		9,500
Total tangible capital assets....................		$169,100
Intangible assets:		
Patents		11,200
Total assets..		$248,900
Liabilities and Shareholders' Equity:		
Current liabilities:		
Accounts payable	14,000	
Wages payable	540	
Interest payable.....................................	2,000	
Income taxes payable.............................	32,600	
Total current liabilities	49,140	
Long-term liabilities:		
Long-term notes payable........................	50,000	
Total liabilities		99,140
Shareholders' equity:		
Common shares	100,000	
Retained earnings..................................	49,760	
Total shareholders' equity.......................		$149,760
Total liabilities and shareholders' equity		$248,900

Raw Materials Inventory

Raw materials inventory refers to the goods a company acquires to use in making products. Materials are used in two ways—directly and indirectly. Most raw materials physically become part of the product and are identified with specific units or batches of product. Raw materials used directly in products are called **direct materials**. For example, the tires, seat, and frame of a mountain bike are direct materials. A mountain bike cannot be produced without direct materials.

The costs of these materials are usually a significant portion of the total cost of producing the bike and therefore must be identified separately.

Other materials used in support of the production process are sometimes not as clearly identified with specific units or batches of product. Examples are lubricants needed for machinery and supplies for cleaning the factory. These materials are called **indirect materials** because they do not become a part of a product and are not clearly identified with specific units or batches of product. Items used as indirect materials often appear on a balance sheet as factory supplies. In other cases, they are included in raw materials.

In addition to the indirect materials as defined above, there may be some direct materials that are actually classified as indirect materials. These are classified this way because of their low (insignificant) values. Examples include screws and nuts used in assembling mountain bikes, or nails and glue used in manufacturing shoes. The costs of these materials are likely to be very low compared to the cost of the other direct materials. Using the materiality principle, it does not make much economic sense to individually trace the cost of each of these materials and classify them separately as raw materials. For example, it is not cost-beneficial to keep detailed records of the amount of glue used in manufacturing one unit of a shoe.

Goods In Process Inventory

Another inventory held by manufacturers is **goods in process inventory**, also called *work in process inventory*. It consists of products in the process of being manufactured but not yet complete. The amount of goods in process inventory depends on the type of production process. If the time required to produce a unit of product is short, the goods in process inventory is likely small. But, if weeks or months are needed to produce a unit, the goods in process inventory is usually larger.

Finished Goods Inventory

A third inventory owned by a manufacturer is finished goods inventory. **Finished goods inventory** consists of completed products ready for sale. This inventory is similar to merchandise inventory owned by a merchandising company. The implementation of JIT can reduce inventory levels quite drastically, thereby lowering the working capital requirements.

Manufacturers often carry unique plant assets such as small tools, factory buildings, and factory equipment. They also frequently invest in *patents*. Companies use these assets to manufacture products. The balance sheet in Exhibit 21.9 shows Rocky Mountain Bikes owns all of these assets. Some manufacturers invest millions or even billions of dollars in production facilities and patents. A recent balance sheet for Magna International, headquartered in Aurora, Ontario, reported a net investment in land, buildings, machinery, and equipment of U.S.$3.9 billion, much of which involves production facilities.

Income Statement of a Manufacturer

LO⁸ Explain differences in the income statements of manufacturing and merchandising companies.

The main difference between income statements of manufacturers and merchandisers is the items making up cost of goods sold. Exhibit 21.10 compares the components of cost of goods sold for a manufacturer and a merchandiser. A merchandiser adds beginning merchandise inventory to cost of goods purchased, and then subtracts ending merchandise inventory to get cost of goods sold. A manufacturer adds beginning finished goods inventory to cost of goods manufactured, and then subtracts ending finished goods inventory to get cost of goods sold.

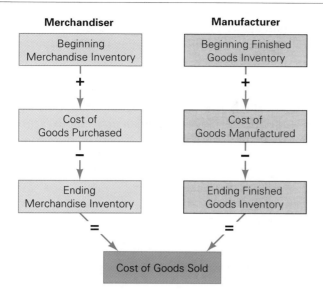

Exhibit 21.10

Cost of Goods Sold
Computation

A merchandiser uses the term *merchandise* inventory while a manufacturer uses the term *finished goods* inventory. The manufacturer's inventories of raw materials and goods in process are not included in finished goods because they are not available for sale. A manufacturer also shows cost of goods *manufactured* instead of cost of goods *purchased*. This difference is because a manufacturer produces its goods instead of purchasing them ready for sale. In the next section, we will show how we derive cost of goods manufactured from the *manufacturing statement*.

We show cost of goods sold sections for a merchandiser (Tele-Mart) and a manufacturer (Rocky Mountain Bikes) in Exhibit 21.11 to highlight these differences. The remaining income statement sections are similar.

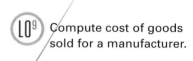 Compute cost of goods sold for a manufacturer.

Exhibit 21.11

Cost of Goods Sold for a Merchandiser and Manufacturer

Merchandising Company		Manufacturing Company	
Cost of goods sold:		Cost of goods sold:	
Beginning *merchandise* inventory	$ 14,200	Beginning *finished goods* inventory	$ 11,200
Total cost of merchandise *purchased*.....	234,150	Cost of goods *manufactured**	170,500
Goods available for sale	248,350	Goods available for sale	181,700
Ending *merchandise* inventory..............	12,100	Ending *finished goods* inventory	10,300
Cost of goods sold.................................	$236,250	Cost of goods sold..................................	$171,400

*The cost of goods manufactured amount is reported in the income statement presented in Exhibit 21.13.

Except for these differences, the cost of goods sold computations are the same. But we need to emphasize the numbers used in these computations reflect different activities. A merchandiser's cost of goods purchased is the cost of buying products to be sold. A manufacturer's cost of goods manufactured is the sum of direct materials, direct labour, and factory overhead costs incurred in producing products. The remainder of this section explains these manufacturing costs, and describes prime and conversion costs.

Direct Materials

Direct materials are tangible components of a finished product. **Direct material costs** are the expenditures for direct materials that are separately and readily traced through the manufacturing process to finished goods. Examples of direct materials in manufacturing a mountain bike include the tires, seat, frame, pedals, brakes, cables, gears, and handlebars. According to a 1999 Industry Canada report on manufacturing costs within the Computer and Electronic Product Manufacturing subsector, the costs of materials and supplies represented a major portion of the total manufacturing costs. Of course, the proportion of direct material costs varies by industry.

Direct Labour

Direct labour refers to efforts of employees who physically convert materials to finished product. **Direct labour costs** are the wages and salaries for direct labour that are separately and readily traced through the manufacturing process to finished goods. Examples of direct labour in manufacturing a mountain bike include operators directly involved in converting raw materials into finished products (welding, painting, forming) and assembly line workers who assemble materials such as tires, seats, pedals, and brakes to mountain bike frames. Costs of other workers on the assembly line who assist direct labourers are classified as **indirect labour**. Efforts of indirect labourers are not linked to specific units or batches of product.

Factory Overhead

Factory overhead involves components of activities that support the manufacturing process and are not direct materials or direct labour. **Factory overhead costs** are the expenditures for factory overhead that cannot be separately or readily traced to finished goods. These costs include indirect materials and indirect labour not directly traceable to the product. Overtime wages paid to direct labourers are also usually included as part of factory overhead. This is because due to delays, interruptions, or constraints they are not necessarily identifiable with a specific product or batch of products.

Factory overhead costs also include maintenance of the mountain bike factory, supervision of its production employees, repairing manufacturing equipment, factory utilities (water, gas, electricity), production manager's salary, factory rent, amortization on factory buildings and equipment, factory insurance, property taxes on factory buildings and equipment, and factory accounting and legal services. Factory overhead does *not* include selling and administrative expenses. This is because selling and administrative expenses are not incurred in manufacturing products; these are called *period costs* and are recorded as expenses on the income statement when incurred.

Prime and Conversion Costs

Direct material costs and direct labour costs are also called **prime costs** —expenditures directly associated with the manufacturing of finished goods. Direct labour costs and overhead costs are also called **conversion costs**—expenditures incurred in the process of converting raw materials to finished goods. Note that direct labour costs often make up both prime costs and conversion costs. Exhibit 21.12 conveys the relation between prime and conversion costs along with their components of direct material, direct labour, and factory overhead.

Exhibit 21.12

Prime and Conversion Costs

Reporting Performance

Exhibit 21.13 shows the income statement for Rocky Mountain Bikes. The cost of goods sold consists of product costs and includes the cost of goods manufactured which is discussed in the next section. Its operating expenses, classified earlier as period costs, include sales salaries, office salaries, and amortization of delivery and office equipment.

Rocky Mountain Bikes **Income Statement** **For the Year Ended December 31, 2004**			
Sales..			$310,000
Cost of goods sold:			
Finished goods inventory, December 31, 2003..........		$ 11,200	
Cost of goods manufactured......................................		170,500	
Goods available for sale...		181,700	
Finished goods inventory, December 31, 2004...........		(10,300)	
Cost of goods sold..			171,400
Gross profit			138,600
Operating expenses:			
Selling expenses:			
Sales salaries expense..	$18,000		
Advertising expense	5,500		
Delivery wages expense..	12,000		
Shipping supplies expense	250		
Insurance expense, delivery equipment..................	300		
Amortization expense, delivery equipment	2,100		
Total selling expenses..		38,150	
General and administrative expenses:			
Office salaries expense	15,700		
Miscellaneous expense	200		
Bad debts expense..	1,550		
Office supplies expense	100		
Amortization expense, office equipment.................	200		
Interest expense..	4,000		
Total general and administrative expenses..............		21,750	
Total operating expenses...			59,900
Income before income taxes			78,700
Less income taxes expenses			(32,600)
Net income...			$46,100
Net income per common share (20,000 shares)............			$2.31

Exhibit 21.13

Income Statement for a Manufacturer

8. What are the three types of inventory on a balance sheet of a manufacturing company?

9. What is the difference between cost of goods sold in merchandising versus manufacturing companies?

Flashback

Answers—p. 1116

Manufacturing Statement

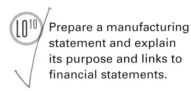

L0¹⁰ Prepare a manufacturing statement and explain its purpose and links to financial statements.

Exhibit 21.14a shows the **manufacturing statement** for Rocky Mountain Bikes. It reports costs of both materials and production activities as described in Exhibit 21.8. The statement is divided into four parts: *direct material, direct labour, overhead,* and *computation of cost of goods manufactured.* We describe each of these parts in this section.

Exhibit 21.14a

Manufacturing Statement

Rocky Mountain Bikes Manufacturing Statement For Year Ended December 31, 2004		
Direct materials:		
Raw materials inventory, December 31, 2003	$ 8,000	
Raw materials purchases	86,500	
Raw materials available for use	94,500	
Raw materials inventory, December 31, 2004	(9,000)	
Direct materials used		$ 85,500
② **Direct labour**		60,000
Factory overhead costs:		
Indirect labour	9,000	
Factory supervision	6,000	
Factory utilities	2,600	
Repairs, factory equipment	2,500	
Property taxes, factory building	1,900	
Factory supplies used	600	
Factory insurance expired	1,100	
Small tools written off	200	
Amortization, factory equipment	3,500	
Amortization, factory building	1,800	
Amortization, patents	800	
Total factory overhead costs		30,000
Total manufacturing costs		$175,500
Add goods in process inventory, December 31, 2003		2,500
Total costs of goods in process		$178,000
Deduct goods in process inventory, December 31, 2004		(7,500)
Cost of goods manufactured		$170,500

Sections labelled ①, ②, ③, ④ at left of table.

Direct Materials ①

The manufacturing statement begins by computing the cost of raw materials used. We start by adding the beginning raw materials inventory of $8,000 to the current period's purchases of $86,500. This yields $94,500 of total raw materials available for use. A physical count of inventory shows $9,000 of ending raw materials inventory. We then compute total cost of raw materials used during the period as $85,500. This is computed by subtracting the $9,000 ending inventory from the $94,500 total direct materials available for use. Many companies substitute the terms **raw materials** for *direct materials.*

Direct Labour ②

The second part of the manufacturing statement reports direct labour costs incurred. Rocky Mountain Bikes had total direct labour cost of $60,000 for the period. This amount includes payroll taxes and fringe benefits.

Overhead ③

The third part of the manufacturing statement reports on overhead costs. The statement lists each important factory overhead item along with its cost. Total factory overhead cost for the period is $30,000. Some companies report only total factory overhead on the manufacturing statement and attach a separate schedule listing individual overhead costs. Total manufacturing costs for the period are $175,500, computed as $85,500 1 $60,000 1 $30,000. This is the sum of direct materials used, direct labour incurred, and overhead costs incurred.

Computation of Cost of Goods Manufactured ⑤

The final section of the manufacturing statement computes and reports the cost of goods manufactured. First, total manufacturing costs are added to beginning goods in process inventory. This gives the total cost of goods in process inventory of $178,000, computed as $175,500 1 $2,500. We then compute the current period's cost of goods manufactured of $170,500 by subtracting the cost of ending goods in process inventory of $7,500 from the total cost of goods in process of $178,000. The amount of $7,500 assigned to the ending goods in process inventory consists of direct materials, direct labour, and factory overhead. The cost of goods manufactured amount is also called net cost of goods manufactured or cost of goods completed. Exhibit 21.13 shows that this item and amount are listed in the cost of goods sold section of Rocky Mountain Bikes' income statement.

Since Rocky Mountain Bikes includes a detailed list of overhead costs in its manufacturing statement, we show the alternative use of a supporting schedule in Exhibit 22.14b. The manufacturing statement includes total factory overhead in its computation of cost of goods manufactured. Costs of goods manufactured is then carried to the income statement and shown as part of costs of goods sold.

Exhibit 21.14b

Overhead Cost Flows Across Accounting Reports

Rocky Mountain Bikes Schedule of Overhead Items For Year Ended December 31, 2004		Rocky Mountain Bikes Manufacturing Statement For Year Ended December 31, 2004		Rocky Mountain Bikes Income Statement For Year Ended December 31, 2004	
Indirect labour	$ 9,000	Direct materials	$ 85,500	Sales	$ 310,500
Supervision	6,000	Direct labour	60,000	Cost of goods sold:	
Other overhead items*	15,000	Factory overhead	30,000	Beginning finished gooods	11,200
Total overhead	$ 30,000	Total manuf. costs	$ 175,500	Cost of goods manufacturing...	$ 170,500
		Beginning goods in process	2,500	Ending finished goods	(10,300)
*Overhead items are listed in Exhibit 21.14a.		Total goods in process	$ 178,000	Cost of goods sold	$ 171,400
		Ending goods in process	(7,500)	Gross profit	$ 133,600
		Cost of goods manufacturing	$ 170,500	Expenses	(59,900)
				Income taxes	(32,600)
				Net Income	$ 46,100

Management uses information in the manufacturing statement when planning and controlling the company's manufacturing activities. To provide timely information for decision-making, the statement is often prepared monthly, weekly, or even daily. While the manufacturing statement contains information useful to external users, it is not a general-purpose financial statement. Most companies view this information as proprietary and potentially harmful to the company if released to competitors. As a result companies rarely publish the manufacturing statement.

Flashback

Answers—p. 1116

10. A manufacturing statement: (a) computes cost of goods manufactured for the period, (b) computes cost of goods sold for the period, (c) reports operating expenses incurred for the period.

11. Does GAAP require companies to report a manufacturing statement?

12. How are both beginning and ending goods in process inventories reported on a manufacturing statement?

(?)   **Did You Know?**   **Automation, Information and Overhead**

Kitchener, Ontario-based PEER Group is a software solution provider specifically to manufacturing companies. For TRW Avionics, one of its clients, the company developed a system that helped TRW's engineers respond to customers' needs in a much more timely manner. With the new system in place, TRW was also able to reduce its manufacturing overhead costs and become more cost competitive.

SOURCE: http://www.peergroup.com

Summary

LO¹ Explain the purpose of managerial accounting. The purpose of managerial accounting is to provide useful information to management and other internal decision makers. It collects, manages, and reports both monetary and nonmonetary information in a manner useful to internal users.

LO² Describe the major characteristics of managerial accounting. Major characteristics of managerial accounting include: (1) focus on internal decision makers, (2) emphasis on planning, implementation, and control, (3) flexibility, (4) timeliness, (5) reliance on forecasts and estimates, (6) focus on segments and projects, and (7) reporting both monetary and nonmonetary information.

LO³ Describe commonly used lean business practices. Today's business environment emphasizes customer satisfaction. To satisfy the customer, companies increasingly focus on quality, flexibility, timely delivery, and cost. Several new practices have emerged to help in this process: total quality management, just-in-time, and theory of constraints.

LO⁴ Describe the different ways of classifying costs. We can classify costs on the basis of their (1) behaviour—fixed vs. variable, (2) traceability—direct vs. indirect, (3) controllability—controllable vs. uncontrollable, (4) relevance—sunk vs. out-of-pocket, and (5) function—product vs. period. It is important to remember that a single cost can be classified in more than one way depending on the purpose for which the cost is being determined. These classifications are useful in understanding cost patterns, analyzing performance, and planning future operations.

LO⁵ Define product and period costs and explain how they impact financial statements. Costs that are capitalized because they are expected to have value in the future are called product costs, whereas costs that are expensed are called period costs. This classification is important because it affects the amount of costs expensed in the income statement and the amount of costs assigned to inventory on the balance sheet. Product costs are commonly made up of direct materials, direct labour, and manufacturing overhead. Period costs include selling and administrative expenses.

LO⁶ Explain manufacturing activities and the flow of manufacturing costs. Manufacturing activities consist of materials, production, and marketing activities. Materials activity consists of the purchase and issuance of materials to production. The production activity consists of converting materials into finished goods. At this stage in the process, materials, labour and overhead costs are incurred, and the manufacturing statement is prepared. Marketing activity consists of selling some or all of the finished goods that are available for sale. The cost of goods sold is determined at this stage in the process.

LO⁷ Explain differences in the balance sheets of manufacturing and merchandising companies. The main difference is that manufacturers usually carry three

Summary

types of inventory instead of one type carried by merchandising companies. These three types of inventories are: raw materials, goods in process, and finished goods.

LO8 **Explain differences in the income statements of manufacturing and merchandising companies.** The main difference between income statements of manufacturers and merchandisers is the items making up cost of goods sold. A merchandiser adds beginning merchandise inventory to cost of goods purchased, and then subtracts ending merchandise inventory to get cost of goods sold. A manufacturer adds beginning finished goods inventory to cost of goods manufactured, and then subtracts ending finished goods inventory to get cost of goods sold.

LO9 **Compute cost of goods sold for a manufacturer.** A manufacturer adds beginning finished goods inventory to cost of goods manufactured, and then subtracts ending finished goods inventory to get cost of goods sold.

LO10 **Prepare a manufacturing statement and explain its purpose and links to financial statements.** The manufacturing statement reports the computation of the cost of goods manufactured during a period. It begins by recording the period's costs for direct materials, direct labour, and overhead, and then adjusts these numbers for the beginning and ending inventories of goods in process to compute the cost of goods manufactured.

GUIDANCE ANSWERS TO Judgement Call

Personal Banker

While someone must pay the bill, it appears that all three of your friends want to pay the bill with someone else's money. David is using money belonging to the tax authorities, Denise is taking money from her company, and Derek is defrauding the government. To prevent such practices, companies have internal audit mechanisms. Also, many companies precisely define the kinds of expenses that can be claimed. Many companies also set up ethical codes of conduct to help guide employees in making decisions. We must recognize that, depending on the circumstances, some entertainment expenses are justifiable and even encouraged. For example, the tax law allows certain deductions for entertainment that have a business purpose. Corporate policies also sometimes allow and encourage reimbursable spending for social activities, and government contracts sometimes include entertainment as allowable costs. Nevertheless, without further details, payments should be made from their personal accounts.

General Manager

You need information from the managerial accounting system to help you decide whether it would be worthwhile establishing an in-house marketing team. Therefore, you must perform a cost-benefit analysis of establishing a marketing team. The costs include the salaries and benefits of the team members, their travel expenses, sales commissions, and space and utility costs (to house the team members). In addition, the company must estimate the costs of marketing activities and budget them (e.g., advertising and sales promotions)—this is a new activity. It is

also important to note that many of the expenses involved in establishing a marketing team will be recurring in nature as opposed to incurring them only when required, as in the case of contracting the marketing function. The benefits of establishing an in-house marketing team are harder to estimate but include factors such as more control over marketing activity, and the increased possibility of developing new customers/services.

Budget Officer

It is always desirable to trace all costs directly to cost objects. But you need to be able to trace costs in an economically feasible manner. In this case, you are able to trace 90% of costs directly to the assembly department. It may not be economical to spend added money on new software to trace the final 10% of costs. You need to make a cost-benefit trade-off. Also, if the software offers benefits beyond tracing the remaining 10% of the assembly department's costs, your decision should take this into account.

Purchase Manager

Opportunity costs refer to the potential quality and delivery benefits given up by not choosing supplier (A) as the preferred supplier. Selecting supplier (B) might involve future costs of poor quality seats (inspection, repairs, and returns). Also, because of potential delivery delays, work might be interrupted and increase manufacturing costs. Your company might also incur sales losses if the product quality of supplier (B) is lower. As purchase manager, you are responsible for these costs and must consider them in making your decision.

GUIDANCE ANSWERS TO  **Flashback**

1. *d.* Managerial accounting information is primarily used by internal users, is flexible to meet the needs of individual users and often focuses heavily on the future (e.g., budgets).

2. Financial accounting information is intended for users external to an organization such as investors, creditors, and government authorities. Managerial accounting, on the other hand, focuses on providing information to managers and other decision makers within the organization.

3. No, generally accepted accounting principles (GAAP) do not control the practice of managerial accounting. Unlike external users, internal users need managerial accounting information for planning and controlling their organization's activities rather than for external comparison. Different types of information may be required depending on the managerial activity. Therefore, it is difficult to standardize managerial accounting systems across companies through the use of GAAP or a similar rigid structure.

4. Companies are adopting lean business practices to become more effective and efficient in running their operations. This is in response to increased customer orientation and global competition.

5. The three lean business practices described in the chapter are Total Quality Management (TQM), Just-in-Time (JIT) and Theory of Constraints (TOC). Although the focus of each of the three practices is slightly different, they all help in improving operations and eliminating waste.

6. Variable cost behaviour causes total costs to increase when the volume of activity increases.

7. By being able to trace the costs to cost objects (e.g., products, departments), managers have a better understanding of the total costs associated with that cost object. This information is very useful when managers are considering making changes to the cost object (say dropping the product or expanding the department).

8. The three different types of inventory that can be found on the balance sheet of a manufacturing company are raw materials inventory, goods in process inventory, and finished goods inventory.

9. The cost of goods sold in merchandising companies includes only the purchase price of the merchandise, whereas the cost of goods sold in manufacturing companies includes the three costs of manufacturing: raw materials, direct labour, and overhead.

10. *a*

11. No.

12. Beginning goods in process inventory is added to total manufacturing costs to give total goods in process. Ending goods in process inventory is subtracted from total goods in process to give the cost of goods manufactured for the period.

Demonstration Problem #1

The balance sheet and income statement for a manufacturing company are different than those for a merchandising or service company. This problem requires that we understand the important differences between the two.

Required

1. Fill in the "[BLANKS]" on the partial balance sheets for both the manufacturing company and merchandising company. Explain why a different presentation is required.

Manufacturing Company

Chip Making Systems Balance Sheet December 31, 2004	
Assets	
Current assets:	
Cash..	$10,000
[BLANK]...	8,000
[BLANK]...	5,000
[BLANK]...	7,000
Supplies..	500
Prepaid insurance.......................................	500
Total current assets..................................	$31,000

Merchandising Company

Joe's Shoe Outlet Balance Sheet December 31, 2004	
Assets	
Current assets:	
Cash..	$ 5,000
[BLANK]...	12,000
Supplies..	500
Prepaid insurance.......................................	500
Total current assets..................................	$18,000

2. Fill in the "[BLANKS]" on the income statements for the manufacturing company and merchandising company. Explain why a different presentation is required. The manufacturer's cost of goods manufactured is the sum of (a) _____, (b) _____, and (c) _____ costs incurred in producing the product.

Manufacturing Company

Chip Making Systems Income Statement For Year Ended December 31, 2004		
Sales..		$200,000
Cost of goods sold:		
Finished goods inventory, December 31, 2003.........................	$ 10,000	
[BLANK]...	120,000	
Goods available for sale..	130,000	
Finished goods inventory, December 31, 2004.........................	(40,000)	
Cost of goods sold		90,000
Gross profit		$110,000

Merchandising Company

Joe's Shoe Outlet Income Statement For Year Ended December 31, 2004		
Sales..		$190,000
Cost of goods sold:		
Merchandise inventory, December 31, 2003	$ 12,000	
[BLANK]...	108,000	
Cost of goods available for sale...	120,000	
Merchandise inventory, December 31, 2004	(40,000)	
Cost of goods sold		80,000
Gross profit		$110,000

SOLUTION TO Demonstration Problem #1

1. *Manufacturing Company*

Chip Making Systems Balance Sheet December 31, 2004	
Assets	
Current assets:	
Cash	$10,000
[Raw materials inventory]	8,000
[Goods in process inventory]	5,000
[Finished goods inventory]	7,000
Supplies	500
Prepaid insurance	500
Total current assets	$31,000

Merchandising Company

Joe's Shoe Outlet Balance Sheet December 31, 2004	
Assets	
Current assets:	
Cash	$ 5,000
[Merchandise inventory]	12,000
Supplies	500
Prepaid insurance	500
Total current assets	$18,000

A different presentation is required for manufacturing and merchandising companies because they handle different types of inventory. A merchandising company handles only one type of inventory, called merchandise inventory, whereas a manufacturing firm handles three types of inventory: raw materials, goods in process, and finished goods. To efficiently manage each type of inventory, a manufacturing firm must record them separately.

2. *Manufacturing Company*

Chip Making Systems Income Statement For Year Ended December 31, 2004		
Sales..		$200,000
Cost of goods sold:		
Finished goods inventory, December 31, 2003	$ 10,000	
[Cost of goods manufactured]...	120,000	
Goods available for sale	130,000	
Finished goods inventory, December 31, 2004	(40,000)	
Cost of goods sold		90,000
Gross profit..		$110,000

Merchandising Company

Joe's Shoe Outlet		
Income Statement		
For Year Ended December 31, 2004		
Sales..		$190,000
Cost of goods sold:		
Merchandise inventory, December 31, 2003..........................	$ 12,000	
[Cost of merchandise purchased]...	108,000	
Goods available for sale	120,000	
Merchandise inventory, December 31, 2004..........................	(40,000)	
Cost of goods sold		80,000
Gross profit...		$110,000

A separate presentation is required because the goods available for sale by a manufacturing company are produced within the company and incur manufacturing costs, whereas the goods available for sale in a merchandising company are purchased from outside and incur purchasing costs. The cost of goods manufactured is the sum of *direct materials*, *direct labour*, and *factory (or manufacturing) overhead* costs.

Demonstration Problem #2

Terms and Reporting for a Manufacturing Business

The following account balances and other information were taken from the accounting records of Sunny Corporation for the year ended December 31, 2004. Use the information to prepare a schedule of factory overhead costs, a manufacturing statement (show only the total factory overhead cost), and an income statement.

Advertising expense..	$ 85,000
Amortization of patents	16,000
Bad debts expense...	28,000
Amortization expense, office equipment	37,000
Amortization of factory building..	133,000
Amortization of factory equipment...	78,000
Direct labour...	250,000
Factory insurance expired	62,000
Factory supervision	74,000
Factory supplies used..	21,000
Factory utilities	115,000
Finished goods inventory, December 31, 2003...........................	15,000
Finished goods inventory, December 31, 2004...........................	12,500
Goods in process inventory, December 31, 2003	8,000
Goods in process inventory, December 31, 2004	9,000
Income taxes expense	53,400
Indirect labour...	26,000
Interest expense	25,000
Miscellaneous expense..	55,000
Property taxes on factory	14,000
Raw materials inventory, December 31, 2003	60,000
Raw materials inventory, December 31, 2004	78,000
Raw materials purchases	313,000
Repairs, factory equipment	31,000
Salaries expense	150,000
Sales..	1,630,000

Planning the Solution

○ Analyze the list of the costs and select those items that are factory overhead.

○ Arrange these costs in a schedule of factory overhead costs for 2004.

○ Analyze the items remaining on the list and select the ones related to production activity for the year; the selected items should include the materials and goods in process inventories and direct labour.

○ Prepare a manufacturing statement for 2004 showing the calculation of the cost of materials used in production, the cost of direct labour, and the total factory overhead cost. When presenting the overhead cost on this statement, show only the total overhead cost from the schedule of overhead costs for 2004. Then, show the costs of the beginning and ending goods in process inventory to determine the total cost of goods manufactured. Be certain to include the proper title.

○ Combine the remaining revenue and expense items from the list into the income statement for 2004. Combine the cost of goods manufactured from the manufacturing statement with the finished goods inventory amounts to compute the cost of goods sold for 2004.

SOLUTION TO Demonstration Problem #2

Sunny Corporation
Schedule of Factory Overhead Costs
For Year Ended December 31, 2004

Amortization of patents	$ 16,000
Amortization of factory building	133,000
Amortization of factory equipment	78,000
Factory insurance expired	62,000
Factory supervision	74,000
Factory supplies used	21,000
Factory utilities	115,000
Indirect labour	26,000
Property taxes on factory	14,000
Repairs, factory equipment	31,000
Total factory overhead	$570,000

Sunny Corporation
Manufacturing Statement
For Year Ended December 31, 2004

Direct materials:		
Raw materials inventory, December 31, 2001	$ 60,000	
Raw materials purchases	313,000	
Raw materials available for use	373,000	
Raw materials inventory, December 31, 2002	(78,000)	
Direct materials used		$ 295,000
Direct labour		250,000
Factory overhead costs		570,000
Total manufacturing costs		1,115,000
Goods in process inventory, December 31, 2001		8,000
Total goods in process		1,123,000
Goods in process inventory, December 31, 2002		(9,000)
Cost of goods manufactured		$1,114,000

Sunny Corporation
Income Statement
For Year Ended December 31, 2004

Sales		$1,630,000
Cost of goods sold:		
Finished goods inventory, December 31, 2003	$ 15,000	
Cost of goods manufactured	1,114,000	
Goods available for sale	1,129,000	
Finished goods inventory, December 31, 2004	(12,500)	
Cost of goods sold		(1,116,500)
Gross profit		513,500
Operating expenses:		
Advertising expense	85,000	
Bad debts expense	28,000	
Amortization expense, office equipment	37,000	
Miscellaneous expense	55,000	
Salaries expense	150,000	
Total operating expenses		(355,000)
Income from operations		158,500
Interest expense		(25,000)
Income before income taxes		133,500
Income taxes expense		(53,400)
Net income		$ 80,100

Glossary

Control The process of monitoring planning decisions and evaluating the organization's activities and employees. (p. 1093)

Controllable or not controllable costs A cost is controllable or not controllable depending on a manager's responsibilities and whether or not they are in a position to make decisions on expenditures. (p. 1100)

Conversion costs Expenditures incurred in the process of converting raw materials to finished goods. They include direct labour costs and factory overhead costs. (p. 1110)

Cost object A product, process, department, or customer to which costs are assigned. (p. 1100)

Direct cost Costs that are incurred for the benefit of one specific cost object. (p. 1100)

Direct labour Efforts of employees who physically convert materials to finished product. (p. 1110)

Direct labour costs Wages and salaries for direct labour that are separately and readily traced through the manufacturing process to finished goods. (p. 1110)

Direct materials Raw materials that physically become part of the product and therefore are clearly identified with specific units or batches of product. (p. 1107)

Direct material costs Expenditures for direct materials that are separately and readily traced through the manufacturing process to finished goods. (p. 1110)

Factory overhead Factory activities supporting the manufacturing process that are not direct materials or direct labour. (p. 1110)

Factory overhead costs Expenditures for factory overhead that cannot be separately or readily traced to finished goods. (p. 1110)

Finished goods inventory Products that have completed the manufacturing process and are ready to be sold by the manufacturer. (p. 1108)

Fixed cost The cost does not change with changes in the volume of an activity. (p. 1099)

Goods in process inventory Products that are in the process of being manufactured but that are not yet complete (also called *work in process inventory*). (p. 1108)

Implementation The process of ensuring that the plans are carried out; involves developing actions, and directing and motivating employees. (p. 1093)

Indirect cost Costs that are incurred for the benefit of more than one cost object. (p. 1100)

Indirect labour Efforts of manufacturing employees who do not work specifically on converting direct materials into finished products and that are not clearly associated with specific units or batches of product. (p. 1110)

Indirect materials Materials that are used in support of the production process but that do not become a part of the product and are not clearly identified with units or batches of product. (p. 1108)

Just-in-time (JIT) A system whereby a company acquires or produces inventory only when needed. (p. 1098)

Lean business practices Includes practices such as just-in-time, total quality management, and theory of constraints which are designed to reduce waste in an organization. (p. 1098)

Management accounting See *managerial accounting.*

Managerial accounting The collecting, managing, and processing of financial and nonfinancial information for use by managers and other internal decision makers of an organization. (p. 1092)

Manufacturing cost A cost that is necessary and integral towards the production of finished goods. (p. 1101)

Manufacturing statement A statement that summarizes the types and amounts of costs incurred by a company during a given period for its manufacturing process; also called the *schedule of manufacturing activities* or the *schedule of goods manufactured.* (p. 1112)

Non-manufacturing cost A cost that is not integral to the production of finished goods. (p. 1101)

Opportunity costs The potential benefit lost by taking a specific action out of two or more alternative choices. (p. 1101)

Out-of-pocket cost A cost requiring a future outlay of cash. (p. 1101)

Period costs Expenditures identified more with a time period than with finished products costs. Includes selling and general administration expenses. (p. 1101)

Planning The process of setting goals and making plans to achieve them. (p. 1092)

Prime costs Expenditures directly associated with the manufacturing of finished goods. They include direct material costs and direct labour costs. (p. 1110)

Product costs Costs that are capitalized as inventory because they produce benefits that are expected to have value in the future. They include direct materials, direct labour, and factory overhead costs. (p. 1101)

Raw materials Materials that are purchased for use in manufacturing a product; those that become an integral part of the finished product are called direct materials, and the others are called indirect materials. (p. 1112)

Raw materials inventory The goods a company acquires to use in making products. (p. 1107)

Relevant Cost A cost that influences or has a bearing on a certain decision. (p. 1100)

Sunk cost A cost already incurred and that cannot be avoided or changed. (p. 1100)

Theory of constraints (TOC) The process of identifying factors that constrain or limit a company's operations. (p. 1098)

Throughput The added value (selling price minus direct material costs) of finished products processed through the system. (p. 1098)

Total Quality Management (TQM) A management process that achieves continuous improvement by relentlessly focusing on improving quality everywhere in the organization. (p. 1098)

Unit contribution margin A product's sale price less its total variable costs per unit. (p. 1099)

Variable cost The cost changes in proportion to changes in the volume of an activity. (p. 1099)

For more study tools, quizzes, and problem material,
refer to the Online Learning Centre at
www.mcgrawhill.ca/college/larson

Questions

1. Discuss the role of the management accountant in planning, implementation, and control.
2. Distinguish between managerial and financial accounting on the elements of:
   a. users and decision makers,
   b. purposes of information,
   c. flexibility of practice,
   d. time dimension, and
   e. focus of information.
3. Explain the difference between a manufacturing company and that of merchandising and service companies.
4. Why is managerial accounting required to work with numerous predictions?
5. Identify the changes a company must make when it decides to adopt lean business practices.
6. Explain why understanding cost behaviour is useful in performance evaluation.
7. Should we evaluate a manager's performance on the basis of controllable or uncontrollable costs? Why?
8. Explain why product costs are capitalized but period costs are expensed in the current accounting period.
9. How do the financial reports of a manufacturing firm differ from those of a merchandising firm?
10. Identify three inventory components that typically appear on the balance sheet of a manufacturer.
11. Besides inventories, what other assets often appear on balance sheets of manufacturers but not on balance sheets of merchandisers?

12. Why does a manufacturing firm require three different inventory categories?
13. Distinguish between direct material and indirect material.
14. Explain the difference between direct labour and indirect labour.
15. Distinguish between factory overhead and selling and administrative overhead.
16. What product cost is listed as both a prime cost and a conversion cost?
17. Assume you complete a tour of **NIKE's** factory where they make basketball shoes for Canadian university teams. List three direct costs and three indirect costs you are likely to see.
18. List examples of factory overhead costs.
19. What is the difference between factory overhead and selling and administrative overhead?
20. List the components of a manufacturing statement for a manufacturer of running shoes and provide specific examples of each component.
21. Does the date of a manufacturing statement match the balance sheet or income statement? Why?
22. Describe the relationships among income statement, the manufacturing statement, and a detailed schedule of factory overhead costs.
23. If **NIKE** were to set up a manufacturing operation in Calgary, what inventories would you expect the company to hold?

Quick Study

Managerial accounting:
a. Must follow generally accepted accounting principles.
b. Is directed at reporting aggregate data on the company as a whole.
c. Provides information that is widely available to all interested parties.
d. Provides information to aid management in planning, implementing, and controlling business operations.

QS 21-1
Managerial accounting defined

LO[1]

State whether each of the following most likely describes financial accounting or managerial accounting:
a. ____ Its principles and practices tends to be very flexible.
b. ____ Its users are company managers.
c. ____ Its primary focus is on the organization as a whole.
d. ____ Its information is available only after an audit is complete.
e. ____ It is directed at external users in making investment, credit, and other decisions.

QS 21-2
Managerial accounting versus financial accounting

LO[2]

QS 21-3
Describing lean business practices

LO³

Match each of the lean business practices with the phrase that best describes it by filling in the blank with the appropriate letter:

1. ____ Total quality management
2. ____ Just-in-time manufacturing
3. ____ Theory of constraints
4. ____ Continuous improvement

a. Focuses on factors that limit business operations.
b. Inventory is acquired or produced only as needed.
c. Every manager and employee constantly looks for ways to improve company operations.
d. Focuses on quality throughout the entire organization.

QS 21-4
Describing fixed and variable costs

LO⁴

Which one of these statements is true regarding fixed and variable costs?
a. Fixed and variable costs stay the same in total as activity volume increases.
b. Fixed and variable cost increase as activity volume increases.
c. Fixed costs stay the same and variable cost increase in total as activity volume increases.
d. Fixed cost increase and variable costs decrease in total as activity volume decreases.

QS 21-5
Describing product and period costs

LO⁵

Which one of these statements is true regarding product and period costs?
a. Sales commission is a product cost and factory rent is a period cost.
b. Factory wages is a product cost and direct materials is a period cost.
c. Factory repair and maintenance is a product cost and sales commission is a period cost.
d. Sales commission is a product cost and amortization on factory equipment is a product cost.

QS 21-6
Identify manufacturing flow

LO⁶

Identify the usual sequence of manufacturing activities by filling in the blank (1, 2, or 3) corresponding to its order: _____ Production activities _____ Marketing activities _____ Materials activities.

QS 21-7
Reporting inventory for manufacturers

LO⁶,⁷

Three inventory categories are reported on a manufacturing company's balance sheet: (1) raw materials, (2) goods in process inventory, and (3) finished goods. Identify the order in which these inventory items are normally reported on the balance sheet.
a. (2)(1)(3)
b. (1)(2)(3)
c. (2)(3)(1)
d. (3)(2)(1)

QS 21-8
Calculate cost of goods sold

LO⁹

For the month end, Book Time recorded its cost of goods manufactured as $6,000. It also has beginning finished goods inventory of $800 and ending finished goods inventory of $950. The cost of goods sold is:
a. $4,800
b. $6,800
c. $5,850
d. $4,950

QS 21-9
Calculate cost of goods sold

LO⁹

Calculate cost of goods sold using the following information:

Finished goods inventory, December 31, 2003	$ 450,100
Goods in process inventory, December 31, 2003	104,370
Goods in process inventory, December 31, 2004	113,680
Cost of goods manufactured, 2004	1,361,283
Finished goods inventory, December 31, 2004	416, 080

Monroe Company's manufacturing statement includes the following information. Determine the cost of goods manufactured.

Direct materials used	$175,650
Direct labour..	66,300
Total factory overhead costs...........................	24,720
Selling and administration expenses..............	24,300
Goods in process, December 31, 2003..........	295,200
Goods in process, December 31, 2004...........	224,210

QS 21-10
Determine Cost of Goods Manufactured

LO^{10}

Exercises

Both managerial accounting and financial accounting provide useful information to decision makers. Indicate in this chart the most likely source of information for each business decision (a decision can require major input from both sources):

Business Decision	Accounting Information Source	
	Managerial	**Financial**
Place more emphasis on precision.		
Prepare financial reports to GAAP.		
Plan the budget for the next quarter.		
Present financial performance to the board of directors.		
Measure profitability of all individual stores.		
Estimate product cost for a new line of ladies purses.		
Determine amount of dividends to pay common shareholders.		
Determine location and size for a new plant.		
Evaluate a purchasing department's performance.		

Exercise 21-1
Sources of accounting information

LO^{1}

Complete the following by filling in the blanks:
1. _____ is the process of setting goals and making plans to achieve them.
2. _____ is a process of monitoring planning decisions and evaluating an organization's activities and its employees.
3. _____ usually covers a period of one, five or ten years.
4. _____ is the process of carrying out action plans.

Exercise 21-2
Planning, implementation and control descriptions

LO^{1}

Complete the chart below comparing financial and managerial accounting. Be specific in your response and *write down* your answer to how both areas of accounting deal with each of the items listed. Experience shows writing out your response increases your likelihood of understanding it.

	Financial Accounting	**Managerial Accounting**
1. Users and decision makers		
2. Purpose of information		
3. Flexibility of practice		
4. Timeliness of information		
5. Time dimension		
6. Focus on information		
7. Nature of information		

Exercise 21-3
Characteristics of financial accounting and managerial accounting

LO^{2}

Exercise 21-4
Identify lean business practices

LO³

The chart below lists recent developments in management accounting systems for four companies (treat each item separately). Match the lean business practice(s) that is (are) likely to be adopted by each company for the recent development identified.

Match	Recent Developments	Lean Business Practices
_____ 1.	The company starts measuring inventory turnover and discontinues elaborate inventory records. Its new focus is to pull inventory through the system.	a. Time quality management (TQM)
_____ 2.	The company starts reporting measures such as the percent of defective products and the number of units scrapped.	b. Theory of constraints (TOC) c. Continuous improvement (CI) d. Just-in-time (JIT)
_____ 3.	The company starts a program focusing on its bottlenecks.	

Exercise 21-5
Focus on the customer

LO³

Customer focus means a company's managers and employees are responding to changing wants and needs of consumers. You are to stop at a restaurant, hotel, or other local business in your area and pick up a customer response card. On the right-hand side of a blank sheet of paper write down the competitive forces: time, quality, cost, and flexibility of service. Attach the customer response card to the left side of the sheet. Draw arrows linking questions of the customer response card to the competitive forces. Identify how the response card provides information to management and employees to better meet competitive forces. Be prepared to form small groups to compare and contrast the type of business and customer response cards across the types of businesses.

Exercise 21-6
Critical thinking about cost classifications

LO⁴

Identify each of the five cost accounting concepts discussed in the chapter. Explain the purposes of identifying these separate cost accounting concepts.

Exercise 21-7
Analyze and identify costs

LO⁴,⁵

The following costs are incurred by Cable & Wireless, a manufacturing company. Classify each cost as either a product or period cost. If a product cost, further classify it as a prime and/or conversion cost and also as a direct or indirect cost.

	Product Cost				
	Prime Cost	Conversion Cost	Direct Cost	Indirect Cost	Period Cost
Direct materials used (example)	×	×			
Provincial and federal income taxes			×		
Payroll taxes for production supervisor					
Amortization of patents on factory machine					
Accident insurance on factory workers*					
Wages to assembly workers**					
Factory utilities					
Small tools used					
Bad debts expense					
Amortization of factory building					
Advertising					
Office supplies used					

Listed below are *product costs* for the production of 1,000 soccer balls. Classify each cost as either fixed or variable and as either direct or indirect. What pattern do you see regarding the relation between costs classified by behaviour and costs classified by traceability?

Product Cost	Cost By Behaviour		Cost By Traceability	
	Variable	Fixed	Direct	Indirect
Wages of assembly workers				
Annual flat fee paid to Security Ltd.				
Water for cooling machine				
Machinery amortization				
Leather cover for soccer balls				
Lace to hold leather together				
Taxes on factory				

Exercise 21-8
Analyze and categorize costs

LO[4,5]

The following partially completed flowchart shows how costs flow through a business as the product is manufactured. Some of the boxes in the flowchart show cost amounts while other boxes contain question marks. Compute the cost that should appear in each box containing a question mark.

Exercise 21-9
Understanding the manufacturing process

LO[6]

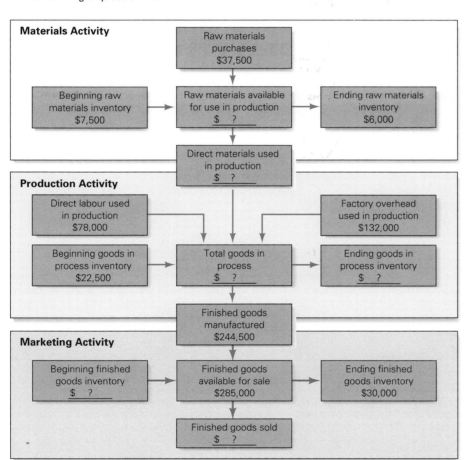

Exercise 21-10
Identify and prepare balance sheets

LO⁷

Current assets for two different companies at the end of 2004 are listed below. One is a manufacturer, Roller Blades Co., and the other, Wholesale Distribution Co., is a grocery distribution company.

Required
1. Identify which set of numbers relates to the manufacturer and which to the merchandiser.
2. Prepare the current asset section of a balance sheet for each company from the following information. Discuss why the current asset sections are different for these two companies.

Account	Company 1	Company 2
Cash	$ 6,000	$ 9,000
Raw materials		65,000
Merchandise inventory	45,000	
Goods in process		45,000
Finished goods		20,000
Prepaid expenses	2,000	1,000
Accounts receivable	54,000	82,000

Exercise 21-11
Identify and prepare income statements

LO⁸, ⁹

Calculate cost of goods sold for each of these two companies for the year ended December 31, 2004:

	Landry Retail Company	Stravka Manufacturing Company
Beginning Inventory:		
Merchandise	$350,000	
Finished goods		$ 700,00
Cost of purchases	644,000	
Cost of goods manufactured		1,240,400
Ending inventory:		
Merchandise	210,000	
Finished goods		201,600

Exercise 21-12
Identify and prepare income statements

LO⁸, ⁹

On January 1, 2004, Ryder Company had no inventories. During January Ryder purchased 9,000 auto batteries at $12 each. A total of 8,200 batteries were taken from the factory storeroom during the month. Eighty of these batteries were placed in autos that were supplied to company sales personnel and the remaining batteries were placed in autos that were being manufactured for sale. Twelve and a half percent of finished autos were still on hand at the end of January. Eighty percent of autos placed into production during January were completed and transferred from goods in process inventory to finished goods inventory.

Required
Calculate the costs of goods sold during January.

Exercise 21-13
Identify and prepare income statements

LO⁸

Refer to exercise 21-12.

Required
How should we account for the cost of the batteries supplied to the sales personnel?

The following information is taken from the accounting records of Jinks Company and O'Neill Company.

	Jinks Company	O'Neill Company
Beginning finished goods inventory	$14,000	$16,600
Beginning goods in process inventory	11,500	19,000
Beginning raw materials inventory	5,400	7,240
Lease on factory equipment	24,000	36,000
Direct labour	12,000	14,000
Ending finished goods inventory	10,300	13,800
Ending goods in process inventory	13,400	16,000
Ending raw materials inventory	4,400	3,600
Factory utilities	7,000	4,400
Factory supplies used	3,500	4,600
General and administrative expenses	34,000	50,000
Indirect labour	1,300	1,910
Repairs, factory equipment	3,290	5,050
Raw materials purchases	28,000	33,600
Sales salaries	30,000	28,000

Compute the cost of goods manufactured and the cost of goods sold for each company.

Exercise 21-14
Computing cost of goods manufactured and cost of goods sold

LO6, 9, 10

For each of the following account balances in a manufacturing company's ledger, indicate by a ✓ in the appropriate column whether it will appear on the balance sheet, the income statement, the manufacturing statement, or a detailed schedule of factory overhead costs. Assume that the income statement shows the calculation of cost of goods sold and the manufacturing statement shows only the total amount of factory overhead.

Note that an account balance may appear on more than one report. For example, the ending inventory of finished goods appears on both the balance sheet and the income statement.

Exercise 21-15
Identifying components of financial statements

LO7, 8, 10

Account	Balance Sheet	Income Statement	Manufacturing Statement	Overhead Schedule
Cash				
Beginning finished goods inventory				
Beginning goods in process inventory				
Beginning raw materials inventory				
Supplies for marketing department				
Accounts receivable				
Amortization of factory building				
Amortization of factory equipment				
Amortization expense, office building				
Amortization expense, office equipment				
Direct labour				
Ending finished goods inventory				
Ending goods in process inventory				
Ending raw materials inventory				
Factory supervision				
Factory supplies used				
Income taxes				
Insurance on factory building				
Insurance expense, office building				
Sales				
Property taxes on factory building				
Raw materials purchases				
Office supplies used				

Exercise 21-16
Preparing a manufacturing statement

LO[10]

After Gabriel Corporation posted its adjusting entries on December 31, 2004, the General Ledger included the following account balances. (Some accounts in the General Ledger have not been listed.)

Raw materials inventory, December 31, 2003	$ 38,000
Goods in process inventory, December 31, 2003	42,525
Sales	912,500
Finished goods inventory, December 31, 2003	55,175
Raw materials purchases	114,825
Direct labour	146,650
Factory supplies used	13,400
Indirect labour	32,200
Repairs, factory equipment	6,000
Rent on factory building	48,500
Advertising expenses	90,300
General and administrative expenses	97,750

The ending inventories are:

Raw materials inventory, December 31, 2004	$34,625
Goods in process inventory, December 31, 2004	33,350
Finished goods inventory, December 31, 2004	44,450

Given this information, prepare a manufacturing statement for Gabriel Corporation. Include the individual overhead account balances in this statement and be certain to begin the statement with the proper title.

Use the information provided in Exercise 21-16 to prepare an income statement for Gabriel Corporation. Assume that the cost of goods manufactured is $365,625.

Exercise 21-17
Preparing a manufacturing company's income statement

LO$^{8,\,10}$

Problems

This chapter begins with a discussion of the objectives of managerial accounting along with a discussion on the current business environment. You are to look through the *automobile* section of your local newspaper. Devote special attention to advertisements of sport utility vehicles and take note of how many manufacturers offer these products and what factors they compete on.

Problem 21-1A
Evaluate management accountant's role

LO^3

Required
Discuss the potential contributions and responsibilities of the managerial accounting professional in helping an automobile manufacturing company. (Hint: Think about estimates a management accountant might provide new entrants into the sports utility market.)

A trip through a drive-up window of any leading fast food restaurant is useful in understanding lean business practices such as total quality management (TQM), just-in-time (JIT), and theory of constraints (TOC). Each restaurant can be viewed as a small manufacturing plant. List two fast food restaurants you are familiar with in the first column of the table below (examples include McDonald's, Taco Bell, Burger King, KFC, and Tim Hortons). Record in the following table how each company is putting each of these principles into action, both favourably and unfavourably.

Problem 21-2A
Lean business practices

LO^3

Restaurant	TQM	JIT	TOC

Problem 21-3A
Compute, classify, and
analyze costs

LO 4, 5, 11

Listed below are costs for the production of 1,000 drum sets manufactured by Big Sound Ltd. They sell for $420 each.

Costs	Cost By Behaviour		Cost By Function	
	Variable	Fixed	Product	Period
Plastic for casing—$16,800	16,800		16,800	
Wages to assembly workers—$85,200				
Taxes on factory—$6,300				
Accounting staff's salary—$40,000				
Drum stands (1,000 stands outsourced)—$35,000				
Lease on equipment for sales staff—$9,800				
Upper-management salaries—$140,000				
Annual flat fee for security service—$12,600				
Sales commission—$10 per unit				
Machinery amortization—$80,000				

Check figure:
Total variable costs: $147,000

Required

Preparation component
1. Classify costs and their amounts as (a) either fixed or variable, and (b) product or period (the first cost is completed as an example).
2. Delete "35%" in the last column of the row showing "sales commission."
3. Insert a new row in between "sales commission" and "contribution margin." In the newly inserted row, write "Total variable costs" in the first column and "35%" in the last column.

Big Sound Ltd. Contribution Margin Income Statement For the Year Ended December 31, 2004			
Sales ($420 × 1000)			100%
Variable costs			
Plastic for casing			
Wages for assembly			
Out-sourced drum stands			
Sales commission			35%
Contribution Margin			Contribution Margin Ratio* %

*contribution ratio = contribution margin/sales

Analysis component
4. What can we interpret from the contribution margin and the contribution margin ratio?

Refer to the Judgement Call entitled "Purchase Manager" in this chapter. Assume you are the managerial accountant for a motorcycle manufacturer. The purchasing manager asks you about preparing an estimate of the related costs for buying motorcycle seats from supplier (B). She tells you this estimate is needed because unless dollar estimates are attached to nonfinancial factors, such as lost production costs, her supervisor does not give it full attention. The purchase manager also shows you the following information:

1. Production output is 1,000 motorcycles per year based on 250 production days a year.
2. Production time per day is 8 hours at a cost of $2,000 per hour to run the production line.
3. Lost production time due to poor quality is 1%.
4. Satisfied customers purchase, on average, three motorcycles during their lifetime.
5. Satisfied customers recommend, on average, the product to five other people.
6. Marketing estimates that moving to seat (B) will result is five lost customers per year from repeat business and referrals.
7. Average contribution margin per motorcycle is $3,000.

Required

Estimate the costs of buying motorcycle seats from supplier (B). This problem requires you to think creatively and make reasonable estimates and, therefore, there is more than one correct answer. [Hint: Re-read the answer to the original Judgement Call, and also think about costs of lost production time, repeat business, and other similar factors.]

Problem 21-4A
Projecting and estimating opportunity costs

LO^4

Check figure:
Cost of lost production, $40,000

Quality Boots Company makes specialty boots for the rodeo circuit. On December 31, 2003, the company had (a) 700 boots in ending inventory valued at $140 per pair and (b) 2,100 heels valued at $7 each in raw materials inventory for boots to be made. During 2004 the company purchased 70,000 heels at $7 each and manufactured 28,000 pairs of boots.

Required

Preparation component
1. Determine the unit and dollar amounts of raw materials inventory of heels at December 31, 2004.

Analysis component
2. Write a one-page memo to the production manager outlining why a just-in-time inventory management program for heels should be considered. Include in your memo the amount of working capital that can be reduced by December 31, 2004, if the ending heel raw material inventory is cut in half.

Problem 21-5A
Calculate and evaluate ending inventory

$LO^{3,7}$

Check figure:
Ending heel inventory, $112,700

Listed below are financial data at December 31, 2004, taken from two different companies.

	Sport World Retail	DuraBlade Manufacturing
Beginning Inventory:		
Merchandise	$210,000	
Finished goods		$420,000
Cost of purchases	350,000	
Cost of goods manufactured		820,400
Ending inventory:		
Merchandise	140,000	
Finished goods		280,000

Required

1. Calculate cost of goods sold at December 31, 2004, for each of the two companies. Include proper title and format in your solution.
2. Write a memo to your instructor (1) identifying the inventory accounts, and (2) describing where each is reported on the income statement and balance sheet.

Problem 21-6A
Calculate and evaluate inventory values

$LO^{7,8,9}$

Check figure:
DuraBlade Cost of goods sold, $960,400

Problem 21-7A
Explaining and contrasting costs

$LO^{5, 9}$

You must make a presentation to the marketing staff explaining the difference between product and period cost. Your supervisor tells you that the staff would like clarification regarding prime and conversion costs and an explanation of how these terms fit with product and period cost. You are told that many of the staff are unable to identify with these terms in their merchandising activities.

Required
Write a one-page memorandum in proper form to your supervisor outlining your presentation to this group.

Problem 21-8A
Preparing manufacturing and income statements

$LO^{8, 10}$

The following alphabetical list of items was taken from the adjusted trial balance and other records of Greer Company before the 2004 year-end closing entries were recorded:

Advertising expense	$ 16,200
Amortization expense, office equipment	6,750
Amortization expense, selling equipment	8,100
Amortization of factory equipment	28,350
Direct labour	523,800
Factory supervision	97,200
Factory supplies used	14,850
Factory utilities	27,000
Income taxes expense	109,350
Indirect labour	47,250
Inventories:	
Raw materials, January 1	132,300
Raw materials, December 31	136,350
Goods in process, January 1	10,700
Goods in process, December 31	11,250
Finished goods, January 1	141,750
Finished goods, December 31	113,400
Miscellaneous production costs	6,750
Office salaries expense	56,700
Raw materials purchases	695,250
Rent expense, office space	18,900
Rent expense, selling space	21,600
Rent on factory building	64,800
Maintenance, factory equipment	24,300
Sales	2,431,350
Sales discounts	45,900
Sales salaries expense	236,250
Transportation-in on raw materials	20,250

Check figure:
Cost of goods manufactured, $1,545,200

Required

Preparation component
1. Prepare a manufacturing statement and an income statement for the company. The income statement should present separate categories for (a) selling expenses and (b) general and administrative expenses.

Analysis component
2. Review what you learned about merchandise turnover (chapter 20) and compute the turnover rates for Greer's raw materials and finished goods inventories. Then, discuss some possible reasons for the differences between the turnover rates for the two inventories.

Park N Shoppe grocery store chain, a market leader, is trying to increase sales to its existing customers by creating a customer orientation in meeting buyer needs and wants. Assume you are hired as a consultant by Park N Shoppe to analyze its operations and suggest improvements. Park N Shoppe wants to increase its contribution margin by $56,000.

Required
1. To increase sales and total contribution margin from existing customers of Park N Shoppe, offer three improvements that you have observed in other stores and feel would be successful at Park N Shoppe.
2. What level of increase in sales is necessary for Park N Shoppe to increase total contribution margin by $56,000? (Hint: With each suggestion in (1), identify the expected sales dollars and contribution margin ratios to meet the $56,000 increase in contribution margin).

Problem 21-9A
Projecting and estimating sales and costs; contribution margin analysis

$LO^{3, 11}$

Alternate Problems

The chapter begins with a discussion of the objectives of management and cost accounting. You are to look through the *home electronics* section of your local newspaper, the weekend paper is often best. Review advertisements of home electronics and take note of how many times manufacturers offer these products and on what factors they compete.

Required
What is the responsibility of the management accountant in helping a home electronics manufacturing company succeed in our current business environment? (Hint: Think about information and estimates a managerial accountant might provide new entrants into the home electronics market.)

Problem 21-1B
Evaluate managerial accountant's role

$LO^{1, 3}$

A trip to the photography store can be used to learn about lean business practices such as total quality management (TQM), just-in-time (JIT), and theory of constraints (TOC). List two photography stores you are familiar with in the first column of the table below. Record in the table how each store is putting each of these principles into action, both favourably and unfavourably. (Hint: To prepare a response to this question you may want to watch how film is processed and prints prepared within one hour).

Problem 21-2B
Lean business practices

LO^3

Photography Store	TQM	JIT	TOC

Problem 21-3B
Compute, classify, and
analyze costs

LO^{4,5}

Listed below are costs for the production of 12,000 CDs manufactured by Down Home Music Inc. They sell for $15 each.

Costs	Cost By Behaviour		Cost By Function	
	Variable	Fixed	Product	Period
Plastic for CDs—$1,000	1,000		1,000	
Wages to assembly workers—$21,700				
Machinery amortization—$15,000				
Rent on factory—$4,500				
Systems staff's salary—$10,000				
Labeling (12,000 outsourced)—$2,500				
Lease on office equipment—$700				
Upper-management salaries—$100,000				
Annual fee for factory cleaning service—$3,000				
Sales commissions—$0.50 per CD				

Check figure:
Total variable costs: $31,200

Required

Preparation component
1. Classify the costs as (a) either fixed or variable and (b) either product or period.
2. Compute the (a) contribution margin and (b) contribution margin ratio by filling in the blanks in the following table.
3. Delete "17%" in the last column of the row showing "sales commission."
4. Insert a new row in between "sales commission" and "contribution margin." In the newly inserted row, write "Total variable costs" in the first column and "17%" in the last column.

Down Home Music Inc. Contribution Margin Income Statement For Year Ended December 31, 2004			
Sales ($15 × 12,000)			100%
Variable costs			
Plastic for CDs			
Wages of assembly workers			
Labels outsourced			
Sales commission			17%
Contribution Margin			Contribution Margin Ratio* %

*contribution ratio = contribution margin/sales

Analysis component
5. What can we interpret from the contribution margin and contribution margin ratio?

Refer to the Judgement Call entitled "Purchase Manager" in this chapter. Assume you are the managerial accountant for the motorcycle company. The purchasing manager asks you about preparing an estimate of the related costs for buying motorcycle seats from supplier (B). She tells you this estimate is needed because unless dollar estimates are attached to nonfinancial factors, such as lost production costs, her supervisor will not give it full attention. The purchase manager also shows you the following information:

1. Production is 1,000 motorcycles per year based on 250 production days a year.
2. Production time per day is 8 hours at a cost of $1,500 per hour to run the production line.
3. Lost production time due to poor quality is 1%.
4. Satisfied customers purchase, on average, three motorcycles during their lifetime.
5. Satisfied customers recommend, on average, the product to four other people.
6. Marketing estimates that moving to seat (B) will result is four lost customers per year from repeat business and referrals.
7. Average contribution margin per motorcycle is $4,000.

Required

Estimate the costs of buying motorcycle seats from supplier (B). This problem requires you to think creatively and make reasonable estimates and, therefore, there is more than one correct answer. [Hint: Re-read the answer to the original Judgement Call, and also think about costs of lost production time, repeat business, and other similar factors.]

Problem 21-4B
Projecting and estimating opportunity costs

LO^{1,4}

Check figure:
Cost of lost production, $30,000

Candle Skate, Inc. makes specialty skates for the ice skating circuit. On December 31, 2003, the company had (a) 2,100 skates in ending inventory valued at $280 per pair and (b) 2,800 blades valued at $21.00 each in raw materials inventory for skates to be made. During 2004 Candle Skate, Inc purchased 63,000 blades at $21.00 each and manufactured 28,000 pairs of skates.

Required

Preparation component
1. Determine the value of the skate raw materials inventory at December 31, 2004.

Analysis component
2. Write a one-page memo to the production manager outlining why a just-in-time inventory management program for blades should be considered. Include in your memo the amount of working capital that can be reduced by December 31, 2004, if the ending blade raw material inventory is cut in half.

Problem 21-5B
Compute and evaluate ending inventory

LO^{3,7}

Check figure:
Ending blade inventory, $205,800

Listed below are financial data at December 31, 2004, taken from two different companies.

	Sasktel Chips Retail	Digital Data Ltd. Manufacturing
Beginning Inventory:		
Merchandise..	$ 70,000	
Finished goods		$280,000
Cost of purchases	420,000	
Cost of goods manufactured...........................		960,400
Ending inventory:		
Merchandise..	35,000	
Finished goods		420,000

Required

1. Calculate cost of goods sold at December 31, 2004, for each of the two companies. Include proper title and format in your solution.
2. Write a memo to your instructor (1) identifying the inventory accounts and (2) describing where each are reported on the balance sheet.

Problem 21-6B
Calculate and evaluate inventory values

LO^{7,8,9}

Check figure:
Digital Data Cost of goods sold, $820,400

Problem 21-7B
Explaining and contrasting costs

LO⁹

You must make a presentation to a client explaining the difference between prime and conversion costs. The client makes and sells bread for 200,000 customers per week. The client tells you that the sales staff would like a clarification regarding product and period cost. She tells you that many on the staff have had financial accounting training but lack training in managerial accounting topics.

Required
Write a one-page memo in good form to your client outlining your planned presentation to the sales staff.

Problem 21-8B
Preparing manufacturing and income statements

LO⁸, ¹⁰

The following list of items was taken from the adjusted trial balance and other 2004 records of Inverness Building Supplies Ltd. before the year-end closing entries were recorded:

Factory utilities...	13,500
Direct labour	255,000
Freight on raw materials...................................	9,175
Income taxes expense......................................	94,560
Indirect labour..	23,625
Inventories:	
Raw materials, January 1	74,050
Raw materials, December 31	64,000
Goods in process, January 1	51,650
Goods in process, December 31	50,125
Finished goods, January 1	70,800
Finished goods, December 31	56,700
Miscellaneous production costs	3,375
Office salaries expense	28,350
Raw materials purchases..................................	347,625
Rent expense, office space	9,450
Rent expense, selling space	10,800
Rent on factory building....................................	32,400
Repairs to machinery..	12,300
Sales	1,312,675
Sales discounts...	23,350
Sales salaries expense......................................	118,125
Factory supervision..	48,600
Advertising expense	8,100
Amortization expense, Machinery	14,175
Amortization expense, Office equipment..........	3,375
Amortization of selling equipment....................	4,050
Factory supplies used.......................................	7,425

Check figure:
Cost of goods manufactured, $778,775

Required

Preparation component
1. Prepare a manufacturing statement and an income statement for the company. The income statement should present separate categories for (a) selling expenses and (b) general and administrative expenses.

Analysis component
2. Review what you learned about merchandise turnover (Chapter 20) and compute the turnover rates for Inverness's raw materials and finished goods inventory. Then, discuss some possible reasons for the differences between the turnover rates for the two inventories.

Delicious Donuts chain, a market leader, is trying to increase sales to its existing customers by creating a customer orientation in meeting buyer needs and wants. Assume you are hired as a consultant by Delicious Donuts to analyze its operations and suggest improvements. Delicious Donuts wants to increase its contribution margin by $14,000.

Required

1. To increase sales and total contribution margin from existing customers of Delicious Donuts offer three improvements that you have observed in other stores and feel would be successful at Delicious Donuts
2. What level of increase in sales is necessary for Delicious Donuts to increase total contribution margin by $14,000? (Hint: With each suggestion in (1), identify the expected sales dollars and contribution margin ratios to meet the $14,000 increase in contribution margin).

Problem 21-9B
Projecting and estimating sales and costs; contribution margin analysis

$LO^{1, 3, 11}$

Analytical and Review Problems

A & R Problem 21-1

Stevens Company has operated its manufacturing business for three years. It sells a single product. Annual sales have increased by 20% and 25% in the last two years but net income increased only by 7% and 15% respectively. The company president, Muctar Clair, has asked you to analyze the situation and tell him why profits have lagged behind sales. Clair is an expert in production but knows very little about accounting. Also, the company bookkeeper has only a limited knowledge of accounting for manufacturing.
   The company's condensed income statements for the past three years show:

	2002	2003	2004
Sales	$1,000,000	$1,200,000	$1,500,000
Cost of goods sold:			
Finished goods inventory, beginning	$ -0-	$ 66,000	$ 99,000
Cost of goods manufactured	330,000	437,500	628,000
Goods available for sale	$ 330,000	$ 503,500	$ 727,000
Finished goods inventory, ending	66,000	99,000	145,200
Cost of goods sold	$ 264,000	$ 404,500	$ 581,800
Gross profit from sales	$ 736,000	$ 795,500	$ 918,200
Selling and administrative expenses	160,000	180,000	217,500
Net income	$ 576,000	$ 615,500	$ 700,700

As you have checked into things, you have uncovered the following additional information:

a. The company sold 5,000 units of its product during the first year it was in business, 6,000 units during the second year, and 7,500 units during the third. All sales were priced at $200 per unit, and no discounts were granted.
b. The finished goods inventory consisted of 500 units at the end of the first year, 750 at the end of the second, and 1,100 at the end of the third.
c. The bookkeeper valued the units in each year's ending finished goods inventory at $132 per unit. The amount reported by the bookkeeper on the income statement as the cost of goods manufactured in each year was the sum of the costs for materials, labour, and overhead incurred in each year.
d. Because the time needed to produce the product is very short, no in-process inventories existed at any of the reporting dates.

Required

Prepare a report for Clair that shows: (1) the number of units of product manufactured each year, (2) each year's cost to manufacture a unit of product, (3) the cost of each year's ending inventory of finished goods (using FIFO), and (4) each year's selling and administrative expenses per unit of product sold. As part of your report, (5) prepare income statements for all three years showing the net income each year. Finally, (6) provide a possible explanation of why the net income has not kept pace with the rising sales volume.

A & R Problem 21-2

Klapstein Watch Company has recently automated its production line. "This automation is great," said Jack Duffy, the company production superintendent. "It has enabled us to reduce our throughput time by about 35 percent. We have been able to rid ourselves of many costs that do not add value to our product."

"I agree," said Ray Klapstein, the company president. "Let's keep in mind that manufacturing time consists of process time, inspection time, move time, and wait time, and it is only process time that adds value to our product."

"I guess that is why the other costs are called nonvalue-added activities?" mumbled Adam Upp, a trainee in the accounting department. Adam is a little overwhelmed at how the new technology seems to be affecting accounting. Adam is unclear on how total costs flow through the system with a just-in-time system in comparison with the traditional job-order system. "I would like to know more about how JIT actually saves costs and how it might affect the accounting system."

Required

Explain to Adam how JIT can save costs and speculate as to how the accounting might differ from traditional accounting.

A & R Problem 21-3

Amortization of plant and equipment is normally considered as a cost attributable to a specific period of time. For example, the cost of a factory is allocated over the service life of that factory with specific amounts charged to each period. In accounting for manufacturing companies, amortization calculated in a particular period may be carried forward to future period(s). Alternatively, more than the calculated amortization for the current period may be included in the current period's income statement.

Required

Do you agree with the above statements? Using a numerical example, prove or disprove the above statements.

Job Order Cost Accounting

Designing Great Rooms

Lethbridge, AB—Roger Worth thought he knew it all. He already has three years work experience with an online service provider as an executive assistant. Yet, since starting his new job as a junior manager with Custom Interiors (CI), a medium-sized custom interior designer, he has felt like a rookie.

The worst occurred during Worth's second week at CI. He was given a cost accounting project termed "high priority" for use in preparing a quote against an enquiry from an upcoming five-star hotel in Hong Kong. Says Worth, "It gave me a chance to show off my quantitative skills."

Worth devoted much time and energy to the company's first major international proposal. He talked to several key people who would potentially be involved in the project, gathered a lot of data and presented a detailed report to his supervisor. After reading the report, his supervisor called him into the office, looked straight into his eyes and said, "This report is seriously incomplete. Details of overhead and their allocation to this job are missing. And don't forget, we are a *custom* designer."

Worth returned to his office, determined to address the supervisor's challenge. "I read everything I could about job order manufacturing, custom designing and job order cost accounting. I learned that custom manufacturers and service providers require special accounting and reports. I also learned about overhead and its potential impact on job order cost accounting."

Two weeks later, Worth submitted his revised report. "The supervisor said my new report was excellent. She said it would help her in preparing a competitive yet profitable quote." Added Worth, "I am still learning but won't make the same mistake again."

Learning Objectives

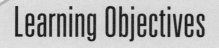

LO¹ Describe job order manufacturing systems.

LO² Explain job cost sheets and how they are used in job order cost accounting.

LO³ Describe and record the flow of materials costs in job order cost accounting.

LO⁴ Describe and record the flow of labour costs in job order cost accounting.

LO⁵ Describe and record the flow of overhead costs in job order cost accounting.

LO⁶ Describe the adjustment of overapplied and underapplied factory overhead.

LO⁷ Describe the closing process for a manufacturer using a general accounting system.

Chapter Preview

In Chapter 21, we described managerial concepts and principles, along with the differences between service, merchandising, and manufacturing companies. We also described the flow of manufacturing activity and discussed the recording of manufacturing costs. In this chapter, we will introduce two different types of manufacturing systems, *job order manufacturing* and *process manufacturing*. The rest of the chapter will focus on describing the *job order cost accounting system.*

The Inventory System and Accounting for Costs

This section explains the accounting methods used to compile the costs reported in the manufacturing statement explained in Chapter 21. We begin with a brief discussion of accounting for manufacturing activities using a general accounting system. But our main emphasis is describing accounting activities using a cost accounting system.

General Accounting System

A general accounting system records manufacturing activities using a **periodic inventory system**. A periodic inventory system measures costs of raw materials, goods in process, and finished goods from physical counts of quantities on hand at the end of each period. This information is used to compute amounts of the product used, finished, and sold during a period.

Some companies still use a periodic inventory system. However, the frequency of a periodic inventory system in practice is declining. Competitive forces and customer demands have increased pressure on companies to better manage inventories. This means an increasing number of companies need more timely and precise information on inventories than is provided by a periodic inventory system.

Cost Accounting System

An ever-increasing number of companies use cost accounting systems to generate timely and precise information. A cost accounting system records manufacturing activities using a **perpetual inventory system**. A perpetual system continuously updates records for costs of materials, goods in process, and finished goods inventories.

A cost accounting system gives us timely information about inventories and changes in inventories. It also gives us more timely information about manufacturing costs per unit of product. This is especially helpful for managers in efforts to control costs and determine selling prices.

Job Order Manufacturing and Cost Accounting System

Generally, manufacturing systems can be classified on a continuum. The system at one end of the continuum is known as a job order (or custom) manufacturing system and at the other end as a process manufacturing system. It is important to understand that many manufacturing companies have *hybrid* systems that combine elements of the two systems mentioned above. *Although the two systems will be described in a manufacturing context, many service companies can also be classified as custom service providers or process type service providers.* In this chapter, we will describe the job order system. The process system is described in the next chapter.

Job Order Manufacturing

Many companies manufacture products designed to meet the unique needs of each customer. **Job order manufacturing**, also called *customized production*, is the production of products in response to special orders.

The production of a unique product is called a **job**. Items that might be produced as jobs include a special machine tool, a building, an airplane, or a piece of custom-made jewellery. They are made to meet the unique demands of specific customers. This type of manufacturing system is likely to be very flexible in the number of different products it can produce.

Bombardier's aerospace division is one example of a job order manufacturing system. Its business activities include: (1) design, development, and integration of space carriers, (2) design, development, manufacture, and support of major airframe components, and (3) joint venture operations in close-air defence systems. Each order is usually unique.

When a job involves producing more than one unit of a unique product, it is often called a **job lot**. Products produced as job lots might include benches for a church, imprinted T-shirts for a 10K race or company picnic, and advertising signs for a chain of stores. Although these orders involve more than one unit, the volume of production is typically low. For example, an order might be placed for 50 benches, 220 T-shirts, or 100 advertising signs.

Another feature of a job order manufacturer is the diversity, often called *heterogeneity*, of the products manufactured. Each customer order is likely different from another in some respect. These variations can be minor or major. T-shirts for a 10K race, for instance, are different from those for a company or family picnic.

It is important to note that the job order system is equally applicable to both manufacturing *and* service companies. Most service companies meet their customers' needs by performing a unique service for each customer. Examples of such services include an accountant's audit of a client's financial statements, an interior designer's remodelling of an office, a wedding consultant's plan and supervision of a reception, and a lawyer's defense of a client in a lawsuit. Whether the setting is manufacturing or service, job order operations involve meeting the needs of customers by producing or performing unique jobs.

LO^1 Describe job order manufacturing systems.

Job Order Caterer

Alexandra Berlingette, the president of 24 Carrot Catering Ltd., a small company based in Nanaimo, British Columbia, has a passion for "cooking up" unique meals for her diverse customers. Just like a custom manufacturer, Alexandra also develops a "custom design" for each order which may range from a wedding dinner for 500 people to a simple working lunch for six. She must understand the specifications of each order to estimate her resource requirements and compute costs. There are at least three important cost items she must consider for each individual order: (1) materials (ingredients) required in cooking the different items for the special event, (2) labour required to fulfill the order, and (3) other resource requirements (e.g., tables and chairs, large vessels, special cooking facility). Finally, she must price competitively, and maintain service quality because a business like hers operates largely on word of mouth. 24 Carrot Catering has done well for itself: it received the 2001 Athena Award as the best home-based business of the year.

SOURCE: http://www.24carrotcatering.bc.ca, and personal conversation with the president of the company.

Did You Know?

Events in Job Order Manufacturing

The initial event in a normal job order manufacturing operation is the receipt of a customer's order for a unique product. This causes the manufacturer to begin work on the job.[1] A less common case is when management decides to begin work on a job before a contract is signed with a customer. This is referred to as *jobs manufactured on speculation.*

The first step in both cases is to predict the cost of completing the job. The cost depends on the design of the product—prepared by the customer or the manufacturer. The second step is to negotiate a sales price and decide whether to pursue the job. Some jobs are priced on a *cost-plus basis.* This means the customer pays the manufacturer for costs incurred on the job plus a negotiated amount or rate of profit. The third step is for the manufacturer to schedule production of the job to meet the customer's needs and to fit within its own production capacity. This work schedule should take into account workplace facilities including tools, machinery, and supplies. Once this schedule is complete, the manufacturer can place orders for raw materials. Under a just-in-time (JIT) system, orders for materials require delivery just in time for use in production. Production occurs as materials and labour are applied to the job.

An overview of job order production activity is shown in Exhibit 22.1. This exhibit shows the March production activity of Road Warriors. Road Warriors manufactures security-equipped cars and trucks. They take any brand vehicle and equip it with a variety of security items. These items include special alarms, reinforced exterior, bulletproof glass, and bomb detectors. The company began by catering to high profile celebrities, but has grown dramatically as it now serves anyone who wants added security in a vehicle.

Exhibit 22.1

Job Order Manufacturing Activities

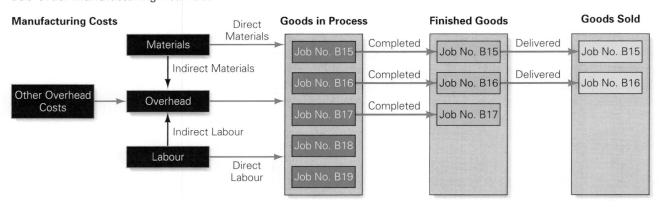

Job order manufacturing for Road Warriors requires direct and indirect materials and labour, and other overhead costs. Recall that direct materials are goods used in manufacturing and clearly identified with a particular job. Similarly, direct labour is efforts devoted to a particular job. Indirect materials and labour are included in factory overhead. Other overhead costs support the production of more than one job. Common overhead items are amortization on

---

[1] This is no different in the case of a service company. The major difference in a service company is that it does not need raw materials; consequently, accounting is simplified. Also, there are no inventory accounts.

factory buildings and equipment, factory supplies, supervision, maintenance, cleaning, and utilities.

Exhibit 22.1 shows that materials, labour, and overhead are added to Job Numbers B15, B16, B17, B18, and B19 during March. Road Warriors completed Jobs B15, B16, and B17 in March, and delivered Jobs B15 and B16 to customers. At the end of March, Jobs B18 and B19 remain in goods in process inventory and Job B17 is in finished goods inventory. Labour and materials are also divided into their direct and indirect components. The indirect costs P. 1100 are added to overhead. Total overhead cost is then allocated to the various jobs.

1. Which of these products are likely to involve job order manufacturing? (a) inexpensive watches, (b) racing bikes, (c) bottled soft drinks.

2. What is the difference between a job and a job lot?

Answers—p. 1161

Management Consultant
You recently joined a management consulting company. One of your first tasks is to control and manage costs for the consulting company. At the end of your first month, you find three consulting jobs are completed and two are 60% complete. Each of the unfinished consulting jobs is estimated to cost $10,000 and to earn revenue of $12,000. You are unsure about how to recognize goods in process inventory and record costs and revenues. First, do you expect to recognize any inventory? If yes, how much? Second, how much revenue is recorded for the unfinished jobs in your first month?

Judgement Call

Answer—p. 1160

Job Order Cost Documents

Much of the accounting information that managers of job order cost operations use to plan and control production activities is not stored in general ledger accounts. This is because the information often involves very detailed data. Instead it is usually stored in subsidiary records controlled by general ledger accounts. Subsidiary records can store information about raw materials, overhead costs, jobs in process, finished goods, and other items. This section describes the use of these records in a job order cost accounting system.

A major aim of **a job order cost accounting system** is to determine the cost of producing each job or job lot. In the case of a job lot it also aims to compute the cost per unit. The accounting system must track each job individually to accomplish this. The system must capture information about costs incurred, and charge these costs to jobs.

A **job cost sheet** is a separate record maintained for each job. Exhibit 22.2 shows a job cost sheet for a basic alarm system that Road Warriors produced for a customer. This job cost sheet identifies the customer, the reference number assigned to the job, the job description, and various dates. Costs incurred on the job are immediately recorded on this sheet. When each job is complete, the supervisor enters the date of completion, records any remarks, and signs the sheet.

LO² Explain job cost sheets and how they are used in job order cost accounting.

Exhibit 22.2

Job Cost Sheet

| Road Warriors | | | •Job Cost Sheet• | | | Toronto, Ontario | | |

Customer's Name _Carroll Connor_   Job No. _B15_

Address _1542 High Point Dr._   City & Province _Vancouver, British Columbia_

Job Description _Level I Alarm System on Ford Expedition_

Date promised _March 15_   Date started _March 3_   Date completed _March 11_

Direct Materials			Direct Labour			Manufacturing Overhead		
Date	Requisition	Cost	Date	Time Ticket	Cost	Date	Rate	Cost
Mar. 3/04	R-4698	100.00	Mar. 3/04	L-3393	120.00	Mar. 11/04	160% of	1,600.00
Mar. 7/04	R-4705	225.00	Mar. 4/04	L-3422	150.00		Direct	
Mar. 9/04	R-4725	180.00	Mar. 5/04	L-3456	180.00		Labour	
Mar. 10/04	R-4777	95.00	Mar. 8/04	L-3479	60.00		Cost	
			Mar. 9/04	L-3501	90.00			
			Mar. 10/04	L-3535	240.00			
			Mar. 11/04	L-3559	160.00			
Total		600.00	Total		1,000.00	Total		1,600.00

REMARKS: Completed job on March 11, and shipped to customer on March 15. Met all specifications and requirements.

Signed: _C. Luther, Supervisor_

SUMMARY:

Materials	600.00
Labour	1,000.00
Overhead	1,600.00
Total cost	3,200.00

The job cost sheet in Exhibit 22.2 classifies costs as direct materials, direct labour, or overhead. It shows direct materials are added to Job B15 on four different dates, with a value totalling $600. The seven entries for direct labour costs total $1,000. Road Warriors allocates (applies, assigns, or charges) overhead costs of $1,600 to this job using an allocation rate of 160% of direct labour cost, computed as 160% × $1,000.

While a job is being manufactured, its accumulated costs are kept in goods in process inventory. The collection of job cost sheets for all of the jobs in process makes up a subsidiary ledger controlled by the Goods in Process Inventory account in the general ledger. Managers use job cost sheets to monitor costs incurred to date and to predict and control costs for each job.

When a job is finished, its job cost sheet is completed and moved from the file of jobs in process to the file of finished jobs awaiting delivery to customers. This latter file acts as a subsidiary ledger controlled by the Finished Goods Inventory account. When a finished job is delivered to the customer, the job cost sheet is moved to a permanent file supporting the total cost of goods sold. This permanent file contains records from both current and prior periods.

Flashback

Answers—p. 1161

3. Which of these statements is correct?

   a. The collection of job cost sheets for unfinished jobs makes up a subsidiary ledger controlled by the Goods in Process account.

   b. Job cost sheets are financial statements provided to investors.

   c. A separate job cost sheet is maintained in the General Ledger for each job in process.

4. What three costs are normally accumulated on job cost sheets?

Materials Cost Flows and Documents

This section and the next two explain the flow of costs and related documents in a job order cost accounting system. We focus on the three cost components: (1) materials, (2) labour, and (3) overhead. Materials cost flows are described in this section, and labour and overhead costs in the following sections.

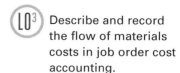

LO³ Describe and record the flow of materials costs in job order cost accounting.

We begin our analysis of the flow of materials cost data through subsidiary records by looking at Exhibit 22.3. When materials are first received from suppliers, the employees count and inspect them. They record the quantity and cost of items on a receiving report. Companies that deal with trustworthy suppliers can reduce some of their costs by eliminating the inspection and counting of incoming raw materials. The receiving report serves as the *source document* for recording materials received in both the materials ledger card and in the general ledger. In nearly all job order cost systems, the **materials ledger cards** are perpetual records that are updated each time units are purchased and each time units are issued for use in production.

Exhibit 22.3

Job Order Materials Cost Flows Through Subsidiary Records

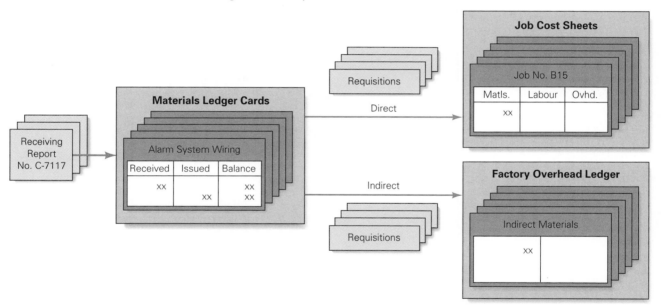

Exhibit 22.3 shows that materials can be requisitioned for use either on a specific job (direct materials) or as overhead (indirect materials). Cost of direct materials flows from the materials ledger card to the job cost sheet. The cost of indirect materials flows from the materials ledger card to the Indirect Materials account in the Factory Overhead Ledger. The factory overhead ledger is a subsidiary ledger controlled by the Factory Overhead account in the general ledger.

Exhibit 22.4 shows a materials ledger card for material used by Road Warriors. The card identifies the item as alarm system wiring. The card also shows the item's stock number, its location in the storeroom, information about the maximum and minimum quantities that should be on hand, and the reorder quantity. Note the issue of alarm system wiring recorded on March 7, 2004. The job cost sheet in Exhibit 22.2 shows this wiring is used in Job No. B15.

Exhibit 22.4

Materials Ledger Card

Road Warriors

Item ___Alarm system wiring___   Stock No. ___M–347___   Location in Storeroom ___Bin 137___

Maximum quantity ___5 units___   Minimum quantity ___1 unit___   Quantity to reorder ___2 units___

	Received				Issued				Balance		
Date	Receiving Report Number	Units	Unit Price	Total Price	Requisition Number	Units	Unit Price	Total Price	Units	Unit Price	Total Price
									1	225.00	225.00
Mar. 4/04	C-7117	2	225.00	450.00					3	225.00	675.00
Mar. 7/04					R–4705	1	225.00	225.00	2	225.00	450.00

When materials are needed in production, a production manager prepares a **materials requisition** and sends it to the materials manager. The requisition shows the job number, the type of material, the quantity needed, and the signature of the manager authorized to make the requisition. Exhibit 22.5 shows the materials requisition for alarm system wiring for Job No. B15. To see how this requisition ties to the flow of costs, compare the information on the requisition with the March 7, 2004, data in Exhibits 22.2 and 22.4.

Exhibit 22.5

Materials Requisition

Road Warriors

MATERIALS REQUISITION NUMBER R–4705

Job No. ___B15___   Date ___March 7/04___

Material Stock No. ___M–347___   Material Description ___Alarm system wiring___

Quantity Requested ___1___   Requested By ___C. Luther___

===

Quantity Provided ___1___   Date Provided ___March 7/04___

Filled By ___M. Bateman___   Material Received By ___C. Luther___

Remarks _____

The use of alarm system wiring on Job No. B15 yields the following journal entry (locate this item in the job cost sheet shown in Exhibit 22.2):

Mar. 7	Goods in Process Inventory - Job No. B15	225	
	Raw Materials Inventory - M-347		225
	To record use of material on Job No. B15.		

This entry is posted to general ledger accounts and to subsidiary records. Posting to subsidiary records includes a debit to a job cost sheet and a credit to a materials ledger card.

An entry to record use of indirect materials is the same as that for direct materials *except* the debit is to Factory Overhead. In the subsidiary factory overhead ledger, this entry is posted to Indirect Materials.

Labour Cost Flows and Documents

Exhibit 22.6 shows the flow of labour costs from clock cards and the Factory Payroll account to subsidiary records of the job cost accounting system. Recall that the costs in subsidiary records give detailed information needed to manage and control operations.

The flow of costs in Exhibit 22.6 begins with **clock cards**. Employees commonly use these cards to record number of hours worked. Clock cards serve as source documents for entries to record labour costs. Clock card data on the number of hours worked is used at the end of each pay period to determine total labour cost. This amount is then debited to the Factory Payroll account. Factory Payroll is a temporary account containing the total payroll cost (both direct and indirect). Payroll cost is later allocated to both specific jobs and overhead.

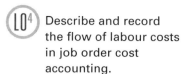

LO⁴   Describe and record the flow of labour costs in job order cost accounting.

Exhibit 22.6

Job Order Labour Cost Flows Through Subsidiary Records

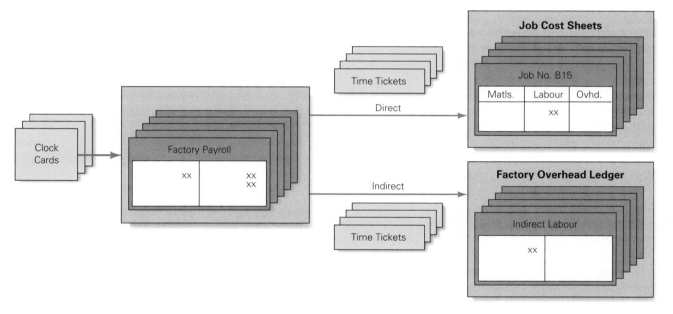

To assign labour costs to specific jobs and to overhead, we must know how each employee's time is used and how much it costs. Source documents called **time tickets** usually capture this data. Employees fill out time tickets each day to report how much time they spent on each job. An employee who works on several jobs during a day completes a separate time ticket for each job. Tickets are also prepared for time that is charged to overhead as indirect labour. A supervisor signs an employee's time ticket to confirm its accuracy.

Exhibit 22.7 shows a time ticket reporting the time a Road Warrior employee spent working on Job No. B15. The employee's supervisor signed the ticket to confirm its accuracy. The hourly rate and total labour cost are computed after the time ticket is turned in. To see the effect of this time ticket on the job cost sheet, look at Exhibit 22.2 for the entry dated March 8, 2004.

Exhibit 22.7

Labour Time Ticket

Road Warriors

TIME TICKET   L–3479

Job No. _____ B15 _____   Date _____ March 8/04 _____

Employee Name ____ T. Zeller ____   Employee Number ____ 3969 ____

TIME AND RATE INFORMATION:

Start Time _____ 9:00 _____   Finish Time _____ 12:00 _____

Elapsed Time _____ 3.0 _____   Hourly Rate _____ $20.00 _____   Total Cost _____ $60.00 _____

Approved By _____ C. Luther _____

Remarks _____

When time tickets report labour used on a specific job, this cost is recorded as direct labour. The following entry records the data from time ticket number L-3479 shown in Exhibit 22.7.

Mar. 8	Goods in Process Inventory - Job No. B15	60	
	Factory Payroll		60
	To record direct labour used on Job No. B15.		

The debit in this entry is posted to both the General Ledger account and to the appropriate job cost sheet.

An entry to record indirect labour is the same as for direct labour *except* it debits Factory Overhead and credits Factory Payroll. In the subsidiary Factory Overhead Ledger, the debit in this entry is posted to the Indirect Labour account.

Overhead Cost Flows and Documents

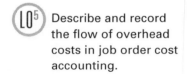

LO⁵ Describe and record the flow of overhead costs in job order cost accounting.

Factory overhead (or simply overhead) cost flows are shown in Exhibit 22.8. Factory overhead includes all manufacturing costs other than direct materials and direct labour. Two of the four sources of overhead costs are indirect materials and indirect labour. These costs are recorded from requisitions for indirect materials and time tickets for indirect labour. The other two sources of overhead are (1) vouchers authorizing payments for items such as supplies or utilities and (2) adjusting entries for costs such as amortization of assets related to production.

Because factory overhead usually includes many different costs, a separate account for each overhead cost is often maintained in a subsidiary factory over-

Exhibit 22.8

Job Order Overhead Cost Flows Through Subsidiary Records

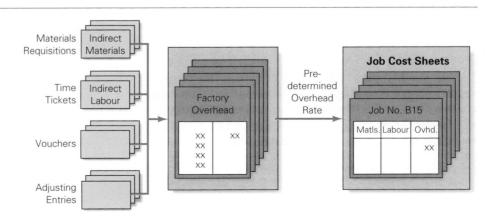

head ledger. This ledger is controlled by the Factory Overhead account in the general ledger. Factory Overhead is a temporary account that accumulates costs until they are allocated to jobs.

Recall that manufacturing overhead costs are recorded with debits to the Factory Overhead account and credits to other accounts such as Cash, Accounts Payable, and Accumulated Amortization—Equipment. In the subsidiary factory overhead ledger, the debits are posted to their proper accounts such as Amortization on Factory Equipment, Insurance on Factory Equipment, or Amortization of Patents.

Exhibit 22.8 shows overhead costs flow from the Factory Overhead account to job cost sheets. Since overhead is made up of costs not directly associated with specific jobs or job lots we cannot determine the dollar amount incurred on a particular job. We know manufacturing overhead costs are necessary in any manufacturing operation. If the total cost of a job is to include all costs needed to manufacture the job, some amount of manufacturing overhead must be included.

We already showed how to allocate overhead by linking it to another factor used in production, such as direct labour or machine hours. In Exhibit 22.2, for instance, overhead is expressed as 160% of direct labour. We then allocated overhead by multiplying 160% by the estimated amount of direct labour costs in both ending inventory and cost of goods sold.[2]

Since perpetual inventory records are used in a job order accounting system, we cannot wait until the end of the period to allocate overhead to jobs. We must predict overhead in advance and assign it to jobs by using a **predetermined overhead allocation rate**, or simply *predetermined overhead rate*. Using a predetermined rate to allocate overhead also allows managers to estimate unit costs at the start of the planning process; doing so will help managers in budgeting. Job order manufacturers who are required to quote prices before an order may be received must estimate job costs, including overhead. The use of a predetermined overhead rate helps managers estimate the job costs. As we will see later in this book, actual overhead costs may be different from estimated costs; however, the estimates are very useful for planning. This rate requires us to estimate total overhead cost and total direct labour cost (or another factor) before the start of the period. Exhibit 22.9 shows the formula for computing a predetermined overhead allocation rate. These estimates are usually based on annual amounts. We then can use this rate during the period to allocate overhead to jobs.

$$\text{Predetermined Overhead Allocation Rate} = \frac{\text{Estimated Overhead Costs}}{\text{Estimated ``Factor'' Costs}}$$

Exhibit 22.9

Predetermined Overhead Allocation Rate Formula

Road Warriors, for instance, allocates overhead by linking it to direct labour. At the start of the current period, management predicted total direct labour cost of $125,000, and total factory overhead costs of $200,000. Using these estimates, management computed its predetermined overhead allocation rate as 160% of direct labour cost ($200,000 ÷ $125,000).

---

[2] By using direct labour as the only overhead allocation base, we are assuming that direct labour costs have a certain relationship with overhead costs or that they *drive* overhead costs. It is unreasonable to assume that direct labour drives overhead costs such as maintenance, rent, and many other operating costs. Although direct labour once accounted for a significant portion of total costs, that is no longer the case. Overhead now forms a large proportion of the total costs. As a result, many companies are beginning to use multiple allocation bases and rates (we discuss this issue further in Chapter 24).

Look back to the job order cost sheet for Job No. B15 in Exhibit 22.2. See that $1,000 of direct labour is assigned to this job. We then use the predetermined overhead allocation rate of 160% to allocate $1,600 of overhead to the job. The journal entry to record this allocation is

Mar. 11	Goods in Process Inventory - Job No. B15	1,600	
	Factory Overhead		1,600
	To assign overhead to Job No. B15.		

Because the allocation rate for overhead is estimated at the start of the period, the total amount assigned to jobs during the period is rarely equal to the amount actually incurred. We explain how this difference is treated at the end of the period later in this chapter.

Judgement Call

Answer—p. 1160

Systems Consultant

Your professional services firm is currently working on seven client engagements. In two of these engagements the clients reimburse your firm for actual costs plus a 10% markup. The other five pay a fixed fee for services. Your firm's costs include overhead allocated at $47 per labour hour. The partner of the firm instructs you to record as many labour hours as possible to the two markup engagements by transferring labour hours from other engagements. She says "this will ensure we'll earn an added $47 markup for each added labour hour recorded." You are the tax manager in charge of these two engagements and your bonus depends on profits generated by the entire seven engagements. What do you do?

Summary of Manufacturing Cost Flows

We showed journal entries for charging Goods in Process inventory—Job No. B15 with the cost of (1) direct materials requisitions, (2) direct labour time tickets, and (3) factory overhead. While we entered separate entries for each of these costs, they are usually recorded in one entry. Specifically, materials requisitions are collected for a day or a week and recorded with a single entry summarizing these requisitions. The same is done with labour time tickets. When summary entries are made, supporting schedules of the jobs charged and the types of materials used provide the basis for postings to subsidiary records.

To show all the manufacturing cost flows for a period and their related entries, we again look at Road Warriors' activities. Exhibit 22.10 shows costs linked to all of Road Warriors' manufacturing activities for March. Road Warriors did not have any jobs in process at the beginning of March but it did apply materials, labour, and overhead costs to five new jobs in March. Job Nos. B15 and B16 are completed and delivered to customers in March, Job No. B17 is completed but not delivered, and Job Nos. B18 and B19 are still in process. Exhibit 22.10 shows purchases of raw materials for $2,750, labour costs incurred for $5,300, and overhead costs of $6,720.

Exhibit 22.10

Job Order Costs of All Manufacturing Activities

			Overhead				
Explanation	**Materials**	**Labour**	**Incurred**	**Assigned**	**Goods in Process**	**Finished Goods**	**Cost of Goods Sold**
Road Warriors — Job Order Manufacturing Costs — For Month Ended March 31, 2004							
Job B15	$ 600	$1,000		$1,600*			$3,200
Job B16	300	800		1,280			2,380
Job B17	500	1,100		1,760		$3,360	
Job B18	150	700		1,120	$1,970		
Job B19	250	600		960	1,810		
Total job costs...............	$1,800	$4,200		$6,720	$3,780	$3,360	$5,580
Indirect materials	550		$ 550				
Indirect labour...............		1,100	1,100				
Other overhead............. .			5,550				
Total costs used in production	$2,350	$5,300	$7,200				
Ending inventory............	1,400						
Materials available	$3,750						
Less beginning inv.	(1,000)						
Purchases....................	$2,750						

*160% × DL$

Exhibit 22.11 shows the flow of these costs through general ledger accounts and the end-of-month balance in the subsidiary records. Arrow lines are numbered to show the flows of costs for March. Each numbered cost flow reflects several entries made in March.

Exhibit 22.11

Flow of All Job Order Costs and Ending Cost Sheets

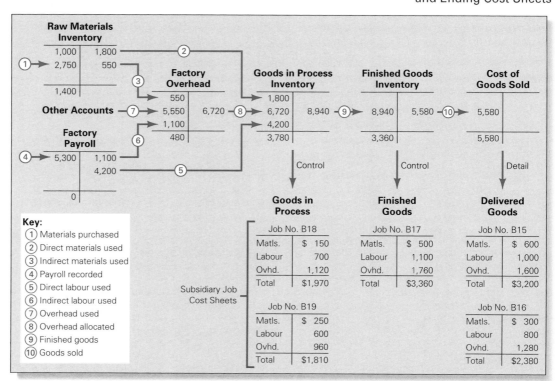

The lower part of Exhibit 22.11 shows the status of job cost sheets at the end of March. The sum of costs assigned to the jobs in process ($1,970 + $1,810) equals the $3,780 balance in Goods in Process Inventory shown in Exhibit 22.10. Also, costs assigned to Job No. B17 equal the $3,360 balance in Finished Goods Inventory. The sum of costs assigned to Job Nos. B15 and B16 ($3,200 + $2,380) equals the $5,580 balance in Cost of Goods Sold.

Exhibit 22.12 shows each cost flow with a single entry summarizing the actual individual entries made in March. Each entry is numbered to link with the arrow lines in Exhibit 22.11.

Exhibit 22.12

Entries for Job Order Manufacturing Costs*

1.	Raw Materials Inventory..................................	2,750	
	Accounts Payable		2,750
	Acquired materials on credit for factory use.		
2.	Goods in Process Inventory............................	1,800	
	Raw Materials Inventory..........................		1,800
	To assign the cost of direct materials used.		
3.	Factory Overhead	550	
	Raw Materials Inventory..........................		550
	To record the use of indirect materials.		
4.	Factory Payroll	5,300	
	Cash (and other accounts)		5,300
	To record salaries and wages of factory workers (including various payroll liabilities).		
5.	Goods in Process Inventory............................	4,200	
	Factory Payroll		4,200
	To assign the cost of direct labour used.		
6.	Factory Overhead	1,100	
	Factory Payroll		1,100
	To record indirect labour costs as overhead.		
7.	Factory Overhead	5,550	
	Cash (and other accounts)		5,550
	To record overhead costs incurred such as insurance on factory equipment, utilities, rent, and amortization.		
8.	Goods in Process Inventory............................	6,720	
	Factory Overhead		6,720
	To apply overhead at 160% of direct labour.		
9.	Finished Goods Inventory...............................	8,940	
	Goods in Process Inventory.....................		8,940
	To record the completion of Job Nos. B15, B16, and B17.		
10.	Cost of Goods Sold..	5,580	
	Finished Goods Inventory........................		5,580
	To record the sale of Job Nos. B15 and B16.		

*Transactions are numbered consistent with the arrow line in Exhibit 22.11

Manufacturing Statement in Job Order Costing

A manufacturing statement prepared using a job order cost accounting system summarizes the total costs of manufacturing activities during the period. The March manufacturing statement for Road Warriors is shown in Exhibit 22.13. (See Exhibit 22.11 to verify the amounts for each item on the statement.)

Road Warriors Manufacturing Statement For Month Ended March 31, 2004		
Direct Materials:		
Raw material inventory, March 1, 2004	$1,000	
Raw materials purchases	2,750	
Raw materials available for use	3,750	
Indirect materials used	(550)	
Raw materials inventory, March 31, 2004	(1,400)	
Direct materials used		$ 1,800
Direct labour		4,200
Factory overhead costs:		
Indirect materials	550	
Indirect labour	1,100	
Other overhead costs	5,070	
Total factory overhead costs		6,720
Total manufacturing costs		$12,720
Add goods in process inventory, March 1, 2004		-0-
Total cost of goods in process		$12,720
Deduct goods in process inventory, March 31, 2004		(3,780)
Unadjusted cost of goods manufactured		$ 8,940
Deduct: underapplied overhead		(480)
Cost of goods manufactured		$ 8,460

Exhibit 22.13

Manufacturing Statement for Road Warriors

Computerized Job Order Costing

Our discussion of job order cost flows and the required documentation indicates a labour-intensive process for tracking costs. This approach seems to be out of place now that many companies are using computerized accounting systems. In fact, many job costing software packages are also available in the market place (some more customized, specialized, and versatile than others). Using such software does not mean our earlier discussion of cost flows is irrelevant—the cost flows still remain. The data are now captured electronically, allowing managers to track information in a timely manner. However, companies must also be more cautious about the possibility of data manipulation and need to put internal controls in place to avoid such undesirable activity.

Answers—p. 1161

5. In job order cost accounting, what account is debited in recording a raw materials requisition? (a) Raw Materials Inventory; (b) Raw Materials Purchases; (c) Goods in Process Inventory if for a job; (d) Goods in Process Inventory if they are indirect materials.

6. What are the four sources of information for recording costs in the Factory Overhead account?

7. Why does job order cost accounting use a predetermined overhead application rate?

8. What events result in a debit to Factory Payroll? What events result in a credit?

Adjusting of Overapplied and Underapplied Overhead

LO⁶ Describe the adjustment of overapplied and underapplied factory overhead.

Overhead costs incurred seldom equal overhead costs assigned. Overhead cost applied is computed using an overhead rate which is determined before the period actually begins, so it is very likely that the actual amount of overhead will be more or less than the amount applied or allocated to manufacturing activity during the period. We see from Exhibit 22.10 that the actual amount incurred is $7,200 but that only $6,720 is assigned to jobs. Refer also to Exhibit 22.11 and observe the debits in the Factory Overhead account. The total cost of factory overhead incurred during March is $7,200, computed as $550+$5,550+$1,100. Also note that only $6,720 is assigned to goods in process inventory (see arrow line in ⑧). It is the applied amounts that are assigned to jobs, not the actual amounts of overhead. In this case overhead applied is lower than the amount of overhead incurred. This section explains what we do when too much or too little overhead is applied to jobs.

Underapplied Overhead

When less overhead is applied than is actually incurred the remaining debit balance in the Factory Overhead account at the end of the period is called **underapplied overhead**. Since Road Warriors actually incurred total overhead cost of $7,200 in March but applied $6,720, the Factory Overhead account is left with a $480 debit balance as shown in the ledger account in Exhibit 22.14.

Exhibit 22.14

Underapplied Overhead in the Factory Overhead Ledger Account

		Factory Overhead			Acct. No. 540	
Date		Explanation	Debit	Credit	Balance	
2004						
Mar.	31	Indirect materials cost............	550		550	
	31	Indirect labour cost	1,100		1,650	
	31	Other overhead costs	5,550		7,200	
	31	Overhead costs applied to jobs.......................		6,720	480	(debit)

The $480 debit balance reflects manufacturing costs not assigned to jobs. This means the balances in Goods in Process Inventory, Finished Goods Inventory, and Cost of Goods Sold do not include all manufacturing costs incurred. Technically, we should allocate this underapplied Factory Overhead balance to these three accounts. However, the underapplied overhead amount is often immaterial and is entirely allocated (or closed) to the Cost of Goods Sold account.[3] The adjusting entry to record this allocation is made as follows:

Mar. 31	Cost of Goods Sold	480	
	Factory Overhead		480
	To adjust for underapplied overhead cost.		

Overapplied Overhead

When the overhead applied in a period exceeds the overhead incurred the resulting credit balance in the Factory Overhead account is called **overapplied overhead**. We treat overapplied overhead at the end of the period in the same way we treat underapplied overhead, except that Factory Overhead is debited and Cost of Goods Sold is credited.

Another method of treating the overapplied or underapplied overhead is to adjust the manufacturing statement by that amount. This adjustment is necessary so that the manufacturing statement reports the actual overhead. The adjustment for over- or underapplied overhead is normally reported as the final line item immediately above the total cost of goods manufactured figure in the manufacturing statement (where underapplied overhead is deducted and overapplied overhead is added to cost of goods manufactured) as shown in Exhibit 22.13. Alternatively, the over- or underapplied overhead can also be reported in the factory overhead section of the manufacturing statement.

9. In a job order cost accounting system, why does the Factory Overhead account usually have an overapplied or underapplied balance at the end of a period?

10. The Factory Overhead account has a debit balance at the end of a period. Does this reflect overapplied or underapplied overhead?

Flashback

Answers—p. 1161

Sales Director

You are the sales director of a product division. Your division's product is facing increasing price competition. Competitors' prices are often lower than your product's price. You learn 53% of total product cost is factory overhead allocated using direct labour hours. You believe product costs from your costing system are distorted and you are wondering if there is a better means to allocate factory overhead and to set product price. What do you do?

Judgement Call

Answer—p. 1160

---

[3] When the underapplied overhead is significant, the amount is usually allocated to the Cost of Goods Sold, Finished Goods Inventory and Goods in Process Inventory accounts. The preferred method of allocating underapplied overhead is one consistent with the allocation method used in the period. For Road Warriors this means underapplied overhead is allocated to jobs based on direct labour. Jobs B15 and B16, which are sold, consumed 42.8% of the total direct labour cost in March 2004. Also, 26.2% of direct labour was consumed by B16 which is in Finished Goods inventory, and the remaining 31% was consumed by jobs B17 and B18 which are in Goods in Process inventory. These percents are multiplied by $480 to compute the amount of underapplied overhead allocated to each account (for example, 42.8% of $480, or $225, is allocated to the Cost of Goods Sold account). An adjusting entry records this allocation:

Mar. 31	Goods in Process Inventory	149	
	Finished Goods Inventory	126	
	Cost of Goods Sold	205	
	Factory Overhead		480
	To adjust the cost of the jobs worked on in		
	March for underapplied overhead cost.		

Summary

LO¹ Describe job order manufacturing systems. Certain manufacturers produce unique products for customers and are called *job order manufacturers*. These unique or special products are manufactured in response to a customer's orders. The products produced by a job order manufacturer are usually different for each customer, and typically manufactured in low volumes. The manufacturing systems of job order companies are flexible, and are not highly standardized.

LO² Explain job cost sheets and how they are used in job order cost accounting. In a job order cost accounting system, the costs of producing each job are accumulated on a separate job cost sheet. Costs of direct materials, direct labour, and manufacturing overhead are accumulated separately on the job cost sheet and then added to determine the total cost of a job. Job cost sheets for jobs in process, finished jobs, and jobs that are sold make up subsidiary records that are controlled by general ledger accounts.

LO³ Describe and record the flow of materials costs in job order cost accounting. Costs of materials flow from receiving reports to materials ledger cards and then to either job cost sheets or the Indirect Materials account in the factory overhead ledger.

LO⁴ Describe and record the flow of labour costs in job order cost accounting. Costs of labour flow from clock cards to the Factory Payroll account and then to either job cost sheets or the Indirect Labour account in the factory overhead ledger.

LO⁵ Describe and record the flow of overhead costs in job order cost accounting. Manufacturing overhead costs are accumulated in the Factory Overhead account that controls the subsidiary factory overhead ledger. Then, using a predetermined overhead application rate, overhead costs are assigned to jobs.

LO⁶ Describe the adjustment of overapplied and underapplied factory overhead. At the end of each period, the Factory Overhead account usually has a residual debit or credit balance. A debit balance reflects underapplied overhead and a credit balance reflects overapplied overhead. If this balance is not material, it is transferred to Costs of Goods Sold. If the balance is material it is transferred to Goods in Process, Finished Goods Inventory, and Cost of Goods Sold.

GUIDANCE   ANSWERS   TO   Judgement Call

Management Consultant

Service companies do not recognize goods in process inventory or finished goods inventory. This is an important difference between service and manufacturing companies. As a result, you will not recognize any amount as goods in process inventory at the end of the month.

For the two jobs that are 60% complete, you could recognize revenues and costs at 60% of the total expected amounts. Therefore, you will recognize revenue of $7,200 (0.60 × $12,000) and costs of $6,000 (0.60 × $10,000), or net income of $1,200.

Systems Consultant

There is a monetary incentive to fudge the numbers and make the two cost-plus engagements appear more costly. This would also reduce costs on the fixed price engagements. While there is an incentive to act in such a manner, it is clearly unethical. As a professional and as an honest person, it is your responsibility to engage in ethical behaviour. You must bring to your supervisor's attention the ethical issue involved in the situa-

tion. You must not comply with the superior's instructions. If the supervisor insists that you act in an unethical manner, you should report the matter to a higher authority in the organization. It often takes a person of strong moral character to do the right thing in such situations because the whistle blower is sometimes the person who gets victimized.

Sales Director

A faulty cost system can lead to distortions in product costs. The sales director should talk to the controller and ask to review the factory overhead costs in detail. Once the different cost elements in the factory overhead account are known, they can be classified into several groups such as material-related, labour-related, or machine-related. Other groups can also be formed (we will discuss more about this in Chapter 24). Once the overhead items are classified into groups, appropriate overhead allocation bases can be established which can be used to compute predetermined overhead rates. These multiple rates can then be used to assign the overhead costs to products. This will likely improve product pricing.

GUIDANCE ANSWERS TO  Flashback

1. *b*

2. A job is a special order for a unique product. A job lot consists of a small quantity of identical, special order items.

3. *a*

4. The three costs normally accumulated are: direct materials, direct labour, and manufacturing overhead.

5. *c*

6. The four sources are materials requisitions, time tickets, vouchers, and adjusting entries.

7. Because a job order cost accounting system uses perpetual inventory records, overhead costs must be assigned to jobs before the end of the period. This requires use of a predetermined overhead application rate.

8. Debits are recorded when wages and salaries of factory employees are paid or accrued. Credits are recorded when direct labour costs are assigned to jobs and when indirect labour costs are transferred to the Factory Overhead account.

9. Overapplied or underapplied overhead exists at the end of a period because application of overhead is based on estimates of overhead and another variable such as direct labour. Those estimates rarely equal the actual amounts incurred.

10. A debit balance reflects underapplied overhead

22A General Accounting Systems for Manufacturing Activities

As explained in the chapter, a general accounting system records manufacturing activities using a periodic inventory system. This system may therefore be referred to sometimes as a *periodic cost accounting system*. Although it is different from a cost accounting system which records activities using a perpetual inventory system—a *perpetual cost accounting system*—the two systems have many features in common. They both account for the three elements of manufacturing cost: direct materials, direct labour, and factory overhead. They also record and report information on the three types of inventory: raw materials, goods in process, and finished goods. The difference is that they do not keep records in the same way. This appendix describes the closing process for a manufacturer using a general (periodic cost) accounting system.

Journalizing in a General Accounting System

LO7 Describe the closing process for a manufacturer using a general accounting system.

Journalizing for both the perpetual and periodic inventory systems of a merchandising company was described in volume 1 of this text. Except for the additional manufacturing inventories and expense accounts, the journalizing process is the same for a manufacturing company. However, the closing entries change slightly for a manufacturer using a general accounting system.

To illustrate, let's assume Rocky Mountain Bikes uses the periodic cost accounting system and reports the information in Exhibit 22A.1 on inventories and manufacturing activities for 2004.

Exhibit 22A.1

Manufacturing Transactions of Rocky Mountain Bikes in 2004

Rocky Mountain Bikes Schedule of Overhead Items For Year Ended December 31, 2004	
Indirect labour	$ 9,000
Supervision	6,000
Other overhead items*	15,000
Total overhead	$30,000

*Overhead items are listed in Exhibit 22.2.

Rocky Mountain Bikes Manufacturing Statement For Year Ended December 31, 2004	
Direct materials	$ 85,500
Direct labour	60,000
Factory overhead	30,000
Total Manuf. costs	$175,500
Beg. goods in process	2,500
Total goods in process	$178,000
End. goods in process	(7,500)
Cost of goods manuf.	$170,500

Rocky Mountain Bikes Income Statement For Year Ended December 31, 2004	
Sales	$310,000
Cost of goods sold:	
Beg. finished goods	$ 11,200
Cost of goods manuf.	170,500
End. finished goods	(10,300)
Cost of goods sold	$171,400
Gross profit	$138,600
Expenses	(59,900)
Income taxes	(32,600)
Net income	$ 46,100

Manufacturing Summary

A general accounting system uses a Manufacturing Summary account to close accounts that appear in the manufacturing statement. This temporary account is similar to the Income Summary account. The Manufacturing Summary account has a zero balance during each period. During the closing process all manufacturing costs are transferred to this account. The account balance is returned to zero when the costs in this account are allocated among the raw materials and goods in process ending inventory accounts and the income summary account.

The first closing entry is to transfer the raw materials and goods in process inventory opening amounts, and the three manufacturing cost amounts, to the manufacturing summary account. Turn back to Exhibit 21.14a to find these amounts.

Dec. 31	Manufacturing Summary	187,000	
	Raw Materials Inventory..........................		8,000
	Goods in Process Inventory.....................		2,500
	Raw Materials Purchases		86,500
	Direct Labour		60,000
	Factory Overhead		30,000
	To close production accounts to		
	Manufacturing Summary.		

When several factory overhead accounts are used, the above closing entry includes a credit to each of them. If a separate account is used for each overhead cost listed in the manufacturing statement then the closing entry is replaced by:

Dec. 31	Manufacturing Summary	187,000	
	Raw Materials Inventory..........................		8,000
	Goods in Process Inventory.....................		2,500
	Raw Materials Purchases		86,500
	Direct Labour		60,000
	Indirect Labour		9,000
	Factory Supervision		6,000
	Factory Utilities.......................................		2,600
	Repairs, Factory Equipment		2,500
	Property Taxes on Factory Building		1,900
	Factory Supplies Used.............................		600
	Factory Insurance expired		1,100
	Small Tools Written Off		200
	Amortization of Factory Equipment..........		3,500
	Amortization of Factory Building..............		1,800
	Amortization of Patents		800
	To close production accounts to		
	Manufacturing Summary.		

The second entry is to record the cost of ending raw materials and goods in process inventories based on the physical count of ending inventories. This entry is:

Dec. 31	Raw Materials Inventory...................................	9,000	
	Goods in Process Inventory............................	7,500	
	Manufacturing Summary		16,500
	To update the raw materials and goods		
	in process inventories.		

The $170,500 cost of completed units temporarily remains as the balance of Manufacturing Summary. Look at Exhibit 21.14a to find this amount as the last line of the Manufacturing Statement. We also see it in the Cost of Goods Sold section of the income statement in Exhibit 21.13.

The third entry is to close the beginning finished goods inventory, the manufacturing summary account and all expense accounts for Rocky Mountain Bikes. Balances of expense accounts are taken from the income statement in Exhibit 21.13.

Dec. 31	Income Summary	274,200	
	Manufacturing Summary		**170,500**
	Finished Goods Inventory..........................		11,200
	Sales Salaries Expense.............................		18,000
	Advertising Expense..................................		5,500
	Delivery Wages Expense...........................		12,000
	Shipping Supplies Expense		250
	Insurance Expense,		
	Delivery Equipment		300
	Amortization Expense,		
	Delivery Equipment.................................		2,100
	Office Salaries Expense.............................		15,700
	Miscellaneous Expense.............................		200
	Bad Debts Expense		1,550
	Office Supplies Expense		100
	Amortization Expense,		
	Office Equipment....................................		200
	Interest Expense		4,000
	Income Taxes Expense..............................		32,600
	To close the Manufacturing Summary		
	and expense accounts, and to clear		
	the Finished Goods Inventory account.		

The fourth closing entry records ending finished goods inventory based on the physical count, and closes the sales account:

Dec. 31	Finished Goods Inventory...................................	10,300	
	Sales	310,000	
	Income Summary		320,300
	To close the Sales account and update		
	the Finished Goods Inventory account.		

After this entry is posted the Income Summary account has a credit balance of $46,100. This equals net income for the year.

The fifth and final entry is to close the Income Summary account and update the Retained Earnings account:

Dec. 31	Income Summary	46,100	
	Retained Earnings.......................................		46,100
	To close the Income Summary and update		
	Retained Earnings.		

This last closing entry is the same whether the company is engaged in merchandising, manufacturing, or service activities.

After the closing process is complete, the T-accounts for the summary accounts appear as follows. (The numbers in parentheses refer to the journal entries above.)

Manufacturing Summary		Income Summary	
(1) Dec. 31 187,000	(2) Dec. 31 16,500	(3) Dec. 31 274,200	(4) Dec. 31 320,200
	(3) Dec. 31 170,500	(5) Dec. 31 46,100	

11. Which of these statements is true about a general accounting system for a manufacturer?

    a. Raw materials purchased are debited to Goods in Process Inventory.

    b. The Goods in Process Inventory account is updated as part of the end-of-period closing process.

    c. FIFO inventory costing method must be used.

12. What is the major difference in journalizing between a general accounting system and a cost accounting system?

13. Identify an account with a function similar to the Manufacturing Summary account.

14. In recording closing entries for a manufacturing company using a general accounting system, the beginning balance of Finished Goods Inventory is:

    a. Debited to Finished Goods Inventory and credited to Income Summary.

    b. Debited to Finished Goods Inventory and credited to Manufacturing Summary.

    c. Credited to Finished Goods Inventory and debited to Income Summary.

15. What accounts are summarized in the Manufacturing Summary account?

16. What accounts are summarized in the Income Summary account?

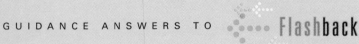

GUIDANCE ANSWERS TO   **Flashback**

11. *b*

12. A cost accounting system continually updates its three inventory accounts, whereas a general accounting system updates them only at the end of each period. A cost accounting system uses a cost of goods manufactured account to capture all the manufacturing expenses, whereas the general accounting system uses a manufacturing summary account to which manufacturing expenses incurred during the period are closed. Finally, a cost accounting system uses the cost of goods sold account to record the manufacturing costs and other expenses incurred during the period, whereas a general accounting system uses an income summary account to which the manufacturing summary, several expense accounts and finished goods inventory are closed.

13. Income summary

14. *c*

15. Accounts that enter into the computation of cost of goods manufactured are summarized in the Manufacturing Summary account. They include the beginning and ending balances of Raw Materials Inventory and Goods in Process Inventory, and the preclosing balances of the raw materials purchases, Direct Labour, and Factory Overhead accounts.

16. Accounts that enter into the computation of the year's net income are summarized in the Income Summary account. They include the beginning and ending balances of the Finished Goods Inventory account, the balance of the Manufacturing Summary account, and the balances of all revenue and expense accounts.

Summary

LO⁷   **Describe the closing process for a manufacturer using a general accounting system.** After end-of-period adjustments are recorded in the closing process, all manufacturing costs are transferred to the manufacturing summary account. Next, the Manufacturing Summary balance is allo-

cated to cost of goods manufactured (Income Summary) and to ending inventories of materials and goods in process. At the same time, the beginning finished goods inventory balance is transferred to Income Summary. Another closing entry records the ending finished goods inventory.

Demonstration Problem

The following information describes the job order manufacturing activities of Peak Manufacturing Company for May:

Raw materials purchases..	$16,000
Factory payroll cost...	15,400
Overhead costs incurred:	
Indirect materials	5,000
Indirect labour	3,500
Other factory overhead..	9,500

The predetermined overhead rate is 150% of the direct labour cost. These costs are allocated to the three jobs worked on during May as follows:

	Job 401	Job 402	Job 403
Balances on April 30:			
Direct materials	$3,600		
Direct labour..	1,700		
Applied overhead..	2,550		
Costs during May:			
Direct materials	3,550	$3,500	$1,400
Direct labour..	5,100	6,000	800
Applied overhead..	?	?	?
Status on May 31	Finished (sold)	Finished (unsold)	In process

Required

1. Determine the total cost of:
   a. April 30 inventory of jobs in process.
   b. Materials used during May.
   c. Labour used during May.
   d. Factory overhead incurred and applied during May and the amount of any over- or underapplied overhead on May 31.
   e. Each job as of May 31, the May 31 inventories of goods in process and finished goods, and the goods sold during May.
2. Prepare summarized journal entries, using a cost accounting system, for the month to record:
   a. Materials purchases (on credit), the factory payroll (paid with cash), indirect materials, indirect labour, and the other factory overhead (paid with cash).
   b. Assignment of direct materials, direct labour, and overhead costs to the Goods in Process Inventory account. (Use separate debit entries for each job.)
   c. Transfer of each completed job to the Finished Goods Inventory account.
   d. Cost of goods sold.
   e. Removal of any underapplied or overapplied overhead from the Factory Overhead account. (Assume the amount is not material.)
3. Prepare a manufacturing statement for May.

Planning the Solution

- ○ Determine the cost of the April 30 in-process inventory by adding up the materials, labour, and applied overhead costs for Job 401.
- ○ Compute the cost of materials used and labour by adding up the amounts assigned to jobs and to overhead.
- ○ Compute the total overhead incurred by adding the amounts of the three components; compute the amount of applied overhead by multiplying the total direct labour cost by the predetermined overhead rate; compute the underapplied or overapplied amount as the difference between the actual cost and the applied cost.
- ○ Determine the total cost charged to each job by adding any costs incurred in April to the materials, labour, and overhead applied during May.
- ○ Group the costs of the jobs according to their status as completed.
- ○ Record the direct materials costs assigned to the three jobs, using a separate Goods in Process Inventory account for each job; do the same thing for the direct labour and the applied overhead.
- ○ Transfer the costs of Jobs 401 and 402 from Goods in Process Inventory to Finished Goods Inventory.
- ○ Record the costs of Job 401 as the cost of goods sold.
- ○ Record the transfer of the underapplied overhead from the Factory Overhead account to the Cost of Goods Sold account.
- ○ On the manufacturing statement, remember to include the beginning and ending in-process inventories, and to deduct the underapplied overhead.

SOLUTION TO **Demonstration Problem**

1. Total cost of:

a. April 30 inventory of jobs in process (Job 401):

Direct materials	$3,600
Direct labour	1,700
Applied overhead	2,550
Total	$7,850

b. Materials used during May:

Direct materials:	
Job 401	$ 3,550
Job 402	3,500
Job 403	1,400
Total direct materials	8,450
Indirect materials	5,000
Total materials	$13,450

c. Labour used during May:

Direct labour:	
Job 401	$ 5,100
Job 402	6,000
Job 403	800
Total direct labour	11,900
Indirect labour	3,500
Total labour	$15,400

d. Factory overhead incurred during May:

Indirect materials	$ 5,000
Indirect labour	3,500
Other factory overhead	9,500
Total actual overhead	18,000
Overhead applied (150% × $11,900)	17,850
Underapplied overhead	$ 150

e. Total cost of each job:

	401	402	403
From April:			
Direct materials	$ 3,600		
Direct labour	1,700		
*Applied overhead............	2,550		
From May:			
Direct materials	3,550	$ 3,500	$1,400
Direct labour	5,100	6,000	800
*Applied overhead............	7,650	9,000	1,200
Total costs	$24,150	$18,500	$3,400

*Equals 150% of the direct labour cost.

Total cost of the May 31 inventory of goods in process (Job 403) = $3,400
Total cost of the May 31 inventory of finished goods (Job 402) = $18,500
Total cost of goods sold during May (Job 401) = $24,150

2. Journal entries:

a.

Raw Materials Inventory....................................	16,000	
Accounts Payable		16,000
To record materials purchases.		
Factory Payroll	15,400	
Cash..		15,400
To record factory payroll.		
Factory Overhead	5,000	
Raw Materials Inventory..........................		5,000
To record indirect materials.		
Factory Overhead	3,500	
Factory Payroll		3,500
To record indirect labour.		
Factory Overhead	9,500	
Cash..		9,500
To record other factory overhead.		

b. Assignment of costs to goods in process:

Goods in Process Inventory (Job 401)............	3,550	
Goods in Process Inventory (Job 402)............	3,500	
Goods in Process Inventory (Job 403)............	1,400	
Raw Materials Inventory..........................		8,450
To assign direct materials to jobs.		
Goods in Process Inventory (Job 401)............	5,100	
Goods in Process Inventory (Job 402)............	6,000	
Goods in Process Inventory (Job 403)............	800	
Factory Payroll....................................		11,900
To assign direct labour to jobs.		
Goods in Process Inventory (Job 401)............	7,650	
Goods in Process Inventory (Job 402)............	9,000	
Goods in Process Inventory (Job 403)............	1,200	
Factory Overhead..................................		17,850
To apply overhead to jobs.		

c.

Finished Goods Inventory..................................	42,650	
Goods in Process Inventory (Job 401)......		24,150
Goods in Process Inventory (Job 402)......		18,500
To record completion of jobs.		

d.

Cost of Goods Sold..	24,150	
Finished Goods Inventory.......................		24,150
To record sale of Job 401.		

e.

Cost of Goods Sold..	150	
Factory Overhead..................................		150
To assign underapplied overhead.		

3.

Peak Manufacturing Company Manufacturing Statement For Month Ended May 31		
Direct materials used		$ 8,450
Direct labour used		11,900
Factory overhead:		
Indirect materials...	$5,000	
Indirect labour...	3,500	
Other factory overhead	9,500	18,000
Total manufacturing costs		38,350
Add goods in process, April 30...		7,850
Total goods in process during the month		46,200
Deduct goods in process, May 31.......................................		(3,400)
Deduct underapplied overhead		(150)
Cost of goods manufactured...		$42,650

Glossary

Clock card A source document that is used to record the number of hours an employee works and to determine the total labour cost for each pay period. (p. 1151)

Job The production of a unique product or service. (p. 1145)

Job cost sheet A separate record maintained for each job. (p. 1147)

Job lot Producing more than one unit of a unique product. (p. 1145)

Job order cost accounting system A cost accounting system that is designed to determine the cost of producing each job or job lot. (p. 1147)

Job order manufacturing The production of special order products, also called *customized production.* (p. 1145)

Materials ledger cards Perpetual records that are updated each time units are purchased and each time units are issued for use in production. (p. 1149)

Materials requisition A source document that production managers use to request materials for manufacturing and that is used to assign materials costs to specific jobs or to overhead. (p. 1150)

Overapplied overhead The amount by which the overhead applied to jobs during a period with the predetermined over-

head application rate exceeds the overhead incurred during the period. (p. 1159)

Periodic inventory system Measures costs of raw materials, goods in process, and finished goods inventories from physical counts of quantities on hand at the end of each period. (p. 1144)

Perpetual inventory system Continuously updates records for costs of raw materials, goods in process, and finished goods inventories. (p. 1144)

Predetermined overhead application rate The rate established prior to the beginning of a period that relates estimated overhead to another variable such as estimated direct labour, and that is used to assign overhead cost to jobs. (p. 1153)

Time ticket A source document used to report how much time was spent working on a job or on overhead activities and that is used to determine the amount of direct labour to charge to the job or the amount of indirect labour to charge to overhead. (p. 1151)

Underapplied overhead The amount by which overhead incurred during a period exceeds the overhead applied to jobs with the predetermined overhead application rate. (p. 1158)

 **Online LearningCentre** *with POWERWEB*

For more study tools, quizzes, and problem material,
refer to the Online Learning Centre at
www.mcgrawhill.ca/college/larson

Questions

1. Why must a company estimate the amount of overhead assigned to individual jobs or job lots?

2. The text used a percentage of labour cost to assign factory overhead to individual jobs. Identify another approach that a company may use to assign factory overhead costs.

3. What types of information are recorded on a job cost sheet? How are job cost sheets used by management and employees?

4. In a job order cost accounting system, what records serve as a subsidiary ledger for Goods in Process Inventory? For Finished Goods Inventory?

5. What journal entry is recorded when a materials manager receives a materials requisition and then issues materials for use in the factory?

6. What role does the materials requisition slip play to safeguard the company's assets?

7. What is the difference between a "clock card" and a "time ticket?"

8. What events cause debits to be recorded in the Factory Overhead account? What events cause credits to be recorded in the account?

9. What accounts are used to eliminate overapplied or underapplied overhead from the Factory Overhead account, assuming the amount is not significant?

10. NIKE just finished production on a batch of 300 football shoes, specially coloured green and gold, for a CFL team. How should they account for this, as 300 individual jobs or as a job lot? Why?

11. Why must a company compute a predetermined overhead allocation rate?

12. How would a hospital apply job order costing?

13.^A In the general accounting system model, all manufacturing accounts are closed to the _____ summary account.

---

^A Identifies assignment material based on Appendix 22A.

Quick Study

QS 22-1
Determine factory overhead rates

LO⁵

Secor Company incurred the following manufacturing costs for the period:

Direct labour	$524,000
Direct materials	655,000
Factory overhead...	131,000

Compute overhead cost as a percentage of (a) direct labour and (b) direct materials.

QS 22-2
Review job and job lot differences

LO¹

Determine which products from the following list would most likely be manufactured as a job and which as a job lot:

1. T-shirts imprinted with a company logo.
2. A hand-crafted table.
3. A custom-designed home.
4. A 30-metre motor yacht.
5. Little League trophies.
6. Wedding dresses for a chain of department stores.

QS 22-3
Determine job cost

LO²

The following information was found on materials requisitions and time tickets for Job 7-1045, which was completed by Copeland Company. The requisitions are identified by code numbers starting with the letter R and the time tickets start with W:

Date	Document	Amount
1/7/04	R-1289	$1,350
1/7/04	W-3103	700
5/7/04	R-4615	1,100
5/7/04	W-3429	450
10/7/04	W-3454	400

Before the year started, management estimated that the overhead cost would equal 130% of the direct labour cost for each job. Determine the total cost on the job cost sheet for Job 7-1045.

QS 22-4
Prepare material journal entries

LO³

During November 2004, Rupert Company, which uses a job order cost accounting system, purchased raw materials for $45,000 cash. It then used $13,000 of the raw materials indirectly as factory supplies and used $28,000 as direct materials. Prepare entries to record these transactions.

QS 22-5
Prepare labour journal entries

LO⁴

During March, Kane Company, which uses a job order cost accounting system, had a monthly factory payroll of $135,000, paid in cash. Of this amount, $28,000 was classified as indirect labour and the remainder as direct. Prepare entries to record these transactions.

QS 22-6
Prepare factory overhead entries

LO⁵

During one month, a company that uses a job order cost accounting system had a monthly factory payroll of $140,000, paid in cash. Of this amount, $30,000 was classified as indirect labour and the remainder as direct for the production of 100 pairs of ice skates. Factory overhead is applied at 140% of direct labour payroll. Prepare the entry to record manufacturing overhead to this job lot.

QS 22-7
Compute overhead allocation rate

LO⁵

Seniors Financial & Management Consulting (SFMC) specializes in offering services to fellow seniors. Sarah Jones, SFMC's controller, estimated its labour and overhead costs for 2005 to be $386,000 and $974,000, respectively. SFMC pays its direct labour at the rate of $19.30 per hour. Compute SFMC's predetermined overhead allocation rate for 2005 using (a) direct labour $ and (b) direct labour hours.

Angela's Detective Service has received a request for a quote from a small business for a private investigation. Angela has determined that this job will likely require 220 hours of investigator time. She pays her investigators $26 an hour. She assigns overhead at the rate of $12 per investigation hour. Compute the expected total cost for the proposed assignment.

QS 22-8
Determine job costs

LO^2

Windsor Company allocates overhead at a rate of 160% of direct labour cost. Actual overhead for the period was $850,000 and direct labour was $500,000. Prepare the closing entry of over- or underapplied overhead to cost of goods sold.

QS 22-9
Prepare over/underapplied overhead entry

LO^6

Complete the following sentences about accounts unique to a manufacturing company:
a. The temporary account that has a zero balance until the closing process starts and is similar to Income Summary is the _____ account.
b. The temporary accounts in which manufacturing costs are recorded throughout the period are _____, _____, and _____.

QS 22-10[A]
Identify general accounting system terms.

LO^7

Felix Company manufactures products and accounts for its activities using a periodic cost accounting system. The following account balances are taken from the company's ledger at the end of the year before closing:

QS 22-11[A]
Prepare general accounting system closing entries

$LO^{3, 4, 7}$

Raw Materials Inventory	$ 18,000
Goods in Process Inventory	16,000
Raw Materials Purchases	85,000
Direct Labour	107,000
Factory Overhead	220,000

Physical counts at the end of the year show:

Raw Materials Inventory	$17,000
Goods in Process Inventory	16,600

Prepare the closing entries that should be made to the Manufacturing Summary account, except for the entry to the Income Summary account.

[A] Identifies assignment material based on Appendix 22A.

Exercises

Exercise 22-1
Documents used in job order cost accounting systems

$LO^{3,4,5}$

The left column below includes the names of several documents used in job order cost accounting systems. The right column presents short descriptions of the purposes of the documents. In the blank space beside each of the numbers in the right column, write the letter of the document that serves the described purpose.

a. Factory Payroll account

b. Materials ledger card

c. Time ticket

d. Voucher

e. Materials requisition

f. Factory Overhead account

g. Clock card

_____ 1. Communicates to the storeroom that materials are needed to complete a job.

_____ 2. Shows only the total amount of time that an employee works each day.

_____ 3. Shows the amount approved for payment of an overhead cost.

_____ 4. Shows the amount of time an employee worked on a specific job.

_____ 5. Temporarily accumulates the cost of incurred overhead until the cost is assigned to specific jobs.

_____ 6. Temporarily accumulates labour costs incurred until they are assigned to specific jobs or to overhead.

_____ 7. Perpetual inventory record of raw materials received, used, and on hand.

Exercise 22-2
Analysis of cost flows

$LO^{3,4,5}$

As of the end of June, the job cost sheets at David's Limited showed that the following total costs had been accumulated on three jobs:

	Job 102	Job 103	Job 104
Direct materials..	$14,000	$30,000	$27,000
Direct labour	9,000	11,200	21,000
Overhead	11,250	14,000	26,250

Job 102 was started in production during May and the following costs were assigned to it in that month: direct materials of $6,000, direct labour of $1,800, and overhead of $2,250. Jobs 103 and 104 were started during June. Overhead cost was applied with a predetermined application rate based on direct labour cost. Only Jobs 102 and 103 were finished during June, and it is expected that Job 104 will be finished in July. No raw materials were used indirectly during June. Using this information, answer the following questions:
a. What was the cost of the raw materials requisitioned during June for the three jobs?
b. How much direct labour cost was incurred during June?
c. What predetermined overhead application rate was used during June?
d. How much cost was transferred to finished goods during June?

Exercise 22-3
Computing overhead application rate; assigning costs to jobs

LO^5

In December 2003, Hi-Tek Marketing's management established the 2004 overhead application rate based on direct labour cost. The information used in setting the rate included the cost accountant's estimates that the company would incur $672,000 of overhead costs and $420,000 of direct labour cost during 2004. During March of 2004, Hi-Tek began and completed Job No. 13-56.

Required
a. Compute the overhead application rate for 2004.
b. Use the information on the following job cost sheet to determine the total cost of the job.

JOB COST SHEET

Customer's Name Clark Co. **Job No.** 13-56

Job Description Market Research

Date	Direct Labour Time-Ticket No.	Direct Labour Amount	Overhead Costs Applied Rate	Overhead Costs Applied Amount
Mar. 8	T-124	730.00		
11	T-176	1,370.00		
18	T-204	1,250.00		
Total				

Newton Company uses a job order cost accounting system that charges overhead to jobs on the basis of direct labour cost. At the end of last year, the company's Goods in Process Inventory account showed the following:

Goods in Process Inventory				Acct. No. 121
Date	Explanation	Debit	Credit	Balance
2004				
Dec. 31	Direct materials cost	1,400,000		1,400,000
31	Direct labour cost	336,000		1,736,000
31	Overhead costs	436,800		2,172,800
31	To finished goods		1,548,000	624,800

Required

1. Determine the overhead application rate (based on direct labour cost) used by the company.
2. Only one job with direct materials of $348,800 was in the goods in process inventory at the end of December 2004. How much direct labour cost must have been assigned to it? How much overhead cost must have been assigned to it?

Exercise 22-4
Analysis of costs assigned to goods in process

LO^5

Maloney Security Company produces special order security products and uses a job order cost accounting system. The system provided the following information:

Exercise 22-5
Understanding cost flows in a job order cost accounting system

LO$^{3, 4, 5}$

	May 31	June 30
Inventories:		
Raw materials	$27,000	$ 46,000
Goods in process	9,200	18,700
Finished goods	60,000	33,300
Information about May:		
Raw materials purchases (paid with cash)		$ 195,000
Factory payroll (paid with cash)		405,000
Factory overhead:		
Indirect materials		15,000
Indirect labour		85,000
Other overhead costs		100,600
Sales (received in cash)		$1,540,000
Predetermined overhead application rate based on direct labour cost		62.5%

Compute the following amounts for the month of June:

a. Cost of direct materials used.
b. Cost of direct labour used.
c. Cost of goods manufactured.
d. Cost of goods sold.
e. Gross profit.

Exercise 22-6

Recording journal entries for a job order cost accounting system

LO 3, 4, 5

Use information provided in Exercise 22-5 to prepare general journal entries to record the following events for June:
a. Raw materials purchases.
b. Direct materials usage.
c. Indirect materials usage.
d. Factory payroll costs.
e. Direct labour usage.
f. Indirect labour usage.
g. Factory overhead other than indirect materials and indirect labour (record the credit in Other Accounts).
h. Application of overhead to goods in process.
i. Transfer of finished jobs to the finished goods inventory.
j. Sale and delivery of finished goods to customers.

Exercise 22-7

Eliminating end-of-period balance in Factory Overhead

LO 5, 6

In December 2003, Frederick Limited established its predetermined overhead application rate during 2004 by using the following predictions:

Overhead costs	$1,260,000
Direct labour costs	840,000

At the end of 2004, the company's records showed that actual overhead costs for the year had been $1,414,000. The actual direct labour cost had been assigned to jobs as follows:

Jobs completed and sold	$588,000
Jobs in goods in process inventory	117,600
Jobs in finished goods inventory	78,400
Total actual direct labour cost	$784,000

Required
1. Compute the predetermined overhead application rate for 2004.
2. Set up a T-account for overhead and enter the overhead costs incurred and the amounts applied to jobs during the year with the predetermined rate.
3. Determine whether overhead was overapplied or underapplied during the year.
4. Prepare the general journal entry to close any over- or underapplied overhead directly to the cost of goods sold.
5. Prepare the adjusting entry to allocate any over- or underapplied overhead to cost of goods sold and the various inventories.

Exercise 22-8

Eliminating end-of-period balance in Factory Overhead

LO 5, 6

In December 2003, Setter Company established its predetermined overhead application rate for jobs produced during 2004 by using the following predictions:

Overhead costs	$900,000
Direct labour costs	600,000

At the end of 2004, the company's records showed that actual overhead costs for the year had been $1,010,000. The actual direct labour cost had been assigned to jobs as follows:

Jobs completed and sold	$420,000
Jobs still in the finished goods inventory	84,000
Jobs in the goods in process inventory	56,000
Total actual direct labour cost	$560,000

Required

1. Compute the predetermined overhead application rate for 2004.
2. Set up a T-account for Factory Overhead and enter the overhead costs incurred and the amounts applied to jobs during the year with the predetermined rate.
3. Determine whether overhead was over-applied or underapplied during the year.
4. Prepare the general journal entry to allocate any over- or underapplied overhead to cost of goods sold.
5. Prepare the general journal entry to allocate any over- or underapplied overhead assuming the amount is material.

The following chart lists seven accounts in general accounting systems used by manufacturers. Fill in the requested facts for each account. The first row is completed for you.

Exercise 22-9[A]
Identifying facts about manufacturing accounts

LO[7]

Account	Balance at Beginning of Year	Entries to Account Prior to Closing	Closing Entries Made to Account	Closed at End of Year?	Financial Statements on Which Balance is Reported
Raw Materials Inventory	Cost of raw materials on hand at end of prior year	None	Credited for beginning balance. Debited for ending balance	No	Manufacturing Statement
Balance Sheet					
Raw Materials Purchases					
Direct Labour					
Factory Overhead					
Goods in Process Inventory					
Finished Goods Inventory					
Manufacturing Summary					

[A] Identifies assignment material based on Appendix 22A.

Exercise 22-10[A]
Closing entries for a manufacturing company

LO[7]

The following account balances are taken from the Helix Co.'s accounting records after adjustments as of December 31, 2004. Also presented are the results of physical counts and valuations of the ending inventories.

Sales	$422,400
Raw materials purchases	67,200
Direct labour	99,120
Factory overhead	81,600
Selling expenses	45,840
General and administrative expenses	41,760
Income taxes expense	47,520
Beginning inventories:	
Raw materials	12,480
Goods in process	17,040
Finished goods	10,320
Ending inventories:	
Raw materials	19,440
Goods in process	25,200
Finished goods	15,840

Prepare closing entries for the company using a general accounting system.

Exercise 22-11[A]
Overhead rate calculation and analysis

LO[5, 7]

Baker Company uses direct labour costs as the base to assign factory overhead to its inventories of goods in process and finished goods. The company incurred the following costs during 2004:

Factory overhead costs	$1,512,000
Direct materials used	1,249,500
Direct labour costs	2,016,000

a. Determine the company's overhead rate for 2004.
b. Under the assumption that the company's $57,000 ending goods in process inventory had $16,000 of direct labour costs, determine the inventory's direct material costs.
c. Under the assumption that the company's $473,000 ending finished goods inventory had $273,000 of direct material costs, determine the inventory's direct labour cost and its factory overhead costs.

Exercise 22-12[A]
Allocating costs to ending inventories

LO[7]

According to physical counts, Monarch Company's ending goods in process inventory consisted of 4,500 units of partially completed product and its finished goods inventory consisted of 11,700 units of product. The factory manager determined that the goods in process inventory included direct materials cost of $10.50 per unit and direct labour cost of $7.00 per unit. Finished goods were estimated to have $12.80 of direct materials cost per unit and $9.00 of direct labour cost per unit. During the period, the company incurred these costs:

Direct materials	$460,000
Direct labour	277,000
Factory overhead	443,200

The company allocates factory overhead to goods in process and finished goods inventories by relating overhead to direct labour cost.
a. Compute the overhead rate.
b. Compute the total cost of the two ending inventories.
c. Because this was Monarch's first year, there were no beginning inventories. Compute the cost of goods sold for the year.

[A] Identifies assignment material based on Appendix 22A.

Roxanne Company's General Ledger included the following items related to its manufacturing activities for 2004. The accounts have been adjusted, but have not yet been closed.

Raw materials inventory	$ 84,600
Goods in process inventory	99,360
Raw materials purchases	311,400
Direct labour	450,000
Indirect labour	194,220
Factory utilities	109,440
Repairs, factory equipment	30,060
Rent on factory building	84,600
Property taxes on factory building	19,260
Factory insurance expired	16,020
Factory supplies used	34,920
Amortization of factory equipment	82,800
Amortization of patents	13,680

In addition, the ending inventory of raw materials is known to be $91,080. The ending inventory of goods in process is not known, but it is known that the company makes a single product and 4,500 units of goods were in process on December 31, 2004. Each unit of the product contained an estimated $18.00 of direct materials and had $7.50 of direct labour cost assigned to it.

Required

Preparation component

1. Compute the overhead rate based on the relationship between total factory overhead cost and total direct labour cost. Then, determine the cost of the ending goods in process inventory.
2. Prepare a manufacturing statement for 2004. Be certain to include a title on this statement.
3. Prepare entries to close the manufacturing accounts to Manufacturing Summary and to close the Manufacturing Summary account.

Analysis component

4. Compute the overhead rate based on the relationship between total factory overhead and total direct materials used. Then, without providing additional calculations, explain how Roxanne Company's manufacturing statement would be affected if this rate were used instead of one based on direct labour cost.

Exercise 22-13A
Allocating costs to goods in process; preparing manufacturing statement

LO5, 7

Check figure:
Overhead rate: 130%

Problems

Beaver Company's inventory of raw materials for June was $140,000. Raw materials purchases in July were $560,000. Factory payroll cost in July is $308,000. Overhead costs incurred during July are: indirect materials, $42,000; indirect labour, $27,440; factory rent, $39,200; factory heat, $23,520; factory equipment amortization, $54,880. The predetermined overhead rate is 60% of the direct labour cost. Job 206 is sold for $532,000 cash during July. Costs allocated to the three jobs worked on during July were:

	Job 206	Job 207	Job 208
Balances on June 30:			
Direct materials	$ 19,600	$ 25,200	
Direct labour	25,200	22,400	
Applied overhead	15,120	13,440	
Costs during July:			
Direct materials	140,000	238,000	$112,000
Direct labour	42,000	78,400	168,000
Applied overhead	?	?	?
Status on July 31	Finished (sold)	Finished (unsold)	In process

Problem 22-1A
Computing and recording manufacturing costs and preparing reports

LO2, 3, 4, 5

A Identifies assignment material based on Appendix 22A.

Check figure:
Cost of goods manufactured,
$705,600

Required

Preparation component

1. Determine the total of each manufacturing cost incurred for July (direct labour, direct materials, allocated overhead), and the total cost assigned to each of the three jobs (including the balances from June 30).
2. Present journal entries for the month to record:
   a. The materials purchases (on credit), the factory payroll (paid with cash), and the actual overhead costs, including indirect materials and indirect labour. (The factory rent and utilities were paid with cash.)
   b. The assignment of direct materials, direct labour, and applied overhead costs to the Goods in Process Inventory.
   c. The transfer of Jobs 206 and 207 to the Finished Goods Inventory.
   d. The cost of goods sold for Job 206.
   e. The revenue from the sale of Job 206.
   f. The assignment of any underapplied or overapplied overhead to the Cost of Goods Sold account. (The amount is not material.)
3. Prepare a manufacturing statement for July (use a single line presentation for direct materials and show the details of overhead cost). Also, present a calculation of gross profit for July and show how the inventories would be presented on the July 31 balance sheet.

Analysis component

4. When the over- or underapplied overhead adjustment is made, you are closing Factory Overhead to Cost of Goods Sold. Discuss how this adjustment affects business decision making regarding individual jobs or batches.

Problem 22-2A
Source documents, journal entries, overhead, and financial statements

LO 3, 4, 5, 6

The following trial balance of Murray Company was generated by the computer system on the morning of December 31, 2004. Lyle Handfield, the company's accountant, knows that something is wrong with the trial balance because it does not show any balance for goods in process inventory and it still shows balances in the Factory Payroll and Factory Overhead accounts:

Cash	$ 48,000	
Accounts receivable	42,000	
Raw materials inventory	24,000	
Goods in process inventory	-0-	
Finished goods inventory	9,000	
Prepaid rent	3,000	
Accounts payable		$ 10,500
Notes payable		13,500
Common shares		30,000
Retained earnings		87,000
Sales		180,000
Cost of goods sold	105,000	
Factory payroll	18,000	
Factory overhead	27,000	
Miscellaneous expenses	45,000	
Total	$321,000	$321,000

After a few moments of searching a cluttered in-box, Handfield found six source documents that needed to be processed to bring the accounting records up to date:

Materials requisition 21-3010:	$3,600	direct materials to Job 402
Materials requisition 21-3011:	$6,600	direct materials to Job 404
Materials requisition 21-3012:	$2,100	indirect materials
Labour time ticket 6052:	$6,000	direct labour to Job 402
Labour time ticket 6053:	$9,000	direct labour to Job 404
Labour time ticket 6054:	$3,000	indirect labour

Jobs 402 and 404 are the only units in process at the end of the year. The predetermined overhead application rate is 210% of direct labour cost.

Required

Preparation component

1. Use the information on the six source documents to prepare journal entries to assign the following costs:
   a. Direct material costs to goods in process inventory.
   b. Direct labour costs to goods in process inventory.
   c. Overhead costs to goods in process inventory.
   d. Indirect material costs to the Overhead account.
   e. Indirect labour costs to the Overhead account.
2. Determine the new balance of the Factory Overhead account after making the entries in requirement 1. Determine whether there is any under- or overapplied overhead for the year. If so, prepare the appropriate adjusting entry to close the overhead account, assuming that the amount is not material.
3. Prepare a revised trial balance.
4. Prepare an income statement for 2004 and a balance sheet as of December 31, 2004.

Analysis component

5. Assume that the $2,100 on materials requisition 21-3012 should have been direct materials charged to Job 404. Without providing specific calculations, describe what impact this error would have on Murray's 2004 income statement and balance sheet.

The predetermined overhead application rate for 2004 was 200% of direct labour costs for Harbison Company. The company's activities related to manufacturing during May 2004 were:

a. Purchased raw materials on account, $100,000.
b. Paid factory wages with cash, $84,000.
c. Paid miscellaneous factory overhead costs with cash, $11,000.
d. Materials requisitions for the month show that the following materials were used on jobs and indirectly:

Problem 22-3A
Source documents and journal entries in job order cost accounting

LO[5, 6]

Job 136	$20,000
Job 137	10,000
Job 138	22,000
Job 139	24,000
Job 140	4,000
Total direct materials	$80,000
Indirect materials	12,000
Total materials used	$92,000

e. Labour time tickets for the month show the following labour was used on jobs and indirectly:

Job 136	$8,000
Job 137	14,000
Job 138	18,000
Job 139	26,000
Job 140	2,000
Total direct labour	$68,000
Indirect labour	16,000
Total	$84,000

f. Overhead was applied to Jobs 136, 138, and 139.
g. Jobs 136, 138, and 139 were transferred to finished goods.
h. Jobs 136 and 138 were sold on account for a total price of $240,000.

i. Overhead costs incurred during the month were as follows. (Credit Prepaid Insurance for the expired factory insurance.)

Amortization of factory building........................	$37,000
Amortization of factory equipment..................	31,000
Expired factory insurance	7,000
Accrued property taxes payable	21,000

j. At the end of the month, overhead is applied to the goods in process (Jobs 137 and 140) using the predetermined rate of 200% of direct labour cost.

Check figure:
Finished goods inventory, $102,000

Required

1. Prepare general journal entries to record the events and transactions *a* through *j*.
2. Set up T-accounts for each of the following general ledger accounts, each of which started the month with a zero balance. Then, post the journal entries to these T-accounts and determine the balance of each account.

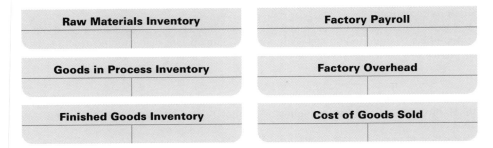

3. Prepare a job cost sheet for each job worked on during the month. Use the following simplified form of the job cost sheet:

Job No.	
Materials	$_____
Labour....................	_____
Overhead	_____
Total cost................	$_____

4. Prepare a schedule showing the total cost of each job in process and proving that the sum of the costs equals the Goods in Process Inventory account balance. Prepare similar schedules for the finished goods inventory and the cost of goods sold.

Problem 22-4A
Allocating overhead using predetermined overhead allocation rate; job cost

LO^{2,5,6}

Beautiful Interiors specializes in designing and implementing custom interior decorations. Its direct labour consists of designers who are paid $32 per hour. During November 2004, Betty Arthur, a staff accountant, estimated the following overhead costs for 2005:

Supervision	$162,000
Indirect labour	146,000
Utilities...	18,300
Miscellaneous	74,100
Total overhead costs	$400,400

She also estimated the total direct labour requirements at 5,500 hours for the year. At the end of 2005, the cost records showed that the company had incurred overhead costs of $402,900. In 2005, the company completed five assignments as follows:

Job Number	Job Description	Direct labour hours
AW1 – 05	Art work & paintings	750
FL 1 – 05	Flower decorations	1,150
PN 1 – 05	Interior painting & wall-paper	2,100
DR 1 – 05	Designer drapes	700
CL 1 – 05	Ceiling & light fixtures	850
		5,550

Required

1. Determine:
   a. The predetermined overhead application rate for 2005 based on direct labour cost.
   b. The total overhead cost applied to each job during 2005.
   c. The over- or underapplied overhead at year-end.
2. Prepare the appropriate journal entry to close the over- or underapplied overhead at year-end.

Check figure:
Overhead, $1,140 credit
overapplied

The Kaplan Company manufactures special variations of its product, a technopress, in response to special orders from its customers. On May 1, the company had no inventories of goods in process or finished goods but held the following raw materials:

Problem 22-5A
Recording manufacturing transactions; subsidiary records

LO 3, 4, 5, 6

Material M	120 units @ $200 =	$24,000
Material R	80 units @ 160 =	12,800
Paint............................	44 units @ 72 =	3,168
Total		$39,968

On May 4, the company began working on two technopresses: Job 102 for Grobe Company and Job 103 for Reynco Company.

Required

Follow the instructions given in the list of activities below and complete them:

a. Purchased raw materials on credit and recorded the following information from the receiving reports and invoices:

> Receiving Report No. 426, Material M, 150 units at $200 each.
> Receiving Report No. 427, Material R, 70 units at $160 each.

(Instructions: Record the purchases with a single general journal entry and post it to the appropriate general ledger T-accounts, using the transaction letter to identify the entries. Also, enter the receiving report information on the materials ledger cards.)

b. Requisitioned the following raw materials for production:

> Requisition No. 35, for Job 102, 80 units of Material M.
> Requisition No. 36, for Job 102, 60 units of Material R.
> Requisition No. 37, for Job 103, 40 units of Material M.
> Requisition No. 38, for Job 103, 30 units of Material R.
> Requisition No. 39, for 12 units of paint.

(Instructions: Enter the amounts for the direct materials requisitions only on the materials ledger cards and the job cost sheets. Enter the indirect material amount on the raw materials ledger card and record a debit to the Indirect Materials account in the subsidiary Factory Overhead Ledger. Do not record a general journal entry at this time.)

Check figure:
Balance in Factory Overhead,
$1,536 credit, overapplied

c. Employees turned in the following time tickets for work in May:

> Time tickets Nos. 1 to 10 for direct labour on Job 102, $40,000.
> Time tickets Nos. 11 to 30 for direct labour on Job 103, $32,000.
> Time tickets Nos. 31 to 36 for equipment repairs, $12,000.

(Instructions: Record the direct labour reported on the time tickets only on the job cost sheets and debit the indirect labour to the Indirect Labour account in the subsidiary Factory Overhead Ledger. Do not record a general journal entry at this time.)

d. Paid cash for the following items during the month:

> Factory payroll, $84,000.
> Miscellaneous overhead items, $36,000.

(Instructions: Record the payments with general journal entries and then post them to the general ledger accounts. Also record a debit in the Miscellaneous Overhead account in the subsidiary Factory Overhead Ledger.)

e. Finished Job 102 and transferred it to the warehouse. The company assigns overhead to each job with a predetermined overhead application rate equal to 70% of direct labour cost.

(Instructions: Enter the allocated overhead on the cost sheet for Job 102, fill in the cost summary section of the cost sheet, and then mark the cost sheet as "Finished." Next, prepare a journal entry to record the job's completion and transfer to finished goods, and then post it to the general ledger accounts.)

f. Delivered Job 102 and accepted the customer's promise to pay $290,000 within 30 days.

(Instructions: Prepare general journal entries to record the sale of Job 102 and the cost of goods sold. Post them to the general ledger accounts.)

g. Applied overhead to Job 103, based on the job's direct labour to date.

(Instructions: Enter the overhead on the job cost sheet but do not make a general journal entry at this time.)

h. Recorded the total direct and indirect materials costs as reported on all the requisitions for the month.

(Instructions: Prepare a general journal entry to record these costs, and post it to the general ledger accounts.)

i. Recorded the total direct and indirect labour costs as reported on all the time tickets for the month.

(Instructions: Prepare a general journal entry to record these costs, and post it to the general ledger accounts.)

j. Recorded the total overhead costs applied to jobs.

(Instructions: Prepare a general journal entry to record the application of these costs and post it to the general ledger accounts.)

k. Determine the balances in the raw materials inventory and goods in process inventory.
l. Determine if the balance of the factory overhead account is over- or underapplied.

Following is the unadjusted trial balance of Tuffs Company as of December 31, 2004:

Problem 22-6A[A]
Adjusting and closing entries,
allocating overhead costs

LO[1, 2, 8]

Cash	$ 52,500	
Accounts receivable	230,000	
Raw materials inventory	200,000	
Goods in process inventory	100,000	
Finished goods inventory	225,000	
Factory equipment	500,000	
Accumulated amortization, factory equipment		$ 112,500
Accounts payable		162,500
Wages payable		
Income taxes payable		
Common shares		397,000
Retained earnings		408,500
Sales		1,562,500
Raw materials purchases	625,000	
Direct labour	232,500	
Indirect labour	87,500	
Factory utilities	67,500	
Repairs, factory equipment	15,000	
Amortization of factory equipment		
Selling expenses	182,500	
General and administrative expenses	125,500	
Income taxes expense		
Total	$2,643,000	$2,643,000

The following adjusting entries need to be made:
a. Amortization on the factory equipment for the year is $80,000.
b. Accrued direct labour wages are $24,500.
c. Accrued indirect labour wages are $7,000.
d. Accrued income taxes are estimated to be $112,000.
The raw materials ending inventory was $210,000. These facts were known about the other ending inventories:

	Materials Cost per Unit	Labour Cost per Unit	Units
Goods in process	$25.00	$10.00	2,500
Finished goods	42.00	22.50	6,000

Required
1. Present the prescribed adjusting entries.
2. Determine the total adjusted overhead cost, the total adjusted direct labour cost, and the overhead cost to direct labour cost ratio.
3. Determine the cost of the ending inventories of goods in process and finished goods.
4. Present the closing entries.

Check figure:
Ending finished goods inventory,
$522,000

[A] Identifies assignment material based on Appendix 22A.

Alternate Problems

Problem 22-1B

Recording manufacturing costs
and preparing financial reports

LO$^{2, 3, 4, 5}$

The following information refers to the job order manufacturing activities of Alliance
Company for April:

The March 31 inventory of raw materials was $5,000. Raw materials purchases
during April were $20,000. Factory payroll cost during April was $11,000. Overhead costs
incurred during the month of April were:

Indirect materials...	$1,500
Indirect labour...	700
Factory rent	1,000
Factory utilities	600
Factory equipment amortization......................	1,400

The predetermined overhead rate was 50% of the direct labour cost. Costs allocated to
the three jobs worked on during April were:

	Job 614	Job 615	Job 616
Balances at March 31:			
Direct materials...	$ 700	$ 900	
Direct labour..	900	800	
Applied overhead...	450	400	
Costs during April:			
Direct materials...	5,000	8,500	$4,000
Direct labour..	1,500	2,800	6,000
Applied overhead...	?	?	?
Status on April 30.	Finished (sold)	Finished (unsold)	In process

Job 614 was sold for $19,000 cash during April.

Required

Preparation component

1. Determine the total of each manufacturing cost incurred for April (direct labour, direct
   materials, allocated overhead), and the total cost assigned to each of the three jobs
   (including the balances from March 31).
2. Present journal entries for the month to record:
   a. The materials purchases (on credit), the factory payroll (paid with cash), and the
      actual overhead costs, including indirect materials and indirect labour. (The factory
      rent and utilities were paid with cash.)
   b. The assignment of direct materials, direct labour, and applied overhead costs to
      the Goods in Process Inventory.
   c. The transfer of Jobs 614 and 615 to the Finished Goods Inventory.
   d. The cost of goods sold for Job 614.
   e. The revenue from the sale of Job 614.
   f. The assignment of any underapplied or overapplied overhead to the Cost of Goods
      Sold account. (The amount is not material.)
3. Prepare a manufacturing statement for April (use a single line presentation for direct
   materials and show the details of overhead cost). Also, present a calculation of gross
   profit for April and show how the inventories would be presented on the April 30 balance sheet.

Analysis component

4. When the over- or underapplied overhead adjustment is made, you are closing
   Factory Overhead to Cost of Goods Sold. Discuss how this adjustment impacts business decision making regarding individual jobs or batches.

The following trial balance of Elroy Company was generated by the computer system on the morning of December 31, 2004. The company's accountant knows that something is wrong with the trial balance because it does not show any balance for the goods in process inventory and it still shows balances in the Factory Payroll and Factory Overhead accounts:

Problem 22-2B
Source documents, journal entries, and preparing financial statements

LO^{3, 4, 5, 6}

Cash	$ 30,000	
Accounts receivable	90,000	
Raw materials inventory	24,000	
Goods in process inventory	-0-	
Finished goods inventory	50,000	
Prepaid rent	4,000	
Accounts payable		$ 16,000
Notes payable		30,000
Common shares		60,000
Retained earnings		33,800
Sales		250,000
Cost of goods sold	140,000	
Factory payroll	20,000	
Factory overhead	9,800	
Miscellaneous expenses	22,000	
Total	$389,800	$389,800

After searching various files, six source documents are found that need to be processed to bring the accounting records up to date:

Materials requisition 94-231:	$ 5,000	direct materials to Job 406
Materials requisition 94-232:	8,000	direct materials to Job 408
Materials requisition 94-233:	700	indirect materials
Labour time ticket 765:	6,000	direct labour to Job 406
Labour time ticket 766:	12,000	direct labour to Job 408
Labour time ticket 777:	2,000	indirect labour

Jobs 406 and 408 are the only units in process at the end of the year. The predetermined overhead application rate is 70% of direct labour cost.

Required

Preparation component

1. Use the information on the six source documents to prepare journal entries to assign the following costs:
   a. Direct materials costs to goods in process inventory.
   b. Direct labour costs to goods in process inventory.
   c. Overhead costs to goods in process inventory.
   d. Indirect materials costs to the Overhead account.
   e. Indirect labour costs to the Overhead account.
2. Determine the new balance of the Factory Overhead account after making the entries in requirement 1. Determine whether there is under- or overapplied overhead for the year. If so, prepare the appropriate adjusting entry to close the overhead account, assuming that the amount is not material.
3. Prepare a revised trial balance.
4. Prepare an income statement for 2004 and a balance sheet as of December 31, 2004.

Analysis component

5. Assume that the $700 indirect materials on materials requisition 94-233 should have been direct materials charged to Job 408. Without providing specific calculations, describe what impact this error would have on Elroy's 2004 income statement and balance sheet.

Check figure:
Net income, $88,100

Problem 22-3B

Source documents and
journal entries in job order
cost accounting

LO[5,6]

Back Pack Company's predetermined overhead application rate during a recent month
was 200% of direct labour cost. The company's activities related to manufacturing during
the month were:

a. Purchased raw materials on account, $49,500.
b. Paid factory wages with cash, $42,750.
c. Paid miscellaneous factory overhead costs with cash, $6,750.
d. Indirect materials used were $9,000 and materials requisitions for the month show
that the following materials were used directly on jobs:

Job 45	$ 9,000
Job 46	4,725
Job 47	8,775
Job 48	9,675
Job 49	1,800
Total direct materials	$33,975

e. Indirect labour costs were $11,250. Labour time tickets for the month show the follow-
ing labour was used on specific jobs:

Job 45	$ 8,550
Job 46	4,950
Job 47	9,000
Job 48	8,100
Job 49	900
Total direct labour	$31,500

f. Jobs 45, 47, and 48 were completed, and overhead was allocated to them.
g. Jobs 45, 47, and 48 were transferred to finished goods.
h. Jobs 45 and 48 were sold on account for a total price of $97,000.
i. Overhead costs incurred during the month were as follows. (Credit Prepaid Insurance
for the expired factory insurance.)

Amortization of factory building	$13,500
Amortization of factory equipment	15,050
Expired factory insurance	2,700
Accrued property taxes payable	4,200

j. At the end of the month, overhead is applied to the goods in process (Jobs 46 and 49)
using the predetermined rate of 200% of direct labour cost.

Required
1. Prepare general journal entries to record the events and transactions *a* through *j*.
2. Set up T-accounts for each of the following general ledger accounts, each of which
started the month with a zero balance. Then, post the journal entries to these
T-accounts and determine the balance of each account:

Raw Materials Inventory	Factory Payroll

Goods in Process Inventory	Factory Overhead

Finished Goods Inventory	Cost of Goods Sold

3. Prepare a job cost sheet for each job worked on during the month. Use the following simplified form of the job cost sheet:

Job No.	
Materials	$_____
Labour	_____
Overhead	_____
Total cost	$_____

4. Prepare a schedule showing the total cost of each job in process and proving that the sum of the costs equals the Goods in Process Inventory account balance. Prepare similar schedules for the finished goods inventory and the cost of goods sold.

Custom Landscaping specializes in designing and implementing landscapes for residential and commercial property. Its direct labour consists of landscape designers who are paid $28 per hour. During November 2004, Kevin Anderson, a staff accountant, estimated the following overhead costs for 2005:

Supervision	$262,000
Indirect labour	246,000
Utilities...	28,300
Miscellaneous	54,100
Total overhead costs	$590,400

He also estimated the total direct labour costs at $210,000 hours for the year. At the end of 2005, the cost records showed that the company had incurred overhead costs of $613,432. In 2005, the company completed five assignments, as follows:

Job Number	Job Description	Direct labour cost
CL – 05-01	Tree design & planting	$ 32,200
CL – 05-02	Rose garden design	40,600
CL – 05-03	Commercial lawn design	58,800
CL – 05-04	Vegetable garden	19,600
CL – 05-05	Complete backyard	51,800
		$203,000

Required
1. Determine:
   a. The predetermined overhead application rate for 2005.
   b. The total overhead cost applied to each job during 2005.
   c. The over- or underapplied overhead at year-end.
2. Prepare the appropriate journal entry to close the over- or underapplied overhead at year-end.

Berry Company manufactures special variations of its product, a megatron, in response to orders from its customers. On March 1, the company had no inventories of goods in process or finished goods but held the following raw materials:

Material M	150	units @ $40 =	$ 6,000
Material R	50	units @ 160 =	8,000
Paint...............................	22	units @ 20 =	400
Total			$14,400

Problem 22-4B
Allocating overhead using predetermined overhead allocation rate; job cost

LO^{2,5,6}

Check figure:
$42,717.80, debit; underapplied

Problem 22-5B
Recording manufacturing transactions; subsidiary records

LO^{3,4,5}

On March 3, the company began working on two megatrons: Job 450 for Ancira Company and Job 451 for Montero, Inc.

Required

Follow the instructions given in the list of activities below and complete them:

a. Purchased raw materials on credit and recorded the following information from the receiving reports and invoices:

> Receiving Report No. 20, Material M, 150 units at $40 each.
> Receiving Report No. 21, Material R, 200 units at $160 each.

(Instructions: Record the purchases with a single general journal entry and post it to the appropriate general ledger T-accounts, using the transaction letter to identify the entries. Also, enter the receiving report information on the materials ledger cards.)

b. Requisitioned the following raw materials for production:

> Requisition No. 223, for Job 450, 60 units of Material M.
> Requisition No. 224, for Job 450, 100 units of Material R.
> Requisition No. 225, for Job 451, 30 units of Material M.
> Requisition No. 226, for Job 451, 75 units of Material R.
> Requisition No. 227, for 10 units of paint.

(Instructions: Enter the amounts for the direct materials requisitions only on the materials ledger cards and the job cost sheets. Enter the indirect material amount on the raw materials ledger card and record a debit to the Indirect Materials account in the subsidiary Factory Overhead Ledger. Do not record a general journal entry at this time.)

c. Employees turned in the following time tickets for work in March:

> Time tickets Nos. 1 to 10 for direct labour on Job 450, $24,000.
> Time tickets Nos. 11 to 20 for direct labour on Job 451, $20,000.
> Time tickets Nos. 21 to 24 for equipment repairs, $4,000.

(Instructions: Record the direct labour reported on the time tickets only on the job cost sheets and debit the indirect labour to the Indirect Labour account in the subsidiary Factory Overhead Ledger. Do not record a general journal entry at this time.)

d. The company paid cash for the following items during the month:

> Factory payroll, $48,000.
> Miscellaneous overhead items, $47,000.

(Instructions: Record the payments with general journal entries and then post them to the general ledger accounts. Also record a debit in the Miscellaneous Overhead account in the subsidiary Factory Overhead Ledger.)

e. Finished Job 450 and transferred it to the warehouse. The company assigns overhead to each job with a predetermined overhead application rate equal to 120% of direct labour cost.

(Instructions: Enter the allocated overhead on the cost sheet for Job 450, fill in the cost summary section of the cost sheet, and then mark the cost sheet as "Finished." Next, prepare a journal entry to record the job's completion and transfer to finished goods, and then post it to the general ledger accounts.)

f. Delivered Job 450 and accepted the customer's promise to pay $130,000 within 30 days.

(Instructions: Prepare general journal entries to record the sale of Job 450 and the cost of goods sold. Post them to the general ledger accounts.)

g. At the end of the month, used the predetermined rate to assign overhead cost to Job 451, based on the direct labour cost used on the job up to that date.

(Instructions: Enter the overhead on the job cost sheet but do not make a general journal entry at this time.)

h. Recorded the total direct and indirect materials costs as reported on all the requisitions for the month.

(Instructions: Prepare a general journal entry to record these costs, and post it to the general ledger accounts.)

i. Recorded the total direct and indirect labour costs as reported on all the time tickets for the month.

(Instructions: Prepare a general journal entry to record these costs, and post it to the general ledger accounts.)

j. Recorded the total overhead costs applied to jobs.

(Instructions: Prepare a general journal entry to record the application of these costs, and post it to the general ledger accounts.)

Following is the unadjusted trial balance of Wright Company as of December 31, 2004:

Problem 22-6B[A]
Adjusting and closing entries,
allocating overhead costs

LO[1, 2, 8]

Cash	$ 227,500	
Accounts receivable	350,000	
Raw materials inventory	420,000	
Goods in process inventory	140,000	
Finished goods inventory	315,000	
Factory equipment	700,000	
Accumulated amortization, factory equipment		$ 157,500
Accounts payable		227,500
Wages payable		
Income taxes payable		
Common shares		555,800
Retained earnings		865,200
Sales		2,187,500
Raw materials purchases	875,000	
Direct labour	325,500	
Indirect labour	122,500	
Factory utilities	94,500	
Repairs, factory equipment	21,000	
Amortization of factory equipment		
Selling expenses	227,500	
General and administrative expenses	175,000	
Income taxes expense		
Total	$3,993,500	$3,993,500

The following adjusting entries need to be made:
a. Amortization on the factory equipment for the year is $103,750.
b. Accrued direct labour wages are $22,750.
c. Accrued indirect labour wages are $6,500.
d. Accrued income taxes are estimated to be $91,000.

———
[A] Identifies assignment material based on Appendix 22A.

The raw materials ending inventory was $294,000. These facts were known about the other ending inventories:

	Materials Cost per Unit	Labour Cost per Unit	Units
Goods in process	$25.00	$10.00	2,500
Finished goods...................	30.00	32.50	6,000

Required
1. Present the prescribed adjusting entries.
2. Determine the total adjusted overhead cost, the total adjusted direct labour cost, and the overhead cost to direct labour cost ratio.
3. Determine the cost of the ending inventories of goods in process and finished goods.
4. Present the closing entries.

Analytical and Review Problems

A & R 22-1

On July 31, 2004, a flood completely damaged all of the work in process inventory of Drake Manufacturing. Neither the materials nor the finished goods inventory was destroyed. Drake uses a job order costing system. Its fiscal year-end is December 31.

Selected information from the June 30 interim financial statements follows:

Materials inventory (includes both direct and indirect materials)	$ 81,690
Work in process inventory...	118,139
Finished goods inventory	42,000
Manufacturing overhead incurred (year to date)	203,840
Manufacturing overhead applied..	198,100
Cost of goods sold (year to date)	596,400
Accounts payable (relates to material purchases only)	26,488

You were also able to obtain the following information for July 31, 2004

Materials inventory...	$ 73,920
Finished goods inventory	56,000
Accounts payable (relates to material purchases only)	67,984
Payroll costs (including $27,910 indirect)	131,390
Cost of goods sold (year to date)	694,400
Manufacturing overhead incurred (year to date)	249,900
Indirect materials used..	4,810
Overapplied overhead (during July)..	2,450
Cash payments to suppliers during July...	50,960

Required
Compute the cost of the work in process inventory lost in the flood.

K. Oppong, accountant for Wolfson Ltd., became ill during the year end closing process. Oppong posted only parts of several transactions to the accounts in the ledger. Following are selected general ledger accounts with balances as of July 2001, along with some parts of the posting entries. In some cases either the debit or credit portion of a particular entry appears in the accounts, but one or more of the offsetting credits or debits is missing. Assume that all entries have been completely posted except for postings to the following accounts.

A & R 22-2

Raw Materials Inventory		
July 1 Bal.	30,000	35,000

Factory Payroll	
65,000	

Goods in Process Inventory		
July 1 Bal.	10,000	100,000
Direct Matl.	25,000	
Direct Labour	50,000	

Factory Overhead	
36,000	

Finished Goods Inventory		
May 1 Bal.	12,500	94,000

Cost of Goods Sold	

Wolfson charges overhead to jobs with an overhead application rate of 125% of direct labour costs. The $36,000 debit in the Factory Overhead account is the sum of all overhead costs for May other than indirect materials and indirect labour.

Required
1. Copy the selected accounts and add the missing debits and credits. Use a code letter to identify the debits and credits of each entry.
2. Answer the following questions before considering any overapplied or underapplied overhead.
   a. What is the July 31 balance in the Finished Goods account?
   b. How much factory labour cost (direct and indirect) was incurred in July?
   c. What was the cost of goods sold for July?
   d. How much overhead was incurred during July?
   e. How much overhead was charged to jobs during July.
3. Was overhead underapplied or overapplied? If yes, then state the amount.

On July 31, 2004, a fire completely destroyed the plant of Balour Co. The following information was recovered from various sources:
- Inventories at July 1, 2004 were as follows: Materials, $7,000; Work in process, $21,000; Finished goods, $38,500.
- The cost of goods completed during July was $72,800.
- The factory overhead rate in use during July was $1.12 per dollar of direct material cost.
- Purchases of materials during July amounted to $42,000. The payroll records show wages accrued during July as $35,000, of which $4,200 was for indirect labour.
- The charges to factory overhead accounts totalled $25,200. Of this, $2,800 was for indirect materials and $4,200 was for indirect labour.
- Underapplied overhead was $560. This amount was not deducted in the computation of the gross profit margin.
- Total sales for the month amounted to $84,000. The gross profit margin was 35% of the selling price.

A & R 22-3

Required
Estimate of the cost assigned to (a) raw materials, (b) work in process, and (c) finished goods at the time of the fire on July 31, 2004.

A & R 22-4

Porter Company uses a job order system and assigns factory overhead using a predetermined overhead rate that relates overhead to direct labour.

The president of Porter Company has hired you as the new accountant and asked you to prepare the financial statements for the year ended December 31, 2004, based on the adjusted trial balance that follows:

Porter Company Adjusted Trail Balance December 31, 2004		
Cash	$ 62,016	
Accounts receivable	89,800	
Raw materials inventory	5,880	
Goods in process inventory	39,900	
Finished goods inventory	66,640	
Store equipment	103,292	
Accumulated amortization, store equipment		$ 37,912
Accounts payable		35,280
Long-term notes payable		97,440
Common shares		100,240
Retained earnings		89,516
Sales		270,200
Sales returns and allowances	3,500	
Cost of goods sold	193,760	
Factory payroll	6,720	
Factory overhead	3,360	
Miscellaneous expenses	55,720	
	$630,588	$630,588

The president has informed you that this trial balance was prepared by the previous accountant and is supposedly ready to be used in preparing the statements.

After taking a brief look at the adjusted trial balance, you suspect that some items of information for the period were not processed, or were processed incorrectly, and that you need some time to research the problem. Explain the basis of your suspicions to the president and describe the nature of the entries that will probably be required to correct the adjusted trial balance.

Process Cost Accounting

Coffee Time

Niagara Falls, On.—Christine Butler, fresh out of college with a business degree, recently joined Coffee Heaven, a processor and distributor of gourmet coffee. Coffee Heaven offers 15 different blends of coffee to gourmet shops in 500 gram bags.

After finishing a two-week training period, Butler and all new employees had to prepare a report on Coffee Heaven's process operations. "The company's expectations for us are high, and the competition is fierce," says Butler.

The report must include identifying the flow of product cost information and estimating total product costs for Coffee Heaven.

Butler's report identified three major processes: roasting coffee beans, blending the different types of coffee beans, and packaging the product. She explained that the roasting and packaging processes are highly automated and computer controlled, but the blending process is more labour intensive.

When Butler looked over her report, she was satisfied it covered all important processes and flows, with one exception. "I just couldn't figure out how to come up with the cost of a package of coffee," says Butler. "It's a simple concept, but implementing it was tough. I had to figure out how much was in process at the beginning and end of each period and estimate their percentages of completion." Butler knew this cost estimate is crucial for setting and maintaining profit margins and planning operations. "The market for our product is very competitive. Our prices are basically set by the market so we have to focus on cost control."

Butler recalled from her training course that companies with continuous processing, such as Coffee Heaven, must use a costing system different from that used by custom manufacturers. She sought out colleagues and additional readings for help with process costing. "It took me about 40 hours of work to get my estimate," says Butler, "and I'm still not entirely confident with it."

Butler obtained her estimate using both process cost accounting methods and process cost summaries. Adds Butler, "Without training in managerial accounting it would have taken me twice as long, with twice as many questions!"

Learning Objectives

LO¹ Explain process operations and how they differ from job order operations.

LO² Compare process cost accounting and job order cost accounting systems.

LO³ Record the flow of direct materials costs in process cost accounting.

LO⁴ Record the flow of direct labour costs in process cost accounting.

LO⁵ Record the flow of factory overhead costs in process cost accounting.

LO⁶ Define, explain, and compute equivalent units.

LO⁷ Explain the four steps in accounting for production activity in a period.

LO⁸ Define, describe, and prepare a process cost summary.

LO⁹ Record the transfer of goods between departments.

LO¹⁰ Record the transfer of goods to Finished Goods Inventory and Cost of Goods Sold.

Chapter Preview

The type of product or service a company offers determines its cost accounting system. We focused on job order cost accounting P. 1147 in Chapter 22. Companies use job order cost accounting to account for costs when each product or job consists of one unit (or a group of units) that is uniquely designed to meet the requirements of a particular customer. Each unit, or group of units, is a distinct product or job requiring unique applications of material, labour, and overhead. But not all products are manufactured in this way. Many products carry standard designs where one unit of product is no different than any other unit. This type of system often produces large numbers of products on a continuous basis, period after period. In this case all units pass through similar manufacturing steps or processes. This chapter describes how to use a process cost accounting system to account for these types of products. We explain how costs are accumulated for each process and then assigned to units passing through processes. This knowledge helps in understanding and estimating the cost of each process. It also helps in finding ways to reduce costs and improve processes.

Process Manufacturing Operations

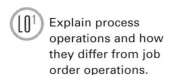

LO¹ Explain process operations and how they differ from job order operations.

There are many manufacturers engaged in continuous processing of similar, often called homogenous, products. **Process manufacturing**, also called *process operations* or *process production*, is the mass production of products in a continuous flow of steps. This means products pass through a series of sequential processes.

Petroleum refining is a common example of a process production system. Crude oil passes through a series of steps before it is processed into three grades of petroleum. The assembly line at the Ford plant in Oakville, Ontario resembles a process production system. An important characteristic of a process production system is its high level of standardization. This is necessary if the system is to produce large volumes of products.

Other examples of products manufactured in a process manufacturing system are carpeting, hand tools, personal computers, standard furniture, skis, television sets, compact discs, building supplies (lumber, doors, paint, etc.), greeting cards, calculators, and small pleasure boats. Michelin, for instance, uses a process manufacturing system and a process cost accounting system for a portion of its operations.

Process operations also extend to services. Examples include mail sorting at Canada Post and order processing in large mail-order firms. Each of these examples of products and services involve operations having a series of processes or production steps. Each process involves a different set of activities. A manufacturing operation that processes chemicals, for instance, might include the four steps as shown in Exhibit 23.1

Exhibit 23.1

Processing of Chemicals

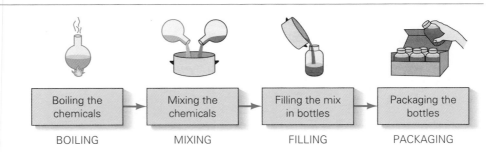

BOILING   MIXING   FILLING   PACKAGING

Comparing Job Order and Process Production

Important features of both job order and process production systems are shown in Exhibit 23.2. While we often describe job order and process operations with manufacturing examples, they also apply to service companies. In a job order costing system the measurement focus is on the individual job or batch. In a process costing system the measurement focus is on the process itself and the standardized output. Examples of products typically accounted for using process costing include cement, flour, glass, and textiles. Typically, in such systems, the output cannot be measured in terms of discrete units because they are continuous flow systems. Job order costing is more applicable to unique and divisible products such as designer furniture, housing, printing projects, and client services such as audit or legal services.

 Compare process cost accounting and job order cost accounting systems.

Job Order Systems	Process Systems
Custom orders	Repetitive operations
Heterogeneous products	Homogenous offerings
Low output volume	High output volume
High flexibility	Low flexibility
Low to medium standardization	High standardization

Exhibit 23.2

Features of Job Order and Process Systems

The ultimate objective of both job order and process costing is the same—to determine the cost per unit of output. We learned in Chapter 22 that the cost object of a job order costing system is a specific job or a job lot; all costs are assigned to this cost object. Typically, a specific job relates to a particular product or service; therefore, costs traced to that job also pertain to the individual product or service. In the case of a job lot, costs per unit can be computed by dividing total costs traced to the job lot by the number of units in that lot. In contrast, a process costing system assigns costs to individual processes or operations that make up the entire process flow; in other words, the individual processes are the cost objects. The cost per unit for each individual process for a given time period can be computed by dividing the total costs assigned to that process by the total output of that process during that period. The costs per unit of a specific product or service can be computed by adding the costs per unit of the different processes which the product or service consumes. We discuss this in greater detail in this chapter.

Organization of Process Manufacturing Operations

In a process manufacturing operation, each process is identified as a separate *production department, workstation,* or *work centre.* A manager is usually responsible for one or more processes. With the exception of the first department or process, each receives the output from the prior department as a partially processed product. Depending on the nature of the process, direct labour P. 1110, manufacturing overhead, and, perhaps, additional direct materials P. 1107 are combined to move the product further toward completion. Only the final department in the series produces finished goods ready for sale to customers.

A product can move through the manufacturing process in a variety of ways. In a typical mass production case costs flow in sequence from one process or department to the next. This is known as sequential processing. Raw materials are placed into process in the first department and flow through every department in the factory. Additional materials may or may not be added in one or more of the other departments or only labour and overhead costs may be added. In the manufacture of chinaware, for example, materials may flow in sequence through the mixing department, moulding department, cleaning department, glazing department, and firing department.

Parallel processing is the simultaneous processing of parts in two or more departments that are brought together later in a subsequent department to form a finished product. For example, various circuit boards may be manufactured at the same time in different departments. These circuit boards flow from these different departments to the assembly department where they are combined to form the finished product. Exhibit 23.3 shows an operation in which components of a final product are manufactured in three parallel processes (shown in horizontal layout) and then combined at different stages of production.

Other patterns of cost flows also exist in process costing. The important point is that cost flows must be identified in order to determine the cost of inventory and the cost of goods sold. This information is also needed for cost control and for pricing and other management decisions.

Exhibit 23.3

Manufacturing Operation with Parallel and Sequential Processes

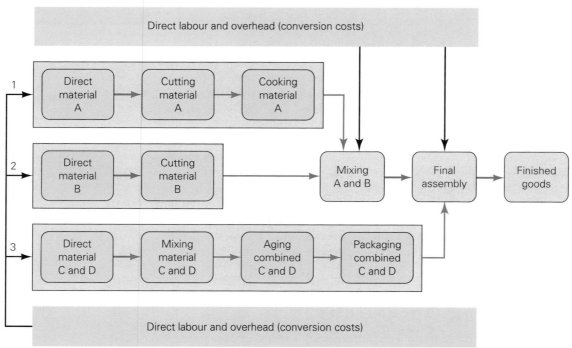

1, 2, and 3 are parallel processes.

GenX Company—An Illustration

We look at **GenX Company** to provide a basis for illustrating process operations. GenX produces Profen, an over-the-counter pain reliever for athletes. GenX sells Profen to wholesale distributors who in turn sell it to retailers.

Profen is produced in two steps. Step one uses a grinding process to pulverize blocks of its active ingredient, Profelene. Step two mixes the resulting powder with flavourings and preservatives, and moulds it into Profen tablets. Step two also packages the Profen tablets.

The flowchart in part A of Exhibit 23.4 shows the production steps for GenX. The table in part B of the exhibit summarizes GenX's manufacturing inventories at the beginning of April, the manufacturing costs GenX incurred during April, and the application of these costs to the grinding and mixing departments. The following sections explain how GenX uses a process cost accounting system to obtain these costs. Many of the explanations refer to the exhibit and its numbered cost flows.

Exhibit 23.4

Process Manufacturing Operations—GenX

A. Process Manufacturing Operations

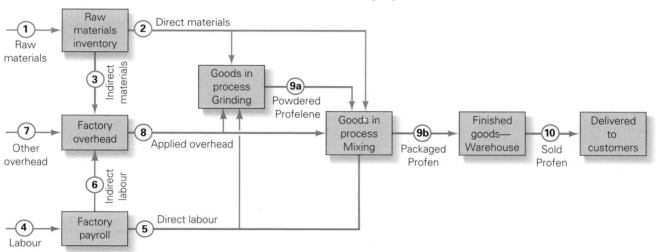

B. Manufacturing Costs During April 2004

	Raw Materials	Factory Payroll	Factory Overhead	Grinding Department	Mixing Department
Beginning balance	$4,000			$4,250	$3,520
Purchases and costs incurred	14,135	$14,020	$880		
Application of costs:					
Direct materials	(11,940)			9,900	2,040
Indirect materials	(1,195)		1,195		
Direct labour		(10,800)		5,700	5,100
Indirect labour		(3,220)	3,220		
Overhead applied			(5,295)	4,275	1,020

1. A process manufacturing operation: (a) is another name for a job order operation; (b) does not use the concepts of direct materials or direct labour; (c) consists of a continuous flow of operations.

2. Under what conditions is a process cost accounting system more suitable for measuring manufacturing costs than a job order cost accounting system?

Answers—p. 1225

Process Cost Accounting

Process and job order manufacturing operations are similar in that they both combine materials, labour, and overhead in the process of producing products. Yet they differ in the way they are organized and managed.

In job order operations, the job order cost accounting system assigns direct materials, direct labour, and overhead to specific jobs. The total job cost is then divided by the number of units to compute a cost per unit for that job.

In a process manufacturing operation, the **process cost accounting system** assigns direct materials, direct labour, and overhead to specific processes. The total costs associated with each process are then divided by the number of units passing through that process to determine the cost per *equivalent unit* (defined later in the chapter) for that process. The costs per equivalent unit for each process are added to determine the total cost per unit of a product.

The differences in how these two accounting systems apply materials, labour, and overhead costs are highlighted in Exhibit 23.5. We explain how to compute unit costs later in the chapter.

Exhibit 23.5

Job Order and Process Cost Accounting

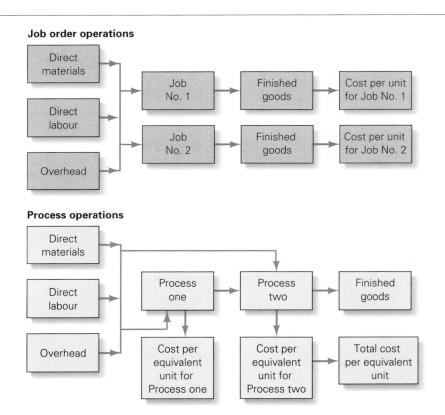

Direct and Indirect Costs

Chapter 21 explained that direct material and direct labour costs are linked with specific units or batches of product. Manufacturing costs that cannot be clearly associated with specific units or batches of product are defined as manufacturing overhead. Chapter 22 explained how the concepts of direct and indirect costs P. 1100 are used in job order cost accounting. In particular, materials and labour used on jobs are charged to the jobs as direct costs. Materials and labour that contribute to manufacturing but that are not linked with specific jobs are indirect costs and are allocated to jobs as manufacturing overhead.

Process cost accounting systems also use the concepts of direct and indirect costs. Materials and labour that are clearly connected with specific processes are assigned to those processes as direct costs. Materials and labour that are not linked with a specific process are indirect costs and are assigned to overhead. Some costs classified as manufacturing overhead in a job order system may be classified as direct costs in process cost accounting. For example, amortization of a machine used entirely by one process is a direct cost of that process. (Remember, whether a cost is classified as direct or indirect depends on the cost object it is being traced to.) The same cost can be a direct cost of a department but an indirect cost with respect to the product. The next three subsections explain the accounting for materials, labour and overhead costs in a process cost accounting system.

Accounting for Materials Costs

In Exhibit 23.4, arrow 1 reflects the arrival of materials at GenX's factory. These materials include Profelene, flavourings, preservatives, and packaging. It also includes supplies for the production support office. GenX uses a perpetual inventory system and makes all purchases on credit. The summary entry for receipts of raw materials during April is:[1]

 Record the flow of direct materials costs in process cost accounting.

1	Raw Materials Inventory..................................	14,135	
	Accounts Payable		14,135
	Acquired materials on credit for factory use.		

The accounting department makes entries to record receipt of materials when it receives copies of receiving reports from the storeroom.

Arrow 2 in Exhibit 23.4 reflects the flow of direct materials to the grinding and mixing departments, where they are used in producing Profen. Most direct materials are physically combined into the finished product. But in process cost accounting, direct materials also include supplies used in a specific process because they can be clearly linked with that process.

The manager of a process usually obtains material for use in a process by submitting a materials requisition to the raw materials storeroom manager. In some situations, materials move continuously from the raw materials inventory to a manufacturing process. Coca-Cola Bottling, for instance, uses a process in which inventory moves through the system continuously. In this case materials requisitions are replaced by a **materials consumption report** that summarizes the quantity of materials used by a department.

The entry to record the use of direct materials by GenX's two production departments during April is:

2	Goods in Process Inventory—Grinding............	9,900	
	Goods in Process Inventory—Mixing	2,040	
	Raw Materials Inventory..........................		11,940
	To assign costs of direct materials used in		
	the grinding and mixing departments.		

The use of two goods in process inventory accounts allows the costs incurred by each process to be separately accumulated. Also, this entry does not increase or decrease the company's assets. It merely transfers costs from one asset account to two other asset accounts.

---

[1] We omit the transaction date in the journal entries for brevity since each of the entries designated 1–10 is dated April 30.

In Exhibit 23.4, arrow 3 shows the flow of indirect materials from the storeroom to factory overhead P.1110. These materials are not clearly linked with either the grinding or the mixing departments. They are used in support of overall production activity. The entry to record the cost of indirect materials used by GenX during April is:

3	Factory Overhead	1,195	
	Raw Materials Inventory..........................		1,195
	To record indirect materials used in April.		

After the entries for both direct and indirect materials are posted, the Raw Materials Inventory account appears as shown in Exhibit 23.6.

Exhibit 23.6

Raw Materials Inventory Ledger Account

Raw Materials Inventory				Acct. No. 132		
Date		**Explanation**	**Debit**	**Credit**	**Balance**	
2004						
Mar.	31	Beginning balance			4,000	
Apr.	30	Materials purchases	14,135		18,135	
	30	Direct materials usage............................		11,940	6,195	
	30	Indirect material usage...........................		1,195	5,000	

The April 30 balance sheet reports a $5,000 Raw Materials Inventory account as a current asset.

Accounting for Labour Costs

LO⁴ Record the flow of direct labour costs in process cost accounting.

Exhibit 23.4 shows the factory payroll cost of GenX as reflected in arrow 4. Total labour costs of $14,020 are paid in cash and are recorded in the Factory Payroll account with this entry:

4	Factory Payroll	14,020	
	Cash..		14,020
	To record factory wages for April.		

This entry is triggered by time reports from the two production departments and the production support office. For simplicity, we do not identify withholdings and additional payroll taxes for the employees.

In a process operation, the direct labour of a production department includes all labour used exclusively by that department. This is the case even if the labour is not applied to the product itself. If a production department in a process operation, for instance, has a full-time manager and a full-time maintenance worker, their salaries are direct labour costs, not factory overhead.

Arrow 5 in Exhibit 23.4 shows GenX's use of direct labour in the grinding and mixing departments. The entry to transfer April's direct labour costs from the Factory Payroll account to the two goods in process accounts is:

5	Goods in Process Inventory—Grinding.............	5,700	
	Goods in Process Inventory—Mixing	5,100	
	Factory Payroll		10,800
	To assign costs of direct labour used in		
	the grinding and mixing departments.		

Arrow 6 in Exhibit 23.4 reflects the indirect labour of GenX. These employees provide the clerical, maintenance, and other services that help the grinding and mixing departments produce Profen more efficiently. For example, they order materials, deliver them to the factory floor, repair equipment, operate and program computers used in production, keep payroll and other production records, clean up, and move the finished goods to the warehouse. The entry to charge these indirect labour costs to factory overhead is:

6	Factory Overhead	3,220	
	Factory Payroll		3,220
	To record indirect labour as overhead.		

After these entries for labour are posted, the Factory Payroll account looks as follows:

Raw Materials Inventory				Acct. No. 132
Date	**Explanation**	**Debit**	**Credit**	**Balance**
2004				
Mar. 31	Beginning balance			-0-
Apr. 30	Total payroll for April...............................	14,020		14,020
30	Direct labour costs		10,800	3,220
30	Indirect material usage...........................		3,220	-0-

Exhibit 23.7

Factory Payroll
Ledger Account

This account is now closed and ready to receive entries for May.

Accounting for Factory Overhead

Overhead costs other than indirect materials and indirect labour are reflected by arrow 7 in Exhibit 23.4. These overhead items include the costs of insuring manufacturing assets, renting the factory building, using factory utilities, and depreciating equipment not directly related to a specific process. The entry to record overhead costs for April is:

LO⁵ Record the flow of factory overhead costs in process cost accounting.

7	Factory Overhead	880	
	Prepaid Insurance.....................................		80
	Accrued Utilities Payable.........................		200
	Cash..		250
	Accumulated Amortization,		
	Factory Equipment		350
	To record overhead items incurred in April.		

After this entry is posted, the Factory Overhead account balance is $5,295, which comprises indirect materials of $1,195, indirect labour of $3,220, and $880 of other overhead costs.

Arrow 8 in Exhibit 23.4 reflects the application of factory overhead to the two production departments. Recall from Chapters 21 and 22 that factory overhead was applied to products or jobs by relating overhead costs to another variable such as direct labour hours or machine hours used in production. Process cost systems use a similar procedure with predetermined application rates. For example, it is common for firms to use total labour hours for allocating overhead costs to products.

In many situations, a single allocation basis such as direct labour hours (or a single rate for an entire plant) fails to provide useful allocations. As a result, management may use different rates for different production departments. Based on an analysis of each department's operations, GenX applies its April overhead on the basis of direct labour cost, but with different rates, as shown in Exhibit 23.8.

Exhibit 23.8

Applying Factory Overhead

Production Department	Direct Labour Cost	Predetermined Rate*	Overhead Applied
Grinding	$5,700	75%	$4,275
Mixing	5,100	20	1,020
Total			$5,295

* Predetermined overhead application rates are 75% of direct labour cost for the grinding department and 20% of direct labour cost for the mixing department.

GenX records its applied overhead with the following entry:

8	Goods in Process Inventory—Grinding.............	4,275	
	Goods in Process Inventory—Mixing	1,020	
	Factory Overhead		5,295
	To allocate factory overhead costs to the grinding department at 75% of direct labour cost and to the mixing department at 20% of direct labour cost.		

After posting this entry, the Factory Overhead account appears as shown in Exhibit 23.9.

Exhibit 23.9

Factory Overhead Ledger Account

	Factory Overhead			Acct. No. 540	
Date		Explanation	Debit	Credit	Balance
2004					
Mar.	31	Beginning balance			-0-
Apr.	30	Indirect materials......................................	1,195		1,195
	30	Indirect labour costs.................................	3.220		4,415
	30	Other overhead costs..............................	880		5,295
	30	Applied to production depts.		5,295	-0-

For GenX, the amount of overhead applied equals the actual overhead incurred during April. In most cases, using a predetermined overhead application rate nearly always leaves an overapplied or underapplied balance in the Factory Overhead account. At the end of the period, this overapplied or underapplied balance should be either closed to the Cost of Goods Sold account or allocated among the cost of goods sold, the goods in process inventory, and the finished goods inventories. Procedures for making this allocation are the same as those described in Chapter 22 for job order cost accounting systems.

Budget Officer

You are working on identifying the direct and indirect costs of a new processing department containing several automated machines. The manager of this department instructs you to classify a majority of the costs as indirect to take advantage of the direct labour-based allocation method and to be charged with a lower amount of overhead (owing to the small direct labour component within the department). You know that this penalizes other departments who will then be hit with higher allocations. It also means the performance ratings of managers in these other departments will suffer. What action(s) do you take?

Judgement Call

Answer—p. 1225

3. When direct materials are assigned and used in both Department X and Department Y, the entry that records the use of direct materials includes:

a. A credit to Goods in Process Inventory—Department X.

b. A debit to Goods in Process Inventory—Department Y.

c. A credit to Goods in Process Inventory—Department Y.

4. What are the three categories of cost incurred by both job order and process manufacturing operations?

5. How many Goods in Process Inventory accounts are needed in a process cost accounting system?

Flashback

Answers—p. 1225

Full Service Accounting

Many service companies use process departments to perform specific tasks for consumers. Hospitals, for instance, have radiology and physical therapy facilities with special equipment and trained employees. When patients need services, they are processed through proper departments and receive prescribed care. Service companies need cost accounting information as much as manufacturers. Managers use information about the cost of providing services to plan future operations, to control costs, and to determine charges to customers. All the basic techniques of process cost accounting are applied equally well to service operations.

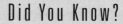

Did You Know?

Computing and Using Equivalent Units of Production

We already explained how materials, labour, and overhead costs for a period are accumulated in separate Goods in Process Inventory accounts for each manufacturing process. But we have not explained the arrows labelled 9a, 9b, and 10 in Exhibit 23.4. These lines reflect the transfer of products from the grinding department to the mixing department, from the mixing department to finished goods inventory, and from finished goods inventory to cost of goods sold. To determine the costs recorded for these flows, we must first determine the cost per unit of product and then apply this result to the number of units transferred.

Accounting for Goods in Process Inventories

If a manufacturing process has no beginning and ending goods in process inventory, the unit cost computation is simple. The unit cost of goods transferred out of a process when there is no beginning and ending goods in process inventory is:

> *Total cost assigned to the process (direct materials, direct labour, and factory overhead)*
> *Total number of units started and finished during the period*

However, if a process has a beginning or ending inventory of partially processed units, the total cost assigned to the process must be allocated to all units worked on during the period. The partially completed units must be converted into a measure equivalent to fully completed units; this measure is called **equivalent units of production (EUP)**. Equivalent units of production refer to the number of units that are *considered* as being 100% processed during a given period.

To illustrate, assume GenX adds (or introduces) 100 units of material into the grinding process during the period. Suppose at the end of the period, the production supervisor determines that the 100 units are 60% processed. The equivalent units of production for that period are 60 units, computed as 100 units × 60%.

In other words, we believe that if we had introduced 60 units into the process, we would have completely processed these 60 units. The EUP measure is used as a denominator in computing the cost per (equivalent) unit of a process to assign costs to finished goods and goods in process inventory.

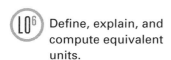

LO⁶ Define, explain, and compute equivalent units.

Differences Between Equivalent Units for Materials and for Labour and Overhead

In many manufacturing processes, the equivalent units of production for materials is not the same as it is for labour and overhead. To illustrate, consider the process operation shown in Exhibit 23.10:

Exhibit 23.10

Process Manufacturing System

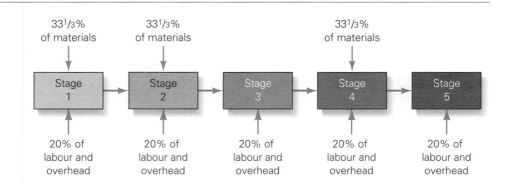

This exhibit shows a single production process consisting of five stages. One-third of the direct material cost is added at each of three stages: Stage 1, Stage 2, and Stage 4. One-fifth of the direct labour cost is added at each of the five stages. Because overhead is applied as a percentage of direct labour, one-fifth of the overhead also is added at each of the five stages. Note that if a different base is used to allocate overhead, the cost system must track the usage of that allocation base by the different processes.

When units finish Stage 1, they are one-third complete with respect to materials but only one-fifth complete with respect to labour and overhead. When they finish Stage 2, they are two-thirds complete with respect to materials, but only two-fifths complete with respect to labour and overhead. When they finish Stage 3, they remain two-thirds complete with respect to materials, but are now three-fifths complete with respect to labour and overhead. When they finish Stage 4, they are 100% complete with respect to materials but only four-fifths complete with respect to labour and overhead.

As an example, if 300 units of product are started and processed through Stage 1 in Exhibit 23.10, they are one-third complete *with respect to materials.* Expressed in terms of equivalent finished units, the processing of these 300 units is equal to finishing 100 units, computed as 300 units × 33 1/3%. But only one-fifth of direct labour and overhead are included in the 300 units at the end of Stage 1. The equivalent units of production with respect to direct labour and overhead is 60 units, computed as 300 units × 20%.

Accounting for GenX's Grinding Department

Exhibit 23.11 shows the information necessary to compute equivalent units of production for GenX's grinding department for the month of April.

Exhibit 23.11

Production Data—Grinding Department

Beginning inventory (March 31):	
Units of product	30,000
Percentage of completion — direct materials...........................	100%
Percentage of completion — direct labour	33 1/3%
Units started during April	90,000
Units transferred from grinding to mixing in April.........................	100,000
Ending inventory (April 30):	
Units of product	20,000
Percentage of completion — direct materials...........................	100%
Percentage of completion — direct labour	25%

In computing equivalent units, we assume that each of GenX's production departments processes units on a first-in, first-out (FIFO) basis. We select the FIFO method because it provides up-to-date information for cost control purposes. FIFO is suitable for cost control purposes because it separates costs of the current period from costs of prior periods. This separation is necessary in order to evaluate current performance.[2] Accounting for the period's activity involves four steps: (1) physical flow, (2) equivalent units, (3) cost per equivalent unit, and (4) cost reconciliation. Each of these steps is described in this section.

---

[2] We assume a FIFO flow for all related computations in this chapter. Weighted-average is sometimes used in practice but this method combines current period activity with the prior periods. Current performance should be measured on the basis of the current period's costs only. However, if inventories are low the two methods would give similar results.

Physical Flow of Units

 LO7 Explain the four steps in accounting for production activity in a period.

Physical flow is a reconciliation of (a) the physical units started in a period with (b) the physical units completed. A physical reconciliation is shown in Exhibit 23.12 for GenX for April.

Exhibit 23.12

Physical Flow—Grinding Department

Units to account for:		Units accounted for as:	
Beginning inventory	30,000 units	Units transferred from grinding to mixing	100,000 units
Units started during April......	90,000 units	Ending inventory:	20,000 units
Total number of units............	120,000 units	Total number of units	120,000 units

The 100,000 units transferred from grinding to mixing during April include the 30,000 units from the beginning goods in process inventory (or simply beginning inventory). The remaining 70,000 units transferred out are started during April. Because 70,000 of these 90,000 units are completed, 20,000 units remain unfinished at the end of the period.

Equivalent Units of Production

The second step is to compute equivalent units of production in the grinding department for direct materials, direct labour, and factory overhead for April. Overhead is applied using direct labour as an allocation base. This means the equivalent units are the same for both labour and overhead in this case.

Equivalent Units—Direct Materials

Direct materials (the Profelene blocks) are added at the beginning of the process. A unit of product is 100% complete with respect to materials as soon as it is started. This means beginning goods in process inventory for April already received all its materials in March and is not assigned any additional materials. The 70,000 units started and completed in April and the 20,000 units in ending goods in process inventory (or simply ending inventory) on April 30 received all their materials in April. With respect to materials, the grinding department's equivalent units of production are computed as shown in Exhibit 23.13.[3]

Exhibit 23.13

Equivalent Units of Production—Grinding Department's Direct Materials

	Units of Product	Percent Added This Period		Equivalent Units
Beginning goods in process	30,000	× 0%	=	-0-
Goods started and completed	70,000	× 100	=	70,000
Ending goods in process	20,000	× 100	=	20,000
Total units	120,000			90,000

---

[3] If a weighted-average were used, the equivalent units for materials would be as follows:

Goods transferred to mixing dept.	$100,000 \times 100\% =$	100,000
Ending goods in process	$20,000 \times 100\% =$	20,000
Total units	120,000	120,000

Equivalent Units—Direct Labour and Factory Overhead

Direct labour and factory overhead, both considered conversion costs, are assigned uniformly throughout the process for GenX.[4] Recall that beginning inventory of 30,000 units are partially completed in March. In April, additional labour and overhead are assigned to these units to complete them. Based on percentage of completion, 33 1/3% of labour and overhead was assigned during March. The remaining 66 2/3% is assigned in April. The 70,000 units started and completed in April are assigned 100% of labour and overhead. The 20,000 units in ending inventory are assigned only 25% of labour at the end of April. Exhibit 23.14 shows us these computations.[5]

	Units of Product		Percent Added This Period		Equivalent Units
Beginning goods in process	30,000	×	66 2/3%	=	20,000
Goods started and completed	70,000	×	100	=	70,000
Ending goods in process	20,000	×	25	=	5,000
Total units	120,000				95,000

Exhibit 23.14

Equivalent Units of Production—Grinding Department's Direct Labour and Factory Overhead

A summary of April's equivalent units of production for the grinding process is shown in Exhibit 23.15.[6]

Activities during April	Direct Materials	Direct Labour	Factory Overhead
Units from beginning inventory processed in current period..	-0-	20,000	20,000
Units started and completed in current period............	70,000	70,000	70,000
Units in ending inventory at end of current period	20,000	5,000	5,000
Equivalent units of production for period....................	90,000	95,000	95,000

Exhibit 23.15

Equivalent Units of Production—Grinding Department's Summary

Cost per Equivalent Unit

The third step is to compute the *cost per equivalent unit* for direct materials, direct labour, and factory overhead. Exhibit 23.4 reported that GenX's grinding department incurred $9,900 in direct materials costs and $5,700 in direct labour costs for April. Factory overhead of $4,275 is also applied to the grinding process. These costs are assigned to the partially completed units from beginning inventory, the units started and completed during the current period, and the units in ending inventory at the end of the period. GenX's cost assignment of direct labour for April is shown in Exhibit 23.16. Similar cost assignments are made for materials and overhead.

---

[4] Note that factory overhead is applied using direct labour as an allocation base. This means the equivalent units is the same for both labour and overhead.

[5] If the weighted-average method were used, the equivalent units for direct labour and overhead would be as follows:

Goods transferred to mixing department	100,000 × 100% =	100,000
Ending goods in process	20,000 × 25% =	5,000
Total units	120,000	105,000

[6] In Exhibits 23.15 and 23.17, the last two columns can be combined and termed Conversion. This practice of combining these two cost items must then be carried over to the other reports as well.

Exhibit 23.16

Grinding Department
Assignment of Direct Labour

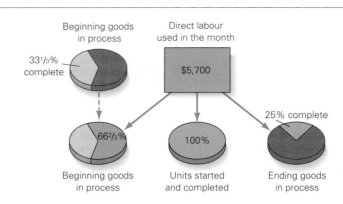

These cost assignments along with the equivalent units computed in the prior section are used in determining the cost per equivalent unit for materials, labour, and overhead. These computations are shown in Exhibit 23.17.[7]

Exhibit 23.17

Cost Per Equivalent
Unit—Grinding
Department

Activities During April	Direct Materials	Direct Labour	Factory Overhead	Total
Costs assigned to grinding in current period...............	$ 9,900	$ 5,700	$ 4,275	$19,875
Equivalent units of production in current period..........	90,000	95,000	95,000	
Cost per equivalent unit for period.............................	$ 0.11	$ 0.06	$ 0.045	$ 0.215

Total cost per equivalent unit for the grinding process amounts to $0.215, computed as $0.11 + $0.06 + $0.045.

Cost Reconciliation

The fourth and final step in this process is to reconcile the *costs to account for* with the *costs accounted for* in the period. We do this by identifying the costs to (1) process beginning inventory, (2) start and complete units transferred from grinding to mixing, and (3) process ending inventory. Exhibit 23.18 shows this cost reconciliation.

Exhibit 23.18

Cost Reconciliation—
Grinding Department

Costs to Account for:		Amount
From beginning inventory (from Exhibit 23.4).......................................		$ 4,250
Assigned in April (from Exhibit 23.17)...		19,875
Total costs to account for..		**$24,125**

Costs Accounted for:		
Beginning inventory completed in April:		
Costs from previous period..		$ 4,250
Costs assigned during current period:		
Direct materials (0 units × $0.11)..	$ -0-	
Direct labour (20,000 units × $0.06)..	1,200	
Factory overhead (20,000 units × $0.045)...	900	2,100
Costs to process beginning inventory in April...................................		$ 6,350
Cost of units started and completed in April (70,000 × $0.215).......		$ 15,050
Ending inventory in April:		
Direct materials (20,000 × $0.11)...	$2,200	
Direct labour (5,000 × $0.06)...	300	
Factory overhead (5,000 × $0.045)...	225	
Cost of ending inventory in April..		$ 2,725
Total costs accounted for..		**$24,125**

---

[7] To compute cost per equivalent unit under the weighted-average method, the previous period's inventory costs are added to current period's costs and then divided by the equivalent units.

The total *costs to account* for must equal the total *costs accounted for* in a cost reconciliation (minor differences can exist due to rounding). Also, the costs of units transferred out from grinding to mixing must include the costs of beginning inventory processed in the current period ($6,350) and the costs of units started and completed in the current period ($15,050). This amounts to $21,400 for 100,000 units transferred out, or $0.214 per unit. This leaves ending inventory, which is valued at $2,725, and that is carried over to the next period.

Exhibit 23.17 showed that total cost per equivalent unit for April is $0.215. But the cost per unit for the units transferred out is $0.214. The difference of $0.001 exists because the total cost per equivalent unit is different for March—recall that $4,250 of the $21,400 is carried forward from March. As we explained earlier, the FIFO method uses only current period's costs and activities in computing the cost per equivalent unit for that period.

Answers—p. 1225

6. Equivalent units are:

  a. A measure of a production department's productivity in using direct materials, direct labour, or overhead.

  b. Units of a product produced by a foreign competitor that are similar to units produced by a domestic company.

  c. Generic units of a product similar to brand-name units of a product.

7. Interpret the meaning of a department's equivalent units of production with respect to direct labour.

8. A department began an accounting period with 8,000 units that were one-fourth complete. It also started and completed 50,000 units, and ended with 6,000 units that were one-third complete. How many equivalent units did it produce during the period?

Process Cost Summary

An important managerial accounting report for a process cost accounting system is the **process cost summary**. A separate process cost summary is prepared for each process or production department. Three purposes of the summary are to: (1) help managers control their departments; (2) help factory managers evaluate department managers' performance; and (3) provide cost information for financial statements. A process cost summary achieves these purposes by describing the costs charged to the department, computing the equivalent units of production achieved by each department, and determining the costs assigned to each department's output.

A summary report is prepared through a combination of Exhibits 23.14, 23.15, 23.17, and 23.18. A common format for the process cost summary is shown in Exhibit 23.19. The summary is divided into three sections. Section 1 lists the total costs charged to the department. This includes direct materials, direct labour, and overhead costs incurred. It also includes the cost of the beginning goods in process inventory.

 Define, describe, and prepare a process cost summary.

Exhibit 23.19

GenX Grinding Department Process Cost Summary

GenX Company
Process Cost Summary for Grinding Department
For Month Ended April 30, 2004

Costs Charged to Department

① {

Direct materials requisitioned	$ 9,900
Direct labour charged	5,700
Overhead allocated (at predetermined rate)...	4,275
Total processing costs for the month..	$19,875
Goods in process at the beginning of the month.......................................	4,250
Total costs to be accounted for	**$24,125**

②

		Equivalent Units	
Equivalent Unit Processing Costs:	**Units of Product**	**Direct Materials**	**Labour and Overhead**
Units processed:			
Beginning goods in process............................	30,000	-0-	20,000
Units started and completed...........................	70,000	70,000	70,000
Ending goods in process.................................	20,000	20,000	5,000
Total..	120,000	90,000	95,000

Total direct materials cost for April...	$9,900
Direct materials cost per equivalent unit ($9,900/90,000 units)	$0.110
Total direct labour cost for the April	$5,700
Direct labour cost per equivalent unit ($5,700/95,000 units)........................	$0.060
Total overhead cost for the April	$4,275
Overhead cost per equivalent unit ($4,275/95,000 units)	$0.045

Assignment of Costs to Output of Department:	**Equivalent Units**	**Cost per Unit**	**Total Cost**
Goods in process, March 31, 2004, and completed during April			
Costs from prior month...................................			$ 4,250
Direct materials added (none)			-0-
Direct labour added..	20,000	$0.060	1,200
Overhead applied..	20,000	0.045	900
Total costs to process			$ 6,350
Goods started and completed during April			
Direct materials added....................................	70,000	0.110	$ 7,700
Direct labour added...	70,000	0.060	4,200
Overhead applied..	70,000	0.045	3,150
Total costs to process			$ 15,050
Total costs transferred to mixing department (unit cost = $21,400/100,000 units = $0.214).....			21,400
Goods in process, April 30, 2004:			
Direct materials added....................................	20,000	0.110	$ 2,200
Direct labour added...	5,000	0.060	300
Overhead applied..	5,000	0.045	225
Total costs to process			$ 2,725
Total costs accounted for			**$24,125**

③ (brace for Goods started and completed during April section)

Section 2 describes the equivalent units of production for the department. Equivalent units for materials and labour, and overhead are often shown in separate columns. GenX reports equivalent units for labour and overhead in one column because it applies overhead using labour as the allocation base. Section 2 also shows direct materials, direct labour, and overhead costs per equivalent unit.

Section 3 allocates total costs among products worked on in the period. Costs of completing beginning inventory units are computed and added to the cost carried forward from March to get total processing cost of $6,350 for beginning inventory units. Also, costs of processing 70,000 units from start to finish are computed and added to get their total processing cost of $15,050. The $6,350 and $15,050 are added to give us $21,400 total cost of goods transferred out of the department. The final part of section 3 computes the $2,725 cost of partially processing the ending inventory units. The assigned costs are then added to show that the total $24,125 cost charged to the department in section 1 is now assigned to the units in section 3.

9. A process cost summary for a department has three sections. What information is presented in each of them?

Flashback
Answer—p. 1225

General Manager
You are the general manager of a new company manufacturing two distinctly different types of tiny electronic components. Both components are produced in very large quantities using the same process consisting of four departments. You are preparing for a meeting with your management accountant to discuss whether to report the cost per equivalent unit for both products together or separately for each product. What do you advise?

Judgement Call
Answer—p. 1225

Transferring Goods Between Departments

Arrow 9a in Exhibit 23.4 reflects the transfer of units (powdered Profelene) from the grinding department to the mixing department. The $21,400 cost of this transfer, as computed in Section 3 of the process cost summary of Exhibit 23.19, is recorded with the following entry:

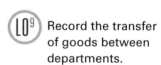

LO⁹ Record the transfer of goods between departments.

9a	Goods in Process Inventory—Mixing	21,400	
	Goods in Process Inventory—Grinding.....		21,400
	To record the transfer of partially completed goods from the grinding department to the mixing department.		

After this entry is posted, the Goods in Process Inventory account for the grinding department appears as shown in Exhibit 23.20.

Exhibit 23.20

Goods in Process Inventory
(Grinding) Ledger Account

Goods in Process Inventory — Grinding				Acct. No. 133	
Date		**Explanation**	**Debit**	**Credit**	**Balance**
2004					
Mar.	31	Beginning balance			4,250
Apr.	30	Direct materials	9,900		14,150
	30	Direct labour costs	5,700		19,850
	30	Applied overhead	4,275		24,125
	30	Transfer to mixing department		21,400	2,725

The $2,725 ending balance in this Goods in Process Inventory account equals the cost assigned to partially completed units as shown in section 3 of the process cost summary.

 **Flashback**

Answer—p. 1225

10. What effect does the transfer of a partially completed product from one production department to another have on the total assets of the company?

Accounting for Second (Mixing) Department

The mixing department begins working on Profelene when it is received from the grinding department. Most of the costs are for labour—for specialists in mixing the compounds and labourers for packaging the product. Direct labour and overhead are added at the same rate as direct materials.

Equivalent Units of Production

The mixing department requires only one computation of equivalent units of production. This is because direct materials, direct labour, and overhead are used at the same rate. Exhibit 23.21 provides the data needed to compute equivalent units of production in the mixing department for April.

Exhibit 23.21

Production Data—Mixing
Department

Beginning inventory (March 31):	
Units of product	16,000
Percentage of completion—Direct materials, direct labour, and overhead...................................	25%
Units received from grinding department	100,000
Units transferred to finished goods	101,000
Ending inventory (April 30):	
Units of product	15,000
Percentage of completion—Direct materials, direct labour, and overhead...................................	33 1/3%

A total of 101,000 units are transferred from the mixing department to finished goods in the period. Based on a first-in, first-out assumption, 16,000 of these units came from beginning goods in process inventory and 85,000 are received and completed in the period. Because 100,000 units are received from the grinding department in the period and only 85,000 of these units are completed, the ending goods in process inventory is 15,000 units.

Exhibit 23.22 computes the mixing department's equivalent units of production for direct materials, direct labour, and overhead for the month of April.

	Units of Product		Percent Added		Equivalent Units
Beginning goods in process	16,000	×	75%	=	12,000
Goods started and completed	85,000	×	100	=	85,000
Ending goods in process	15,000	×	33 1/3	=	5,000
Total units	116,000				102,000

Exhibit 23.22

Equivalent Units of Production—Mixing Department

Process Cost Summary

Exhibit 23.23 shows the process cost summary for the mixing department. The costs charged to the department in section 1 include $21,400 transferred in from the grinding department. Section 2 shows the equivalent units of production for the direct materials, direct labour, and overhead added by the mixing department. Section 2 also computes the costs per equivalent unit. Section 3 shows how costs charged to the department are assigned to the output of the department. The $29,470 cost of the units transferred to finished goods is computed as the combined cost of the beginning units in process and the units received and completed in the period.

The beginning goods in process inventory for the mixing department is 100% complete with respect to Profelene. None of the Profelene transferred in during April is used to complete the beginning inventory. Instead, the $21,400 cost transferred in during April relates to the 100,000 units that the mixing department began to process in April. In section 3 of Exhibit 23.23, $18,190 of the $21,400 is assigned to the 85,000 units received and completed in April (85,000 × $0.214). The remaining $3,210 is assigned to the 15,000 units in ending inventory of the mixing department (15,000 × $0.214).

Exhibit 23.23

GenX Mixing Department Process Cost Summary

GenX Company
Process Cost Summary for Mixing Department
For Month Ended April 30, 2004

Costs Charged to Department

①

Direct materials requisitioned	$ 2,040
Direct labour charged	5,100
Overhead allocated (at predetermined rate)	1,020
Total processing costs for the month	$ 8,160
Goods in process at the beginning of the month	3,520
Costs transferred in from the grinding department (100,000 units at $0.214 each)	21,400
Total costs to be accounted for	**$33,080**

②

Equivalent Unit Processing Costs:	Units of Product	Equivalent Units of Production
Units processed:		
Beginning goods in process	16,000	12,000
Units started and completed	85,000	85,000
Ending goods in process	15,000	5,000
Total	116,000	102,000

Total direct materials cost for April	$2,040
Direct materials cost per equivalent unit ($2,040/102,000 units)	$0.020
Total direct labour cost for April	$5,100
Direct labour cost per equivalent unit ($5,100/102,000 units)	$0.050
Total overhead cost for April	$1,020
Overhead cost per equivalent unit ($1,020/102,000 units)	$0.010

③

Assignment of Costs to Output of Department:	Equivalent Units	Cost per Unit	Total Cost	
Goods in process, March 31, 2004, and completed during April				
Costs from prior month			$ 3,520	
Direct materials added	12,000	$0.020	240	
Direct labour added	12,000	0.050	600	
Overhead applied	12,000	0.010	120	
Total costs to process			$ 4,480	
Goods started and completed during April				
Costs transferred in (85,000 × $0.214)			$ 18,190	
Direct materials added	85,000	0.020	1,700	
Direct labour added	85,000	0.050	4,250	
Overhead applied	85,000	0.010	850	
Total costs to process			$ 24,990	
Total costs transferred to finished goods (unit cost = $29,470/101,000 units = $0.2918)				$ 29,470
Goods in process, April 30, 2004:				
Costs transferred in (15,000 × $0.214)			$ 3,210	
Direct materials added	5,000	0.020	100	
Direct labour added	5,000	0.050	250	
Overhead applied	5,000	0.010	50	
Total costs to process				$ 3,610
Total costs accounted for				**$33,080**

11. A ski manufacturer's total processing costs are $262,500 for its waxing department in the month of December. To complete beginning goods in process, this department added 20,000 equivalent units of materials, labour, and overhead. This department also started and completed 70,000 units during the month and had 15,000 equivalent units remaining in process at month end. Costs transferred in from the sanding department for December totals $300,000, of which 25% relates to units the waxing department had not finished by month-end. For the waxing department's process cost summary, what is reported as the total costs to process goods received and completed?

Flashback

Answer—p. 1225

Mid-Chapter Demonstration Problem

A production department in a process manufacturing system of Golden Company completed 500,000 units of product and transferred them to finished goods during a recent week. Of these units, 150,000 were in process at the beginning of the week. The other 350,000 units were started and completed during the week. At the end of the period, 60,000 units were in process.

Required

Compute the department's equivalent units of production with respect to direct materials under each of the following unrelated assumptions:

a. All direct materials are added to the products when processing begins.

b. The direct materials are added to the products evenly throughout the process. The beginning goods in process inventory was 30% complete and the ending goods in process inventory was 60% complete.

c. One quarter of the direct materials are added to the products when the process begins and the other three quarters is added when the process is 75% complete as to direct labour. The beginning goods in process inventory was 40% complete as to direct labour and the ending goods in process inventory was 80% complete as to direct labour.

SOLUTION TO Mid-Chapter Demonstration Problem

a. Ending inventory is 100% complete with respect to materials.

	Units of Product		Percent Added		Equivalent Units
Beginning goods in process	150,000	×	0%	=	-0-
Goods started and completed	350,000	×	100	=	350,000
Ending goods in process	60,000	×	100	=	60,000
Total units	560,000				410,000

b. Beginning inventory is 30% complete with respect to materials, so 70% must be added. Ending inventory is 60% complete with respect to materials.

	Units of Product		Percent Added		Equivalent Units
Beginning goods in process	150,000	×	70%	=	105,000
Goods started and completed	350,000	×	100	=	350,000
Ending goods in process	60,000	×	60	=	36,000
Total units	560,000				491,000

c. Beginning inventory is 25% complete with respect to materials so the additional 75% must be added in the current week. Ending inventory is 100% complete with respect to materials because direct labour has passed the 75% level.

	Units of Product		Percent Added		Equivalent Units
Beginning goods in process	150,000	×	75%	=	112,500
Goods started and completed	350,000	×	100	=	350,000
Ending goods in process	60,000	×	100	=	60,000
Total units	560,000				522,500

Transferring Costs to Finished Goods Inventory and Cost of Goods Sold

LO10 Record the transfer of completed goods to Finished Goods Inventory and Cost of Goods Sold.

Arrow 9b in Exhibit 23.4 reflects the transfer of finished products from the mixing department to Finished Goods Inventory. The process cost summary for the mixing department shows 101,000 units of finished Profen are assigned a cost of $29,470. The following entry records the transfer:

9b	Finished Goods Inventory..................................	29,470	
	Goods in Process Inventory—Mixing		29,470
	To record transfer of completed units of Profen.		

After this entry is posted, the mixing department's Goods in Process Inventory account appears as shown in Exhibit 23.24.

Goods in Process Inventory — Mixing			Acct. No. 134		
Date		Explanation	Debit	Credit	Balance
2004					
Mar.	31	Beginning balance			3,520
Apr.	30	Direct materials	2,040		5,560
	30	Direct labour costs	5,100		10,660
	30	Applied overhead	1,020		11,680
	30	Transfer from grinding dept.	21,400		33,080
	30	Transfer to warehouse		29,470	3,610

Exhibit 23.24

Goods in Process Inventory
(Mixing) Ledger Account

The ending balance of the Goods in Process Inventory—Mixing account equals the cost assigned to the partially completed units in section 3 of Exhibit 23.23.

GenX sells 106,000 units of Profen in April. The beginning inventory of finished goods consists of 23,000 units with a cost of $6,440. All of these 23,000 units are sold in April. The remaining 83,000 units sold are from the 101,000 units completed in April. Ending finished goods inventory amounts to 18,000 units remaining.

Section 3 of Exhibit 23.23 shows that the total cost per unit of finished goods in April is $0.2918 ($29,470÷101,000 units). Using this information we can compute cost of goods sold for April as shown in Exhibit 23.25.

23,000 units from the beginning inventory*		$ 6,440
83,000 units manufactured during April (83,000 × $0.2918)		24,219
Total cost of goods sold..		$30,659

Exhibit 23.25

GenX Cost of Goods Sold

* Computations assume a FIFO inventory system.

The entry to record the cost of goods sold for April:

10	Cost of Goods Sold..	30,659	
	Finished Goods Inventory..........................		30,659
	To record cost of goods sold during April.		

After this entry is posted, the Finished Goods Inventory account appears as shown in Exhibit 23.26.

Finished Goods Inventory			Acct. No. 135		
Date		Explanation	Debit	Credit	Balance
2004					
Mar.	31	Beginning balance			6,440
Apr.	30	Transfer from mixing dept.	29,470		35,910
	30	Transfer to warehouse		30,659	5,251

Exhibit 23.26

Finished Goods Inventory
Ledger Account

Summary of GenX's Manufacturing Cost Flows

Exhibit 23.27 shows manufacturing cost flows of GenX for April. Each of these cost flows and the entries to record them are explained in the prior sections. The flow of costs through accounts reflects the flow of manufacturing activities and products in its operations.

Exhibit 23.27

Cost Flows Through GenX

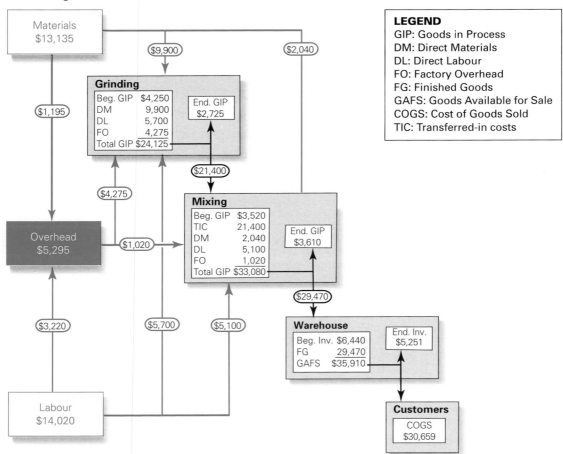

Lean Business Model and Job Order/ Process Cost Accounting Systems

We described several lean business practices in Chapter 21. These practices are applicable regardless of the type of organization. Businesses with job order or process cost accounting systems can benefit from adopting these practices. Typical benefits of adopting lean business practices include higher efficiency, improved quality, and lower inventory, all of which can translate into lower costs.

Typically, cost accounting systems do not track costs that arise due to poor quality. Instead, these costs are absorbed by the "good" units produced, thereby inflating the cost per "good" unit. By tracking the costs incurred due to poor quality, managers can get a better idea of the savings that can result from improved quality. Details of tracking costs that arise due to poor quality are left for advanced texts.

Manufacturing companies that adopt the "just-in-time" (JIT) philosophy typically end up reducing inventories. In a perfect JIT setting, there would be zero inventories (of all three kinds); this means that there would be no need to maintain the three inventory accounts (raw materials, goods in process, and finished goods). All the materials purchased would be used up in the current period and all the finished goods produced would be sold in the current period. This means that all the product costs can be directly debited to the Cost of Goods Sold account.

Flashback

Answer—p. 1225

12. A company successfully uses just-in-time manufacturing and essentially eliminates its goods in process inventories. How does this affect its computations of equivalent units of production?

Judgement Call

Answer—p. 1225

Process Manager
You are the manager of a crucial process in your company's manufacturing system. During the recent quarter, your process generated an unusually high percent of defective units. Yet, the monthly process cost report doesn't show the cost of these defects. You want to submit a proposal to top management to obtain resources for implementing process improvement measures and you need information on the cost of defects to include in your proposal. What do you do?

Summary

LO¹ Explain process operations and how they differ from job order operations. Process operations produce large quantities of identical products or services by passing them through a series of processes or steps. Like job order operations, they combine direct materials, direct labour, and overhead in the operations. The focus is on the series of processes, not jobs.

LO² Compare process cost accounting and job order cost accounting systems. Process and job order manufacturing operations are similar in that they both combine materials, labour, and other manufacturing overhead items in the process of producing products. They differ in the way they are organized and managed. In job order operations, the job order cost accounting system assigns materials, labour, and overhead to specific jobs. The total job cost is then divided by the number of units to compute a cost per unit for that job. In process manufacturing operations, the process cost accounting system assigns materials, labour, and overhead to specific manufacturing processes. The total costs associated with each process are then divided by the number of units passing through that process to determine

the cost per equivalent unit for that process. The costs per equivalent unit for all processes are added to determine the total cost per unit of a product.

LO³ Record the flow of direct materials costs in process cost accounting. Materials purchased are debited to a Raw Materials Inventory account. As direct materials are issued to processes, they are separately accumulated to a Goods in Process Inventory account for that process.

LO⁴ Record the flow of direct labour costs in process cost accounting. Direct labour costs are initially debited to the Factory Payroll account. The total amount in Factory Payroll is then assigned to the Goods in Process Inventory account pertaining to each process.

LO⁵ Record the flow of factory overhead costs in process cost accounting. The different factory overhead items are first accumulated in the Factory Overhead account and then allocated, using a predetermined overhead rate, to the different processes. The allocated amount is debited to the Goods in Process Inventory account pertaining to each process.

LO⁶ Define, explain, and compute equivalent units. Equivalent units of production measure the activity of a process as the number of units that are considered as being 100% processed during a given period. This measure of production activity is used in computing the cost per equivalent unit. It is also used to assign costs to finished goods and goods in process inventory. To compute equivalent units, first determine the number of units that are fully processed. For the partially completed units, determine their percentage of completion. Multiply the units in GIP inventory by their percentage completion and add the quantity of the fully completed units. This total quantity represents the equivalent units of production for the period. The costs incurred by a process are divided by its equivalent units of production to determine cost per unit.

LO⁷ Explain the four steps in accounting for production activity in a period. The four steps involved in accounting for production activity in a period are (1) recording the physical flow of units, (2) computing the equivalent units of production, (3) computing the cost per equivalent unit of production and (4) reconciling costs. The last step involves assigning the costs to finished goods and goods in process inventory for the period. These four steps are helpful in preparing the process cost summary report.

LO⁸ Define, describe, and prepare a process cost summary. A process cost summary is a managerial accounting report that summarizes the activity of a production process or department during a period. Three purposes of the report are to: (a) help managers control their departments; (b) help factory managers evaluate department managers' performance; and (c) provide cost information for financial statements. A process cost summary achieves these purposes by describing the costs charged to the department, the equivalent units of production achieved by the department, and the costs assigned to the output. A process cost summary can be prepared by including the physical flow of units, equivalent units of production, costs per equivalent unit, and cost reconciliation in one summary report. The report shows the units and costs to account for during the period and how these were accounted for during the period. In terms of units, the report includes the beginning goods in process inventory and the units received during the month. These are accounted for in terms of goods completed and transferred out and ending goods in process inventory. With respect to costs, the report includes the materials, labour, and overhead costs assigned to the process during the period. It shows how these costs were assigned to goods completed and transferred out and goods in process inventory at the end of the period.

LO⁹ Record the transfer of goods between departments. As units of product are transferred from one process to the next, the accumulated cost of those units is transferred from one goods in process account to the next. Once the goods are completed in the preceding process, they are transferred out to the next process in the sequence. Costs associated with the goods completed in the preceding process are then debited to the goods in process inventory of the next process. With this procedure, the costs of the preceding process are accumulated in the next process.

LO¹⁰ Record the transfer of goods to Finished Goods Inventory and Cost of Goods Sold. As units complete the last process and are eventually sold, their accumulated cost is transferred to Finished Goods Inventory and finally to Cost of Goods Sold.

GUIDANCE ANSWERS TO Judgement Call

Budget Officer

By instructing you to classify a majority of the costs as indirect, the manager is passing on some of his department's costs to a common overhead pool that will be partially absorbed by other departments within the company. Since overhead costs are allocated on the basis of direct labour for this company and the new department has a relatively low direct labour component, the new department will be assigned less overhead. Such action suggests unethical behaviour by the department manager. You have a responsibility to bring this to the attention of the department manager. If this manager refuses to listen, you must inform someone in a more senior position of authority.

General Manager

Both components are produced using the same process. This means the conversion activity is likely to be very similar for both products. Therefore, the conversion cost per equivalent

unit can be computed for both products combined. However, it is likely that the materials consumed by each component are different. If they are different, then the materials cost per equivalent unit must be computed and reported separately for each component; but the labour and overhead costs per equivalent unit can still be combined.

Process Manager

It is important for you to meet with the management accountant and explain the situation. Assuming you can collect information on the defects, you should compute the total equivalent units produced including defects and recompute the cost per equivalent unit. The new cost per equivalent unit will be lower than what was previously computed. You can then multiply the new cost per equivalent unit by the number of defective units to determine the cost of defects. This cost should be reported to top management to inform them about the financial implications of poor quality.

GUIDANCE ANSWERS TO Flashback

1. *c*

2. When a company produces large quantities of identical products, a process cost accounting system is more suitable.

3. *b*

4. The costs are direct materials, direct labour, and overhead.

5. One Goods in Process Inventory account is needed for each production department.

6. *a*

7. Equivalent units with respect to direct labour is the number of units that would have been produced if all of the labour had been used on units that were started and finished during the period.

8.

	Units of Product		Percent Added		Equivalent Units
Beginning inventory..............	8,000	×	75%	=	6,000
Units started and finished	50,000	×	100	=	50,000
Ending inventory..................	6,000	×	33 1/3	=	2,000
Equivalent units					58,000

9. The first section shows the costs charged to the department. The second section describes the equivalent units produced by the department. The third section shows how the total costs are assigned to units worked on during the period.

10. The transfer decreases one Goods in Process Inventory account and increases another. Therefore, the transfer has no effect on total assets.

11. Equivalent unit processing cost:

$$\frac{\$262,500}{20,000 + 70,000 + 15,000} = \$2.50$$

Goods started and completed:

Costs transferred in	$225,000
Total costs added (70,000 × $2.50)	175,000
Total costs to process	$400,000

12. If goods-in-process inventories are eliminated, equivalent units of production is the number of units started and completed during the period.

Demonstration Problem

Brandon Processing Company produces a product by passing it through a moulding process and then through an assembly process. Information related to manufacturing activities during July follows:

Raw materials:		Moulding department:	
Beginning inventory	$100,000	Beginning goods in process inventory (units)	5,000
Raw materials purchased on credit	300,000	Percentage completed—materials	100%
Direct materials used in moulding	(190,000)	Percentage completed—labour and overhead	60%
Direct materials used in assembling	(88,600)	Units started and completed	17,000
Indirect materials used	(51,400)	Ending goods in process inventory (units)	8,000
Ending inventory	$ 70,000	Percentage completed—materials	100%
Factory payroll:		Percentage completed—labour and overhead	25%
Direct labour used in moulding	$ 42,000	Costs:	
Direct labour used in assembling	55,375	Beginning in process inventory	$ 53,000
Indirect labour used	50,625	Direct materials added	190,000
Total payroll cost (paid with cash)	$148,000	Direct labour added	42,000
Factory overhead incurred:		Overhead applied (150% of direct labour)	63,000
Indirect materials used	$ 51,400	Total costs	$348,000
Indirect labour used	50,625	**Assembling department:**	
Other overhead costs	71,725	Beginning goods in process inventory	$154,800
Total factory overhead incurred	$173,750	Ending goods in process inventory	108,325
Factory overhead applied:		**Finished goods inventory:**	
Moulding (150% of direct labour)	$ 63,000	Beginning inventory	$ 96,400
Assembling (200% of direct labour)	110,750	Costs transferred in from assembling	578,400
Total factory overhead applied	$173,750	Cost of goods sold	(506,100)
		Ending inventory	$168,700

Required

1. Compute the equivalent units of production for the moulding department for July, and determine the costs per equivalent unit for direct materials, direct labour, and overhead.
2. Compute the cost of the units transferred from moulding to assembling during the month and the cost of the ending goods in process inventory for the moulding department.
3. Prepare summary journal entries to record the events of July.

Planning the Solution

○ Compute the moulding department's equivalent units of production and cost per unit with respect to direct materials.

○ Compute the moulding department's equivalent units of production with respect to direct labour and overhead and determine the cost per unit for each.

○ Compute the total cost of the goods transferred to the assembly department by using the equivalent units and unit costs to determine: (a) the cost of the beginning in-process inventory, (b) the materials, labour, and overhead costs added to the beginning in-process inventory, and (c) the materials, labour, and overhead costs added to the units that were started and completed in the month.

○ Use the information to record entries for (a) raw materials purchases, (b) direct materials usage, (c) indirect materials usage, (d) factory payroll costs, (e) direct labour usage, (f) indirect labour usage, (g) other overhead costs (credit Other Accounts), (h) application of overhead to the two departments, (i) transferring partially completed goods from moulding to assembling, (j) transferring finished goods out of assembling, and (k) the cost of goods sold.

SOLUTION TO Demonstration Problem

1. Equivalent units of production—direct materials:

	Units of Product		Percent Added		Equivalent Units
Beginning goods in process	5,000	×	0%	=	-0-
Goods started and completed	17,000	×	100	=	17,000
Ending goods in process	8,000	×	100	=	8,000
Total units	30,000				25,000

Materials cost per equivalent unit $= \frac{\$190,000}{25,000} = \$7.60$ per unit

Equivalent units of production—direct labour and overhead:

	Units of Product		Percent Added		Equivalent Units
Beginning goods in process	5,000	×	40%	=	2,000
Goods started and completed	17,000	×	100	=	17,000
Ending goods in process	8,000	×	25	=	2,000
Total units	30,000				21,000

Labour cost per equivalent unit $= \frac{\$42,000}{21,000} = \$2$ per unit

Overhead cost per equivalent unit $= \frac{\$63,000}{21,000} = \$3$ per unit

2. Cost of units transferred from moulding to assembling during the month:

	Equivalent Units	Cost per Unit	Total Cost
Beginning goods in process:			
Costs from prior month			$ 53,000
Direct materials added..................................	-0-	$7.60	-0-
Direct labour added	2,000	2.00	4,000
Overhead applied..	2,000	3.00	6,000
Total cost to process....................................			$ 63,000
Units started and completed:			
Direct materials added..................................	17,000	$7.60	$ 129,200
Direct labour added	17,000	2.00	34,000
Overhead applied..	17,000	3.00	51,000
Total cost to process....................................			$ 214,200
Cost of transferred units.....................			**$277,200**

Costs of July goods in process inventory for the moulding department

	Units of Product	Cost per Unit	Equivalent Units
Direct materials added......................................	8,000	$7.60	$ 60,800
Direct labour added..	2,000	2.00	4,000
Overhead applied..	2,000	3.00	6,000
Cost of ending goods in process inventory			**$70,800**

3. Summary general journal entries for July:

a. Raw materials purchases:

Raw Materials Inventory	300,000	
Accounts Payable		300,000

b. Direct materials usage:

Goods in Process Inventory—Moulding	190,000	
Goods in Process Inventory—Assembling	88,600	
Raw Materials Inventory		278,600

c. Indirect materials usage:

Factory Overhead	51,400	
Raw Materials Inventory		51,400

d. Factory payroll costs:

Factory Payroll	148,000	
Cash		148,000

e. Direct labour usage:

Goods in Process Inventory—Moulding	42,000	
Goods in Process Inventory—Assembling	55,375	
Factory Payroll		97,375

f. Indirect labour usage:

Factory Overhead	50,625	
Factory Payroll		50,625

g. Other overhead costs:

Factory Overhead	71,725	
Other Accounts		71,725

h. Application of overhead:

Goods in Process Inventory—Moulding	63,000	
Goods in Process Inventory—Assembling	110,750	
Factory Overhead		173,750

i. Transferring partially completed goods from moulding to assembling:

Goods in Process Inventory—Assembling	277,200	
Goods in Process Inventory—Moulding		277,200

j. Transferring finished goods:

Finished Goods Inventory	578,400	
Goods in Process Inventory—Assembling		578,400

k. Cost of goods sold:

Cost of Goods Sold	506,100	
Finished Goods Inventory		506,100

Glossary

Equivalent units of production (EUP) The number of units that are considered as being 100% processed during a given period. (p. 1208)

Materials consumption report A document that summarizes the materials used by a department during a reporting period and that replaces materials requisitions. (p. 1203)

Process cost accounting system A system of assigning direct materials, direct labour, and overhead to specific processes. The total costs associated with each process are then divided by the number of units passing through that process to determine the cost per equivalent unit. (p. 1202)

Process cost summary A primary managerial accounting report for a process cost accounting system. The report describes the costs charged to a department, the equivalent units of production by the department, and how the costs were assigned to the output. (p. 1213)

Process manufacturing The processing of products in a continuous flow of steps (also called process operations or process production); this means products pass through a series of sequential processes. (p. 1198)

For more study tools, quizzes, and problem material,
refer to the Online Learning Centre at
www.mcgrawhill.ca/college/larson

Questions

1. Can services be delivered by process operations? Support your answer with an example.

2. This book has described two main types of cost accounting systems up to this point: job order and process costing. What is the main factor for a company in selecting between these two cost accounting systems? Give two likely applications of each system.

3. Identify the control document for materials flow when a material requisition slip is not used.

4. The focus in a job order costing system is the job or batch. Identify the two main focuses in process costing.

5. Are the journal entries that match cost flows to product flows in process costing primarily the same or much different than in job order costing? Explain.

6. Explain in laymans terms the notion of equivalent units of production (EUP). Why is it necessary to use EUP in process costing?

7. Why is it possible for direct labour in a process manufacturing operation to include the labour of employees who do not work specifically on products or services?

8. Assume a manufacturing company produces a single product by processing it first through a mixing

department and next through a cutting department. Direct labour costs flow through what accounts in this company's process cost system?

9. After all labour costs for a period are allocated, what balance should remain in the Factory Payroll account?

10. Is it possible to have underapplied or overapplied overhead costs in a process cost accounting system?

11. Explain why equivalent units of production for direct labour and overhead may be the same and why they can differ from equivalent units for direct materials.

12. List the four steps in accounting for production activity in a period.

13. What purposes are served by a process cost summary?

14. Assume that you are the production manager of a shoe manufacturing operation in Kitchener, Ontario. Your company has taken on a special order to produce the shoes for all the employees of Canadian Tire stores across the country. Draw the production process assuming three production departments: cutting, Canadian Tire design set to the material, and assembly. Your picture should begin with the delivery of raw materials and finish with the shipment of goods.

Quick Study

For each of the following, indicate whether it is most likely to be produced in a process operation or a job-order operation:

a. Pianos.
b. Wall clocks.
c. Cut flower arrangements.
d. Bolts and nuts.
e. House paint.
f. Folding chairs.
g. Custom tailored suits.
h. Sport shirts.
i. Concrete swimming pools.
j. Door hinges.

QS 23-1
Match product to cost system

LO[1]

QS 23-2
Matching cost flows to
product flows

LO^{3,4,5}

Comeau Company manufactures a product requiring two processes: cutting and sewing.
During July, partially completed units with a cost of $285,500 were transferred from cutting
to sewing. Record this transaction.

QS 23-3
Matching cost flows to
product flows

LO^{3,4,5}

Refer to QS 23-2. The sewing department requisitioned $56,300 of direct materials and
incurred direct labour of $92,000. Record these two events.

QS 23-4
Matching cost flows to
product flows

LO^{3,4,5}

Refer to QS 23-2. Overhead is applied to the sewing department at 100% of direct labour.
Prepare a journal entry to record application of the overhead.

QS 23-5
Matching cost flows to
product flows

LO^{3,4,5}

Prepare a journal entry to record the completion and transfer of goods costing $99,400 to
finished goods.

QS 23-6
Computing equivalent units
of production

LO^{6}

The following information pertains to units processed in the binding department of Lowe
Printing Company during March:

	Units of Product	Percent of Labour Added
Beginning goods in process............	130,000	25%
Goods started and completed.........	290,000	100
Ending goods in process................	110,000	45

Compute the total equivalant units of production with respect to labour for March, under
(a) FIFO method, and (b) Weighted-average method.

QS 23-7
Computing equivalent units
of production

LO^{6}

The following information pertains to the sorting department of Wings International, a
fully automated courier company.

	Number of units	Percentage of overhead added
Beginning units in process	70,000	40
Units started and completed	370,000	100
Ending units in process	88,000	60

Compute the total equivalent units of production with respect to overhead, using
(a) weighted-average method, and (b) FIFO method.

QS 23-8
Computing EUP cost

LO^{8}

The cost of beginning inventory plus the costs added during the period should equal the
cost of units _____ plus the cost of _____.

Refer to QS 23-7. Assume the following overhead cost information for the month of March:

	Amount
Cost of beginning units in process	$110,000
Costs incurred in March	600,000

Compute the cost per equivalent unit for March, using (a) weighted-average method, and (b) FIFO method.

Prepare a journal entry that shows the transfer of $145,000 of goods in process from the fabricating department to the assembly department for Abdol Manufacturing Company.

Match each of the following items with the appropriate description of its purpose:
a. Equivalent units
b. Materials consumption report
c. Process cost summary
d. Equivalent units of production
e. Factory overhead account
f. Materials requisition
g. Finished goods inventory account
h. Raw materials inventory account
i. Goods in Process Inventory—Department A

_____ 1. Holds costs for indirect materials, indirect labour, and other similar costs until assigned to production departments.
_____ 2. Describes the direct materials used in a production department.
_____ 3. Notifies the materials manager that materials should be sent to a production department.
_____ 4. Holds costs of materials until they are used in production departments or as factory overhead.
_____ 5. Holds costs of direct materials, direct labour, and applied overhead until products are transferred from Department A.
_____ 6. A periodic report that describes the activity and output of a production department.
_____ 7. Partially completed units standardized to completed units
_____ 8. Holds costs of finished products until sold to customers.

Jewers Company manufactures products with two processes: sanding and painting. Prepare entries to record the following activities for July:
a. Purchased raw materials on credit at a cost of $42,000.
b. Used direct materials with costs of $12,600 in the sanding department and $21,000 in the painting department.
c. Used indirect materials with a cost of $14,700.
d. Incurred total labour cost of $105,000, all of which was paid in cash.
e. Used direct labour with costs of $42,000 in the sanding department and $33,600 in the painting department.
f. Used indirect labour with a cost of $29,400.
g. Incurred other overhead costs of $33,600 (credit Cash).
h. Applied overhead at the rates of 125% of direct labour in the sanding department and 75% of direct labour in the painting department.
i. Transferred partially completed products with a cost of $97,860 from the sanding department to the painting department.
j. Transferred completed products with a cost of $189,000 from the painting department to the finished goods inventory.
k. Sold products on credit for $400,000. Their accumulated cost was $197,000.

Exercise 23-3

Interpreting journal entries in process cost accounting

LO 3, 4, 5

The following journal entries were recorded by Semour Company's process cost accounting system. The company produces its products by passing them through a cutting department and a moulding department. Overhead is applied to production departments based on the direct labour cost during the period. Provide a brief explanation for each entry.

a.	Factory Overhead	4,000	
	Accounts Payable		4,000
b.	Finished Goods Inventory	39,000	
	Goods in Process Inventory—Moulding ...		39,000
c.	Factory Payroll	15,000	
	Cash...		15,000
d.	Raw Materials Inventory...................................	31,000	
	Accounts Payable		31,000
e.	Goods in Process Inventory—Cutting..............	11,500	
	Goods in Process Inventory—Moulding	8,500	
	Raw Materials Inventory...........................		20,000
f.	Goods in Process Inventory—Cutting..............	9,000	
	Goods in Process Inventory—Moulding	5,000	
	Factory Payroll		14,000
g.	Cost of Goods Sold..	50,000	
	Finished Goods Inventory........................		50,000
	Accounts Receivable	125,000	
	Sales		125,000
h.	Goods in Process Inventory—Moulding	30,000	
	Goods in Process Inventory—Cutting		30,000
i.	Factory Overhead	5,500	
	Raw Materials Inventory...........................		5,500
j.	Goods in Process Inventory—Cutting..............	6,750	
	Goods in Process Inventory—Moulding	7,000	
	Factory Overhead		13,750
k.	Factory Overhead	4,000	
	Factory Payroll		4,000

Exercise 23-4

Recording cost flows in a process cost system

LO 3, 4, 5

Doule Company specializes in shredding government documents in a two-step process. The system begins by processing documents through the shredding department and then through the packing department. The following information describes the manufacturing operations for the month of June 2004:

	Shredding Department	Packing Department
Direct materials used..	$252,000	$378,000
Direct labour used	47,250	78,850
Predetermined overhead application rate		
(based on direct labour)	120%	180%
Goods transferred from shredding to packing................	$(362,250)	$362,250
Goods transferred from packing to finished goods		(633,150)

Service revenue for the month totalled $960,000 on credit and cost of good sold was $454,000.

Required

Prepare summary general journal entries to record the June activities.

During November 2004, a production department in a process manufacturing system for Drake Company completed a number of units of product and transferred them to finished goods. Of these units, 70,000 were in process in the department at the beginning of the month and 308,000 were started and completed during the month. The beginning inventory units were 75% complete with respect to materials and 80% complete with respect to labour when the month began. At the end of the month, 92,400 additional units were in process in the department and were 30% complete with respect to materials and 10% complete with respect to labour.

Required
Compute (a) the number of physical units transferred to finished goods and (b) the number of equivalent units with respect to materials and with respect to labour produced in the department during the month, both using the FIFO and weighted-average methods.

Exercise 23-5
Computing equivalent units of production

LO^6

Refer to Exercise 23-5. Drake Company had $918,372 of direct materials and $728,728 of direct labour costs charged to it during the month. Compute the direct materials cost and the direct labour cost per equivalent unit in the department and allocate the costs among the units in the goods in process inventories and the units started and completed during the month, using the FIFO method.

Exercise 23-6
Assigning costs to inventories

LO^{6,7,8}

Abraham Company has a production department in a process manufacturing system that completed 86,400 units of product and transferred them to finished goods during a recent week. Of these units, 21,600 were in process at the beginning of the week. The other 64,800 units were started and completed during the week. At the end of the period, 18,000 units were in process, three-fifths processed.

Required
Compute the department's equivalent units of production with respect to direct materials under each of the following separate assumptions:
a. All direct materials are added to the products when processing begins.
b. The direct materials are added to the products evenly throughout the process. The beginning goods in process was one-third complete.
c. One half the direct materials are added to the products when the process begins and the other half is added when the process is 75% complete as to direct labour.

Exercise 23-7
Computing equivalent units

LO^{6,8}

The following flowchart shows the production activity of the punching and bending departments of Laker Company for August. Use the amounts shown on the flowchart to compute the missing numbers identified by question marks.

Exercise 23-8
Completing a flowchart for a process system

LO^{3,4,5,9}

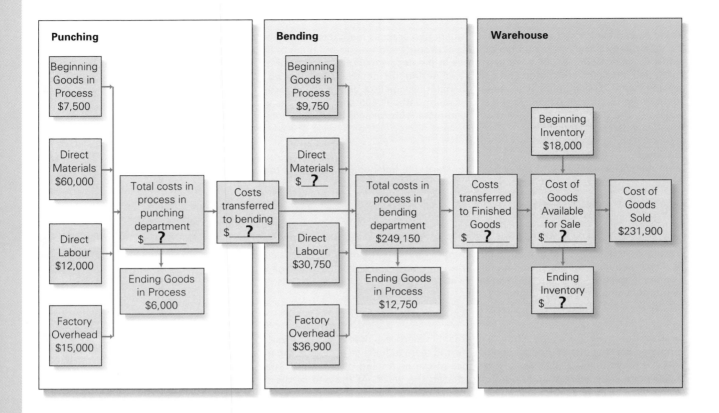

Exercise 23-9

Completing a process cost summary

LO 6, 8

The following partially completed process cost summary describes the July activities of the slicing department of Sneider Company. The output of the slicing department is sent to the canning department, which sends the finished goods to the warehouse for shipping. A partially completed process cost summary for the slicing department follows:

Costs Charged to Department

Direct materials requisitioned	$173,600
Direct labour charged	54,600
Overhead allocated (at 150% of labour predetermined rate)	81,900
Total processing costs for the month..	310,100
Goods in process at the beginning of the month...	25,200
Total costs to be accounted for	$335,300

		Equivalent Units	
Equivalent Unit Processing Costs:	**Units of Product**	**Direct Materials**	**Labour and Overhead**
Beginning goods in process...............................	2,240	1,120	1,680
Units started and completed	14,000	14,000	14,000
Ending goods in process..................................	3,360	2,240	2,520
Total	19,600	17,360	18,200

Prepare the process cost summary for the slicing department by completing the Equivalent Unit Processing Costs section and the Assignment of Costs to the Output of the Department section.

Caper Designs Company manufactures blankets by passing the products through a weaving department and a sewing department. The following information has been gathered about its inventories for October, 2004:

	Beginning Inventory	Ending Inventory
Raw materials	$ 120,000	$ 105,000
Goods in process—Weaving	300,000	330,000
Goods in process—Sewing	570,000	705,000
Finished goods	1,266,000	1,150,000

Problem 23-1A
Measuring production costs and preparing journal entries

LO³, ⁴, ⁵, ⁹, ¹⁰

The following information describes the company's activities during October:

Raw materials purchases (on credit)	$420,000
Factory payroll cost (paid with cash)	1,200,000
Other overhead cost (credit Other Accounts)	156,000
Materials used:	
Direct—Weaving	240,000
Direct—Sewing	75,000
Indirect	120,000
Labour used:	
Direct—Weaving	600,000
Direct—Sewing	180,000
Indirect	420,000
Overhead rates as a percentage of direct labour:	
Weaving	80%
Sewing	120%
Sales (on credit)	$2,700,000

Required

1. Compute (a) the cost of products transferred from weaving to sewing, (b) the cost of products transferred from sewing to finished goods, and (c) the cost of goods sold.
2. Prepare summary general journal entries to record the activities during May.

Check figure:
Cost of goods sold, $1,742,000

Jude Company passes its product through several departments, the last of which is the carving department. Direct labour is added evenly throughout the process in this department. One-fourth of direct materials are added at the beginning of the process and the remaining three-fourths is added when the process is 50% complete with respect to direct labour. During June, 475,000 units of product were transferred to finished goods from the carving department. Of these units, 100,000 units were 40% complete with respect to labour at the beginning of the period and 375,000 were started and completed during the period. At the end of June, the goods in process inventory consisted of 225,000 units that were 30% complete with respect to labour.

The carving department's direct labour cost for June was $854,250 and direct materials cost was $556,875.

Problem 23-2A
Computing costs per equivalent unit and assigning costs to products

LO⁶

Required

Preparation component:

1. Determine the carving department's equivalent units of production with respect to direct labour and with respect to direct materials.
2. Compute the direct labour cost and the direct materials cost per equivalent unit.
3. Compute the amount of direct labour cost and the amount of the direct materials cost assigned to the beginning goods in process inventory, to the units started and completed, and to the ending goods in process inventory.

Check figure:
Direct labour cost per equivalent unit, $1.70

Analysis component:
4. Jude sells and ships all units to customers as soon as they are completed. Assume that an error was made in determining the percentage of completion for the units in ending inventory. Instead of being 30% complete with respect to labour, they were actually 60% complete. Write a brief essay describing how this error would affect Jude's June financial statements.

Problem 23-3A
Journal entries in a process cost accounting system and using equivalent units

LO 3, 4, 5, 6

Barker Company produces large quantities of a product that goes through two processes —spinning and cutting. These facts are known about the factory's activities for August:

Raw materials:

Beginning inventory	$ 35,000
Raw materials purchased (on credit)	218,120
Direct materials used in spinning	(160,000)
Direct materials used in cutting	(37,120)
Indirect materials used	(40,560)
Ending inventory	$15,440

Factory payroll:

Direct labour used in spinning	$ 71,400
Direct labour used in cutting	58,464
Indirect labour used	37,000
Total payroll cost (paid with cash)	$166,864

Factory overhead incurred:

Indirect materials used	$ 40,560
Indirect labour used	37,000
Other overhead costs	92,000
Total factory overhead incurred	$169,560

Factory overhead applied:

Spinning (125% of direct labour)	$ 89,250
Cutting (150% of direct labour)	87,696
Total factory overhead applied	$176,946

The following facts are known about the inventory in the spinning department:

Units:

Beginning in process inventory	4,000
Started and completed	12,000
Ending in process inventory	8,000

Percentage completed:

Beginning in process inventory	
Materials	100%
Labour and overhead	25%
Ending in process inventory	
Materials	100%
Labour and overhead	25%

Costs:

Beginning in process inventory	$ 41,000
Direct materials added	160,000
Direct labour added	71,400
Overhead applied (125% of direct labour)	89,250
Total costs	$361,650
Transferred out to cutting department	(278,750)
Ending in process inventory	$ 82,900

These facts are known about the goods in process inventories for the cutting department:

Beginning in process inventory	$174,000
Ending in process inventory	168,570

These facts are known about the finished goods:

Beginning inventory..	$155,820
Cost transferred in from cutting	467,460
Cost of goods sold	(556,500)
Ending inventory...	$ 66,780

During the month, 10,000 units of finished goods were sold for cash at the price of $130 each.

Required

Preparation component:

1. Prepare entries to record the activities of August.

2. Compute the equivalent units of production for the spinning department for August, and compute the costs per equivalent unit for direct materials, direct labour, and overhead.

3. Compute the cost of the ending goods in process inventory for the spinning department.

Analysis component:

4. Barker provides incentives to managers of the processing departments by paying monthly bonuses based on their success in controlling costs per equivalent unit of production. Assume that the spinning department underestimated the percentage of completion for the units in ending inventory, with the result that the equivalent units of production in ending inventory for August were understated. What impact would this error have on the bonuses paid to the manager of the spinning department and the manager of the cutting department? What impact, if any would this error have on September bonuses?

Check figure:
Cost per equivalent unit:
materials, $8.00; labour, $4.20;
overhead, $5.25

Problem 23-4A
Preparing a process
cost summary

LO⁶, ⁸

Scotia Company produces its product by passing it through a single processing department. Direct materials, direct labour, and overhead are added to the product evenly throughout the process. The company uses month-long reporting periods for its process cost accounting system.

The Goods in Process Inventory account appears as follows after posting entries for direct materials, direct labour, and overhead costs during October:

Goods in Process Inventory				Acct. No. 133
Date	**Explanation**	**Debit**	**Credit**	**Balance**
Oct. 1	Beginning balance			40,800
31	Direct materials	92,250		133,050
31	Direct labour costs	307,500		440,550
31	Applied overhead	123,000		563,550

During October, the company finished and transferred 150,000 units of the product to finished goods. Of these units, 30,000 were in process at the beginning of the month and 120,000 were started and completed during the month. The beginning goods in process inventory was 40% complete. At the end of the month, the goods in process inventory consisted of 22,500 units that were 70% complete.

Required

1. Compute the number of equivalent units of production for October.

2. Prepare the department's process cost summary for October.

3. Prepare an entry to transfer the cost of the completed units to finished goods inventory.

Check figure:
Total cost transferred to
finished goods, $510,000

Problem 23-5A
Preparing a process cost summary

LO[6, 8, 9]

Alphonse Company manufactures a single product in one department. All direct materials are added at the beginning of the manufacturing process. Direct labour and overhead are added evenly throughout the process. The company uses month-long reporting periods for its process cost accounting system.

During May, the company completed and transferred 22,200 units of product to the finished goods inventory. The beginning goods in process inventory consisted of 3,000 units that were 100% complete with respect to direct materials and 40% complete with respect to direct labour and overhead. The other 19,200 completed units were started during the month. In addition, 2,400 units were in process at the end of the month. They were 100% complete with respect to direct materials and 80% complete with respect to direct labour and overhead.

After posting the entries to record direct materials, direct labour, and overhead during May, the company's Goods in Process Inventory account appears as follows:

Goods in Process Inventory				Acct. No. 133		
Date		Explanation	Debit	Credit	Balance
May	1	Beginning balance			190,386
	31	Direct materials	521,640		712,026
	31	Direct labour costs	1,244,880		1,956,906
	31	Applied overhead	995,904		2,952,810

Check figure:
Total cost transferred to finished goods, $2,707,026

Required
1. Compute the department's equivalent units of production for May.
2. Compute the cost per equivalent unit.
3. Prepare the department's process cost summary for May.
4. Prepare the entry to transfer the cost of the completed units to finished goods inventory.

Analysis component:
5. Throughout the course you have been exposed to the fact that accountants rely upon estimates.
   a. Identify the two major estimates that influence the cost per equivalent unit.
   b. In what direction do you anticipate a bias from the management team for each estimate in part (a)? (Assume management compensation is based on maintaining low inventory values.) Explain.

Alternate Problems

Problem 23-1B
Measuring production costs and preparing journal entries

LO[3, 4, 5, 9, 10]

Bardeau Company manufactures plaques by passing the products through a carving department and an assembly department. This information is known about its inventories for June:

	Beginning Inventory	Ending Inventory
Raw materials	$ 36,000	$ 31,000
Goods in process—Carving........................	100,000	110,000
Goods in process—Assembly....................	190,000	235,000
Finished goods...	422,000	402,000

The following information describes the company's activities during June:

Raw materials purchases (on credit)	$140,000
Factory payroll cost (paid with cash)	400,000
Other overhead cost (credit Other Accounts)	50,000
Materials used:	
Direct—Carving	$ 80,000
Direct—Assembly	25,000
Indirect	40,000
Labour used:	
Direct—Carving	$200,000
Direct—Assembly	60,000
Indirect	140,000
Overhead rates as a percentage of direct labour:	
Carving	80%
Assembly	120%
Sales (on credit)	$905,000

Required

1. Compute (a) the cost of products transferred from carving to assembly, (b) the cost of products transferred from assembly to finished goods, and (c) the cost of goods sold.
2. Prepare entries to record the activities during June. Any over- or underapplied overhead is charged to cost of goods sold.

Check figure:
Cost of goods sold, $562,000

Parsons Company passes its product through several departments. The last of these is the bagging department. Direct materials are added evenly throughout the process. Also, one-half of the direct labour is added at the beginning of the process and the other half is added when the process is 50% complete with respect to materials. During October, 70,000 units of product were transferred to finished goods from the bagging department. Of these units, 16,000 units were 60% complete at the beginning of the period and 54,000 were started and completed during the period. The bagging department's direct materials cost for October was $682,000 and direct labour cost was $1,705,200. At the end of October, the goods in process inventory consisted of 8,000 units that were 20% complete with respect to materials.

Problem 23-2B
Computing costs per equivalent unit and allocating costs to products

LO[7]

Required

Preparation component:
1. Determine the bagging department's equivalent units of production with respect to (a) direct labour and (b) direct materials.
2. Compute both the direct labour cost and the direct materials cost per equivalent unit.
3. Compute the amounts of both direct labour cost and direct materials cost assigned to the (a) beginning goods in process inventory, (b) units started and completed, and (c) ending goods in process inventory.

Analysis component:
4. Parsons sells and ships all units to customers as soon as they are completed. Assume an error is made in determining the percentage of completion for the units in ending inventory. Instead of being 20% complete with respect to materials, they were actually 75% complete. Write a brief essay describing how this error would affect Parson's October financial statements.

Check figure:
Direct labour cost per equivalent unit, $29.40

Problem 23-3B

Journal entries in a process cost accounting system and using equivalent units

LO 3, 4, 5, 6

Forgeron Company produces large quantities of a product that goes through two processes—tooling and machining. These facts are known about the factory activities for May:

Raw materials:

Beginning inventory	$117,600
Raw materials purchased (on credit)	700,000
Direct materials used in tooling	(347,480)
Direct materials used in machining	(249,480)
Indirect materials used	(142,240)
Ending inventory	$ 78,400

Factory payroll:

Direct labour used in tooling	$445,200
Direct labour used in machining	49,896
Indirect labour used	64,904
Total payroll cost (paid with cash)	$560,000

Factory overhead incurred:

Indirect materials used	$142,240
Indirect labour used	64,904
Other overhead costs	68,728
Total factory overhead incurred	$275,872

Factory overhead applied:

Tooling (40% of direct labour)	$178,080
Machining (200% of direct labour)	99,792
Total factory overhead applied	$277,872

The following facts are known about the inventory in the tooling department:

Units:

Beginning in process inventory	40,000
Started and completed	120,000
Ending in process inventory	20,000

Beginning in process Inventory:

Materials—percent completed	80%
Labour and overhead—percent completed	40%

Ending in process inventory

Materials—percent completed	90%
Labour and overhead—percent completed	75%

Costs:

Beginning in process inventory	$ 138,880
Direct materials added	347,480
Direct labour added	445,200
Overhead applied (40% of direct labour)	178,080
Total costs	$1,109,640
Transferred out to machining department	(1,008,000)
Ending in process inventory	$ 101,640

Information about the goods in process inventories for the machining department follows: beginning goods in process inventory, $348,600; and ending goods in process inventory, $321,048, Also, these facts are available regarding finished goods:

Beginning inventory	$ 51,240
Cost transferred in from cutting	1,434,720
Cost of goods sold	(1,400,560)
Ending inventory	$ 85,400

During May, 80,000 units of finished goods were sold for cash at the price of $28 each. Any over- or underapplied overhead is adjusted to cost of goods sold.

Required

Preparation component:
1. Prepare entries to record the activities of May.
2. Compute the tooling department's equivalent units of production for May. Calculate the costs per equivalent unit for direct materials, direct labour, and overhead, assuming all product costs are added evenly throughout the process.
3. Compute the cost of the ending goods in process inventory for the tooling department.

Analysis component:
4. Forgeron provides incentives to managers of the processing departments by paying monthly bonuses based on their success in controlling costs per equivalent unit of production. Assume that the tooling department overestimated the percentage of completion for the units in ending inventory, with the result that the equivalent units of production in ending inventory for May was overstated. What effect would this error have on the bonuses paid to the manager of the tooling department and the manager of the machining department? What effect, if any, does this error have on June bonuses?

Manitoba Company produces its product by passing it through a single processing department. Direct materials, direct labour, and overhead are added to the product evenly throughout the process. The company uses monthly reporting periods for its process cost accounting system. The Goods in Process Inventory account appears as follows after posting entries for direct materials, direct labour, and overhead costs:

Problem 23-4B
Preparing a process cost summary

LO^{6,8}

Goods in Process Inventory					Acct. No. 140
Date		**Explanation**	**Debit**	**Credit**	**Balance**
Nov.	1	Beginning balance			60,000
	31	Direct materials	104,130		164,130
	31	Direct labour costs	381,810		545,940
	31	Applied overhead	496,353		1,042,293

During November, the company finished and transferred 90,000 units of the product to finished goods. Of these units, 7,500 were in process at the beginning of the month, and 82,500 were started and completed during the month. The beginning goods in process inventory was 75% complete. At the end of the month, the goods in process inventory consisted of 12,000 units that were 20% completed.

Required
1. Compute the number of equivalent units of production for November.
2. Prepare the department's process cost summary for November.
3. Prepare an entry to transfer the cost of the completed units to Finished Goods Inventory.

Jiffy Manufacturing Company manufactures a single product in one department. Direct labour and overhead are added evenly throughout the process. Direct materials are added as needed. The company uses month-long reporting periods for its process cost accounting system. During January, the company completed and transferred 220,000 units of product to the finished goods inventory. The beginning in process inventory consisted of 20,000 units that were 75% complete with respect to direct materials and 60% complete with respect to direct labour and overhead. The other 200,000 completed units were started during the month. In addition, 40,000 units were in process at the end of the month. They were 50% complete with respect to direct materials and 30% complete with respect to direct labour and overhead. After posting entries for direct materials, direct labour, and overhead for January, the company's Goods in Process Inventory account appears as follows:

Problem 23-5B
Preparing a process cost summary

LO^{6,8,9}

Goods in Process Inventory				Acct. No. 133
Date	Explanation	Debit	Credit	Balance
Jan. 1	Beginning balance			41,100
31	Direct materials	112,500		153,600
31	Direct labour costs	176,000		329,600
31	Applied overhead	440,000		769,600

Required
1. Compute the equivalent units of production for direct materials and for direct labour and factory overhead.
2. Compute the cost per equivalent unit for direct materials, direct labour, and factory overhead.
3. Prepare the department's process cost summary for January.
4. Prepare an entry to transfer the cost of the completed units to finished goods inventory.

Analysis component:
5. Throughout the course you have been exposed to the fact that accountants rely upon estimates.
   a. Identify the two major estimates that influence the cost per equivalent unit.
   b. In what direction would you anticipate a bias from the operations management team for each estimate, given you know their compensation is based on maintaining low inventory values? Explain.

Comprehensive Review Problem

Sawler Company produces a product by sending it through two processes, one of which takes place in Department One and the other in Department Two. All the Department One's output is transferred to Department Two. In addition to the goods in process inventories in Departments One and Two, Sawler maintains inventories of raw materials and finished goods. Sawler uses raw materials as direct materials in Departments One and Two and as indirect materials. Its factory payroll costs include direct labour for each department and indirect labour.

Required
In the problem, you are to maintain certain records and produce various measures of the inventories to reflect the events of July. Round all calculations of unit costs to the nearest penny and all other dollar amounts to the nearest whole dollar. To begin, set up the following general ledger accounts and enter their June 30 balances:

Raw Materials Inventory	$ 64,000
Goods in Process Inventory—Department One	128,440
Goods in Process Inventory—Department Two.......................	50,000
Finished Goods Inventory	220,000
Sales	- 0 -
Cost of Goods Sold	- 0 -
Factory Payroll..	- 0 -
Factory Overhead..	- 0 -

1. Prepare entries to record the following events that occurred in July:
   a. Purchased raw materials for $200,000 cash (use a perpetual inventory system).
   b. Used raw materials as follows:

Department One...................................	$72,000
Department Two...................................	89,600
Indirect materials	42,000

c. Incurred factory payroll cost of $360,000, paid with cash (ignore income and other taxes).

d. Assigned factory payroll costs as follows:

Department One	$200,000
Department Two	100,000
Indirect labour	60,000

e. Incurred additional factory overhead costs of $48,000, paid in cash.

f. Allocated factory overhead to Department One and Two as percentage of the direct labour costs. (To make this entry, you must first compute the overhead allocation rate using direct labour and overhead costs incurred during July.)

2. Information about the units of product on hand or worked on during July follows:

	Department One	Department Two
Units in beginning inventory	500	1,000
Percent completed with respect to:		
Materials	50%	40%
Labour and overhead	40%	62%
Units started and finished in July	2,000	1,800
Percent completed with respect to:		
Materials	100%	100%
Labour and overhead	100%	100%
Units in ending inventory	1,000	1,600
Percent completed with respect to:		
Materials	15%	25%
Labour and overhead	20%	20%

Use this information and the facts from part 1 to make the following calculations:

a. Equivalent units of production in Department One and the per unit costs for labour, materials, and overhead.

b. Equivalent units of production in Department Two and the per unit costs for labour, materials, and overhead.

3. Using the results from requirement 2 and previously given information, make the following calculations, and prepare general journal entries to record:

a. Total cost of units transferred from Department One to Department Two during July.

b. Total cost of units transferred from Department Two to finished goods during July.

c. Sale of finished goods that cost $535,600 for $1,300,000 cash.

4. Post the journal entries from parts 1 and 3 to the ledger accounts that you set up at the beginning of the problem.

5. Compute the amount of gross profit from the sales in July.

Analytical and Review Problems

A & R 23-1

Deveau Company uses a process cost system. The following selected information is for the month of June 2004.

	Physical Units	% Complete
Beginning work in process.................	4,200	50%
Units started.......................................	16,800	
Units in ending work in process..........	7,000	30%

The total cost of the beginning work in process was $25,900, of which $4,900 represented direct labour costs. Overhead is applied on the basis of direct labour costs.

All direct materials are added at the beginning of the process, and the conversion costs are incurred uniformly through the process. During August, the company added $48,720 of direct materials and $35,000 of direct labour, and applied $42,700 of overhead to work in process.

Required
1. What is the overhead rate?
2. Show the direct materials, the direct labour, and the overhead components of the beginning work in process.
3. What is the number of equivalent units used to establish the cost for direct materials, direct labour, and overhead?
4. What is the cost of ending work in process inventory for direct materials, direct labour, and overhead? Show each component separately.

A & R 23-2

Vancouver Canners ltd. has recently modernized its canning process by installing updated, more efficient machines. The process has become much less labour intensive.

Required
Indicate what changes you would expect to see in the company's process costing system as a result of the modernization.

A & R 23-3

Tsoi Company uses process costing for its two manufacturing departments—smelting and turning. Overhead is applied on the basis of 100% of direct labour for smelting and 180% for the turning department. The following costs were reported for July 2004:

	Smelting	Turning
Raw materials	$140,000	$227,500
Direct labour	52,500	77,000
Factory Overhead applied	52,500	138,600
Totals...	$245,000	$443,100

Tsoi Company has no beginning or goods in process inventories. Goods are delivered to customers as soon as they are processed so there is also no inventory of finished goods.

Two employees who work in the turning department incorrectly coded their time sheets. As a result, labour charges of $8,750 were charged to the smelting department that should have been charged to the turning department.

Required
Explain how the coding error affects Tsoi Company's financial statements and process cost summaries.

Cost Allocation and Performance Measurement

Chasing Costs and Finding Gold

Montreal, Que.—Karla Sellers, a department manager for AeroTech—a small aerospace manufacturer—was recently confronted with several strategic initiatives launched by top management. These initiatives were directed at improving AeroTech's competitive position. Its managers pursue a policy of continuous improvement, and aim to strategically identify specific areas for improvement. Says Sellers, "My department was the guinea pig, and I was leery, to put it politely."

To identify opportunities for improvement, Sellers' supervisors examined cost data based on an analysis of processes and activities. This required designing an accounting system to track cost information for the flow of materials, labour, and overhead in the processes at AeroTech. Management considered this necessary to obtain reliable data useful in targeting and measuring its policy of continuous quality improvement.

Sellers' department—the Small Aircraft Division—was the target of the process and activity analysis project. Its aim is to implement an activity-based cost system to meet management's information demands. Sellers and her team identified four main goals of AeroTech's activity-based cost system:

1. Identify costs, especially when processes cross departments.
2. Identify major cost drivers for analysis and prediction of cost behaviour.
3. Improve tracing of overhead costs.
4. Identify activities that add value to the product and those that do not.

"I felt uneasy about the whole project," says Sellers. "I'd never participated in such a major overhaul of an information system." Before beginning, Sellers needed to get a better understanding of how costs are traced to processes, how they're accumulated, and how costs per unit are computed for each process.

"It all eventually came together," says Sellers. She admits her team's lack of knowledge in activity-based costing slowed its progress. "In the end, we cut costs by nearly 12%, which drove price reductions. Our competitors didn't react and we gained 9% in market share." Sellers' reward? She's now Vice-President of Strategic Operations with a hefty salary to boot! Adds Sellers, "Our effective use of cost accounting data was the key."

Learning Objectives

LO¹ Assign overhead costs using two-stage cost allocation.

LO² Assign overhead costs using activity-based costing.

LO³ Describe allocation of joint costs across multiple outputs.

LO⁴ Explain segmentation and the role of segmented reporting.

LO⁵ Distinguish between direct and indirect expenses.

LO⁶ Identify bases for allocating indirect expenses to departments.

LO⁷ Prepare segmented income statements.

LO⁸ Prepare departmental contribution reports.

LO⁹ Explain controllable costs and responsibility accounting.

Chapter Preview

The three prior chapters focused on measuring the costs of products or services, including reporting and analyzing the results in managerial reports. This chapter discusses further the issue of cost allocation. It describes how we allocate common costs among multiple cost objects (e.g., multiple services or products). The chapter then describes activity-based costing and the tracing of costs of individual activities. This knowledge helps us better understand how resources are assigned as illustrated in the opening article. The chapter introduces additional managerial accounting reports useful in managing a company's activities. It also explains how and why management divides companies into segments.

Additional Methods of Overhead Cost Allocation

An organization typically incurs many different kinds of overhead costs, which must be allocated (or assigned) to cost objects in some manner. We introduced one extreme method of assigning these costs in Chapter 22 where we lumped all overhead costs together into one *cost pool* and allocated them using a plant-wide predetermined overhead rate. A **cost pool** is like a bucket in which we accumulate costs. We now consider other possible methods of overhead allocation.

Two-Stage Cost Allocation

 LO¹ Assign overhead costs using two-stage cost allocation.

As we move away from lumping all overhead costs into a single cost pool, we must decide how many cost pools we must consider. A common method of overhead allocation is based on lumping overhead costs into multiple cost centres; each cost centre represents an *operating* department of the organization. An **operating department** carries out activities that directly contribute to the main purpose of the organization. For example, the audit, taxation, and business advisory services departments of an accounting firm would be considered operating departments because these are the main services that accounting firms provide to their clients. However, an organization also consists of *service* departments which also incur costs. A **service department** provides support function to one or more operating and other service departments within the organization. Typical service departments in a manufacturing company would include maintenance, factory accounting, janitorial, legal, information systems, and human resources.

Recall that each operating department represents a separate cost centre. This means that we must separately capture all the direct costs incurred by individual operating departments. However, an operating department may also use the services of one or more service departments to carry out its activities. A critical issue, therefore, is to decide how to allocate the costs of service departments to the operating departments they serve.

We use a **two-stage cost allocation method** to assign the total overhead costs to desired cost objects. In the first stage, costs incurred by the service departments are assigned to operating departments (or production departments in the case of a manufacturing company). In the second stage, costs accumulated within each operating department are assigned to the desired cost objects. Managers have the important task of identifying appropriate **allocation bases** to assign costs from service departments to operating departments, and then from the operating departments to the desired cost objects.

Illustration of Two-Stage Cost Allocation

We use Exhibit 24.1 to explain the two-stage procedure. This exhibit illustrates cost allocation for AutoGrand, a custom automobile manufacturer. AutoGrand employs five manufacturing-related departments: janitorial, maintenance, factory accounting, machining, and assembly. Expenses incurred by each department are considered a product cost.

The three service departments—janitorial, maintenance, and factory accounting—expect to incur $10,000, $15,000, and $8,000 (total $33,000) of expenses, respectively, for a recent month that are not directly traceable to a department. Another $28,000 of expenses is directly traceable to the two operating departments (machining and assembly). This means a total of $61,000 of overhead expenses must be allocated to the desired cost objects (jobs 236, 237 & 238 in this example).

The two operating departments as shown in the exhibit use the resources of the service departments. To illustrate the first stage of cost allocation, let us look at janitorial. Its cost is allocated to machining and assembly in the ratio of 60:40. This means 60% or $6,000 of the janitorial costs is assigned to the machining department and 40% or $4,000, to the assembly department. The allocation method used here, known as the direct method, is very simplistic and assumes that service departments cater only to the operating departments. However, this is not true. For example, the Factory Accounting department will likely provide a portion of its services to the Maintenance department. Therefore, we must ensure that a service department's costs are appropriately allocated among other service departments as well as operating departments. Two methods are available to correct any potential cost distortions created by the use of the direct method: (1) the sequential or step method, and (2) the reciprocal method (we will not discuss these advanced cost allocation methods in this text).

To determine total costs assigned to each operating department, the costs directly incurred by the operating department ($10,000 in the case of machining) are added to those assigned from service departments. This yields total costs of $25,000 assigned to machining and $36,000 to assembly.

In the second stage, predetermined overhead rates P. 1153 for each operating department are computed. For machining, this rate is computed using machine hours as the allocation base. For assembly, the rate is computed using labour hours as the allocation base. The predetermined overhead rates are computed as $2.50 per machine hour for machining and $1.80 per labour hour for assembly. The predetermined overhead rates are then used to assign overhead to jobs (the desired cost objects).

Exhibit 24.1

Two-Stage Cost Allocation

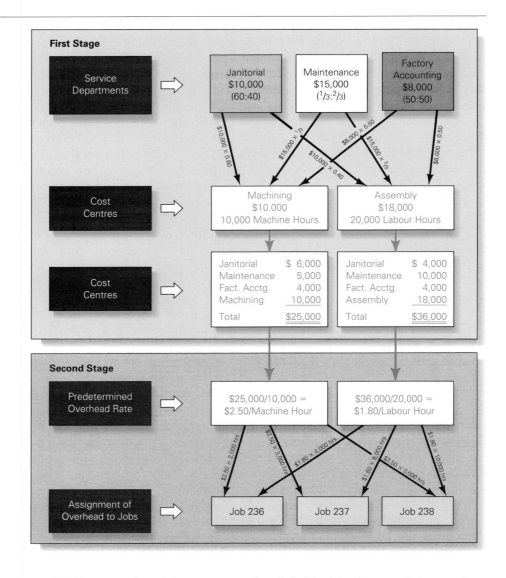

To illustrate, three jobs were started and finished in the month in question. These jobs consumed resources as follows: Job 236—2,000 machine hours in machining and 4,000 labour hours in assembly; Job 237—3,000 machine hours and 6,000 labour hours; Job 238—5,000 machine hours and 10,000 labour hours. The overhead assigned to these three jobs is shown in Exhibit 24.2. Total overhead assigned to each job is $12,200, $18,300, and $30,500 respectively. This adds to $61,000, which is the total amount of overhead with which we began.

Exhibit 24.2

Assignment of Overhead to Jobs

Overhead Assignment	Job 236	Job 237	Job 238
Machining:			
$2.50 × 2,000............................	$ 5,000		
$2.50 × 3,000............................		$ 7,500	
$2.50 × 5,000............................			$12,500
Assembly:			
$1.80 × 4,000............................	$ 7,200		
$1.80 × 6,000............................		10,800	
$1.80 × 10,000..........................			18,000
Total overhead assigned	$12,200	$18,300	$30,500

Activity-based Costing

As we mentioned earlier, identifying appropriate allocation bases to assign overhead costs is critical in ensuring that costs are allocated accurately. Ideally, overhead costs must be assigned using allocation bases that have some kind of a cause–effect relationship with the overhead cost that is being allocated. It does not take a rocket scientist to figure out that overhead cost items such as rent, supervisor's salary and machine depreciation are not caused by the same cost driver. A **cost driver** is a factor that causes a particular overhead cost to go up or down. It is equally easy to recognize that direct labour hours or even machine hours cannot drive all the overhead costs.[1]

Lumping overhead costs into one cost pool or even two or three cost centres as we have done so far is certainly a less costly way of allocating overhead costs, but it can lead to cost distortions. Increased competition has created a tremendous sense of urgency to understand costs better. A better understanding of costs allows managers to avoid making poor decisions; as we will see in later chapters, cost information is crucial in making a number of key decisions.

Overhead Kills

Did You Know?

Futura Computer Company faced two opportunities. First, bankruptcy of a competitor offered it an opportunity to pick up half a million units of incremental sales of its seemingly best product on top of existing sales of 3 million units. Second, it had an opportunity to outsource 2 million units of a money-losing product to a Korean firm that submitted an attractive bid. The senior vice president of production recommended manufacturing the less profitable product in Korea and retooling its own domestic plant to produce the extra units of the better product. This strategy aimed to convert the company's current $11 million loss to a $17.5 million profit. But profits never materialized, and losses ballooned to $20 million! What went wrong? It turns out the "best" product was a loser, while the "worst" product was a consistent moneymaker. The root of the problem was allocation of overhead items like amortization on the basis of direct labour cost. This meant a product using, say, 20% of total labour was assigned 20% of amortization. But where labour was being used, machinery wasn't. Labour-heavy products should've been assigned less amortization. Poor cost allocation brought this company to its knees.

SOURCE: "Overhead Can Kill You," *Forbes*, October 2, 1997.

Activity-based costing (ABC) attempts to better allocate costs to the desired cost objects by focusing on the *activities* consumed by the cost objects. An **activity** is a set of tasks that consumes resources, thereby incurring overhead costs. Examples of activities may include purchasing, invoicing, quality inspection, product design, customer contact, and order-entry.

---

[1] The proportion of direct labour costs has gone down significantly due to technological advances leading to automation. In such situations, it is clear that direct labour hours have no cause–effect relationship with the overhead costs.

Exhibit 24.3 illustrates the two-step activity-base cost allocation method. The first step includes identifying activities involved in carrying out the manufacturing and forming activity cost *pools* by combining activities into sets. The second step involves computing predetermined overhead cost allocation rates for each cost pool and assigning costs to jobs.

Exhibit 24.3

Activity-based Cost Allocation

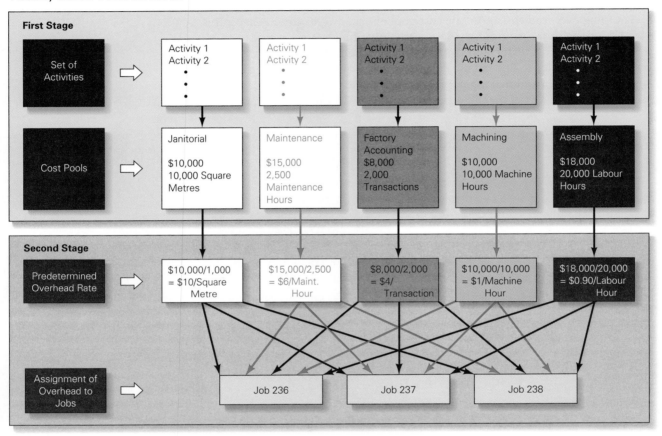

We begin our explanation at the top of Exhibit 24.3. Costs of individual activities of overhead items or *resources* are collected in separate temporary accounts. The cost of each activity is driven by what is called a cost driver. A cost driver causes the cost of an activity to go up or down. The cost driver for a purchase order processing activity, for instance, is the number of purchase orders processed. The essential idea is that activities cause costs and to understand cost behaviour we must understand the activities that drive the costs.

Activities are then pooled in a logical manner into **activity cost pools**. An activity cost pool is a temporary account accumulating costs a company incurs to support an identified set of activities. Costs accumulated in an activity cost pool include variable and fixed costs of the activity. Variable costs pertain to resources acquired as needed (such as materials) whereas fixed costs pertain to resources acquired in advance (such as equipment).

An activity cost pool account is handled like a manufacturing overhead account. After all activity costs are accumulated in an activity cost pool account, users of the activity, called *cost objects*, are assigned a portion of the total activity cost. This is done using a cost driver or allocation base.

Illustration of Activity-based Costing

To illustrate, let's return to the three jobs of AutoGrand. Assume resources are consumed by Jobs 236, 237, and 238 as shown in Exhibit 24.4.

 LO² Assign overhead costs using activity-based costing.

Exhibit 24.4

Activity Resource Consumption

Resource Use	Job 236	Job 237	Job 238
Square metres of space	500	300	200
Maintenance hours	1,250	750	500
Number of transactions	500	700	800
Machine hours	2,000	3,000	5,000
Direct labour hours	4,000	6,000	10,000

We then assign overhead to these three jobs using activity-based costing as shown in Exhibit 24.5.

Exhibit 24.5

Activity-based Overhead Assignment

Overhead Assignment	Job 236	Job 237	Job 238
Janitorial			
$10.00 × 500	$ 5,000		
$10.00 × 300		$ 3,000	
$10.00 × 200			$ 2,000
Maintenance			
$6.00 × 1,250	7,500		
$6.00 × 750		4,500	
$6.00 × 500			3,000
Factory Accounting			
$4.00 × 500	2,000		
$4.00 × 700		2,800	
$4.00 × 800			3,200
Machining			
$1.00 × 2,000	2,000		
$1.00 × 3,000		3,000	
$1.00 × 5,000			5,000
Assembly			
$0.90 × 4,000	3,600		
$0.90 × 6,000		5,400	
$0.90 × 10,000			9,000
Total overhead assigned	$20,100	$18,700	$22,200

Comparing Two-Stage and Activity-Based Cost Allocation

Exhibit 24.6 shows that the overhead amounts assigned to the three jobs vary markedly depending on whether traditional two-stage cost allocation or activity-based costing is applied. These differences in amounts assigned result from more accurately tracing overhead resource use to each job. This increase in accuracy results because activity-based costing uses allocation bases reflecting actual cost drivers.

Exhibit 24.6

Cost Comparisons

Cost Allocation Method	Job 236	Job 237	Job 238
Traditional two-stage allocation	$12,200	$18,300	$30,500
Activity-based allocation	20,100	18,700	22,200
Difference	($ 7,900)	($ 400)	$ 8,300

Did You Know?

Broad Application

Activity-based costing is used in many settings. ABC has been used by banks such as the Bank of Nova Scotia, automotive manufacturers such as Volkswagon Canada and in many other organizations such as universities, health care providers, and computer manufacturers. The only requirements are the existence of overhead costs and the need to determine the activities that cause overhead costs. Results of using ABC include more accurate costing that enables management to make better resource allocation decisions leading to improved profitability.

Differences between traditional allocation methods and activity-based costing are mainly due to how many cost drivers are used and how many allocations are made. Traditional cost systems commonly accumulate overhead in one overhead pool or a small number of overhead pools. Companies then assign these overhead costs to desired cost objects using a single allocation base such as direct labour. In addition, service department costs are often allocated to operating departments separately (see Exhibit 24.1).

Under activity-based costing, the costs of resources are assigned to activities that consume the resources. These activities are then accumulated into activity cost pools. A company selects an allocation base for each activity pool. It uses this base to assign the accumulated activity costs to cost objects (such as jobs or products) benefiting from the activity.

It is common for an activity-based costing system to involve 6 to 12 (or more) times as many allocations as in a traditional cost system. As one example, a Montreal-based manufacturer currently uses nearly 20 different activity cost drivers to assign overhead costs to its products.

An activity-based cost system was recently set-up at Perkin-Elmer, a maker of analytical instruments for the global market. The company's controller reports that at first they tried to analyze too many cost drivers. Eventually, they set up cross-functional teams able to identify the important cost drivers for each pool.

Exhibit 24.7 lists examples of overhead cost pools and their cost drivers. We use these cost drivers to assign activity costs to cost objects and then to products produced.

Exhibit 24.7

Costs and Cost Drivers in Activity-based Costing

	Cost	Cost Driver
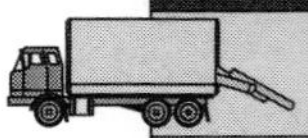	Materials purchasing	Number of purchase orders
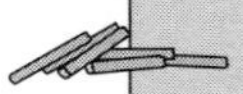	Materials handling	Number of materials requisitions
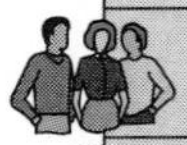	Personnel	Number of employees
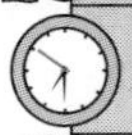	Equipment amortization	Number of products produced or hours of use
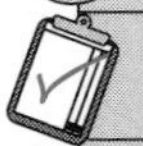	Quality inspection	Number of units inspected
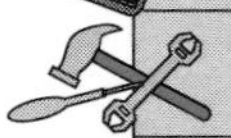	Indirect labour in setting up equipment	Number of setups required
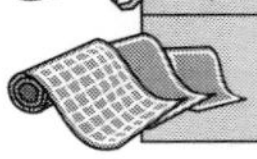	Engineering costs for product modifications	Number of modifications (engineering change orders)

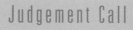

Director of Operations

You are the director of operations for a promotional company. Two department managers approach you with a complaint. Both feel they are unduly assigned high overhead costs. Overhead is currently assigned on the basis of labour hours for artwork designers. These managers argue overhead doesn't only depend on the designers' hours and that many overhead items are unrelated to these hours. How do you respond?

Judgement Call

Answer—p. 1274

Activity-based costing is especially effective when many different kinds of products or services are offered by companies. Some products produced in a department might be simple, while others are more complex. More complex products likely require more help from service departments such as engineering, maintenance, and materials handling. If the same amount of direct labour is applied to the complex and simple products, a traditional overhead allocation system assigns the same amount of overhead costs to them. But with activity-based costing, the complex products are assigned a greater portion of overhead because they cause greater amounts of overhead costs than do simple products.

Cost-Benefits of an ABC System

Companies are increasingly attracted to ABC because it offers the potential for more accurate cost allocation, thereby increasing decision-making accuracy. For example, cost information is useful for pricing decisions. ABC works very well in organizations that adopt the lean business model. By understanding key activities and the resources they consume, managers and employees can attempt to identify sources of waste in the system and eliminate them. This concept of improvement using information provided by an ABC system is known as activity-based management (ABM). Note that ABM is not possible in a traditional cost allocation system—improving a convenience-based cost allocation base such as direct labour will not reduce overhead costs because no cause-effect relationship exists between direct labour and most overhead costs.

However, implementing an ABC system is not possible without considering key implementation issues. We mentioned in Chapter 21 that managerial accounting is not governed by GAAP. Therefore, there is no standard for the number of activities that an organization must have as part of its cost system. Managers must decide, then, how many activities and allocation bases they wish to include in the ABC system. Clearly, a more complex costing system (with many activities) will be more expensive to implement and maintain because more information must be tracked and maintained. On the other hand, a less complex system (with few activities) will definitely be less costly but can lead to cost distortions; moreover, such a simple system will provide little useful information for the purposes of ABM. Another key challenge for management is overcoming any resistance to change from the employees, particularly if employees perceive that the information produced by an ABC system may adversely affect them.

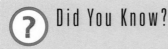

Judgement Call

Answer—p. 1274

Accounting Officer

You are an accounting officer working for a company producing expensive women's footwear, the production of which involves many complicated and specialized activities. The company's general manager recently learns about activity-based costing (ABC) and thinks it might be appropriate to use. But your current supervisor doesn't want to disturb the existing cost accounting system and instructs you to prepare a report stating, "The implementation of ABC is a complicated process involving too many steps and may not be worth the effort." You actually believe ABC will help the company in identifying sources of costs and controlling them. What action do you take?

Flashback

Answers—p. 1274

1. What is a cost driver?
2. When activity-based costing is used rather than traditional allocation methods:
   a. Managers must identify cost drivers for various overhead cost items.
   b. Individual overhead cost items are assigned to the activities that consume the overhead resources.
   c. Managers can direct their attention to the activities that drive overhead cost.
   d. All of the above.
3. Service departments: (a) manufacture products; (b) make sales directly to customers; (c) produce revenues; (d) assist operating departments.

Joint Costs

LO³ Describe the allocation of joint costs across multiple outputs.

We have talked about the allocation of overhead costs across cost objects. Another case of allocation deals with the concept of *joint costs*. Consider a situation where Solutions Specialists (SS), an independent marketing research firm, carries out a study pertaining to children's hygiene which leads to the publication of three separate reports that can be potentially useful to providers of children's hygiene products or services. The costs associated with carrying out this study are joint costs (they are common to all three publications). A **joint cost** includes individual cost items incurred for the purposes of carrying out a joint process (or series of joint processes) leading to multiple outputs (three separate reports in our example). As another example, a petroleum refining company incurs a joint cost when it buys crude oil that it separates into multiple products, such as gasoline, lubricating oil, kerosene, paraffin and ethylene (see Exhibit 24.8). The point at which the separate outputs are identifiable is called the split-off point.

Whenever a joint cost is incurred, the main question once again is how to allocate them to the different cost objects (i.e. the different outputs of the joint process). Broadly speaking, there are two general methods of allocating joint costs to the outputs: physical basis or value basis. The physical basis involves allocating joint costs using measures representing physical characteristics of outputs such as weight, volume, or any other measure. In the case of the reports published by SS, this could be the number of pages. If all three reports are nearly equal in size, we would simply divide the joint costs equally among the three reports.

Although this method is easy, it does not reflect the market values generated by the different outputs. Allocation on the basis of value assumes that the relative market values of the individual outputs are easily available. For example, two of the three reports published by SS may have market values of less than $250, whereas the third report may have a value of over $1,000. In such a situation, two of the three reports will absorb only a third of the total joint costs, whereas the third will absorb the remaining two-thirds. This method allocates costs on the basis of the benefits received from the individual outputs (benefits received is measured in terms of potential revenues generated from the sale of the reports).

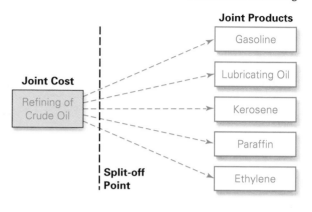

Exhibit 24.8

Joint Products from Petroleum Refining

Illustrating Physical Allocation of Joint Cost

To illustrate a physical measure of allocating a joint cost, let's consider a sawmill that bought logs for $30,000. When cut, these logs produce 30,000 cubic metres of lumber in the grades and amounts shown in Exhibit 24.9. The logs produce 6,000 cubic metres of No. 3 Common lumber, which is 20% of the total. With physical allocation, the No. 3 Common lumber is assigned 20% of the $30,000 cost of the logs, or $6,000 ($30,000 × 20%). Because this low-grade lumber sells for $4,000, this allocation gives a $2,000 loss from its production and sale. The physical basis for allocating joint costs does not reflect the extra value flowing into some products or the inferior value flowing into others. The portion of a log that produces Structural grade lumber is worth more than the portion used to produce the three grades of Common lumber.

Grade of Lumber	Board Metres Produced	Percent of Total	Allocated Cost	Selling Price	Gross Profit
Structural...............	3,000	10.0%	$ 3,000	$12,000	$ 9,000
No. 1 Common	9,000	30.0	9,000	18,000	9,000
No. 2 Common	12,000	40.0	12,000	16,000	4,000
No. 3 Common	6,000	20.0	6,000	4,000	(2,000)
Total	30,000	100.0%	$30,000	$50,000	$20,000

Exhibit 24.9

Allocating Joint Costs on a Physical Basis

Illustrating Value-based Allocation of Joint Cost

Exhibit 24.10 reflects the value basis method of allocation. Here, the percents of the total cost allocated to each grade are determined by the ratio of each grade's sales value to the total sales value of $50,000 (sales value is the unit selling price multiplied by the number of units produced). The Structural grade lumber receives 24%

of the total cost ($12,000/$50,000) instead of the 10% portion based on a physical measure. The No. 3 Common lumber receives only 8% of the total cost, or $2,400, which is much less than the $6,000 assigned to it with the physical basis.

An outcome of value-based allocation is that *every* grade produces exactly the same 40% gross profit on its sales value. This 40% rate equals the gross profit rate from selling all the lumber made from the $30,000 logs for a combined price of $50,000.

Exhibit 24.10

Allocating Joint Costs on a Value Basis

Grade of Lumber	Sales Value	Percent of Total	Allocated Cost	Gross Profit
Structural......................................	$12,000	24.0%	$ 7,200	$ 4,800
No. 1 Common........................	18,000	36.0	10,800	7,200
No. 2 Common........................	16,000	32.0	9,600	6,400
No. 3 Common........................	4,000	8.0	2,400	1,600
Total..	$50,000	100.0%	$30,000	$20,000

 **Flashback**

Answer—p. 1274

4. A company produces three products: B1, B2, and B3. The joint cost incurred for the current month for these products is $180,000. The following data relate to this month's production:

Product	Units Produced	Unit Sales Price
B1	96,000	$3.00
B2	64,000	6.00
B3	32,000	9.00

The amount of joint cost allocated to B3 using the value basis allocation is: (a) $30,000; (b) $54,000; (c) $90,000.

Mid-Chapter Demonstration Problem

Leonard Company produces two products: Zig and Zag. Overhead is estimated at $600,000 and the company expects to use 1,000 labour hours to produce Zig and 3,000 hours to produce Zag. Overhead is caused by purchase orders costing $120,000, inspections costing $270,000, and materials handling costing $210,000. The company estimates the following activity information:

	Zig	Zag	Total
Number of purchase orders......................	1,000	500	1,500
Number of inspections	1,000	500	1,500
Number of times material is handled	1,500	500	2,000

Required

a. Compute the amount of overhead assigned to each product using direct labour hours as the base.

b. Compute the amount of overhead assigned to each product using ABC.

c. What insight does ABC provide?

Planning the Solution

○ Determine the total overhead costs and divide this amount by the total estimated labour hours.

○ Allocate the overhead to each product by multiplying the overhead rate by the number of labour hours used by each product.

○ Establish a separate overhead rate for each activity that causes the overhead cost. To assign overhead to each product multiply each separate rate by the quantity of the activity consumed by each product.

SOLUTION TO Mid-Chapter Demonstration Problem

a.

Overhead rate based on direct labour hours $= \dfrac{\$600,000}{4,000 \text{ DHL}} = \$150$ per hour

Overhead assigned to Zig:	$150 × 1,000	=	$150,000
Overhead assigned to Zag:	$150 × 3,000	=	$450,000
Total			$600,000

b. Purchase order overhead = $120,000 ÷ 1,500 = $80 per purchase order

Inspection rate = $270,000 ÷ 1,500 = $180 per inspection

Materials handling rate = $210,000 ÷ 2,000 = $105 per handling

Allocation Using ABC:

			Zig	Zag
Purchase order overhead				
Zig	1,000 × $80	=	$ 80,000	
Zag	500 × $80	=		$ 40,000
Inspection overhead				
Zig	1000 × $180	=	180,000	
Zag	500 × $180	=		90,000
Materials handling				
Zig	1,500 × $105	=	157,500	
Zag	500 × $105	=		52,500
	Total		$417,500	$182,500

c. Using labour hours as the overhead base assigned too little overhead to Zig and too much overhead costs to Zag. ABC gives a more accurate assignment of overhead to the products. Since Zig uses more of the activities that cause overhead it should be assigned more of the overhead costs. A more accurate determination of overhead costs will help management make better decisions regarding the employment of resources and lead to better product pricing decisions.

Segmented Reporting

 LO⁴ Explain segmentation and the role of segmented reporting.

Many organizations divide their operations into individual segments for various reasons. For example, if an organization grows too large, it must be broken down into smaller, more manageable subunits or segments. Organizations providing multiple services may also be organized by segments. For example, a large merchandiser like Zellers is segmented in at least three different ways: by region, by location, and by type of merchandise sold. Exhibit 24.11 presents the possible segmentation of Zellers. A common term often used to identify a level-1 segment is a *division*; similarly, each segment *within* an individual store may be called a *department*; e.g., clothing department. Other examples include the operating and service departments that we introduced earlier in this chapter.

Exhibit 24.11

Segmentation Levels

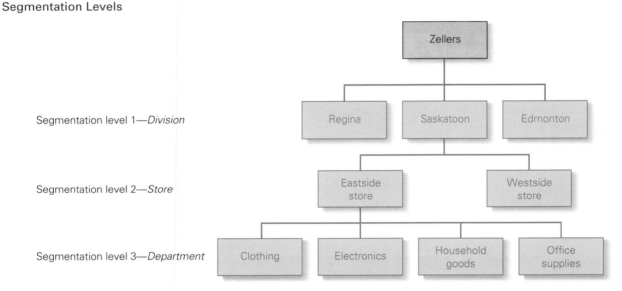

Segmentation level 1—*Division*

Segmentation level 2—*Store*

Segmentation level 3—*Department*

Segment Evaluation

It is reasonable to assume that top management at Zellers would be interested in getting information about each level-1 segment; similarly, top management of the level-1 segments would be interested in information about their level-2 segments, and top management of each of the level-2 segments would be interested in information about their level-3 segments.

The type of information required depends upon how each segment will be evaluated. A segment can be evaluated either as a (1) cost centre, (2) profit centre, or (3) investment centre. A **cost centre** manager is responsible only for controlling its costs; she is not expected to generate revenues. An example of a cost centre is the production department of a manufacturing company, or the accounting, purchasing, legal, and human resource departments of any organization. A **profit centre** manager is expected to influence both costs and revenues, and is therefore evaluated on the basis of profits. Each level-3 segment in Exhibit 24.11 would likely be classified as a profit centre. An **investment centre** manager is responsible for costs, revenues, and the efficient use of assets, and is evaluated on the basis of return on assets (or return on investment). An example of an investment centre may be the Saturn Division of General Motors.

Managerial Accounting Systems
for Segmented Reporting

Managerial accounting systems must be designed in such a way that they can provide segmented information to the managers at the different levels. This information can then be used for the purposes of cost management and performance evaluation. In the case of cost centres, the system is designed to capture costs, whereas in the case of profit centres, the system must be designed to capture both costs and revenues. The rest of this section will focus on key cost allocation issues as they pertain to profit centre reporting at a department level, i.e. a departmental accounting system.

Direct Expenses

Direct expenses are readily traced to a department because they are incurred for the sole benefit of that department. They require no allocation across departments. For example, the salary of an employee who works in only one department is directly traceable to that department and should therefore be charged directly to it.

 Distinguish between direct and indirect expenses.

The concept of direct expense is similar to the concept of direct cost introduced in Chapter 21. We used the term *direct cost* in the context of a manufacturer where all manufacturing costs are assigned to products. This was different from period costs P. 1101 that are immediately expensed. In *non*manufacturing departments, costs are charged to expense as they are incurred. In these situations, the term *direct expense* is used instead of *direct cost*.

Indirect Expenses

Indirect expenses (like *indirect costs*) are incurred for the joint benefit of more than one department. For example, if two or more departments share a single building, they both enjoy the benefits of the expenses of rent, heating, and lighting. These expenses are indirect because they cannot be readily traced to one department.

When we need information about department profits, indirect expenses are allocated across departments benefiting from them. Ideally we allocate indirect expenses by using a cause-effect relation. Identifying cause-effect relations is not always possible. In these latter situations, each indirect expense is allocated on a basis approximating the relative benefit received by each department. However, measuring the benefit each department receives from an indirect expense is often difficult or even impossible. Even when a reasonable allocation basis is chosen, considerable doubt exists regarding the amount allocated to each department.

Illustration of Indirect Expense Allocation

To illustrate how an indirect expense is allocated, let's consider a jewellery store that purchases janitorial services from an outside company. Management allocates this cost across the store's three departments according to the floor space each occupies. Costs of janitorial services for a recent month are $300. Exhibit 24.12 shows the square metres of floor space occupied by each department. The store computes the proportion of the total square metres taken up by each department, and then allocates the $300 cost using these proportions.

Exhibit 24.12

Indirect Expense Allocation

Department	Square Metres	Percent of Total	Allocated Cost
Jewellery	400	25.0%	$ 75
Watch repair	240	15.0	45
China and silver	960	60.0	180
Total	1,600	100.0%	$300

When the allocation process is complete, these and other allocated costs are deducted from gross profits for each department to determine the net income for each.

We can apply the concepts of direct and indirect expenses (and costs) in a variety of cases. We can readily link direct costs or expenses with a *cost object*. Here, the relevant cost object is a department. Other cost objects may be relevant for other decisions. For job order cost systems (Chapter 22) the cost object is a job or job lot. For process cost systems (Chapter 23) the cost object is a process.

One consideration in allocating costs is to motivate managers and employees toward desired behaviour. This means a cost incurred in one department might be best allocated to another department because the latter department caused the cost and can control it. For example, the controller of AeroTech (introduced in the opening article) captures the costs of purchasing, maintenance, and IT services in separate accounts. These costs are then allocated to the individual departments that caused the costs. This reassignment of costs ensures that department managers become aware of the costs they cause, and are able to control them.

Allocation of Indirect Expenses

 LO⁶ Identify bases for allocating indirect expenses to departments.

This section describes how to allocate indirect expenses across departments and identifies the bases used. There is no standard rule about what basis is best. This is because expense allocation involves several factors, and the relative importance of these factors varies across departments. Judgement is required, and people don't always agree. In our discussion, note the parallels between activity-based costing and the allocation procedures described here.

Wages and Salaries

Employees' wages and salaries can be either direct or indirect expenses. If employee time is spent entirely in one department, their wages are a direct expense of that department. But if employees work in more than one department, their wages are an indirect expense and must be allocated across the departments benefited. An employee's contribution to a department usually depends on the hours worked in that department. A reasonable basis then for allocating employees' wages and salaries is the *relative amount of time spent in each department*. But a supervisory employee often manages more than one department and it is sometimes not practical to record a supervisor's time spent in each department. In this case, a company can allocate supervisory salaries to departments on the basis of the number of employees in each department. This basis is reasonable if a supervisor's main task is managing people. Another basis of allocation is on sales across departments. This basis is reasonable if a supervisor's job focuses on generating departmental sales.

Rent and Related Building Expenses

Rent expense for a building is reasonably allocated to departments on the basis of floor space occupied by each department. However, some floor space is often more valuable than other space because of location. If so, the allocation method charges departments with more valuable space a higher expense per square metre. Ground floor retail space, for instance, is often more valuable than basement or upper-floor space because all customers pass departments near the entrance while fewer go beyond the first floor. When there are no precise measures of floor space values, it is helpful to base allocations on data such as customer traffic and real estate assessments. When a company owns a building, then its expenses for amortization, taxes, insurance, and other building-related expenses are allocated in the same way as rent expense.

Advertising

Effective advertising of a department's products increases customer traffic and sales. Customers also often buy unadvertised products during their visit. Advertising of products for some departments often helps sales of all departments, so many stores treat advertising as an indirect expense. Advertising is often allocated on the basis of each department's proportion of total sales. For example, a department with 10% of a store's total sales is assigned 10% of advertising expense. Another method is to analyze each advertisement to compute the newspaper space or TV/radio time devoted to the products of different departments. A department is then charged with the proportional costs of advertisements. Management must consider whether this more detailed and costly method is justified.

Equipment and Machinery Amortization

Amortization on equipment and machinery used only in one department is a direct expense of that department. Amortization on equipment and machinery used by more than one department is an indirect expense to be allocated across those departments that use the equipment. Accounting for each department's equipment amortization expense requires a company to keep records showing which departments use specific assets. The number of hours equipment and machinery are used by departments is a reasonable basis for allocating amortization.

Utilities

Utilities expenses such as heating and lighting are usually allocated on the basis of floor space occupied by departments. This practice assumes their use is uniform across departments. When this is not the case, a more involved allocation may be necessary. There is often a trade-off between the usefulness of more precise allocations and the effort in computing them.

Services

To generate product and service revenues, operation departments require services (support) by departments such as personnel, payroll, advertising, and purchasing. Because these service departments do not produce revenues, they are evaluated as cost centres. A departmental accounting system can accumulate and report costs incurred directly by each service department for this purpose. It then allocates a service department's indirect expenses and costs to operating departments benefiting from them. This is done, for example, using traditional two-stage cost allocation (see Exhibit 24.1). The costs of service departments are shared indirect expenses of operation departments. If management wants to evaluate operating departments as profit centres using net income instead of gross profit, service department costs are also allocated to them. Exhibit 24.13 shows some commonly used bases for allocating service department costs and operating departments.

Exhibit 24.13

Allocation Bases for Services

Service Departments	Common Allocation Bases
Office	Number of employees or sales in each department
Personnel	Number of employees in each department
Payroll	Number of employees in each department
Advertising	Sales or amounts of advertising charged directly to each department
Purchasing	Dollar amounts of purchases or number of purchase orders processed
Cleaning	Square metres of floor space occupied
Maintenance	Square metres of floor space occupied

A Word About Allocations

A careful reading of the above section on allocation of indirect expenses suggests that department managers usually make a sincere effort to identify the real cost drivers of their department's expenses and use these drivers to allocate the expenses to other "user" departments. In identifying true cost drivers, managers are following the notion of cause-effect relationships between expenses and drivers. Other examples in the above section suggest that, in some cases, managers allocate indirect expenses on the basis of the benefits received by a "user" department from the indirect expense. Once again this suggests that managers try to find some meaningful way of allocating the indirect expenses.

Sometimes, it is very difficult to identify an appropriate allocation base. For example, it is usually not easy to identify a base to allocate corporate expenses to other departments. It is difficult to track the consumption of corporate services by other departments or even to measure the benefits received by other departments from the services provided by the corporate office. In such situations, some companies may choose to not allocate such expenses to departments, or may use some arbitrary method to allocate them. Managers must understand how indirect expenses from other parts of the organization are allocated to their departments, if they want to reduce their share of the allocation.

Segmented Income Statements

Segment reports are useful to segment managers to evaluate performance, plan for the next period, and manage operations. We introduced multiple levels of segmentation earlier in this chapter. We can therefore prepare reports pertaining to segments at the different levels. Let us once again focus on departmental-level reports. It is important to remember that we prepare income statements only for segments that are classified as a profit centre. In the case of a cost centre, we will simply prepare a report showing the budgeted versus actual costs (we present this report in Chapter 27).

To illustrate the steps in preparing departmental income statements, let's look at Acer Hardware, a merchandiser with five departments. Two of them (office and purchasing) are service departments and the other three (hardware, housewares, and appliances) are operating (selling) departments. There are four steps in allocating costs to its operating departments and preparing departmental income statements.

Step One

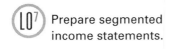

Prepare segmented income statements.

Step one is to accumulate direct expenses for each service and operating department as shown in Exhibit 24.14. Direct expenses include salaries and other expenses each department incurs but does not share with any other department. This information is accumulated in departmental expense accounts.

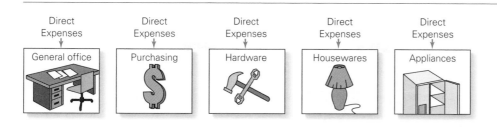

Exhibit 24.14

Step 1: Direct Expense Accumulation

Step Two

Step two is to allocate indirect expenses across all departments using the allocation base identified for each expense. This step is shown in Exhibit 24.15.

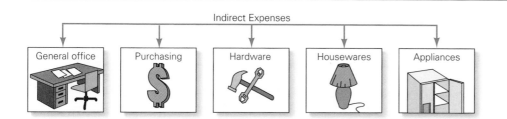

Exhibit 24.15

Step 2: Indirect Expense Allocation

Indirect expenses can include items such as amortization, rent, advertising, and any other expenses that cannot be directly assigned to a department. Indirect expenses are recorded in expense accounts, and can be allocated using a *departmental expense allocation spreadsheet.* We describe this spreadsheet in the next step.

Step Three

Step three is to allocate expenses of the two service departments (office and purchasing) to the three operating departments. Exhibit 24.16 reflects the process of step three for both service departments. Service department expenses are allocated using one of the bases described in the prior section. Computations for both steps two and three are made on a departmental expense allocation spreadsheet as shown in Exhibit 24.17.[2]

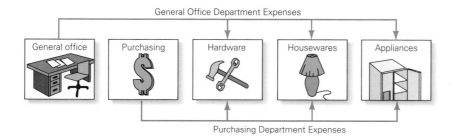

Exhibit 24.16

Step 3: Service Department Expense Allocation

---

[2] In some cases, we might allocate costs of a service department to other service departments because they also use its services. For example, costs of a payroll office benefit all service and operating departments and some of its costs can be assigned to all departments. Nearly all examples and assignment materials in this book allocate service cost only to operating departments for simplicity.

Exhibit 24.17

Departmental Expense Allocation Spreadsheet

Acer Hardware
Departmental Expense Allocations
For Year Ended December 31, 2004

			Allocation of Expenses to Departments				
	Allocation Base	Expense Account Balance	General Office Dept.	Purchasing Dept.	Hardware Dept.	House-wares Dept.	Appliances Dept.
Direct expenses:							
Salaries expense	Payroll records	$51,900	$13,300	$8,200	$15,600	$7,000	$7,800
Amortization on equipment	Amortization records	1,500	500	300	400	100	200
Supplies expense	Requisitions	900	200	100	300	200	100
Indirect expenses:							
Rent expense	Amount and value of space	12,000	600	600	4,860	3,240	2,700
Utilities expense	Floor space	2,400	300	300	810	540	450
Advertising expense	Sales	1,000			500	300	200
Insurance expense	Value of insured assets	2,500	400	200	900	600	400
Total department expenses		$72,200	$15,300	$9,700	$23,370	$11,980	$11,850
Service department expenses:							
General office department	Sales		$15,300		7,650	4,590	3,060
Purchasing department	Purchase orders			$9,700	3,880	2,630	3,190
Total expenses allocated to							
selling departments		$72,200			$34,900	$19,200	$18,100

The top two-thirds of column one in Exhibit 24.17 lists both direct and indirect expenses. The lower part of column one lists service departments. The allocation bases are identified in the second column, and total expense amounts are in the third column.

The departmental expense allocation spreadsheet is useful in implementing the first three steps. First, the three direct expenses of salaries, amortization, and supplies are accumulated in each of the five departments. Second, the four indirect expenses of rent, utilities, advertising, and insurance are allocated to all departments using the allocation bases identified. To illustrate how this is done, let's look at allocation of rent. Exhibit 24.18 lists the five departments' square metres of space occupied.

Exhibit 24.18

Departments' Square Metres

General office	500
Purchasing	500
Hardware	1,350
Housewares	900
Appliances	750
Total	4,000

The two service departments (office and purchasing) occupy 25% of the total space (1,000 sq. metres/4,000 sq. metres). But they're located near the back of the building, which is of lower value than space near the front occupied by operating departments. Management estimates that space near the back accounts for $1,200 (or 10%) of the total rent expense of $12,000. Exhibit 24.19 shows how we allocate the $1,200 rent expense between these two service departments in proportion to the space they occupy.

Exhibit 24.19

Allocating Indirect (Rent)
Expense to *Service*
Departments

Department	Square Metres	Percent of Total	Allocated Cost
General office	500	50.0%	$ 600
Purchasing	500	50.0	600
Total	1,000	100.0%	$1,200

We then allocate the remaining $10,800 (or 90%) of rent expense to the three operating departments as shown in Exhibit 24.20.

Exhibit 24.20

Allocating Indirect (Rent)
Expense to *Selling*
Departments

Department	Square Metres	Percent of Total	Allocated Cost
Hardware..................	1,350	45.0%	$ 4,860
Housewares..............	900	30.0	3,240
Appliance..................	750	25.0	2,700
Total.........................	3,000	100.0%	$10,800

We continue step two in allocating the $2,400 of utilities expense to all departments based on the square metres occupied as shown in Exhibit 24.21.

Exhibit 24.21

Allocating Indirect (Utilities)
Expense to All Departments

Department	Square Metres	Percent of Total	Allocated Cost
General office...........	500	12.50%	$ 300
Purchasing	500	12.50	300
Hardware	1,350	33.75	810
Housewares..............	900	22.50	540
Appliances................	750	18.75	450
Total	4,000	100.00%	$2,400

The rows in Exhibit 24.17 for rent and utilities expenses show the amounts from Exhibits 24.19, 24.20, and 24.21. The allocations of the two other indirect expenses of advertising and insurance are similarly computed. Note that since advertising expense is allocated on the basis of sales, and since service departments don't have sales, advertising expense is allocated to only the three operating departments.

The third step allocates total expenses from the two service departments to the three operating departments. Whereas the general office department expenses are allocated using sales dollars, expenses incurred by the purchasing department are assigned on the basis of the number of purchase orders. The relevant information for this allocation process is given in Exhibit 24.22.

Exhibit 24.22

Operating Departments'
Sales and Purchase Orders

	Hardware Department	Housewares Department	Appliances Department	Total
Sales	$119,500	$71,700	$47,800	$239,000
Purchase orders	776	526	638	1,940

Step Four

When the departmental expense spreadsheet is complete, the amounts in the departmental columns are used to prepare departmental income statements as shown in Exhibit 24.23. This exhibit draws on the departmental expense allocation spreadsheet for data on operating expenses. Information on sales and cost of goods sold is taken from departmental records.

Exhibit 24.23

Departmental Income Statements

		Acer Hardware Departmental Income Statements For Year Ended December 31, 2004		
	Hardware Department	Housewares Department	Appliances Department	Combined
Sales....................................	$119,500	$71,700	$47,800	$239,000
Cost of goods sold	73,800	43,800	30,200	147,800
Gross profit on sales	$ 45,700	$27,900	$17,600	$ 91,200
Operating expenses:				
Salaries expense	$ 15,600	$ 7,000	$ 7,800	$ 30,400
Amortization expense, equipment	400	100	200	700
Supplies expense	300	200	100	600
Rent expense	4,860	3,240	2,700	10,800
Utilities expense..............	810	540	450	1,800
Advertising expense.........	500	300	200	1,000
Insurance expense	900	600	400	1,900
Share of general office expenses	7,650	4,590	3,060	15,300
Share of purchasing expenses	3,880	2,630	3,190	9,700
Total operating expenses .	$ 34,900	$19,200	$18,100	$ 72,200
Net income (loss)................	$ 10,800	$ 8,700	$ (500)	$ 19,000
Analysis:				
Gross profit as percent of sales	38.2%	38.9%	36.8%	38.2%

Flashback

Answers—p. 1274

5. Explain the difference between a cost centre and a profit centre, and give an example of each.

6. If a company has two operating departments (shoes and hats) and two service departments (payroll and advertising), which of the following statements is correct?

   a. Wages incurred in the payroll department are direct expenses of the shoe department.

   b. Wages incurred in the payroll department are indirect expenses of the operating departments.

   c. Advertising department expenses are allocated to the other three departments.

7. Which of the following bases can be used to allocate salaries of supervisors across production departments?

   a. Hours spent in each department.

   b. Number of employees in each department.

   c. Sales achieved in each department.

   d. Any of the above, depending on which is most relevant.

8. What are the three steps in allocating expenses to profit centres?

Departmental Contribution to Overhead

Departmental income statements are not always best for evaluating each department's performance. This is especially true when indirect expenses are a large portion of total expenses, and when weaknesses in assumptions and decisions in allocating indirect expenses can materially affect net income. In these and other cases we might look to evaluate departmental performance using departmental contributions to overhead. The **departmental contribution to overhead** is a report of the amount of revenues less *direct* expenses.[3]

(LO[8]) Prepare departmental contribution reports.

Exhibit 24.24 shows a departmental contribution report in the upper portion of the income statement for Acer Hardware. This type of presentation format is common when reporting departmental contributions to overhead.

Acer Hardware Income Statement Showing Departmental Contributions to Overhead For Year Ended December 31, 2004				
	Hardware Department	Housewares Department	Appliances Department	Combined
Sales	$119,500	$71,700	$47,800	$239,000
Cost of goods sold	73,800	43,800	30,200	147,800
Gross profit on sales	$ 45,700	$27,900	$17,600	$ 91,200
Direct expenses:				
Salaries expense	$ 15,600	$ 7,000	$ 7,800	$ 30,400
Amortization expense, equipment	400	100	200	700
Supplies expense	300	200	100	600
Total direct expenses	$ 16,300	$ 7,300	$ 8,100	$ 31,700
Departmental contributions to overhead	$ 29,400	$20,600	$ 9,500	$ 59,500
Indirect expenses:				
Rent expense				$ 10,800
Utilities expense				1,800
Advertising expense				1,000
Insurance expense				1,900
General office department expense				15,300
Purchasing department expense				9,700
Total indirect expenses				$ 40,500
Net income				$ 19,000
Contribution percents	24.6%	28.7%	19.9%	24.9%

Exhibit 24.24

Departmental Contributions to Overhead

Using the information in Exhibits 24.23 and 24.24, we can perform a more complete evaluation of the profitability of the three operating departments. For instance, let's compare the performance of the appliances department as described in these two exhibits. Exhibit 24.23 shows a net loss of $500 resulting from the department's operations, whereas Exhibit 24.24 shows a positive contribution to overhead of $9,500, which is 19.9% of sales. While the contribution of the appliances department is not as large as the other selling departments, a $9,500 contribution to overhead is better than a $500 loss. This tells us that the appliances department is not a money loser. On the contrary, it is contributing $9,500 towards defraying total indirect expenses of $40,500.

---

[3] A department's contribution is said to be "to overhead" because of the traditional practice of considering all indirect expenses as overhead. This meant the excess of a department's revenues over direct expenses was a contribution to paying total overhead.

Answer—p. 1274

> **9.** On an income statement showing departmental and combined contributions to overhead: (a) indirect expenses are subtracted from each department's revenues; (b) only direct costs and expenses are subtracted from each department's revenues; (c) net income is shown for each department.

Responsibility Accounting

Departmental accounting reports are often used to evaluate a department's performance. But are these reports useful in assessing how well a department *manager* performs? The answer is that neither departmental income nor its contribution to overhead may be useful because many expenses are outside the control of a manager. Instead, we evaluate a manager's performance using responsibility accounting reports that describe a department's activities in terms of **controllable costs**.[4] Chapter 21 explained that a cost is controllable if a manager has the authority to determine or at least strongly influence the amounts incurred. **Uncontrollable costs** are not within the manager's control or influence.

LO⁹ Explain controllable costs and responsibility accounting.

Controllable versus Direct Costs

Controllable costs are not always the same as direct costs. Direct costs are readily traced to a department, but their amounts may or may not be under the control of the department manager. For example, department managers often have little or no control over amortization expense because they can't affect the amount of equipment assigned to their departments. Department managers also usually have no control over their salaries. But department managers can control or influence items such as the cost of goods sold and supplies used in the department. When evaluating managers' performances, we should use data describing their departments' outputs along with managers' controllable costs and expenses. A manager's performance is then often judged by comparing current period's results with planned levels and those of prior periods.

Identifying Controllable Costs

Controllable and uncontrollable costs are identified with a particular manager and a definite time period. Without defining these two reference points, we don't know whether a cost is controllable or not. For example, the cost of property insurance is usually not controllable at the department manager's level, but it is controllable by the executive responsible for obtaining the company's insurance coverage. Likewise, this executive may not have any control over costs resulting from insurance policies already in force. But, when a policy expires, this executive is free to renegotiate a replacement policy and now controls these costs. This means all costs are controllable at some level of management if the time period is sufficiently long. We must use good judgement in identifying controllable costs.

Responsibility Accounting System

The concept of controllable costs provides the basis for a **responsibility accounting system**. A responsibility accounting system assigns managers the responsibility

---

[4] The terms cost and expense are often used interchangeably, but they're not the same. A cost is the monetary value of acquiring some resource that may have present and future benefit. An expense is an expired cost; i.e., as the benefit of a resource expires, a portion of the cost is written off as an expense.

for costs and expenses under their control. Prior to each reporting period, a company prepares plans that identify costs and expenses under the control of each manager. These plans are called **responsibility accounting budgets**. To ensure cooperation of managers and the reasonableness of budgets, the managers are involved in preparing their budgets.

A responsibility accounting system also prepares performance reports. A **responsibility accounting performance report** accumulates costs and expenses for which a manager is responsible. This report shows actual costs and expenses alongside budgeted amounts. Managers use performance reports to focus attention on differences between budgeted amounts and actual costs and expenses. This information often results in corrective or strategic actions. Upper-level management uses performance reports to evaluate the effectiveness of lower-level managers in controlling costs and keeping them within budgeted amounts. Chapter 27 further explains the nature and use of performance reports.

A responsibility accounting system must recognize that control over costs and expenses belongs to several levels of management. To illustrate, let's consider the organization chart in Exhibit 24.25. The lines in this chart connecting the managerial positions reflect channels of authority. This means that while the four provincial sales managers are responsible for the controllable costs and expenses incurred in their segments, these same costs are subject to the overall control of the western region's marketing manager. Similarly, the western region's costs are subject to the control of the vice president of marketing, the president, and ultimately the board of directors.

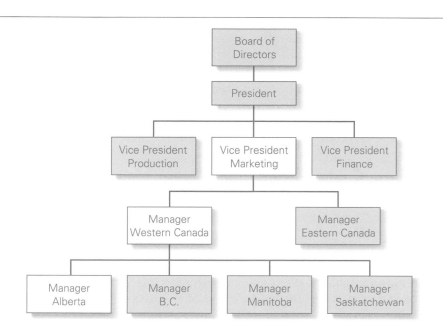

Exhibit 24.25

Organizational Responsibility

At lower levels, managers have limited responsibility and relatively little control over costs and expenses. Performance reports for this management level cover only the few controllable costs. Responsibility and control broaden at higher levels. Reports to higher-level managers therefore span a wider range of costs. But reports to higher-level managers often don't contain the details reported to their subordinates. These details are summarized for two reasons: (1) lower-level managers are often responsible for these detailed costs and (2) detailed reports can obscure important points. Detailed reports to higher-level managers can detract attention from the broader, more important issues facing a company.

Exhibit 24.26 shows summarized performance reports for the three management levels identified in Exhibit 24.25. Exhibit 24.26 shows that costs under the control of Alberta's sales manager are totaled and included among the controllable costs of the western region's marketing manager. Also, costs under the control of the region's marketing manager are totaled and included among controllable costs of the vice president for marketing. In this way, a responsibility accounting system provides relevant information for each management level.

Exhibit 24.26

Responsibility Accounting Performance Reports

Vice President, Marketing		For July	
Controllable Costs	Budgeted Amount	Actual Amount	Over (Under) Budget
Salaries, Regional managers	$ 80,000	$ 80,000	$ -0-
Advertising	21,000	22,400	1,400
Office costs	29,500	28,800	(700)
Western Canada	276,700	279,500	2,800
Eastern Canada	390,000	380,600	(9,400)
Total	$797,200	$791,300	$(5,900)

Marketing Manager, Western Canada		For July	
Controllable Costs	Budgeted Amount	Actual Amount	Over (Under) Budget
Salaries, Provincial managers	$ 75,000	$ 78,000	$3,000
Travel	10,600	10,600	-0-
Office expenses	6,800	6,300	(500)
Alberta	79,600	79,900	300
B.C.	61,500	60,200	(1,300)
Manitoba	24,300	24,700	400
Saskatchewan	18,900	19,800	900
Total	$276,700	$279,500	$2,800

Sales Manager, Alberta		For July	
Controllable Costs	Budgeted Amount	Actual Amount	Over (Under) Budget
Salaries, sales reps.	$26,500	$25,900	$ (600)
Travel	32,000	33,500	1,500
Sales promotions	7,200	7,000	(200)
After-sales service	4,000	3,900	(100)
Other controllable costs	9,900	9,600	(300)
Total	$79,600	$79,900	$ 300

We must recognize that technological advances increase means our ability to produce vast amounts of information that often exceed our ability to use that information. Good managers select relevant data for planning and controlling the areas under their responsibility. A good responsibility accounting system reflects this need and makes every effort to get relevant information to the right person at the right time. The right person is the one who controls the cost, and the right time is before a cost gets out of control.

Let's return to the case of AeroTech in the opening article to illustrate responsibility accounting. Its controller changed the basis for computing commissions paid to salespersons this past year. Sales revenues previously were the sole basis for computing commissions. But the new system reduced these sales revenues by the raw materials, direct labour, delivery, and reinstallation costs of reworking aerospace components. The new system combines the concepts of cost allocation, controllable costs, and responsibility accounting to motivate salespersons to control reworking costs. Because salespersons are now rewarded on sales net of the cost of controllable errors, their behaviour changed. They verified specifications before submitting component orders. This led to reduced costs and an income increase of more than 20%.

10. Are departmental net income and contribution to overhead useful when assessing the performance of a department manager? Explain.

11. Performance reports used to evaluate managers should: (a) include data about controllable expenses; (b) compare actual results with planned levels; (c) both a and b.

Flashback

Answers—p. 1274

Summary

LO¹ Assign overhead costs using two-stage cost allocation. In a traditional two-stage cost allocation procedure, service department costs are first assigned to operating departments (or cost centres). In the second stage, the total overhead costs accumulated in each cost centre are then used to compute a predetermined overhead allocation rate for that cost centre. This rate is used to assign costs from each cost centre to the desired cost objects.

LO² Assign overhead costs using activity-based costing. In activity-based costing, the costs of separate activities of overhead items or resources are first collected in separate temporary accounts. Then the activities are pooled together in some logical manner into activity cost pools. After all activity costs have been accumulated in an activity cost pool account, users of the activity, termed cost objects, are assigned a portion of the total activity cost using an appropriate cost driver or allocation base.

LO³ Describe allocation of joint costs across multiple outputs. A joint cost includes individual cost items incurred for the purposes of carrying out joint processes, leading to multiple outcomes. A joint cost can be allocated using two methods: physical basis or value basis.

LO⁴ Explain segmentation and the role of segmented reporting. For various reasons, companies are often divided into smaller segments, such as divisions or departments. Companies design their managerial accounting systems such that they capture information about individual segments to generate segment reports. Such a report is useful to its manager for planning, decision making, and evaluation purposes.

LO⁵ Distinguish between direct and indirect expenses. Direct expenses are traced to a specific department and are incurred for the sole benefit of one department. Indirect expenses benefit more than one department. If departmental net incomes are measured, indirect expenses are allocated to the departments on some reasonable basis.

LO⁶ Identify bases for allocating indirect expenses to departments. There is no standard rule about what allocation base is best to allocate indirect expenses to departments. Ideally we allocate indirect expenses by using a cause-effect relation. But identifying cause-effect relations is not always possible. In these situations, each indirect expense is allocated on a basis approximating the relative benefit received by each department.

LO⁷ Prepare segmented income statements. Each profit centre (department) is assigned its full expenses to yield its own income statement. These costs include the department's own direct expenses and its share of indirect expenses. The departmental income statement begins by listing the revenues and the cost of goods sold of the department to determine the gross profit. The operating expenses (direct expenses and indirect expenses allocated to the departments) are deducted from the gross profit to yield the department's net income

LO⁸ Prepare departmental contribution reports. The departmental contribution report is similar to the departmental income statement in terms of computing the gross profit for each department. But then the direct operating expenses for each department are deducted from gross profit to determine the contribution generated by each department. The indirect operating expenses are not allocated to individual departments. Instead, they are deducted in total from the total contribution generated by the company.

LO⁹ Explain controllable costs and responsibility accounting. A controllable cost is one influenced by a specific level of management and a specific time period. The total expenses of operating a department often include items that are not controllable by the department manager. Responsibility accounting systems provide information for evaluating the performance of departmental managers and should include only the expenses (and revenues) controllable by the managers.

GUIDANCE ANSWERS TO Judgement Call

Director of Operations

You should collect details of the overhead items and review them to see if direct labour does indeed drive these costs. If it does not, then the department managers are correct in pointing out that the overhead was unduly assigned to their departments. The situation also provides an opportunity to consider other overhead allocation bases, including the use of activity-based costing.

Accounting Officer

You should not write a report as required by your supervisor if you disagree with it. It also appears the report may be misrepresenting the situation. It is your responsibility to ascertain all the facts regarding activity-based costing (the implementation procedure to be followed, advantages and disadvantages of ABC, costs involved). You should then approach your supervisor with all the facts and suggest that you would like to modify the report to request a pilot implementation of the system. The pilot test will allow you to further assess the suitability of ABC in your company. You should realize your suggestion may be rejected, at which time you may wish to speak to some other person with more senior authority.

GUIDANCE ANSWERS TO

1. A cost driver is a factor that causes an overhead cost to go up or down.

2. *d*

3. *d*

4. *b*

5. A cost centre, such as a service department, incurs costs without directly generating revenue. A profit centre, such as a selling department, incurs costs but also generates revenues.

6. *b*

7. *d*

8. 1. Assign the direct expenses to each department.
   2. Allocate indirect expenses to all departments.
   3. Allocate the service department expenses to the operating departments.

9. *b*

10. No, because many of the expenses that enter into these calculations are beyond the control of the manager, and managers should not be evaluated using costs they do not control.

11. *c*

Use the following information to prepare departmental income statements for Hacker's Haven, a computer store. The store has five departments. Three of them are operating departments (hardware, software, and repairs), and two are service departments (general office and purchasing).

Some accounting information about the five departments' activities for 2004 follows:

	General Office	Purchasing	Hardware	Software	Repairs
Sales	—	—	$960,000	$600,000	$840,000
Cost of goods sold	—	—	500,000	300,000	200,000
Direct expenses:					
Payroll	$60,000	$45,000	80,000	25,000	325,000
Amortization	6,000	7,200	33,000	4,200	9,600
Supplies	15,000	10,000	10,000	2,000	25,000

In addition, several indirect expenses are incurred in the departments. In preparing an income statement, these indirect expenses are allocated among the five departments. Then, the expenses of the two service departments are allocated to the three production departments. The total amounts and the allocation bases for each expense are as follows:

Type of Indirect Expense	Total Cost	Allocation Basis
Rent	$150,000	Square metres occupied
Utilities	50,000	Square metres occupied
Advertising	125,000	Dollars of sales
Insurance	30,000	Value of assets insured
Service departments:		
General office	?	Number of employees
Purchasing	?	Dollars of cost of goods sold

The following information is needed for the allocations:

Department	Square Metres	Sales	Insured Assets	Employees	Cost of Goods Sold
General office	500		$ 60,000		
Purchasing	500		72,000		
Hardware	4,000	$ 960,000	330,000	5	$ 500,000
Software	3,000	600,000	42,000	5	300,000
Repairs	2,000	840,000	96,000	10	200,000
Total	10,000	$2,400,000	$600,000	20	$1,000,000

Required

1. Complete a departmental expense allocation worksheet for Hacker's Haven.

2. Prepare a departmental income statement reporting net income for each operating department and for all operating departments combined.

Planning the Solution

- ○ Set up and complete four schedules to allocate the indirect expenses for rent, utilities, advertising, and insurance.
- ○ Allocate the departments' indirect expenses with a six-column worksheet like the one in Exhibit 24.17. Enter the given amounts of the direct expenses for each department. Then enter the allocated amounts of the indirect expenses that you computed.
- ○ Complete two schedules for allocating the general office and purchasing department costs to the three operating departments. Enter these amounts on the worksheet and determine the total expenses allocated to the three operating departments.
- ○ Prepare a four-column departmental income statement like the one in Exhibit 24.23. Show sales, cost of goods sold, the gross profit from sales, the individual direct and indirect expenses, and net income for each of the three operating departments and for the combined company.

SOLUTION TO **Demonstration Problem**

Allocations of indirect expenses among the five departments:

Rent	Square Metres	Percent of Total	Allocated Cost
General office...........	500	5.0%	$ 7,500
Purchasing	500	5.0	7,500
Hardware	4,000	40.0	60,000
Software	3,000	30.0	45,000
Repairs	2,000	20.0	30,000
Total	10,000	100.0%	$150,000

Utilities	Square Metres	Percent of Total	Allocated Cost
General office...........	500	5.0%	$ 2,500
Purchasing	500	5.0	2,500
Hardware	4,000	40.0	20,000
Software	3,000	30.0	15,000
Repairs	2,000	20.0	10,000
Total	10,000	100.0%	$50,000

Advertising	Sales Dollars	Percent of Total	Allocated Cost
Hardware..............	$ 960,000	40.0%	$ 50,000
Software..............	600,000	25.0	31,250
Repairs	840,000	35.0	43,750
Total.....................	$2,400,000	100.0%	$125,000

Insurance	Assets Insured	Percent of Total	Allocated Cost
General office...........	$ 60,000	10.0%	$ 3,000
Purchasing	72,000	12.0	3,600
Hardware	330,000	55.0	16,500
Software	42,000	7.0	2,100
Repairs	96,000	16.0	4,800
Total	$600,000	100.0%	$30,000

| Departmental Expense Allocation Spreadsheet
For Year Ended December 31, 2004 | | | | | | | |
Expense	Allocation Bases	Expense Account Balance	General Office	Purchasing	Hardware Dept.	Software Dept.	Repairs Dept.
Direct expenses:							
Payroll..		$ 535,000	$60,000	$45,000	$ 80,000	$ 25,000	$325,000
Amortization		60,000	6,000	7,200	33,000	4,200	9,600
Supplies......................................		62,000	15,000	10,000	10,000	2,000	25,000
Indirect expenses:							
Rent...	Square metres	150,000	7,500	7,500	60,000	45,000	30,000
Utilities.......................................	Square metres	50,000	2,500	2,500	20,000	15,000	10,000
Advertising	Sales	125,000	—	—	50,000	31,250	43,750
Insurance....................................	Assets	30,000	3,000	3,600	16,500	2,100	4,800
Total...		$1,012,000	$94,000	$75,800	$269,500	$124,550	$448,150
Service dept. expenses:							
General office............................	Employees		$94,000		23,500	23,500	47,000
Purchasing.................................	Goods sold			$75,800	37,900	22,740	15,160
Total expenses allocated to operating departments...........................		$1,012,000			$330,900	$170,790	$510,310

General Office:	Employees	Percent of Total	Allocated Cost
Hardware...............	5	25.0%	$23,500
Software...............	5	25.0	23,500
Repairs..................	10	50.0	47,000
Total......................	20	100.0%	$94,000

Purchasing:	Cost of Goods Sold	Percent of Total	Allocated Cost
Hardware...............	500,000	50.0%	$37.900
Software...............	300,000	30.0	22,740
Repairs..................	200,000	20.0	15,160
Total......................	1,000,000	100.0%	$75,800

| Hacker's Haven Computer Store
Departmental Income Statement
For Year Ended December 31, 2004 | | | | |
	Hardware	Software	Repairs	Combined
Sales...	$960,000	$600,000	$840,000	$2,400,000
Cost of goods sold..................	500,000	300,000	200,000	1,000,000
Gross profit..............................	$460,000	$300,000	$640,000	$1,400,000
Expenses:				
Payroll.......................................	$80,000	$25,000	$325,000	$430,000
Amortization	33,000	4,200	9,600	46,800
Supplies	10,000	2,000	25,000	37,000
Rent...	60,000	45,000	30,000	135,000
Utilities......................................	20,000	15,000	10,000	45,000
Advertising................................	50,000	31,250	43,750	125,000
Insurance..................................	16,500	2,100	4,800	23,400
General office	23,500	23,500	47,000	94,000
Purchasing................................	37,900	22,740	15,160	75,800
Total expenses.........................	$330,900	$170,790	$510,310	$1,012,000
Net income...............................	$129,100	$129,210	$129,690	$ 388,000

Glossary

Activity A set of tasks that consume resources, thereby incurring overhead costs. (p. 1251)

Activity-based costing (ABC) A two-stage allocation system. The two stages are: (1) identify activities involved in the manufacturing (or service) process and form cost pools by combining activities and (2) compute the predetermined overhead cost allocation rate for each cost pool and assign costs. (p. 1251)

Activity cost pool A temporary account that accumulates the costs a company incurs to support an activity. (p. 1252)

Allocation base The activity or volume measure used to charge the cost from one department to another. (p. 1248)

Controllable costs Costs that a manager has the authority to determine or at least strongly influence. (p. 1270)

Cost centre A segment that incurs costs alone, such as the accounting or legal department. (p. 1260)

Cost driver A variable that causes the cost of an activity to go up or down; a causal factor. (p. 1251)

Cost pool A bucket in which costs are accumulated. (p. 1248)

Departmental contribution to overhead The amount by which a department's revenues exceed its direct expenses. (p. 1269)

Direct expenses Expenses traced to a specific department because they are incurred for the sole benefit of that department. (p. 1261)

Indirect expenses Expenses incurred for the joint benefit of more than one department. (p. 1261)

Investment centre A segment of business whose manager is responsible for profitability and the efficient use of assets. (p. 1260)

Joint cost Includes individual cost items incurred for the purposes of carrying out joint processes, leading to multiple outcomes. (p. 1256)

Operating department Carries out activities that directly contribute to the main purpose of an organization. (p. 1248)

Profit centre A unit of a business that incurs costs and generates revenues. (p. 1260)

Responsibility accounting budget A plan that specifies the expected costs and expenses under the control of a manager. (p. 1271)

Responsibility accounting performance report A responsibility accounting report that compares actual costs and expenses for a department with the budgeted amounts. (p. 1271)

Responsibility accounting system An accounting system that provides information that management can use to evaluate the performance of a department's manager. (p. 1270)

Service department Provides support function to one or more operating and other service departments within an organization. (p. 1248)

Two-stage cost allocation method A method of allocating overhead costs, wherein service department costs are first assigned to operating departments, and the total costs within each operating department are then assigned to desired cost objects. (p. 1248)

For more study tools, quizzes, and problem material,
refer to the Online Learning Centre at
www.mcgrawhill.ca/college/larson

Questions

1. Why are businesses divided into segments?

2. Identify the two stages in a two-stage allocation system by completing the following: In the first stage, costs are assigned to _____ departments such as machining and assembly. Then, in the second stage, a predetermined overhead allocation rate is computed for each cost centre which is used to assign overhead to _____.

3. What is the difference between operating departments and service departments?

4. What is activity-based costing?

5. Identify five typical cost pools for activity-based costing.

6. In activity-based costing, costs in a cost pool are allocated to _____?

7. Why would a business use activity based costing?

8. What is a joint cost? How are joint costs usually allocated among the products produced from them?

9. Give two examples of products with joint costs. Explain with examples.

10. What are the two primary goals for managerial accounting for segments?

11. Is it possible to evaluate the profitability of a cost centre? Explain?

12. What is the difference between direct and indirect expenses?

13. Suggest a reasonable basis for allocating each of the following indirect expenses to departments: (a) salary of a supervisor who manages several departments, (b) rent, (c) heat, (d) electricity used for lighting, (e) janitorial services, (f) advertising, (g) expired insurance on equipment, and (h) property taxes on equipment.

14. How is a department's contribution to overhead measured?

15. What are controllable costs?

16. Controllable and uncontrollable costs must be identified with a particular _____ and a definite _____ period.

17. Why should managers be closely involved in preparing their responsibility accounting budgets?

18. In responsibility accounting, who is the proper person to be given timely reports and specific cost information?

19. Nike receives orders for merchandise sold in different types of stores, such as sporting goods super stores and specialty running shoe stores. Why is it useful to (a) collect information for the each particular store category and (b) treat each category as a profit centre?

20. Reebok delivers its products to many different locations in Canada and around the world. List three controllable and three uncontrollable costs for Reebok's delivery department.

Quick Study

Jarvis Company uses three activity cost pools. The company has provided the following data concerning its costs and its activity-based costing system:

QS 24-1
Activity Based Costing

LO²

Costs:

Manufacturing overhead	$400,000
Selling and administration expenses	200,000
Total	$600,000

Activity Cost Pools	Orders	Customer Support	Other*	Total
Manufacturing overhead...................	35%	55%	10%	100%
Selling and admin. expense	50%	30%	20%	100%

*The "other" activity cost pool consists of idle capacity costs and organization-sustaining costs.

Required
1. Compute the total product costs allocated to the "orders" activity cost pool.
2. Compute the total cost allocated to the "customer support" activity cost pool.

The following is taken from Foster's internal financial reports of a factory with two operating departments:

QS 24-2
Activity-based costing

LO²

	Number of Orders	Hours of Machine Use
Department 1	$1,316	840
Department 2	924	1,400
Totals	$2,240	2,240

Activity Cost Pools	
Production	$ 8,540
Maintenance..	3,780
Order-entry	2,380
Invoicing	2,100
Purchasing...	1,260
Total overhead...	$18,060

Compute the total amount of overhead cost that would be allocated to Department 1 for Foster if activity-based costing is used. The cost driver for order-entry, purchasing, and invoicing is number of orders, and the cost driver for the remaining activity cost pools is hours of machine use.

QS 24-3
Joint cost allocation

LO³

A 7,014 square metre commercial building was purchased for $1,575,000. An additional $70,000 was spent to split the space into two separate rental units and to get it ready to rent. Unit A, which has the desirable location on the corner and contains 2,338 square metres, will be rented out for $4.20 per square metre. Unit B contains 4,676 square metres and will be rented out for $3.60 per square metre. How much of the joint cost should be assigned to Unit B?

QS 24-4
Allocation and measurement terms

LO⁴,⁵,⁶,⁷,⁸,⁹

In each of the blanks next to the following terms, place the identifying letter of the description that best matches each term.
1. _____ Cost centre
2. _____ Segmented reporting system
3. _____ Operating department
4. _____ Investment centre
5. _____ Profit centre
6. _____ Responsibility accounting system
7. _____ Service department
a. Incurs costs without directly generating revenues.
b. Incurs costs but also generates revenues.
c. Manager is responsible for revenues, costs, and investments
d. Provides information used to evaluate the performance of a department.
e. Provides information used to evaluate the performance of a department manager.
f. Does not directly manufacture products, but contributes to the profitability of the entire company.
g. Engages directly in manufacturing or in making sales directly to customers.

QS 24-5
Basis for allocation

LO⁶

For each of the following types of indirect and service department expenses, name one possible allocation basis that could be used to distribute it to the departments indicated:
a. Advertising expense to the selling department:

_____

b. Electric utility expense to all departments:

_____

c. Purchasing department expenses to the operating departments:

_____

d. General office department expenses to the operating departments:

_____

QS 24-6
Departmental contributions to overhead

LO⁸

Using the following information, compute each department's contribution to overhead (both in dollars and as a percent). Which department contributes the highest dollar amount to total overhead? Which department's contribution percent is the highest?

	Dept. L	Dept. M	Dept. N
Sales...	$74,200	$238,000	$117,600
Cost of goods sold	47,859	145,180	69,384
Gross profit..............................	26,341	92,820	48,216
Total direct expenses...............	8,904	51,884	12,230
Contribution to overhead..........	$ _____	$ _____	$ _____
Contribution percent.................	_____ %	_____ %	_____ %

Home Decorating Store pays $384,000 rent every year for its two-story building. The building space is occupied by five departments as follows:

> Paint department .... 1,390 square metres of first-floor space
> Engine department .... 3,410 square metres of first-floor space
> Window department..................... 2,040 square metres of second-floor space
> Electrical department.................... 960 square metres of second-floor space
> Auto Accessory department.......... 1,800 square metres of second-floor space

The company allocates 65% of the total rent expense to the first floor and 35% to the second floor. It then allocates the rent expense for each floor to the departments on that floor on the basis of the space occupied. Determine the rent to be allocated to each department. (Round all percents to the nearest one-tenth and all dollar amounts to the nearest whole dollar.)

Exercise 24-1
Allocating rent expense
to departments

$LO^{1,6}$

Fraser Corporation has four departments: materials, personnel, manufacturing, and packaging. In a recent month, the four departments incurred three shared indirect costs. The amounts of these expenses and the bases used to allocate them are:

Expense	Cost	Allocation Base
Supervision...........	$ 75,000	Number of employees
Utilities	60,000	Square metres occupied
Insurance..............	16,500	Value of assets in use
Total expense	$151,500	

Exercise 24-2
Departmental expense
allocations

$LO^{1,6}$

These quantities are to be used in allocating the costs for the month:

Department	Employees	Square Metres	Assets Value
Materials................	9	3,000	$ 12,000
Personnel..............	3	500	2,400
Manufacturing	33	5,000	75,600
Packaging	15	1,500	30,000
Total	60	10,000	$120,000

Using this information, prepare allocations of each of the three indirect expenses among the four departments. Then, prepare a table that shows the total expenses assigned to the four departments.

Thibault Company sells to two different customer groups. The two groups consist of 1,400 and 1,800 customers respectively. The company uses activity-based costing to assign costs to its two customer groups and then determines the average cost per customer within each group. Thibault has identified three activity cost pools: (1) order getting ($109,440)—allocated on the basis of number of orders received, (2) after-sales service ($15,120)—allocated on the basis of the number of service calls, and (3) sales promotion costs ($84,000)—allocated on the basis of sales revenues. Data relating to the activity levels for the previous year are given below.

Exercise 24-3
Activity-based costing

LO^2

Activity Volume	Customer Group A	Customer Group B	Total
Orders received.........................	510	1,010	1,520
Service calls	80	100	180
Sales revenue...........................	$240,000	$360,000	$600,000

Required
1. Allocate the activity costs to the two different customer groups.
2. Compute the average cost per customer within each group.

Exercise 24-4
Activity-based costing

LO²

Gilbert Company manufactures two products, hinges and fasteners, on the same production line. Last month, the company experienced the following costs and results:

	Hinges	Fasteners	Total
Direct materials	$ 9,500	$21,600	$ 31,100
Direct labour	6,100	11,900	18,000
Overhead (300% of labour)	18,300	35,700	54,000
Total cost	$33,900	$69,200	$103,100
Quantity produced	10,500	14,100	
Average cost per unit..........................	$3.23	$4.91	

Several of the managers have approached the cost accounting department for help in understanding activity-based costing. Their specific request is that ABC be applied to the production results to see whether the average cost per unit is significantly changed. The following additional information is extracted from the production records for the month:
- The overhead cost for supervision was $2,160. The cost driver for supervision is direct labour cost.
- The overhead cost for machinery amortization was $28,840. The cost driver for this cost is hours of use. The machinery was used 300 hours for hinges and 700 hours for fasteners.
- The overhead cost for preparing the line to manufacture products was $23,000. The cost driver for this cost is number of set up times. The line was set up 31 times to produce different kinds of hinges and 94 times to produce different kinds of fasteners.

Required
Use this information to:
a. Assign the overhead cost to the products using activity-based costing.
b. Determine the average cost per unit of the two products using direct materials, direct labour, and overhead allocated under ABC.
c. Compare and explain the average per unit cost under ABC to the average cost per unit found in the data section of this problem.

Exercise 24-5
Assigning joint real estate costs

LO³

Capital Properties just completed developing a subdivision that contains 40 building lots, of which 32 lots are for sale at $36,000 each. The remaining 8 lots are larger and have a panoramic view. The latter lots sell for $72,000 each. The land for the subdivision originally cost the developer $264,000, and the company spent $312,000 on street and utilities improvements. Assign the joint land and improvement costs to the lots using the value basis of allocation and determine the average cost per lot. (Round all amounts to the nearest whole dollar).

Exercise 24-6
Assigning joint product costs

LO³

Clearwater Company purchases lobsters and processes them into tails and flakes. It then sells the lobster tails for $42.00 per kilogram and sells the flakes for $28.00 per kilogram. On average, 100 kilograms of lobster can be processed into 52 kilograms of tails and 22 kilograms of flakes, with 26 kilograms of waste.

Assume that 2,400 kilograms of lobster are purchased for $15.75 per kilogram. The lobsters are then processed with additional labour cost of $2,200. No materials or labour costs are assigned to the waste. If 1,096 kilograms of tails and 324 kilograms of flakes are sold, what is what is the allocated cost of the sold items and the cost of the remaining inventory?

The following partially completed lower section of a departmental allocation spreadsheet is being prepared for Early Bird Bookstore. At this stage it shows only the amounts of direct and indirect expenses that have been allocated to the five departments:

Exercise 24-7
Allocating service department expenses to operating departments

LO⁷

Expense	Allocation Bases	Expense Account Balance	Advertising Office	Purchasing Dept.	Book Dept.	Magazine Dept.	Newspaper Dept.
Total..........................		$654,000	$22,000	$30,000	$425,000	$86,000	$91,000
Service dept. expenses:							
Advertising..................	Sales		?		?	?	?
Purchasing...................	Purchase orders			?	?	?	?
Total expenses allocated to selling departments................		?			?	?	?

Complete the spreadsheet by allocating the two service departments' expenses to the three selling departments. These amounts were known about the allocation bases for the three selling departments:

Orders	Sales	Purchase Orders
Books..............................	$ 896,000	424
Magazines.......................	288,000	312
Newspapers....................	416,000	264
Total...............................	$1,600,000	1,000

Ramona Wright works in both the jewellery department and the hosiery department of Fine's Department Store. Wright assists customers in both departments and also straightens and stocks the merchandise in both departments as needed. The store allocates Wright's annual wages of $30,720 between the two departments based on a sample of the time worked in the two departments. The sample was obtained from a diary that Wright kept of hours worked in a randomly chosen two-week period. The diary showed that the following hours were spent in these activities:

Exercise 24-8
Allocating indirect payroll expense to departments

LO⁶·⁷

Selling in the jewellery department..	32
Straightening and rearranging merchandise in the jewellery department........................	3
Selling in the hosiery department	7
Straightening and stocking merchandise in the hosiery department	6
Idle time spent waiting for a customer to enter one of the selling departments.............	2

Required
Prepare calculations to allocate Wright's wages between the departments. Round all percents to the nearest tenth of a percent and all dollar amounts to the nearest whole dollar.

Exercise 24-9

Departmental expense allocation spreadsheet

LO[6,7]

The Wheel Shoppe has two service departments (advertising and administrative), and two sales departments (motorcycles and clothing). During 2004, the departments had the following direct expenses:

Advertising department	$14,784
Administrative department	17,836
Motorcycle department	142,240
Clothing department	16,660

The departments occupy the following square metres of floor space:

Advertising department	170
Administrative department	180
Motorcycle department	990
Clothing department	660

The advertising department developed and distributed 50 ad pieces during the year. Of these, 38 promoted motorcycles and 12 promoted clothing. The store sold $351,400 of merchandise during the year. Of this amount, $284,634 was from the motorcycle department while the remainder was from the clothing department.

Required

Prepare an expense allocation sheet for the Wheel Shoppe that assigns the direct expenses to all four departments and the year's $89,600 of utilities expense to the four departments on the basis of floor space occupied. In addition, allocate the advertising department expenses on the basis of the number of ads placed and the administrative department expenses based on the amount of sales. Provide supplemental schedules showing how you computed the expense allocations. (Round all percents to the nearest one-tenth and all dollar amounts to the nearest whole dollar.)

Exercise 24-10

Evaluating managerial performance

LO[9]

Helen Cruickshanks manages the auto stereo department of a large department store. This is the 2004 income statement for her department:

Revenues:		
Sales of parts	$343,000	
Sales of services	238,000	$581,000
Costs and expenses:		
Cost of parts sold	$109,200	
Wages (hourly)	203,000	
Manager's salary	39,200	
Payroll taxes	26,700	
Supplies	53,100	
Building amortization	30,800	
Utilities	47,600	
Interest on long-term debt	24,000	
Income taxes allocated to department	15,400	
Total costs and expenses		$549,000
Department net income		$ 32,000

Required

Analyze the items on the income statement to identify those that clearly should be included on a performance report used to evaluate Helen's performance. List them and explain why you have chosen them. Then, list and explain the items that should clearly be excluded. Finally, list the items that are not clearly included or excluded and explain why they fall in that category.

Alpine Limited has several departments that occupy both floors of a two-story building. Alpine's accounting system has a single account in the ledger called Building Occupancy Cost. These types and amounts of costs were recorded in this account for last year:

Amortization, building	$ 36,000
Interest, building mortgage	29,700
Taxes, building and land	11,100
Heating expense	5,000
Lighting expense	6,400
Maintenance expense	25,200
Total	$113,400

The building has 350 square metres on each floor. For simplicity, the accountant merely divided the $113,400 occupancy cost by 700 square metres to find an average cost of $162 per square metre. Then, each department was charged with a building occupancy cost equal to this rate times the number of square metres that it occupies.

Elsie MacNeil manages a second-floor department that occupies 170 square metres of floor. Ned Carver manages a ground floor department that also occupies 170 square metres. Elsie cited a recent real estate board study that showed average rental charges for similar space, including heat and lights, cleaning and maintenance. She found that ground-floor space is worth $360 per square metre while second-floor space is worth only $240 per square metre. Both managers question whether the same rate per square metre should be charged to each department because the space on the ground floor has more market value.

Required
Use the preceding information to:
1. Allocate the occupancy cost to the two departments by the bookkeeper's method.
2. Allocate the occupancy cost to the two departments in proportion to the relative market values of the space, except for the heating, lighting, and maintenance costs, which should be allocated on an equal basis per square metre occupied. Round costs per square metre to the nearest cent.

Analysis component
3. If you were a manager of a second floor department, which method would you prefer, and why?

Problem 24-1A
Allocation of building occupancy costs

LO^{1,7}

Check figure:
2. Total occupancy cost to Elsie, $23,810.20

Surgery Centre, Inc. is a growing outpatient surgery centre that has enjoyed excess profits for many years. However, now the government is beginning to cut reimbursement by as much as 50%. As a result the centre is trying to get a better understanding of its cost of resources. You are to prepare an activity-based cost analysis with the following data. It is important to estimate the average cost of both general surgery and orthopedic surgery. The company's three cost centres and their drivers are:

Problem 24-2A
Activity based costing

LO^2

Activity Centre	Cost	Driver	Quantity
Professional salaries	$1,800,000	Professional hours	12,000
Service patients/supplies	30,000	Number of patients	600
Building cost	180,000	Square metres*	500

The professional services:

Service	Prof. Hours	Square metres*	# of Patients
General surgery	3,000	200	480
Orthopedic	9,000	300	120

*Orthopedic surgeries requires more space for patients, supplies, and special equipment.

Required

1. Compute the cost per driver.
2. Compute the average cost for a general and an orthopedic surgery.

Analysis component

3. Without computation, would the average cost of a general surgery be more or less if activity centres cost were allocated on number of surgeries alone. Why?

Problem 24-3A
Allocating joint costs

LO^3

Elwood and Darlene Snerd own a farm that produces potatoes. After preparing the following 2004 income statement, Elwood remarked to Darlene that they should have fed the No. 3 potatoes to the pigs and saved a lot of money and trouble.

Elwood and Darlene Snerd Income from Potatoes For Year Ended December 31, 2004				
	No. 1	**No. 2**	**No. 3**	**Combined**
Sales (by grade):				
No. 1: 202,500 kgs. @ $0.30	$60,750			
No. 2: 360,000 kgs. @ $0.25		$90,000		
No. 3: 135,000 kgs. @ $0.20			$27,000	
Total sales..				$177,500
Costs:				
Land preparation @ $0.0948/kg........	$19,197	$34,128	$12,798	$ 66,123
Harvesting @ $0.79kg.	15,998	28,440	10,665	55,103
Marketing @ $0.027666/kg.	5,602	9,960	3,735	19,297
Total costs	$40,797	$72,528	$27,198	$140,523
Net income (loss)	$19,953	$17,472	$ (198)	$ 37,227

    In preparing the statement, Elwood and Darlene allocated the joint costs among the grades as an equal amount per kilogram. They did this because, with the exception of marketing costs, their records did not show the costs per grade. Records about the marketing cost show that $18,687 of the $19,297 was the cost of placing the No. 1 and No. 2 potatoes in bags and hauling them to the buyer. Bagging and hauling costs were the same for both grades. The remaining $610 of marketing costs was the cost of loading the No. 3 potatoes into trucks belonging to a potato starch factory that bought these potatoes in bulk and picked them up at the farm

Required

Preparation component

1. Prepare allocation schedules showing how the costs would be allocated on the basis of the relative sales values of the three grades. Separate the marketing cost into the amounts directly identifiable to the grades. (Round all percents to the nearest one-tenth and all dollar amounts to the nearest whole dollar.)
2. Using your answers to requirement 1, prepare an income statement that shows the results of producing and delivering the potatoes.

Analysis component

3. Do you think the marketing cost is a true joint cost? Explain your answer.

Great Wall Limited began operating in January 2004 with two selling departments and one office department. The 2004 departmental net incomes are:

Problem 24-4A
Departmental income statement

LO[7]

Great Wall Limited Departmental Income Statement For Year Ended December 31, 2004	Clocks	Mirrors	Combined
Sales	$122,500	$52,500	$175,000
Cost of goods sold	60,000	32,000	92,000
Gross profit from sales	$ 62,500	$20,500	$ 83,000
Direct expenses:			
Sales salaries	$ 20,000	$ 7,000	$ 27,000
Advertising	1,200	500	1,700
Store supplies used	900	400	1,300
Amortization of equipment	1,500	300	1,800
Total direct expenses	$ 23,600	$ 8,200	$ 31,800
Allocated expenses:			
Rent expense	$ 7,020	$ 3,780	$ 10,800
Utilities expense	2,600	1,400	4,000
Share of office department expenses	10,500	4,500	15,000
Total allocated expenses	$ 20,120	$ 9,680	$ 29,800
Total expenses	43,720	17,880	61,600
Net income	$ 18,780	$ 2,620	$ 21,400

Starting in January 2005, Great Wall plans to open a third department that will sell paintings. Management predicts that the new department will produce $35,000 in sales with a 55% gross profit margin and that it will require the following direct expenses: sales salaries, $8,000; advertising, $800; store supplies, $500; and equipment amortization, $200.

Since opening, the store has rented space in a building. It will be possible to fit the new department into the same overall space by taking some square metres from the other two departments. When the new painting department is opened, it will fill one-fifth of the space presently used by the clock department and one-sixth of the space used by the mirror department. Management does not predict any increase in utilities costs, which are allocated among the departments in proportion to occupied space.

The company allocates its office department expenses among the selling departments in proportion to their sales. It expects the painting department to increase office department expenses by $7,000. Because the painting department will bring new customers into the store, management expects sales in the clock and mirror departments to increase by 7%. Those departments' gross profit percents are not expected to change. No changes are expected in their direct expenses, except for store supplies used, which will increase in proportion to sales.

Required

Prepare a departmental income statement that shows the company's predicted results of operations for 2005 with three selling departments. (Round all percents to the nearest one-tenth and all dollar amounts to the nearest whole dollar.)

Check figure:
Forecasted combined net income, $29,815

Josey Madinski, the manager of Royal Manufacturing Company's Alberta plant, is responsible for all costs of the plant's operation other than her own salary. The plant has two production departments and one service department. The camper and trailer departments manufacture different products and have their own managers. The office department provides services equally to the two production departments. Madinski manages the office department. A budget is prepared for each production department and the office department. The responsibility accounting system must assemble the information to present budgeted and actual costs in performance reports for each of the production department managers and the plant manager.

Problem 24-5A
Responsibility accounting performance reports

LO[8, 9]

Each performance report includes only those costs that the particular manager can control. The production department managers control the costs of raw materials, wages, supplies used, and equipment amortization. The plant manager is responsible for the department managers' salaries, utilities, building rent, office salaries other than her own, other office costs, plus all the costs controlled by the two production department managers.

The annual departmental budgets and cost accumulations for the two production departments were as follows:

	Budget			Actual		
	Campers	Trailers	Combined	Campers	Trailers	Combined
Raw materials	$154,000	$255,000	$ 409,000	$159,400	$246,500	$ 405,900
Wages.................................	99,000	191,000	290,000	102,300	193,700	296,000
Department manager salary	40,000	44,000	84,000	40,000	45,100	85,100
Supplies used......................	34,000	83,000	117,000	31,900	84,600	116,500
Equipment amortization......................	58,000	110,000	168,000	58,000	110,000	168,000
Utilities	2,800	4,200	7,000	2,500	3,800	6,300
Building rent.......................	4,800	7,200	12,000	4,800	7,200	12,000
Office department costs...............................	54,000	54,000	108,000	52,000	52,000	104,000
Total.................................	$446,600	$748,400	$1,195,000	$450,900	$742,900	$1,193,800

Office department budget and actual costs consisted of the following:

	Budget	Actual
Plant manager salary	$ 57,000	$ 57,100
Other office salaries........	29,000	27,700
Other office costs	22,000	19,200
Total.................................	$108,000	$104,000

Check figure:
3. Alberta plant controllable costs, $1,300 under budget

Required

Prepare responsibility accounting performance reports that list the costs controlled by the following managers:

1. Manager of the camper department.
2. Manager of the trailer department.
3. Manager of the Alberta plant.

In each report, include the budgeted and actual costs and show the amount that each actual cost is over or under the budgeted amount.

Analysis component

4. Who did a better job of managing cost assuming that the budget and actual costs are based on the same activity level, the plant manager or the production department managers? Explain.

Alternate Problems

Problem 24-1B
Allocation of building occupancy costs

LO[1,7]

Hanna's has several departments that occupy all three floors of a two-story building with a basement. The store has rented this building under a long-term lease negotiated when rental rates were much lower. The departmental accounting system has a single account in the ledger called Building Occupancy Cost. These types and amounts of costs were recorded in this account for last year:

Building rent..	$324,000
Lighting expense..	12,000
Cleaning expense...	60,000
Total...	$396,000

The building has 1,000 square metres on each floor. For simplicity, the bookkeeper merely divided the $396,000 occupancy cost by 3,000 square metres to find an average cost of $132.00 per square metre. Then, each department was charged with a building occupancy cost equal to this rate times the number of square metres that it occupies.

Patty Hanna manages a department that occupies 300 square metres of floor space in the basement. In discussing the departmental reports with other managers, Hanna has questioned whether using the same rate per square metre for all departments makes sense considering the fact that different floors have different values. Looking further into the issue, Hanna checked a recent real estate study of average rental costs for similar space. The amounts do not include costs for lighting and cleaning. The report shows that ground-floor space is worth $300.00 per square metre while second-floor space is worth $200.00 and basement space is worth only $100.00.

Required

Use the preceding information to:

1. Allocate the occupancy cost to Hanna's department by the bookkeeper's method.
2. Allocate the occupancy cost to Hanna's department in proportion to the relative market value of the space, except for the lighting and cleaning costs, which should be allocated on an equal basis per square metre occupied.

Analysis component

3. If you were a manager of a basement department, which method would you prefer, and why?

Check figure:
2. Total occupancy cost to Patty, $23,400

Bill's Landscaping Centre, Inc. is a growing landscaping business that has enjoyed excess profits for many years. However, now competition is beginning to cut service revenue by as much as 30%. As a result the centre is trying to get a better understanding of its cost of resources. You have been hired to prepare an activity based cost analysis with the following data. The key question is what is the average cost to offer general landscaping services compared to custom designed (with water flow) landscaping services?

The cost centres and respective drivers are:

Problem 24-2B
Activity based costing

LO^2

Activity Centre	Cost	Driver	Quantity
Professional salaries	$700,000	Professional hours	10,000
Customer supplies	175,000	Number of customers	700
Building cost	210,000	Square metres*	420

The professional services:

Service	Prof. Hours	Square metres*	# of Patients
General services	2,500	140	400
Water services	7,500	280	100

*Landscaping services including water flow requires more space for equipment, supplies, and planning.

Required

1. Compute the cost per driver.
2. Compute the average cost for a general and a water flow landscaping service.

Analysis component

3. Without computation, would the average cost of a general landscaping service be more or less if activity centre cost were allocated on number of customers alone. Why?

Problem 24-3B

Allocating joint costs

LO^3

Bill Goggins owns a pear farm. After preparing the following income statement, Bill remarked that he should have fed the No. 3 pears to the pigs and saved a lot of money and trouble.

	Bill Goggins Income from Pears For Year Ended December 31, 2004			
	No. 1	**No. 2**	**No. 3**	**Combined**
Sales (by grade):				
No. 1: 120,000 kg @ $0.50	$60,000			
No. 2: 120,000 kg @ $0.35		$42,000		
No. 3: 60,000 kg @ $0.20			$12,000	
Total sales...				$114,000
Costs:				
Tree pruning @ $0.10/kg.......................	$12,000	$12,000	$ 6,000	$ 30,000
Fruit picking, grading, and sorting @ $0.038/kg..................	15,000	15,000	7,500	37,500
Delivery @ $0.038/kg............................	4,560	4,560	2,280	11,400
Total costs.	$31,560	$31,560	$15,780	$ 78,900
Net income (loss)	$28,440	$10,440	$(3,780)	$ 35,100

In preparing the statement, Bill allocated the joint costs among the grades as an equal amount per kilogram. Records about the delivery cost show that $10,600 of the $11,400 was the cost of crating the No. 1 and No. 2 fruit in boxes and hauling them to the buyer. The remaining $800 of delivery cost was the cost of crating the No. 3 pears and hauling them to a fruit juice manufacturer who bought this grade of fruit in bulk.

Required

Preparation component
1. Prepare allocation schedules showing how the costs would be allocated on the basis of the relative sales values of the three grades. Separate the delivery cost into the amounts directly identifiable to the grades. Then, allocate any shared delivery cost on the basis of the relative sales values of the grades. (Round all percents to the nearest one tenth and all dollar amounts to the nearest whole dollar.)
2. Using your answers to requirement 1, prepare an income statement that shows the results of producing and delivering the pears.

Analysis component
3. Do you think the delivery cost is a true joint cost? Explain your answer.

Tremblay Company began operating in January 2004 with two selling departments and one office department. The 2004 departmental net incomes are shown below:

Tremblay Company Ltd. Departmental Income Statement For Year Ended December 31, 2004			
	Dept. K	Dept. L	Combined
Sales	$270,000	$120,000	$390,000
Cost of goods sold	132,000	93,000	225,000
Gross profit from sales	$138,000	$ 27,000	$165,000
Direct expenses:			
Advertising	$6,000	$2,700	$8,700
Store supplies used	2,400	1,800	4,200
Amortization of equipment	4,500	2,250	6,750
Total direct expenses	$ 12,900	$ 6,750	$ 19,650
Allocated expenses:			
Rent expense	9,600	7,200	16,800
Sales salaries	67,500	13,500	81,000
Bad debts expense	1,500	1,200	2,700
Office salaries	18,750	18,750	37,500
Insurance expense	2,250	800	3,050
Share of office department expenses	1,650	600	2,250
Total allocated expenses	$101,250	$ 42,050	$143,300
Total expenses	$114,150	$ 48,800	$162,950
Net income (loss)	$ 23,850	$ (21,800)	$ 2,050

If Department L is eliminated:

a. The company has one office worker who earns $37,500 per year and three sales clerks each of whom earns $2,250 per month, or $27,000 per year. At present the salaries of two and one-half salesclerks are charged to Department K and one-half salesclerk to Department L. The sales salaries presently assigned to Department L can be avoided if the department is eliminated and the office worker's salary could be reduced from full time to one-half time. It is the opinion of management that one salesclerk may be dismissed if Department L is eliminated, leaving only two full-time salesclerks in Department K and making up the difference by assigning the office worker to half-time sales work in the department. The office work could be squeezed into the remaining half-time.

b. Since opening, the store has rented space in a building. This is a long-term lease that cannot be changed; therefore, the space presently occupied by Department L will have to be charged to Department K. Also, Department K will have to make whatever use of Department L's equipment it can, since the equipment has little or no sales value.

c. The elimination of Department L will eliminate the Department L advertising expense, losses from bad debts, and store supplies used. It will also eliminate 75% of the insurance expense allocated to the department (the portion on merchandise) and 50% of the miscellaneous office expenses presently allocated to Department L.

Required

1. Under the assumption that Department K's sales and gross profit will not be affected by the elimination of Department L, prepare an income statement showing what the company can expect to earn from the operation of Department K after Department L is eliminated. Assume that the plan of assigning part of the office worker's time to the sales force is used and the salary reduction occurs.

Problem 24-5B

Responsibility accounting
performance reports

LO[8, 9]

Leslie Baker, the manager of a manufacturing company's Quebec plant, is responsible for all costs of the plant's operation other than her own salary. The plant has two production departments and one service department. The webbing and dalite departments manufacture different products and have their own managers. The office department provides services equally to the two production departments. Leslie manages the office department. A monthly budget is prepared for each production department and the office department. After the end of each month, the responsibility accounting system must assemble the information to present budgeted and actual costs in performance reports for each of the production department managers and the plant manager.

Each performance report includes only those costs that the particular manager can control. The production department managers control the costs of raw materials, wages, supplies used, and equipment amortization. The plant manager is responsible for the department managers' salaries, utilities, building rent, office salaries other than her own, other office costs, plus all the costs controlled by the two production department managers.

The May departmental budgets and cost accumulations for the two production departments were as follows:

	Budget			Actual		
	Webbing Dept.	Dalite Dept.	Combined	Webbing Dept.	Dalite Dept.	Combined
Raw materials	$138,000	$168,000	$306,000	$134,100	$172,560	$306,660
Wages.................................	100,800	118,800	219,600	104,340	115,740	220,080
Dept. mgr. salary.................	15,600	16,800	32,400	16,500	16,800	33,300
Supplies used......................	4,500	4,800	9,300	5,760	5,520	11,280
Equipment amortization......	8,400	6,000	14,400	8,400	6,600	15,000
Utilities...............................	9,600	14,400	24,000	11,660	17,500	29,160
Building rent........................	6,000	9,000	15,000	6,000	9,000	15,000
Office dept. costs	39,000	39,000	78,000	41,700	41,700	83,400
Total...................................	$321,900	$376,800	$698,700	$328,460	$385,420	$713,880

Office department budget and actual costs for May consisted of the following:

	Budget	Actual
Plant manager salary.......	$ 80,000	$ 85,000
Other office salaries........	36,000	37,200
Other office costs	9,600	13,800
Total.................................	$125,600	$136,000

Check figure:

3. Quebec plant controllable costs, $15,180 over budget

Required

Prepare responsibility accounting performance reports that list the costs controlled by the following managers:
1. Manager of the webbing department.
2. Manager of the dalite department.
3. Manager of the Quebec plant.
In each report, include the budgeted and actual costs for the month, and show the amount that each actual cost is over or under the budgeted amount.

Analysis component
4. Who did a better job of managing cost, the plant manager or the production department managers? Why?

Analytical and Review Problems

Many accountants and analysts hold that whatever method is used for common cost or joint cost allocation is arbitrary and an exercise in futility. Allocation obscures rather than illuminates the essential data on which evaluation and decision must be made. Consequently, allocation of costs should only be made where it is absolutely necessary; for example, amount of cost to be matched with the current period (cost of goods sold) and the amount of cost to be carried to future period(s) as inventory. Allocation for evaluation of performance should, however, not be made because such allocations are at best meaningless and at worst misleading and obscure the facts of a situation.

A & R 24-1

Required
Do you agree with the view expressed? Discuss your answer.

It has been stated that in eliminating a profit centre you eliminate all of the revenue but not all the costs.

A & R 24-2

Required
Do you agree? Support your answer with an illustration.

To allocate or not to allocate; that is the question.

A & R 24-3

Required
Make a case for allocation and a case against allocation of common and/or joint costs.

Goldberg Corporation retails two models of specialized engines. The company's operations produced these results in the year just ended:

A & R 24-4

	E550	E850
Units sold	600	500
Selling price per unit	$15,000	$ 22,000
Cost per unit	$10,000	$ 14,000
Sales commission per unit	$ 300	$ 440
Indirect selling and administrative expenses per unit	$712.50	$1,045.00

The total indirect selling and administrative expenses were $950,000. They were allocated to the models on the basis of their relative sales. The E550 model produced $9,000,000 revenue and the E850 model produced $11,000,000. Thus, the E550 model was assigned 45% of the $960,000 of indirect expenses, or $427,500. Then this amount was divided by the number of units to get $712.50 per unit. The same calculations produced the $1,045.00 per unit indirect cost for the E850 model.

Andrew Goldberg, the company vice president of operations, is in the process of selecting among three management strategies for the next quarter. The three alternatives are: (1) do no special advertising, in which case sales of each model will continue at present levels; (2) increase the sales of the E550 model by a special advertising effort; or (3) increase the sales of the E850 model by a special advertising effort. Because the demand for these engines is stable, an increase in the unit sales of one model will cause an equal decrease in unit sales of the other model. By spending $50,000 on advertising for the E550, the company can sell 100 additional units for the E550 and lose 100 units of sales of the E850. Or, the opposite effect will occur if the company advertises the E850 model.

On February 19 Goldberg asks you to compare the three alternative strategies on the basis of contribution to overhead and net income. You are to report your findings to him in a memo the next day. You should recommend the best action for Goldberg and support your recommendation with income statements for each alternative. (Assume that the indirect expenses do not change.)

A & R 24-5

Super View Corporation wholesales high-quality slide projectors that are designed for professional usage. Operations of the company during the past year resulted in the following:

	Standard	Deluxe
Units sold	300	100
Selling price per unit	$600	$800
Cost per unit	$320	$420
Sales commission per unit	$ 90	$120
Indirect selling and administrative expenses per unit	$150	$200

Indirect selling and administrative expenses totalled $65,000 and were allocated between the sales of Standard and Deluxe units on the basis of their relative sales volumes. The Standard model produced $180,000 of revenue, and the Deluxe model produced $80,000; thus, the Standard model was assigned 18/26 of the $65,000 of indirect expenses and the Deluxe model was assigned 8/26. After allocating the total indirect expenses to the two models, the indirect expenses per unit were determined by dividing the total by the number of units sold. Hence, the Standard model's cost per unit was $150, and the Deluxe model's cost per unit was $200.

Management of Super View Corporation is attempting to decide among three courses of action and asks you to evaluate which of the three courses is most desirable. The three alternatives are: (1) through advertising push the sales of the Standard model; (2) through advertising push the sales of the Deluxe model; or (3) do no additional advertising, in which case sales of each model will continue at present levels. The demand for slide projectors is fairly stable, and an increase in the number of units of one model sold will cause an equally large decrease in unit sales of the other model. However, through the expenditure of $2,000 for advertising, the company can shift the sale of 50 units of the Standard model to the Deluxe model, or vice versa, depending upon which model receives the advertising attention. Should the company advertise; and if so, which model? Prepare income statements to support your position.

CHAPTER 25

Cost-Volume-Profit Analysis

High and Dry

Victoria, B.C.—Cara McKey is the marketing manager for Maxum, a leading manufacturer of sealant for water sports equipment and gear. This past year, McKey helped close one of the company's biggest deals ever. But the big deal came close to being the big bust.

Maxum had been working with Sport Marine over the past two years supplying goods and services to its water sports division. "Then," says McKey, "they asked about a long-term contract that'd nearly double yearly sales. I was ecstatic." McKey quickly put things in motion. But, McKey next got a call from Maxum's controller. He wanted to go over the proposed contract with her.

"I knew he was a numbers person," says McKey, "so I prepared and came armed with accounting reports." She pointed out the new contract wouldn't impact any current business, and that the new business would require no added advertising or servicing costs. "Then, to top it off," adds McKey, "I proposed we offer Sports Marine a contract price 10% to 12% lower than normal. And I showed him we'd cover current inventory costs and maintain our 15% gross profit margin."

Now it was the controller's turn. McKey says he pointed out that current inventory product cost was an average of current manufacturing costs at today's sales level. He said that such a major shift in sales would result in many changes in cost behaviour.

"The next thing I knew," adds McKey, "he and I are running cost-volume-profit analyses on the contract." In the end, Maxum got the contract, but not at the price cut McKey originally thought. Maxum did slice about 3% off the price and still maintained its 15% margin. "If it were not for cost-volume-profit analysis, I'd be looking at about a 5% gross margin today," and, adds McKey, "a new job."

Learning Objectives

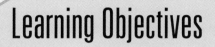

LO¹ Describe different types of cost behaviour in relation to output volume.

LO² Determine cost estimates using three different methods.

LO³ Compare the scatter diagram, high-low, and least-squares regression methods of estimating costs.

LO⁴ Compute a break-even point for a single-product company.

LO⁵ Graph costs and revenues for a single-product company.

LO⁶ Identify assumptions in cost-volume-profit analysis and explain how they impact the analysis.

LO⁷ Describe several applications of cost-volume-profit analysis.

LO⁸ Compute the break-even point for a multi-product company.

Chapter Preview

This chapter describes different kinds of costs and shows how they are affected by changes in the operating volume of a business. This chapter also analyzes the costs and revenues of a company to understand how different operating strategies affect profit or loss. Managers use this kind of analysis to forecast what will happen if changes are made in costs, sales volume, selling prices, or product mix. They then use these forecasts to select the best strategy for the future such as whether to price a special order below the usual selling price, as seen with Maxum in the opening article.

Cost-Volume-Profit Analysis and Cost Behaviour

Planning a company's future activities and events is a crucial phase in successful management. One of the first steps in planning is predicting the volume of activity, the costs to be incurred, revenues to be received, and income (or profit) to be earned. An important tool to help managers carry out this step is **cost-volume-profit (CVP) analysis.**

Cost-volume-profit analysis helps managers predict how income is affected by changes in costs and sales levels. In its basic form, CVP analysis involves computing the sales level at which a company neither earns an income nor incurs a loss. This is called the break-even point. For this reason, this basic form of cost-volume-profit analysis is often called *break-even analysis.* But managers use many other applications of this analysis to answer questions like:

- What sales volume is needed to earn a target income?
- What is the change in income if selling prices are reduced and sales volume increases?
- How much will income increase if we install a new machine to reduce labour costs?
- What is the income effect if we change the sales mix of our products?

The phrase *cost-volume-profit analysis* is better than break-even analysis as a description of this tool when it is used to address such questions.

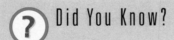

Breaking Even

Compaq Computer got its start when Rod Canion, Jim Harris, and Bill Murto, previously all senior managers at Texas Instruments, had a good plan and a solid product. They eventually raised start-up capital of $20 million using cost-volume-profit analysis showing break-even volumes attainable within the first year after product development. Sales in Compaq's first year totaled more than $100 million.

We can see from the above discussion that CVP analysis ultimately focuses on sales volume and the corresponding costs, revenues, and profitability at different sales levels. For example, consider a fund-raising event organized by your local student society. An important goal of the organizing committee would be to ensure that the event does not incur losses. This means that it has to sell enough tickets to cover all its costs, and perhaps some more to generate additional revenues. The organizing committee must have a good understanding of how the different cost items behave with respect to the corresponding activity base, i.e.

attendance volume. We now expand our discussion of cost behaviour as it relates to CVP analysis using volume as the activity base of interest.[1]

Fixed Costs

When a company increases its volume of activity (e.g., production volume) it must incur additional costs. In other words, higher volume causes higher costs. However the percentage increase in costs is often less than the increase in volume. This is due to the presence of fixed costs. The amount of a **fixed cost** incurred each period remains unchanged even when volume varies from period to period within a relevant range. The **relevant range of operation** is the range of volume within which our assumptions regarding cost behaviour are valid. An example of fixed costs is rent cost. For example, $5,000 rent paid for a factory building remains the same each month, whether the factory operates with a single eight-hour shift or around the clock with three shifts. This also means rent cost is the same each month at any level of output from zero on up to the full production capacity of the plant.

While *total* fixed cost remains constant as the level of production changes, the fixed cost *per unit* of product decreases as volume increases. For instance, if 20 units are produced, the average monthly factory building rent cost per unit is $250 (computed as $5,000 ÷ 20 units). When production increases to 200 units per month, the average cost per unit decreases to $25 (computed as $5,000 ÷ 200 units). The average cost decreases to $2.50 per unit if production increases to 2,000 units per month. Other examples of fixed costs include amortization, property taxes, office salaries, and many service department costs.

The graph in Exhibit 25.1 shows that fixed costs are represented as a horizontal line because their total amount remains constant at $32,000 at all production levels up to the factory's monthly capacity of 2,000 units of output. The *relevant range* for fixed costs in Exhibit 25.1 is 0 to 2,000 units. If the relevant range changes (i.e., production capacity increases or decreases), it is likely the amount of fixed costs will change.

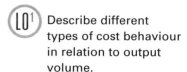 Describe different types of cost behaviour in relation to output volume.

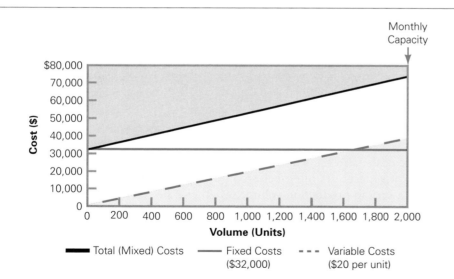

Exhibit 25.1

Relations of Fixed and Variable Costs to Volume

---

[1] In the case of a manufacturing company, output refers to production/sales, whereas in the case of a service company it refers to the service level (number of service orders completed).

Variable Costs

A **variable cost** changes in proportion to changes in activity volume. The direct material cost of a product is one example of a variable cost. If one unit of product requires material costing $20, total material costs are $200 when 10 units of product are manufactured, $400 for 20 units, $600 for 30 units, and so on. The variable cost *per unit* produced remains constant while the *total* amount of variable cost changes with the level of production. Other variable costs include direct labour P.1110 (if workers are paid for completed units), some overhead costs such as supplies and lubricants, and some expense such as selling commissions and shipping costs.

When variable costs are plotted on a graph of cost and volume, it appears as an upward sloping straight line starting at the zero cost level (see Exhibit 25.1). The line rises as production volume increases. The variable cost of $20 per unit is also known as the slope of the line.

Mixed Costs

Mixed costs are those that include a combination of fixed and variable costs. Compensation for sales representatives often includes a fixed monthly salary and a variable commission based on sales. The total cost line in Exhibit 25.1 represents a mixed cost. Total cost increases in the same direction as volume but increases less than proportionately with changes in volume. Like fixed costs, mixed costs are greater than zero when volume is at zero. The mixed cost line starts on the vertical axis at the $32,000 fixed cost point. This means that at the zero level of output, total cost equals only the fixed costs. Total cost increases, however, as output volume increases. The amount of the increase equals the variable cost per unit for each additional unit produced (slope of the line) and is the highest when production volume is 2,000 units (the end point of our graph).

The simplest way to include mixed costs in a CVP analysis is to separate them into fixed and variable components. The fixed component is added to other fixed costs for the planning period, and the variable component is added to other variable costs.

Recall the opening article involving Maxum. In analyzing the potential sales order, the controller's first course of action was to separate all manufacturing and selling costs into variable and fixed categories. The controller concluded that only raw materials and sales commissions were variable costs. Direct labour was added in eight-hour shifts and was called a *step-wise cost* (see below). All other manufacturing costs were categorized as fixed costs.

Step-Wise Costs

Step-wise costs, also known as *stair-step costs*, reflect a step pattern. Salaries of production supervisors often behave in a step-wise manner. Their salaries are fixed for a certain production volume, whether it be zero or the maximum produced in a shift. But when another shift is added to increase production, additional supervisors must be hired. Then the total cost for supervisory salaries goes up by a lump-sum amount. Total supervisory salaries remain fixed at this new, higher level until a third shift is added. A third shift increases cost by another lump sum.

A step-wise cost is graphed in Exhibit 25.2. Notice that the graph is flat within narrow ranges (steps). Then it jumps up to the next higher level and stays there over another range (step). In a conventional CVP analysis, a step-wise cost is treated as either a fixed cost or a variable cost. This treatment involves judgement on the part of the manager and mostly depends on the width of the range and the expected volume level.

To illustrate, suppose after the production of every 25 snowboards the operator must add special oil to the finishing machine. The cost of this oil reflects a step-wise pattern. Also suppose that after the production of every 1,000 units, a maintenance person must replace the snowboard cutting tool. Again, this is a step-wise cost. But note the range of 25 snowboards is much narrower than the range of 1,000 snowboards. This means some managers might treat the cost of the oil as a variable cost and the cost of the cutting tool as a fixed cost.

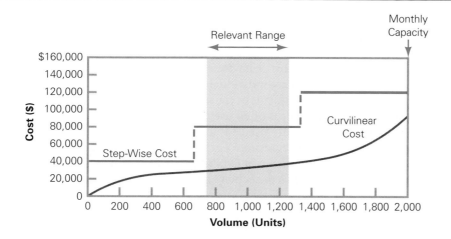

Exhibit 25.2

Step-Wise and Curvilinear Costs

Curvilinear Costs

A variable cost, as explained above, is a *linear* cost represented by a straight line. This means it increases at a constant rate as the activity base (e.g., production volume) increases. **Curvilinear costs**, also called *nonlinear costs*, increase as the activity base increases but not at a constant rate like variable costs. When graphed, curvilinear costs appear as a curved line. Exhibit 25.2 shows a curvilinear cost begins at zero when production is zero and then increases at different rates. Its highest rate is where sales volume reaches the maximum for the month.

An example of a curvilinear cost is total direct labour cost when workers are paid by the hour. At low levels of production, adding more workers allows each of them to specialize by doing the same task over and over again instead of doing several different tasks. The work crew becomes more efficient and is able to produce additional units for lower costs. But a point is eventually reached where adding more workers begins to create inefficiencies. For instance, a large crew may demand more time and effort in communicating or coordinating their efforts. While adding workers increases output, the labour cost per unit increases and the total labour cost goes up with a steeper slope. This pattern is seen in Exhibit 25.2 where the curvilinear cost curve starts at zero, rises, flattens out, and then increases at a faster rate as output nears the maximum for the month.

Another good example of curvilinear costs is the cost of utilities. It is common for utility costs to increase at an increasing rate resulting in curvilinear cost behaviour. For example a firm may be charged $1,000 flat fee for the first 1,000,000 litres of water consumed but pay $0.003 for the next 10,000 litres, $0.005 for the next 10,000 litre increment, $0.008 for the subsequent 10,000 litres, etc. However, curvilinear costs are often approximated to represent a linear pattern and are even treated as variable costs.

1. Which of the following statements is typically true?
   a. Variable cost per unit increases as volume increases.
   b. Fixed cost per unit decreases as volume increases.
   c. A curvilinear cost includes both fixed and variable elements.
2. Describe the behaviour of a fixed cost.
3. If a raw material cost per unit remains constant (fixed), why is it called a variable cost?

Measuring Cost Behaviour

 Determine cost estimates using three different methods.

Identifying and measuring cost behaviour requires careful analysis and judgement. We first want to identify individual costs that can be classified as either fixed or variable. When it is difficult to classify a cost as either fixed or variable, an analysis of past cost behaviour is often useful.

Three methods are usually used in analyzing past costs: scatter diagrams, high-low, and least-squares regression. Each method is discussed in this section using the sales and cost data shown in Exhibit 25.3 taken from a start-up company. Sales volume in units is used as the activity base in estimating cost behaviour.

Exhibit 25.3

Data for Estimating Cost Behaviour

Month	Sales Volume (Units)	Total Cost ($)
January	17,500	$20,500
February	27,500	21,500
March	25,000	25,000
April	35,000	21,500
May	47,500	25,500
June	22,500	18,500
July	30,000	23,500
August	52,500	28,500
September	37,500	26,000
October	57,500	26,000
November	62,500	31,000
December	67,500	29,000

Scatter Diagrams

Scatter diagrams display data about past costs in graphical form (see Exhibit 25.4). In Exhibit 25.4, the prior 12 months' figures are graphed. Each point reflects total costs incurred and sales volume for one of those months. For instance, the point labelled March had sales of 25,000 units and costs of $25,000.

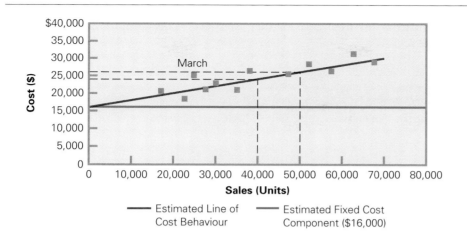

Exhibit 25.4

Scatter Diagram

The **estimated line of cost behaviour** is drawn on a scatter diagram to reflect the past relation between cost and sales volume; it is the line that best "fits" visually the points in a scatter diagram. Fitting this line requires judgement. This is a drawback because different analysts using the same data are likely to draw different cost estimation lines. The line drawn in Exhibit 25.4 intersects the vertical axis at approximately $16,000. This amount reflects the fixed cost estimate.

To compute the variable cost per unit (or the slope of the estimated cost behaviour line), we perform three steps. *First*, we select any two points on the horizontal axis (say, 40,000 and 50,000 units). *Second*, we draw vertical lines from these two points so that they intersect the estimated cost behaviour line. You will see that the corresponding costs on the vertical axis at which the lines drawn from the 40,000 and 50,000 points intersect the estimated cost behaviour line are $24,000 and $26,000 respectively. *Third*, we compute the slope of the line as the change in cost on the vertical axis divided by the change in sales volume on the horizontal axis; this computation is shown in Exhibit 25.5. Now that we have computed the fixed and variable portions of the total mixed costs, we can write the cost equation as follows: total costs (Y) = fixed costs (a) + variable cost per unit (b) times the number of units sold (X), and we can use this equation to predict total costs at different sales levels within the relevant range. For this example, we can write the equation as $Y = \$16,000 + \$0.20X$.

$$\frac{\text{Change in cost}}{\text{Change in sales units}} = \frac{\$26,000 - \$24,000}{50,000 - 40,000} = \frac{\$2,000}{10,000} = \$0.20 \text{ per sales unit}$$

Exhibit 25.5

Variable Cost per Unit
(Scatter diagram method)

High-Low Method

The **high-low method** is another means to estimate the cost equation. To apply this method, we connect the two cost amounts in the diagram representing the highest and lowest sales volumes. This method involves the following steps:

First, we identify the highest and lowest sales volume levels within our data set, and their corresponding cost levels. Using the data set in Exhibit 25.3, we find that the lowest and highest sales levels (and their corresponding costs) are 17,500 ($20,500) and 67,500 ($29,000) respectively. *Second*, we compute the slope of the line by dividing the difference between the two cost levels by the difference between the two sales levels; this computation is shown in Exhibit 25.6. *Finally*, we compute the fixed portion of the total cost by multiplying the variable cost per unit by either the low or the high sales level and then deducting this resulting amount from the total cost for that sales level. This computation is shown in Exhibit 25.7.

Exhibit 25.6

Variable Cost per Unit (High-Low Method)

$$\frac{\text{Change in cost}}{\text{Change in sales units}} = \frac{\$29,000 - \$20,500}{67,500 - 17,500} = \frac{\$8,500}{50,000} = \$0.17 \text{ per unit of sales}$$

Exhibit 25.7

Computation of Fixed Costs (High-Low Method)

Total variable cost at the low sales level = $0.17 \times 17,500$ units = \$2,975

Fixed cost = Total cost at the low sales level − total variable cost at low sales level
       = \$20,500 − \$2,975 = \$17,525

The cost equation used to estimate costs at different sales levels within the relevant range is: $17,525 plus $0.17 per unit sold ($Y = \$17,525 + \$0.17X$). This cost equation is slightly different from that determined using the scatter diagram method. One deficiency of the high-low method is that it ignores all sales points except the highest and lowest. Although the difference in this example is slight we could have gotten very different results if we had more extreme high and low points. The result is less precise because it uses the most extreme points rather than the more usual conditions likely to occur in future periods.

Least-Squares Regression

Least-squares regression is a statistical method of identifying cost behaviour. This method directly estimates cost behaviour by fitting the estimated line to the observations. For our purposes we will use the cost equation estimated from this method but leave the details of this method for more advanced cost accounting courses. The computations for least-squares regression are easily made on most spreadsheet programs and calculators.

The regression cost equation for the data presented in Exhibit 25.3 is: $16,947 plus $0.19 per unit sold ($Y = \$16,947 + \$0.19X$). This means fixed cost is estimated as $16,947 and variable cost as $0.19 per unit sold. Both costs are reflected in the diagram shown in Exhibit 25.8.

Exhibit 25.8

Least-Squares Regression

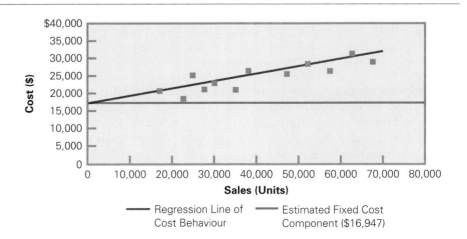

Regression Line of Cost Behaviour

Estimated Fixed Cost Component ($16,947)

Comparing Cost Estimation Methods

The three cost estimation methods result in slightly different estimates of fixed and variable costs as summarized in Exhibit 25.9. Estimates from the scatter diagram are based on a visual fit of the cost line and are subject to interpretation. Estimates from the high-low method use only two values corresponding to the lowest and highest sales volumes. Estimates from least-squares regression are based on a statistical technique that uses all the available data points. Many users consider least-squares regression superior to the other two methods.

 Compare the scatter diagram, high-low, and least-squares regression methods of estimating costs.

Estimation Method	Fixed Cost	Variable Cost
Scatter Diagram	$16,000	$0.20 per unit sold
High-Low	$17,525	$0.17 per unit sold
Least-Squares Regression	$16,947	$0.19 per unit sold

Exhibit 25.9

Comparison of Cost Estimation Methods

We must remember all three methods use *past data*. Cost estimates resulting from any of these methods are only as good as the data used for estimation. Managers must establish that the data are reliable and can be used to derive cost estimates useful in predicting future costs.

4. Which of the following is likely to yield the more precise estimated line of cost behaviour? (a) High-low method; (b) Least-squares method; (c) Scatter diagram.

5. What is the primary weakness of the high-low method?

6. Using conventional CVP, a mixed cost should be: (a) disregarded; (b) treated as a fixed cost; (c) separated into fixed and variable components.

Answers—p. 1320

Mid-Chapter Demonstration Problem

Total factory overhead costs for Landry Company has been fluctuating considerably from year to year in relation to increases and decreases in the number of direct labour hours worked in the factory.

The factory overhead costs consist of indirect materials, rent, and maintenance. The company has analyzed these costs at the 50,000-hour level of activity and has determined that at this activity level these costs exist in the following proportions:

Indirect materials (V)	$25,000
Rent (F)	80,000
Maintenance (M)	35,000
Total factory overhead costs	$140,000

V = variable; F = fixed; M = mixed.

Total factory overhead costs at high and low levels of activity for recent years are:

	Level of Activity	
	Low	**High**
Direct labour hours	50,000	80,000
Total factory overhead costs..................	$140,000	$170,000

To have data available for planning, the company wants to break down the maintenance cost into its variable and fixed cost elements.

Required

1. Determine how much of the $170,000 factory overhead cost at the high level of activity above consists of maintenance cost.

2. By means of this high-low method of cost analysis, determine the cost formula for maintenance.

3. Express the company's maintenance costs in the linear equation form $Y = a + bX$

4. What *total* factory overhead costs would you expect the company to incur at an operating level of 75,000 direct labour hours? Show computations.

Planning the Solution

1. Find the periods of the highest and lowest activity. In this problem these activity points are given.

2. Next, determine maintenance costs by first deducting the costs of all other overhead items from the total overhead costs.

3. Determine the change in the maintenance cost and the change in activity between the high and low points.

4. Compute the variable maintenance cost per unit by dividing the change in maintenance costs by the change in activity.

5. Compute the fixed maintenance cost by deducting the variable maintenance cost from the total maintenance costs at either the high or low activity level.

6. Combine the variable and fixed components of maintenance costs and express this relationship as a formula.

7. Using the formula from step (6) determine maintenance costs at the 75,000 hour level of activity and add the other component overhead costs to arrive at total overhead costs.

SOLUTION TO Mid-Chapter Demonstration Problem

1. Maintenance cost at the low and high levels of direct labour hour activity can be isolated as follows:

	Level of Activity	
	50,000 DLH	80,000 DLH
Total factory overhead cost	$140,000	$170,000
Deduct:		
Indirect materials @ $0.50 per DLH*....	(25,000)	(40,000)
Rent..	(80,000)	(80,000)
Maintenance cost..................................	$ 35,000	$ 50,000

*$25,000 ÷ 50,000 DLH = $0.50 per DLH

2. High-low analysis of maintenance cost:

	Direct Labour Hours	Maintenance Cost
High level of activity	80,000	$50,000
Low level of activity	50,000	35,000
Change observed	30,000	$15,000

Variable cost element:

$$\frac{\text{Change in cost}}{\text{Change in activity}} = \frac{\$15,000}{30,000 \text{ DLH}} = \$0.50 \text{ per DLH}$$

Fixed cost element:

Total cost at the high level of activity	$50,000
Less variable cost element ($0.50 × 80,000 DLH)	40,000
Fixed cost element	$10,000

Therefore, the cost formula for maintenance is: $10,000 per year plus $0.50 per direct labour hour.

3. $Y = \$10,000 + \$0.50X$

4. Total factory overhead cost at 75,000 direct labour hours would be:

Maintenance:		
Variable cost element (75,000 DLH × $0.50)........	$37,500	
Fixed cost element...	10,000	$47,500
Indirect materials (75,000 DLH × $0.50)		37,500
Rent...		80,000
Total factory overhead cost		$165,000

It is important to note that 75,000 labour hours is within the relevant range of activity.

Break-Even Analysis

We now explain a special case of cost-volume-profit analysis known as break-even analysis. This section describes break-even analysis including computation of the break-even point and preparing a CVP (or break-even) chart.

Computing Break-Even Point

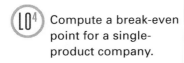
Compute a break-even point for a single-product company.

The **break-even point** is the sales level at which a company neither earns a profit nor incurs a loss. The break-even point can be expressed either in units or in dollars of sales.

    To illustrate break-even analysis let's look at Rydell Limited that sells footballs for $100 per unit and incurs $70 of variable costs per unit sold. Rydell's fixed costs are $24,000 per month and it has the capacity to produce 1,800 footballs per month. Rydell breaks even for the month when it sells 800 footballs at a sales volume of $80,000. We compute this break-even point using the formula in Exhibit 25.10.[2]

Exhibit 25.10

Formula for Computing Break-Even Sales (in units)

$$\text{Break-even point in units} = \frac{\text{Fixed costs}}{\text{Contribution margin per unit}}$$

    The **contribution margin per unit** is the difference between the selling price and the variable cost per unit. For Rydell, the contribution margin per unit is $30 ($100 − $70). Break-even sales volume is computed as $24,000 ÷ $30, or 800 units per month. At a price of $100 per unit, monthly sales of 800 units generate revenues of $80,000 (break-even sales dollars).

    The break-even sales volume of $80,000 can also be computed without computing sales units. This involves using the formula shown in Exhibit 25.11.

Exhibit 25.11

Formula for Computing Break-Even Sales (in dollars)

$$\text{Break-even point in dollars} = \frac{\text{Fixed costs}}{\text{Contribution margin ratio}}$$

---

[2] The mathematics of this formula are shown here:

Define: S = sales in units   R = revenue per unit
         F = fixed costs per month   V = variable cost per unit
         S × R = dollar sales   S × V = total variable cost

Then: Contribution margin per unit = R − V

At break-even: Sales = Fixed Costs + Variable Costs
                  (S × R) = F + (S × V)
                  (S × R) − (S × V) = F
                  S × (R − V) = F
                  S = F/(R − V)
                  S = F/Contribution margin per unit

Also: Contribution margin ratio = (R − V)/R

At break-even: S = F/(R − V)
                  S × R = (F × R)/(R − V)
                  S × R = F × [R/(R − V)]
                  S × R = F/[(R − V)/R]
                  S × R = F/Contribution margin ratio

The **contribution margin ratio** (or contribution margin percentage) is the *proportion* of a unit's selling price that exceeds total unit variable cost. It is computed as the unit contribution margin divided by the unit selling price.

For Rydell the contribution margin ratio is 30% ($30 ÷ $100). Break-even sales dollars is computed as $24,000 ÷ 0.30, or $80,000 of monthly sales.

To verify that Rydell's break-even point equals $80,000 (or 800 units), we prepare a simple income statement as shown in Exhibit 25.12. It shows the $80,000 revenue from sales of 800 units exactly equals the sum of fixed and variable costs. Note that the break-even point can also be defined as the point at which total contribution margin equals total fixed costs.

Rydell Company Forecasted Income Statement	
Sales (800 units @ $100 each)	$80,000
Variable costs (800 units @ $70 each)	56,000
Contribution margin	$24,000
Fixed costs	24,000
Net income	$ -0-

Exhibit 25.12

Income Statement at Break-Even

Exhibit 25.12 shows the *contribution margin income statement.* This statement differs only in format from the income statement. First, it separately classifies costs and expenses as variable or fixed. Second, it reports contribution margin, which is sales less variable costs and variable expenses (this example assumes no variable expenses). It is easier to use the contribution format income statement for applying CVP analysis; we will therefore use this format throughout this chapter.

Preparing a Cost-Volume-Profit Chart

Exhibit 25.13 is a graph of the cost-volume-profit relations for Rydell Limited. This graph is called a **cost-volume-profit (CVP) chart**, also called a *break-even graph* or *break-even chart*. The horizontal axis is the number of units sold and the vertical axis is dollars of sales and costs. We assume straight lines depict both costs and revenues on the graph. To prepare a CVP chart, we complete the following steps:[3]

 Graph costs and revenues for a single-product company.

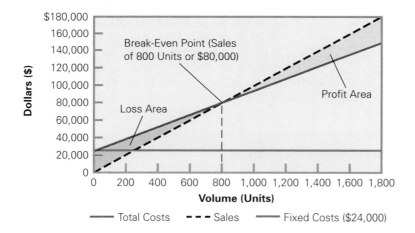

Exhibit 25.13

Cost-Volume-Profit Chart

---

[3] These instructions are provided to guide you through a manual drafting process. The graph can also be drawn with computer assistance, including spreadsheet programs that can convert numeric data to graphs.

1. Plot fixed costs on the vertical axis (i.e. $24,000). Draw a horizontal line at this level to show that fixed costs remain unchanged regardless of sales volume. Exhibit 25.13 includes this line, although the fixed cost line is not essential to the analysis.

2. Draw a line reflecting total costs (variable costs plus fixed costs). For any sales level, this line shows the sum of both fixed and variable costs for that level. This line starts at the fixed costs on the vertical axis because total costs equal fixed costs at the zero sales level. The slope of the total cost line equals the variable cost per unit ($70). To draw the line, compute the total costs for any sales level, and connect this point with the vertical axis intercept ($24,000). Do not draw this line beyond the productive capacity for the planning period (1,800 units for Rydell).

3. Draw a sales line starting at the origin (zero units and zero dollars of sales). The slope of this line equals the selling price per unit ($100). To draw the line, compute the total revenues for any sales level, and connect this point with the origin. Do not extend this line beyond the productive capacity for the planning period. The total revenue is at its highest level at maximum capacity. It is likely that the relevant range is near the middle of the graph.

The total cost line and the sales line intersect at 800 units of product in Exhibit 25.13. This intersection is the break-even point. It is the point where total sales revenue of $80,000 equals the sum of both fixed and variable costs ($80,000).

On either side of the break-even point, the vertical distance between the sales line and the total cost line at any specific sales volume represents the profit or loss expected at that volume. At volume levels to the left of the break-even point, the vertical distance is the amount of the loss because the total cost line is above the total sales line. At volume levels to the right of the break-even point, the vertical distance represents the amount of profit because the total sales line is above the total cost line.

Assumptions Underlying Cost-Volume-Profit Analysis

LO6 Identify assumptions in cost-volume-profit analysis and explain how they impact the analysis.

Cost-volume-profit analysis assumes relations can be expressed as straight lines similar to those in Exhibits 25.1 and 25.13. This assumption allows users of CVP to classify all costs as either fixed or variable. CVP analysis also treats revenues as variable, with all units of a product being sold at the same unit price. These assumptions allow users to answer several important questions. But the usefulness of these answers depends on the validity of at least three of these assumptions for the planning period:

1. Selling price per unit is constant.
2. Variable costs per unit are constant.
3. Total fixed costs are constant.

While these assumptions are not always realistic, they don't necessarily limit the usefulness of CVP as a first step in forecasting the effects of an operating plan. This section discusses these and other assumptions of CVP analysis.

Production Output versus Sales Volume

We normally define variable costs and fixed costs in terms of the level of *output produced*. But CVP analysis usually describes the planning period's level of activity in terms of *sales volume* rather than production output. Sales volume can be described as either the number of units sold or the dollars of sales generated.

To simplify analysis, users often assume the level of production will be the same as the level of sales. This means we don't have to be concerned with costs flowing into inventory instead of being sold or with costs flowing into cost of goods sold from the prior period's inventory. This assumption is justified because CVP analysis provides only rough estimates.

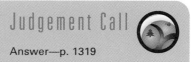

Manager of Operations

You are the manager of operations for a new manufacturing plant set up to produce a variety of gift articles. One of your immediate and important tasks is to coordinate with the accountant to identify the behaviour of manufacturing costs to develop a production cost budget. You know three methods can be used to identify cost behaviour from past data. But past data is not available as this is a new plant. What do you do?

Judgement Call

Answer—p. 1319

Working with Assumptions

The behaviour of individual costs and revenues often is not perfectly consistent with CVP assumptions. If the expected cost and revenue behaviour is different from the assumptions, the results of a CVP analysis may be limited. Still, there are several reasons why we can perform useful analyses using these assumptions.

Summing Costs Can Offset Deviations

Deviations from assumptions with individual costs are often minor when these costs are summed. For instance, while the individual variable cost items may not be perfectly variable, when we sum all variable costs their individual deviations can offset each other. This means the assumption of variable cost behaviour may be proper for total variable costs even when it is not valid for individual variable cost items. Similarly, an assumption that total fixed costs are constant may be proper even when individual fixed cost items are not exactly constant.

Relevant Range of Operations

Revenues, variable costs, and fixed costs often are reasonably reflected in straight lines on a graph when the assumptions are applied only over a relevant range of operations. The relevant range of operations is the normal operating range for a business. Assumptions about fixed and variable costs are valid within this range. Except for unusually difficult or prosperous times, management typically plans for operations within a range of volume neither close to zero nor maximum capacity. The relevant range for planning excludes extremely high and low operating levels that are unlikely to occur. The validity of assuming a specific cost is fixed or variable is more acceptable when operations are within the relevant range. As shown in Exhibit 25.2, a curvilinear cost can be treated as variable and linear if the relevant range covers volumes that have a near constant slope.

A relevant range may not be applicable to all cost items. For example, production supervisory salaries will increase as more production shifts are added. If production in each shift is 1,000 units, the initial relevant range for supervisory salaries is 0 to 1,000 and increases in steps of 1,000. But factory rent increases only when a company rents more space. Rental cost remains the same up to a production level of, say, 3,000 units from the three shifts. The initial relevant range for this cost item is 0 to 3,000 units of production and increases in steps of 3,000. A company cannot keep track of all these different relevant ranges. Management must plan according to the normal relevant range of activity. If the normal range of activity changes, some costs may need reclassification.

Estimates from Cost-Volume-Profit Analysis

CVP analysis yields approximate answers to questions about costs, volumes, and profits. These answers do not have to be precise because the analysis makes rough estimates about the future. As long as managers understand that CVP analysis gives estimates, then it can be a useful tool for starting the planning process.

Recall the opening article and the decision by the controller at Maxum's to use CVP analysis. While Maxum's variable costs per unit appeared to be stable, the proposed volume was well beyond the current relevant range of its production capacity. Maxum was already near capacity during its peak months. After including the new fixed costs necessary to expand capacity, Maxum set a rough price to recover all relevant costs and contribute 15% to overhead and income.

CVP analysis is only a starting point. Other qualitative factors must be considered. The large capital outlay for a second manufacturing facility would increase Maxum's fixed costs. These fixed costs would leverage the company and make it vulnerable in a business downturn. This is because fixed costs do not decline if volume decreases. Also, the proposal would mean about 50% of Maxum's business is with one buyer. Maxum could end up being a captive supplier for Sport Marine. This would make it vulnerable to pressure for future price concessions.

Flashback

Answers—p. 1320

7. Fixed cost divided by the contribution margin ratio yields the:

   a. Break-even point in dollars.

   b. Contribution margin per unit.

   c. Break-even point in units.

8. A company sells a product for $90 per unit with variable costs of $54 per unit. What is the contribution margin ratio?

9. Refer to Flashback number 8 above. If fixed costs for the period are $90,000, what is the break-even point in dollars?

10. What are the three basic assumptions used in CVP analysis?

Applying Cost-Volume-Profit Analysis

Describe several applications of cost-volume-profit analysis.

Managers consider a variety of strategies in planning business operations. These strategies often affect costs and revenues for the company. Cost-volume-profit analysis is useful in helping managers evaluate the likely effects of these strategies. This section explains several applications of cost-volume-profit analysis.

Computing Income from Sales

Managers need to answer the important question, "What is the amount of income from a predicted level of sales?" To answer this, we look at four factors in the CVP analysis. These variables and their relations to pre-tax income are shown in Exhibit 25.14. We use these relations to compute income from predicted sales and cost levels.

Pre-tax income = Sales − [Fixed costs + Variable costs]
or
Pre-tax income = Sales − Fixed costs − Variable costs

Exhibit 25.14

Income Relations in
CVP Analysis

To illustrate, let's assume the management of Rydell expects to sell 1,500 product units this month. What is the amount of income if this monthly sales level is achieved? At this level, revenues are $150,000, computed as 1,500 units 3$100. Rydell's fixed costs are $24,000 per month. Its variable costs per unit are $70 per unit, and total variable costs for 1,500 units of product are $105,000 (1,500 units 3$70). Using the relations from Exhibit 25.14, and substituting these amounts, we compute Rydell's income as shown in Exhibit 25.15.

Pre-tax income = [1,500 units × $100] − [1,500 units × $70] − $24,000 = $21,000

Exhibit 25.15

Computing Expected Income
from Expected Sales

The $21,000 income does not include the effects of income taxes. Recall that corporations must pay income taxes. If management wants to find the amount of *after-tax* income from selling 1,500 units, they must apply the proper tax rate to the $21,000. If the tax rate is 25%, the income tax is $5,250 and net income is $15,750. Management would then determine whether this net income is an adequate return on the assets invested. Management should also look at whether sales and income can be increased by raising or lowering prices. CVP analysis is a good tool for addressing these kinds of "what if" questions.

Computing Sales for a Target Income

Many companies' annual plans are based on certain income targets. Rydell's income target for year 2005 is to increase 2004 income by 10%. When 2004 income is known, Rydell easily computes its target income for 2005. CVP analysis helps us in determining the sales level needed to achieve the target income. Computing this target sales level is important because planning for the year is then based on this level. We use the formula shown in Exhibit 25.16 to compute sales for a target after-tax income.[4]

"How many units must I sell to earn $50,000?"

---

[4] The mathematics of this formula are shown here:

Define: S = sales in units R = revenue per unit
         F = fixed costs per month V = variable cost per unit
         N = target net income T = income taxes
         $S \times R$ = dollar sales $S \times V$ = total variable cost

Recall that: Contribution margin ratio = $(R - V)/R$

Then: $N = (S \times R) - F - (S \times V) - T$
         $(S \times R) - (S \times V) = F + N + T$
         $S \times (R - V) = F + N + T$
         $S = (F + N + T)/(R - V)$
         $S \times R = [(F + N + T) \times R]/(R - V)$
         $S \times R = (F + N + T) \times [R/(R - V)]$
         $S \times R = (F + N + T)/[(R - V)/R]$
         $S \times R = (F + N + T)/$Contribution margin ratio

Exhibit 25.16

Computing Sales (dollars)
for a Target Income

$$\text{Dollar sales} = \frac{\text{Fixed costs + Target income + Income taxes}}{\text{Contribution margin ratio}}$$

To illustrate, we return to Rydell, which has monthly fixed costs of $24,000 and a 30% contribution margin ratio. Let's assume it sets a target monthly after-tax income of $9,000 when the tax rate is 25%. This means the before-tax income is targeted at $12,000 [$9,000/(120.25)] with a tax expense of $3,000. Using the formula in Exhibit 25.16 we find $120,000 of sales is needed to produce an $9,000 income after-taxes. We show this computation in Exhibit 25.17.

Exhibit 25.17

Rydell's Sales for a
Target Income

$$\text{Dollar sales at target income} = \frac{\$24,000 + \$9,000 + \$3,000}{30\%}$$
$$= \$120,000$$

We can alternatively use the formula in Exhibit 25.16 to compute *unit sales* instead of dollar sales. To do this we need only substitute the *contribution margin per unit* in place of the contribution margin ratio as the denominator. This gives us the unit sales needed to reach the target income level. Exhibit 25.18 illustrates this application to Rydell Company. The two computations in Exhibits 25.17 and 25.18 correspond to each other because 1,200 units at $100 per unit equal $120,000 of sales.

Exhibit 25.18

Computing Sales (units)
for a Target Income

$$\text{Unit sales} = \frac{\text{Fixed costs + Net income + Income taxes}}{\text{Contribution margin per unit}}$$
$$= \frac{\$24,000 + \$9,000 + \$3,000}{\$30}$$
$$= 1{,}200 \text{ units}$$

Judgement Call

Answer—p. 1319

Management Trainee

You are part of a management trainee group debating a proposed product launch. A crucial factor is the range of income levels from different sales projections. Sales projections are very subjective given the product has not before been produced. One team member suggests they pick numbers producing favourable income numbers because any estimate is "as good as any other." Another crucial factor is fixed and variable cost predictions that are being estimated from a scatter diagram of 20 months' production on a comparable product. But these cost predictions do not support the investment. A team member asks whether less favourable data points can be dropped from the analysis to see if the cost picture is improved. Your role is to do a cost-volume-profit analysis to reflect these suggestions. What do you do?

Computing the Margin of Safety

All companies desire to earn income by selling more than the break-even number of units. The excess of expected sales over break-even sales is a company's **margin of safety**. The margin of safety is the amount sales can drop before the company incurs a loss. It can be expressed in units, in dollars, or even as a percent of the predicted level of sales.

To illustrate, if Rydell's expected sales are $100,000, the margin of safety is $20,000 above break-even sales of $80,000. As a percent, the margin of safety is 20% of expected sales as shown in Exhibit 25.19.

$$\text{Margin of safety, percent} = \frac{\text{Expected sales} - \text{Break-even sales}}{\text{Expected sales}}$$
$$= \frac{\$100,000 - \$80,000}{\$100,000} = 20\%$$

Exhibit 25.19

Computing Margin of Safety (in Percent)

Management needs to assess whether this margin of safety is adequate in light of various factors. These factors include sales variability, competition, consumer tastes, and economic conditions.

Did You Know?

Food For Thought

In The Zone Delivery, a food service business that delivers tasty yet nutritious meals inspired by the popular diet, has seen a growing list of clientele from all walks of life within Canada. People not only enjoy filling meals, they also end up dropping pounds. In addition, the price charged to all the common folk is much lower than it would be to Hollywood-based celebrities. The company's owner admits that at the current price and volume levels, the business just about breaks even, because the meals cost a considerable amount due to the quality of the ingredients used to prepare the food.

SOURCE: In The Zone Delivery Web site: http://www.inthezonedelivery.com/articles.html. February 20, 2003. Adapted from Rob Salem's How I Fell For the Diet of the Stars.@ Toronto Star. October 21, 2001.

Sensitivity Analysis

It is often useful to know the effects of changing some *estimates* used in CVP analysis. This is because they are estimates and not actual values. For instance, we may want to know what happens if we reduce a product's selling price to increase sales. Or, we may want to know what happens to income if we automate an existing manual process that increases fixed costs but reduces variable costs. If we can describe how these changes affect a company's fixed costs, variable costs, selling price, and volume, we can use CVP to predict income.

"Will automation lower break-even sales?"

To illustrate, assume Rydell Company is looking into buying a new machine that would increase monthly fixed costs from $24,000 to $30,000, but decrease variable costs from $70 per unit to $60 per unit. The product's selling price will remain unchanged at $100. This results in increases in both the unit contribution margin and the contribution margin ratio. The new contribution margin per unit is $40 per unit ($100 − $60) and the new contribution margin ratio is 40% of selling price ($40/$100). The manager wants to know what the break-even point is if the machine is bought.

We use CVP analysis to help answer the question. If Rydell buys the machine, its new break-even point in dollars is $75,000. This is computed as shown in Exhibit 25.20.

Exhibit 25.20

Computing Break-Even When Changes Occur

$$\text{New break-even point in dollars} = \frac{\text{New fixed costs}}{\text{New contribution margin ratio}} = \frac{\$30,000}{40\%} = \$75,000$$

The new fixed costs and the new contribution margin ratio can also be used to address other issues including computation of (a) expected income for a given sales level, and (b) the sales level needed to earn a target income. Another use of sensitivity analysis is to generate three different sets of revenue and cost estimates that are: optimistic, pessimistic, and most likely. Different CVP analysis based on these estimates provide management with different scenarios that they can analyze and use in planning business strategy.

Flashback

Answers—p. 1320

11. A company has fixed costs of $50,000 and a 25% contribution margin ratio. How many dollars of sales are necessary for the company to achieve a net income of $120,000 if the tax rate is 20%? (a) $800,000; (b) $680,000; (c) $600,000.

12. If the contribution margin ratio decreases from 50% to 25%, what can be said about unit sales needed to achieve a target income level?

13. What is a company's margin of safety?

Computing Multi-Product Break-Even Point

LO⁸ Compute the break-even point for a multi-product company.

To this point we have looked only at cases where the company produces a single product. This was to keep the basic CVP analysis simple. We can modify CVP analysis for use when a company produces and sells several products.

An important assumption in a multi-product setting is that the sales mix of different products is known and remains constant in the planning period. **Sales mix** is the ratio (proportion) of the sales volumes for various products. For instance, if a company normally sells 10,000 footballs, 5,000 baseballs, and 4,000 basketballs, then its sales mix is said to be 10:5:4 for footballs, baseballs, and basketballs.

To apply multi-product CVP analysis, we estimate the break-even point by using a composite unit. A **composite unit** is defined as a specific number of units of each product in proportion to the expected sales mix. Multi-product CVP analysis treats this composite unit like a single product.

To illustrate, let's look at Hair-Today, a stylist salon, that offers three cuts: basic, ultra, and budget in the ratio of 4 units of basic to 2 units of ultra to 1 unit of budget (expressed as 4:2:1). Management wants to estimate its break-even point for the next year. Unit selling prices for the three cuts are: basic, $10; ultra, $16; and budget, $8. Using the 4:2:1 sales mix, the selling price of a composite unit of the three products is computed as:

4 units of basic @ $10 per unit...............................	$40
2 units of ultra @ $16 per unit..............................	32
1 unit of budget @ $8 per unit	8
Selling price of a composite unit...........................	**$80**

The fixed costs of Hair-Today are $96,000 per year and the variable costs of the three products are: basic, $6.50; ultra, $9.00; and budget, $4.00. Therefore, variable costs for a composite unit of these products are:

4 units of basic @ $6.50 per unit............................	$26
2 units of ultra @ $9.00 per unit............................	18
1 unit of budget @ $4.00 per unit	4
Variable costs of a composite unit........................	**$48**

Once we compute the variable costs and selling price of a composite unit of the company's products, we calculate the contribution margin for a composite unit. This is computed as $32 determined by subtracting the variable costs ($48) of a composite unit from its selling price ($80).

We can use the $32 contribution margin to determine Hair-Today's break-even point in composite units as shown in Exhibit 25.21.

$$\text{Break-even point in composite units} = \frac{\text{Fixed costs}}{\text{Contribution margin per composite unit}}$$

$$= \frac{\$96,000}{\$32} = 3,000 \text{ composite units}$$

Exhibit 25.21

Break-Even Point in Composite Units

This computation shows that Hair-Today breaks even when it sells 3,000 composite units of its products. To determine how many units of each product must be sold to break even, we multiply the number of units of each product in the composite by 3,000:

Basic: 4 × 3,000....................................	12,000 units
Ultra: 2 × 3,000....................................	6,000 units
Budget: 1 × 3,000....................................	3,000 units

The schedule in Exhibit 25.22 verifies these results by showing Hair-Today's revenues and costs at the break-even point.

Hair-Today Forecasted Product Income Statement at Break-Even Point				
	Basic	**Ultra**	**Budget**	**Combined**
Revenues:				
Basic (12,000 @ $10.00)	$120,000			
Ultra (6,000 @ $16.00)		$96,000		
Budget (3,000 @ $8.00)			$24,000	
Total revenues				$240,000
Variable costs:				
Basic (12,000 @ $6.50)	78,000			
Ultra (6,000 @ $9.00)		54,000		
Budget (3,000 @ $4.00)			12,000	
Total variable costs				144,000
Contribution margin............................	$ 42,000	$42,000	$12,000	$ 96,000
Fixed costs				96,000
Net income				$ -0-

Exhibit 25.22

Multi-Product Break-Even Income Statement

A CVP analysis using composite units can be used to answer a variety of planning questions. Once a product mix is set, all answers are based on the assumption it remains constant at all sales levels, just like other factors in the analysis. Caution should be exercised because the sales mix may change due to changes in consumer tastes and buying habits resulting in a different composite contribution margin and different break-even level of sales. But we can vary the sales mix to see what happens under alternative strategies.

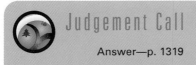

Judgement Call

Answer—p. 1319

Marketing Manager

You are the marketing manager of medium-sized communications firm, responsible for marketing cellular phones and accessories. A CVP analysis indicates that with the current sales mix and price levels, the product line will just break even. You want to earn at least 10% more income than you earned last year. What alternatives do you have for achieving the desired income level?

Flashback

Answers—p. 1320

14. The sales mix of a company's two products, X and Y, is 2:1. Unit price and variable cost data are:

	X	Y
Unit sales price	$5	$4
Unit variable cost	2	2

What is the contribution margin per composite unit? (a) $5; (b) $10; (c) $8.

15. What additional assumption about sales mix must be made in doing a conventional CVP analysis for a company that produces and sells more than one product?

Summary

LO1 **Describe different types of cost behaviour in relation to output volume.** A cost's behaviour is described in terms of how its amount changes in relation to output volume within a relevant range. Fixed costs remain constant even when sales increase or decrease. Total variable costs change in direct proportion to sales volume changes. Mixed costs display the effects of fixed and variable components. Step-wise costs remain constant over a small volume range, then change by a lump-sum amount and remain constant over another volume range, and so on. Curvilinear costs change in a nonlinear relation to volume changes.

LO2 **Determine cost estimates using three different methods.** The three different methods used to estimate costs are the scatter graph method, the high-low method, and the least-squares regression method. All three methods use past data to estimate costs.

LO3 **Compare the scatter diagram, high-low, and least-squares regression methods of estimating costs.** Cost estimates from the scatter diagram are based on a visual fit of the cost line and are subject to interpretation. Estimates from the high-low method are based only on two sets of values corresponding to the lowest and highest sales volumes. The least-squares regression method is a statistical technique that uses all the data points. The regression method is usually considered superior to the other two methods.

LO4 **Compute a break-even point for a single-product company.** A company's break-even point for a period is the sales volume at which total revenues equal total costs. To compute a break-even point in terms of sales units, divide total fixed costs by the contribution margin per unit. To compute a break-even point in terms of sales dollars, divide total fixed costs by the contribution margin ratio.

LO⁵ Graph costs and revenues for a single product company. The costs and revenues for a company can be graphically illustrated. This type of presentation is called a CVP chart. In this chart, the horizontal axis represents the number of units sold and the vertical axis represents dollars of sales and costs. Straight lines are used to depict the costs and revenues on the CVP chart.

LO⁶ Identify assumptions in cost-volume-profit analysis and explain how they impact the analysis. Conventional cost-volume-profit analysis is based on assumptions that the selling price of the product remains constant and that variable and fixed costs behave in a manner consistent with their variable and fixed classifications. These assumptions are not likely to hold at volume levels outside the relevant range of operations of the business. If the assumptions do not lead to valid predictions of future costs, the CVP analysis is less helpful.

LO⁷ Describe several applications of cost-volume-profit analysis. Cost-volume-profit analysis can be used to develop initial predictions of what can happen under alternative strategies concerning sales volume, selling prices, variable costs, or fixed costs. Applications include "what if" analysis, computing sales for a target income, and break-even analysis.

LO⁸ Compute the break-even point for a multi-product company. CVP can be applied to a multi-product company by expressing the predicted sales volume in terms of composite units of product. A composite unit consists of a specific number of units of each product in proportion to their expected sales mix. Multi-product CVP analysis treats this composite unit like a single product and it is assumed that the product mix will not change over the relevant range.

GUIDANCE ANSWERS TO Judgement Call

Manager of Operations

Without the availability of past data, none of the three methods described in the chapter can be used to measure cost behaviour. In this situation, the manager must investigate if s/he can get access to such data from similar manufacturing systems, such as from other plants within the company. If not, the manager can attempt to get this information from other companies. But this is difficult due to the sensitive nature of the data. In the absence of any data the manager should develop a list of the different production inputs and identify input-output relations. This understanding will provide preliminary guidance to the manager in measuring cost behaviour. After several months, actual cost data will be available for analysis.

Management Trainee

Your dilemma is whether to go along with the suggestion to "manage" the numbers to make the project look like it will achieve sufficient profits to allow it to be approved. You should not succumb to this suggestion. Many people will likely be affected negatively if you manage the predicted numbers and the project eventually is unprofitable. Moreover, if it does fail, it is likely an investigation would reveal that the data in the proposal were "fixed" to make it look good. Probably the only benefit from managing the numbers is some short-term payoff from pleasing the manager who proposed the project. One way to deal with this dilemma and comply with one's professional responsibilities is to prepare several analyses showing results under different assumptions, and then let senior management decide whether to go ahead in light of the information about the uncertainties of success. A point to remember is that it seldom makes sense for groups within an organization to attempt to deceive each other. Major decisions often affect many people in addition to those who make them, and their effects can linger for a long time.

Marketing Manager

You must first compute the level of sales required to achieve the desired net income. Then you must conduct sensitivity analyses by varying the price, sales mix, and cost estimates. Results from the sensitivity analysis will provide information that you can use to assess the possibility of reaching the target sales levels based on the price and sales mix estimates. For instance, you may then have to pursue aggressive marketing strategies to push the high margin products, or you may have to cut prices to increase sales and profits, or some other suggested strategy may emerge.

GUIDANCE ANSWERS TO  Flashback

1. *b*

2. A fixed cost remains unchanged in total amount regardless of changes in volume within a relevant range.

3. The cost of raw materials is a variable cost because the total cost changes in proportion to volume changes.

4. *b*

5. The high-low method ignores all of the cost/volume data points except those corresponding to the high and low extremes.

6. *c*

7. *a*

8. ($90 − $54)/$90 = 40%

9. $90,000/40% = $225,000

10. The three basic assumptions are: (1) selling price per unit is constant; (2) variable costs per unit are constant; and (3) fixed costs are constant.

11. *a* Before-tax income = $120,000/(1 − .20) = $150,000

$$\frac{\$50,000 + \$120,000 + (\$150,000 \times 20\%)}{25\%} = \$800,000$$

12. If the contribution margin ratio decreases by half, unit sales would have to double.

13. The margin of safety is the excess of the predicted sales level over its break-even sales level.

14. *c* Selling price of a composite unit:

2 units of X @ $5 per unit	$10
1 unit of Y @ $4 per unit	4
Selling price of a composite unit......................	$14

Variable costs of a composite unit:

2 units of X @ $2 per unit	$ 4
1 unit of Y @ $2 per unit	2
Variable costs of a composite unit	$ 6
Contribution margin per composite unit.................	$ 8

15. It must be assumed that the sales mix remains unchanged at all sales levels in the relevant range.

Demonstration Problem

Sporting Caps Co. produces and sells sporting caps for different sports activities. The fixed costs of operating the company are estimated at $150,000 per month, and the variable costs for caps are $5 per unit. The caps are sold at $8 per unit. The fixed costs provide a production capacity of up to 100,000 caps per month.

Required

1. Use formulas to compute the following:
   a. Contribution margin per cap.
   b. Break-even point in terms of the number of caps sold.
   c. Amount of profit at 30,000 caps sold per month (ignore income taxes).
   d. Amount of profit at 85,000 caps sold per month (ignore income taxes).
   e. Quantity of caps to be produced and sold to provide $45,000 of after-tax profits, assuming an income tax rate of 25%.

2. Draw a CVP chart for the company, showing cap sales on the horizontal axis. Identify the break-even point and the amount of pre-tax profit when the level of cap production is 75,000. (Omit the fixed cost line.)

3. Use formulas to compute the following:

   a. Contribution margin ratio.

   b. Break-even point in terms of sales dollars.

   c. Amount of net income at $250,000 of sales per month (ignore income taxes).

   d. Amount of net income at $600,000 of sales per month (ignore income taxes).

   e. Dollars of sales needed to provide $45,000 of after-tax income, assuming an income tax rate of 25%.

Planning the Solution

○ Find the formulas in the chapter for the required items concerning volumes expressed in units and solve them using the original data given in the problem.

○ Draw a CVP chart that reflects the facts given in the problem. The horizontal axis should plot the volume in units up to 100,000, and the vertical axis should plot the total dollars up to $800,000. Plot the total cost line as upward-sloping, starting at the fixed cost level ($150,000) on the vertical axis and increasing until it reaches $650,000 at the maximum volume of 100,000 units. Verify that the break-even point (where the two lines cross) equals the amount you computed in Part 1.

○ Find the formulas in the chapter for the required items concerning volumes expressed in dollars and solve them using the original data given in the problem.

SOLUTION TO Demonstration Problem

1. a. Contribution margin per cap $= $ Selling price per unit $-$ Variable cost per unit
      $= \$8 - \$5 = \$3$

   b. Break-even point in caps $= \dfrac{\text{Fixed costs}}{\text{Contribution margin per cap}} = \dfrac{\$150,000}{\$3} = 50,000$ caps

   c. Net income at 30,000 caps sold $=$ (Units $\times$ Contribution margin per unit) $-$ Fixed costs
      $= (30,000 \times \$3) - \$150,000 = -\$60,000$ (a loss)

   d. Net income at 85,000 caps sold $=$ (Units $\times$ Contribution margin per unit) $-$ Fixed costs
      $= (85,000 \times \$3) - \$150,000 = \$105,000$ net income

   e. Pre-tax income $= \dfrac{\$45,000}{75\%} = \$60,000$

   Income taxes $= \$60,000 \times 25\% = \$15,000$

   Units needed for $45,000 income $= \dfrac{\text{Fixed costs} + \text{Net income} + \text{Income taxes}}{\text{Contribution margin per cap}}$

   $= \dfrac{\$150,000 + \$45,000 + \$15,000}{\$3}$

   $= 70,000$ caps

2. CVP chart:

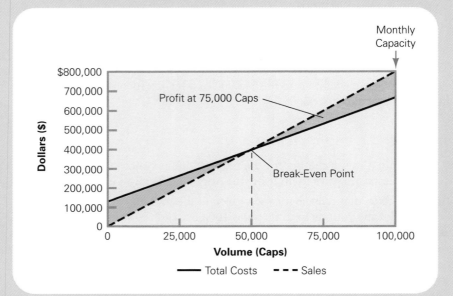

3. a. Contribution
margin ratio $= \dfrac{\text{Contribution margin per unit}}{\text{Selling price per unit}} = \dfrac{\$3}{\$8} = .375$, or 37.5%

b. Break-even point
in dollars $= \dfrac{\text{Fixed costs}}{\text{Contribution margin ratio}} = \dfrac{\$150{,}000}{37.5\%} = \$400{,}000$

c. Net income at
sales of \$250,000 $= (\text{Sales} \times \text{Contribution margin ratio}) - \text{Fixed costs}$
$= (\$250{,}000 \times 37.5\%) - \$150{,}000$
$= -\$56{,}250 \text{ (loss)}$

d. Net income at
sales of \$600,000 $= (\text{Sales} \times \text{Contribution margin ratio}) - \text{Fixed costs}$
$= (\$600{,}000 \times 37.5\%) - \$150{,}000$
$= \$75{,}000 \text{ income}$

e. Dollars of sales
to have \$45,000
income after taxes $= \dfrac{\text{Fixed costs} + \text{Net income} + \text{Income taxes}}{\text{Contribution margin ratio}}$

$= \dfrac{\$150{,}000 + \$45{,}000 + \$15{,}000}{37.5\%} = \$560{,}000$

Glossary

Break-even point The unique sales level at which a company neither earns a profit nor incurs a loss. (p. 1308)

Composite unit A specific number of units of each product in proportion to the expected sales mix. Multi-product CVP analysis treats this composite unit like a single product. (p. 1316).

Contribution margin per unit The amount that the sale of one unit contributes toward recovering fixed costs and profit. (p. 1308)

Contribution margin ratio The contribution margin per unit expressed as a percentage of the product's selling price. (p. 1309)

Cost-volume-profit analysis The first step in the planning phase is predicting the volume of activity, the costs to be incurred, revenues to be received, and profits to be earned. (p. 1298)

Cost-volume-profit chart A graphic representation of the cost-volume-profit relationships. (p. 1309)

Curvilinear cost A cost that changes with volume but not at a constant rate like pure variable costs. (p. 1301)

Estimated line of cost behaviour A line on a scatter diagram drawn to identify the historical relationship between cost and sales volume. (p. 1303)

Fixed cost A cost that remains unchanged in total amount regardless of changes in output volume within a relevant range. (p. 1299)

High-low method A method for drawing an estimated line of cost behaviour which uses cost data corresponding to the high and low sales volumes. (p. 1303)

Least-squares regression A statistical method for deriving an estimated line of cost behaviour that is more precise than the high-low method. (p. 1304)

Margin of safety The excess of expected sales over break-even sales. (p. 1315)

Mixed cost A cost that acts like a combination of a fixed and a variable cost. (p. 1300)

Relevant range of operation A business' normal operating range; excludes extremely high and low volumes that are not likely to be encountered. (p. 1299)

Sales mix The ratio of the volumes of the various products sold by a company. (p. 1316)

Scatter diagram A graph used to display data about past cost behaviours and volumes for each period as points on a diagram. (p. 1302)

Step-wise cost A cost that remains fixed over limited ranges of volumes but increases by a lump sum when volume increases beyond maximum amounts. (p. 1300)

Variable cost A cost that changes in proportion to changes in activity volume. (p. 1300)

Online **LearningCentre** with POWERWEB

For more study tools, quizzes, and problem material,
refer to the Online Learning Centre at
www.mcgrawhill.ca/college/larson

Questions

1. Why is cost-volume-profit analysis used?

2. What is a variable cost? Identify two variable costs.

3. When volume increases, do variable costs per unit increase, decrease, or stay the same within the relevant range of activity? Why?

4. When volume increases, do fixed costs per unit increase, decrease, or stay the same within the relevant range of activity? Why?

5. How do step-wise costs and curvilinear costs differ?

6. In performing a conventional CVP analysis for a manufacturing company, what simplifying assumption is usually made about the volume of production and the volume of sales?

7. What two factors tend to justify classifying all costs as either fixed or variable even though individual costs might not behave perfectly consistently with these classifications?

8. How does assuming a relevant range affect cost-volume-profit analysis?

9. List three ways to identify cost behaviour.

10. How can a scatter diagram be used in identifying the behaviour of a company's costs?

11. In CVP analysis, what is the estimated profit at the break-even point?

12. Assume that a straight line on a CVP chart intersects the vertical axis at the level of fixed costs and has a positive slope, such that it rises with each additional unit of volume by the amount of the variable costs per unit. What would this line represent?

13. Why are fixed costs depicted as a horizontal line on a CVP chart?

14. Two similar companies each have sales of $20,000 and total costs of $15,000 for a month. Company A's total costs include $10,000 of variable costs and $5,000 of fixed costs. If Company B's total costs include $4,000 of variable costs and $11,000 of fixed costs, which company will enjoy a greater profit if sales double?

15. _____ ___ _____ measures the expected sales in excess of the sales at the break-even point.

16. Consider the process of manufacturing hats for sale during the Olympic games. Identify some of the variable and fixed product costs associated with that process. [Hint, your costs are limited to product costs.]

17. Reebok is thinking of expanding production of it most popular walking shoe by 65%. Do you expect its variable costs to stay within the relevant range? Explain.

Quick Study

QS 25-1
Identify cost behaviour

LO[1]

Following are four series of costs measured at various volume levels. Examine each series and identify which is fixed, variable, and step-wise.

Volume (Units)	Series 1	Series 2	Series 3
0	$ -0-	$450	$ 800
100	800	450	800
200	1,600	450	800
300	2,400	450	1,600
400	3,200	450	1,600
500	4,000	450	2,400
600	4,800	450	$2,400

QS 25-2
Identify cost behaviour

LO[1]

For each of the following, determine whether it would best be described as a fixed, variable, or mixed cost:
a. Taxes on factory building.
b. Shipping expense.
c. Wages of an assembly-line worker paid on the basis of acceptable units produced.
d. Factory supervisor's salary.
e. Maintenance of factory machinery
f. Rubber used in manufacture of tennis shoes.

QS 25-3
Identify cost behaviour

LO[1]

Wilford Company produced 1,600 units of its product in July and 1,700 units in August. The following information relates to three different classifications:

Classification	July	August
1	$18,500	$18,500
2	49,000	50,400
3	67,200	71,400

State whether each of the above classifications of costs are fixed, variable, or mixed.

QS 25-4
Identify cost behaviour

LO[1,2]

The following scatter diagram reflects past maintenance hours and corresponding maintenance costs:

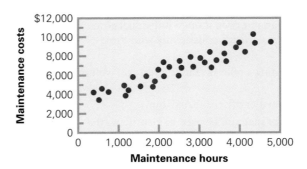

Draw an estimated line of cost behaviour and determine the fixed and variable components of maintenance costs.

Given the cost formula Y = $15,000 + $6X compute the total cost at an activity level of 9,000 units.

Brennen Company manufactures and sells a product for $50 per unit. Fixed costs for the period total $225,000 and variable costs are $30 per unit. Determine the (a) contribution margin per unit and (b) the break-even point in units.

QS 25-6
Find contribution margin and
BE in units

LO^4

Refer to QS 25-6. Determine the (a) contribution margin ratio and (b) the break-even point in dollars.

QS 25-7
Find contribution margin ratio
and BE in dollars

LO^4

Which of the following is one of the assumptions that underlie cost-volume-profit analyses?
a. Selling price per unit must change in proportion to the number of units sold during the planning period.
b. All costs have approximately the same relevant range.
c. For costs classified as variable, the actual costs per unit of output must change constantly.
d. For costs classified as fixed, the actual costs per unit of output must remain constant.

Refer to QS 25-6. Assume that Brennen Company is subject to a combined federal and provincial income tax rate of 40%. Compute the units of product that must be sold to earn after-tax income of $630,000.

Pepper Company manufactures and sells two products, toasters and mixers, in the ratio of 5:3. Fixed costs are $835,125 and the contribution margin per composite unit is $85. What is the number of mixers that will be sold at the break-even point?

Exercises

Exercise 25-1
Identifying categories of cost behaviour

LO[1]

The left column presents the names of several categories of costs. The right column presents short definitions of those costs. In the blank space beside each of the numbers in the right column, write the letter of the cost described by the definition.

a. Fixed cost

b. Mixed cost

c. Variable cost

d. Curvilinear cost

e. Step variable cost

f. Total cost

_____ 1. This cost is the combined amount of all the other costs.

_____ 2. This cost increases in direct proportion to increases in volume because its amount is constant for each unit produced.

_____ 3. This cost increases when volume increases, but the increase is not constant for each unit produced.

_____ 4. This cost remains the same over all volume levels within the productive capacity for the planning period.

_____ 5. This cost has a component that remains the same over all volume levels and another component that increases in direct proportion to increases in volume.

_____ 6. This cost remains constant over a limited range of volume that is less than the total productive capacity; when it reaches the end of its limited range, it increases by a lump sum and remains at that level until another limited range is exceeded.

Exercise 25-2
Recognizing cost behaviour patterns

LO[1]

Fill in the missing items:

Sales	Variable Cost	Fixed Cost	Total Cost	Net Income	Contribution Margin
$4,000		$600		$400	
$2,800	$1,960		$2,800	-0-	
$6,200			$1,800	$4,400	$5,240

Exercise 25-3
Recognizing cost behaviour patterns

LO[1]

Following are five series of costs measured at various volume levels. Examine each series and identify which is fixed, variable, mixed, step-wise, and curvilinear:

Volume (Units)	Series A	Series B	Series C	Series D	Series E
0	$ 2,000	$3,200	$ -0-	$2,000	$4,200
400	3,000	3,700	3,200	2,000	4,200
800	6,000	4,200	6,400	2,000	4,200
1,200	11,000	4,700	9,600	4,000	4,200
1,600	17,500	5,200	12,800	4,000	4,200
2,000	19,500	5,700	16,000	6,000	4,200
2,400	20,000	6,200	19,200	6,000	4,200

The following five graphs represent various cost behaviours.

Exercise 25-4
Recognizing cost behaviour
in graphs

LO¹

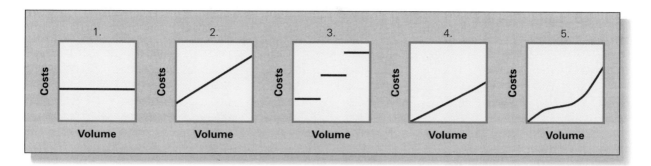

Required

a. Identify the type of cost behaviour that each graph represents—mixed, step-wise, fixed, variable, or curvilinear.

b. For each of the following items, identify the graph that best illustrates the cost behaviour described:

   (1) Plant security requires one guard for every 20 factory workers.
   (2) An addition of hourly paid workers that provides substantial gains in efficiency as a few workers are added, but gradually smaller gains in efficiency as more workers are added.
   (3) Insurance on factory machinery.
   (4) Commissions to salespersons.
   (5) Electricity charge in total that includes the standard monthly charge plus a charge for each kilowatt hour.

A company's accounting system provides the following information about its monthly sales and the amount of a specific cost in those months. Each unit sells for $500.

Exercise 25-5
Measuring cost behaviour
using a scatter diagram

LO²

Month	Sales	Cost
1	$15,000	$8,100
2	10,500	5,500
3	10,500	7,000
4	7,500	5,500
5	9,000	6,000
6	12,500	6,500

Use this data to prepare a scatter diagram. Then, draw an estimated line of cost behaviour and determine whether the cost appears to be variable, fixed, or mixed.

Exercise 25-6
Scatter diagram and cost
behaviour—15 data points

LO^2

Use the following information about monthly sales volume and the amount of a specific cost to prepare a scatter diagram. Then, draw a cost line that reflects the behaviour displayed by this cost. Finally, determine whether the cost is variable, step-wise, fixed, mixed, or curvilinear.

Period	Sales	Cost	Period	Sales	Cost
1	$38,000	$29,500	9	29,000	$19,500
2	40,000	28,000	10	16,500	12,000
3	10,000	11,500	11	12,500	12,250
4	20,500	20,000	12	36,000	27,500
5	24,500	19,500	13	14,000	13,000
6	31,500	27,500	14	22,000	20,500
7	34,000	29,500	15	19,000	13,250
8	27,500	21,500			

Exercise 25-7
High-low method of analysis

LO^2

Keating Ltd. produces a product that is becoming increasingly more popular throughout Canada. Below are the company's income statements for November and December.

	November	December
Sales...	$420,000	$450,000
Cost of goods sold	226,000	235,000
Gross margin	$194,000	$215,000
Selling and administrative expenses	106,000	108,000
Income before taxes	$ 88,000	$107,000
Income taxes (35% rate)	30,800	37,450
Net income...	$ 57,200	$ 69,550

Required
Compute the fixed and variable components of the cost of goods sold using the high-low method of analysis.

Exercise 25-8
High-low method of analysis

LO^2

Refer to Exercise 25-7. Compute the fixed and variable components of selling and administrative expenses using the high-low method of analysis.

Exercise 25-9
High-low method of analysis

$LO^{2,4}$

Refer to Exercise 25-7. Sales for January are forecasted at $500,000. Prepare an income statement for Keating Company using the contribution format.

Exercise 25-10
Computing contribution margin and break-even point

$LO^{4,5}$

Monroe Company manufactures a single product that sells for $117.60 per unit. The total variable costs of the product are $88.20 per unit and the company's annual fixed costs are $441,000. Compute each of the following for Monroe Company:
a. contribution margin per unit.
b. contribution margin ratio.
c. break-even point in units.
d. break-even point in dollars of sales.

Refer to exercise 25-10. Prepare an income statement for Monroe Company's operations showing sales, variable costs, and fixed costs at the break-even point. What amount of sales (in dollars) would be needed to break even if Monroe's fixed costs increase by $63,000?

Exercise 25-11
Income reporting and break-even analysis

LO⁷

Refer to exercise 25-10. Monroe Company's management wants to earn an annual after-tax income of $530,000. The company is subject to a combined federal and provincial income tax rate of 40%. Compute:
a. The units of product that must be sold to earn the target after-tax net income.
b. The dollars of sales that must be reached to earn the target after-tax net income.

Exercise 25-12
Computing sales required to achieve target income

LO⁷

Refer to exercise 25-10. Monroe Company's management wants to earn a **pre-tax** income of 18% of sales. Compute:
a. The dollars of sales that must be achieved to earn the target pre-tax income.
b. The units of products that must be sold to earn the target pre-tax income.

Exercise 25-13
Computing sales required to achieve target income

LO⁷

In looking ahead, the sales manager of Monroe Company (in Exercise 25-10) predicts that the annual sales of the company's product will soon reach 60,000 units even though the price will increase to $175 per unit. According to the production manager, the variable costs are expected to increase to $100 per unit but fixed costs will remain at $441,000. The company's tax adviser expects that the combined federal and provincial income tax rate will still be 40%. What amounts of before-tax and after-tax income can the company expect to earn from selling units at this expected level with these expected costs?

Exercise 25-14
Forecasted income statement

LO⁷

In predicting the events of the upcoming quarter, the management of the Techno Company thinks that it will incur a total of $375,000 of variable costs and $600,000 of fixed costs while earning a pre-tax income of $150,000. The management predicts that the contribution margin per unit will be $75. Using this information, determine (a) the total expected dollar sales for the quarter and (b) the number of units expected to be sold in the quarter.

Exercise 25-15
Unit and dollar sales using contribution margin

LO⁷

Driskel Company expects to sell 80,000 units of its product next year, which should produce total revenues of $12 million. Management predicts that the pre-tax net income for the year will be $2,400,000 and that the contribution margin per unit will be $40.

Required
Using this information, compute (a) the total expected variable costs and (b) the total expected fixed costs for next year.

Exercise 25-16
Computing variable and fixed costs

LO⁵

The management of Waterloo Company predicts that it will incur fixed costs of $600,000 next year and that the pre-tax income will be $240,000. The expected contribution margin ratio is 75%. Use this information to compute the amounts of (a) total dollar sales and (b) total variable costs.

Exercise 25-17
Computing sales and variable costs using contribution margin ratio

LO⁷

Exercise 25-18
CVP analysis using composite units

LO^8

The AA Hardware Company sells windows and doors in the ratio of 10:3 (10 windows for every 3 doors). The selling price of each window is $70 and the selling price of each door is $450. The variable cost of a window is $40 and the variable cost of a door is $290. Next year's fixed costs are expected to be $975,000. Use this information to determine:

a. the selling price of a composite unit of these products.
b. the variable costs per composite unit.
c. the break-even point in composite units.
d. the number of units of each product that will be sold at the break-even point.

Problems

Problem 25-1A
Scatter diagram and estimating cost behaviour

LO^2

Jubilee Co.'s monthly sales and cost data for its operating activities of the past year are shown below. The management of the company wants to use these data to predict future fixed and variable costs.

Period	Sales	Total Cost
1..................................	$250,000	$170,000
2..................................	190,000	130,000
3..................................	234,000	200,000
4..................................	210,000	160,000
5..................................	300,000	230,000
6..................................	210,000	170,000
7..................................	270,000	200,000
8..................................	250,000	190,000
9..................................	170,000	130,000
10.................................	200,000	180,000
11.................................	180,000	140,000
12.................................	170,000	150,000

Check figure:
Approximate slope of cost line, $0.66 per sales dollar

Required
1. Prepare a scatter diagram for Jubilee Co. with sales volume (in $) plotted on the horizontal (scale this axis in $40,000 intervals) and with total cost plotted on the vertical axis.
2. Estimate the line of cost behaviour by a visual inspection and draw it on the scatter diagram. (Assume a linear relationship, which means that you should draw a straight line on the graph.)
3. Using the estimated line of cost behaviour and the assumption that the future will be like the past, predict the amount of monthly fixed costs for Jubilee Co. Also, predict future variable cost per sales dollar.
4. Use the estimated line of cost behaviour to predict future total costs when the sales volume is (a) $200,000 and (b) $280,000.

Problem 25-2A
Completing CVP analyses, including a chart

$LO^{4,5}$

Grove Company manufactures and markets a number of rope products. Management is considering the future of Product XT, a special rope for hang gliding, which has not been as profitable as planned. Because this product is manufactured and marketed independently from the other products, its total costs can be precisely measured. The plan for the next year calls for a selling price of $480 per unit. The fixed costs for the year are expected to be $300,000, up to the maximum capacity of 2,500 units. The forecasted variable costs are $180 per unit.

Check figure:
Requirement 4: Pre-tax target income, $330,000

Required
1. Predict the break-even point for Product XT in terms of (a) units and (b) dollars of sales.
2. Prepare a CVP chart for Product XT. Use 2,500 as the maximum number of units sold on the graph and $1,200,000 as the maximum number of sales dollars.
3. Prepare an income statement showing sales, fixed costs, and variable costs for Product XT at the break-even point.
4. Determine the sales volume in dollars that the company must achieve to earn a $231,000 income from Product XT, after income taxes are assessed at 30%.
5. Determine the after-tax income that the company would earn from sales of $1,200,000.

In 2004, Morgan Company sold 15,000 units of its only product and incurred a $84,000 loss (ignoring income taxes), as follows:

Morgan Company Income Statement For Year Ended December 31, 2004	
Sales	$750,000
Variable costs	450,000
Contribution margin	$300,000
Fixed costs	384,000
Net loss	$ (84,000)

During a planning session for 2005's activities, the production manager has pointed out that variable costs can be reduced 50% by installing a machine that automates several operations presently being done by hand. To obtain these savings, the company must increase its annual fixed costs by $120,000. The maximum capacity of the system would be 30,000 units per year.

Required

1. Compute the 2004 break-even point in dollar sales.
2. Compute the dollar break-even point for 2005 under the assumption that the new machine is installed.
3. Prepare a CVP chart for 2005 under the assumption that the new machine is installed.
4. Prepare a forecasted income statement for 2005 that shows the expected results with the new machine installed. Assume that there will be no change in the selling price and no change in the number of units sold. The combined federal and provincial income tax rate is 30%.
5. Compute the sales level required to earn $147,000 of after-tax income in 2005 with the new machine installed and with no change in the selling price.
6. Prepare a forecasted income statement that shows the results at the sales level computed in part 5.

Problem 25-3A
Income statements to confirm projections

LO^7

Check figure:
Requirement 5: Unit sales, 20,400 units

OMR Company produces and sells two products, A and B. These products are manufactured in separate factories and marketed through completely different channels. Thus, they do not have any shared costs. Last year OMR sold 50,000 units of each product. The following income statements describe the financial results:

Problem 25-4A
Break-even analysis comparing different cost structures

LO^7

	Product A	Product B
Sales	$800,000	$800,000
Costs:		
Fixed costs	$100,000	$560,000
Variable costs	560,000	100,000
Total costs	$660,000	$660,000
Income before taxes	$140,000	$140,000
Income taxes (32% rate)	44,800	44,800
Net income	$ 95,200	$ 95,200

Required

Preparation component:

1. Compute the break-even point in dollars for each product.
2. Prepare a CVP chart for each product. Use 80,000 as the annual capacity for each factory.
3. Assume that the company expects the sales of each product to decline to 33,000 units in the upcoming year, even though the price will remain unchanged. Prepare a forecasted income statement that shows the expected profits from the two products. Follow the format of the preceding statement and assume that any loss before taxes results in a tax savings.
4. Assume that the company expects the sales of each product to increase to 64,000 units in the upcoming year, even though the price will remain unchanged. Prepare a forecasted income statement that shows the expected profits from the two products. Follow the format of the preceding statement.

Analysis component:

5. If sales were to greatly decrease, which of these products would experience the greater loss? Why?
6. Describe some factors that might have created the different cost structures for these two products.

Problem 25-5A
Analyzing the effects of price and volume changes on profits

LO⁷

This year, Kirby Company sold 35,000 units of product at $16 per unit. Manufacturing and selling the product required $120,000 of fixed manufacturing costs and $180,000 of fixed selling and administrative expenses. This year's variable costs and expenses per unit were:

Material	$4.00
Direct labour (paid on the basis of completed units)	3.00
Variable manufacturing overhead costs..................................	0.40
Variable selling and administrative expenses	0.20

Next year the company will use new raw material that is easier to work with and cheaper than the old material. A switch to the new material will decrease material costs by 60% and direct labour costs can be decreased by 40%. The new material will not affect the product's quality or marketability. The next set of decisions concerns the marketing strategy to be used. Because the factory's output is creeping up to its annual capacity of 40,000 units, some consideration is being given to increasing the selling price to reduce the number of units sold. At this point, two strategies have been identified. Under Plan 1, the company will keep the price at the current level and sell the same volume as this year. This plan increases profits because of the materials change. Under Plan 2, the product's price will be increased by 25%, but unit sales volume will fall only 10%. Under both Plan 1 and Plan 2, all of the fixed costs and variable costs (per unit) will be exactly the same.

Required

1. Compute the break-even point in dollars for Plan 1 and Plan 2.
2. Prepare CVP charts for both Plan 1 and Plan 2.
3. Prepare side-by-side condensed forecasted income statements showing the anticipated results of Plan 1 and Plan 2. The statements should show sales, total fixed costs, total variable costs and expenses, income before taxes, income taxes (30% rate), and net income.

The following budgeted income statement has been prepared for Boutlier Corporation based on a 15% sales commission paid to independent sales agents. The independent sales agents are seeking to raise the sales commission from the current 15% to 20% and Boutlier is considering the option of hiring its own sales agents.

Problem 25-6A
Break-even analysis with decision

LO⁷

Boutlier Corporation Budgeted Income Statement For Year Ending December 31, 2004		
Sales		$1,400,000
Cost of goods sold (all variable)		840,000
Gross profit		$560,000
Selling and administrative:		
Variable (commission only)	$210,000	
Fixed	14,000	224,000
Income before taxes		$336,000
Income tax expense (25%)		84,000
Net income		$252,000

If Boutlier chooses to hire its own sales agents the company expects to pay an annual salary of $84,000 to a sales manager and $42,000 to each of three salespeople. The sales people will also each receive a commission of 5% of sales. The company is expected to operate within the relevant range.

Required

1. Calculate the break-even point in sales dollars for Boutlier for the year ending December 31, 2004.
2. If Boutlier employs its own salespeople, what would be the break-even point in sales dollars for the year ending December 31, 2004?
3. Calculate the volume of sales dollars required for the year ending December 31, 2004, to yield the same net income as reported on the projected income statement if Boutlier continues to use the independent sales agents and agrees to their demand for a 20% sales commission.
4. Compute the estimated dollar sales volume at which Boutlier would be indifferent between employing its own salespeople or continuing to use the independent sales agents paying them a 20% commission.

Check figure:
Requirement 1: Estimated break-even point, $56,000

Barton Manufacturing manufactures products only when a customer's order is received and then it is shipped immediately after it is made. Barton's break-even point was $1,890,000. On sales of $1,680,000, their income statement showed a gross profit of $140,000, direct materials cost of $560,000, and direct labour costs of $700,000. The contribution margin was $140,000 and variable manufacturing overhead was $140,000.

Problem 25-7A
Break-even with decision

LO³,⁷

Required

Calculate:
a. Variable selling and administrative expense.
b. Fixed manufacturing overhead.
c. Fixed selling and administrative expense.
d. Assume that fixed manufacturing overhead was $140,000 and the fixed selling and administrative expense was $112,000. The marketing vice president feels that if the company increased its advertising, sales could be increased by 25%.What is the maximum increased advertising cost the company can incur and still report the same income as before the advertising expenditure?

Check figure:
Part b: Fixed manufacturing overhead, $140,000

Problem 25-8A
Break-even analysis with composite units

LO⁸

Check figure:
New plan break-even point, 639 composite units

Peabody Company manufactures and sells three products, Red, White, and Blue. Their individual selling prices are: Red, $55 per unit; White, $85 per unit; and Blue, $110 per unit. The variable costs of manufacturing and selling these products are: Red, $40 per unit; White $60 per unit; and Blue, $80 per unit. Their sales mix is a ratio of 5:4:2 (Red:White:Blue). Annual fixed costs shared by all three products are $150,000. One item of raw materials is used in manufacturing all three products. Management has learned that a new material is of equal quality and less costly. The new material would reduce the variable costs as follows: Red by $10; White by $20, and Blue by $10. But, the new material requires new equipment, which will increase annual fixed costs by $20,000. (In preparing your answers always round up to the nearest whole composite unit.)

Required
1. If the company continues to use the old material, determine the company's break-even point in dollars and units of each product that would be sold at the break-even point.
2. If the company decides to use the new material, determine the company's new break-even point in dollars and units of each product that would be sold at the break-even point.

Analysis component:
3. What insight does this analysis offer to management in long-term planning?

Alternate Problems

Problem 25-1B
Scatter diagram with estimating cost behaviour

LO²

Inland Co.'s monthly sales and cost data for its operating activities of the past year are shown below. The management of the company wants to use these data to predict future fixed and variable costs.

Period	Sales	Total Cost
1	$390	$194
2	250	174
3	210	146
4	310	178
5	190	162
6	430	220
7	290	186
8	370	210
9	270	170
10	170	130
11	350	190
12	230	158

Required
1. Prepare a scatter diagram with sales volume (in $) plotted on the horizontal axis and with total cost plotted on the vertical axis.
2. Estimate the line of cost behaviour by a visual inspection and draw it on the scatter diagram. (Assume a linear relation, which means that you should draw a straight line on the graph.)
3. Using the estimated line of cost behaviour and the assumption that the future will be like the past, predict the amount of monthly fixed costs for Inland Co. Also, predict future variable cost per sales dollar.
4. Use the estimated line of cost behaviour to predict future total costs when the sales volume is (a) $150 and (b) $250.

Saskatoon Company manufactures and markets a number of products. Management is considering the future of one product, electronic keyboards, which has not been as profitable as planned. Because this product is manufactured and marketed independently from the other products, its total costs can be precisely measured. The plan for the next year calls for a selling price of $225 per unit. The fixed costs for the year are expected to be $30,000, up to the maximum capacity of 700 units. The forecasted variable costs are $150 per unit.

Required
1. Predict the break-even point for keyboards in terms of (a) units and (b) dollars of sales.
2. Prepare a CVP chart for keyboards. Use 700 as the maximum number of units on the graph and $180,000 as the maximum number of sales dollars.
3. Prepare an income statement showing sales, fixed costs, and variable costs for keyboards at the break-even point.

Problem 25-2B
Completing CVP analyses, including a chart

$LO^{4,5}$

Capital Company sold 50,000 units of its only product, and incurred a $200,000 loss (ignoring taxes), for the year shown below:

Problem 25-3B
Targeting and forecasting income

LO^7

Capital Company Income Statement For Year Ended December 31, 2004	
Sales	$ 800,000
Variable costs	900,000
Contribution margin	$(100,000)
Fixed costs	100,000
Net loss	$(200,000)

During a planning session for 2005's activities, the production manager has pointed out that variable costs can be reduced 72.22% by installing a machine that automates several operations presently being done by hand. To obtain these savings, the company must increase its annual fixed costs by $200,000. The maximum capacity of the system would be 80,000 units per year.

Required
1. Compute the break-even point in dollar sales for 2004.
2. Compute the break-even point in dollar sales for 2005 assuming the machine is installed. (Round the change in variable cost to a whole number.)
3. Prepare a forecasted income statement for 2005 that shows the expected results with the new machine installed. Assume that there will be no change in the selling price and no change in the number of units sold. The combined federal and provincial income tax rate is 40%.
4. Compute the sales level required to earn $300,000 of after-tax income in 2005 with the new machine installed and and no change in the selling price.
5. Prepare a forecasted income statement that shows the results at the sales level computed in part (4).

Check figure:
Requirement 4: Required sales, 72,728 units

Problem 25-4B
Break-even analysis comparing different cost structures

LO⁷

Model Co. produces and sells two products, L and M. These products are manufactured in separate factories and marketed through different channels. This year, Model Co. sold 120,000 units of each product. The following income statements describe the financial results:

	Product L	Product M
Sales	$3,000,000	$3,000,000
Variable costs	1,800,000	600,000
Contribution margin	$1,200,000	$2,400,000
Fixed costs	600,000	1,800,000
Income before taxes	$ 600,000	$ 600,000
Income taxes (35% rate)	210,000	210,000
Net income	$ 390,000	$ 390,000

Required

Preparation component:
1. Compute the break-even point in dollars for each product.
2. Assume that the company expects the sales of each product to decline to 104,000 units in the upcoming year, even though the price will remain unchanged. Prepare a forecasted income statement that shows the expected profits from the two products. Follow the format of the preceding statement.
3. Assume that the company expects the sales of each product to increase to 190,000 units in the upcoming year, even though the price will remain unchanged. Prepare a forecasted income statement that shows the expected profits from the two products. Follow the format of the preceding statement.

Analysis component:
4. If sales were to greatly increase, which of these products would experience the greater increase in profit? Why?
5. Describe some factors that might have created the different cost structures for these two products.

Problem 25-5B
Analyzing the effects of price and volume changes on profits

LO⁷

This year, White Company earned a disappointing 4.2% after-tax return on sales from marketing 100,000 units of its only product, watch bands. The company buys watch bands in bulk and repackages them in bags for resale at the price of $25 per unit. White incurred these costs this year:

Cost of bulk product for 100,000 packages	$1,000,000
Packaging materials and other variable packaging costs	100,000
Fixed costs	1,250,000
Income tax rate	30%

The marketing manager has reported that next year's results will be the same as this year's unless some changes are made. The manager predicts the company can increase the number of units sold by 80% if it reduces the selling price by 20% and upgrades the packaging. The change would increase variable packaging costs by 25%. Increased sales would allow the company to take advantage of a 20% quantity purchase discount on the cost of the bulk purchase price. Neither the packaging nor the volume change would affect fixed costs, which provide an annual capacity of 200,000 units.

Check figure:
Net income under new strategy, $479,500

Required
1. Compute the dollar break-even points for selling watch bands under the (a) existing price strategy and (b) new strategy that alters both selling price and variable costs.
2. Prepare side-by-side condensed forecasted income statements showing the anticipated results of (a) continuing the existing strategy and (b) changing to the new strategy. Determine whether the after-tax return on sales will be changed by the new strategy.

The following budgeted income statement has been prepared for Gautier Corporation based on a 12% sales commission paid to independent sales agents. The independent sales agents are seeking to raise the sales commission from the current 12% to 15% and Gautier is considering the option of hiring its own sales agents.

Problem 25-6B
Break-even analysis decision

LO^{3,7}

Gautier Corporation Pro Forma Income Statement For Year Ending December 31, 2004		
Sales		$1,960,000
Cost of goods sold (all variable)		1,176,000
Gross profit		$784,000
Selling and administrative:		
Variable (commission only)	$235,200	
Fixed	21,100	256,300
Income before taxes		$527,700
Income tax expense (25%)		131,925
Net income		$395,775

If Gautier chooses to hire its own sales agents the company expects to pay an annual salary of $107,600 to a sales manager and $48,000 to each of three salespeople. Thee sales people will also each receive a commission of 4% of sales. The company is expected to operate within the relevant range.

Required

1. Calculate the break-even point in sales dollars for Gautier for the year ending December 31, 2004.
2. If Gautier employs its own salespeople, what would be the break-even point in sales dollars for the year ending December 31, 2004?
3. Calculate the volume of sales dollars required for the year ending December 31, 2004, to yield the same net income as reported on the projected income statement if Gautier continues to use the independent sales agents and agrees to their demand for a 15% sales commission.
4. Compute the estimated dollar sales volume at which Gautier would be indifferent between employing its own salespeople or continuing to use the independent sales agents paying them a 15% commission.

Reeves Company has a policy of not carrying inventories. The company's breakeven point is $1,050,000. Reeves reported a gross profit of $910,000 at a sales level of $910,000. Direct material costs were $280,000 and direct labour costs amounted to $350,000. Variable manufacturing overhead was $70,000 and the contribution margin was $182,000.

Problem 25-7B
Break-even with decision

LO^{3,7}

Required

Calculate:
a. Variable selling and administrative expense.
b. Fixed manufacturing overhead.
c. Fixed selling and administrative expense.
d. Assume that the fixed manufacturing overhead was $98,000 and the fixed selling and administrative expense was $91,000. The vice president of marketing feels that if the company increased its advertising, sales could be increased by 30%. What is the maximum increased advertising cost the company can incur and still report the same income as before the advertising expenditure if advertising is expected to increase sales by 30%?

Problem 25-8B
Break-even analysis with composite units

LO⁸

Hudgens Company manufactures and sells three products, Product 1, Product 2, and Product 3. Their individual selling prices are: Product 1, $225 per unit; Product 2, $150 per unit; and Product 3, $120 per unit. The variable costs of manufacturing and selling the products are: Product 1, $120 per unit; Product 2, $102 per unit; and Product 3, $75 per unit. Their sales mix is a ratio of 2:5:8, and the annual fixed costs shared by all three products are $793,800.

    Management is considering purchasing a new machine that will be used in the manufacture of Products 2 and 3. If the machine is purchased, fixed manufacturing costs will increase by $81,000. However, variable costs of Product 2 will decrease by $18 per unit, and the variable costs of Product 3 will decrease by $9 per unit.

Check figure:
New plan break-even point, 980 composite units

Required
1. If the company continues to use the old machine, determine the company's break-even point in both sales dollars and sales units of each individual product.
2. If the company purchases the new machine, determine the company's new break-even point in both sales dollars and sales units of each individual product.

Analysis component:
3. What insight does this problem offer management in planning for long term planning?

Analytical and Review Problems

A & R 25-1

Scott Company has decided to introduce a new product that can be manufactured by either a computer-assisted manufacturing system (CAMS) or a labour-intensive production system (LIPS). The manufacturing method will not affect the quality of the product. The estimated manufacturing costs of each system are as follows:

	CAMS	LIPS
Direct material.........................	$7.00	$7.84
Direct labour............................	0.5DHL @ $16.80 = $8.40	0.8DHL @ $12.60 = $10.08
Variable overhead....................	0.5DHL @ $8.40 = $4.20	0.8DHL @ $8.40 = $6.72
Fixed overhead........................	$3,416,000	$1,848,000

    These costs are directly traceable to the new product line. They would not be incurred if the new product were not produced. The company's marketing research department has recommended an introductory unit sales price of $42. Selling expenses are estimated to be $700,000 annually plus $2.80 for each unit sold. (Ignore income taxes.)

Required
a. Calculate the estimated break-even point in annual unit sales of the new product if the company uses the (i) computer-assisted manufacturing system, or (ii) labour-intensive production system.
b. Determine the annual unit sales volume at which the firm would be indifferent between the two manufacturing methods.

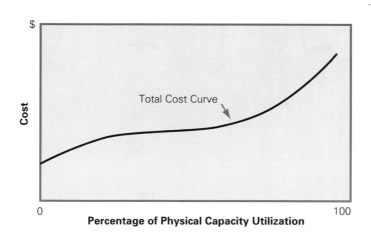

Required

Utilizing the above diagram of cost/volume relationship, demonstrate your understanding of (a) the relevant range and (b) cost behaviour. (Hint: Identify the relevant ranges by lettering the appropriate points on the diagram.)

Fixed and variable costs are also viewed as capacity and activity costs.

Required

Discuss the basis for the alternate view of fixed and variable costs.

Both Nike and Reebok make basketball shoes that are widely sold in Canada and throughout the world, yet one company is often more profitable than the other in sales of these shoes. We want to understand how this is possible. Each company makes decisions about purchasing assets to produce basketball shoes, similar to the decisions described in the chapter. In particular, fixed asset and variable cost decisions determine the break-even point and profitability of the company.

Required

1. Using the data below, compute the monthly cost per pair of basketball shoes for Nike and Reebok. (Assume sales equals production volume.)

	NIKE	Reebok
Estimated pair sales	10,000 @ $60.	10,000 @ $60.
Material/unit	$10/unit	$10/unit
Direct labour/unit	$30/unit	$34/unit
Factory rent/month	$30,000	$10,000
Factory equipment (amortization)	$50,000	$60,000

2. Compare and explain why one company is more profitable than the other.
3. If sales sharply decline, which company will be more profitable (computations are unnecessary)?

Master Budgets and Planning

Easy Rider

Edmonton—Biker is a high-tech and unconventional manufacturer of coil springs. Its target customers are domestic and international manufacturers of sports bikes, both bicycles and motorcycles. Biker has developed and patented a unique spring design that substantially cushions the jolts of on- and off-road biking. The growth in mountain bikes has further fueled its double-digit sales growth over the past five years.

Candy Bergman, with brother Michael, launched the company from her parents' garage only 8 short years ago. "Dad loved off-road biking, and really got us hooked," says Bergman, now 29. "But the ride was horrible, and we started tinkering with the springs. Dad was an auto mechanic and got us on the right track."

But Biker came close to folding. "We didn't run a profit until our fourth year," complains Bergman. "Both Michael and I had other jobs, and the money demands were almost too much."

It wasn't until Biker's fourth year that they turned a profit. Bergman points to several problems, but one was budgeting. "Our goal is to give our customers a better ride, at less cost," says Bergman, "but this demands careful budgeting and planning. And we didn't do either well."

But Bergman learned fast. "We now run budgets for everything," says Bergman. "Estimates of the demand for sports bikes, and our sales in particular, enable us to forecast sales and prepare budgets for the next three years. We know things change, but at least we know what happens when they change." While Bergman is far from a numbers person, she knows the importance of income and cash flow. She points to the sales budget as the starting point. "I don't pay employees, customers do. If we don't serve customers, none of us gets paid," adds Bergman. "What's the use of other budgets or plans if there's no sales? The sales budget is key." For now, Biker's ride is smooth and fast.

Learning Objectives

LO1 Explain the importance and benefits of budgeting.

LO2 Describe the process of budget administration.

LO3 Describe a master budget and the process of preparing it.

LO4 Prepare each component of a master budget and link them to the budgeting process.

LO5 Link both operating and capital expenditure budgets to budgeted financial statements.

LO6 Analyze expense planning using zero-based budgeting.

LO7 Prepare production and manufacturing budgets.

Chapter Preview

After management applies cost-volume-profit analysis in devising a strategy for future periods, it then looks to turn this strategy into action plans. These action plans are usually compiled in a master budget. The budgeting process serves several purposes, including motivating employees and effectively communicating with them. The budget process also helps coordinate a company's activities toward common goals, and is useful for evaluating actual results and management performance.

In this chapter, we explain how to prepare a master budget and use it as a formal plan for the future activities of a company. One's ability to prepare this kind of formal plan is of enormous help in starting and operating a company. It gives us a glimpse into the future and attempts to translate plans into actions. As described in the opening article, this kind of planning was crucial to the success of BIKER.

Budgeting Process

LO1 Explain the importance and benefits of budgeting.

In Chapter 21, we introduced the Planning-Implementation-Control cycle. Generally, companies formulate long-term (strategic) plans that usually span a five- to ten-year horizon, and then refine them using medium- and short-term plans. A common term used to specify the planning process is called **budgeting**. A **budget** is a formal statement of a company's plans expressed in monetary terms. Budgeting is not limited to businesses but is also undertaken by not-for-profit, government, educational, and other types of organizations.

A budget is a forward-looking document in that it attempts to capture the future activities of an organization. A focus on the future is important because management often gets consumed by day-to-day problems. A good budgeting system counteracts this tendency by formalizing the planning process. Budgeting makes planning an explicit management responsibility.

Role of Budgeting

Budgeting is a good tool for the purposes of planning, communication, and coordination, as a guide to implementation, and a basis for evaluation. For planning, managers use the budgeting process to outline the details of their ideas. A budget typically includes detailed plans with respect to sales, expenses, capital investments, and the potential impact of these plans on future financial performance.

Managers can also use the budget as a tool to communicate their plans to other employees within the organization. The use of the budget as a communication tool is important in both small and large organizations. Even though communication is much easier in a smaller organization, the use of a budget helps to ensure that every individual within the organization has the same information. As for a large organization, it serves as a tool for both communication and coordination.

Coordination is important because the different segments must carry out their activities so they are consistent with the overall objectives of the organization. Budgeting provides a way to achieve this coordination. For example, the purchasing department of a large automaker like Toyota Canada must align its purchasing plans with the plans of the production departments.

We introduced the concept of long-term, medium-term and short-term plans. A long-term plan provides a strategic road map for the future, and contains information about potential opportunities (new markets, products, investments).

A long-term plan usually covers a five- to ten-year horizon and typically includes rough estimates of future activity. On the other hand, medium- and short-term plans are much more precise; they are operational in nature and translate strategic plans into actions. Budgets, which are typically annual plans, are fairly concrete, consist of defined objectives and goals, and serve as a guide to implementing long-term plans.

Basis for Evaluation

Managers find it useful to review whether their actions are providing the results that are consistent with their plans. The budget once again provides a basis against which management can evaluate the organization's performance and take any necessary corrective actions.

Budgeted performance is potentially superior to past performance as a benchmark in deciding whether actual results trigger a need for corrective actions. Past performance is often inferior as a standard for evaluation as it fails to take into account several changes that may affect current activities. Changes in economic conditions, shifts in competitive advantages within the industry, new product developments, increased or decreased advertising, and other factors all reduce the usefulness of comparisons with past results. This is particularly true for industries that encounter rapid technological changes.

Budgeted performance levels are computed after careful analysis and research that attempts to anticipate and adjust for changes in important company, industry, and economic factors. This usually means budgets provide a superior basis for evaluating performance. This gives management a more effective control and monitoring system.

Employee Motivation

Budgeting provides standards for evaluating performance; it can affect the attitudes of employees who are evaluated. The budgeting process can be used to have a positive effect on employees' attitudes, but it can also yield a negative one if the process is handled without care. Budgeted levels of performance, for instance, must be realistic to avoid discouraging employees. Also, personnel who will be evaluated should be consulted and involved in preparing the budget to increase their commitment to meeting it. This practice of involving employees in the budgeting process is known as participatory budgeting. Evaluations of performance also must allow the affected employees to explain the reasons for apparent performance deficiencies. Accounting reports don't tell the whole story.

We can identify three important guidelines in the budgeting process:

1. Employees affected by a budget should be consulted when it is prepared.
2. Goals reflected in a budget should be attainable.
3. Evaluations of performance should be made carefully with opportunities to explain any failures.

Budgeting can be a positive motivating force when these guidelines are followed. Budgeted performance levels can provide goals for employees to attain or even exceed as they carry out their responsibilities.

Regardless of how well the budgeting process is carried out, an exclusive focus on the budget can sometimes lead managers to become myopic.

Judgement Call

Answer—p. 1362

Budgeting Staffer

You are working in the budget office of a company. You learn that earnings for the current quarter are going to be far below the budgeted amount announced in the press. You learn that one of your superiors, who is also aware of the impending news of the earnings shortfall, has decided to accept a management position with a competitor. Before his departure is announced to the public, he decides to sell all shares of the company that you and he are working for. His leaving will hurt your company's ability to improve earnings. Does this situation present ethical concerns or responsibilities to you? Is there anything you would do?

Budget Administration

Annual planning is an important activity in most organizations. Budgeting is usually an integral part of this annual planning process, and therefore requires careful administration.

Budget Committee

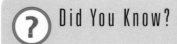

Describe the process of budget administration.

In a small business the owner-manager has full responsibility for preparing the budget. Often the owner-manager will consult with an accountant about how to go about the budgeting process. The owner-manager can explain goals to employees and quickly obtain feedback about any matters that might need adjusting.

In larger organizations the task of preparing a budget should not be the sole responsibility of any one department. Similarly, the budget should not be simply handed down as top management's final word. Instead, budget figures and budget estimates usually are more useful if developed through a *bottom up* process. Without active employee involvement in preparing budget figures, there is a risk these employees will feel as if the numbers fail to reflect their special problems and needs.

While most budgets should be developed by a bottom up process, the budgeting system also requires central guidance. This guidance is provided by a budget committee of department heads and other executives responsible for ensuring that budgeted amounts are realistic. Communication between the originating department and the budget committee should continue as needed to ensure that both parties accept the budget as reasonable, attainable, and desirable. Budgeting can often consume a large amount of management's time. Therefore, it is very important to find ways to improve the budgeting process.

The budget committee is responsible for settling any disputes that may occur between different units within an organization. Sometimes fear and distrust lead to internal conflict as business segments compete for limited budgeted resources. An awareness of potential turf battles among segment managers is an important step in preventing any dysfunctional behaviour that might otherwise occur.

(?) Did You Know?

Budgeting for Safety

For 2003, the City of Calgary budgeted an amount of $1.5 billion for its operating expenses. Over 50% of the budgeted expenses pertained to three categories: safety (police, fire, and EMS—21.6%), transportation (public transportation and roads—17.3%) and water (wastewater and waterworks—12.6%). The remaining amount was allocated among nine other expense categories.

SOURCE: http://www.calgary.ca/DocGallery/BU/finance/2003budget_finalization_present.pdf

Budget Horizon

One important decision pertains to an organization's budget horizon or budgeting cycle. The most common budgeting cycle is one year. This means that an organization reviews its budget at least annually. Managers use a report such as the one in Exhibit 26.1 to compare actual performance with the budget. This report shows actual results, budgeted numbers, and any differences or *variances*, which we discuss in Chapter 27.

Eccentric Music Income Statement with Variations from Budget For Month Ended April 30, 2004			
	Actual	**Budget**	**Variance**
Sales	$63,500	$60,000	$+3,500
Less:			
Sales returns and allowances	1,800	1,700	+100
Sales discounts	1,200	1,150	+50
Net sales	60,500	57,150	+3,350
Cost of goods sold:			
Merchandise inventory, April 1, 2001	42,000	44,000	−2,000
Purchases, net	39,100	38,000	+1,100
Transportation-in	1,250	1,200	+50
Goods available for sale	82,350	83,200	−850
Merchandise inventory, April 30, 2001	41,000	44,100	−3,100
Cost of goods sold	41,350	39,100	+2,250
Gross profit	$19,150	$18,050	$+1,100
Operating expenses:			
Selling expenses:			
Sales salaries	6,250	6,000	+250
Advertising	900	800	+100
Store supplies	550	500	+50
Amortization, store equipment	1,600	1,600	
Total selling expenses	9,300	8,900	+400
General and administrative expenses:			
Office salaries	2,000	2,000	
Office supplies used	165	150	+15
Rent	1,100	1,100	
Insurance	200	200	
Amortization, office equipment	100	100	
Total general and administrative expenses	3,565	3,550	+15
Total operating expenses	12,865	12,450	+415
Income from operations	$ 6,285	$ 5,600	$ +685

Exhibit 26.1

Comparing Actual Performance with Budgeted Performance

Many organizations choose to use different budgeting cycles. For example, Codman & Shurtleff, a division of Johnson & Johnson, prepares a five-year outlook, a two-year plan, and an annual budget.[1] Every time the budget is reviewed, managers take a look at the numbers in all three budgets and revise them as necessary. Preparing a two-year outlook allows managers to think about the coming year to stay ahead in the planning process.

---

[1] Robert Simons, "Codman & Shurtleff, Inc.: Planning and Control System," Harvard Business School Case, 1987.

Many companies also break their annual budgets into quarterly or monthly budgets to provide more specific details for shorter periods. These short-term budgets allow management to evaluate actual performance against budgets more quickly, thereby enabling managers to take appropriate corrective actions if necessary. Consider a company that prepares quarterly budgets and reviews performance on a quarterly basis. At the time of the quarterly review, it revises its entire budget for the remaining three quarters and adds a new one. This type of budgeting process is known as **continuous budgeting** wherein managers prepare **rolling budgets** so that at any time quarterly budgets are available for the next four quarters.

Exhibit 26.2 shows five rolling budgets. The first set of budgets is prepared in December 2003 and covers the next four calendar quarters of the year 2004. In March 2004, the company prepares another rolling budget for the next four quarters through March 2005. This same process is repeated every three months. As a result, management is continuously planning ahead.

Exhibit 26.2 reflects an annual budget composed of four quarters that is drawn up four times per year using the most recent information available. For example the budget for the fourth quarter of 2004 is prepared in December 2003 and revised in March, June, and September 2004. When continuous budgeting is not used, the fourth-quarter budget is nine months old and, perhaps, out of date when applied.

Exhibit 26.2

Rolling Budgets

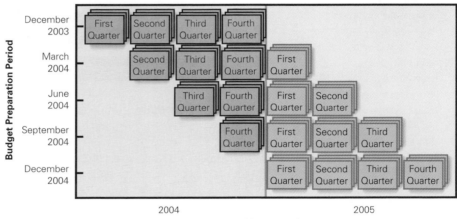

Answers—p. 1362

1. What are the major benefits of budgeting?
2. What is the responsibility of the budget committee?
3. What is the usual time period covered by a budget?
4. What are rolling budgets?

Master Budget

A **master budget** is a formal, comprehensive plan for the future of a company. To include definite plans for all activities, a master budget contains several individual budgets. These individual budgets are linked with each other to form a coordinated plan for the company.

Master Budget Components

The master budget typically includes individual budgets for sales, purchases, production, various expenses, capital expenditures, and cash. Managers often express the expected financial results of these planned activities with both a budgeted income statement for the budget period and a budgeted balance sheet as of the last day of the budget period.

 LO³ Describe a master budget and the process of preparing it.

The usual number and types of budgets included in a master budget depend on the size and complexity of the company. A master budget should include, at a minimum, the budgets listed in Exhibit 26.3. In addition to these individual budgets, managers often include supporting calculations and schedules along with the master budget.

---

1. **Operating budgets.**
   a. *Sales budget.*
   b. For merchandisers: *Merchandise purchases budget* (specifying units to be purchased).
      For manufacturers:
         (i) *Production budget* (specifying units to be produced).
         (ii) *Manufacturing budget* (specifying planned manufacturing costs).
   c. *Selling expense budget.*
   d. *General and administrative expense budget.*
2. **Capital expenditures budget** (specifying budgeted expenditures for plant and equipment).
3. **Financial budgets.**
   a. *Cash budget* (specifying budgeted cash receipts and disbursements).
   b. *Budgeted income statement.*
   c. *Budgeted balance sheet.*

Exhibit 26.3

Basic Components of the Master Budget

Some budgets require the input of other budgets. For example, the merchandise purchases budget cannot be prepared until after the sales budget is prepared. This is because the number of units to be purchased depends on how many units are expected to be sold. As a result, we must prepare budgets within the master budget in a sequence. A typical sequence is that followed by HON Company, an office products manufacturer, in its quarterly budgeting process.[2] Its quarterly budget consists of five steps as shown in Exhibit 26.4 and is completed over a six-week period.

Exhibit 26.4

Master Budget Sequence for a Manufacturing Company

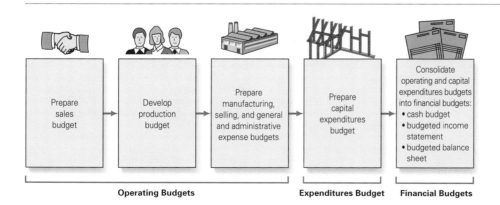

| Prepare sales budget | Develop production budget | Prepare manufacturing, selling, and general and administrative expense budgets | Prepare capital expenditures budget | Consolidate operating and capital expenditures budgets into financial budgets:
• cash budget
• budgeted income statement
• budgeted balance sheet |

Operating Budgets   **Expenditures Budget**   **Financial Budgets**

---

[2] Drtina, R., S. Hoeger and J. Schaub, "Continuous Budgeting at the HON Company," *Management Accounting*, January 1996, pp. 20–24.

At any stage in this budgeting process, undesirable outcomes might be revealed. This means that changes must be made to prior budgets, and the previous steps repeated. For instance, an early version of the cash budget might show an insufficient amount of cash unless cash outlays are reduced. This might yield a reduction in planned equipment purchases. Or a preliminary budgeted balance sheet may reveal too much debt due to an ambitious expenditures budget. Such findings often result in revised plans.

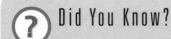

Did You Know?

Budgeting and Acquisition

Budgeting is a crucial part of management's analysis at Koch Industries for potential acquisitions. Analysis begins by projecting annual sales volume, prices, and total revenues. Managers then estimate cost of sales for each revenue item along with selling, general, and administrative expenses. These are combined to form projected net income of the potential acquisition for the next several years. They also predict expenditures and other costs. By comparing the budgeted cost of a potential acquisition with its expected future income, they decide the price to offer for the potential acquisition.

Flashback

Answers—p. 1362

5. What is a master budget?
6. A master budget:
   a. Always includes a manufacturing budget specifying the number of units to be produced.
   b. Is prepared with a process starting with the operating budgets and continuing with the capital expenditures budget, the cash budget, and the budgeted financial statements.
   c. Is prepared with a process ending with the budgeted income statement.
7. What are the three primary categories of budgets in the master budget?

LO⁴ Prepare each component of a master budget and link them to the budgeting process.

The remainder of this section explains how the master budget for Hockey Den (HD), a retailer of youth hockey sticks, is prepared. The company's master budget includes operating, capital expenditure, and cash budgets for each month in a quarter. It also includes a budgeted income statement for each quarter and a budgeted balance sheet as of the last day of each quarter. We will show how HD's budgets are prepared for October, November, and December 2004. Exhibit 26.5 presents HD's balance sheet at the start of this budgeting period. We will often refer to it as we prepare individual operating budgets.

Exhibit 26.5

Balance Sheet Prior to the
Budgeting Periods

Hockey Den Balance Sheet September 30, 2004		
Assets		
Cash		$ 20,000
Accounts receivable	$ 42,000	
Less allowance for doubtful accounts..................................	420	41,580
Inventory (9,000 units @ $6)..		54,000
Equipment*..	$200,000	
Less accumulated amortization..	(36,000)	164,000
Total assets		$279,580
Liabilities and Shareholders' Equity		
Liabilities:		
Accounts payable	$ 58,200	
Income taxes payable (due 31/10, 2004)	20,000	
Note payable to bank	10,000	$ 88,200
Shareholders' equity:		
Common shares..	150,000	
Retained earnings	41,380	191,380
Total liabilities and shareholders' equity		$279,580

*Equipment is amortized on a straight-line basis over 10 years where salvage value is $20,000.

Operating Budgets

This section explains the preparation of operating budgets for Hockey Den. Operating budgets consist of the sales budget, merchandise purchases budget, selling expense budget, and general and administrative expense budget. Hockey Den does not prepare production and manufacturing budgets because it is a merchandiser. The preparation of a production budget and related manufacturing budgets are also described in this section.

Sales Budget

In Chapter 25 we studied the relationships between costs, volume, and profits. Estimated sales volume is vital to the whole budgeting process and the first step in preparing the master budget is planning the **sales budget**. This budget shows the planned sales units and the revenue derived from these sales. The sales budget is the starting point in the budgeting process because plans for most departments are linked to sales. The sales budget should emerge from a careful analysis of forecasted economic and market conditions, operating capacity, proposed selling expenses (such as advertising), and predictions of unit sales. Because people normally feel a greater commitment to goals they have had a hand in setting, the sales personnel of a company are usually asked to develop predictions of sales for each territory and department. Another advantage of using this *participatory budgeting* approach is that it draws on knowledge and experience of people involved in the activity.

In September 2004, Hockey Den sold 700 hockey sticks at $100 per unit. After considering sales predictions and market conditions, Hockey Den's sales budget is prepared for the next quarter (three months) plus one extra month, see Exhibit 26.6. The sales budget includes January 2005 because the purchasing department relies on estimated January sales in estimating December 2004 purchases.

Exhibit 26.6

Sales Budget Showing
Planned Unit and Dollar
Sales

Hockey Den Monthly Sales Budget October 2004–January 2005	Budgeted Unit Sales	Budgeted Unit Price	Budgeted Total Sales
September 2004 (actual)	700	$100	$ 70,000
October 2004	1000	$100	$100,000
November 2004...	800	100	80,000
December 2004..	1400	100	140,000
Total for the quarter.......................................	3,200	$100	$320,000
January 2005...	900	$100	$ 90,000

The sales budget in Exhibit 26.6 includes forecasts of both unit sales and unit prices. While some companies prepare a sales budget expressed only in total sales dollars, most sales budgets are more detailed. Management finds it useful to know budgeted units and unit prices for many different products, regions, departments, and sales representatives.

This chapter's opening article described budgets and planning at Biker. In prior years, Biker had classified its sales budget by the type of coil (steel vs. titanium). This past year it expanded the classifications by type of bike. It used the planning process to identify industries other than sports bikes that can benefit from the high tensile strength and lightweight properties of titanium coil springs. It identified and successfully marketed a new coil spring to NASCAR racing vehicles. Both strength and weight are crucial in this sport, and important enough to justify the added expense of titanium coil springs. By using the budgeting and planning process, Biker successfully increased its sales. Projections for the next two years have titanium coil spring sales increasing by 30% to 50%. The majority of this growth comes from NASCAR parts.

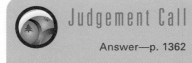

Judgement Call

Answer—p. 1362

Sales Manager

You are a sales manager for a designer clothes manufacturer. Business is highly seasonal and you find that fashions and designs are continuously changing. How do you prepare annual sales budgets?

Merchandise Purchases Budget

Various methods are used to help managers make merchandise inventory purchasing decisions. All these methods recognize that the number of units added to inventory depends on budgeted sales volume. Whether a company manufactures or purchases the product it sells, budgeted future sales volume is the primary factor in most inventory management decisions. The **merchandise purchases budget** provides detailed information about the amount of purchases necessary to fulfill the sales budget and to provide adequate inventories.

Just-in-Time Inventory Systems

Managers of *just-in-time* (JIT) inventory systems use sales budgets for covering short periods (often as few as one or two days) to order just enough merchandise or materials to satisfy the immediate sales demand. As a result, the level of inventory on hand is held to a minimum (or zero in an ideal situation). A just-in-time system minimizes the costs of maintaining inventory. But just-in-time systems are practical only if customers are content to order in advance or if managers can accurately determine short-term sales demand. Also, suppliers must be able and willing to ship small quantities regularly and promptly.

Safety Stock Inventory Systems

Market conditions and manufacturing processes for many products may not allow a just-in-time system to be used. Instead, many companies keep enough inventory on hand to reduce the risk of running short. This practice requires enough purchases to satisfy the budgeted sales amounts and to maintain an additional quantity of inventory as a **safety stock**. The safety stock provides protection against lost sales caused by unfulfilled demands from customers or delays in shipments from suppliers.

Merchandise Purchases Budget

Companies usually express a merchandise purchases budget in both units and dollars. Exhibit 26.7 shows the general layout for computing purchases in equation form. If this formula is expressed in units and only one product is involved, we can compute the number of dollars of inventory to be purchased for our budget by multiplying the units to be purchased by the cost per unit.

Exhibit 26.7

Formula for a Merchandise Purchases Budget

After Hockey Den assessed the cost of keeping inventory along with the risk of a temporary inventory shortage, it decided the number of units in its inventory at the end of each month should equal 90% of next month's predicted sales. For example, inventory at the end of October should equal 90% of budgeted November sales, and the November ending inventory should equal 90% of budgeted December sales, and so on.

Hockey Den's suppliers expect the September 2004 per unit cost of $60 to remain unchanged through January 2005. This information, along with knowing 900 units are on hand at September 30 (see Exhibit 26.5), allows the company to prepare the merchandise purchases budget shown in Exhibit 26.8.

Hockey Den Merchandise Purchases Budget October, November, and December 2004			
	October	November	December
Next month's budgeted sales (units)	800	1,400	900
Ratio of inventory to future sales	× 90%	× 90%	× 90%
Budgeted ending inventory (units)	720	1,260	810
Add budgeted sales for the month (units)	1,000	800	1,400
Required units of available merchandise	1,720	2,060	2,210
Deduct beginning inventory (units)	(900)	(720)	(1,260)
Number of units to be purchased	820	1,340	950
Budgeted cost per unit	$ 60	$ 60	$ 60
Budgeted cost of merchandise purchases	$49,200	$80,400	$57,000

Exhibit 26.8

Merchandise Purchases Budget

The first three lines of Hockey Den's merchandise purchases budget compute the required ending inventories. Budgeted unit sales are then added to the desired ending inventory to give us the required units of available merchandise. We then subtract beginning inventory to determine the budgeted number of units to be purchased. The last line is the budgeted cost of the purchases, computed by multiplying the units to be purchased by the predicted cost per unit.

We already indicated that some budgeting systems describe only the total dollars of budgeted sales. Likewise, a system can express a merchandise purchases budget only in terms of the total cost of merchandise to be purchased, omitting the number of units to be purchased. This method assumes a constant relation between sales and cost of goods sold. Hockey Den, for instance, might assume the expected cost of goods sold to be 60% of sales, computed from the budgeted unit cost of $60 and the budgeted sales price of $100. Here its cost of goods sold can be budgeted in dollars on the basis of budgeted sales without requiring information on the number of units involved. But it is still necessary to consider the effects of beginning and ending inventories in determining the amounts to be purchased.

Selling Expense Budget

The **selling expense budget** is a plan listing the types and amounts of selling expenses expected during the budget period. Its initial responsibility usually rests with the vice president of marketing or an equivalent sales manager. The selling expense budget is normally created to provide sufficient selling expenses to meet sales goals reflected in the sales budget. Predictions of selling expenses are based on both the sales budget and on the experience of previous periods. After the entire master budget (or a portion thereof) is prepared, management may decide that projected sales volume is inadequate. If so, subsequent adjustments to the sales budget may require corresponding adjustments to the selling expense budget.

Hockey Den's selling expense budget is shown in Exhibit 26.9. Hockey Den's selling expenses consist of commissions paid to sales personnel and a $2,000 monthly salary paid to the sales manager. Sales commissions equal 10% of total sales and are paid in the month sales occur. Sales commissions are variable with respect to sales volume whereas the sales manager's salary is fixed. No advertising expenses are budgeted for this particular quarter.

Exhibit 26.9

Selling Expense Budget

Hockey Den Selling Expense Budget October, November, and December 2004				
	October	November	December	Total
Budgeted sales	$100,000	$80,000	$140,000	$320,000
Sales commission percentage	× 10%	× 10%	× 10%	× 10%
Sales commissions	$ 10,000	$ 8,000	$ 14,000	$ 32,000
Salary for sales manager	2,000	2,000	2,000	6,000
Total selling expenses	$ 12,000	$10,000	$ 16,000	$ 38,000

General and Administrative Expense Budget

The **general and administrative expense budget** is a plan showing the predicted operating expenses not included in the selling expenses budget. General and administrative expenses may consist of items that are variable or fixed with respect to sales volume. Both cash and non-cash expenses are included in this budget. The office manager, or the person responsible for general administration, often is responsible for preparing the initial general and administrative expense budget.

While interest expense and income tax expense are often classified as general and administrative expenses in published income statements, they normally cannot be planned for at this stage of the budgeting process. The prediction of interest expense follows the preparation of the cash budget and the decisions regarding debt. The predicted income tax expense depends on the budgeted amount of pre-tax income. Also, both interest and income taxes are usually beyond the control of the office manager. As a result, they should not be used in evaluating that person's performance in comparison to the budget.

Exhibit 26.10 shows the general and administrative expense budget for Hockey Den. General and administrative expenses include salaries of $54,000 per year, or $4,500 per month. Salaries are paid each month when they are earned. Using the information in Exhibit 26.5, the amortization on equipment is $18,000 per year [($200,000 − $20,000) ÷ 10 years], or $1,500 per month ($18,000 ÷ 12 months).

Hockey Den **General and Administrative Expense Budget** **October, November, and December 2004**				
	October	November	December	Total
Administrative salaries............................	$4,500	$4,500	$4,500	$13,500
Amortization of equipment......................	1,500	1,500	1,500	4,500
Total general and administrative expenses.........................	$6,000	$6,000	$6,000	$18,000

Exhibit 26.10

General and Administrative Expense Budget

8. In preparing monthly budgets for the third quarter, a company budgeted 120 unit sales for July and 140 unit sales for August. The June 30 merchandise inventory consists of 50 units and management wants each month's ending inventory to be 60% of next month's sales. How many units of product should the merchandise purchase budget for the third quarter specify for July? (a) 84; (b) 120; (c) 154; (d) 204.

9. How does a just-in-time inventory system differ from a safety stock system?

Flashback

Answers—p. 1362

Capital Expenditures Budget

The **capital expenditures budget** lists dollar amounts to be received from the sale of any capital equipment and to be spent on acquiring additional equipment required to carry out an organization's plans. In the case of a manufacturing company, capital equipment would relate to production and other types of equipment. In the case of a merchandiser, no production equipment is required, but the firm may buy equipment needed for repair, materials handling, or storage. The capital expenditures budget is typically affected by the company's long-range plans because the life of capital equipment extends beyond just a single year.

Planning for capital expenditures is an important task of management because these expenditures often involve long-term commitments of large amounts. Also, capital expenditures often have a major effect on predicted cash flows and the company's need for debt or equity financing. This means the capital expenditures budget is often linked with management's evaluation of the company's ability to take on more debt.

In the case of Hockey Den, the company doesn't anticipate any disposals of equipment through December 2004. But it does plan to acquire additional equipment for $25,000 cash near the end of December 2004. Since this is the only budgeted capital expenditure from October 2004 through January 2005, no separate budget is shown. The cash budget in Exhibit 26.11 reflects this $25,000 planned expenditure.

Financial Budgets

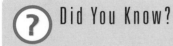 Link both operating and capital expenditure budgets to budgeted financial statements.

After preparing the operating and capital expenditures budgets, a company uses information from these budgets to prepare three financial budgets: a cash budget, a budgeted income statement, and a budgeted balance sheet.

Cash Budget

After developing budgets for sales, merchandise purchases, expenses, and capital expenditures, the next step is preparing the cash budget. The **cash budget** shows expected cash inflows and outflows during the budget period. It is especially important to maintain a cash balance necessary to meet a company's obligations. By preparing a cash budget, management can prearrange loans to cover any anticipated cash shortages before they are needed. A cash budget also helps management avoid a cash balance that is too large. Too much cash is undesirable because it earns a relatively low rate of return.

(?) Did You Know?   **Managing Cash**

Businesses are now able to access wireless Internet-based cash management products that give real-time account information through Web-enabled phones. Employees who provide raw information for the budgeting process can update the information immediately. Advances in technology help make budgeting a less arduous task. However, having access to more information more quickly does not necessarily make budgets more useful. We must remember that budgets are only as good as the underlying assumptions and that forecasts seldom turn out exactly as anticipated.

When preparing a cash budget, we add expected receipts to the beginning cash balance and then deduct expected cash expenditures. If the expected final cash balance is inadequate, any additional cash requirements appear in the budget as planned increases from short-term loans. If the expected final cash balance exceeds the desired balance, the excess is used to repay loans or to acquire temporary investments. Information for preparing the cash budget is primarily taken from the operating and capital expenditures budgets. But further data and calculations are sometimes necessary to compute the final amounts.

Exhibit 26.11 presents the cash budget for Hockey Den. The beginning cash balance for October is taken from the September 30, 2004 balance sheet in Exhibit 26.5. The remainder of this section describes the computations in the cash budget.

Exhibit 26.11

Cash Budget

Hockey Den Cash Budget October, November, and December 2004	October	November	December
Beginning cash balance....................................	$ 20,000	$ 20,000	$ 21,248
Cash receipts from customers			
(Exhibit 26.12)..	81,580	91,400	103,520
Total cash available...	$101,580	$111,400	$124,768
Cash disbursements			
Payments for merchandise			
(Exhibit 26.13)...	58,200	49,200	80,400
Sales commissions (Exhibit 26.9)................	10,000	8,000	14,000
Salaries:			
Sales (Exhibit 26.9).................................	2,000	2,000	2,000
Administrative (Exhibit 26.10)..................	4,500	4,500	4,500
Income taxes payable (Exhibit 26.5).............	20,000		
Dividends ($150,000 × 2%).........................		3,000	
Interest on bank loan:			
October ($10,000 × 1%)...........................	100		
November ($23,220 × 1%)........................		232	
Purchase of equipment.................................			25,000
Total cash disbursements............................	$ 94,800	$ 66,932	$125,900
Preliminary balance	6,780	44,468	(1,132)
Additional loan from bank..............................	13,220		21,132
Repayment of loan from bank.........................		(23,220)	
Ending cash balance.......................................	$ 20,000	$ 21,248	$ 20,000
Loan balance, end of month...........................	$ 23,220*	$ -0-	$ 21,132

*Recall from Exhibit 26.5 that Hockey Den owed $10,000 to the bank as of September 30, 2004.

Budgeted sales of Hockey Den are shown in Exhibit 26.6. Analysis of past sales records indicates 40% of Hockey Den's sales are for cash. The remaining 60% are credit sales of which 1% is expected to be uncollectible. Customers are expected to pay the remaining 99% of credit sales in full during the month following the sales. We can compute the budgeted cash receipts from customers as shown in Exhibit 26.12.

Exhibit 26.12

Computing Budgeted
Cash Receipts

	September	October	November	December
Sales.................................	$70,000	$100,000	$80,000	$140,000
Ending accounts				
receivable (60%).........................	$42,000	$ 60,000	$48,000	$ 84,000
Cash receipts from:				
Cash sales (40%).........................		$ 40,000	$32,000	$ 56,000
Collections of prior				
month's receivables................		41,580	59,400	47,520
Total cash receipts..........................		$ 81,580	$91,400	$103,520

The amount of cash collected will be less than sales because of bad debts. Allowance for uncollectible accounts should be built into the cash receipts budget. Exhibit 26.16 shows October's budgeted cash receipts consist of $40,000 from expected cash sales ($100,000 × 40%) plus the anticipated collection of

$41,580 (computed as $42,000 × 99%) of accounts receivable from the end of September. Each month's cash receipts from customers are listed on the second line of Exhibit 26.11.

Hockey Den's purchases of merchandise are entirely on account. Full payments are made during the month following these purchases. This means cash disbursements for purchases are computed from the September 30, 2004 balance sheet (Exhibit 26.5) and from the merchandise purchases budget (Exhibit 26.8). This computation is shown in Exhibit 26.13.

Exhibit 26.13

Computing Cash
Disbursements for Purchases

October payments (September 30 balance)	$58,200
November payments (October purchases)	49,200
December payments (November purchases)	80,400

Because sales commissions and all salaries are paid monthly, the budgeted cash disbursements for these expenses come from the selling expense budget (Exhibit 26.9) and the general and administrative expense budget (Exhibit 26.10). The cash budget is unaffected by amortization expense in the general and administrative expenses budget.

As shown in the September 30, 2004, balance sheet (Exhibit 26.5), income taxes are due and payable in October. The cash budget in Exhibit 26.11 shows this $20,000 expected expenditure in October. Predicted income tax expense for the quarter ending December 31 is 40% of net income and is due in January 2005. It is therefore not reported in the October–December 2004 cash budget. But it does appear in the budgeted income statement as income tax expense and on the budgeted balance sheet as income tax liability.

Hockey Den also pays a cash dividend equal to 2% of the recorded value of common shares in the second month of each quarter. The cash budget in Exhibit 26.11 shows a November payment of $3,000 for this purpose (2% of $150,000; see Exhibit 26.5).

Hockey Den has an agreement with its bank that promises additional loans at the end of each month if necessary to keep a minimum cash balance of $20,000. Interest is paid at the end of each month at the rate of 1% of the beginning balance of these loans. If the cash balance exceeds $20,000 at the end of a month, the company uses the excess to repay loans. The interest payments in Exhibit 26.11 equal 1% of the prior month's ending loan balance. For October, this payment is 1% of the $10,000 amount reported in the balance sheet of Exhibit 26.5. For November, the company expects to pay interest of $232 (rounded), computed as 1% of the $23,220 expected loan balance at October 31. No interest is budgeted for December because the company expects to repay the loans in full at the end of November.

Exhibit 26.11 shows the October 31 cash balance falls to $6,720 (before any loan-related activity). This amount is less than the $20,000 minimum. Hockey Den expects to bring this balance up to the minimum by borrowing $13,320 with a short-term note. At the end of November, the budget shows an expected cash balance of $44,467 before any loan activity. This means the company expects to repay the $23,220 debt. The equipment purchase budgeted for December reduces the expected cash balance to negative $1,233, far below the $20,000 minimum. This means the company expects to borrow $21,233 in that month reach the minimum desired ending balance.

Budgeted Income Statement

One of the final steps in preparing the master budget is summarizing the income effects of the plans. The **budgeted income statement** is a managerial accounting report showing predicted amounts of revenues and expenses for the budget period. Information needed for preparing a budgeted income statement comes primarily from already prepared budgets.

The volume of information summarized in the budgeted income statement is so large for some companies that spreadsheets are often used to accumulate the budgeted transactions and classify them by their effects on income. We condense the budgeted income statement for Hockey Den and show it in Exhibit 26.14. All information in this exhibit is taken from earlier budgets.

From this budget, we can predict the amount of income tax expense for the quarter, computed as 40% of the budgeted pre-tax net income. This amount is included in the cash budget and/or the budgeted balance sheet as necessary.

Hockey Den Budgeted Income Statement For Three Months Ended December 31, 2004		
Sales (Exhibit 26.6, 3,200 units @ $100)		$320,000
Cost of goods sold (3,200 units @ $60)		192,000
Gross profit		128,000
Operating expenses:		
Sales commissions (Exhibit 26.9)	$32,000	
Sales salaries (Exhibit 26.9)	6,000	
Administrative salaries (Exhibit 26.10)	13,500	
Amortization on equipment (Exhibit 26.10)	4,500	
Bad debts expense ($320,000 × 60% × 1%)	1,920	
Interest expense (Exhibit 26.11)	332	(58,252)
Net income before income taxes		69,748
Income tax expense ($69,747 × 40%)		(27,899)
Net income		$41,849

Exhibit 26.14

Budgeted Income Statement

Did You Know?

Budgeted Balance Sheet

The final step in preparing the master budget is summarizing the company's financial position. The **budgeted balance sheet** shows predicted amounts for the company's assets, liabilities, and shareholders' equity as of the end of the budget period. The budgeted balance sheet of Hockey Den is prepared using information from the other budgets. The sources of amounts shown in its budgeted balance sheet are listed in Exhibit 26.15.

Exhibit 26.15

Sources of Amounts in
Budgeted Balance Sheet

Item	Amount	Explanation
Cash	$ 20,000	Ending balance for December from the cash budget in Exhibit 26.11.
Accounts receivable	$ 84,000	60% of $140,000 sales budgeted for December from the sales budget in Exhibit 26.6.
Allowance for doubtful accounts	$ 840	Accounts receivable balance times 1%.
Inventory	$ 48,600	810 units in budgeted December ending inventory at the budgeted cost of $60 per unit (from the purchases budget in Exhibit 26.8).
Equipment	$225,000	September 30 balance of $200,000 from the beginning balance sheet in Exhibit 26.5 plus $25,000 cost of new equipment from the cash budget in Exhibit 26.11.
Accumulated amortization	$ 40,500	September 30 balance of $36,000 from the beginning balance sheet in Exhibit 26.5 plus $4,500 expense from the general and administrative expense budget in Exhibit 26.10.
Accounts payable	$ 57,000	Budgeted cost of merchandise purchases for December from the purchases budget in Exhibit 26.8.
Income taxes payable	$ 27,899	Budgeted income tax expense from the budgeted income statement for the fourth quarter in Exhibit 26.14.
Bank loan payable	$ 21,132	Budgeted December 31 balance from the cash budget in Exhibit 26.11.
Common shares	$150,000	Unchanged from the beginning balance sheet in Exhibit 26.5.
Retained earnings	$ 80,229	September 30 balance of $41,380 from the beginning balance sheet in Exhibit 26.5 plus budgeted net income of $41,849 from the budgeted income statement in Exhibit 26.10 minus budgeted cash dividends of $3,000 from the cash budget in Exhibit 26.11.

    The resulting budgeted balance sheet is shown in Exhibit 26.16. An eight-column spreadsheet, or work sheet, can be used to prepare the budgeted balance sheet (and income statement). The first two columns would show the post-closing trial balance as of the last day of the period prior to the budget period. The budgeted transactions and adjustments are entered in the third and fourth columns in the same manner as end-of-period adjustments are entered on an ordinary work sheet. After all budgeted transactions and adjustments are entered, the post-closing trial balance amounts in the first two columns are combined with the budget amounts in the third and fourth columns and sorted to the proper income statement (fifth and sixth columns) and balance sheet columns (seventh and eight columns). Balances in these columns are used to prepare the budgeted income statement and balance sheet.

Hockey Den
Budgeted Balance Sheet
December 31, 2004

Exhibit 26.16

Budgeted Balance Sheet

Assets

Cash		$ 20,000
Accounts receivable	$ 84,000	
Less allowance for doubtful accounts	(840)	83,160
Inventory (810 units @ $60)		48,600
Equipment	$225,000	
Less accumulated amortization	(40,500)	184,500
Total assets		$336,260

Liabilities and Shareholders' Equity

Liabilities:

Accounts payable	$ 57,000	
Income taxes payable	27,899	
Bank loan payable	21,132	$106,031
Shareholders' equity:		
Common shares	150,000	
Retained earnings	80,229	230,229
Total liabilities and shareholders' equity		$336,260

Exhibit 26.16

Budgeted Balance Sheet

10. In preparing a budgeted balance sheet:

a. Plant assets are determined by analyzing the capital expenditures budget and the balance sheet from the beginning of the budget period.

b. Liabilities are determined by analyzing the general and administrative expense budget.

c. Retained earnings are determined from information contained in the cash budget and the balance sheet from the beginning of the budget period.

11. What sequence is followed in preparing the budgets comprising the master budget?

Flashback

Answers—p. 1362

Zero-based Budgeting

This chapter focused on the preparation of budgets within an organization. In most cases, annual budgets are based on figures from the previous year, and adjusted for changes in operating conditions. But in some cases companies encounter totally new circumstances that demand a different budgeting process.

Consider, for example, the marketing department of a company that plans to promote its products for the very first time at a trade show. How does it prepare a budget for the trade show? One solution to this situation is zero-based budgeting (ZBB).

Companies using zero-based budgeting start each budgeting period at "ground zero." They assume no previous history for the set of activities being planned. Instead, they prepare a detailed list of activities to be carried out, the resources required to carry out these activities, and the expenses of acquiring these resources. This type of expense planning requires managers to justify the amounts budgeted for each activity to top management.

 LO[6] Analyze expense planning using zero-based budgeting.

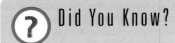

Did You Know?

Activity-Based Budgeting

Activity-based budgeting (ABB) is a tool that uses the concepts of activity-based costing to enhance the budgeting process. Rather than using a single cost allocation base to budget overhead costs, ABB focuses on budgeting for resources using activities as a base. Proponents (and of course consultants) claim that this can improve the accuracy of budgeting. Note that an ABB system can provide a strong basis for zero-based budgeting.

Zero-based budgeting is sometimes put in place to counter a natural tendency to continue to fund certain activities. Zero-based budgeting forces managers to ask questions as if the activity were being proposed for the very first time. Under this system each unit of the organization prepares a detailed list of budget requests commonly called *decision packages*. The manager is required to rank each request in terms of importance and fully document the costs and benefits of each activity.

Zero-based budgeting is particularly popular among government and nonprofit organizations that have large amounts of discretion in decisions about how funds should be spent. Preparation of decision packages is time consuming and uses a lot of resources during the budgeting period. Many managers believe that annual zero-based budgets are too costly but that zero-based reviews should be done occasionally.

Judgement Call

Answer—p. 1362

Environmental Manager

You are the new manager responsible for environmental control of a chemical company. This is a new position within the company. You are asked to develop a budget for your job and its responsibilities. How do you proceed?

Human Relations

Budgeting involves interactions among people and this inevitably can lead to conflict. Ideally the goals of individual managers should harmonize with the mission of the company. This is known as goal congruence. In practice, goal congruence is difficult to achieve because of inherent conflicts. For example, marketing will want inventory to be high to meet any unexpected sales demand but production will want to keep stocks low to save costs.

One way of achieving goal congruence is to ensure that managers at various levels of the organization play a role in the budgeting process and that budgets are not simply imposed on them by senior management. If budgets are imposed morale may suffer leading to a lack of management commitment to work within the budget. This lack of commitment may be due to the feeling by subordinate managers that their perceived right to participate in the budgeting process has been ignored. Lack of commitment could also be due to failure to fully understand a budget that they were not instrumental in developing. There may also exist a feeling that the budget is unfair simply because it is being imposed upon them.

Problems may also arise when budgets are used too rigidly to assess managerial performance. This may lead some managers to build slack into their estimates. **Slack** allows managers to use their private information about costs and revenues to distort the budget so that budget targets will be easier to achieve. For example, they may overstate estimated expenses or understate estimated revenues. Managers should be called upon to justify any proposed budget increases in cost estimates.

Budgets should not be set in stone. They should be set in an atmosphere of trust with the implicit assumption that managers will do their best to achieve budget targets but that targets are subject to adjustment due to unforeseen changes in budget assumptions. Managers should focus attention on significant deviations from budget when evaluating performance and seek not to place blame but to find explanations for these deviations. This principle of concentrating on significant deviations from budget is known as management by exception, a principle that we will talk more about in Chapter 27.

Summary

LO¹ Explain the importance and benefits of budgeting. Planning is a management responsibility of crucial importance to business success. Budgeting is the process used by management to formalize its plans. Budgeting promotes analysis by management and focuses its attention on the future. Budgeting also provides a basis for evaluating performance, serves as a source of motivation, is a means of coordinating business activities, and communicates management's plans and instructions to employees.

LO² Describe the process of budget administration. Budgeting is a detailed activity that requires administration. At least two aspects are important: budget committee and budget horizon. A budget committee oversees the preparation of the budget. The budget horizon refers to the time period for which the budget is prepared such as a year, quarter, or month.

LO³ Describe a master budget and the process of preparing it. A master budget is a formal overall plan for a company. It consists of specific plans for business operations, capital expenditures, and the financial results of those activities. The budgeting process begins with preparing a sales budget. Based on expected sales volume, merchandisers can budget merchandise purchases, selling expenses, and administrative expenses. Next, the capital expenditures budget is prepared, followed by the cash budget, and budgeted financial statements.

LO⁴ Prepare each component of a master budget and link them to the budgeting process. In the process of preparing a master budget, each component budget is designed to provide guidance for persons responsible for activities covered by that budget. The master budget shows how much revenue is to be received from sales and how much expense is to be incurred. Budgets are designed to reflect the activities of one area (such as sales) impacting the activities of others (such as purchasing). The various components of a company are directed to pursue activities consistent with and supportive of its overall objectives.

LO⁵ Link both operating and capital expenditure budgets to budgeted financial statements. The operating budgets, capital expenditures budget, and cash budget contain much of the information to prepare a budgeted income statement for the budget period and a budgeted balance sheet at the end of the budget period. Budgeted financial statements show the expected financial consequences of the planned activities described in the budgets.

LO⁶ Analyze expense planning using zero-based budgeting. Companies often budget for the next year based on the current year's budgets. This may not be possible if there are no historical data available as a base. In such situations, zero-based budgeting can be used for expense planning. Managers following the zero-based budgeting approach must prepare a detailed list of the activities to be carried out, the resources required to carry out these activities, and the expenses of acquiring these resources.

GUIDANCE ANSWERS TO Judgement Call

Budget Staffer

The action of your superior is unethical. This is because he is using private information for personal gain. His action also hurt the company and its shareholders. As a budget staffer, you are low in the company's hierarchical structure and probably unable to directly confront this superior. Yet you should inform an individual with a position of authority in the organization about your discovery. You might also enlist a colleague and explain the situation. The information might be considered more credible if it comes from two people rather than one.

Sales Manager

There are two issues you must deal with. First, given that fashions and designs are constantly changing, you cannot rely heavily on previous budgets, because they may be irrelevant. As a result, you must carefully analyze the market to understand what designs are in vogue and how long they will last. This information will help you plan the product mix of designs you are willing to offer and estimate demand for your designs. The second issue has to do with the budgeting period. Because of continuous change, you may not be able to prepare an annual sales budget. Your best bet may be to prepare monthly and quarterly sales budgets that you continuously monitor and revise if necessary.

Environmental Manager

Given that yours is a new position, you probably have no historical data to draw on in preparing your budget. In this situation, you must use zero-based budgeting to develop your budget. This requires you to develop a list of activities you plan to conduct, the resources required to carry out these activities, and the expenses associated with these resources. You should challenge yourself to be absolutely certain that the listed activities are necessary and the listed resources are required. This process will strengthen your budget and its likelihood of funding.

GUIDANCE ANSWERS TO  Flashback

1. Major benefits include: (1) promoting a focus on the future; (2) providing a basis for evaluating performance; (3) providing a source of motivation; (4) coordinating the departments of an organization; and (5) communicating plans.

2. The budget committee's responsibility is to provide central guidance to ensure that budget figures are realistic and coordinated.

3. Budget periods usually coincide with accounting periods and therefore cover a month, quarter, or a year. Budgets can also be prepared to cover a long-range period, such as five years.

4. Rolling budgets are budgets that are periodically revised in the process of continuous budgeting.

5. A master budget is a comprehensive or overall plan for a business.

6. *b*

7. The master budget includes operating budgets, the capital expenditures budget, and financial budgets.

8. *c* $(0.60 \times 140) + 120 - 50 = 154$

9. With a just-in-time system, the level of inventory is kept to a minimum and orders for merchandise or materials are intended to meet immediate sales demand. A safety stock system maintains an inventory that is large enough to meet sales demands plus an amount to satisfy unexpected sales demands and an amount to cover delayed shipments from suppliers.

10. *a*

11. (1) Sales budget (and any other operating budget), (2) Capital expenditures budget, (3) Financial budgets—cash budget, budgeted income statement, and budgeted balance sheet.

Production and Manufacturing Budgets

26A

APPENDIX

In merchandising companies, the merchandise purchases budget provides information to decision makers about the quantities to be purchased. For accounting purposes, this budget contains information about the cost of goods sold. In contrast, manufacturing companies must prepare a different set of budgets to provide the same type of information to decision makers and accountants.

Production Budget

In a manufacturing company, a **production budget** must be prepared to provide information regarding budgeted production activities. Exhibit 26A.1 shows a production budget for Toronto Supply Company (TSC), a manufacturer of hockey sticks and exclusive supplier to Hockey Den. Given that TSC supplies only to Hockey Den, its managers use information from Hockey Den's sales budget (Exhibit 26.6) to prepare TSC's production budget. The production budget is similar to the merchandise purchases budget in Exhibit 26.8 except that the numbers are expressed in units, which represent the number of hockey sticks to be produced. The production budget forms the basis of preparation for other **manufacturing budgets**.

 LO7 Prepare production and manufacturing budgets.

TSC Production Budget October, November, and December 2004			
	October	November	December
Next month's budgeted sales (units)	800	1,400	900
Ratio of inventory to future sales	× 90%	× 90%	× 90%
Budgeted ending inventory (units)	720	1,260	810
Add budgeted sales for the month (units)	1,000	800	1,400
Required units of available production	1,720	2,060	2,210
Deduct beginning inventory (units)	(900)	(720)	(1,260)
Number of units to be produced	820	1,340	950

Exhibit 26A.1

Production Budget

Manufacturing Budgets

Manufacturers need inputs to produce their final products. These inputs are materials, labour, and other overhead resources. For planning purposes, it is important that managers prepare individual budgets for each of these three resources. Information contained in these three budgets is required to estimate the budgeted cost of goods sold for TSC. Exhibits 26A.2–26A.4 present the three individual budgets.

The *direct materials budget* shown in Exhibit 26A.2 contains information about the materials required for budgeted production. We first compute the materials needed to satisfy each month's production requirement, then add the desired ending inventory requirements.

The desired ending inventory of direct materials as shown in Exhibit 26A.2 is 50% of next month's budgeted material requirements of wood. For instance, in the month of October 2004, an ending inventory of 335 units of material is desired (50% of November's 670 units). The desired ending inventory for December 2004 is 225 units, computed from the direct material requirement of 450 units for a production level of 900 units in January 2005.

Exhibit 26A.2

Direct Materials Budget

TSC Direct Materials Budget October, November, and December 2004	October	November	December
Budgeted production (units)................................	820	1,340	950
Material requirements for production	× 0.5	× 0.5	× 0.5
Materials needed for production (units)	410	670	475
Add desired ending inventory (units)	335	237.5	225
Total materials requirements (units)..................	745	907.5	700
Deduct beginning inventory (units)	(205)	(335)	(237.5)
Units of materials to be purchased	540	572.5	462.5
Material price per unit	$ 6	$ 6	$ 6
Total cost of direct materials purchases............	$3,240	$3,435	$2,775

The total material requirements are computed by adding the desired ending inventory figures to that month's budgeted production material requirements. From Exhibit 26A.2, we see that for October 2004, the total material requirement is 745 units (335+410). From the total material requirement we then subtract the units of materials available in beginning inventory. For October 2004, the materials available from September 2004 are computed as 50% of October's material requirements to satisfy production, or 205 units (50% of 410). This means the direct materials purchases in October 2004 is budgeted at 540 units (740 − 205).

The *direct labour budget* for TSC is shown in Exhibit 26A.3. About 15 minutes of labour time is required to produce one unit for TSC. Labour is paid at the rate of $12 per hour. Budgeted labour hours are computed by multiplying the budgeted production level for each month by one quarter (0.25) of an hour. Direct labour cost is then computed by multiplying budgeted labour hours by the labour rate of $12 per hour.

Exhibit 26A.3

Direct Labour Budget

TSC Direct Labour Budget October, November, and December 2004	October	November	December
Budgeted production (units)................................	820	1,340	950
Labour requirements per unit (hours)	× 0.25	× 0.25	× 0.25
Total labour hours needed	205	335	237.5
Labour rate (per hour)	$ 12	$ 12	$ 12
Labour dollars..	$2,460	$4,020	$2,850

The *manufacturing overhead budget* for TSC is shown in Exhibit 26A.4. The variable portion of overhead is assigned at the rate of $2.50 per unit of production for TSC. The fixed portion stays constant at $1,500 per month for TSC. We show a condensed manufacturing overhead budget in Exhibit 26A.4. Most overhead budgets are more detailed, listing each overhead cost item.

TSC Manufacturing Overhead Budget October, November, and December 2004			
	October	November	December
Budgeted production (units)	820	1,340	950
Variable manufacturing overhead rate	× $ 2.50	× $ 2.50	× $ 2.50
Budgeted variable overhead	$2,050	$3,350	$2,375
Budgeted fixed overhead	$1,500	$1,500	$1,500
Total manufacturing overhead	$3,550	$4,850	$3,875

Exhibit 26A.4

Manufacturing Overhead Budget

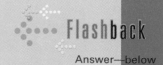

12. What is the difference between operating budgets for a merchandising and a manufacturing firm?

Flashback

Answer—below

GUIDANCE ANSWERS TO  **Flashback**

12. Merchandisers prepare merchandise purchases budgets, whereas manufacturers prepare production and manufacturing budgets. The three manufacturing budgets include the direct materials budget, the direct labour budget, and the manufacturing overhead budget.

Summary

LO7 **Prepare production and manufacturing budgets.** Unlike merchandisers who prepare a merchandise purchases budget to reflect the cost of goods sold, manufacturing companies must prepare four different budgets: (1) production budget, (2) direct materials budget, (3) direct labour budget, and (4) manufacturing overhead budget. The figures in the production budget are derived from sales estimates just as in the case of the merchandise purchases budget.

Demonstration Problem #1

The management of Wood Company has asked you to prepare a master budget for the company from the following information. The budget is to cover the months of April, May, and June of 2004.

Wood Company **Balance Sheet** **March 31, 2004**		
Assets		
Cash	$ 50,000	
Accounts receivable	175,000	
Inventory	126,000	
Total current assets		$351,000
Equipment	480,000	
Accumulated amortization..	(90,000)	390,000
Total assets..		$741,000
Liabilities and Shareholders' Equity		
Accounts payable	$156,000	
Short-term notes payable	12,000	
Total current liabilities...		$168,000
Long-term note payable		200,000
Total liabilities		368,000
Common shares..	235,000	
Retained earnings..	138,000	
Total shareholders' equity..		373,000
Total liabilities and shareholders' equity		$741,000

a. Unit sales for March are 10,000 units. Each month's sales are expected to exceed the prior month's results by 5%. The selling price of the product is $25 per unit.

b. The company's policy calls for the ending inventory of a given month to equal 80% of the next month's expected unit sales. The March 31 inventory is 8,400 units, which is in compliance with the policy. The purchase price is $15 per unit.

c. Sales representatives' commissions are 12.5% and are paid in the month of the sales. The sales manager's salary will be $3,500 in April and $4,000 thereafter.

d. The general and administrative expenses include administrative salaries of $8,000 per month, amortization of $5,000 per month, and 0.9% monthly interest on the long-term note payable.

e. Thirty percent of the company's sales are expected to be for cash and the remaining 70% will be on credit. Receivables are collected in full in the month following the sale (none is collected in the month of the sale).

f. All purchases of merchandise are on credit, and no payables arise from any other transactions. The purchases of one month are fully paid in the next month.

g. The minimum ending cash balance for all months is $50,000. If necessary, the company will borrow enough cash to reach the minimum. The resulting short-term note will require an interest payment of 1% at the end of each month. If the ending cash balance exceeds the minimum, the excess will be applied to repaying the short-term notes payable.

h. Dividends of $100,000 are to be declared and paid in May.

i. No cash payments for income taxes are to be made during the second quarter. Income taxes will be assessed at 35% in the quarter.

j. Equipment purchases of $55,000 are scheduled for June.

Required

Prepare the following budgets and other financial information:

1. Sales budget, including sales for July.
2. Purchases budget, the budgeted cost of goods sold for each month and the quarter, and the cost of the June 30 budgeted inventory.
3. Selling expense budget.
4. General and administrative expense budget.
5. Expected cash receipts from customers and the expected June 30 balance of accounts receivable.
6. Expected cash payments for purchases and the expected June 30 balance of accounts payable.
7. Cash budget.
8. Budgeted income statement.
9. Budgeted statement of retained earnings.
10. Budgeted balance sheet.

Planning the Solution

○ The sales budget shows the expected sales for each month in the quarter. Start by multiplying March sales by 105%, and do the same for the remaining months. July's sales are needed for the purchases budget. To complete the budget, multiply the expected unit sales by the selling price of $25 per unit.

○ Using these results, apply the 80% inventory policy to budget the ending inventory for April, May, and June. Add the budgeted sales to these numbers, and subtract the actual or expected beginning inventory for each month. The result will be the number of units to be purchased in each month. Multiply these numbers by the per unit cost of $15. Find the budgeted cost of goods sold by multiplying the unit sales in each month by the $15 cost per unit. Compute the cost of the June 30 ending inventory by multiplying the units expected to be on hand at that date by the $15 cost per unit.

○ The selling expense budget has only two items. Find the amount of the sales representatives' commissions by multiplying the expected dollar sales in each month by the 12.5% commission rate. Then, add the sales manager's salary of $3,500 in April and $4,000 in May and June.

○ The general and administrative expense budget should show three items. Administrative salaries are fixed at $8,000 per month and amortization is to be $5,000 per month. Budget the monthly interest expense on the long-term note by multiplying its $200,000 balance by the 0.9% monthly interest rate.

○ Determine the amounts of cash sales in each month by multiplying the budgeted sales by 30%. Add to this amount the credit sales of the prior month, which you can compute as 70% of the prior month's sales. April's cash receipts from collecting receivables will equal the March 31 balance of $175,000. The expected June 30 accounts receivable balance equals 70% of June's total budgeted sales.

○ Determine expected cash payments on accounts payable for each month by making them equal to the merchandise purchases in the prior month. The payments for April equal the March 31 balance of accounts payable shown on the beginning balance sheet. The June 30 balance of accounts payable equals merchandise purchases for June.

○ Prepare the cash budget by combining the given information and the amounts of cash receipts and payments on account that you just computed. Complete the cash budget for each month by either borrowing enough to raise the preliminary balance up to the minimum or paying off the short-term note as much as the balance will allow without falling below the minimum. Also show the ending balance of the short-term note in the budget.

○ Prepare the budgeted income statement by combining the budgeted items for all three months. Determine the income before income taxes and multiply it by the 35% rate to find the quarter's income tax expense.

○ The budgeted statement of retained earnings should show the March 31 balance plus the quarter's net income minus the quarter's dividends.

○ The budgeted balance sheet includes updated balances for all the items that appear in the beginning balance sheet and an additional liability for unpaid income taxes. The amounts for all asset, liability, and equity accounts can be found either in the budgets and schedules or by adding amounts found there to the beginning balances.

SOLUTION TO **Demonstration Problem #1**

1. The sales budget:

	April	May	June	July
Prior month's sales............................	10,000	10,500	11,025	11,576
Plus 5% growth	500	525	551	579
Projected unit sales...........................	10,500	11,025	11,576	12,155

	April	May	June	Quarter
Projected unit sales	10,500	11,025	11,576	
Selling price per unit.....................	× $ 25	× $ 25	× $ 25	
Projected sales revenue	$262,500	$275,625	$289,400	$827,525

2. The purchases budget:

	April	May	June	Quarter
Next month's unit sales....................	11,025	11,576	12,155	
Ending inventory percentage...	× 80%	× 80%	× 80%	
Desired ending inventory.................	8,820	9,261	9,724	
This month's unit sales....................	10,500	11,025	11,576	
Units to be available	19,320	20,286	21,300	
Beginning inventory..........................	(8,400)	(8,820)	(9,261)	
Units to be purchased	10,920	11,466	12,039	
Budgeted cost per unit....................	$ 15	$ 15	$ 15	
Projected purchases	$163,800	$171,990	$180,585	$516,375

Budgeted cost of goods sold:

	April	May	June	Quarter
This month's unit sales.................	10,500	11,025	11,576	
Budgeted cost per unit.................	× $ 15	× $ 15	× $ 15	
Projected cost of goods sold	$157,500	$165,375	$173,640	$496,515

Budgeted inventory for June 30:

Units	9,724
Cost per unit	× $ 15
Total	$145,860

3. Selling expense budget:

	April	May	June	Quarter
Budgeted sales	$262,500	$275,625	$289,400	$827,525
Commission percentage	× 12.5%	× 12.5%	× 12.5%	× 12.5%
Sales commissions	$ 32,813	$ 34,453	$ 36,175	$103,441
Manager's salary	3,500	4,000	4,000	11,500
Projected selling expenses	$ 36,313	$ 38,453	$ 40,175	$114,941

4. General and administrative expense budget:

	April	May	June	Quarter
Administrative salaries	$ 8,000	$ 8,000	$ 8,000	$24,000
Amortization	5,000	5,000	5,000	15,000
Interest on long-term note payable (0.9% × $200,000).............	1,800	1,800	1,800	5,400
Projected expenses.........................	$14,800	$14,800	$14,800	$44,400

5. Expected cash receipts from customers:

	April	May	June	Quarter
Budgeted sales	$262,500	$275,625	$289,400	
Ending accounts receivable (70%)	$183,750	$192,938	$202,580	
Cash receipts:				
Cash sales (30%)	$ 78,750	$ 82,687	$ 86,820	$248,257
Collections of prior month's receivables	175,000	183,750	192,938	551,688
Total cash to be collected...............	$253,750	$266,437	$279,758	$799,945

6. Expected cash payments to suppliers:

	April	May	June	Quarter
Cash payments (equal to prior month's purchases).................	$156,000	$163,800	$171,990	$491,790
Expected June 30 balance of accounts payable (June purchases)			$180,585	

7. Cash budget:

	April	May	June
Beginning cash balance	$ 50,000	$ 89,517	$ 50,000
Cash received from customers	253,750	266,437	279,758
Total cash available	$303,750	$355,954	$329,758
Cash payments:			
Payments for merchandise	$156,000	$163,800	$171,990
Sales commissions	32,813	34,453	36,175
Salaries:			
Sales	3,500	4,000	4,000
Administrative	8,000	8,000	8,000
Interest on long-term note	1,800	1,800	1,800
Dividends		100,000	
Equipment purchase			55,000
Interest on short-term notes:			
April ($12,000 × 1.0%)	120		
June ($6,099 × 1.0%)			61
Total	$202,233	$312,053	$277,026
Preliminary balance	101,517	43,901	52,732
Additional loan		6,099	
Loan repayment	(12,000)		(2,732)
Ending cash balance	$ 89,517	$ 50,000	$ 50,000
Ending short-term notes	$ -0-	$ 6,099	$ 3,367

8.

Wood Company Budgeted Income Statement Quarter Ended June 30, 2004		
Sales		$827,525	(part 1)
Cost of goods sold		(496,515)	(part 2)
Gross profit		$331,010	
Operating expenses:			
Sales commissions	$103,441		(part 3)
Sales salaries	11,500		(part 3)
Administrative salaries	24,000		(part 4)
Amortization	15,000		(part 4)
Interest on long-term note	5,400		(part 4)
Interest on short-term notes	181		(part 7)
Total operating expenses		(159,522)	
Income before income taxes		171,488	
Income taxes (35%)		(60,021)	
Net income		$111,467	

9.

Wood Company Budgeted Statement of Retained Earnings For the Quarter Ended June 30, 2004		
Beginning retained earnings	$138,000	(given)
Net income	111,467	(income statement)
Total	$249,467	
Dividends	(100,000)	(given)
Ending retained earnings	$149,467	

10.

Wood Company Budgeted Balance Sheet June 30, 2004		
Assets		
Cash	$ 50,000	(part 7)
Accounts receivable	202,580	(part 5)
Inventory	145,860	(part 2)
Total current assets	$398,440	
Equipment	535,000	(given plus purchase)
Accumulated amortization	(105,000)	430,000 (given plus expense)
Total assets	$828,440	
Liabilities and Shareholder's Equity		
Accounts payable	$180,585	(part 6)
Short-term notes payable	3,367	(part 7)
Estimated income taxes payable	60,021	(income statement)
Total current liabilities	$243,973	
Long-term note payable	200,000	(given)
Total liabilities	$443,973	
Common shares	235,000	(given)
Retained earnings	149,467	(retained earnings statement)
Total shareholders' equity	384,467	
Total liabilities and equity	$828,440	

Demonstration Problem #2

A sales budget for the first six months of 2004 is given below for Clarke Manufacturing Ltd.

Month	Budgeted Sales (units)
January	7,000
February	10,000
March	16,000
April	9,000
May	7,000
June	7,500

The finished goods inventory on hand at the end of each month is engineered to equal 30 percent of the budgeted sales for the subsequent month. Each unit of product requires 6 metres of material A. In an effort to minimize cost Clarke Company's policy is to carry materials inventory not in excess of 10 percent of the next month's production needs. Assume goods in process are not material in amount. On January 1, there were 2,000 units of product on hand.

Required

Prepare a budget showing the quantity of material A to be purchased for each month in the first quarter.

Planning the Solution

○ First prepare a production budget. Start with the budgeted sales for January and add the desired ending inventory. The desired ending inventory is determined by multiplying February budgeted sales by 30%. Deduct the number of units in the beginning inventory (2,000) to arrive at the units to be produced.

○ Repeat this same sequence for February, March, and April.

○ Prepare a materials purchases budget by taking the units to be produced in January and multiplying this number by 6 metres to arrive at the total material needs for the month. Add the desired ending inventory in metres needed to arrive at the required metres to be purchased in January. Repeat this sequence for February and March.

○ Add the rows together to arrive at the figures for the quarter.

SOLUTION TO **Demonstration Problem #2**

Production Budget

	January	February	March	April	May
Budgeted Sales..............................	7,000	10,000	16,000	9,000	7,000
Add: Desired ending inventory	3,000	4,800	2,700	2,100	
Total needs............................	10,000	14,800	18,700	11,100	
Less: Beginning inventory	2,000	3,000	4,800	2,700	
Units to be produced	8,000	11,800	13,900	8,400	

Purchases Budget

	January	February	March	Quarter
Units to be produced	8,000	11,800	13,900	33,700
Material A needed per unit (m).............	6	6	6	6
Material needs in metres......................	48,000	70,800	83,400	202,200
Add: Desired ending inventory	7,080	8,340	5,040*	5,040
Total metres needed	55,080	79,140	88,440	207,240
Less: Beginning inventory	4,800	7,080	8,340	4,800
Required metres to be purchased	50,280	72,060	80,100	202,440
Material price per metre ($5)	5	5	5	5
Total cost of material purchased...........	$251,400	$360,300	$400,500	$1,012,200

*(8,400 × 6 = 50,400 × 0.10)

Glossary

Budget A formal statement of future plans, usually expressed in monetary terms. (p. 1342)

Budgeted balance sheet A managerial accounting report that presents predicted amounts of the company's assets, liabilities, and shareholders' equity as of the end of the budget period. (p. 1357)

Budgeted income statement A managerial accounting report that presents predicted amounts of the company's revenues and expenses for the budget period. (p. 1357)

Budgeting The process of planning future business actions and expressing them as formal plans. (p. 1342)

Capital expenditures budget A plan that lists dollar amounts to be received from disposing of equipment and dollar amounts to be spent on purchasing additional equipment if the proposed production program is carried out. (p. 1353)

Cash budget A plan that shows the expected cash inflows and outflows during the budget period, including receipts from loans needed to maintain a minimum cash balance and repayments of such loans. (p. 1354)

Continuous budgeting The practice of preparing budgets for each of several future periods and revising those budgets as each period is completed; as one period is completed, a new budget period is added, with the result that the budget always covers the same number of future periods. (p. 1346)

General and administrative expense budget A plan that shows the predicted operating expenses not included in the selling expenses budget. (p. 1352)

Manufacturing budget A plan that shows the predicted costs for materials, direct labour, and overhead to be incurred

in manufacturing the units in the production budget. (p. 1363)

Master budget A comprehensive or overall formal plan for a business that includes specific plans for expected sales, the units of product to be produced, the merchandise (or materials) to be purchased, the expenses to be incurred, the long-term assets to be purchased, and the amounts of cash to be borrowed or loans to be repaid, as well as a budgeted income statement and balance sheet. (p. 1346)

Merchandise purchases budget A plan that shows the units or costs of merchandise to be purchased by a merchandising company during the budget period. (p. 1350)

Production budget A plan showing the number of units to be produced each month. (p. 1363)

Rolling budgets As each budget period goes by, a firm adds a new set of budgets for the next period to replace the ones that have lapsed. (p. 1346)

Safety stock Inventory on hand to reduce the risk of running out; a quantity of merchandise or materials over the minimum needed to satisfy budgeted demand. (p. 1351)

Sales budget A plan showing the units of goods to be sold and the revenue to be derived from sales; the starting point in the budgeting process because the plans for most departments are related to sales. (p. 1349)

Selling expense budget A plan that lists the types and amounts of selling expenses expected during the budget period. (p. 1352)

Slack The deliberate overstatement of estimated expenses or understatement of estimated revenue to make budget targets easier to reach. (p. 1360)

For more study tools, quizzes, and problem material,
refer to the Online Learning Centre at
www.mcgrawhill.ca/college/larson

Questions

1. Identify the three roles budgeting plays in helping managers control a business.
2. Budgeting promotes good decision making by requiring managers to conduct _____ and by focusing their attention on the _____.
3. What two alternative norms or objectives can be used to evaluate actual performance? Which of the two is generally more useful?
4. What is the benefit of continuous budgeting?
5. Identify the three typical short-term planning time horizons for budgets.
6. Why should each department participate in preparing its own budget?
7. How does budgeting help management coordinate business activities?
8. Why is the sales budget so important to the budgeting process?
9. What is a selling expense budget? What is a capital expenditure(s) budget?
10. What is a cash budget? Why do operating budgets and the capital expenditures budget need to be prepared before the cash budget?

11.ᴬ What is the difference between a production budget and a manufacturing budget?

12.ᴬ As the accountant for the athletic apparel division of a major international manufacturer you are charged with the responsibility of preparing the rolling budget. Identify the participants (for example, the sales manager for the sales budget) you would contact and describe the information each person would provide in preparing the master budget.

13.ᴬ Does the manager of a local fast food restaurant participate in long-term budgeting?

Quick Study

QS 26-1 Effective budget guidelines LO¹	What are three guidelines that should be followed if budgeting is to serve effectively as a source of motivation?
QS 26-2 Budget committee LO²	Explain why the *bottom up* approach to budgeting is viewed as more successful and provide an example.
QS 26-3 Identify types of budgets LO³	Which of the following comprise the master budget: **a.** Sales budget, operating budgets, historical financial budgets. **b.** Operating budgets, budgeted income statement, budgeted balance sheet. **c.** Sales budgets, capital expenditures budget, financial budgets. **d.** Operating budgets, financial budgets, capital expenditures budget.
QS 26-4 Preparing a purchases budget LO⁴	The July sales budget of the Penrose Company calls for sales of $325,000. The store expects to begin July with a $50,000 inventory and to end the month with a $55,000 inventory. The cost of goods sold is typically about 70% of sales. Determine the cost of goods that should be purchased during July.
QS 26-5 Preparing a cash budget LO²,⁴	Use the following information to prepare a cash budget for the Chase Company. The budget should show expected cash receipts and disbursements for the month of May and the balance expected on May 31. **a.** Cash receipts from sales, $402,000 **b.** Beginning cash balance on March 1, $72,000. **c.** Budgeted cash payments for purchases, $121,300 **d.** Budgeted cash disbursements for salaries, $81,300 **f.** Repayment of bank loan, $40,000. **e.** Other budgeted cash expenses, $64,000.
QS 26-6 Computing ending accounts receivable LO⁵	Evans Company's cash sales are normally 60% of total sales. Anticipated sales for April and May are $588,000 and $550,000 respectively. Of the credit sales, 10% are collected in the same month as the sale, 70% are collected during the first month after the sale, and the remaining 20% are collected in the second month. Determine the accounts receivable balance that should be reported on Evans' budgeted balance sheet as of May 31.
QS 26-7 Zero-based budgeting LO⁶	Why is zero-based budgeting usually more time consuming for management and employees?

ᴬ Identifies assignment material based on Appendix 26A.

Wyatt Company manufactures Product X and has a policy that requires ending inventory to equal 30% of the next month's sales. Sales for July, August, and September are estimated to be 475,000, 565,000 and 600,000 units respectively. Prepare a production budget for July and August. Wyatt estimates that June's ending inventory will consist of 170,000 units.

QS 26-8A
Production budget

LO7

Use the information in QS 26-8A. Assume that 0.8 units of raw material M are required to produce one unit of Product X. The company's inventory policy states that ending raw materials inventory should equal 20% of next month's production. The raw materials inventory at the end of June was 95,000 units. Each unit of raw material M costs $3.75. Prepare a direct materials budget for July.

QS 26-9A
Direct materials budget

LO7

Use the information in QS 26-8A. Each unit of Product X requires 0.4 hours of direct labour at the rate of $9.20 per hour. Prepare a direct labour budget for July and calculate the budgeted direct labour cost per unit of Product X.

QS 26-10A
Direct labour budget

LO7

Use the information in QS 26-8A. The company applies variable manufacturing overhead at the rate of $0.75 per direct labour hour. Fixed manufacturing overhead is budgeted at $505,000 per month. Prepare a manufacturing overhead budget for July.

QS 26-11A
Manufacturing overhead budget

LO7

Exercises

MacPhee Company prepared monthly budgets for the current year. The budgets planned for a July ending inventory of 22,500 units. The company follows a policy of ending each month with merchandise inventory on hand equal to a specified percentage of the budgeted sales for the following month. Budgeted sales and merchandise purchases for three months were as follows:

Exercise 26-1
Merchandise purchases budget for three months

LO3, 4

	Sales (Units)	Purchases (Units)
May	60,000	65,625
June	82,500	90,000
July	112,500	106,875

1. Based on this information, compute the following amounts:
   a. The percentage relationship between a month's ending inventory and sales budgeted for July.
   b. The units budgeted to be sold in August.
   c. The units budgeted for May's beginning inventory.
2. Show the merchandise purchases budgets for May, June, and July.

Holmes Company budgeted the following cash receipts and cash disbursements from operations for the first quarter of the next year:

Exercise 26-2
Cash budget for three months

LO3, 5

	Receipts	Disbursements
January	$435,000	$416,400
February	525,000	467,780
March	600,000	631,500

A Identifies assignment material based on Appendix 26A.

According to a credit agreement with the company's bank, Holmes promises to have a minimum cash balance of $30,000 at the end of each month. In return, the bank has agreed that the company can borrow up to $150,000 with interest of 12% per year, paid on the last day of each month. The interest is computed on the beginning balance of the loan for the month. The company is expected to have a cash balance of $30,000 and a loan balance of $60,000 on January 1.

Required
Prepare monthly cash budgets for the first quarter.

Exercise 26-3
Cash budget from transaction data

LO^{3,5}

Use the following information to prepare a cash budget for Tait Company. The budget should show expected cash receipts and disbursements for the month of June and the balance expected on June 30.

a. Beginning cash balance on June 1: $94,500.

b. Cash receipts from sales: 40% are collected in the month of sale, 50% in the next month, 5% in the second month, and 5% are uncollectible. The following actual and budgeted amounts of sales are known:

April (actual)	$540,000
May (actual)	720,000
June (budgeted)	630,000

c. Payments on purchases: 50% in the month of purchase and 50% in the month following purchase. The following actual and budgeted amounts of merchandise purchases are known:

May (actual)	$270,000
June (budgeted)	405,000

d. Budgeted cash disbursements for salaries in June: $180,000.
e. Budgeted amortization expense for June: $9,000.
f. Other cash expenses budgeted for June: $48,000.
g. Accrued income taxes due in June: $101,250.
h. Bank loan interest due in June: $6,750.

Exercise 26-4
Budgeted income statement and balance sheet

LO^{3,5}

Based on the information provided in Exercise 26-3 and the additional information that follows, prepare a budgeted income statement for the month of June and a budgeted balance sheet for June 30 for Tait Company:

a. Cost of goods sold is 50% of sales.
b. The inventory at the end of May was $121,500.
c. Salaries payable on May 31 were $31,500 and are expected to be $18,000 on June 30.
d. The Equipment account has a balance of $922,500 on June 30. On June 1, accumulated amortization was $236,250.
e. The $6,750 cash payment of interest represents the 1% monthly expense on a bank loan of $675,000.
f. Income taxes payable on May 31 were $101,250, and the income tax rate applicable to the company is 40%. Use this information to check the net income value.
g. Ending June 30 Accounts Receivable and Allowance are $450,000 and $67,500 respectively. The 5% of sales that prove to be uncollectible are debited to Bad Debts Expense and credited to the Allowance for Doubtful Accounts during the month of sale.
h. The only other balance sheet accounts are Common Shares, which has a balance of $225,000, and Retained Earnings, which has a balance of $157,500 on May 31.

Rubert Company's cost of goods sold is consistently 40% of sales. All merchandise is purchased on credit, and 50% of the purchases made during a month are paid in that month. Another 35% is paid for during the first month after purchase, and the remaining 15% is paid for during the second month after purchase. The company plans to have a merchandise inventory at the beginning of each month with a cost equal to 30% of that month's budgeted cost of goods sold.

Use the following sales budgets to compute the expected cash payments to be made during October:

August..	$250,000
September	200,000
October	300,000
November	360,000

Exercise 26-5
Calculations of budgeted cash payments

LO$^{3, 5}$

Tucker Company purchases all of its camping merchandise on credit. It has recently budgeted the following accounts payable balances and merchandise inventory balances:

	Accounts Payable	Merchandise Inventory
January 31	$224,000	$560,000
February 28	280,000	672,000
March 31	246,400	627,200
April 30	319,200	554,400

Cash payments on accounts payable during each month are expected to be:

January..	$1,340,000
February	1,540,000
March	1,300,000
April...	1,580,000

a. Calculate the budgeted amounts of purchases for February, March, and April.
b. Calculate the budgeted amounts of cost of goods sold for February, March, and April.

Exercise 26-6
Budgeting monthly cost of goods sold

LO$^{3, 5}$

Thornton Company specializes in home computer speakers. It budgets its monthly cost of goods sold to equal 70% of sales. The inventory policy calls for a beginning inventory in each month equal to 25% of the budgeted cost of goods sold for that month.

All purchases are on credit, and 20% of the purchases in any month are paid for during the same month. Another 50% is paid during the first month after purchase, and the remaining 30% is paid in the second month after purchase. The following sales budgets have been established:

July..	$600,000
August..	480,000
September	540,000
October	480,000
November	420,000

a. Calculate the budgeted purchases for July, August, September, and October.
b. Calculate the budgeted payments on accounts payable for September and October.
c. Calculate the budgeted ending balances of accounts payable for September and October.

Exercise 26-7
Budgeting accounts payable balances

LO$^{2, 4}$

Exercise 26-8
Zero-based budgeting

LO$^{2, 6}$

Jimmy John's foot-long, ballpark franks are sold at sporting events around the country. Each year management and employees begin preparing the master budgets for each region. The process requires the budget committee to merge several hundred regional budgets into one consolidated budget to begin production planning at the manufacturing plant. This is a challenging process because new regions are added and other regions drop out each year.

Required
As the chair of the budget committee, fill in the following chart by identifying the budget process (continuous or zero-based) you would use for each category of region and then justify your selection. Regions are defined as new and existing. A new region represents a new customer base, where the market size must be estimated from available data. An existing region is one that has a stable, predictable market.

Region	Budget process (Continuous or Zero-based)	Justification
New region		
Existing region		

Exercise 26-9^A
Production budget for two quarters

LO^7

Jacks Company manufactures an innovative automobile transmission for electric cars. Management's policy calls for the ending inventory of a quarter to equal 60% of the next quarter's budgeted sales.

Management predicts an ending inventory for the first quarter of 140,000 units. Forecasted unit sales for the remaining three quarters are 280,000, 400,000, and 700,000 respectively.

Required
Prepare a production budget showing the transmissions that should be manufactured during the year's second and third quarters.

Problems

Problem 26-1A
Merchandise purchases budget

LO$^{3, 4}$

Zed Corporation retails three products that it buys ready for sale. The company's February 28 inventories are:

Product A	20,580 units
Product B	68,700 units
Product C	35,700 units

The company's management has realized that excessive inventories have accumulated for all three products. As a result, the managers have created a new policy that the ending inventory in any month should equal 25% of the expected unit sales for the following month.

Expected sales in units for March, April, May, and June are as follows:

	Budgeted Sales in Units			
	March	April	May	June
Product A	21,000	29,400	37,800	46,200
Product B	66,000	90,000	114,000	78,000
Product C	36,000	30,000	24,000	18,000

---

^{A} Identifies assignment material based on Appendix 26A.

Required

Preparation component:
Prepare separate merchandise purchases budgets (in units) for each of the three products covering March, April, and May.

Analysis component:
Your answer to the preparation component of this problem should reflect much smaller purchases of all three products in March compared to April and May. What factor caused these smaller purchases to be planned? Suggest some conditions in the business that would cause this factor to affect Zed like it apparently has.

NewSound Company has a cash balance of $60,000 on June 1. The company's product sells for $125 per unit. Actual and projected sales are:

	Units	Dollars
April (actual)	8,000	$1,000,000
May (actual)	4,000	500,000
June (budgeted)	12,000	1,500,000
July (budgeted)	6,000	750,000
August (budgeted)	7,600	950,000

Problem 26-2A
Cash budgets with supporting schedules

LO^{3,5}

All the sales are on credit. Recent experience shows that 20% of the revenues are collected in the month of the sale, 30% in the next month after the sale, 48% in the second month after the sale, and 2% prove to be uncollectible.

The purchase price of the product is $100 per unit. All purchases are payable within 12 days. Thus, 60% of the purchases made in a month are paid in that month and the other 40% are paid in the next month. Management has a policy of maintaining an ending monthly inventory of 25% of the next month's unit sales plus a safety stock of 100 units. The March 31 and May 31 actual inventory levels were consistent with this policy.

Cash selling and administrative expenses for the year are $1,200,000, and are paid evenly throughout the year.

The company's minimum cash balance for the end of a month is $60,000. This minimum is maintained, if necessary, by borrowing cash from the bank. If the balance goes over $60,000, the company repays as much of the loan as it can without going below the minimum. This loan carries an annual 9% interest rate. On May 31, the balance of the loan was $44,800.

Required

Preparation component
1. Prepare a schedule that shows how much cash will be collected in June and July from the credit customers.
2. Prepare a schedule that shows the budgeted ending inventories for April, May, June, and July.
3. Prepare a schedule showing the purchases budgets for the product for May, June, and July. Present the calculation in units and then show the dollar amount of purchases for each month.
4. Prepare a schedule showing the cash to be paid out during June and July for product purchases.
5. Prepare monthly cash budgets for June and July, including any loan activity and interest expense. Also, show the loan balance at the end of each month.

Analysis component:
6. Refer to your answer to part 5. Note that NewSound's cash budget indicates that the company will need to borrow over $40,000 in June and over $60,000 in July. Suggest some reasons why knowing this information in May would be helpful to NewSound's management.

Check figure:
Budgeted ending loan balance for July, $149,775

Problem 26-3A
Monthly cash budgets

LO³, ⁵

During the last week of August, the owner of Jazz Company approached the bank for a $80,000 loan to be made on September 1 and repaid on November 30 with annual interest of 12%, or a total of $2,400. The owner planned to increase the store's inventory by $60,000 during September and needed the loan to pay for the merchandise in October and November. The bank's loan officer needed more information about Keller's ability to repay the loan and asked the owner to forecast the store's November 30 cash position.

On September 1, Keller was expected to have a $3,000 cash balance, $120,000 of accounts receivable, and $100,000 of accounts payable. Its budgeted sales, purchases, and cash expenditures for the coming three months are as follows:

	September	October	November
Sales	$220,000	$300,000	$360,000
Merchandise purchases	230,000	160,000	200,000
Payroll	16,000	17,000	18,000
Rent	6,000	6,000	6,000
Other cash expenses	64,000	8,000	7,000
Repayment of bank loan			21,000
Interest on the loan plus bank charges			2,100

The budgeted September purchases include the inventory increase. All sales are on account. The company's regular past experience shows that 25% is collected in the month of the sale, 45% is collected in the month following the sale, 20% in the second month, 9% in the third, and the remainder is not collected. Applying these percentages to the September 1 accounts receivable balance shows that $81,000 of the $120,000 will be collected during September, $36,000 during October, and $16,200 during November. All merchandise is purchased on credit. Eighty percent of the balance is paid in the month following a purchase and the remaining 20% is paid in the second month. The $100,000 of accounts payable at the end of August will be paid as follows: $80,000 in September and $20,000 in October.

Check figure:
Budgeted total disbursements for November, $299,400

Required
Prepare cash budgets for September, October, and November for Jazz Company. Provide additional supplemental schedules as needed.

Problem 26-4A
Preparation and analysis of budgeted income statements

LO³, ⁵

Perkins Company buys one kind of graduation ring at $64 per unit and sells it at $120 per unit. The company's sales representatives receive an 8% commission on each sale. The December income statement shows the following information:

Perkins Company Income Statement For Month Ended December 31	
Sales	$1,200,000
Cost of goods sold	640,000
Gross profit	$ 560,000
Expenses:	
Sales commissions	$ 96,000
Advertising	160,000
Store rent	24,000
Administrative salaries	40,000
Amortization	50,000
Other	12,000
Total	$ 382,000
Net income	$ 178,000

The company's management believes that the December results would be repeated during January, February, and March without any changes in strategy. However, some changes are being considered. Management believes that unit sales will increase at a rate of 10% each month during the next quarter (including January) if the item's selling price is reduced to $112 per unit and if advertising expenses are increased by 25% and remain at that level for all three months. Even if these changes are made, the purchase price will remain at $64 per unit. Under this plan, the sales representatives would continue to earn a 8% commission and the remaining expenses would remain unchanged.

Required

Using a three-column format, prepare budgeted income statements for January, February, and March that show the expected results of implementing the proposed changes. Based on the information in the budgeted income statements, recommend whether management should implement the plan.

Check figure:
Budgeted net income for
February, $146,384

Shortly before the end of 2004, the management of Lam Corporation prepared the following budgeted balance sheet for December 31, 2004:

Problem 26-5A
Preparing a complete
master budget

$LO^{2,3,4}$

Lam Corporation Budgeted Balance Sheet As of December 31, 2004		
Cash		$ 36,000
Accounts receivable		112,500
Inventory		187,500
Total current assets		336,000
Equipment	$450,000	
Accumulated amortization	45,000	405,000
Total		$741,000
Accounts payable	$ 60,000	
Loan from bank	36,000	
Taxes payable (due March 15, 2005)	90,000	
Total liabilities		$186,000
Common shares	$375,000	
Retained earnings	180,000	
Total shareholders' equity		555,000
Total		$741,000

In anticipation of preparing a master budget for January, February, and March 2005, management has gathered the following information:

a. Lam's single product is purchased for $10 per unit and resold for $15 per unit. The expected inventory level on December 31 (18,750 units) is smaller than management's desired level for 2005 of 80% of the next month's expected sales (in units). Budgeted sales are:

January	75,000 units
February	67,500
March	90,000
April	90,000

b. Cash sales are 50% of total sales and credit sales are 50% of total sales. Of the credit sales, 80% are collected in the first month after the sale and 20% in the second month after the sale. Eighty percent of the December 31, 2004, balance of accounts receivable will be collected during January and 20% will be collected during February.

c. Merchandise purchased by the company is paid for as follows: 70% in the month after purchase, and 30% in the second month after purchase. Seventy percent of the Accounts Payable balance on December 31, 2004, will be paid during January, and 30% will be paid during February.

d. Sales commissions of 10% of sales are paid each month. Additional sales salaries are $90,000 per year.

e. General and administrative salaries are $810,000 per year. Repair expenses equal $3,750 per month and are paid in cash.

f. The equipment shown in the December 31, 2004, balance sheet was purchased in January 2004. It is being amortized over 10 years under the straight-line method with no salvage value. The following new purchases of equipment are planned in the coming quarter:

January	$ 82,800
February.....................................	43,200
March..	108,000

This equipment also will be amortized with the straight-line method over ten years, with no salvage value. A full month's amortization is taken for the month in which the equipment is purchased.

g. The company plans to acquire some land at the end of March at a cost of $750,000. The purchase price will be paid with cash on the last day of the month.

h. Lam has a working arrangement with the bank to obtain additional loans as needed. The interest rate is 12% per year, and the interest is paid at the end of each month based on the beginning balance. Partial or full payments on these loans can be made on the last day of the month. Lam has agreed to maintain an minimum ending cash balance of $36,000 in every month.

i. The income tax rate applicable to the company is 40%. However, income taxes on the first quarter's income will not be paid until April 15.

Check figure:
Budgeted total assets March 31, $2,906,310

Required

Prepare a master budget for the first quarter of 2005. It should include the following component budgets:

1. Monthly sales budgets (showing both budgeted unit sales and dollar sales)
2. Monthly merchandise purchases budgets
3. Monthly selling expense budgets
4. Monthly general and administrative expense budgets
5. Monthly capital expenditures budgets
6. Monthly cash budgets
7. Budgeted income statement for the first quarter
8. Budgeted balance sheet as of March 31, 2005

Provide as many supplemental schedules as you need. Round all amounts to the nearest dollar.

Problem 26-6A[A]

Production budget and materials purchases budget

LO[7]

Sportworld Company produces exercise machines. One particular machine requires two kilograms of steel. The company's management predicts that there will be 6,000 unit of the product and 12,000 kilograms of steel on June 30 of the current year, and that 100,000 exercise machines will be sold during the next quarter. Because the peak selling season will be over, management wants to end the third quarter with only 4,000 finished exercise machines and 5,000 kilograms of steel in the materials inventory. Steel can be purchased for approximately $6.00 per kilogram.

Check figure:
Cost of steel purchases, $1,134,000

Required

Prepare a third-quarter production budget and a third-quarter steel purchases budget for the company (include the dollar cost of the purchases).

Alternate Problems

Problem 26-1B

Merchandise purchases budget

LO[3, 4]

Cecil Corporation retails three products that it buys ready-for-sale. The company's May 31 inventories are:

Product X	23,400 units
Product Y	15,000 units
Product Z	30,000 units

[A] Identifies assignment material based on Appendix 26A.

The company's management has realized that excessive inventories have accumulated for all three products. As a result, the managers have created a new policy that the ending inventory in any month should equal 20% of the expected unit sales for the following month. Expected sales in units for June, July, August, and September are as follows:

	Budgeted Sales in Units			
	June	July	August	September
Product X	30,000	27,600	30,000	22,800
Product Y	16,800	16,800	20,400	21,600
Product Z	36,000	32,400	31,200	34,800

Required

Preparation component
Prepare separate merchandise purchases budgets (in units) for each of the three products covering June, July, and August.

Analysis component
Your answer to the preparation component of this problem should reflect much smaller purchases of Product Y in July compared to June and August. What factor caused these smaller purchases to be planned? Suggest business conditions in the business that would cause this factor to affect Cecil as it has.

Link Company's product sells for $50 per unit. Actual and projected sales are:

Problem 26-2B
Preparing and analyzing cash budgets with supporting inventory and purchases schedules

LO³, ⁵

	Units	Dollars
September (actual)	11,520	$576,000
October (actual)	7,680	384,000
November (budgeted)...........................	9,120	456,000
December (budgeted)...........................	11,040	552,000
January (budgeted)	10,080	504,000

The company has a cash balance of $96,000 on October 31. All the sales are on credit. Recent experience shows that 40% of the revenues are collected in the month of the sale, 40% in the next month after the sale, 18% in the second month after the sale, and 2% prove to be uncollectible.

The purchase price of the product is $35 per unit. Approximately one-fourth of the merchandise purchased is paid during the month of purchase. The remaining three-fourths is paid for in the following month. Link Company's management has a policy of maintaining an ending monthly inventory of 60% of the next month's unit sales plus a safety stock of 750 units. The October 31, inventory is consistent with this policy.

Cash selling and administrative expenses for the year are $1,396,800 (excluding amortization), and are paid evenly throughout the year. The October 31, cash balance is $96,000.

Required
Prepare a monthly cash budget for November and December, with supporting schedules showing cash receipts from collections of receivables and cash payments for merchandise purchases.

Check figure:
November cash payments for purchases $314,160

Problem 26-3B
Preparing cash budgets for three periods

LO3, 5

During the last week of September, the owner of the Jessome Company approached the bank for a $175,000 loan to be made on October 1 and repaid in 60 days with annual interest of 8% plus bank charges. The owner planned to increase the store's inventory by $140,000 during October and needed the loan to pay for the merchandise in November and December. The bank's loan officer needed more information about Jessome's ability to repay the loan and asked the owner to forecast the store's December 31 cash position. On October 1 Jessome was expected to have a $16,800 cash balance, $189,000 of accounts receivable, and $126,000 of accounts payable. Its budgeted sales, purchases, and cash expenditures for the coming three months are as follows:

	October	November	December
Sales	$490,000	$700,000	$770,000
Merchandise purchases	350,000	280,000	266,000
Payroll	31,500	42,000	52,500
Rent	16,800	16,800	16,800
Other cash expenses	12,600	18,900	23,100
Repayment of bank loan			175,000
Interest on the loan plus bank charges			4,725

The budgeted October purchases include the inventory increase. All sales are on account. The company's past experience shows that 10% is collected in the month of the sale, 60% in the month following the sale, 25% in the second month, 3% in the third, and the remainder is uncollectible. Applying these percentages to the October 1 accounts receivable balance shows that $113,400 of the $189,000 will be collected in October, $47,250 in November, and $5,670 in December. All merchandise is purchased on credit. Eighty percent of the balance is paid in the month following a purchase and the remaining 20% is paid in the second month. For example, of the $126,000 of accounts payable at the end of September, $100,800 will be paid in October and $25,200 in November.

Check figure:
Ending cash balance, October $192,500

Required
Prepare cash budgets for October, November, and December for Jessome Company. Provide additional supplemental schedules as needed.

Problem 26-4B
Preparation and analysis of budgeted income statements

LO3, 5

Wolfson Company buys merchandise at $70 per unit and sells it at $126 per unit. The company's sales representatives receive an 8% commission on sales. Its September 2004 income statement is as follows:

Wolfson Company Income Statement For Month Ended September 30, 2004	
Sales	$1,134,000
Cost of goods sold	630,000
Gross profit	$ 504,000
Expenses:	
Sales commissions	$ 90,720
Advertising	80,640
Store rent	25,200
Administrative salaries	30,240
Amortization	15,120
Other	37,800
Total	$ 279,720
Net income	$ 224,280

The company's management believes that the September results will be repeated during the fourth quarter without any changes in strategy. Management also believes that unit sales will increase at a rate of 10% each month during the fourth quarter of 2004 if the item's selling price is reduced to $112 per unit and if advertising expenses are increased by 40% and remain at that level for all three months. Whatever changes are made, the purchase price will remain at $70 per unit. Under this plan, the sales staff would continue to earn an 8% commission and the remaining expenses would stay the same.

Required

Preparation Component
1. Using a three-column format, prepare budgeted income statements for October, November, and December that show the expected results of implementing the proposed changes.

Analysis Component
2. Use the budgeted income statements to recommend whether management should implement the plan.

Check figure:
Budgeted net income for November, $138,550

During March 2005, Shafai Corporation's management prepared the following budgeted balance sheet for March 31, 2005:

Problem 26-5B
Preparing a complete master budget

LO^{2,4}

Shafai Corporation Budgeted Balance Sheet As of March 31, 2005		
Cash		$ 18,000
Accounts receivable		54,000
Inventory		90,000
Total current assets		$162,000
Equipment	$216,000	
Accumulated amortization	21,600	194,400
Total		$356,400
Accounts payable	$ 28,800	
Loan from bank	18,000	
Taxes payable (due June 15, 2005)	43,200	
Total liabilities		$ 90,000
Common shares	$180,000	
Retained earnings (deficit)	86,400	
Total shareholders' equity		266,400
Total		$356,400

In anticipation of preparing a master budget for April, May, and June 2005, management has gathered the following information:
a. Shafai Corporation's single product is purchased for $10 per unit and resold for $15 per unit. Although the inventory level on March 31 is smaller than desired (9,000 units) management has established a new inventory policy that month-end inventory should be 80% of the following month's expected sales. Budgeted unit sales are:

April	36,000 units
May	32,400
June	43,200
July	43,200

b. Cash sales are 50% of total sales and credit sales are 50% of total sales. Of the credit sales, 80% are collected in the first month after the sale and 20% in the second month after the sale. Eighty percent of the March 31, 2005, balance of accounts receivable will be collected during April and 20% will be collected during May.
c. Merchandise purchases are paid for as follows: 70% in the month after purchase, and 30% in the second month after purchase. For example, 70 percent of the Accounts Payable balance on March 31, 2005, will be paid during April, and 30% will be paid during May.
d. Sales commissions of 10% of sales are paid each month. Additional sales salaries are $43,200 per year.

e. General and administrative salaries are $388,800 per year. Repair expenses equal $1,800 per month and are paid in cash.

f. The equipment shown in the March 31, 2005, balance sheet was purchased one year ago. It is being amortized over 10 years under the straight-line method with no salvage value. The following new purchases of equipment are planned in the coming quarter:

April	$36,000
May	18,000
June	54,000

This equipment will also be amortized with the straight-line method over ten years, with no salvage value. A full month's amortization is taken for the month in which the equipment is purchased.

g. The company plans to acquire some land at the end of June at a cost of $360,000. The purchase price will be paid with cash on the last day of the month. Thus if a bank loan is necessary the first payment will be made at the end of July.

h. Shafai Corporation has a working arrangement with the bank to obtain additional loans as needed. The interest rate is 10% per year, and the interest is paid at the end of each month based on the beginning balance. Partial or full payments on these loans can be made on the last day of the month. Shafai Corporation has agreed to maintain a minimum ending cash balance of $18,000 in every month.

i. The income tax rate applicable to the company is 40%. However, income taxes on the first quarter's income will not be paid until July 15.

Required
Prepare a master budget for the second quarter of 2005 with the operating budgets, capital expenditures budget, and the cash budget prepared on a monthly basis. The budgeted income statement should show operations for the second quarter, and the budgeted balance sheet should be prepared as of June 30, 2005. The operating budgets included in the master budget should include a sales budget (showing both budgeted unit sales and dollar sales), a merchandise purchases budget, a selling expense budget, and a general and administrative budget. (Round to the nearest dollar.)

Problem 26-6B[A]
Production budget and materials purchases budget

LO7

Check figure:
Cost of aluminum purchases, $1,423,800

Leverne Company produces baseball bats. Each bat requires 2 kilograms of aluminum alloy. Aluminum alloy can be purchased for approximately $7.00 per kilogram. The company's management predicts that there will be 14,000 bats and 18,000 kilograms of aluminum alloy on hand on March 31 of the current year, and that 120,000 bats will be sold during the year's second quarter. Because the peak selling season will have passed, management wants to end the second quarter of the year with only 4,000 finished bats and only 1,400 kilograms of aluminum alloy in the materials inventory.

Required
Prepare a second-quarter production budget and a second-quarter aluminum alloy purchases budget for the company (include the dollar cost of the purchases).

[A] Identifies assignment material based on Appendix 26A.

Analytical and Review Problems

A & R 26-1

Fei Abella and Cammy Tam were invited by the Racket family for a weekend of tennis during the spring break. During the weekend, Mr. Racket made good on his promise to give Fei another "lesson" on the computer. The lesson was really a demonstration of how the computer is used to plan four or five years ahead under a variety of assumptions. Mr. Racket loaded a spreadsheet program into his microcomputer and loaded the financial statements of Assumed Company. Once the statements appeared on the screen, Mr. Racket explained the assumptions he was using in his calculations and, with the press of a button, projected five-year income statements as well as balance sheets at the end of each year appeared on the screen. He had these printed out and repeated the process with a set of different assumptions. Mr. Racket also demonstrated projections with graphs and bar charts. Amazed and astonished at the speed and the alternatives in presenting financial data, Fei and Cammy thanked Mr. Racket for the demonstration.

On the way back to the university, Fei and Cammy contemplated Mr. Racket's remark at the conclusion of the demonstration which was, "The computer is nothing; the assumptions made are king."

Required

What do you think Mr. Racket meant by the above remark? Explain fully.

A & R 26-2

Donnelly purchases its rubber on account, and the resulting payables are paid in cash as follows: 40% during the month after purchase and 60% during the second month after purchase. This rubber is used to produce bicycle tires that require 3 kilograms of rubber per unit. The owner of the company is negotiating with the bank for approval to obtain loans as they are needed. An important item in the discussion has been the question of how much cash will be required to pay for purchases of rubber.

The company plans to manufacture enough tires to maintain an ending monthly inventory equal to 30% of the next month's sales. Sufficient rubber is to be purchased each month to maintain an ending monthly inventory equal to 20% of the next month's production requirements. During the coming months, budgeted unit sales are as follows:

June	112,000 units
July	168,000
August	210,000
September	70,000

The following data are available on May 31:

Tires on hand	42,000 units
Kilograms of rubber on hand	184,800 units
Accounts payable due in June	$ 840,000
Accounts payable due in July	$1,260,000

Recent prices of rubber have varied substantially and the owner speculates that the price could range from $8 to $20 per kilogram during the next few months. You are asked to assist the owner by predicting the cash payments to be made in the months of June, July, and August. Prepare separate predictions based on a low price of $8 and a high price of $20.

A & R 26-3

Beleveau Corporation's inventory policy is to maintain an ending monthly finished goods inventory of 20% of the next month's budgeted sales plus a safety stock of 14,000 units. The company has budgeted the following monthly sales volumes:

February	392,000 units
March	336,000
April	280,000
May	350,000

The February 1 inventory was 72,800 units. As analysis of Tam's manufacturing costs shows:

Material	$ 7.00 per unit
Direct labour cost	$ 2.80 per unit
Variable overhead cost	$15.40 per unit
Fixed overhead cost	$500,000 per month

Required

Prepare production budgets and manufacturing budgets for the months of February, March, and April. The manufacturing budgets should show the total manufacturing costs expected in each of the three months.

A & R 26-4

Calvert Company projects sales at $492,800 and $537,600 respectively for January and February of 2005. The company's balance sheet contains the following balances on December 31, 2005:

Cash	$ 35,840
Accounts receivable	
(net allowance for doubtful accounts of $8,960)	170,240
Inventory	71,680
Capital assets (net of accumulated amortization of $268,800)	179,200
	$456,960
Accounts payable (for inventory purchases)	$369,600
Common shares	56,000
Retained earnings	31,360
	$326,400

Cash collections for accounts receivable are estimated to be 50% in the month of sale, 48% in the following month, and 2% are uncollectible. Gross margin is 25%.

Purchases of inventory each month are 75% of the next month's projected sales and the balance owed is paid in the following month. Amortization is $22,400 per month and other expenses amount to $73,920 per month, and are paid in cash in the month incurred.

Required

Prepare a projected cash budget and income statement for January 2005.

Flexible Budgets and Standard Costs

A Hole in One

Toronto, Ontario—In the shadow of a high-rise building in downtown Toronto, G-Max could be just another trinket shop for wandering tourists. But rolls of twine, fabrication equipment, and a driving range make it clear that this is a local success story with a difference. This collection is all part of the G-Max manufacturing process.

G-Max makes specialty golf equipment and accessories for individual consumers and organizations. It specializes in golf balls, with simple colour changes to an entirely new design. In six years, G-Max made a name for itself and is quickly becoming the leader in this quirky market. For its most recent fiscal year, earnings are up more than 23%, to $455,000.

Nancy Stricker, 25, is the founder of G-Max. "When I was in high school, I caddied at a golf course in Mesa. I was amazed at what golfers would do to dazzle friends and clients," says Stricker. "They were always looking for that special item or gag gift." Stricker began by taking golf balls and dressing them up to a buyer's liking. "Names, colours, logos, whatever. I'd fix them up any way they liked."

Stricker was soon overwhelmed by more than one hundred requests that led her to set up a small manufacturing facility in an old service garage. "People requested all kinds of things. And they were willing to pay for it." Stricker quickly launched into specialty manufacturing of golf balls. "But within a year I was losing control of costs and revenues," says Stricker. "The business was growing so fast that I didn't know what I was doing right and what I was doing wrong. I needed a way to assess how I was doing."

With help from a financial advisor, Stricker implemented an accounting system with budgets and standard costs. "It literally saved my business. It gave me information I needed to make good decisions. Budget reports and cost variances quickly identified problems," says Stricker, "and I quickly moved to solve them."

And the strangest order? "That's easy," says Stricker. "Square, pink golf balls! A consulting firm ordered them for clients in one of those 'think out of the box' sessions. I guess the firm wanted to make a point."

Learning Objectives

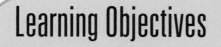

LO¹ Compare fixed and flexible budgets.

LO² Prepare a flexible budget and interpret a flexible budget performance report.

LO³ Define standard costs and explain their computation and uses.

LO⁴ Compute material and labour variances.

LO⁵ Describe variances and what they reveal about performance.

LO⁶ Compute overhead variances.

LO⁷ Explain how standard cost information is useful for management by exception.

LO⁸ Record journal entries for standard costs and account for price and quantity variances.

Chapter Preview

In Chapter 26 we explained how budgeting helps organize and formalize management's planning activities. We also explained how budgets provide a basis for evaluating actual performance. This chapter extends that discussion to look more closely at how budgets are used to evaluate performance. Evaluations are important for monitoring business activities. We also describe and illustrate the use of standard costs and variance analyses. This includes explanation of revenue variances. These managerial tools are useful for both evaluation and control of organizations and in the planning of future activities. Application of these tools can greatly affect the performance of a company as evidenced by G-Max in the opening article.

Section 1—Flexible Budgets

Section 1 introduces fixed budgets and fixed budget performance reports. It then introduces flexible budgets and flexible budget performance reports. The advantages of flexible budgets and reports are illustrated with comparisons to fixed budgets and reports.

Budgetary Process

A master budget P. 1346 reflects management's planned objectives for a future period. We explained in Chapter 26 how a master budget is prepared based on a predicted level of activity such as sales volume for the budget period. This section discusses the usefulness of budget reports when the actual level of activity is different from the predicted level.

Budgetary Control and Reporting

Budgetary control is the use of budgets by management to review the operations of a company. Essentially, this consists of comparing the actual activity to planned (or budgeted) activity.

The *process of budgetary control* involves at least four steps: (1) develop the budget from planned objectives, (2) compare actual results to budgeted amounts and analyze the differences, (3) take corrective and strategic actions, and (4) establish new planned objectives and prepare a new budget. Exhibit 27.1 shows this continual process of budgetary control.

Budget reports contain information that compares actual results to planned objectives. This comparison is motivated by a need to both monitor performance and control activities. Budget reports are sometimes viewed as progress reports, or *report cards*, on management's performance in achieving planned objectives. These reports can be prepared at any time and for any period. Three common periods for a budget report are a month, quarter, and year.

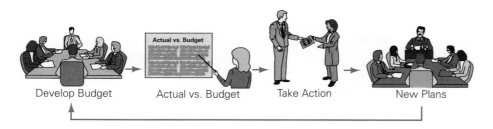

Exhibit 27.1

Process of Budgetary Control

Develop Budget   Actual vs. Budget   Take Action   New Plans

Budget reports and related documents are effective tools for managers in getting the greatest benefits from this process.

Fixed Budget Performance Report

In a fixed budgetary control system, the master budget is based on a single prediction for sales volume or other activity level. The budgeted amount for each cost essentially assumes a specific (or *fixed*) amount of sales will occur. A **fixed budget**, also called a *static budget*, is one based on a single predicted amount of sales or production volume, or some other relevant activity measure (e.g., student enrolment in an educational institution).

We explained in Chapter 26 that one benefit of a budget is its usefulness in comparing actual results with planned activities. A **fixed budget performance report** is shown in Exhibit 27.2; this report compares the actual results of Optel for November 2003 with the results expected under its fixed budget that predicted 10,000 (composite) units of sales. Optel is a manufacturer of inexpensive eyeglasses, frames, contact lens, and related supplies. For this report, its production volume equals sales volume (meaning the amount of inventory did not change).

This type of performance report designates the differences between budgeted and actual results as variances. We see the letters *F* and *U* located beside the numbers in the third column of this report. Their meanings are:

> *F* = ***Favourable variance***—When compared to budget, the actual cost or revenue contributes to a *higher* income. This means actual revenue (cost) is greater (lower) than budgeted revenue (cost).
>
> *U* = ***Unfavourable variance***—When compared to budget, the actual cost or revenue contributes to a *lower* income. This means actual revenue (cost) is lower (greater) than budgeted revenue (cost).

This convention is common in practice and is used throughout this chapter.

Exhibit 27.2

Fixed Budget Performance
Report

	Optel Fixed Budget Performance Report For Month Ended November 30, 2003		
	Fixed Budget	Actual Performance	Variances
Sales: In units	10,000	12,000	
In dollars	$100,000	$125,000	$25,000 F
Cost of goods sold:			
Direct materials	10,000	13,000	3,000 U
Direct labour	15,000	20,000	5,000 U
Overhead:			
Factory supplies	2,000	2,100	100 U
Utilities	3,000	4,000	1,000 U
Amortization of machinery	8,000	8,000	
Supervisory salaries	11,000	11,000	
Selling expenses:			
Sales commissions	9,000	10,800	1,800 U
Shipping expenses	4,000	4,300	300 U
General and administrative expenses:			
Office supplies	5,000	5,200	200 U
Insurance expense	1,000	1,200	200 U
Amortization of office equipment	7,000	7,000	
Administrative salaries	13,000	13,000	
Total expenses	88,000	99,600	11,600 U
Income from operations	$ 12,000	$ 25,400	$13,400 F

F = Favourable variance; and U = Unfavourable variance

The primary use of budget reports is for management in monitoring, controlling, and evaluating operations. A manager seeing Optel's report will definitely be happy with the $13,400 increase in income. The report also shows a $25,000 increase in sales which is also news. However, the report does not explain why sales increased and also does not answer questions about input efficiency (materials, labour, and other resources).

An increase in sales should result in a corresponding increase in some variable costs (those that vary with sales level). But it is also possible that the increase in these variable costs could be higher or lower than they should be. The performance report in Exhibit 27.2 provides little help in verifying the effects of sales increase on cost items. This inability to reflect changes in costs due to changes in activity levels is a major limitation of the fixed budget performance report.

Flexible Budget Reports

This section explains the purpose of both a flexible budget and a flexible budget performance report. We also describe the preparation of the flexible budget and the presentation of the flexible budget performance report.

Purpose of Flexible Budgets

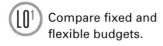
Compare fixed and
flexible budgets.

To help management address questions that arise with the fixed budget performance report, we look to a **flexible budget**. A flexible budget, also called a *variable budget*, is a report based on predicted amounts of revenues and expenses corresponding to the actual level of output. Unlike fixed budgets, a flexible budget is prepared after a period's activities are complete. A flexible budget can be viewed as a fixed budget at an activity level corresponding to the actual level of activity. Many companies prepare and use flexible budgets. The primary purpose of a flexible budget is to help managers evaluate *past* performance.

Preparing Flexible Budgets

A flexible budget is designed to reveal the effects of volume on the level of revenues and costs. To prepare a flexible budget, management relies on the distinctions between fixed costs P. 1299 and variable costs P. 1300. Fixed and variable costs were described under cost-volume-profit analysis in Chapter 25, and also in Chapter 21. Recall that the cost per unit of activity remains constant for variable costs. This means the total amount of a variable cost changes in direct proportion to a change in level of activity. For fixed costs, the total amount of cost remains unchanged regardless of changes in the level of activity within a relevant (normal) operating range.[1]

When we create the numbers comprising a flexible budget, we need to express each variable cost as either a constant amount per unit of sales or as a percent of sales dollars. In the case of a fixed cost, we need to express its budgeted amount as the total amount expected to occur at any sales volume within the relevant range.

Exhibit 27.3 shows a set of flexible budgets for Optel for November 2003. Seven of its expenses are classified as variable costs. Its remaining five expenses are fixed costs. These classifications result from management's investigation of each of the company's expenses using the cost estimation methods we explained

> **LO²** Prepare a flexible budget and interpret a flexible budget performance report.

Exhibit 27.3

Flexible Budgets

	Flexible Budget — Variable Amount per Unit	Flexible Budget — Total Fixed Cost	Flexible Budget for Unit Sales of 10,000	Flexible Budget for Unit Sales of 12,000	Flexible Budget for Unit Sales of 14,000
Optel Flexible Budgets For Month Ended November 30, 2003					
Sales	$10.00		$100,000	$120,000	$140,000
Variable costs:					
Direct materials	1.00		10,000	12,000	14,000
Direct labour	1.50		15,000	18,000	21,000
Factory supplies	0.20		2,000	2,400	2,800
Utilities	0.30		3,000	3,600	4,200
Sales commissions	0.90		9,000	10,800	12,600
Shipping expenses	0.40		4,000	4,800	5,600
Office supplies	0.50		5,000	6,000	7,000
Total variable costs	$ 4.80		$ 48,000	$ 57,600	$ 67,200
Contribution margin	$ 5.20		$ 52,000	$ 62,400	$ 72,800
Fixed costs:					
Amortization, machinery		$ 8,000	8,000	8,000	8,000
Supervisory salaries		11,000	11,000	11,000	11,000
Insurance expense		1,000	1,000	1,000	1,000
Amortization, office equipment		7,000	7,000	7,000	7,000
Administrative salaries		13,000	13,000	13,000	13,000
Total fixed costs		$40,000	$ 40,000	$ 40,000	$ 40,000
Income from operations			$ 12,000	$ 22,400	$ 32,800

---

[1] We assume here that all costs can be reasonably classified as either variable or fixed within a relevant range.

in Chapter 25. Variable and fixed expense categories are not the same for every company, and we must avoid drawing conclusions from specific cases. For example, depending on the nature of a company's operations, office supplies expense can be either fixed or variable with respect to sales.

The layout for the flexible budgets in Exhibit 27.3 reports sales followed by variable costs and then fixed costs. Both individual and total variable costs are reported and then subtracted from sales. As we explained in Chapter 25, the difference between sales and variable costs equals contribution margin P. 1308. The expected amounts of fixed costs are listed next, followed by the expected income from operations before taxes.

The first and second columns of Exhibit 27.3 show the flexible budget amounts for variable and fixed costs applied to any volume of sales in the relevant range. The third, fourth, and fifth columns show the flexible budget amounts computed for three different sales volumes. For instance, the third column's flexible budget is based on 10,000 units. These numbers are the same amounts appearing in the fixed budget of Exhibit 27.2 because the expected volumes are the same for these two budgets.

Recall that Optel's actual sales volume for November is 12,000 units. This sales volume is 2,000 units more than the 10,000 units originally predicted in the master budget. When differences arise between actual and predicted volume, the usefulness of a flexible budget is apparent. For instance, compare the flexible budget for 10,000 units in the third column (which is the same as the fixed budget in Exhibit 27.2) with the flexible budget for 12,000 units in the fourth column. The higher levels for both sales and all variable costs reflect nothing more than the increase in sales activity. Any budget analysis comparing actual with planned results that ignores this information is less useful to management.

To illustrate, when we evaluate the performance of Optel, we need to prepare a flexible budget showing actual and budgeted values at 12,000 units. As part of a complete profitability analysis, managers could compare the actual income of $25,400 (from Exhibit 27.2) with the $22,400 income expected at the actual sales volume of 12,000 units (from Exhibit 27.3). This results in a total income of $3,000 to be explained and understood. This variance is markedly different from the $13,400 variance identified in Exhibit 27.2 using a fixed budget. After receiving the flexible budget based on November's actual volume, management's next step is to determine what caused this $3,000 difference (recall that the difference of $10,400 can be attributed to the increase in sales of 2,000 units). The next section describes a flexible budget performance report that provides guidance for answering this and similar questions.

Flexible Budget Performance Report

A **flexible budget performance report** lists differences between actual performance and budgeted performance based on actual sales volume or other level of activity. This report helps direct management's attention to those costs or revenues that differ substantially from budgeted amounts.

Exhibit 27.4 shows the flexible budget performance report of Optel for November. We prepare this report after the actual volume is known to be 12,000 units.

This report shows a $5,000 favourable variance in total dollar sales. Because actual and budgeted volumes are both 12,000 units, the $5,000 sales variance must have resulted from a selling price that was higher than expected. Further analysis of the facts surrounding this $5,000 sales variance reveals a favourable sales variance per unit of nearly $0.42 as shown here:

Actual average price per unit	$125,000/12,000	=	$10.42
Budgeted price per unit	$120,000/12,000	=	10.00
Favourable sales variance per unit	$ 5,000/12,000	=	$ 0.42

Optel **Flexible Budget Performance Report** **For Month Ended November 30, 2003**	Flexible Budget	Actual Performance	Variances	
Sales (12,000 units)	$120,000	$125,000	$5,000	F
Variable costs:				
Direct materials	$ 12,000	$ 13,000	$1,000	U
Direct labour	18,000	20,000	2,000	U
Factory supplies	2,400	2,100	300	F
Utilities	3,600	4,000	400	U
Sales commissions	10,800	10,800		
Shipping expenses	4,800	4,300	500	F
Office supplies	6,000	5,200	800	F
Total variable costs	$ 57,600	$ 59,400	$1,800	U
Contribution margin	$ 62,400	$ 65,600	$3,200	F
Fixed costs:				
Amortization of machinery	$ 8,000	$ 8,000		
Supervisory salaries	11,000	11,000		
Insurance expense	1,000	1,200	$ 200	U
Amortization of office equipment	7,000	7,000		
Administrative salaries	13,000	13,000		
Total fixed costs	$ 40,000	$ 40,200	$ 200	U
Income from operations	$ 22,400	$ 25,400	$3,000	F

Exhibit 27.4

Flexible Budget
Performance Report

F = Favourable variance; and U = Unfavourable variance

The other variances computed in Exhibit 27.4 also direct management's attention to areas where corrective actions can help them control Optel's operations. Each variance is analyzed like the previous sales variance. We can think of each expense as the joint result of using a given number of units of an expense item and paying a specific price per unit.

Each variance in Exhibit 27.4 is due in part to a difference between *actual price per unit* of input and *budgeted price per unit* of input. This is a **price variance**. A variance can also be due in part to a difference between actual quantity of input used and *budgeted quantity* of input. This is a **quantity variance**. We explain more about this breakdown, known as **variance analysis**, in the section on standard costs later in the chapter.

Budget Officer

You are the budget officer for a management consulting firm. The heads of both the strategic consulting and tax consulting divisions complain to you about the negative variances on their recent quarterly performance reports. "We worked on more consulting assignments than planned. It's not surprising our costs are higher than expected. But this report characterizes our work as poor!" How do you respond?

Judgement Call

Answer—p. 1415

Answers—p. 1415

1. A flexible budget:
   a. Shows fixed costs as constant amounts of cost per unit of activity.
   b. Shows variable costs as constant amounts of cost per unit of activity.
   c. Is prepared based on one expected amount of budgeted sales or production.
2. What is the initial step in preparing a flexible budget?
3. What is the difference between a fixed and a flexible budget?
4. What is contribution margin?

Mid-Chapter Demonstration Problem

Wei Tian Enterprises presents you with the following incomplete flexible budget for overhead costs:

Overhead Costs	Cost Formula (per hour)	Machine Hours 15,000	Machine Hours 20,000	Machine Hours 25,000
Variable costs:				
Indirect labour			$ 16,000	
Indirect materials			10,000	
Maintenance			24,000	
Utilities			20,000	
Total variable costs			$ 70,000	
Fixed costs:				
Management salaries			$200,000	
Factory rent			40,000	
Insurance			25,000	
Maintenance			10,000	
Total fixed overhead			$275.000	
Total overhead			$345,000	

Required

a. Complete the flexible budget for Wei Tien Enterprises. Assume that cost relationships are valid within the range of machine-hours specified by the budget.

b. Estimate the total overhead costs at 28,000 machine hours.

Planning the Solution

o Determine the cost formula for each variable overhead item by dividing each dollar figure under the 20,000 machine-hours column by 20,000 machine-hours. Note that overhead costs have already been separated into fixed and variable components.

o Using the formula for the variable portion of the costs, multiply each formula by the number of machine-hours given in each column (i.e.) 15,000 × $0.80 = $12,000 indirect labour costs.

o Total each column to arrive at the total variable cost at each level of activity.

o Fill in the fixed overhead costs for each column.

○ Add the total fixed overhead to the total variable overhead costs for each column

○ For part (b) multiply 28,000 machine hours by the variable overhead costs per machine-hours and add the total fixed costs to this amount.

SOLUTION TO Mid-Chapter Demonstration Problem

a.

Overhead Costs	Cost Formula (per hour)	Machine Hours		
		15,000	20,000	25,000
Variable costs:				
Indirect labour........................	$0.80	$ 12,000	$ 16,000	$ 20,000
Indirect materials..................	0.50	7,500	10,000	12,500
Maintenance..........................	1.20	18,000	24,000	30,000
Utilities...................................	1.00	15,000	20,000	25,000
Total variable costs....................	$3.50	$ 52,500	$ 70,000	$ 87,500
Fixed costs:				
Management salaries............		$200,000	$200,000	$200,000
Factory rent...........................		40,000	40,000	40,000
Insurance..............................		25,000	25,000	25,000
Maintenance..........................		10,000	10,000	10,000
Total fixed overhead..................		$275,000	$275,000	$275,000
Total overhead costs:................		$327,500	$345,000	$362,500

b. Total overhead costs equal $3.50 variable costs per machine hours plus total fixed costs of $275,000.

(28,000 machine-hours × $3.50) + $275,000 = $373,000 total estimated overhead costs.

Section 2—Standard Costs

We described job order cost accounting P.1147 and process cost accounting P.1202 systems in Chapters 22 and 23. The costs described in these chapters are historical costs. Historical costs are the dollar amounts paid by a company in past transactions. These historical (or actual) costs provide useful information for many analyses.

 LO³ Define standard costs and explain their computation and uses.

To decide whether these historical cost-based amounts are reasonable or excessive, management needs a measure of comparison. Standard costs offer one basis for these comparisons. **Standard costs** are preset costs for delivering a product or service under normal conditions. These costs are established through personnel, engineering, and accounting studies using past experiences and other data. Most people believe that standards should be challenging but attainable. Standards that are unrealistically high (called stretch goals) may discourage employees and harm motivation. Management uses standard costs to assess the reasonableness of actual costs incurred for providing a product or service. When actual costs vary from standard costs, management follows up to identify potential problems and take corrective actions.

Standard costs are often used in preparing budgets because they are the anticipated costs incurred under normal conditions. Terms such as *standard material cost*, *standard labour cost*, and *standard overhead cost* are often used to refer to amounts budgeted for direct materials P.1107, direct labour P.1110, and overhead.

Materials and Labour Standards

This section explains how we set materials and labour standards. It also shows us how to prepare a standard cost card.

Identifying Standard Costs

Managerial accountants, engineers, personnel administrators, and other managers combine their efforts in setting the amounts for standard costs. To identify standards for direct labour costs, we can conduct time and motion studies for each labour operation in the process of providing a product or service. From these studies, management can learn the best way to perform the operation. It then sets the standard labour time required for the operation under normal conditions. In a similar way, standards for materials are set by studying the quantity, grade, and cost of each material used. Standards for overhead costs are explained later in the chapter.

Regardless of the care used in setting standard costs and in revising them as conditions change, actual costs frequently differ from standard costs. These differences often are due to more than one factor.

For instance, the actual quantity of material used may differ from standard, and the price paid per unit of material also may differ from standard. Quantity and price differences from standard amounts can also occur for labour. For instance, the actual labour time and actual labour rate may vary from what was expected. Additional factors can cause actual overhead cost to differ from standard.

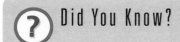 **Did You Know?**   **Standard in Cars**

Toyota Motor Manufacturing Canada, Inc. (TMMC), home of the Corolla, Matrix, Solara, and soon the Lexus, produced 220,000 vehicles in 2001 in its 2.3 million square metre manufacturing facility located in Cambridge, Ontario. Imagine the task of setting standard costs for the hundreds of different parts and components required for its vehicles, and the different categories of labour comprising the 3,200 people who were employees of TMMC in 2002!

Setting Standard Costs

To illustrate setting a standard cost, we consider the case of a baseball bat manufactured by ProBat. Engineers of ProBat have determined that one bat requires 0.90 kg of high-grade wood. They also recognize there can be loss of material as part of the process, due to inefficiencies and waste. This results in adding an **allowance** of 0.10 kg. This means the standard requirement is 1.0 kg of wood for each bat.

The requirement of 0.90 kg is called an ideal standard. An *ideal standard* is the quantity of material required if the process were 100% efficient without any loss or waste. Reality suggests there is usually some loss of material associated with any manufacturing process. The revised standard of 1.0 kg is known as the practical standard. A *practical standard* is the quantity of material required under normal application of the process. Through the use of lean business principles,

ProBat could strive to reduce the gap between the ideal and practical standards by focusing on reducing inefficiencies and waste.

High-grade wood can be purchased at a standard price of $25 per kilogram. This is the price the purchasing department determines as the expected price for the budget period. To determine this price, the purchasing department considers factors such as the quality of materials, future economic conditions, supply factors (shortages and excesses), and any available discounts.

The engineers also decide that two hours of labour time (after including allowances) is required to manufacture a bat. The wage rate is $20 per hour (better than average skilled labour is required). ProBat assigns all overhead at the rate of $10 per labour hour. The standard costs of direct materials, direct labour, and overhead for one bat are as shown in Exhibit 27.5 in what's called a *standard cost card*.

Exhibit 27.5

Standard Cost Card

STANDARD COST CARD

Production factor	Cost factor	Total
Direct materials (wood)	1 kg @ $25 per kg	$25
Direct labour	2 hours @ $20 per hour	40
Overhead	2 labour hours @ $10 per hour	20
	Total cost	$85

These amounts can be used to prepare the manufacturing budgets for the budgeted level of production. Note that if ProBat implements an activity-based costing system to allocate overhead, the standard cost for overhead may be different than the $10 shown in Exhibit 27.5 (labour hours has been used as the allocation base for convenience and simplicity).

Standards in Service Functions

Setting standard costs is not limited to manufacturing companies. Standards can also be set for service functions that involve routine tasks, such as data entry, filing, customer follow-up, or invoicing. It is, however, difficult to set standards for non-routine tasks such as those performed by a senior marketing executive or the president of a university. Nonetheless, given that service organizations also establish budgets, it is useful for them to prepare periodic performance reports to evaluate performance and take appropriate corrective actions that will provide desired results in future periods.

Did You Know?

5. Standard costs:
  a. Change in direct proportion to changes in the level of activity.
  b. Are amounts incurred at the actual level of production for the period.
  c. Are amounts expected to be incurred under normal conditions to provide a product or service.

Flashback

Answers—p. 1415

Variances

A **cost variance**, also simply called a *variance*, is the difference between actual and standard costs. A cost variance can be favourable or unfavourable. A variance from standard cost is considered favourable if actual cost is less than standard cost. It is considered unfavourable if actual cost is more than standard cost.[2] This section discusses variance analysis and computation.

Cost Variance Analysis

Variances are usually identified in performance reports. When a variance occurs, management wants to determine the factors causing it. This often involves analysis, evaluation, and explanation. The results of these efforts should allow management to assign responsibility for the variance. It can then take actions to correct the problem.

To illustrate, Optel's standard material cost for producing 12,000 units of a product is $12,000 (see Exhibit 27.3). But its actual material cost for December proved to be $13,000. The $1,000 unfavourable variance raises questions. These questions call for answers that, in turn, can lead to changes designed to correct the situation and eliminate this variance in the next period. A performance report can often identify the existence of a problem, but we need to follow up with further investigation to see what can be done to improve future results.

Exhibit 27.6 shows the flow of events in the effective management of variance analysis. Four steps are shown: (1) preparation of a standard cost performance report, (2) computation and analysis of variances, (3) investigation of the causes of variances, and (4) corrective and strategic actions.

Exhibit 27.6

Variance Analysis

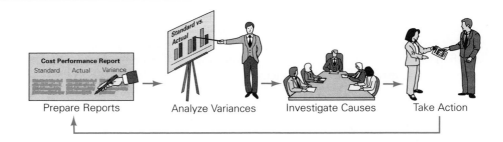

Prepare Reports   Analyze Variances   Investigate Causes   Take Action

These variance analysis steps are interrelated and are applied frequently in well-run organizations.

Computing Cost Variances

Management needs information about the factors causing a cost variance. But it must first know how to compute a variance. In its most simple form, a cost variance (CV) is computed as the difference between actual cost (AC) and standard cost (SC) as shown in Exhibit 27.7.

---

[2] We must recognize that short-term favourable variances can sometimes lead to long-term unfavourable variances. For instance, if management spends less than the budgeted amount on maintenance or insurance, the performance report would identify the difference as a favourable variance. But cutting these expenses can lead to major losses in the long run if machinery wears out prematurely or insurance coverage proves inadequate.

Exhibit 27.7

Cost Variance Formula

Cost Variance (CV) = **Actual Cost** (AC) − **Standard Cost** (SC)
where:
Actual Cost (AC) = **Actual Quantity** (AQ) × **Actual Price** (AP)
Standard Cost (SC) = **Standard Quantity** (SQ) × **Standard Price** (SP)

A cost variance is further defined by its components. Actual quantity (AQ) is the input (material or labour) used in manufacturing the quantity of output. Standard quantity (SQ) is the input expected to be used for the actual quantity of output. Actual price (AP) is the amount paid for acquiring the input (material or labour), and standard price (SP) is the expected price during the budget period.

Two main factors cause a cost variance. (1) The difference between actual price and standard price results in a *price* (or rate) *variance.* (2) The difference between actual quantity and standard quantity results in a quantity (or usage or efficiency) variance.

To assess the effects of these two factors on a cost variance, we use the formula in Exhibit 27.8.

Exhibit 27.8

Price Variance and Quantity Variance Formulae

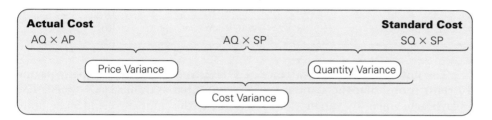

The results from applying the formulae in Exhibits 27.8 and 27.9 are identical. These formulae precisely identify the source of the cost variance. Managers sometimes find it useful to apply an alternate computation for the price and quantity variance as shown in Exhibit 27.9.

Exhibit 27.9

Alternative Price Variance and Quantity Variance Formulas

Price Variance (PV) = [**Actual Price** (AP) − **Standard Price** (SP)] × **Actual Quantity** (AQ)
Quantity Variance (QV) = [**Actual Quantity** (AQ) − **Standard Quantity** (SQ)] × **Standard Price** (SP)

Material and Labour Variances

 Compute material and labour variances.

We illustrate computation of the material and labour cost variances using data from G-Max, the company described in this chapter's opening article. This company has set the following standard quantities and prices for materials and labour per unit for its hand-crafted golf clubhead.

Direct materials (0.5 kg per unit at $2 per kg)	$1.00
Direct labour (1 hr per unit at $6 per hr)	6.00
Total standard direct cost per unit	$7.00

Material Cost Variances

During May 2001, G-Max budgeted to produce 4,000 clubheads (units). It actually produced only 3,500 units. It used 1,800 kilograms of direct material costing $2.10 per kilogram. This means its total material cost was $3,780. This information

allows us to compute both actual and standard direct material costs for
G-Max's 3,500 units along with its direct material cost variance:

Actual cost..	1,800 kg @ $2.10 per kg	= $3,780
Standard cost	1,750 kg @ $2.00 per kg	= 3,500
Direct material cost variance (unfavourable)...........		= **$ 280**

The material price and quantity variances for these G-Max clubheads are
computed and shown in Exhibit 27.10.

Exhibit 27.10

Material Price and Quantity
Variances

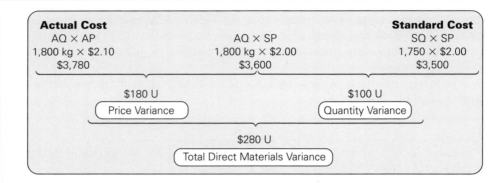

L0⁵ Describe variances and
what they reveal about
performance.

The unfavourable price variance of $180 is caused by the company paying
10 cents more than the standard price, computed as 1,800 kg × $0.10. The
unfavourable quantity variance of $100 is due to the company using 50 kg more
than the standard quantity, computed as 50 kg × $2.00 The total direct material
variance is $280 and is unfavourable. This information allows management to go
to the responsible individuals for explanations and corrective actions.

The purchasing department is usually responsible for the price paid for
materials. Responsibility for explaining the situation rests with the purchasing
manager if the variance is caused by a price higher than standard. The production
department is usually responsible for the amount of material used. The production department manager is responsible for explaining why the process used
more than the standard amount of materials.

But variance analysis can present challenges. For instance, the production
department may have used more than the standard amount of material because
the quality of material didn't meet specifications and led to excessive waste. In
this case the purchasing manager is responsible for explaining why inferior materials were acquired. But the production manager is responsible for explaining
what happened if our analysis shows that waste was due to inefficiencies and not
poor quality material.

In evaluating price variances, managers must recognize that a favourable
cost price variance may indicate a problem with product quality. Moosehead
Breweries, for example, may be able to save 10% to 15% in material prices by buying six-row barley malt instead of two-row for its better ales. But it is unlikely that
the company would gamble on quality.

Labour Cost Variances

Labour cost for a specific product or service depends on the number of hours
worked (quantity) and the wage rate paid to employees (price). This means when
actual amounts for a task differ from standard, the labour cost variance can be
divided into a rate (price) variance and an efficiency (or usage) variance.

To illustrate, G-Max's direct labour standard for 3,500 units of its hand-crafted clubheads is one hour per unit, or 3,500 hours at $6 per hour. Since only 3,400 hours at $6.30 per hour were actually used to complete the units, the actual and standard labour costs for these units are:

Actual cost...	3,400 hr	@ $6.30 per hr	= $21,420
Standard cost	3,500 hr	@ $6.00 per hr	= 21,000
Direct material cost variance (unfavourable)...........			= **$ 420**

This analysis shows actual cost is merely $420 over the standard and suggests no immediate concern. But computing the quantity and price variances reveals a slightly different picture as shown in Exhibit 27.11.

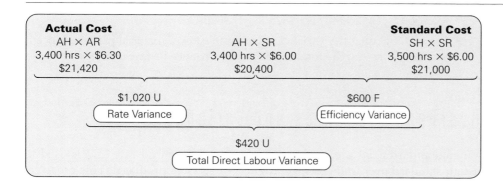

Exhibit 27.11

Labour Rate and Efficiency Variances

Where AH is actual direct labour hours, AR is actual wage rate, SH is standard direct labour hours allowed for actual output, and SR is standard wage rate.

The analysis in Exhibit 27.11 shows that the favourable efficiency variance of $600 results from using 100 fewer direct labour hours than standard for the units produced. But this favourable variance is more than offset by a wage rate that is $0.30 more than standard. The personnel administrator, or possibly the production manager, needs to explain why the wage rate is higher than expected. Also, the production manager should explain how the labour hours were reduced. If this experience can be repeated and transferred to other departments, more savings are possible.

One possible explanation of these labour rate and efficiency variances might be the use of workers with various skill levels. If so, it is the responsibility of the production manager to assign each task to workers with the appropriate skill level. In this case, an investigation might show higher skilled workers were used to produce 3,500 units of hand-crafted clubheads. As a result, fewer labour hours were required for the work. But the wage rate paid to such workers would be higher than standard because of their greater skills. In G-Max's situation, the effect of this strategy would be a higher than standard total cost. This would require actions to remedy this situation or adjust the standard.

Human Resources Manager

You are the human resource manager of an electronics assembly plant. You receive the manufacturing variance report for June 2004 and discover a large unfavourable labour efficiency variance. What factors do you investigate to identify the possible causes of this variance?

Judgement Call

Answer—p. 1415

Answers—p. 1415

6. What is a cost variance?

7. The following information is available for York Co.:

Actual hours worked per unit	2.5
Standard direct labour hours per unit	2.0
Actual production (units)...	2,500
Budgeted production (units)	3,000
Actual rate per hour...	$3.10
Standard rate per hour...	$3.00

The direct labour efficiency variance is: (a) $3,750 U; (b) $3,750 F; (c) $3,875 U; (d) $3,875 F.

8. Refer to the previous Flashback question. The direct labour rate variance is: (a) $500 U; (b) $500 F; (c) $625 F; (d) $625 U.

9. If a material quantity variance is favourable and a material price variance is unfavourable, can the total material cost variance be favourable?

Overhead Standards and Variances

When standard costs are used, a predetermined overhead rate P. 1154 is used to assign standard overhead costs to products or services produced. This predetermined rate is often based on the relation between standard overhead and either standard labour cost, standard labour hours, standard machine hours, or another measure of production (which we call the overhead allocation base).

Setting Overhead Standards

Standard overhead costs are the amounts expected to occur at a predicted level of activity. Unlike direct materials and direct labour, overhead includes both variable and fixed costs. This results in the average overhead cost per unit changing as the predicted volume changes.

Because standard costs are also budgeted costs, they must be established before the reporting period begins. This means standard overhead costs are average per unit costs based on the predicted level of activity.

To establish the standard overhead cost rate, management uses the same cost structure that is used to construct a flexible budget at the end of a period. This cost structure identifies the different overhead cost components and classifies them as variable or fixed. To get the standard overhead rate, management selects a level of activity (volume) and predicts total overhead cost. It then divides this total by the allocation base to get the standard rate. Standard direct labour hours expected to be used to produced the predicted volume is a common allocation base and is used in this section.

Exhibit 27.12 shows the overhead cost structure used in developing flexible budgets for May 2004 for G-Max. It sets the predetermined standard overhead rate for May before the month begins. The first column lists the per unit amounts of variable costs and the monthly amounts of fixed costs. The next four columns show the total costs expected to occur at four different levels of activity. The predetermined overhead rate per labour hour gets smaller as volume of activity increases. This occurs because fixed costs remain constant.

Exhibit 27.12

Flexible Overhead Budget

G-Max Overhead Costs Scenarios For Month Ended May 31, 2003	Flexible Budget Amounts	Different Production Levels (Percent of Monthly Capacity)			
		70%	80%	90%	100%
Production in units..................	1 unit	3,500	**4,000**	4,500	5,000
Factory overhead:					
Variable costs (per unit):					
Indirect labour..................	$ 0.40	$1,400	**$1,600**	$1,800	$2,000
Indirect materials.............	0.30	1,050	**1,200**	1,350	1,500
Utilities............................	0.20	700	**800**	900	1,000
Maintenance....................	0.10	350	**400**	450	500
Total................................	$ 1.00	$3,500	**$4,000**	$4,500	$5,000
Fixed costs (per month):					
Building rent	$1,000	$1,000	**$1,000**	$1,000	$1,000
Amortization, machinery..	1,200	1,200	**1,200**	1,200	1,200
Supervisory salaries.........	1,800	1,800	**1,800**	1,800	1,800
Total................................	$4,000	$4,000	**$4,000**	$4,000	$4,000
Total factory overhead		$7,500	**$8,000**	$8,500	$9,000
Standard direct labour hours....	1 hr/unit	3,500	**4,000**	4,500	5,000
Predetermined overhead rate per standard direct labour hour..........................		$ 2.14	**$ 2.00**	$ 1.89	$ 1.80
Variable overhead rate		1.00	**1.00**	1.00	1.00
Fixed overhead rate		1.14	**1.00**	0.89	0.80

In setting the standard overhead budget for May, managers of G-Max predicted an 80% activity level. This expected level of activity is sometimes called the *denominator level* of activity. This yields a predicted production volume of 4,000 clubheads. At this volume, they budget $8,000 as the total overhead for May. This choice implies a $2 per unit (labour hour) average overhead cost, computed as $8,000 divided by the denominator activity of 4,000 units.

Since G-Max has a standard of one direct labour hour for each unit, the predetermined standard overhead application rate for May is $2 per standard direct labour hour. The variable overhead rate remains constant at $1 per direct labour hour regardless of the budgeted production level. The fixed overhead rate changes according to the budgeted production volume. For instance, for the predicted level of 4,000 units of production, the fixed rate is $1 per hour—computed as $4,000 fixed costs divided by 4,000 units. But for a production level of 5,000 units, the fixed rate is $0.80 per hour.

When choosing the predicted activity level for a company, management looks at many factors. The level can be set as high as 100% of capacity. But this is rare. Factors causing the activity level to be less than full capacity include difficulties in scheduling work, equipment under repair or maintenance, and insufficient product demand. Good long-run management practices often call for some plant capacity in excess of current operating needs to allow for special opportunities and demand changes.

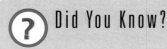

Measuring Up

In the spirit of continuous improvement, leading companies are setting new standards (benchmarks) for performance. Competitors are comparing their processes and performance standards against these benchmarks established by the leaders. This implies continuous revision of standards in all areas of an organization to improve productivity. Corporations such as Xerox Canada, Motorola, and Magna International use benchmarking to stay one step ahead of competitors.

Overhead Cost Variance Analysis

 Compute overhead variances.

When standard costs are used, the cost accounting system applies overhead to the good units produced using the predetermined standard overhead rate. At the end of the period, the difference between the total overhead cost applied to products and the total overhead cost actually incurred is called **overhead cost variance**. This variance is computed as shown in Exhibit 27.13.

Exhibit 27.13

Overhead Cost Variance Formula

> **Overhead Cost Variance = Actual Overhead Incurred − Standard Overhead Applied**
> **OVC   =   AOI   −   SOA**

To help management identify factors causing the overhead cost variance, we analyze this variance separately for variable and fixed overhead. The results provide information useful to management for taking strategic actions to improve company performance.

Similar to our analysis of direct material and direct labour variances, both the variable and fixed overhead variances can be separated into useful components as shown in Exhibit 27.14.

Exhibit 27.14

Variable and Fixed Overhead Variances

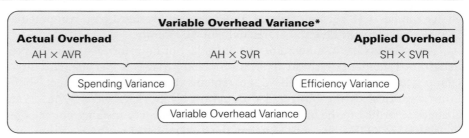

*Where: AH = actual hours; AVR = actual variable overhead rate; SH = standard hours; SVR = standard variable overhead rate.

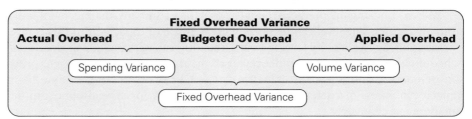

A **spending variance** occurs when management pays an amount different than the standard price to acquire an overhead item. For instance, the actual wage rate paid to indirect labour might be higher than the standard rate. Similarly, actual supervisory salaries might be less than expected. Spending variances such as these cause management to investigate the reasons why the amount paid is different than the standard. Both variable and fixed overhead costs yield their own spending variances.

The analysis of variable overhead includes computation of an **efficiency variance**. An efficiency variance occurs when standard direct labour hours (the allocation base) expected for actual production are different from the actual direct labour hours used. This efficiency variance is unrelated to whether variable overhead is used efficiently. Instead, this variance results from whether or not the overhead allocation base is used efficiently.

We can combine the variable overhead spending variance, the fixed overhead spending variance, and the variable overhead efficiency variance to get **controllable variance**, see Exhibit 27.15. The controllable variance is so named because it is generally under the control of management. Generally production managers of various responsibility centres are responsible for overhead spending variances. A total controllable variance can hide situations in which some overhead items are over budget and others are under budget because they are netted together in the total. Control can only be achieved if the variance from standard for each overhead component is analyzed. Overhead components such as indirect materials, indirect labour, utilities, and maintenance should be individually examined. Control is improved by focusing attention on individual overhead variances that can be controlled. For example, it may be possible to improve the utilization of indirect materials but some overhead costs such as rent, insurance, and property taxes may be allocated costs that are not within the control of a particular responsibility centre manager. Using an activity-based overhead allocation method will force managers to conduct a more detailed overhead variance analysis.

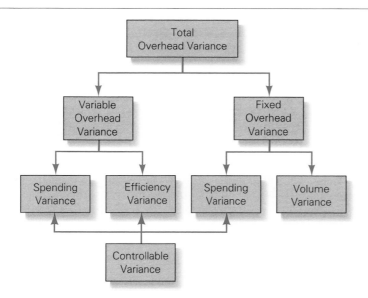

Exhibit 27.15

Framework for Understanding Total Overhead Variance

A **volume variance** occurs when there is a difference between the actual volume of production and the standard volume of production. The budgeted fixed overhead amount remains the same regardless of the actual volume of production (within the relevant range). This budgeted amount is computed based on standard direct labour hours that are allowed for the budgeted production volume. But the applied overhead is based on the standard direct labour hours allowed for with the actual volume of production. This means if there is a difference between budgeted and actual production volumes, there is a difference in the standard direct labour hours allowed for these two production levels. Such a situation yields a volume variance different from zero.

A volume variance is not included as part of controllable variance. The actual production level depends upon many factors after a budget is established, such as the number of orders received. But management must strive to accurately predict the volume of activity. The practice of continuous budgeting and the use of shorter budgeting periods, as discussed in the previous chapter, are helpful in arriving at accurate budget estimates.

Computing Overhead Cost Variances

To illustrate how we compute overhead variances we return to the data from G-Max. We know that 3,500 units are actually produced while 4,000 units were budgeted. Additional data from G-Max show that actual overhead incurred is $7,650, with the variable portion equal to $3,650 of the $7,650. Using this information we compute variances for variable and fixed overhead.

Variable Overhead Cost Variances

Recall that overhead is applied by G-Max based on direct labour hours as the allocation base. We know that 3,400 direct labour hours were used to produce 3,500 units. This compares favourably to the standard requirement of 3,500 direct labour hours at one labour hour per unit. We compute and separate the variable overhead variances of G-Max as shown in Exhibit 27.16.

Exhibit 27.16

Computing Variable
Overhead Cost Variances

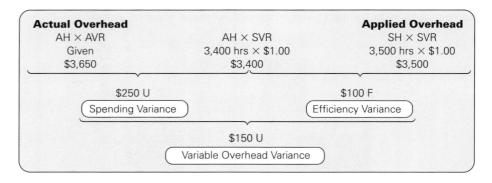

The actual variable overhead amount of $3,650 is available from G-Max's cost records. We use this amount to compute the actual variable overhead rate of $1.07 per direct labour hour, computed as $3,650 divided by 3,400 units. This reveals that, on average, G-Max incurred $0.07 more per direct labour hour in variable overhead, compared to the standard rate. The middle column of Exhibit 27.16 is computed by multiplying the actual direct labour hours (3,400) by the standard rate of $1 per direct labour hour. The right-hand column is the applied overhead. It is computed by multiplying the standard hours allowed for actual production (3,500) by the standard rate of $1 per direct labour hour.

Fixed Overhead Cost Variances

G-Max reports that it incurred $4,000 in actual fixed overhead, computed as $7,650 minus $3,650 of variable overhead costs. This $4,000 amount is equal to the budgeted fixed overhead for May 2004. G-Max's budgeted fixed overhead application rate is $1 per hour, computed as $4,000 divided by 4,000 direct labour hours. But the actual production level for G-Max is only 3,500 units. Using this information, we can compute the fixed overhead variances as shown in Exhibit 27.17.

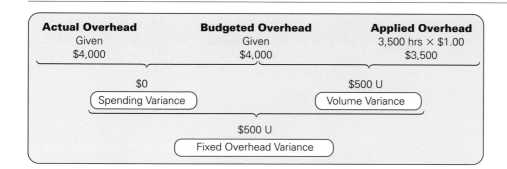

Exhibit 27.17

Computing Fixed Overhead
Cost Variances

The applied fixed overhead is computed by multiplying standard hours allowed for actual production (3,500) by the fixed overhead allocation rate ($1). Exhibit 27.17 reveals the fixed overhead spending variance is zero and the volume variance is $500. The volume variance occurs because 500 fewer units were produced than budgeted. This is because 80% of the manufacturing capacity was budgeted but only 70% was used.

We also show the volume variance graphically in Exhibit 27.18. The upward sloping line reflects the amount of fixed overhead costs applied to the units produced in May using the predetermined fixed overhead rate. The uppermost horizontal line reflects the $4,000 of total fixed costs budgeted for May. These two lines cross at the planned operating volume of 4,000 units. When the volume is 3,500 units, the overhead costs applied line falls $500 below the budgeted overhead line. This shortfall is the volume variance.

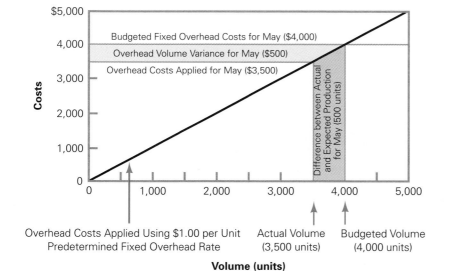

Exhibit 27.18

Volume Variance

An unfavourable volume variance implies the company did not reach its predicted operating level. Of course, management would already know this result. More important, management needs to know why the volume is different from the expected level. The main purpose of the volume variance is that it identifies what portion of the total variance is caused by failing to meet the expected level. This permits management to focus on the controllable variance.

A complete overhead variance report provides managers with information about specific overhead costs and how they differ from budgeted amounts. Exhibit 27.19 shows G-Max's overhead variance report for May. It reveals that: (1) fixed costs and maintenance cost were incurred as expected; (2) costs for indirect labour and utilities were higher than expected; and (3) indirect materials cost was less than expected.

Exhibit 27.19

Overhead Variance Report

G-Max **Factory Overhead Variance Report** **For Month Ended May 31, 2004**			
Volume Variance:			
Expected production level..................................		80% of capacity	
Production level achieved		70% of capacity	
Volume variance..		$500 (unfavourable)	
Controllable Variance:			
	Flexible Budget	**Actual Results**	**Variances**
Variable overhead costs:			
Indirect labour	$1,400	$1,525	$ 125 U
Indirect materials	1,050	1,025	$ 25 F
Utilities..	700	750	50 U
Maintenance	350	350	
Total variable costs...	$3,500	$3,650	$ 150 U
Fixed overhead costs:			
Building rent..	$1,000	$1,000	
Amortization, machinery	1,200	1,200	
Supervisory salaries	1,800	1,800	
Total fixed costs	$4,000	$4,000	$ 0
Total overhead costs	$7,500	$7,650	**$150** U

F = Favourable variance; and U = Unfavourable variance

The sum of the controllable and uncontrollable overhead variances equals the difference between the total actual variable and fixed overhead ($7,650 = $3,650 VOH + $4,000 FOH) and the total variable and fixed overhead ($7,000 = $3,500 VOH + $3,500 FOH) applied. Using information from Exhibits 27.16 and 27.17, we see that the difference between total actual overhead costs and total overhead applied is $650 ($7,650 − $7,000). Again using Exhibits 27.16 and 27.17, we compute the total controllable variance as $150 unfavourable ($250 U + $100 F + $0). This amount can also be computed from the variances for the variable overhead cost; see Exhibit 27.19. The overhead variance report shows the total volume variance as $500 unfavourable (shown at the top). The sum of the controllable variance and the volume variance equals the total (fixed and variable) overhead variance of $650 unfavourable.

10. Under what conditions is overhead volume variance considered favourable?

Flashback

Answer—p. 1415

Extending Standard Costs

This section describes the application of standard costs for use in control systems, for use by service companies, and for use in the accounting system.

Standard Costs for Control

To control business activities, top management must be able to affect the actions of lower-level managers responsible for the company's revenues, costs, and expenses. After a budget is prepared and standard costs are established, management should take actions to gain control when actual costs differ from the standard or budgeted amounts.

 Explain how standard cost information is useful for management by exception.

Reports like the ones illustrated in this chapter call management's attention to variances from business plans and other standards. When managers use these reports to focus on problem areas, the budgeting process contributes to the control function. In using budget performance reports, it is often useful for management to practice management by exception.

Management by exception means that managers focus attention on the most significant variances and give less attention to areas where performance is reasonably close to the standard. This practice leads management to concentrate on the exceptional or irregular situations. It also means deferring any serious analysis of areas showing actual results that are reasonably close to the plan. Management by exception is especially useful when directed at controllable items. Managers should investigate a variance if corrective action can be taken that will reduce costs by a greater amount than the cost of the investigation. Companies frequently use rules of thumb that consider the absolute size of a variance or the percentage of the variance to the standard cost. For example, a manager of a small responsibility centre may not investigate a $100 total overhead variance but would look closely at a $1,000 variance. The percentage of standard costs is usually considered a more important gauge in deciding whether further investigation is warranted. For example, if the standard cost were $500, then a $100 variance would be 20% of standard costs and would warrant a close look by management.

Internal Auditor

You are an internal auditor reviewing your company's records. You discover one manager who always spends exactly what is budgeted for supplies and equipment. You also find about 30% of the annual budget is spent just before the end of the period. A talk with this manager reveals she always spends what is budgeted, whether or not supplies and equipment are needed. She offers three reasons for her actions. First, she doesn't want her budget cut. Second, the company's practice of management by exception calls attention to deviations from the budget. Third, she feels the money was budgeted to be spent. Do you mention these findings in your report?

Judgement Call
Answer—p. 1415

11. To use management by exception with standard costs:

a. A company must record standard costs in its accounts.

b. Variances from flexible budget amounts should be computed to allow management to focus its attention on significant differences between actual and budgeted performance.

c. Only variances for direct materials and direct labour should be analyzed.

Flashback
Answers—p. 1415

Summary

LO¹ Compare fixed and flexible budgets. A fixed budget shows the revenues, costs, and expenses expected to occur at the specified production and sales volume. But if the actual production and sales volume is at some other level, the amounts in the fixed budget do not provide a reasonable basis for evaluating actual performance. A flexible budget expresses variable costs in per unit terms so that it can be used to develop budgeted amounts for any production and sales volume within the relevant range. This means managers compute budgeted amounts after a period for the volume that actually occurred. A flexible budget is more useful in evaluating the actual performance.

LO² Prepare a flexible budget and interpret a flexible budget performance report. To prepare a flexible budget, management depends on the distinctions between fixed and variable costs. In generating the numbers to be used in preparing a flexible budget, we express each variable cost as a constant amount per unit of sales (or as a percentage of a sales dollar). In contrast, the budgeted amount of each fixed cost is expressed as the total amount expected to occur at any sales volume within the relevant range. The flexible budget is then prepared using these computations and amounts for fixed and variable costs at the expected sales volume.

LO³ Define standard costs and explain their computation and uses. Standard costs are the normal costs that should be incurred to produce a product or perform a service. Standard costs are budgeted before the period and used in evaluations. They should be based on a careful examination of the processes used to produce a product or perform a service along with the quantities and prices that should be incurred in carrying out those processes. On a performance report, standard costs (which are flexible budget amounts) are compared to actual costs and the differences are presented as variances.

LO⁴ Compute material and labour variances. Material and labour variances are due to the differences

between the actual costs incurred and the budgeted costs. The price (or rate) variance is computed by comparing the actual cost with the flexible budget amount that should have been incurred to acquire the actual quantity of resources. The quantity (or efficiency) variance is computed by comparing the flexible budget amount that should have been incurred to acquire the actual quantity of resources versus the flexible budget amount incurred that should have been incurred to acquire the standard quantity of resources.

LO⁵ Describe variances and what they reveal about performance. Variances can be used by management to monitor and control activities. They are also used to identify problem areas. Total cost variances can be broken into price and quantity variances to direct management's attention to the actions of the lower-level managers responsible for quantities used or prices paid.

LO⁶ Compute overhead variances. Overhead variances are due to the differences between the actual overhead costs incurred and the overhead applied to production. An overhead spending variance arises when the actual amount incurred is different than the budgeted amount of overhead. An overhead efficiency or volume variance arises when the flexible overhead budget amount is different than the overhead applied to production. It is important to realize that overhead is not directly traced to a cost object. Instead it is assigned using an overhead allocation base. This means an overhead efficiency variance (in the case of variable overhead) is a result of the use of the overhead application base.

LO⁷ Explain how standard cost information is useful for management by exception. Standard cost accounting provides management with information about costs that differ from budgeted (expected) amounts. Performance reports disclose the costs or areas of operations that have significant variances from normal or budgeted amounts. This disclosure of differences from expected levels allows managers to devote attention to the exceptions and pay less attention to areas in which operations are proceeding normally.

GUIDANCE ANSWERS TO Judgement Call

Budget Officer

From the complaints, it appears that the performance report compared the actual results with the fixed budget. While this comparison is useful in determining whether the amount of work actually performed was more or less than what was planned, it is not useful in determining whether the divisions were more or less efficient than planned. If the two consulting divisions worked on more assignments than expected, some of their costs will increase. Therefore, the budgeting department should prepare a flexible budget using the actual number of consulting assignments and compare the actual performance to the flexible budget.

Human Resources Manager

As the HR manager, you may not be directly responsible for labour efficiency variance. However, you should still investigate the causes for any labour related variances because labour issues generally fall under Human Resource Management. An unfavourable labour efficiency variance occurs because more labour hours than standard are used during the period. There are at least three possible reasons for this. First, materials quality may be poor, resulting in more labour consumption due to

rework. Second, there could have been unplanned interruptions during the period (e.g., strike, breakdowns, accidents). Third, the production manager may have used a different labour mix to expedite orders. This new labour mix may have consisted of a larger proportion of untrained labour resulting in more labour hour consumption.

Internal Auditor

This is a situation where the manager of the department is "playing it safe" with regard to the practice of management by exception. It may not be appropriate to classify this manager's action as unethical. However, this action is undesirable and senior management should be informed about it. It is the internal auditor's duty to bring such behaviour to management's attention. Perhaps a good way in which the internal auditor can deal with the situation is to mention this behaviour in an indirect manner in the report. In addition, the internal auditor can recommend that for the purchase of such discretionary items, the individual department managers must provide a report once every three years and any future budgetary requests must be done using a zero-based budgeting process. The internal auditor must be given full authority to verify this budget request.

GUIDANCE ANSWERS TO  Flashback

1. *b*

2. The first step is classifying each cost as variable or fixed.

3. A fixed budget is prepared using an expected volume of sales or production, and a flexible budget compares actual costs with the costs that should have been incurred at the actual activity level.

4. Contribution margin equals sales less variable costs.

5. *c*

6. It is the difference between actual cost and standard cost

7. a; Total actual hours: 2,500 × 2.5 = 6,250

    Total standard hours: 2,500 × 2.0 = 5,000

    QV = (6,250 − 5,000) × $3.00 = $3,750 U

8. d; Rate variance = ($3.10 − $3.00) × 6,250 = $625 U

9. Yes, this will occur when the quantity variance is greater than the materials price variance.

10. The overhead volume variance is favourable when the actual operating level is higher than the expected level.

11. *b*

Demonstration Problem

Pacific Company provides the following information about its budgeted and actual results for June 2004. Although the expected volume for June was 25,000 units produced and sold, the company actually produced and sold 27,000 units.

Budget data—25,000 units
(asterisks identify factory overhead items):

Actual results during June—
27,000 units produced:

Selling price	$5.00 per unit
Variable costs (per unit of output):	
Direct materials	1.24 per unit
Direct labour	1.50 per unit
*Factory supplies	0.25 per unit
*Utilities	0.50 per unit
Selling costs	0.40 per unit
Fixed costs (per month):	
*Amortization of machinery	$3,750
*Amortization of building............................	2,500
General liability insurance...........................	1,200
Property taxes on office equipment............	500
Other administrative expense	750

Selling price (per unit of output)	$5.23 per unit
Variable costs (per unit of output):	
Direct materials	1.12 per unit
Direct labour	1.40 per unit
*Factory supplies	0.37 per unit
*Utilities	0.60 per unit
Selling costs	0.34 per unit
Fixed costs (per month):	
*Amortization of machinery	$3,710
*Amortization of building............................	2,500
General liability insurance...........................	1,250
Property taxes on office equipment............	485
Other administrative expense	900

Standard manufacturing costs based on expected output of 25,000 units:

	Per Unit of Output	Quantity to Be Used	Total Cost
Direct materials, 4 grams @ $0.31/g	$1.24/unit	100,000 g	$31,000
Direct labour, 0.25 hr @ $6.00/hr.	1.50/unit	6,250 hr	37,500
Overhead..	1.00/unit		25,000

Actual costs incurred to produce 27,000 units:

	Per Unit of Output	Quantity to Be Used	Total Cost
Direct materials, 4 grams @ $0.28/g	$1.12/unit	108,000 g	$30,240
Direct labour, 0.20 hr @ $7.00/hr.	1.40/unit	5,400 hr	37,800
Overhead..	1.20/unit		32,400

Standard costs based on expected output of 27,000 units:

	Per Unit of Output	Quantity to Be Used	Total Cost
Direct materials, 4 grams @ $0.31/g	$1.24/unit	108,000 g	$33,480
Direct labour, 0.25 hr @ $6.00/hr.	1.50/unit	6,750 hr	40,500
Overhead..			26,500

Required

1. Prepare flexible budgets for June showing expected sales, costs, and income under assumptions of 20,000, 25,000, and 30,000 units of output produced and sold.

2. Prepare a flexible budget performance report that compares actual results with the amounts budgeted if the actual volume had been expected.

3. Apply variance analyses for direct materials, direct labour, and overhead.

Planning the Solution

○ Prepare a table showing the expected results at the three specified possible levels of output. Compute the variable costs by multiplying the per unit variable costs by the expected volumes. Include fixed costs at the given amounts. Combine the amounts in the table to show the total variable costs, the total contribution margin, total fixed costs, and income from operations.

○ Prepare a table that shows the actual results and the amounts that should be incurred at 27,000 units. Show any differences in the third column, and label them with either an F for favourable if they increase income or a U for unfavourable if they decrease income.

○ Using the variance format from the chapter, compute these total variances and the individual variances:

   • Total materials variance (including the direct materials quantity variance and the direct materials price variance).

   • Total direct labour variance (including the direct labour efficiency variance and the direct labour rate variance).

   • Total overhead variance (including the overhead volume variance and the overhead controllable variance).

SOLUTION TO Demonstration Problem

1. Flexible budgets:

	20,000 Units	25,000 Units	30,000 Units
Sales	$100,000	$125,000	$150,000
Variable costs:			
Direct materials	24,800	31,000	37,200
Direct labour	30,000	37,500	45,000
Factory supplies	5,000	6,250	7,500
Utilities	10,000	12,500	15,000
Selling costs	8,000	10,000	12,000
Total variable costs	$ 77,800	$ 97,250	$116,700
Contribution margin	$ 22,200	$ 27,750	$ 33,300
Fixed costs:			
Amortization of machinery	3,750	3,750	3,750
Amortization of building	2,500	2,500	2,500
General liability insurance	1,200	1,200	1,200
Property taxes on office equipment	500	500	500
Other administrative expense	750	750	750
Total fixed costs	$ 8,700	$ 8,700	$ 8,700
Income from operations	$ 13,500	$ 19,050	$ 24,600

2.

The Pacific Company Flexible Budget Performance Report For Month of June 2004	Flexible Budget	Actual Results	Variance	
Sales (27,000 units)	$135,000	$141,210	$6,210	F
Variable costs:				
Direct materials	33,480	30,240	3,240	F
Direct labour	40,500	37,800	2,700	F
Factory supplies	6,750	9,990	3,240	U
Utilities	13,500	16,200	2,700	U
Selling costs	10,800	9,180	1,620	F
Total variable costs	$105,030	$103,410	$1,620	F
Contribution margin	$ 29,970	$ 37,800	$7,830	F
Fixed costs:				
Amortization of machinery	$ 3,750	$ 3,710	$ 40	F
Amortization of building	2,500	2,500		
General liability insurance	1,200	1,250	50	U
Property taxes on office equipment	500	485	15	F
Other administrative expense	750	900	150	U
Total fixed costs	$ 8,700	$ 8,845	$ 145	U
Income from operations	$ 21,270	$ 28,955	$7,685	F

F = Favourable variance; and U = Unfavourable variance

3. Variance analyses of manufacturing costs:

Material variances:			
Actual cost	108,000 grams @ $0.28	$30,240	
Standard cost	108,000 grams @ $0.31	33,480	
Direct material cost variance (favourable)			$(3,240)
Quantity variance:			
Actual units at standard price	108,000 grams @ $0.31	$33,480	
Standard units at standard price	108,000 grams @ $0.31	33,480	
Variance (none)			-0-
Price variance:			
Actual units at actual price	108,000 grams @ $0.28	30,240	
Actual units at standard price	108,000 grams @ $0.31	33,480	
Variance (favourable)	108,000 grams @ ($0.03)		$(3,240)
Direct material cost variance (favourable)			$(3,240)

Labour variances:

Actual cost	5,400 hr @ $7.00	$37,800	
Standard cost	6,750 hr @ $6.00	40,500	
Direct labour cost variance (favourable)..			$ 2,700
Quantity variance:			
Actual hours at standard price.........	5,400 hr @ $6.00	$32,400	
Standard hours at standard price	6,750 hr @ $6.00	40,500	
Variance (favourable)	(1,350) hr @ $6.00		$(8,100)
Rate variance:			
Actual hours at actual price.............	5,400 hr @ $7.00	37,800	
Actual hours at standard price.........	5,400 hr @ $6.00	32,400	
Variance (unfavourable)	5,400 hr @ $1.00		5,400
Direct labour cost variance (favourable).....................................			$(2,700)

Overhead variances:

Total overhead cost incurred...........	27,000 units @ $1.20	$32,400	
Total overhead applied	27,000 units @ $1.00	27,000	
Overhead cost variance (unfavourable)			$ 5,400 U
Variable overhead variance (factory supplies and utilities):			
Variable overhead cost incurred (given)		$26,190	
Variable overhead cost applied (6,750 × $3/hr)		20,250	
Variable overhead variable cost variance		$ 5,940 U	
Volume variance:			
Budgeted overhead at 27,000 units		$26,500	
Standard overhead applied to production (6,750 hours @ $4.00 per hour rate)		27,000	
Variance (favourable)...		$ 500 F	
Controllable variance:			
Actual overhead incurred...		$32,400	
Overhead budgeted at operating level achieved		26,500	
Variance (unfavourable)...		$ 5,900 U	
Total overhead variance (unfavourable).......................................		$ 5,400 U	

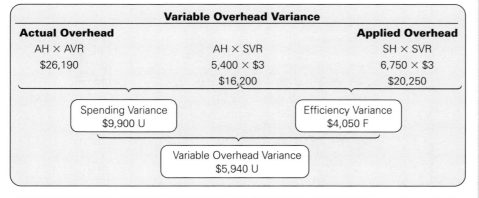

Variable Overhead Variance

Actual Overhead		Applied Overhead
AH × AVR	AH × SVR	SH × SVR
$26,190	5,400 × $3	6,750 × $3
	$16,200	$20,250

Spending Variance $9,900 U

Efficiency Variance $4,050 F

Variable Overhead Variance $5,940 U

Fixed Overhead Variance

Actual Overhead	Budgeted Overhead	Applied Overhead
$6,210	$6,250	6,750 × $1

Spending Variance $40 F

Volume Variance $500 F

Fixed Overhead Variance $540 F

27A Standard Cost Accounting System

LO⁸ Record journal entries for standard costs and account for price and quantity variances.

In the main body of this chapter we have shown how companies use standard costs in management reports. Most standard cost systems also record these costs and variances in accounts. This practice simplifies recordkeeping and helps in preparation of reports.

We don't need knowledge of standard cost accounting practices to understand standard costs and how they are used. But we do need to know how to interpret accounts in which standard costs and variances are recorded. The entries in this section briefly illustrate the important aspects of this process for G-Max's standard costs and variances for May.

The first of these entries is the one to record standard materials cost incurred in May. It is recorded in the Goods in Process Inventory account. This part of the entry is similar to the usual accounting entry but the amount of the debit equals the standard cost ($3,500) instead of the actual cost ($3,780). This entry credits Raw Materials Inventory for actual cost. The difference between standard and actual costs is recorded with debits to two separate materials variance accounts (recall Exhibit 27.10). Both the materials price and quantity variances are recorded as debits because they reflect additional costs greater than the standard cost (if actual costs were less than the standard, they would be recorded as credits). This treatment reflects their unfavourable effect because they represent higher costs and lower net income.

May 31	Goods in Process Inventory	3,500	
	Direct Materials Price Variance	**180**	
	Direct Materials Quantity Variance	**100**	
	Raw Materials Inventory		3,780
	To charge production for standard quantity of materials used (1,750 kg) at the standard price ($2 per kg) and to record direct material price and quantity variances.		

The second entry is the one to debit Goods in Process Inventory for the standard labour cost of the goods manufactured during May ($21,000). Actual labour cost ($21,420) is recorded with a credit to the Factory Payroll account. The difference between standard and actual costs is explained by two variances (see Exhibit 27.11). The direct labour rate variance is unfavourable and is debited to that account. The direct labour efficiency variance, which is favourable, is credited.

May 31	Goods in Process Inventory.............................	21,000	
	Direct Labour Rate Variance	**1,020**	
	Direct Labour Efficiency Variance		**600**
	Factory Payroll		21,420
	To charge production with 3,500 standard		
	hours of direct labour at the standard		
	$6 per hour rate and to record the direct		
	labour rate and efficiency variances.		

The direct labour efficiency variance is favourable because it represents a lower cost and a higher net income.

The entry to assign standard predetermined overhead to the cost of goods manufactured must debit the predetermined amount ($7,000) to the Goods in Process Inventory account. The actual overhead costs incurred of $7,650 are debited to the Factory Overhead account. This means when Factory Overhead is applied to Goods in Process Inventory, the amount applied is debited to the Goods in Process Inventory account and credited to the Factory Overhead account. To account for this difference between actual and standard costs the entry includes a debit of $250 to the Variable Overhead Spending Variance account, a credit of $100 to the Variable Overhead Efficiency Variance account, and a debit of $500 to the Volume Variance account (recall Exhibits 27.16 and 27.17). An alternative approach, which we show here, is to record the difference with a debit of $150 to the Controllable Variance account and a debit of $500 to the Volume Variance account (recall from Exhibit 27.15 that controllable variance is the sum of both variable overhead variances and the fixed overhead spending variance).

May 31	Goods in Process Inventory.............................	7,000	
	Controllable Variance	**150**	
	Volume Variance	**500**	
	Factory Overhead		7,650
	To apply overhead at the standard rate of		
	$2 per standard direct labour hours		
	(3,500 hours) and to record		
	overhead variances.		

The balances of these six different variance accounts accumulate until the end of the accounting period. This results in unfavourable variances of some months offsetting favourable variances of others.

These account balances, which reflect results of transactions in the period, are closed at the end of the period. Since their balances represent differences between actual and standard costs, they must be added to or subtracted from the manufacturing costs recorded in the period. In this way the recorded manufacturing costs equal the actual costs incurred in the period.

A company must use these actual amounts in external financial statements prepared in accordance with generally accepted accounting principles. If the variances are material, they need to be added to or subtracted from the balances of the Goods in Process Inventory, the Finished Goods Inventory, and the Cost of Goods Sold accounts. If the amounts are immaterial, they are typically added to or subtracted from the balance of the Cost of Goods Sold account.[3]

Flashback

Answers—below

12. A company uses a standard cost system. Prepare the journal entry to record these material variances:

Direct materials cost actually incurred............................	$73,200
Direct material quantity variance (favourable).................	3,800
Direct material price variance (unfavourable)...................	1,300

13. If standard manufacturing costs are recorded in the accounts, how are recorded variances treated at the end of an accounting period?

Summary of Appendix 27A

LO⁹ Record journal entries for standard costs and account for price and quantity variances. When a company records standard costs in its accounts, the standard costs of materials, labour, and overhead are debited to the Goods in Process Inventory account. Based on an analysis of the material, labour, and overhead costs, each quantity variance, price variance,

volume variance, and controllable variance is recorded in a separate account. At the end of the period, if the variances are material, they are allocated among the balances of the Goods in Process Inventory, Finished Goods Inventory, and Cost of Goods Sold accounts. If they are not material, they are simply debited or credited to the Cost of Goods Sold account.

GUIDANCE ANSWERS TO  Flashback

12.

Goods in Process Inventory...................	75,700	
Direct Material Price Variance................	1,300	
Direct Materials Quantity Variance.....		3,800
Raw Materials Inventory....................		73,200

13. If the variances are material, they should be prorated among the Goods in Process Inventory, Finished Goods Inventory, and Cost of Goods Sold accounts. If they are not material, they can be closed to Cost of Goods Sold.

---

[3] This process is similar to that shown in Chapter 22 for eliminating an underapplied or overapplied balance in the Factory Overhead account.

Glossary

Allowance The quantity of material that is expected to be lost due to normal inefficiencies or waste associated with a manufacturing process; used when setting a standard cost for a process. (p. 1400)

Budgetary control The use of budgets by management to monitor and control the operations of a company. (p. 1392)

Budget reports Documents that compare actual results to planned objectives. (p. 1392)

Controllable variance Both overhead spending variances (variable and fixed), and the variable overhead efficiency variance combined together. (p. 1409)

Cost variance The difference between the actual incurred cost and the standard amount. (p. 1402)

Efficiency variance Efficiency variance indicates how efficiently inputs are used, and is computed as the standard price per unit times the difference between the actual quantity used and the standard quantity that should be used for actual output. (p. 1409)

Favourable variance A deviation from the budget that contributes to a higher income. (p. 1393)

Fixed budget A planning budget based on a single predicted amount of sales or production volume; unsuitable for evaluations if the actual volume differs from the predicted volume. (p. 1393)

Fixed budget performance report An internal report that compares actual revenue and cost amounts with fixed budgeted amounts and identifies the differences between them as favourable or unfavourable variances. (p. 1393)

Flexible budget A budget prepared after an operating period is complete to help managers evaluate past performance; uses fixed and variable costs in determining total costs. (p. 1394)

Flexible budget performance report An internal report that helps management analyze the difference between actual performance and budgeted performance based on the actual sales volume (or other level of activity); presents the differences between actual and budgeted amounts as variances. (p. 1390)

Management by exception An analytical technique used by management to focus on the most significant variances and give less attention to areas where performance is close enough to the standard to be satisfactory. (p. 1413)

Overhead cost variance The difference between the total overhead cost applied to products and the total overhead cost actually incurred at the end of a cost period. (p. 1408)

Price variance A difference between actual and budgeted revenue or cost caused by the difference between the actual price per unit and the budgeted price per unit. (p. 1397)

Quantity variance The difference between actual and budgeted revenue or cost caused by the difference between the budgeted and actual number of units sold or inputs used. (p. 1397)

Spending variance The difference between the actual price of an overhead item and its standard price (p. 1408)

Standard costs The costs that should be incurred under normal conditions to produce a specific product or component or to perform a specific service. (p. 1399)

Unfavourable variance A deviation from the budget that contributes to a lower income. (p. 1393)

Variance analysis A process of examining the differences between actual and budgeted revenues or costs and describing them in terms of the amounts that resulted from price and quantity differences. (p. 1397)

Volume variance The difference between two dollar amounts of fixed overhead cost. The first amount equals the total budgeted overhead cost. The second number is the overhead cost allocated to products using the predetermined fixed overhead rate. (p. 1409)

For more study tools, quizzes, and problem material, refer to the Online Learning Centre at **www.mcgrawhill.ca/college/larson**

Questions

1. What limits the usefulness of fixed budget performance reports?

2. Identify the primary purpose of a flexible budget.

3. In what sense can a variable cost be considered constant?

4. What type of analysis does a flexible budget performance report help management conduct?

5. What is a price variance? What is a quantity variance?

6. What is the purpose of using standard costs?

7. What department is usually responsible for a direct labour cost variance? What department is usually responsible for a direct labour efficiency variance?

8. What is the predetermined standard overhead rate? How is it computed?

9. In an analysis of the fixed overhead cost variances, what is the volume variance?

10. In an analysis of the overhead cost variances, what is the controllable variance and what causes it?

11. If a company is budgeted to operate at 80% of capacity and actually operates at 75% of capacity, what effect will the 5% reduction have on the controllable variance? The volume variance?

12. Variance analysis, in general, provides, information about _____ and _____ variances.

13. If a company's overhead costs consist of only variable costs and the actual sales volume is 10% higher than the budgeted sales volume, what kind of volume variance would the company experience?

14. What is the relationship among standard costs, flexible budgets, variance analysis, and management by exception?

15. Assume NIKE has a standard shoe cost for a particular line of women's running shoes sold in Canada. List several factors that might cause the actual cost incurred to vary from the standard cost.

Quick Study

QS 27-1

Preparing a flexible budget performance report

LO^2

Berard Company showed the following results for May:

Sales (160,000 units)	$1,320,000
Variable costs	732,500
Fixed costs	280,000

For this level of sales, revenues were budgeted to be $1,440,000; variable costs, $800,000; and fixed costs, $280,000.
Prepare a flexible budget performance report for May.

QS 27-2

Preparing flexible budgets

LO^2

Callagan Company sells its product at $20 per unit and variable costs are $7 per unit. Fixed costs are budgeted at $175,000 for production volumes up to 25,000 units and $230,000 for production volumes exceeding 25,000 units. Prepare a flexible budget if sales are expected to be 20,000 units during the first quarter of 2004.

QS 27-3

Preparing flexible budgets

LO^2

Refer to QS 27-2. Prepare a flexible budget if sales are estimated at 40,000 units during the second quarter of 2004.

QS 27-4

Computing material cost

LO^{4,5}

Regan Company's output for the period required a standard direct material cost of $140,000. During the period, the direct material variances included a favourable price variance of $8,000 and a favourable quantity variance of $3,700. What was the actual total direct materials cost for the period?

QS 27-5

Calculate labour cost

LO^{4,5}

Parker Company's output for the period had an unfavourable direct labour rate variance of $25,130 and an unfavourable direct labour efficiency variance of $8,110. The goods produced during the period required a standard direct labour cost of $412,100. What was the actual total direct labour cost incurred during the period?

QS 27-6

Computing materials used

LO^{4,5}

During a recent period, Harvey Company's manufacturing operations experienced a favourable price variance of $16,800 on its direct materials usage. The actual price per kilogram of material was $82.00 while the standard price was $82.60. How many kilograms of material were used during the period?

QS 27-7

Computing actual overhead

LO^6

Klapstein Company's output for the period had a favourable overhead volume variance of $25,000 and an unfavourable overhead controllable variance of $49,600. Standard overhead charged to production during the period amounted to $260,000. What was the actual total overhead cost incurred during the period?

QS 27-8
Management by exception
LO⁷

Explain the concept of management by exception and the reason why standard costs assist managers in applying this concept.

QS 27-9ᴬ
Preparing overhead journal entries
LO⁸

Refer to the information presented in QS 27-7. Klapstein records standard costs in its accounts. Prepare the journal entry to charge overhead costs to the Goods in Process Inventory account and to record the variances.

Exercises

Exercise 27-1
Classifying costs as fixed or variable
LO²

A company manufactures and sells bicycles. It normally operates eight hours a day, five days per week. On the basis of this general information, classify each of the following costs as fixed or variable. If certain facts would affect your choice, describe at least one reason that would cause you to change your conclusion.

a. Office supplies
b. Direct labour
c. Screws
d. Repair expense for power tools
e. Wheels
f. Incoming shipping expenses
g. Natural gas for heating
h. Amortization on power tools
i. Insurance on property
j. Pension cost
k. Management salaries

Exercise 27-2
Preparing flexible budgets
LO²

Stockhauser Company prepared the following fixed budget for the first quarter of 2004.

Sales (10,000 units)		$2,000,000
Cost of goods sold:		
Direct materials	$550,000	
Direct labour	340,000	
Production supplies	264,000	
Plant manager's salary	60,000	1,124,000
Gross profit		$ 786,000
Selling expenses:		
Sales commissions	$160,000	
Packaging	210,000	
Advertising	100,000	(470,000)
Administrative expenses:		
Administrative salaries	$ 60,000	
Amortization, office equipment	30,000	
Insurance	18,000	
Office rent	12,000	(120,000)
Income from operations		$ 196,000

Following the format of Exhibit 27.3, prepare a schedule that shows the amounts of the variable costs per unit and the fixed costs per quarter and three possible flexible budgets for sales volumes of 7,500, 10,000, and 12,500 units.

ᴬ Identifies assignment material based on Appendix 27A.

Exercise 27-3

Preparing a flexible budget performance report

$LO^{1,2}$

Zapata Company's fixed budget performance report for a recent month shows this information:

	Fixed Budget	Actual Results	Variance	
Unit sales	8,400	10,800		
Sales	$693,000	$891,000	$198,000	U
Expenses	480,000	586,200	106,200	F
Income from operations	$213,000	$304,800	$ 91,800	U

    The budgeted expenses of $480,000 included $420,000 of variable expenses and $60,000 of fixed expenses. The actual expenses included $58,000 of fixed expenses.

    Prepare a flexible budget performance report that shows any variances between the budgeted results and the actual results. (List the fixed and variable expenses separately.)

Exercise 27-4

Preparing a flexible budget performance report

$LO^{1,2}$

Shipiro Company's fixed budget performance report for a recent month shows this information:

	Fixed Budget	Actual Results	Variance	
Unit sales	12,400	15,500		
Sales	$297,600	$383,625	$86,025	F
Expenses	260,400	312,150	51,750	U
Income from operations	$ 37,200	$ 71,475	$34,275	F

    The budgeted expenses of $260,400 included $186,000 of variable expenses and the remainder were fixed expenses. The actual expenses included $70,400 of fixed expenses.

    Prepare a flexible budget performance report that shows any variances between the budgeted results and the actual results. (List the fixed and variable expenses separately.)

Exercise 27-5

Computing and interpreting material variances

$LO^{4,5}$

Kitchen Company has just finished making 6,000 bookshelves using 31,000 square metres of wood that cost $570,400. The company's direct material standards for one bookshelf are 5 square metres of wood at $19.50 per square metre.

Required
1. Measure the direct material variances incurred in manufacturing these bookshelves.
2. Interpret the variances

Exercise 27-6

Computing and interpreting labour variances

$LO^{4,5}$

The management of Reviene Company recently reviewed its manufacturing process and decided to establish standards of 1.2 hours of direct labour per unit of product, and $12.00 per hour for the labour rate.

    The company used 4,650 hours of direct labour during November at a total cost of $56,265 to produce 4,000 units of product. In December, the company used 6,060 hours of direct labour at a total cost of $74,235 to produce 5,000 units of product.

Required
1. Compute the rate variance, the efficiency variance, and the total direct labour cost variance for each of these two months.
2. Interpret the December variances.

Martin Company established the following standard costs for one unit of its product for 2004:

Direct material (1.5 litres @ $3.20 per unit)	$ 4.80
Direct labour (2 hr @ $6.40 per hr.)..	12.80
Factory variable overhead (2 hr @ $5.60 per hr.)	11.20
Standard cost	$28.80

Exercise 27-7
Computing and interpreting
overhead variances

LO[5, 6]

The $5.60 overhead rate per direct labour hour is based on an expected operating level equal to 80% of the factory's capacity and the following monthly flexible budget information applies to the situation:

	Operating Levels		
	70%	**80%**	**85%**
Budgeted output (units)	11,250	12,000	12,750
Budgeted labour (standard hours)..............	22,500	24,000	25,500
Budgeted overhead:			
Variable overhead..	$ 63,000	$ 67,200	$ 71,400
Fixed overhead..	67,200	67,200	67,200
Total overhead...	$130,200	$134,400	$138,600

During the past month, the company operated at 70% of capacity, employees worked 20,000 hours and incurred the following actual overhead costs:

Variable overhead costs	$67,500
Fixed overhead costs	67,200
Total overhead costs	$134,700

Required

1. Show how the company computed the predetermined overhead application rate of $5.60 per hour for total overhead, variable overhead, and fixed overhead.
2. Compute the variable overhead spending and efficiency variances and interpret each.
3. Compute the fixed overhead spending and volume variances and interpret each.

Exercise 27-8
Computing volume and
controllable overhead variances

LO[6]

Presse Company expected to operate last month at 70% of its productive capacity, which requires 3,500 standard direct labour hours to produce 3,500 units per month. At this planned level, the overhead budget includes $21,000 fixed overhead plus $13,650 of variable overhead. Overhead is allocated to products using a predetermined standard rate based on direct labour hours. During the current month, the company incurred $34,800 of actual overhead and 3,000 actual hours while producing 3,000 units of product. Compute (1) the total overhead variance, (2) the overhead volume variance, and (3) the overhead controllable variance.

Exercise 27-9[A]
Recording material variances in the accounts

LO[8]

Refer to the facts in Exercise 27-5 in working on this exercise.

Kitchen Company records standard costs in its accounts. Thus, it records its material variances in separate accounts when it assigns raw materials costs to the Goods in Process Inventory account.

Required
1. Show the general journal entry that would be made to charge the direct materials costs to the Goods in Process Inventory account and to record the material variances in their accounts.
2. Assume that the material variances created by the facts in Exercise 27-5 were the only variances accumulated in the accounting period and that they are not considered material. Show the adjusting journal entry that would be made to close the variance accounts at the end of the period.
3. Which variance should be investigated according to the management by exception concept and why?

Problems

Problem 27-1A
Preparing and using a flexible budget

LO[2]

Lawrence Company's master budget for 2004 included the following fixed budget performance report. It was based on an expected production and sales volume of 20,000 units.

Lawrence Company Fixed Budget For Year Ended December 31, 2004		
Sales		$3,080,000
Cost of goods sold:		
Direct materials	$1,180,000	
Direct labour	260,000	
Machinery repairs (variable cost)	57,200	
Amortization on plant equipment (annual)	240,000	
Utilities (variable cost is 25%)	200,000	
Supervisory salaries	140,000	(2,077,200)
Gross profit		$1,102,800
Selling expenses:		
Packaging	60,000	
Shipping	116,000	
Sales salary (a fixed annual amount)	180,000	(356,000)
General and administrative expenses:		
Insurance expense	80,800	
Salaries	241,600	
Entertainment expense	108,400	(430,800)
Income from operations		$ 216,000

Check figure:
Budgeted income at 24,000 units, $487,360

Required
1. Classify the items in the fixed budget as variable or fixed and determine their amounts per unit or for the year, as appropriate.
2. Prepare one schedule showing two possible flexible budgets for the company for sales and production volumes of 18,000 and 24,000 units.
3. The president of the company is aware of the fluctuations in the marketplace and suggests being prepared for the worst-case and best-case scenarios. A consultant's report suggests the worst-case prediction is 14,000 units of sales and the best-case is 28,000 units. Compute the income from operations under the two extreme scenarios. Assume that the best-case scenario is within the relevant range of operations.

[A] Identifies assignment material based on Appendix 27A.

Refer to the facts in Problem 27-1A in working this problem. Lawrence Company's actual statement of income for 2004 follows:

Problem 27-2A
Preparing and analyzing a flexible budget performance report

LO[1, 2]

Lawrence Company Statement of Income from Operations For Year Ended December 31, 2004		
Sales (24,000 units)..		$3,840,000
Cost of goods sold:		
Direct materials..	$1,400,000	
Direct labour...	360,000	
Machinery repairs (variable cost)	46,400	
Amortization on plant equipment (annual)	240,000	
Utilities (fixed cost is $154,000)........................	218,000	
Supervisory salaries	150,000	(2,414,400)
Gross profit		1,425,600
Selling expenses:		
Packaging...	84,000	
Shipping	124,000	
Sales salary (annual)......................................	182,000	(390,000)
General and administrative expenses:		
Advertising expense	104,000	
Salaries...	232,000	
Entertainment expense....................................	108,000	(444,000)
Income from operations...................................		$ 591,600

Required

Preparation component:

1. Using the flexible budget prepared for Problem 27-1, present a flexible budget performance report for 2004.

Analysis component:

2. Explain the sales variance and the direct materials variance.

Check figure:
Total variance in income, $104,240 favourable

Harbour Company has established the following standard costs per unit for the product it manufactures:

Problem 27-3A
Computing and reporting material, labour, and overhead variances

LO[3, 4, 5]

Direct material (6 kg @ $4.00 per kg)	$24.00
Direct labour (2 hr @ $7.20 per hr)..	14.40
Overhead (2 hr @ $5.00 per hr)	10.00
Total standard cost	$48.40

The overhead rate was based on an expectation that the operating volume would equal 85% of the productive capacity per month. The following additional flexible budget information is available:

| | Operating Levels | | |
	80%	85%	90%
Production in units	2,720	2,890	3,060
Standard direct labour hours	5,440	5,780	6,120
Budgeted overhead:			
Variable costs:			
Indirect materials	$ 6,528	$ 6,936	$ 7,344
Indirect labour	2,176	2,312	2,448
Power	870	925	979
Maintenance	3,482	3,699	3,917
Total variable costs............................	$13,056	$13,872	$14,688
Fixed costs:			
Rent of factory building......................	$ 5,600	$ 5,600	$ 5,600
Amortization, machinery	3,880	3,880	3,880
Taxes and insurance...........................	1,156	1,156	1,156
Supervisory salaries	4,392	4,392	4,392
Total fixed costs	$15,028	$15,028	$15,028
Total overhead costs	$28,084	$28,900	$29,716

During May, the company operated at 90% of capacity and produced 3,060 units. The following actual costs were incurred:

Direct material		
(16,830 kg @ $3.80 per kg).................		$ 63,954
Direct labour		
(6,730 hr @ $7.20 per hr).....................		48,456
Overhead costs:		
Indirect materials................................	$8,190	
Indirect labour	2,940	
Power...	1,100	
Maintenance	3,670	
Rent of factory building.......................	5,600	
Amortization, machinery	3,880	
Taxes and insurance............................	1,280	
Supervisory salaries	4,800	31,460
Total costs		$143,870

Check figure:
Total overhead controllable variance, $1,744 unfavourable

Required
1. Compute the direct material variances, including the price and quantity variances.
2. Compute the direct labour variances, including the rate and efficiency variances.
3. Prepare a factory overhead variance report that shows the total volume and controllable variances.
4. Prepare a detailed factory overhead variance report (like Exhibit 27.19) that shows the variances for the individual items of overhead.

Laguna Company established the following standard unit costs for its single product:

Problem 27-4A
Computing material, labour,
and overhead variances

LO 3, 4, 5

Direct material (32 kg @ $3.60 per kg)	$115.20
Direct labour (8 hr @ $7.00 per hr)...	56.00
Factory overhead (8 hr @ $9.00 per hr)	72.00
Total standard cost	$243.20

The overhead rate was based on an expectation that the operating volume would equal 80% of the productive capacity of 60,000 units per quarter. The following additional flexible budget information is available:

	Operating Levels		
	70%	80%	90%
Production in units	42,000	48,000	54,000
Standard direct labour hours	336,000	384,000	432,000
Budgeted overhead:			
Fixed factory overhead..........................	$2,000,000	$2,000,000	$2,000,000
Variable factory overhead......................	1,274,000	1,456,000	1,638,000

During a recent quarter, the company actually operated at 70% of capacity and produced 42,000 units of product, and actual direct labour totaled 352,000 hours. These units were assigned the following standard costs:

Direct material (1,344,000 kg @ $3.60 per kg)	$ 4,838,400
Direct labour (336,000 hr @ $7.00 per hr)	2,352,000
Factory overhead (336,000 hr @ $9.00 per hr)	3,024,000
Total standard cost...	$10,080,000

Actual costs incurred during the quarter were:

Direct material (1,360,000 kg @ $3.45 per kg)	$ 4,692,000
Direct labour (352,000 hr @ $6.75 per hr)	2,376,000
Fixed factory overhead costs	1,960,000
Variable factory overhead costs	1,300,000
Total actual cost	$10,328,000

Required
1. Compute the total direct material cost variance and the price and quantity variances.
2. Compute the total direct labour variance and the rate and quantity variances.
3. Compute the variable overhead spending and efficiency variances and compute the fixed overhead spending and volume variances.

The Zimmerman Company has established the following standard costs for one unit of its product:

Problem 27-5A
Preparing a flexible budget,
computing variances, and
preparing an overhead report

LO 2, 3, 5

Direct material (6 kg @ $1.20 per kg)................................	$ 7.20
Direct labour (1 hr @ $8.00 per hr)...................................	8.00
Overhead (1 hr @ $7.68 per hr)...	7.68
Total standard costs..	$22.88

The predetermined overhead application rate ($7.68 per direct labour hour) is based on a normal 80% capacity operating level. At this level the company's monthly output is 9,600 units. Thus, the expected monthly output is 5,000 units. Following are the company's budgeted overhead costs for one month at the 80% level:

Zimmerman Company
Monthly Factory Overhead Budget
(at 80% of capacity)

Variable costs:		
Indirect materials	$8,448	
Indirect labour	9,984	
Power	6,144	
Repairs and maintenance	6,912	
Total variable costs		$31,488
Fixed costs:		
Amortization, building	$9,216	
Amortization, machinery	13,824	
Taxes and insurance	3,840	
Supervision	15,360	
Total fixed costs		42,240
Total overhead costs		$73,728

The company incurred the following actual costs when it operated as expected at 70% of capacity during August:

Direct material		
(50,000 kg @ $1.16 per kg)		$ 58,000
Direct labour		
(8,550 hr @ $8.40 per hr)		71,820
Overhead costs:		
Indirect materials	$7,728	
Indirect labour	10,080	
Power	5,040	
Repairs and maintenance	5,960	
Amortization, building	9,216	
Amortization, machinery	13,824	
Taxes and insurance	4,080	
Supervision	16,000	71,928
Total costs		$201,748

Check figure:
Material quantity variance,
$480 favourable

Required
1. Classify the items in the overhead budget as variable or fixed and determine their amounts per unit or for the month, as appropriate.
2. Prepare flexible overhead budgets for August showing the amounts of each variable and fixed cost at the 70%, 80%, and 90% levels.
3. Compute the direct material cost variance, including its price and quantity variances.
4. Compute the direct labour cost variance, including its rate and efficiency variances.
5. Compute (a) the variable overhead spending and efficiency variances, (b) the fixed overhead spending and volume variances, and (c) the total overhead variance.
6. Prepare a detailed factory overhead variance report (like Exhibit 27.19) that shows the variances for individual items of overhead.

Tompkins Company established the following standard unit costs for its single product that sells for $80 per unit:

Direct material (2 kg @ $4.00 per kg)	$ 8.00
Direct labour (2.5 hr @ $12.00 per hr)..	30.00
Variable factory overhead costs ($3.00 per direct labour hr)	7.50
Fixed factory overhead costs ($4.80 per direct labour hr)	12.00
Total actual cost...	$57.50

The overhead rate was based on an expectation that the operating volume would equal 14,000 units per month. The following additional information is also available for January 2004:

Units sold	11,000
Units produced..	12,500
Units of direct materials purchased	28,000
Direct materials purchased	$140,000
Units of direct materials used	26,500
Direct labour paid	$378,125
Direct labour hours worked..	30,250
Actual fixed overhead costs	$170,000
Variable overhead costs incurred	$87,250
Total sales...	$880,000
Total expenses	$150,000

Required
1. Prepare a condensed budgeted income statement based on the actual level of units produced.
2. Compute the total direct material cost variance including its price and quantity variances.
3. Compute the total direct labour variance including its rate and efficiency variances.
4. Compute (a) the variable overhead spending and efficiency variances, (b) the fixed overhead spending and volume variances, and (c) the total overhead controllable variance.
5. Prepare an income statement showing the standard gross profit, variances added or deducted from gross profit, and the actual net income or loss for January 2004.

Problem 27-6A
Preparation of budgeted
income statement and
computation of variances

LO 2, 4, 6

Check figure:
Labour quantity variance,
$12,000 favourable

Patton Company's standard cost accounting system recorded the following information concerning its operations during April:

Standard direct material cost	$125,000
Direct material quantity variance (unfavourable)	5,250
Direct material price variance (favourable)	1,000
Actual direct labour cost...	62,500
Direct labour efficiency variance (favourable).........	7,500
Direct labour rate variance (unfavourable)..............	800
Actual overhead cost..	249,000
Volume variance (unfavourable)	11,000
Controllable variance (unfavourable)	8,800

Required

Preparation component:
1. Prepare general journal entries dated April 30 to record the company's costs and variances for the month.

Analysis component:
2. Identify areas that would attract the attention of a manager who uses management by exception. Explain what action the manager should take.

Problem 27-7A[A]
Recording and analyzing material,
labour, and overhead variances

LO 7, 8

Check figure:
Goods in Process Inventory
(for overhead), $229,200

[A] Identifies assignment material based on Appendix 27A.

Alternate Problems

Problem 27-1B
Preparing and using a flexible budget

LO²

In the process of preparing a master budget for the first six months of 2004, Lee Company assumed a sales volume of 6,750 units. The resulting fixed budget performance report included the following items that comprise income from operations:

Lee Company Fixed Budget For Six Months Ended June 30, 2004		
Sales		$421,875
Cost of goods sold:		
Direct materials	$58,500	
Direct labour	46,800	
Factory supplies	4,650	
Amortization of plant (annual)	8,750	
Utilities (fixed cost is $6,750)	13,200	
Salary of plant manager	82,750	(214,650)
Gross profit		$207,225
Selling expenses:		
Packaging	$26,250	
Sales commissions	27,750	
Shipping	15,900	
Salary of vice president marketing	72,000	
Promotion (variable)	12,600	(154,500)
General and administrative expenses:		
Amortization	$ 7,800	
Consultant's fees (annual retainer)	8,400	
Administrative salaries	38,250	(54,450)
Loss from operations		$ (1,725)

Check figure:
Budgeted income for 7,500 units, $23,037.

Required
1. Classify the items in the fixed budget as variable or fixed. Also, determine their amounts per unit or for the period, as appropriate.
2. Prepare flexible budgets for the company for sales and production volumes of 7,500 and 8,250 units.
3. The president of the company is aware of the fluctuations in the marketplace, and suggests being prepared for the worst-case and best-case scenarios. A consultant's report suggests the worst-case prediction is 5,670 units of sales and the best-case is 8,775 units. Compute the income from operations under the two extreme scenarios. Assume that the best-case scenario is within the relevant range of operations.

Refer to the facts in Problem 27-1B in working this problem. Lee Company's actual statement of income for the first six months of 2004 follows:

Problem 27-2B
Flexible budget performance report

LO[1, 2]

Lee Company Statement of Income from Operations For Six Months Ended June 30, 2004		
Sales (7,500 units)		$495,000
Cost of goods sold:		
Direct materials	$64,350	
Direct labour	55,125	
Factory supplies	5,513	
Amortization of plant	8,775	
Utilities (of which 50% is a fixed cost)	13,950	
Salary of plant manager	82,750	(230,463)
Gross profit		264,537
Selling expenses:		
Packaging	$28,875	
Sales commissions	35,100	
Shipping	16,818	
Salary of vice president marketing	70,500	
Promotion (variable)	17,400	(168,693)
General administrative expenses:		
Amortization	$ 7,800	
Consultant's fee	8,940	
Administrative salaries	37,500	(54,240)
Income from operations		$ 41,604

Required

Preparation component:
1. Using the flexible budget prepared for Problem 27-1B, present a flexible budget performance report for six months ended June 30, 2004.

Analysis component:
2. Analyze and interpret (a) the sales variance (b) the direct materials variance.

Check figure:
Direct materials variance, $650 favourable.

Vacon Company has established the following standard costs per unit for the product it manufactures:

Problem 27-3B
Computing and reporting material, labour, and overhead variances

LO[3, 4, 5]

Direct material (3 kg @ $4 per kg)	$12.00
Direct labour (1 hr @ $13.50 per hr)	13.50
Overhead (1 hr @ $10.50 per hr)	10.50
Total standard cost	$36.00

The overhead rate was based on an expectation that the operating volume would equal 80% of the productive capacity of 3,000 units per month. The following additional flexible budget information is also available:

| | Operating Levels | | |
	75%	80%	85%
Production in units	3,000	3,200	3,400
Standard direct labour hours	3,000	3,200	3,400
Budgeted overhead:			
Variable costs:			
Indirect materials	$ 4,500	$ 4,800	$ 5,100
Indirect labour	6,750	7,200	7,650
Power...	2,025	2,160	2,295
Maintenance	900	960	1,020
Total variable costs....................................	$14,175	$15,120	$16,065
Fixed costs:			
Amortization, building	$6,750	$6,750	$6,750
Amortization, machinery	5,400	5,400	5,400
Taxes and insurance...................................	1,830	1,830	1,830
Supervisory salaries	4,500	4,500	4,500
Total fixed costs	$18,480	$18,480	$18,480
Total overhead costs	$32,655	$33,600	$34,545

During August 2005, the company operated at 75% of capacity and produced 3,000 units. The following actual costs were incurred:

Direct material		
(8,860 kg @ $4.15 per kg)....................		$ 36,769
Direct labour		
(3,120 hr @ $13.10 per hr)...................		40,872
Overhead costs:		
Indirect materials.................................	$4,920	
Indirect labour	7,005	
Power..	1,785	
Maintenance	540	
Amortization, building..........................	6,750	
Amortization, machinery	5,400	
Taxes and insurance.............................	2,175	
Supervisory salaries	4,500	33,075
Total costs		$110,716

Check figure:
Controllable variance,
$420 unfavourable

Required
1. Compute the direct material variances, including the price and quantity variances.
2. Compute the direct labour variances, including the rate and efficiency variances.
3. Prepare a factory overhead variance report that shows the total volume and controllable variances.
4. Prepare a detailed factory overhead variance report that shows the variances for the individual items of overhead.

Madden Company established the following standard unit costs for its single product:

Problem 27-4B
Computing material, labour, and overhead variances

LO3, 4, 5

Direct material (2.5 kg @ $28.00 per kg)	$70.00
Direct labour (3 hr @ $21.00 per hr)	63.00
Variable factory overhead (3 hr @ $7.00 per hr)	21.00
Fixed factory overhead (3 hr @ $4.20 per hr)	12.60
Total standard cost	$166.60

The overhead rate was based on an expectation that the operating volume would equal 90% of the productive capacity of 40,000 units per quarter. The following additional flexible budget information is also available:

	Operating Levels		
	80%	90%	100%
Production in units	32,000	36,000	40,000
Standard direct labour hours	96,000	108,000	120,000
Budgeted overhead:			
Fixed factory overhead	$453,600	$453,600	$453,600
Variable factory overhead	$672,000	$756,000	$840,000

During a recent quarter, the company actually operated at 80% of capacity and produced 32,000 units of product and 96,000 direct labour hours worked. These units were assigned the following standard costs:

Direct material (80,000 kg @ $28.00 per kg)	$2,240,000
Direct labour (96,000 hr @ $21.00 per hr)	2,016,000
Factory overhead (96,000 hr @ $11.20 per hr)	1,075,200
Total standard cost	$5,331,200

Actual costs incurred during the quarter were:

Direct material (77,500 kg @ $28.50)	$2,208,750
Direct labour (100,000 hr @ $19.60)	1,960,000
Fixed factory overhead costs	518,000
Variable factory overhead costs	672,000
Total actual costs	$5,358,750

Required

Check figure:
Variable overhead efficiency variance, $28,000

1. Compute the total direct material cost variance including its price and efficiency variances.
2. Compute the total direct labour variance including its rate and efficiency variances.
3. Compute (a) the variable overhead spending and efficiency variances, (b) the fixed overhead spending and volume variances, and (c) the total overhead controllable variance.

Power Company has established the following standard costs for one unit of its product:

Problem 27-5B
Flexible budget, variance analysis, and report for overhead costs

LO2, 3, 5

Direct material (2 kg @ $1.20 per kg)	$2.40
Direct labour (1/2hr @ $8.80 per hr)	4.40
Overhead (1/2 hr @ $4.80 per hr)	2.40
Total standard cost	$9.20

The predetermined overhead application rate ($4.80 per direct labour hour) is based on an expected volume of 95% of the factory's capacity. At this level the company's monthly output is 3,800 units. Following are the company's budgeted overhead costs for one month at the 95% level:

Power Company Monthly Factory Overhead Budget (at 95% of capacity)		
Variable costs:		
Indirect materials.............................	$1,064	
Indirect labour..................................	912	
Power	608	
Repairs and maintenance	456	
Total variable costs		$3,040
Fixed costs:		
Amortization, building.......................	$1,920	
Amortization, machinery...................	1,440	
Taxes and insurance	960	
Supervision	1,760	
Total fixed costs...............................		6,080
Total overhead costs........................		$9,120

During July 2002, the company operated at 85% of capacity and incurred the following actual costs:

Direct material (7,050 kg)	$ 9,024
Direct labour (1,750 hr)...	14,700
Overhead costs:	
Indirect materials...	960
Indirect labour	800
Power...	600
Repairs and maintenance...	320
Amortization, building...	1,920
Amortization, machinery	1,440
Taxes and insurance	920
Supervision...	1,760
Total costs	$32,444

Check figure:
Overhead volume variance,
$640 unfavourable

Required
1. Classify all items in the overhead budget as either variable or fixed. Also, determine their amounts per unit or their amounts for the month, as appropriate.
2. Prepare a flexible overhead budget for the company showing the amount of each fixed and variable cost at the 75%, 85%, and 95% levels.
3. Compute the direct materials cost variance, including its price and efficiency variances
4. Compute the direct labour cost variance, including its rate and efficiency variances.
5. Compute the factory overhead volume variance and factory overhead controllable variance.
6. Prepare a detailed factory overhead variance report (like Exhibit 27-19) that shows the variances for the individual items of overhead.

Crane Limited established the following standard unit costs for its single product that normally sells for $112 per unit:

Direct material (3 kg @ $5.60 per kg)	$16.80
Direct labour (2.5 hr @ $16.80 per hr)	42.00
Variable factory overhead ($4.20 per direct labour hour)	10.50
Fixed factory overhead ($6.70 per direct labour hour)	16.75
Total standard cost	$86.05

Problem 27-6B
Preparation of budgeted income statement and computation of variances

LO[2, 4, 6]

The overhead rate was based on an expectation that the operating volume would equal 18,000 units per month. The following additional information is also available for January 2004:

Units sold	12,000
Units produced	13,500
Kilograms of direct materials purchased	42,000
Direct materials purchased	$ 239,400
Units of direct materials used	39,000
Direct labour paid	$ 547,800
Direct labour hours worked	33,000
Actual fixed overhead costs	$ 140,000
Variable overhead costs incurred	$ 300,000
Total sales	$1,500,000
Total expenses	$ 170,000

Required
1. Prepare a condensed budgeted income statement based on the actual level of units produced.
2. Compute the total direct material cost variance including its price and quantity variances.
3. Compute the total direct labour variance including its rate and efficiency variances.
4. Compute (a) the variable overhead spending and efficiency variances, (b) the fixed overhead spending and volume variances, and (c) the total overhead controllable variance.
5. Prepare an income statement showing the standard gross profit, variances added or deducted from gross profit, and the actual net income or loss for January 2004.

Check figure:
Total labour variance,
$19,200 favourable

Curtis Company uses a standard cost system to account for its manufacturing operations and provides the following information concerning its operations during the month of March:

Standard material cost of goods produced	$24,000
Direct material quantity variance (favourable)	2,000
Direct material price variance (unfavourable)	2,700
Direct Labour cost actually incurred	37,000
Direct labour quantity variance (unfavourable)	4,500
Direct Labour price variance (favourable)	2,600
Actual overhead cost incurred	16,000
Volume variance (unfavourable)	500
Controllable variance (favourable)	900

Problem 27-7B[A]
Recording material, labour, and overhead variances

LO[7, 8]

Required

Preparation component:
1. Prepare general journal entries dated March 31 to record the company's costs and variances for the month.

Analysis component:
2. Identify areas that would attract the attention of a manager who uses management by exception. Describe what action the manager should take.

Check figure:
Goods in process
(for overhead), $16,400

[A] Identifies assignment material based on Appendix 27A.

Analytical and Review Problems

A & R 27-1

While on vacation, Ms. Roberts, president of Roberts Works, took in a seminar on "Reporting to Top Management." One of the seminars was on the use of profit-volume charts, which Ms. Roberts thought would have applicability to her firm.

Upon returning, Ms. Roberts summoned the controller, Mr. Titus, to her office, told him of the seminar, and asked for a report on how soon such a reporting procedure could be implemented at Roberts Works. The next day a memorandum arrived accompanied by a break-even chart (reproduced below) based on standard budgeted costs and representative of the cost breakdown and the cost-volume-profit relationship under the current selling price and cost structure.

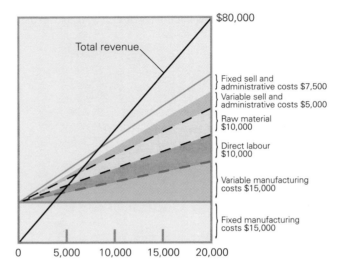

The president studied the chart and filed it away for reference at month-end. On April 3, on arrival at work, the president found the March Income Statement on her desk (reproduced below). It was not long before Mr. Titus was in the office trying to explain the apparent discrepancy between the income statement and the break-even chart.

Roberts Works Limited Income Statement For the Month Ended March 31, 2004		
Sales 14,000 units @ $4		$56,000
Cost of sales at standard $2.50		35,000
		$21,000
Selling and administrative costs		11,000
"Normal" net income		$10,000
Variances:		
Material price and usage	$500 cr.	
Labour rate and efficiency	300 dr.	
Budget variance...................................	800 cr.	1,000
		$11,000

Ms. Roberts was heard saying, "I don't know what kind of accounting you are practising—I can't understand how when the break-even chart indicates that at 14,000 unit sales volume net income should be $5,500 and you show in the income statement an amount that is double—you expect me to have confidence in your reporting. You had better go back to your office and examine the figures and come back with an explanation—and it had better be good, short, and to the point."

Required

As Mr. Titus's assistant, you have been asked to prepare the short (1/2 page) report to reconcile the income statement and break-even chart net incomes.

Doyle Company recently prepared a fixed budget for the coming year based on an expected volume of 200,000 units. At this volume, the fixed costs were expected to be $300,000 and the variable costs also were expected to be $300,000.

Required

1. What amount would be expected for the fixed, variable, and total costs at 100,000 units? At 400,000 units?
2. Explain why the amount of total expected costs at 100,000 units is not 25% of the amount of total expected costs at 400,000 units.
3. Suppose that the company could reduce fixed costs by 25% while increasing variable costs by 50%. What would be the expected amounts of fixed, variable, and total costs at 100,000 units? At 200,000 units? At 400,000 units?
4. Explain why knowledge of the fixed and variable nature of a company's costs is essential for preparing useful plans for the future and useful evaluations of the past.

Springdale Company manufactures a product with a seasonal demand and a short shelf life. As a result, the product cannot be accumulated in advance of its sale, and the number of units manufactured in different quarters varies a great deal.

The company's cost accounting system operates on a quarterly cycle, and adds actual costs to the Goods in Process Inventory. In turn, these costs flow into the Cost of Goods Sold account for each quarter or into the Finished Goods Inventory account. At the end of last year, which reflected a typical set of seasonal variations, this summarized cost report was prepared for the company manager:

Springdale Company Quarterly Reports of Average Product Costs For Year Ended December 31, 2004				
	First Quarter	Second Quarter	Third Quarter	Fourth Quarter
Direct materials	$264,000	$1,046,400	$2,187,500	$ 791,100
Direct labour	94,500	384,000	812,500	297,000
Variable overhead costs	146,700	600,000	1,262,500	445,500
Fixed overhead costs	400,000	400,000	400,000	400,000
Total costs	$905,200	$2,430,400	$4,662,500	$1,933,600
Units of output	7,500	30,000	62,500	22,500
Average cost per unit	$120.69	$81.01	$74.60	$85.94

Because of some difficulty in interpreting the report, the manager has asked you to explain why the average cost per unit varies so much from quarter to quarter. The manager also has asked you to suggest any improvements in the cost accounting system that could lead to more useful information. The manager believes that quarterly reports are needed for a timely response to apparent control problems, so your suggestion should include a schedule showing how last year's material, labour, and overhead costs per unit would have been reported under your suggestion.

Capital Budgeting and Managerial Decisions

Gee-Whiz

Montreal, Que.—At the end of grade ten, Greg Cass left school to work as an auto mechanic. He learned that he hated mechanical work, but he loved electronics. "I found myself tinkering with circuits and other gadgets on cars after work hours," says Cass. He eventually went back to school and earned his high school equivalency and then a diploma in computer electronics.

What Cass is now doing is running Gee-Whiz, a small computer electronics manufacturer. "It's really tough competing in this industry. With all the changes in what customers want, it's amazing I have any hair left at all." But Gee-Whiz is bucking the odds and making a name for itself by living on the edge. "We try to be the company with the newest hip thing," says Cass.

While he admits getting burned once or twice, such as with his video pager, he is getting it right more times than not. Cass mixes computer savvy with sound techniques to analyze potential opportunities. These methods include capital budgeting, payback period, and net present value. "I needed some structure in making decisions," says Cass. "There are a lot of techniques out there to help. If the numbers don't add up, I don't do it."

Gee-Whiz Jeans is the new investment for Cass—a jeans manufacturing company in Montreal. "I'm creating wearable computers woven into jeans," says Cass. "If this works, I'll be merging two industries—electronics and jeans manufacturing." But he admits the development is slow. "I'm over budget and when I'll make a profit is anyone's guess. But I will cut my losses if I have to. I can't hide from the numbers." But don't count Cass out. So far the numbers for Gee-Whiz are pretty rosy.

Learning Objectives

LO¹ Explain the importance of capital budgeting.

LO² Compute the payback period and describe its use.

LO³ Compute accounting rate of return and explain its use.

LO⁴ Compute net present value and describe its use.

LO⁵ Compute internal rate of return and discuss its use.

LO⁶ Describe selection of a hurdle rate for an investment.

LO⁷ Describe the importance of relevant costs for short-term decisions.

LO⁸ Evaluate short-term managerial decisions using relevant costs.

Chapter Preview

Business decisions involve choosing between alternative courses of action. Although many factors affect business decisions, our analysis typically begins by looking for alternatives that appear to have some business potential. Some decisions are based on little more than an intuitive understanding of the situation because available information is too limited to allow a more systematic analysis. In other cases, intangible factors such as convenience, prestige, and environmental considerations are more important than strictly quantitative factors. But even in these situations, we can reach a sounder decision if we identify the consequences of alternative choices in financial terms. The ideal situation is one where we can accurately quantify the relevant costs and benefits of the different alternatives, and analyze the numbers using sound financial techniques. This chapter explains several methods of analysis that help managers such as Greg Cass (see opening article) make long-term and short-term decisions.

Section 1—Capital Budgeting

We described the *capital expenditures budget* in Chapter 26. It is management's plan for acquiring and selling capital assets. **Capital budgeting** is the process of analyzing alternative long-term investments and deciding which assets to acquire or sell. These decisions can involve developing a new product or process, buying a new machine or a new building, or acquiring an entire company. An objective for capital budgeting decisions is to earn a satisfactory return on investment. However capital budgeting decisions are also undertaken by not-for-profit organizations such as public hospitals, universities, and a variety of government organizations that seek to choose projects that produce the maximum output or cost reductions for a given amount of resources invested in the project. Via Rail's investment in computer technology is an example of a capital investment.

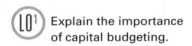
Explain the importance of capital budgeting.

    Capital budgeting decisions require careful analysis because they are usually the most difficult and risky decisions that managers make. These decisions are difficult because they require predictions of events that will not occur until well into the future. Many of these predictions are tentative and potentially unreliable. Specifically, a capital budgeting decision is risky because (1) the outcome is uncertain, (2) large amounts of money are usually involved, (3) the investment involves a long-term commitment, and (4) the decision may be difficult or impossible to reverse, no matter how poor it turns out to be.

    Capital budgeting covers a wide range of decisions. Shaw Communications, for instance, has invested over $800 million in cable and telecommunications distribution systems. Managers use several methods in evaluating capital budgeting decisions. Nearly all of these methods involve predicting after-tax cash inflows and cash outflows of proposed investments, assessing the riskiness of a return on those flows, and then choosing the investments to be made.

    A capital investment is expected to provide benefits over more than one period. To decide whether to invest or not, management must decide at the present time whether to make such an investment. Given that the cash flows are generated in the future, management often restates future cash flows in terms of their present value. This approach applies the time value of money—a dollar today is worth more than a dollar tomorrow. Similarly, a dollar tomorrow is worth less than a dollar today. The process of restating future cash flows in terms of their present value is called **discounting**. While it is important to consider the time value of money when evaluating capital investments, managers sometimes apply evaluation methods that do not explicitly consider it.

This chapter describes four methods for comparing alternative investments. These methods call for computing the *payback period*, the *accounting rate of return*, the *net present value*, and the *internal rate of return*. The first two methods do not consider the time value of money whereas the latter methods do.

Methods Not Using Time Value of Money

All investments, whether they involve the purchase of a machine or another long-term asset, are expected to produce cash inflows and cash outflows. *Net cash flow* is the cash inflows minus the cash outflows for a period. There are methods available for management to perform simple analyses of the financial feasibility of an investment without using the time value of money. This section explains two of the most common methods in this category: (1) payback period and (2) accounting rate of return.

Payback Period

The **payback period (PBP)** of an investment is the time expected to recover the initial investment amount. Managers prefer investing in assets with shorter payback periods to reduce the risk of an unprofitable investment over the long run. Acquiring assets with short payback periods reduces a company's risk due to potentially inaccurate long-term predictions of future cash flows.

 Compute the payback period and describe its use.

Computing Payback Period

This section explains how we compute the payback period with either equal or unequal cash flows.[1]

Equal Cash Flows

To illustrate use of the payback period with equal cash flows, we look at data from FasTrac, a manufacturer of exercise equipment and supplies. FasTrac is considering several different capital investments, one of which is the purchase of a machine used in manufacturing a new product. This machine costs $16,000 and is expected to have an eight-year life with no salvage value. Management predicts this machine will produce 1,000 units of product each year and that the new product will be sold for $30 per unit.

Exhibit 28.1 shows the annual cash flows this asset is expected to generate over its life. It also shows the expected annual revenues and expenses (including amortization and income taxes) from investing in this machine.

---

[1] Equal cash flows means cash flows are the same each and every year. Unequal cash flows means that not all cash flows are equal in amount.

Exhibit 28.1

Cash Flow Analysis

FasTrac Cash Flow Analysis — New Machinery January 15, 2004	Expected Net Income	Expected Cash Flows
Annual sales of new product	$30,000	$30,000
Deduct annual expenses:		
Cost of materials, labour, and overhead (except amort.).......	(15,500)	(15,500)
Amortization...	(2,000)	
Additional selling and administrative expenses	(9,500)	(9,500)
Annual pre-tax income	$3,000	
Income taxes (30%)...	(900)	(900)
Annual net income..	$2,100	
Annual net cash flow		**$4,100**

The amount of net cash flows from the machinery is computed by subtracting expected cash outflows from expected cash inflows. The cash flow column excludes all noncash revenues and expenses. For FasTrac, amortization is the only noncash item. Alternatively, some managers adjust the projected net income for revenue and expense items that do not affect cash flows. For FasTrac this means taking the net income of $2,100 and adding back the $2,000 amortization.

The formula for computing the payback period of an investment is shown in Exhibit 28.2.

Exhibit 28.2

Payback Period Formula

$$\text{Payback period} = \frac{\text{Cost of investment}}{\text{Annual net cash flow}}$$

The payback period is the time it will take the investment to generate enough net cash flow to return (or pay back) the cash initially invested to purchase it.

In the case of FasTrac the payback period is just under four years as follows:

$$\text{Payback period} = \frac{\$16,000}{\$4,100} = 3.9 \text{ years}$$

At 3.9 years the initial investment is fully recovered, just before we reach the halfway point of this machinery's useful life of eight years.

Unequal Cash Flows

Computation of the payback period ratio in the prior section assumes equal net cash flows. But what if the net cash flows are unequal? In this case the payback period is computed using the cumulative total of net cash flows. Cumulative refers to the adding of each additional period's net cash flows as we progress through time.

To illustrate, let's look at data for another potential investment that FasTrac is considering. This machine is predicted to produce unequal, or uneven, net cash flows over the next eight years. The relevant data along with computation of the payback period are shown in Exhibit 28.3.

Period	Expected Net Cash Flows	Cumulative Net Cash Flows
Year 0.............	$(16,000)	$(16,000)
Year 1.............	3,000	(13,000)
Year 2.............	4,000	(9,000)
Year 3.............	4,000	(5,000)
Year 4.............	4,000	(1,000)
Year 5.............	5,000	4,000
Year 6.............	3,000	7,000
Year 7.............	2,000	9,000
Year 8.............	2,000	11,000
		Payback period = 4.2 years

Exhibit 28.3

Payback Period with Unequal Cash Flows

Year 0 refers to the time of initial investment, and is reflected in the $16,000 cash outflow to acquire the machinery. By the end of Year 1, the cumulative net cash flow is reduced to $(13,000)—computed as the $(16,000) initial cash outflow plus Year 1's $3,000 cash inflow. This process continues throughout the asset's life.

The cumulative net cash flow amount changes from negative to positive in Year 5. Specifically, at the end of Year 4, the cumulative net cash flow is $(1,000). This means that as soon as FasTrac receives a net cash flow of $1,000 in the fifth year, the investment is fully recovered. If we assume cash flows are received uniformly *within* each year, then receipt of the $1,000 occurs about one-fifth of the way through the year. This is computed as $1,000 divided by Year 5's total net cash flow of $5,000, or 0.20. This gives us our payback period of 4.2 years, computed as 4 years plus 0.20 of Year 5.

Let's return to the opening article and the decision by Gee-Whiz to acquire a jeans fabric processing plant. Gee-Whiz's group put together a five-year forecast of cash flows from this acquisition. While a major reason to acquire it was for the processing technology, Gee-Whiz continued the plant's current operations. Revenue was projected to grow annually based on an assumed increasing market share and stable prices for the current mix of products. Projected cash outflows reflected an increasing advertising budget believed necessary to increase market share and sales revenue. Projected outflows also assumed stable raw material costs with modest increases in plant, administrative, and sales costs. Gee-Whiz assumed the fabric could be sold and administered by existing sales and administrative staff. It then compared these cash flows with estimated net cash flows from investing in a start-up fabric processing plant. Cash flows of the start-up alternative were used to set a ceiling on the amount to be paid for the plant.

Using the Payback Period

Companies desire a short payback period to increase return and reduce risk. The more quickly cash is received, the sooner it is available for other uses, and the less time its cash investment is at risk of loss. A shorter payback period also improves the company's ability to respond to unanticipated changes and lessens its risk of having to keep an unprofitable investment.

Payback period should never be the only consideration in evaluating investments. This is because it ignores at least two important factors. First, it fails to reflect differences in the timing of net cash flows within the payback period. In Exhibit 28.3, FasTrac's net cash flows in the first five years were $3,000, $4,000, $4,000, $4,000 and $5,000. If another asset had predicted cash flows of $9,000, $3,000, $2,000, $1,800 and $1,000 in these five years, its payback period would also be 4.2 years. But this second alternative is more desirable because it provides cash more quickly.

The second important factor is that the payback period ignores *all* cash flows after the point where its costs are fully recovered. For example, one investment may pay back its cost in three years but stop producing cash after four years. But a second investment might require five years to pay back its cost yet continue to produce net cash flows for another 15 years. A focus on only the payback period would mistakenly lead one to choose the first investment over the second.

Flashback

Answers—p. 1474

1. Capital budgeting is:
   a. Concerned with analyzing alternative sources of capital, including debt and equity.
   b. An essential activity for all companies as they consider what assets to acquire or sell.
   c. Best done by intuitive assessments of the value of assets and their potential usefulness.
2. Why are capital budgeting decisions often difficult?
3. A company is considering the purchase of new equipment costing $75,000. Annual net cash flows from this equipment are $30,000, $25,000, $15,000, $10,000, and $5,000. The payback period is: (a) 4 years, (b) 3.5 years, (c) 3 years.
4. If amortization is an expense, why is it added back to net income from an investment to compute the net cash flow from this investment?
5. If two investments have the same payback period, are they equally desirable? Explain.

Accounting Rate of Return

Another method used by managers in capital budgeting decisions is to compute and apply the accounting rate of return. This section explains the method.

LO³ Compute accounting rate of return and explain its use.

Computing Accounting Rate of Return

The **accounting rate of return**, also called *return on average investment*, is computed by dividing the after-tax net income from a project by the average amount invested in the project.[2] To illustrate, let's return to the $16,000 machinery investment by FasTrac described in Exhibit 28.1. Our first step is to compute the after-tax net income and the second is to compute the average amount invested. The after-tax net income of $2,100 is already available from Exhibit 28.1. We then compute the average amount invested.

We begin by assuming net cash flows are received evenly throughout each year. This means the average investment for each year is computed as the average of its beginning and ending book values. If FasTrac's $16,000 machine is amortized $2,000 each year, then the average amount invested in the machine for each year is computed as shown in Exhibit 28.4. The average for any year is the average of the beginning and ending book values.

---

[2] Accounting rate of return is sometimes calculated by dividing after-tax net income by net investment instead of average investment. This usually yields very different results so one should adopt one method and apply it consistently.

	Beginning Book Value	Annual Amortization	Ending Book Value	Average Book Value
Year 1..............	$16,000	$ 2,000	$14,000	$ 15,000
Year 2..............	14,000	2,000	12,000	13,000
Year 3..............	12,000	2,000	10,000	11,000
Year 4..............	10,000	2,000	8,000	9,000
Year 5..............	8,000	2,000	6,000	7,000
Year 6..............	6,000	2,000	4,000	5,000
Year 7..............	4,000	2,000	2,000	3,000
Year 8..............	2,000	2,000	-0-	1,000
Total...............		$16,000		$64,000/8 years

Exhibit 28.4

Computing Average
Amount Invested

Next, we need the average book value for the asset's entire life. This amount is computed by taking the average of the individual yearly averages. This average equals $8,000, computed as $64,000 (the sum of the individual years' averages) divided by eight years (see the last column of Exhibit 28.4).

If a company uses straight-line amortization, we can find the average book value for the eight years as the sum of the beginning and ending book values divided by 2 as shown in Exhibit 28.5.

$$\text{Annual average investment} = \frac{\text{Beginning book value} + \text{Ending book value}}{2}$$

$$= \frac{\$16,000 + \$0}{2} = \$8,000$$

Exhibit 28.5

Average Amount Invested
Under Straight-Line
Amortization

If an investment carries a salvage value, then the average amount invested when using straight-line amortization is computed as (Beginning book value + Salvage value) ÷ 2.

Once we determine the after-tax net income and the average amount invested, the accounting rate of return on the investment can be computed. This is done by dividing the estimated annual after-tax net income by the average amount invested as shown in Exhibit 28.6.

$$\text{Accounting rate of return} = \frac{\text{Annual after-tax net income}}{\text{Annual average investment}}$$

Exhibit 28.6

Accounting Rate of
Return Formula

This yields an accounting rate of return for FasTrac of:

$$\text{Accounting rate of return} = \frac{\$2,100}{\$8,000} = 26.25\%$$

Using Accounting Rate of Return

Management uses the accounting rate of return to decide whether or not 26% is a satisfactory rate of return. To make this decision we must factor in the riskiness of the investment. For instance, we cannot say an investment with a 26% return is preferred over one with a lower return unless we recognize differences in risk.

This means an investment's return is satisfactory or unsatisfactory only when it is related to returns from other investments with similar lives and risk.

When accounting rate of return is used to select between capital investments, the one with the least risk, the shortest payback period, and the highest return for the longest time is often identified as the best. But this analysis is sometimes challenging because different investments often yield different rankings depending on the measure used.

Perhaps because accounting rate of return is readily computed, it is often used in evaluating investment opportunities. But its usefulness is limited because its use of the amount invested is based on book values for future periods. Amortization methods are used to allocate costs among years, not to predict market values of assets. The accounting rate of return is also limited when an asset's net incomes are expected to vary from year to year. This requires that the rate be computed using *average* annual net incomes. Yet this accounting rate of return fails to distinguish between two investments that have the same average annual net income but one yields higher amounts in early years and the other in later years.

Flashback

Answers—p. 1474

6. The following data relate to a machinery purchase that a company is considering:

Cost..	$180,000
Salvage value	15,000
Annual income	40,000

The company's accounting rate of return on this machinery purchase, assuming net cash flows from the investment are received evenly throughout the year and straight-line amortization is used, is: (a) 22% (b) 41% (c) 21%

7. Is a 15% accounting rate of return for a machine a good rate?

Methods Using Time Value of Money

This section describes methods that help managers with capital budgeting decisions and that also use the time value of money. The two methods described are (1) net present value and (2) internal rate of return.

To apply the methods in this section, we need a basic understanding of the concept of present value. An expanded explanation of present value concepts is in Appendix IV. We can use the present value tables in Appendix IV to solve several of the problems at the end of this chapter.

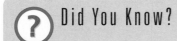

Did You Know?

The Winner Is?

How do we choose among the methods for evaluating capital investments? Management surveys consistently show the internal rate of return (IRR) as the most popular method. This is followed by the payback period and net present value (NPV). The internal rate of return measures the return of a project and is easily understood, while payback period is a quick measure of when an investment is fully recovered. Few companies use the accounting rate of return (ARR). Nearly all companies use more than one of these methods.

Net Present Value

Investment in a plant asset is expected to produce future net cash flows. A company should not acquire an asset unless its expected net cash flows are sufficient to provide a satisfactory return on investment and recover the amount initially invested. One way to make this decision is to compare the cost of the asset to the projected cash flows at a single point in time. Net present value (NPV) is one such method that compares cost to projected cash flows.

Computing Net Present Value

A NPV analysis uses the time value of money applied to future cash inflows and cash outflows so that management can evaluate the benefit and cost of a project at one point in time. To illustrate, let's return to the proposed machinery purchase by FasTrac described in Exhibit 28.1. Does this machine provide a satisfactory return while recovering the amount invested? Recall this machine requires a $16,000 investment. Its annual net cash flows are expected to be $4,100 for the next eight years. If we know the annual return that FasTrac requires on its investments, we can then compute the net present value of this investment.

Net present value is computed by discounting the future net cash flows from the investment at the required rate of return and then subtracting the initial amount invested as shown in Exhibit 28.7. We assume net cash flows from this machine are received at the end of each year and that FasTrac requires a 12% annual return.[3,4]

LO[4] Compute net present value and describe its use.

	Net Cash Flows	Present Value of $1 at 12%*	Present Value of Net Cash Flows
Year 1	$ 4,100	0.8929	$ 3,661
Year 2	4,100	0.7972	3,269
Year 3	4,100	0.7118	2,918
Year 4	4,100	0.6355	2,606
Year 5	4,100	0.5674	2,326
Year 6	4,100	0.5066	2,077
Year 7	4,100	0.4523	1,854
Year 8	4,100	0.4039	1,656
Total	$32,800		$20,367
Amount invested			(16,000)
Net present value			$ 4,367

Exhibit 28.7

Net Present Value with Equal Cash Flows

*Present Value of $1 factors are taken from Table IV in Appendix IV.

The first column of Exhibit 28.7 shows the annual net cash flows. Present value of $1 factors, also called *discount factors*, are shown in the second column. They are taken from Table IV.1 in Appendix IV and assume net cash flows are received at the end of each year. *To simplify present value computations and for assignment material at the end of this chapter, we assume net cash flows are received at the end of each year.*

Annual net cash flows from the first column of Exhibit 28.7 are multiplied by the discount factors in the second column to give present values shown in the third column. The final three rows of this exhibit show the final net present value computations. The asset's $16,000 initial cost is deducted from the $20,367 total present value of all future net cash flows to give us this asset's net present value of

---

[3] This assumption simplifies computations and is commonly made in practice.
[4] A discussion of how the rate of return is determined is left for advanced courses.

$4,367. This means the machine is expected to (1) recover its cost, (2) provide a 12% compounded return, and (3) generate another $4,367. We can summarize the analysis by saying the value of this machine's future net cash flows to FasTrac exceed the $16,000 investment by $4,367.

Net Present Value Decision Rule

The decision rule in applying the net present value method is: When the expected cash flows from an asset are discounted at the required rate and yield a *positive* net present value, the asset should be acquired. This decision rule is reflected in the following chart:

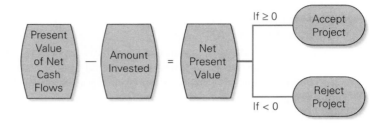

When comparing several investment opportunities of about the same cost and the same risk, the one with the highest positive net present value is preferred.

Judgement Call

Answer—p. 1474

Systems Manager

You are a systems manager. Top management recently adopted new policies to control equipment purchases. The new policy says all proposals for purchases in excess of $5,000 must be submitted with cash flow predictions to the financial analysis group for capital budget analysis. This group has authority to approve or disapprove a proposal. Another systems manager, who is a friend, wants to upgrade his department's computers at a $25,000 cost. Your friend is considering submitting several purchase orders all under $5,000 to avoid the proposal process. He says the computers will increase profits, and wants to avoid a delay. How do you advise your friend?

Simplifying Computations

The computations in Exhibit 28.7 use separate present value of $1 factors for each of the eight years. Then, each year's net cash flow is multiplied by its present value of $1 factor to determine its present value. The individual present values for each of the eight net cash flows are added to give us the total present value of the asset.

This computation can be simplified in two ways when annual net cash flows are equal in amount. One simplification is to add the eight annual present values of $1 factors for a total of 4.9676. This amount is multiplied by the annual net cash flow of $4,100 to get the $20,367 total present value of the net cash flows.[5] A second simplification is to use a calculator with compound interest functions or a spreadsheet program. But, whatever procedure is chosen, it is important to understand the concepts behind these computations. We can use discretion about what technique we choose provided as we apply it properly.

---

[5] We can simplify this computation even further using Table IV.3 which gives the cumulative present value of 1 to be received periodically for a number of periods. To determine the present value of these eight annual receipts discounted at 12%, go down the 12% column of Table IV.3 to the factor on the eighth line. This factor is 4.9676. We then compute the $20,367 present value for these eight annual $4,100 receipts, computed as 4.9676 × $4,100.

Unequal Cash Flows

Net present value analysis can also be applied when net cash flows are unequal. To illustrate, let's assume FasTrac can choose only one capital investment from among *Projects A, B,* and *C.* Each project requires the same $12,000 initial investment. Future net cash flows for each project are shown in the first three columns of Exhibit 28.8.

	Net Cash Flows			Present Value of $1 at 10%	Present Value of Net Cash Flows		
	A	**B**	**C**		**A**	**B**	**C**
Year 1	$ 5,000	$ 8,000	$ 1,000	0.9091	$ 4,546	$ 7,273	$ 909
Year 2	5,000	5,000	5,000	0.8264	4,132	4,132	4,132
Year 3	5,000	2,000	9,000	0.7513	3,757	1,503	6,762
Total	$15,000	$15,000	$15,000		$12,435	$12,908	$11,803
Amount invested .					(12,000)	(12,000)	(12,000)
Net present value					**$ 435**	**$ 908**	**$ (197)**

Exhibit 28.8

Net Present Value with Unequal Cash Flows

All three projects in Exhibit 28.8 have the same expected total cash flows of $15,000. Project A is expected to produce equal amounts of $5,000 each year. Project B is expected to produce a larger amount in the first year. Project C is expected to produce a larger amount in the third year.

The fourth column of Exhibit 28.8 shows the present value of $1 factors from Table IV.1 of Appendix IV. Since the net annual cash flows are different, we expect these projects will generate different net present values.

Computations in the right-most columns show that Project A has a $435 positive net present value. Project B has the largest net present value of $908 because it brings in cash more quickly. Project C has a $197 *negative* net present value because its larger cash flows are delayed. If FasTrac requires a 10% return, then Project C should be rejected because its net present value implies a return *under* 10%. If only one project can be accepted, then Project B appears best because it yields the highest net present value.

Salvage Value and Accelerated Amortization

FasTrac predicted the $16,000 machine to have zero salvage value at the end of its useful life (recall Exhibit 28.1). But in many cases an asset is expected to have a salvage value. If so, this amount is an additional net cash inflow received at the end of the final year of the asset's life. All other computations remain the same.

Let's again return to the opening article's discussion of Gee-Whiz's acquisition of a jeans processing plant. Gee-Whiz's analysis used predicted cash flows *and* assumed the ability to sell the processing plant at about 10 times earnings at the end of five years. In this analysis, the plant's expected selling price was treated like salvage value.

Amortization computations also affect net present value analysis. FasTrac computes amortization using the straight-line method. But accelerated amortization is also commonly used, especially for income tax reports. Amortization for tax purposes is called capital cost allowance (CCA). The Canada Customs and Revenue Agency (CCRA) specifies maximum rates that companies may use for tax purposes. For example, automobiles may be amortized at 30% declining balance and office furniture may be amortized at 20%. It is common for Canadian companies that use accelerated amortization to use the rates that are specified by the CCRA. Accelerated amortization produces larger amortization deductions in the early years of an asset's life and smaller deductions in later years. This pattern results in smaller income tax payments in early years and larger payments in later years. Tax savings from CCA can be computed with a formula that is taught in more advanced accounting and finance courses.

Accelerated amortization does not change the basics of a present value analysis, but it can change the result. Using accelerated amortization for tax reporting affects the net present value of an asset's cash flows because it produces larger net cash inflows in the early years of the asset's life and smaller ones in later years. Because early cash flows are more valuable than later ones, being able to use accelerated amortization for tax reporting always makes an investment more desirable.

Using Net Present Value

In deciding whether to proceed with a capital investment project, we go ahead if the NPV is positive and reject the proposal if the NPV is negative. If there are several projects of similar investment amounts and risk levels, we can compare the net present values of the different projects and rank them on the basis of their NPVs. But if the amount invested differs substantially across projects, then NPV is of limited value for comparison purposes.

To illustrate, suppose Project X requires an investment of $1 million and provides a NPV of $100,000. But Project Y requires an investment of only $100,000 and returns a NPV of $75,000. Ranking on the basis of NPV puts Project X ahead of Y. Yet X's NPV is only 10% of the investment whereas Y's NPV is 75% of its investment.

We must also remember that when reviewing projects with different risks, the NPVs of the individual projects are computed using different discount rates. The greater the risk, the higher the discount rate.

Internal Rate of Return

LO⁵ Compute internal rate of return and discuss its use.

Another means to evaluate capital investments is to use the internal rate of return. The **internal rate of return (IRR)** is the rate that equates the net present value of a project's cash inflows and outflows to zero. This means if we compute the total present value of a project's net cash flows using the IRR as the discount rate and then subtract the initial investment from this total present value, we get a zero NPV.

Computing Internal Rate of Return

To illustrate, we use the data for Project A of FasTrac from Exhibit 28.8 to compute its IRR. Exhibit 28.9 shows the two-step process in computing IRR.

Exhibit 28.9

Computing Internal Rate of Return

Step 1: Compute present value factor for FasTrac's three-year project.

$$\text{Present value factor} = \frac{\text{Amount invested}}{\text{Net cash flows}} = \frac{\$12,000}{\$5,000} = 2.4000$$

Step 2: Identify present value factor of 2.4000 in Table IV.3 for the three-year row. The factor is approximately equal to the 12% discount rate factor of 2.4018. This implies the IRR is approximately 12%.*

* Since the present value factor of 2.4000 is not exactly equal to the 12% factor of 2.4018, we can more precisely estimate the IRR as follows:

Discount rate	Present value factor
12%	2.4018
15%	2.2832
	0.1186 = difference

$$\text{IRR} = 12\% + \left[(15\% - 12\%) \times \frac{2.4018 - 2.4000}{0.1186} \right] = 12.05\%$$

When cash flows are equal such as with Project A, we can compute the present value factor by dividing the initial investment by its net cash flows. We then look up in an annuity[6] table to determine the discount rate equal to this present value factor. For Project A of FasTrac, we look across the three-period row of Table IV.3 and find that the discount rate corresponding to the present value factor of 2.4000 is roughly equal to the 2.4018 value for the 12% rate. This row is reproduced here:

Periods	Rate				
	1%	5%	10%	12%	15%
3	2.9410	2.7232	2.4869	2.4018	2.2832

The 12% rate is the Project's IRR. A more precise estimate of the IRR can be computed following the procedure shown in the note to Exhibit 28.9. Spreadsheet software and calculators can also compute the IRR.

Unequal Cash Flows

If net cash flows are unequal, we must use trial and error to compute the IRR. We do this by selecting any reasonable discount rate and computing the NPV. If the amount is positive (negative), we recompute the NPV using a higher (lower) discount rate. We continue these steps until we reach a point where two consecutive computations result in a NPV having different signs (positive and negative). Since the NPV is zero using IRR, we know that the IRR lies between these two discount rates. We can then estimate its value. Spreadsheet programs and calculators can do these computations for us.

Using Internal Rate of Return

When we use the IRR to evaluate a project, we compare the IRR with a predetermined hurdle rate. A **hurdle rate** is a minimum acceptable rate of return and is applied as follows:

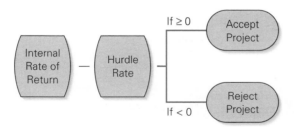

Top management selects the discount rate used as the hurdle in evaluating capital investments. While financial formulas aid in this selection, the choice of a minimum rate is subjective and left to management.

In the case of projects financed from borrowed funds, the hurdle rate must exceed the interest rate paid on these funds. This is because the return on an investment must cover interest and provide an additional profit to reward the company for its risk. For instance, if money is borrowed at 10%, a required after-tax return of 15%(or 5% above the borrowing rate) is often required by the management of industrial companies with average risk. We must remember that lower risk investments require a lower rate of return compared with higher risk investments.

Describe selection of a hurdle rate for an investment.

---

[6] Recall that an annuity is an equal amount of money received at equal time periods (i.e., monthly or annually).

If the project is internally financed, the hurdle rate is often based on actual returns from comparable projects. If the IRR is higher than the hurdle rate, the project is accepted. In the case of multiple projects, they are often ranked by the extent to which IRR exceeds the hurdle rate. The hurdle rate for individual projects is often different depending on the risk involved. IRR is not subject to the limitations of NPV when comparing projects with different amounts invested. This is because the IRR is expressed as a percent rather than an absolute dollar value as in net present value.

In analyzing its jeans processing plant acquisition, Gee-Whiz used an 18% required return on investment. Based on this rate, its competitor accepted the bid price and the processing plant became Gee-Whiz Jeans.

Capital budgeting decisions involve estimates not certainties. This became apparent to Gee-Whiz Jeans less than two years after acquisition when it admitted that it failed to fully take into account changes in customer and distribution channels. This led to higher administrative, delivery, and sales costs than anticipated. The expected increase in market share also had not occurred. Its share actually had declined, as it had under previous ownership. This was despite increased advertising and marketing.

Judgement Call
Answer—p. 1474

R&D Manager
You are the Research and Development manager of a hi-tech company. For a new product currently being developed under your management, you decide to use a 12% discount rate to compute its NPV. The controller expresses concern that your discount rate is too low. How do you respond?

Comparing Capital Budgeting Methods

We explained four methods managers use to evaluate capital investment projects. But how do they compare with each other? That question is addressed in this section.

The accounting rate of return does not consider the time value of money. The payback method only crudely considers the time value of money. On the other hand, both net present value and the internal rate of return do. Exhibit 28.10 identifies this and other differences.

Exhibit 28.10

Comparing Methods of Analyzing Capital Investments

	Payback Period	Accounting Rate of Return	Net Present Value	Internal Rate of Return
Basis of measurement	Cash flows	Accrual income	Cash flows Profitability	Cash flows Profitability
Measure expressed as	Number of years	Percent	Dollar amount	Percent
Strengths	Easy to understand	Easy to understand	Considers time value of money	Considers time value of money
	Allows comparison across projects	Allows comparison across projects	Accommodates different risk levels over a project's life	Allows comparisons of dissimilar projects
Limitations	Doesn't fully consider time value of money	Doesn't consider time value of money	Difficult to compare dissimilar projects	Doesn't reflect varying risk levels over the life of a project
	Doesn't consider cash flows after payback period	Doesn't give annual rates over the life of a project		

The payback period is probably the simplest method. It gives managers an estimate of how soon they will recover their initial investment. Managers sometimes use this method when they have limited cash to invest and a number of projects to choose from.

The accounting rate of return yields a percent measure. It is computed using accrual accounting instead of cash flows. The accounting rate of return is an average rate for the entire investment period.

Net present value considers all estimated after-tax net cash flows for the expected life of the project. It can be applied to equal and unequal cash flows, and can reflect changes in the level of risk over the life of a project. The choice of what discount rate to use requires judgement and should reflect the risk level of the cash flows. A higher discount rate should be used for riskier projects. Because net present value is a dollar measure, a comparison of projects of unequal sizes is more difficult.

The internal rate of return considers all cash flows from a project. It is readily computed when the cash flows are equal, but requires some trial and error estimation in the more typical cases in which cash flows are unequal. Since the internal rate of return is a percent measure, it can be more easily used to compare projects with different investment amounts. But changes in risks over the life of a project are not reflected in the internal rate of return.

Capital budgeting is complex in the sense that many estimates have to be made regarding the amount, timing, and uncertainty of cash flows, salvage values, and choice of discount rate. Sometimes managers find it useful to prepare what-if analyses by changing the assumptions regarding these input variables and gain insight into how change might affect the final outcome of a capital budgeting project. Although capital budgeting techniques are quantitative they involve many qualitative judgements that reflect the attitudes and experience of management. Behavioural factors frequently influence which projects managers focus on. For example, if managers are compensated based on short-term performance they may not pay attention to projects that might provide long-term benefits.

Investment Manager

You are an investment manager for a company. Management asks you to evaluate three alternative investments. Investment recovery time is crucial because cash is scarce. Also, the time value of money is important in your decision. Which methods do you use to evaluate these investments?

Judgement Call

Answer—p. 1474

Answers—p. 1474

8. A company can invest in only one of two projects. Each project requires a $20,000 investment and is expected to generate end-of-period cash flows as follows:

	Annual Cash Flows	
	Project A	**Project B**
Year 1	$12,000	$ 4,500
Year 2	8,500	8,500
Year 3	4,000	13,000
	$24,500	$26,000

Assuming a discount rate of 10%, which project has the greater net present value?

9. Two investment alternatives are expected to generate annual cash flows with the same net present value (assuming the same discount rate applied to each). Using this information, can you conclude that the two alternatives are equally desirable?

10. When two investment alternatives have the same total expected cash flows but differ in the timing of those flows, which method of evaluating those investments is superior? (a) Accounting rate of return, or (b) Net present value.

A Note on Cash Flows

The example of FasTrac pertains to investing in a machine that will produce a new product in order to generate additional revenues. In this example, the annual revenues are cash inflows and annual expenses are cash outflows. In certain other investment decisions, we may not be able to define the cash flows so easily.

Consider Via Rail Canada's investment in computer technology for internal operations as well as to allow customers to purchase tickets on-line and download schedules and other customer information. The annual cash inflows resulting from such an investment are hard to capture. Management expects some improvement in efficiencies which will likely lead to cost savings, and hopes that improved customer service and marketing (through on-line access to customers) will result in higher sales. In many situations, such improvements through technology may, at best, help a company maintain its current sales level and market share, rather than increase these metrics (remember that Greyhound Canada, Air Canada, WestJet and other transportation companies also offer on-line services to customers!).

In this example, a cost saving is like a cash inflow; similarly, being able to avoid a drop in sales revenues might also be considered a cash inflow. The relevant cash outflows will be the expenses incurred to operate and maintain the new technology. To whatever extent possible, it is important that managers identify relevant cash flows for the analysis (the concept of relevant costs and revenues is discussed in the next section).

Mid-Chapter Demonstration Problem

Davenport Company is considering three investment opportunities that would involve purchasing Asset X, Asset Y, or Asset Z. Straight-line amortization would be used in each case, and the salvage value would be received at the end of the life of the investment. In estimating the periodic net incomes from each asset, the only non-cash expense is amortization. The following predictions are available about these investments:

	Asset		
	X	Y	Z
Purchase price................................	$40,000	$40,000	$40,000
Salvage...	$ 1,000	$ -0-	$10,000
Useful life.......................................	6 years	8 years	8 years
Expected net incomes (losses)			
Year 1	$ 3,500	$11,000	$ (3,750)
Year 2	3,500	9,000	4,250
Year 3	3,500	7,000	8,250
Year 4	3,500	5,000	16,250
Year 5	3,500	3,000	(1,750)
Year 6	3,500	1,000	(1,750)
Year 7	-0-	(1,000)	(1,750)
Year 8	-0-	(3,000)	21,250
Total income...................................	$21,000	$32,000	$41,000

Required

Rank the three investments from first to third, based on each of the following analytical techniques:

a. Payback period, assuming that the cash flows from each investment are received evenly throughout each year.

b. Return on average investment, assuming that the net income from each investment is received evenly throughout each year.

c. Net present value, using 8% per year as the discount rate. For this analysis, assume that the cash flows are received at the end of each year.

Planning the Solution

o Begin by calculating the annual amortization cost for each of the three assets. Then, predict the annual net cash flows for the three alternatives for each of the eight years by adding the predicted net income, the amortization expense, and the salvage value (only in the asset's final year).

o Find the payback period for each of the three assets. The calculation for Asset X can be found as a ratio. The payback periods for Assets Y and Z must be found by calculating their cumulative cash flows. Then rank the three opportunities, with the shortest payback period receiving the highest rank.

o Find the return on average investment for each of the three assets. To begin, find each asset's average annual net income by dividing the total income by the number of years in its life. Next, find the average investment over that life by dividing the average annual income by the annual investment to get a percentage. Finally, rank the three alternatives, with the highest rate of return getting the highest ranking.

○ Find the net present value of the future net cash flows from the three investments. Set up a three-column table for each asset. The first column should show the net cash inflow for each year in the asset's life. The second column should show table values for the present value of $1 discounted at 8%. The third column should be the product of the future cash flow and the present value factor. Then take the sum of the yearly present values and subtract the initial cost. The result is the net present value of each project. Finally, rank the three projects, with the largest net present value getting the highest ranking.

Annual amortization and cash flows from each of the three investments:

Annual amortization expense:

Cost..	$40,000	$40,000	$40,000
Salvage value	(1,000)	-0-	(10,000)
Amortizable base...........................	$39,000	$40,000	$30,000
Life	6 years	8 years	8 years
Annual amortization........................	$ 6,500	$ 5,000	$ 3,750

Annual cash flows (net income plus amortization plus salvage in final year):

	X	Y	Z
Year 1	$10,000	$16,000	$ -0-
Year 2	10,000	14,000	8,000
Year 3	10,000	12,000	12,000
Year 4	10,000	10,000	20,000
Year 5	10,000	8,000	2,000
Year 6	11,000	6,000	2,000
Year 7	-0-	4,000	2,000
Year 8	-0-	2,000	35,000
Total...	$61,000	$72,000	$81,000

SOLUTION TO **Mid-Chapter Demonstration Problem**

a. Payback method:

Investment X:

$$\text{Payback period} = \frac{\text{Cost of assets}}{\text{Annual net cash flows}}$$

$$= \frac{\$40,000}{\$10,000} = 4 \text{ years}$$

Investment Y:

	Annual Net Cash Flows	Cumulative Net Cash Flows
Year 1	$16,000	$16,000
Year 2	14,000	30,000
Year 3	12,000	42,000

Thus, the $40,000 cost is paid back in slightly less than three years.

Investment Z:

	Annual Net Cash Flows	Cumulative Net Cash Flows
Year 1	$ -0-	$ -0-
Year 2	8,000	8,000
Year 3	12,000	20,000
Year 4	20,000	40,000

Thus, the $40,000 cost is paid back in four years.

Ranking: Investment Y is ranked first because it will pay back the cost in the least time. Investments X and Z are tied for second with payback periods of four years.

b. Return on average investment:

Because the cash flows are spread evenly throughout each period, the average investment is calculated as the average of the original cost and the salvage value.

Average net income per year:			
Total income over life	$21,000	$32,000	$41,000
Estimated useful life	6 years	8 years	8 years
Average annual net income.........	$3,500	$4,000	$5,125
Average investment:			
Purchase price			
(initial book value)...................	$40,000	$40,000	$40,000
Salvage value			
(final book value)	1,000	-0-	10,000
Sum...	$41,000	$40,000	$50,000
Average (sum/2)	$20,500	$20,000	$25,000
Average return on investment.........	17.1%	20.0%	20.5%
Rank	Third	Second	First

c. Net present value (using 8% per year as the discount rate):

Investment X:

	Net Cash Flows	Present Value of $1 at 8%	Present Value of Cash Flows
Year 1..	$10,000	0.9259	$ 9,259
Year 2..	10,000	0.8573	8,573
Year 3..	10,000	0.7938	7,938
Year 4..	10,000	0.7350	7,350
Year 5..	10,000	0.6806	6,806
Year 6..	11,000	0.6302	6,932
Total...	$61,000		$46,858
Original cost of asset....................			(40,000)
Net present value			$ 6,858

Investment Y:

	Net Cash Flows	Present Value of $1 at 8%	Present Value of Cash Flows
Year 1..	$16,000	0.9259	$14,814
Year 2..	14,000	0.8573	12,002
Year 3..	12,000	0.7938	9,526
Year 4..	10,000	0.7350	7,350
Year 5..	8,000	0.6806	5,445
Year 6..	6,000	0.6302	3,781
Year 7..	4,000	0.5835	2,334
Year 8..	2,000	0.5403	1,081
Total..	$72,000		$56,333
Original cost of asset.....................			(40,000)
Net present value..........................			$16,333

Investment Z:

	Net Cash Flows	Present Value of $1 at 8%	Present Value of Cash Flows
Year 1..	$ -0-	0.9259	$ -0-
Year 2..	8,000	0.8573	6,858
Year 3..	12,000	0.7938	9,526
Year 4..	20,000	0.7350	14,700
Year 5..	2,000	0.6806	1,361
Year 6..	2,000	0.6302	1,260
Year 7..	2,000	0.5835	1,167
Year 8..	35,000	0.5403	18,911
Total..	$81,000		$53,783
Original cost of asset.....................			(40,000)
Net present value..........................			$13,783

On the basis of the net present value, the investments are ranked as follows:

Y..........................	$16,333	First
Z..........................	13,783	Second
X..........................	6,858	Third

Section 2—Managerial Decisions

This section focuses on the use of management and cost accounting information for several important managerial decisions. The emphasis is on the use of quantitative measures to help managers make decisions. Most of these involve short-term decision-making. Methods for long-term managerial decisions are described in the first section of this chapter and in several other chapters of this book. A primary goal of this section is to explain what costs and other financial factors are most relevant to short-term decisions. We provide a framework to help structure an analysis of these decision situations.

Decisions and Information

This section explains how managers make decisions and the information relevant to these decisions.

Decision Making

Managerial decision making involves five steps. (1) define the decision problem, (2) identify alternative courses of action, (3) collect relevant information to evaluate each alternative, (4) select the preferred course of action, and (5) analyze and assess decisions made. These five steps are illustrated in Exhibit 28.11.

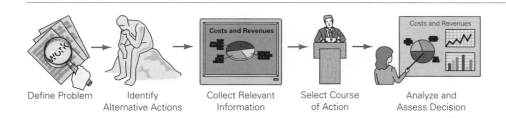

Define Problem   Identify Alternative Actions   Collect Relevant Information   Select Course of Action   Analyze and Assess Decision

Exhibit 28.11

Managerial Decision Making

Both managerial and cost accounting information play an important role in most management decisions. The accounting system is expected to provide primarily *financial* information such as performance reports and budget analyses for decision making. But *nonfinancial* information is also relevant. This includes information on environmental effects, political sensitivities, and social responsibility.

Relevant Costs

Most financial measures of revenues and costs from cost accounting systems are based on historical costs. While historical costs are important and useful for many tasks such as product pricing and the control and monitoring of business activities, they may not be relevant for analyzing individual business decisions. **Relevant costs** are costs that meet two criteria: (1) they are expected future costs; and (2) they differ between alternatives. For example, if Jones Company is choosing between investing in Project A that requires $10,000 of direct labour P.1110 or Project B that requires $12,000 of direct labour, only $2,000 of direct labour will be relevant to the decision.

Three types of costs were identified and explained in Chapter 21 that are pertinent to our discussion of relevant costs: sunk costs, out-of-pocket costs, and opportunity costs P.1101.

LO⁷ Describe the importance of relevant costs for short-term decisions.

A **sunk cost** is a cost that has already been incurred from a past decision. Therefore it cannot be avoided or changed by any decision made today or in the future. Sunk costs are *not relevant* to future decisions. All historical costs are sunk costs. The cost of computer systems purchased by Tango is a sunk cost. Most of a company's *allocated* costs, including fixed overhead such as amortization and administrative expenses, are sunk costs.

An **out-of-pocket cost** requires a future outlay of cash and is relevant for current and future decision-making. These costs are usually the direct result of management's decisions. For instance, future purchases of production equipment involve out-of-pocket costs.

Analysis of relevant costs must consider **opportunity costs**. An opportunity cost is not a cash outlay but is the potential benefit lost or given up by taking a specific action when two or more alternative choices are available. An example is a student giving up wages from a job to attend summer school. Companies are continually faced with alternative courses of action from which they must choose. For instance, a company making standardized products might be approached by a customer with a request to supply a special (nonstandard) product. A decision to accept or not accept the special order must consider not only the profit to be made from the special order but also the profit given up by devoting time and resources to this order instead of pursuing an alternative project. The profit given up is an opportunity cost.

Consideration of opportunity costs is important. The implications extend to internal resource allocation decisions. For instance, a computer manufacturer must decide between internally manufacturing a chip versus buying it externally. In another case, management of a multi-division company must decide whether to continue operating or discontinue a particular division.

Besides relevant costs, management must also consider the relevant benefits associated with a decision. **Relevant benefits** refer to the additional or *incremental* revenue that is generated by selecting a particular course of action over another. For instance, a student must decide the relevant benefits of enrolling in one course of study over another. In summary, both relevant costs and relevant benefits are crucial to managerial decision making.

Managerial Decision Tasks

LO⁸ Evaluate short-term managerial decisions using relevant costs.

Managers confront many business challenges that require analyzing alternative actions and making decisions. We describe several different types of decisions in this section; *we treat each of these decision tasks as separate from each other.*

Additional Business

Consider Mama's Sandwich Kitchen, a sandwich outlet serving primarily downtown businesses. Assume that this company normally operates at 80% of its full capacity. At this level, it can supply 1,600 sandwiches per week. Its operating costs are as shown in Exhibit 28.12:

Exhibit 28.12

Current Accounting Performance Report

	Per Unit	Total
Sales (1,600 units)	$3.00	$4,800
Direct materials	$1.00	$1,600
Direct labour	0.60	960
Overhead	0.65	1,040
Selling expenses	0.45	720
Total expenses	$2.70	$4,320
Operating income	$0.30	$ 480

An existing commercial customer down the street wants to buy additional sandwiches for a week-long training program. This customer offers to buy 300 additional sandwiches at $2.50 per sandwich, which is $0.50 below the regular price. While the price offer is low, this is the single largest order for this company from a single customer, and is not likely to affect the company's current sales.

To determine whether this order should be accepted or not, management needs to know whether net income will increase if the offer is accepted. The analysis in Exhibit 28.13 shows that if management relies on the per unit average historical costs, this sale would be rejected because it results in a loss of $60.

	Per Unit	Total
Sales (300 units)	$ 2.50	$750
Direct materials	$ 1.00	$300
Direct labour	0.60	180
Overhead	0.65	195
Selling expenses	0.45	135
Total expenses	$ 2.70	$810
Operating loss	$(0.20)	$(60)

Exhibit 28.13

Analysis of Additional
Business Using
Historical Costs

Historical costs are *not* relevant to this decision. Instead, the relevant costs are the additional or incremental costs associated with this decision. **Incremental costs**, also called *differential costs*, are the additional costs incurred if a company pursues a certain course of action. Mama's incremental costs are costs related to the added volume that the new order would bring.

To make its decision, Mama's must analyze the costs of this additional business in a different way. Assume that the following information is available:

● Supplying 300 additional sandwiches still requires the same materials and labour costs as other sandwiches.

● Additional overhead required for the 300 additional sandwiches amounts to $90 (variable overhead).

● Incremental selling expenses would be $75 (all variable).

We use this information as shown in Exhibit 28.14 to access how accepting this new business affects Mama's income.

	Current Business	Additional Business	Combined
Sales	$4,800	$ 750	$5,550
Direct materials	$1,600	$ 300	$1,900
Direct labour	960	180	1,140
Overhead	1,040	90	1,130
Selling expenses	720	75	795
Total expenses	$4,320	$ 645	$4,965
Operating income	$ 480	$105	$ 585

Exhibit 28.14

Analysis of Additional
Business Using
Relevant Costs

The analysis of relevant costs in Exhibit 28.14 suggests the additional business should be accepted. The additional business would provide $750 of added revenue while incurring only $645 of added costs. This would yield $105 of additional pre-tax income (profit margin of 14%).

An analysis of incremental costs of additional volume is always relevant for this type of decision. But we must proceed cautiously when the additional volume approaches or exceeds the existing available capacity. If the additional volume requires the company to expand its capacity by obtaining more resources, the incremental costs could quickly exceed the incremental revenue.

Another cautionary note is the effect on existing sales. If accepting additional business causes existing sales to decline, then this information must be included in our analysis. The contribution margin P. 1308 lost from a decline in regular sales is an opportunity cost. Also, if future cash flows over several time periods are affected, then their net present value is computed and used in making this analysis.

The key point is that management must not blindly use historical costs, especially allocated overhead costs. Instead, the accounting system needs to provide information about the incremental costs to be incurred if the additional business is accepted.

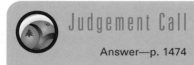

Judgement Call

Answer—p. 1474

Construction Supervisor
You are the supervisor for a construction contractor. A new customer inquires about a special project that your company has never undertaken. The controller asks you to provide information relevant to this decision. What information do you provide?

Make or Buy

Incremental costs are used in deciding whether to make or buy a component of a product. To illustrate, FasTrac (the company we introduced earlier in this chapter), has excess productive capacity that can be used to manufacture Part #417. This part is a component of the main product it sells. The component is currently purchased and delivered to the plant at a cost of $1.20 per unit. FasTrac estimates that to make Part #417 would cost $0.45 for direct materials P. 1107, $0.50 for direct labour, and an undetermined amount for factory overhead P. 1110.

Our task is to figure out how much overhead should be added to these costs so we can decide whether to make or buy Part #417. If FasTrac's normal predetermined overhead application rate is 100% of direct labour cost, we would perhaps conclude that overhead cost is $0.50 per unit, computed as 100% of the $0.50 direct labour cost. We would then conclude that total cost is $1.45, computed as $0.45 of materials plus $0.50 of labour plus $0.50 of overhead. Our decision in this case would be that the company is better off buying the part at $1.20 each than making it for $1.45 each.

But as we explained earlier, only incremental overhead costs are relevant in this situation. This means we must compute an *incremental overhead rate*. Incremental overhead costs might include, for example, power for operating machines, extra supplies, added cleanup costs, materials handling, and quality control. These are the overhead cost items that will be incurred over and above the overhead costs already being incurred. We can prepare a per unit analysis in this case such as the following:

Exhibit 28.15

Make or Buy Analysis

	Make	Buy
Direct materials......................	$0.45	—
Direct labour............................	0.50	—
Overhead costs.................	**[?]**	—
Purchase price	—	$ 1.20
Total incremental costs	**$0.95 + [?]**	**$1.20**

If incremental overhead costs are less than $0.25 per unit, then the total cost of making the component is less than the purchase price of $1.20. This implies FasTrac should make the part.

FasTrac's decision rule in this case is any amount of overhead less than $0.25 per unit yields a total cost for Part #417 that is less than the $1.20 purchase price. But FasTrac must consider several factors in deciding whether to make or buy the part. These include product quality, timeliness of delivery (especially in a just-in-time P. 1098 setting), reactions of customers and suppliers, and other intangibles such as employee morale and workload. It must also consider whether making the part requires incremental fixed costs to expand plant capacity. When these added factors are considered, small cost differences may not matter. It is also possible that FasTrac's management may have consciously decided to keep some excess capacity to deal with potential market fluctuations.

Did You Know?

Outsourcing

Firms engage in outsourcing of services such as accounting, billing, customer service, human resource management, and logistics to cut costs, obtain access to world-class capabilities, and allow company to focus on its core competencies. Outsourcing also makes sense when risks need to be shared or when resources are not available internally. Canada's outsourcing market is estimated to be in the $15–$20 billion range and is engaged in by firms of all sizes. To work well, outsourcing should be part of a firm's strategic planning and the firm should have a clear picture of what it wants to accomplish.

Scrap or Rework Defects

Costs already incurred in manufacturing the units of a product that do not meet quality standards are sunk costs. This means these costs have been incurred and cannot be changed. These costs are irrelevant in any decision on whether to sell the substandard units as scrap or rework them so they meet quality standards.

To illustrate, let's assume FasTrac has 10,000 defective units of a product that has already cost $1 per unit to manufacture. These units can be sold as is, or as scrap, for $0.40 each. Alternatively, they can be reworked for $0.80 per unit, and then sold for their full price of $1.50 each. Should FasTrac sell the units as scrap or rework them?

To make this decision, management must recognize the original manufacturing costs of $1 per unit are sunk, or unavoidable. This means these costs are *entirely irrelevant* to the decision. In addition, we must be certain that all costs of reworking defects, including interfering with normal operations, are accounted for in our analysis. For instance, suppose reworking the defects means FasTrac is unable to manufacture 10,000 *new* units with an incremental cost of $1 per unit and a selling price of $1.50 per unit. The company incurs an opportunity cost equal to the lost $5,000 net return from making and selling new units. This opportunity cost is the difference between the $15,000 revenue (10,000 units × $1.50) from selling these new units and their $10,000 manufacturing costs (10,000 units × $1). Our analysis of this situation is shown in Exhibit 28.16.

Exhibit 28.16

Scrap or Rework Analysis

	Scrap	Rework
Sale of defects	$4,000	$15,000
Less rework of defects		(8,000)
Less opportunity cost of not making new units		**(5,000)**
Incremental net income	**$4,000**	**$2,000**

The analysis yields a $2,000 difference in favour of scrapping the defects, yielding a net incremental return of $4,000. If we had failed to include the opportunity costs of $5,000, the rework option would show a return of $7,000 instead of $2,000. This would mistakenly make reworking appear more favourable than scrapping.

Flashback

Answers—p. 1475

11. A company receives a special order for 200 units of its product. This order requires the buyer's name be stamped on each unit, causing the company to incur an additional fixed cost of $400 above its normal manufacturing costs. Without the order, the company is operating at 75% of capacity and produces 7,500 units of product at the following costs:

Direct materials	$37,500
Direct labour	60,000
Factory overhead (30% variable)	20,000
Selling expenses (60% variable)	25,000

The special order will not affect normal unit sales and will not increase fixed overhead and selling expenses. Variable selling expenses on the special order are reduced to one-half the normal amount. The price per unit necessary to earn $1,000 on this order is: (a) $14.80, (b) $15.80, (c) $19.80, (d) $20.80, (e) $21.80.

12. What are the incremental costs of accepting additional business?

Sell or Process Further

Relevant costs are an important part of the decision to sell partially completed products as is or to process them further for sale. To illustrate, let's suppose FasTrac has 40,000 units of partially finished Product Q. FasTrac has already spent $0.75 per unit to manufacture these 40,000 units of Product Q at a total cost of $30,000. The 40,000 units can be sold to another manufacturer as raw material for $50,000. Alternatively, FasTrac can process them further and produce finished products X, Y, and Z at an incremental cost of $2 per unit. The added processing yields the products and revenues shown in Exhibit 28.17. FasTrac must decide whether the added revenues from selling finished products X, Y, and Z exceed the cost of finishing them.

Product	Price	Units	Revenue
X............................	$4.00	10,000	$ 40,000
Y............................	6.00	22,000	132,000
Z............................	8.00	6,000	48,000
Spoilage................	—	2,000	-0-
Total......................		40,000	**$220,000**

Exhibit 28.17

Revenues from
Processing Further

Exhibit 28.18 shows a two-step analysis for this decision. First, FasTrac needs to compute its incremental revenue from further processing Q into products X, Y and Z. This amount is the difference between the $220,000 revenue from the further processed products and the $50,000 FasTrac will give up from not selling Q as is (the $50,000 is an opportunity cost). Second, FasTrac needs to compute its incremental cost from further processing Q into X, Y, and Z. This amount is the $80,000, computed as 40,000 units × $2 incremental cost. This analysis shows FasTrac can earn incremental net income of $90,000 from a decision to further process Q.

Revenue if processed............	$ 220,000
Revenue if sold as is..............	(50,000)
Incremental revenue..............	$ 170,000
Cost if processed..................	(80,000)
Incremental income.........	**$90,000**

Exhibit 28.18

Sell or Process Further

The earlier $30,000 manufacturing cost for the 40,000 units of Product Q does not appear in Exhibit 28.18. This cost is a sunk cost and is irrelevant to the decision because it has already been incurred.

13. A company has already incurred a cost of $1,000 in partially producing its four products. Selling prices for these products are listed below when partially and fully processed. Also shown are additional costs necessary to finish these partially processed units:

Answers—p. 1475

Product	Unfinished Selling Price	Finished Selling Price	Further Processing Costs
Alpha	$300	$600	$150
Beta.......................	450	900	300
Gamma.................	275	425	125
Delta......................	150	210	75

Which of these product(s) should not be processed further? (a) Alpha, (b) Beta, (c) Gamma, (d) Delta

14. Under what conditions is a sunk cost relevant to decision making?

Selecting Sales Mix

When a company sells a mix of products, some are likely more profitable than others. Management is often wise to concentrate sales efforts on more profitable products. But if production facilities or other factors are limited, an increase in the production and sale of one product usually requires a company to reduce the production and sale of others. In this case, management must identify the most profitable combination, or *sales mix*, of products. Attention is then focused on selling this sales mix of products.

To identify the best sales mix, management must know the contribution margin of each product. It must also know what resources are required to produce these products, any constraints on these resources, and the markets for the products.

To illustrate, let's assume FasTrac makes and sells two products, A and B. The same machines are used to produce both products. The products have the following selling prices and variable costs P. 1099 per unit:

	Product A	Product B
Selling price	$ 5.00	$ 7.50
Variable costs	3.50	5.50
Contribution margin	**$1.50**	**$2.00**

The variable costs are included in the analysis because they are the incremental costs of producing these products within the existing capacity of 100,000 machine hours per month. Three separate cases are reviewed.

Case 1: Assume (a) each product requires one machine hour per unit for production and (b) the markets for these products are unlimited. Under these conditions, FasTrac should produce as much of Product B as it can because of its larger contribution margin per unit. At full capacity, FasTrac would produce $200,000 of total contribution margin per month, computed as $2 per unit times 100,000 machine hours.

Case 2: Assume (a) Product A requires one machine hour per unit, (b) Product B requires two machine hours per unit, and (c) the markets for these products are unlimited. Under these conditions, FasTrac should produce as much of Product A as it can because it generates $1.50 of contribution margin per machine hour while Product B provides only $1 per machine hour. Exhibit 28.19 shows the relevant analysis.

Exhibit 28.19

Sales Mix Analysis

	Product A	Product B
Selling price	$ 5.00	$ 7.50
Variable costs	3.50	5.50
Contribution margin	$ 1.50	$ 2.00
Machine hours per unit	1.0	2.0
Contribution margin per machine hour	**$1.50**	**$1.00**

At its full capacity of 100,000 machine hours, FasTrac would produce 100,000 units of Product A. This would yield $150,000 of contribution margin per month. In contrast, if all 100,000 hours were used to produce Product B, only 50,000 units would be produced with a contribution margin of $100,000. These results suggest that when a company has no excess capacity, only the most profitable product per unit of constraining resource should be manufactured.

Case 3: The need for a mix of different products arises when market demand is not sufficient to allow a company to sell all that it produces. For instance, assume (a) Product A requires one machine hour per unit, (b) Product B requires two machine hours per unit, and (c) the market for Product A is limited to 80,000 units. Under these conditions, FasTrac should produce no more than 80,000 units of Product A. This would leave another 20,000 machine hours of capacity for making Product B. FasTrac should use this spare capacity to produce 10,000 units of Product B. This sales mix maximizes FasTrac's contribution margin per month at $140,000.[7]

Eliminating a Segment

When a segment such as a department or division is performing poorly, management may consider eliminating it. But segment information on net income (loss) or its contribution to overhead is not sufficient for this decision. Instead, we must look at the segment's avoidable expenses and unavoidable expenses. **Avoidable expenses**, also called *escapable expenses,* are amounts that would not be incurred if the segment were eliminated. **Unavoidable expenses**, also called *inescapable expenses,* are amounts that would continue to be incurred even if the segment were eliminated.

To illustrate, FasTrac is considering eliminating its treadmill division because total expenses of $48,300 are greater than its sales of $47,800. Analysis of this division's operating expenses is shown in Exhibit 28.20.

	Total	Avoidable Expenses	Unavoidable Expenses
Cost of goods sold	$ 30,200	$ 30,200	—
Direct expenses:			
Salaries expense	7,900	7,900	—
Amortization expense, Equipment	200	—	$ 200
Indirect expenses:			
Rent and utilities expense	3,150	—	3,150
Advertising expense	200	200	—
Insurance expense	400	300	100
Service department costs:			
Share of office department expenses	3,060	2,200	860
Share of purchasing expenses	3,190	1,000	2,190
Total	$48,300	$41,800	$6,500

Exhibit 28.20

Classification of Segment Operating Expenses

FasTrac's analysis shows it can avoid expenses of $41,800 if it eliminates the treadmill division. Since this division's sales are $47,800, FasTrac will lose $6,000 of income if it eliminates the segment. *Our decision rule is that a segment is a candidate for elimination if its revenues are less than its avoidable expenses.* Avoidable expenses can be viewed as the costs of generating this segment's revenues. Sometimes it is not possible in the short term to avoid service department costs. In Exhibit 28.20 we assume, for example, that $2,200 of office department expenses can be avoided. This could be, for example, the wages of a part-time clerk no longer needed if the division is eliminated.

---

[7] A mathematical technique called *linear programming* is useful for finding the optimal sales mix for several products subject to many market and production constraints. This method is explained in advanced courses.

Another approach to the elimination of a segment decision is to prepare income statements using the contribution format. To illustrate, the management of Spartan Company, a local retailer, is considering dropping two of its three stores (S2 and S3) based on the information shown in Exhibit 28.21.

Exhibit 28.21

Contribution Format Income Statement: Common Cost Allocated

	Total	S1	S2	S3
Sales....................................	$190,500	$78,000	$56,250	$56,250
Variable expenses	88,875	27,375	26,250	35,250
Contribution margin......................	101,625	50,625	30,000	21,000
Direct fixed expenses	76,200	24,800	28,500	22,900
Common expenses, allocated.........	20,300	8,900	8,000	3,400
Operating income (loss)	$ 5,125	$16,925	$ (6,500)	$ (5,300)

These income statements can be recast by calculating a **segment margin** as shown in Exhibit 28.22. A segment margin is computed by deducting directly traceable fixed costs P. 1099 from a segment's contribution margin. In deciding whether to drop stores S2 and S3 we do not allocate the common expenses. These common costs cannot be eliminated even if a store is discontinued so we should exclude them from our analysis. When we remove the common costs we can clearly see that only Store S3 should be eliminated. From examining Exhibit 28.22 we see that Store S2 should not be eliminated because it produces a positive segment margin but S3 should be considered for elimination because its segment margin is negative.

Exhibit 28.22

Contribution Format Income Statement: Common Cost Not Allocated

	Stores			
	Total	S1	S2	S3
Sales....................................	$190,500	$78,000	$56,250	$56,250
Variable expenses	88,875	27,375	26,250	35,250
Contribution margin......................	101,625	50,625	30,000	21,000
Direct fixed expenses	76,200	24,800	28,500	22,900
Segment margin............................	25,425	$25,825	$ 1,500	$ (1,900)
Common expenses	20,300			
Operating income (loss)	$ 5,125			

When considering elimination of a segment we must assess its impact on other segments. While a segment may be unprofitable on its own, it might still contribute to the sales and profits of other segments. This means it is possible to continue a segment even when its revenues are less than its avoidable expenses. Similarly, a profitable segment might be discontinued if its space, assets, or staff can be more profitably used by expanding existing segments or by creating new ones. Our decision to keep or eliminate a segment requires a more complex analysis than simply looking at a segment's performance report. While such reports provide useful information, they do not provide all the information necessary for this decision.

Flashback

Answers—p. 1475

15. What is the difference between avoidable and unavoidable expenses?

16. A segment is a candidate for elimination if: (a) Its revenues are less than its avoidable expenses; (b) It has a net loss; (c) Its unavoidable expenses are greater than its revenues.

Qualitative Decision Factors

Managers must also consider qualitative factors in making managerial decisions. To illustrate, consider a make-versus-buy decision where a manager must choose between buying from an outside supplier instead of continuing to make a component. Several qualitative decision factors must be considered. For example, the quality, delivery, and reputation of the proposed supplier are important. Also, the effects from discontinuing the manufacturing of the component can include potential layoffs and affect worker morale.

Consider another situation where a company is examining a one-time additional sale to a customer at a special low price. Qualitative factors to consider include the effects of a low price on the image of the company and the threat of other regular customers demanding a similar price. The company must also consider whether this sale is really a one-time event. If not, can it continue to offer this low price in the long-term? In summary, management cannot rely solely on financial data to make managerial decisions.

Summary

LO1 Explain the importance of capital budgeting. Capital budgeting is the process of analyzing alternative investments and deciding which assets to acquire or sell. Generally, capital budgeting involves predicting the cash flows to be received from alternative possibilities, evaluating their merits, and then choosing which ones to pursue.

LO2 Compute the payback period and describe its use. One method of comparing possible investments computes and compares their payback periods. The payback period is an estimate of the expected time before the cumulative net cash inflow from the investment equals its initial cost. A payback period analysis is limited because it fails to reflect the riskiness of the cash flows, differences in the timing of cash flows within the payback period, and all cash flows that occur after the payback period.

LO3 Compute accounting rate of return and explain its use. A project's expected accounting rate of return is computed by dividing the periodic after-tax net income by the average investment in the project. When the net cash flows are received evenly throughout each period and straight-line amortization is used, the average investment is computed as the average of the investment's initial book value and its salvage value. One major limitation of the accounting rate of return is its dependence on predictions of future value derived from amortization methods. It also fails to reflect year-to-year variations in expected net incomes.

LO4 Compute net present value and describe its use. The net present value of an investment is determined by predicting the future cash flows that it is expected to generate, discounting them at a rate that represents an acceptable return, and then subtracting the initial cost of the investment from the sum of the present values. This

technique can deal with any pattern of expected cash flows and applies a superior concept of return on investment. However, it is limited by the subjectivity inherent in predicting future cash flows and in selecting the discount rate.

LO5 Compute internal rate of return and discuss its use. The internal rate of return (IRR) is the discount rate that results in a zero net present value. When the cash flows are equal, we can compute the present value factor corresponding to the IRR by dividing the initial investment by the annual cash flows. We then use annuity tables to determine the discount rate corresponding to our present value factor. If the cash flows are uneven, we must use trial and error to compute the IRR.

LO6 Describe selection of a hurdle rate for an investment. Top management should select the hurdle (discount) rate to be used for evaluating capital investments. Although financial formulas can aid this selection, the choice of a satisfactory (minimum) rate is largely subjective. The required earnings rate should be at least higher than the rate at which money can be borrowed because the return on an investment must cover the interest and provide an additional profit to reward the company for its risk.

LO7 Describe the importance of relevant costs for short-term decisions. In the case of short-term decision making, a company must rely on the relevant costs pertaining to alternative courses of action rather than historical costs. Out-of-pocket expenses and opportunity costs are relevant because these are avoidable, whereas sunk costs are irrelevant because they result from past decisions and are therefore unavoidable. In addition to the relevant costs, managers must also consider the relevant benefits associated with an alternative course of action.

LO⁸ Evaluate short-term managerial decisions using relevant costs. Examples of these decisions can be classed as accepting additional business, make or buy, and sell as is or process further. Relevant costs are useful in making these decisions. For example, in deciding whether to produce and sell additional units of product, the relevant factors are the incremental costs and revenues from the additional volume.

GUIDANCE ANSWERS TO **Judgement Call**

Systems Manager

The dilemma faced by your friend and fellow manager is whether to abide by rules that are designed to prevent abuse or to bend those rules to acquire an investment that he believes will benefit the firm. This situation is realistic, and representative of the business world. Because breaking up the entire order into small components is fundamentally dishonest, you should advise your friend against this action. You should point out the consequences of being caught at a later stage, particularly the potential embarrassment in front of peers and subordinates. You should encourage your friend to develop a proposal for the entire package and then do all that he can to expedite its processing, particularly by pointing out the significant benefits associated with the investment. When faced by an internal control system that isn't working, there is virtually never a legitimate reason to overcome its shortcomings by dishonesty. Rather, a direct assault on those limitations is more sensible, and is the ethical thing to do.

R&D Manager

The controller is probably concerned that new products are risky and should therefore be evaluated using a higher rate of return. As the R&D manager, you should conduct a thorough technical analysis and obtain detailed market data and information about similar products available in the market. These factors might provide sufficient information to support the use of a lower return. You must be able to convince the controller (and yourself) that the risk level is consistent with the discount rate used. You should also be confident that the company has the capacity and the resources to handle the new product.

Investment Manager

Given that the time value of money is crucial, you want to use methods that reflect time value. Also, since recovery time is important, your attention should probably be directed at either the payback period. Your analysis should include the use of both methods to evaluate alternative investment opportunities.

Construction Supervisor

As the person who will most likely be responsible for the special project (if it is accepted), you should identify as many details as possible regarding the implementation of the project—direct resources such as manpower, materials, and equipment. Listing as many details as possible will help to more precisely estimate the direct costs. You must also identify any capacity constraints for indirect resources (such as supervision and shared equipment) that may potentially affect existing projects. All of these details will allow the controller to estimate the relevant costs associated with the special project, and determine a price to be quoted to the potential client.

GUIDANCE ANSWERS TO  **Flashback**

---

1. *b*

2. They are usually based on predictions of events that might occur well into the future.

3. *b*

4. Amortization expense is subtracted from revenues in computing net income. However, it does not use cash and should be added back to net income to compute net cash flows.

5. Not necessarily. One investment may continue to generate cash flows beyond the payback period for a longer time than the other. Also, the timing of their cash flows within the payback period may differ.

6. *b* Average investment 5($180,0001$15,000)/25$97,500

   Return on average investment = $40,000/$97,500 = 41%

7. It cannot be determined without comparing it to the returns expected from alternative investments with similar risk.

8. Project A

Year	Present Value of $1 at 10%	Project A		Project B	
		Net Cash Flows	Present Value of Net Cash Flows	Net Cash Flows	Present Value of Net Cash Flows
1	.9091	$12,000	$10,909	$ 4,500	$ 4,091
2	.8264	8,500	7,024	8,500	7,024
3	.7513	4,000	3,005	13,000	9,767
Total		$24,500	$20,938	$26,000	$20,882
Amount to be invested			(20,000)		(20,000)
Net present value of investment			**$ 938**		**$ 882**

9. No, the information is too limited to draw that conclusion. One investment may have more risk than the other.

10. Net present value.

11. *e.* Variable costs per unit for special order:

Direct materials ($37,500/7,500)	$ 5.00
Direct labour ($60,000/7,500)	8.00
Variable factory overhead [(0.30 × $20,000)/7,500]	0.80
Variable selling expenses [(0.60 × $25,000 × 0.5)/7,500]	1.00
Total	$14.80

Cost to produce special order:
(200 × $14.80) + $400 = $3,360

Required price per unit:
($3,360 + $1,000)/200 = $21.80

12. They are the additional costs that will result from accepting the additional business.

13. *d*

14. It is never relevant because it results from a past decision.

15. Avoidable expenses are those that the company will not incur if a segment of a business is eliminated, whereas unavoidable expenses are those that will continue even after the segment is eliminated.

16. *a*

Demonstration Problem

Determine the appropriate action in each of the following decision situations:

a. Packer Company is operating at 80% of its manufacturing capacity of 100,000 units per year. A chain store has offered to buy an additional 10,000 units at $22 each and sell them in an area where Packer currently has no outlet. The following facts are available:

	Per Unit	Total
Costs at 80% capacity:		
Direct materials	$ 8.00	$ 640,000
Direct labour	7.00	560,000
Total (fixed and variable) overhead	12.50	1,000,000
Totals	$27.50	$2,200,000

In producing 10,000 additional units, fixed overhead costs would remain at their current level but incremental variable overhead costs of $3.00 per unit would be incurred. Should the company accept or reject this order?

b. Green Company uses Part JR3 in manufacturing its products. In the past, it has always purchased this part from a supplier at $40 each. It recently upgraded its own manufacturing capabilities and has enough excess capacity (including trained workers) to begin manufacturing Part JR3 instead of buying it. The accountant has prepared the following cost projections of making the part, assuming that overhead is allocated to the part at the normal predetermined application rate of 200% of the direct labour cost.

Direct materials	$11.00
Direct labour	15.00
Overhead (fixed and variable) (200% of direct labour)	30.00
Total	$56.00

The required volume of output to produce the part will not require any incremental fixed overhead. Fifty-five % of the overhead per unit is variable. Should the company make or buy this part?

c. Electrasteel Company's manufacturing process causes a relatively large number of defective parts to be produced. The defective parts can be (1) sold for scrap, (2) melted down to recover the metal for reuse, or (3) reworked to be good units. If defective parts are reworked, the output of other good units is reduced because there is no excess capacity. Each unit reworked means that one new unit cannot be produced. The following information is available about 500 defective parts currently on hand:

Proceeds of selling as scrap	$2,500
Additional cost of melting down all defective parts	$ 400
Cost of purchases avoided by using recycled metal from defects	$4,800
Cost to rework 500 defective parts:	
Direct materials	$ -0-
Direct labour	1,500
Incremental overhead	1,750
Cost to produce 500 new parts:	
Direct materials	$6,000
Direct labour	5,000
Incremental overhead	3,200
Selling price of good unit	$ 40

Should the company melt down the parts, sell them as scrap, or rework them?

d. White Company can invest in one of two projects, TD1 or TD2. Each project would require an initial investment of $100,000 and produces the following end-of-year cash flows:

	TD1	TD2
Year 1	$ 20,000	$ 40,000
Year 2	30,000	40,000
Year 3	70,000	40,000
Total	$120,000	$120,000

Use net present values to determine which project, if any, should be acquired. Assume the company requires a 10% return from its investments.

Planning the Solution

○ Determine whether the Packer Company should accept the additional business by finding the incremental costs of materials, labour, and overhead that will be incurred if the order is accepted. Leave out fixed costs that will not be increased by the order. If the incremental revenue will exceed the incremental cost then accept the order.

○ Determine whether Green Company should make or buy the component by finding the incremental cost of making each unit. If the incremental cost exceeds the purchase price, the component should be purchased.

○ Determine whether Electrasteel Company should sell the defective parts, melt them down and recycle the metal, or rework them. To compare the three choices, examine all costs incurred and benefits received from the alternatives for the 500 defective units. For the scrapping alternative, include the costs of producing 500 new units and subtract the $2,500 proceeds from selling the old ones. For the melting alternative, include the costs of melting the defective units, add the net cost of new materials in excess over those obtained from recycling, and add the direct labour and overhead costs. For the reworking alternative, add the costs of direct labour and incremental overhead as well as the opportunity cost arising from not being able to produce and sell 500 units. Select the alternative that has the lowest cost. The cost assigned to the 500 defective units is sunk and not relevant in choosing among the three alternatives.

○ Compute the net present value of each investment using a 10% discount rate.

SOLUTION TO **Demonstration Problem**

a. This decision concerns accepting additional business. Because the current unit costs are $27.50, it initially appears as if the offer to sell for $22.00 should be rejected. However, the $27.50 cost includes fixed costs. When the analysis includes only the *incremental* costs, the per unit cost is:

Direct materials	$ 8.00
Direct labour	7.00
Variable overhead	3.00
Total incremental cost	$18.00

The offer should be accepted because it will produce $4.00 of additional contribution margin per unit (computed as $22 price less $18 incremental cost), which yields a total profit of $40,000 for the 10,000 additional units.

b. This is a make-or-buy decision. The analysis should include only the variable overhead of $16.50 (55% of $30). The relevant unit cost of manufacturing the part is:

Direct materials	$11.00
Direct labour	15.00
Variable overhead	16.50
Total incremental cost	$42.50

It would be better to continue buying the part for $40 instead of making it for $42.50, unless there are strong nonfinancial/qualitative factors that affect the decision.

c. This is a scrap-or-rework decision. The goal is to identify the alternative that produces the greatest net benefit to the company. To compare the alternatives we determine the net cost of obtaining 500 marketable units as follows:

	Sell As Is	Melt and Recycle	Rework Units
Incremental cost to produce 500 marketable units:			
Direct material:			
Cost of new materials..	$ 6,000	$6,000	
Value of recycled metal...		(4,800)	
Net materials cost..		1,200	
Melting costs...		400	
Total direct material cost...	6,000	1,600	
Direct labour	5,000	5,000	$1,500
Incremental overhead...	3,200	3,200	1,750
Total cost to produce 500 marketable units..............	$14,200	$9,800	$3,250
Less proceeds of selling defective units as scrap	(2,500)		
Opportunity costs*...			5,800
Net cost	$11,700	$9,800	$9,050

* The opportunity cost of $5,800 is the lost contribution margin from not being able to produce and sell 500 units because of reworking, computed as ($40 − $28.40) × 500 units. The $28.40 is computed by dividing $14,200 total cost by 500 marketable units.

The incremental cost of obtaining 500 marketable parts is smallest if the defective parts are reworked.

d. TD1

	Net Cash Flows	Present Value of $1 at 10%	Present Value of Net Cash Flows
Year 1	$ 20,000	0.9091	$ 18,182
Year 2	30,000	0.8264	24,792
Year 3	70,000	0.7513	52,591
Total......................................	$120,000		95,565
Amount invested.......................			(100,000)
Net present value			**$ (4,435)**

TD2

	Net Cash Flows	Present Value of $1 at 10%	Present Value of Net Cash Flows
Year 1	$ 40,000	0.9091	$ 36,364
Year 2	40,000	0.8264	33,056
Year 3	40,000	0.7513	30,052
Total......................................	$120,000		99,472
Amount invested.......................			(100,000)
Net present value			**$ (528)**

White Company should not invest in either project. Both are expected to yield negative net present values, and only positive net present value projects should be considered.

Glossary

Accounting rate of return A rate used to evaluate a potential investment; equals the after-tax periodic income from the project divided by the average investment in the asset; also called *return on average investment*. (p. 1448)

Avoidable expense An expense (or cost) that is relevant for decision making; an expense that is not incurred if a segment, product, or service is eliminated. (p. 1471)

Capital budgeting The process of analyzing alternative investments and deciding which assets to acquire or sell. (p. 1444)

Discounting The process or restating future cash flows in terms of their present value. (p. 1444)

Hurdle rate A minimum acceptable rate of return; used when interpreting the internal rate of return. (p. 1455)

Incremental cost An additional cost incurred when a company pursues a certain course of action; also called a *differential cost*. (p. 1465)

Internal rate of return (IRR) The rate that equates the net present value of a project's cash inflows and outflows to zero. (p. 1454)

Net present value A dollar amount used to evaluate a potential investment; an estimate of an asset's value to the company, computed by discounting the future cash flows from the investment at a satisfactory rate and then subtracting the initial cost of the investment. (p. 1451)

Opportunity cost The costs that represent the potential benefits lost by choosing an alternative course of action. (p. 1464)

Out-of-pocket cost A cost incurred or avoided as a result of management's decisions; requires a future outlay of cash. (p. 1464)

Payback period A time-based measure used to evaluate a potential investment; the time expected to pass before the net cash flows from an investment equal its initial cost. (p. 1445)

Rate of return on average investment See *accounting rate of return*.

Relevant benefits The differential revenue that is generated by selecting a particular course of action over another. (p. 1464)

Relevant cost A future cost that differs between alternatives in a particular business decision; also called an avoidable cost or differential cost. (p. 1463)

Segment margin Contribution margin less traceable or direct fixed costs. (p. 1472)

Sunk cost A cost that cannot be avoided or changed in any way because it arises from a past decision; irrelevant to future decisions. (p. 1464)

Unavoidable expense An expense (or cost) that is not relevant for decision making; an expense that would continue regardless of the decision made. (p. 1471)

 Online **Learning**Centre with POWERWEB

For more study tools, quizzes, and problem material,
refer to the Online Learning Centre at
www.mcgrawhill.ca/college/larson

Questions

1. What is capital budgeting?
2. Capital budgeting decisions require careful analysis because they are generally the _____ _____ and _____ decisions that management faces.
3. Identify four reasons why capital budgeting decisions are risky.
4. Why is an investment more attractive if it has a short payback period?
5. Identify two disadvantages of the payback period method of comparing investments.
6. What is the average amount invested in a machine during its life if it costs $200,000 and has a predicted five-year life with a $20,000 salvage value? Assume that the net income is received evenly throughout each year and straight-line amortization is used.
7. Why is the present value of $100 that you expect to receive one year from now less than $100 received

today? What is the present value of $100 that you expect to receive one year from now, discounted at 12%?
8. If the present value of the expected net cash flows from a machine, discounted at 10%, exceeds the amount to be invested, what can you say about the expected rate of return on the investment? What can you say about the expected rate of return if the present value of the net cash flows, discounted at 10%, is less than the amount of the investment?
9. Why is the value of an investment increased by using accelerated amortization (instead of straight-line) for income tax reporting?
10. Why should the required rate of return always be higher than the rate at which money can be borrowed when making a typical capital budgeting decision?
11. What are the two main criteria in assessing whether a cash flow is relevant?

12. A company manufactures and sells 500,000 units of product at $30 per unit in domestic markets. The product costs $20 per unit to manufacture ($13 variable cost per unit, $7 fixed cost per unit). Can you describe a situation under which the company may be willing to sell an additional 25,000 units of the product in an international market at $15 per unit?

13. What is an out-of-pocket cost? What is an opportunity cost? Are opportunity costs recorded in the accounting records?

14. Why are sunk costs irrelevant in deciding whether to sell the product in its present condition or to make it into a new product through additional processing?

15. Comment on the following statement: Only the variable costs identified with a product are relevant in a decision about which of two alternatives to choose.

16. Identify the incremental costs incurred by NIKE for shipping one additional pair of running shoes to a national retail sporting goods store, along with the normal order of 1,000 pairs of dress shoes.

Quick Study

QS 28-1
Payback period
LO^2

Bray Company is considering investing in a project that requires immediate payment of $15,000 and provides expected cash inflows of $6,000 annually for four years. What is the investment's payback period?

QS 28-2
Analyzing payback alternatives
LO^2

Brewer Company is considering two alternative investments. Investment A has a payback period of 4 years and Investment B has a payback period of 5.2 years. Why might Brewer's analysis of the two alternatives lead to the selection of B over A?

QS 28-3
Computing accounting rate of return
LO^3

Chester Company is considering two investments, each of which is expected to generate an average net income after taxes of $5,000 for three years. Each investment costs $30,000. Investment M has no salvage value but N has an expected salvage value of $10,000. The cash flows from Investment M are received evenly throughout the year and the cash flows from Investment N are received at the end of each year. Compute the accounting rate of return on each investment.

QS 28-4
Computing net present value
LO^4

If Fox Company invests $62,000 now; it can expect to receive $12,000 at the end of each year for seven years plus $5,000 at the end of the seventh year. What is the net present value of the investment, assuming Fox requires an 8% return on the investment?

QS 28-5
Determining relevant costs
$LO^{7,8}$

Burns Company is considering accepting or rejecting a special 1,000 unit order for one of its products. State whether each of the following is relevant to the decision:
a. Direct material cost, $10 per unit.
b. Variable overhead, $6 per unit.
c. Common fixed overhead that will continue if the special order is rejected, $1,500.
d. Fixed overhead that will be avoided if the special order is accepted, $1,000.

QS 28-6
Determining relevant costs
$LO^{7,8}$

Brutis Corporation has 1,000 obsolete units of product Z100 that are carried in inventory at a manufacturing cost of $16,000. If they are reworked for $5,000, they could be sold for $9,000. Alternatively, the product could be sold for scrap for $1,500. Which alternative is more desirable and what are the total relevant costs for that alternative?

QS 28-7
Analyzing incremental costs
LO^8

Gill Company incurs the following per unit costs related to one of the products it currently manufactures and sells for $11.20 per unit: The per unit costs and expenses assigned to the product amount to $8.40. Instead of manufacturing and selling this product, Gill can purchase a similar product for $7 and sell it for $9.80. If this is done, unit sales would remain unchanged and $6.30 of the costs assigned to the product would be eliminated. Should Gill continue to manufacture the product or purchase the alternative product?

Kyle Company can sell all the units of computer memory X and Y, but has limited production capacity. It can produce two units of X per hour or four units of Y per hour and has 6,000 production hours available. Product X has a contribution margin of $5.60 and Product Y has a contribution margin of $4.20. What is the most profitable sales mix for Kyle Company?

QS 28-8
Selecting a sales mix

LO^8

A study has been conducted to determine if one of the departments in Parry Company should be discontinued. The contribution margin in the department is $55,000 per year. Fixed expenses charged to the department are $65,000 per year. It is estimated that $38,000 of these fixed expenses could be eliminated if the department is discontinued. What will be the effect on the company's overall net operating income if the department is discontinued?

QS 28-9
Discontinuing a department

LO^8

Exercises

Compute the payback periods for these two unrelated investments:
a. A new sophisticated networking system costs $33,000 and is expected to have a useful life of six years. The system should save $7,500 (after 40% taxes) each year, after deducting straight-line amortization on the system. The predicted salvage value of the system is $6,000.
b. A new product packaging system costs $210,000 and has an expected useful life of 10 years. The system should save $65,250 per year after taxes. Estimated salvage value at the end of the useful life is $18,000.

Exercise 28-1
Computing payback period; equal cash flows

LO^2

Champ Company is considering the purchase of an asset for $90,000. The asset is expected to produce the following net cash flows:

Exercise 28-2
Computing payback period, unequal cash inflows

LO^2

	Year 1	Year 2	Year 3	Year 4	Year 5	Total
Net cash flows	$35,000	$37,500	$46,000	$60,000	$10,000	$188,500

The cash flows would occur evenly throughout each year. Compute the payback period for this investment.

A machine can be purchased for $240,000 and used for five years to generate these net incomes:

Exercise 28-3
Computing payback period; declining balance amortization

LO^2

	Year 1	Year 2	Year 3	Year 4	Year 5
Net incomes	$34,000	$67,200	$100,400	$133,600	$166,800

In projecting the expected net incomes, double-declining balance amortization was deducted, based on a five-year life and a salvage value of $22,000. Compute the payback period for the machine. Ignore income taxes.

Jet Courier plans to invest in a scanner to further improve its speed and accuracy in sorting packages. The scanner is expected to cost $500,000 and generate after-tax savings of $21,000 each year. Management predicts that the scanner will have a five-year useful life and a $100,000 salvage value. Compute the average return on investment for the scanner.

Exercise 28-4
Computing accounting rate of return

LO^3

Exercise 28-5
Payback and return on average investment

LO^{2,3}

Link Company is considering the purchase of equipment that would allow the company to add a new product to its line. The equipment is expected to cost $210,000 with a six-year life and no salvage value. It will be amortized on a straight-line basis. The company expects to sell 96,000 units of the equipment's product each year, approximately 8,000 per month. The expected end-of-year income statement related to this equipment is as follows:

Sales	$174,720
Costs:	
Materials, labour, and overhead (except for amortization on new equipment)	$114,240
Amortization on new equipment	28,000
Selling and administrative expenses	16,000
Total expenses	$158,240
Operating income	$ 16,480
Income taxes (30%)	4,944
Net income	$ 11,536

Required
Compute (a) the payback period and (b) the return on average investment for this equipment.

Exercise 28-6
Computing net present value

LO^4

After evaluating the risk of the investment described in Exercise 28-5, the Link Company concludes that it must earn at least an 8% return on the investment in the equipment. Use this rate to determine the net present value of the investment in the equipment.

Exercise 28-7
Computing and interpreting net present value and internal rate of return

LO^{4,5}

Tremble Company can invest in each of three cheese making projects, C1, C2, and C3. Each project would require an initial investment of $265,000 and would produce the following annual cash flows:

	C1	C2	C3
Year 1	$ 28,000	$115,000	$252,000
Year 2	112,000	115,000	70,000
Year 3	205,000	115,000	23,000
Total	$336,000	$345,000	$345,000

Required
1. Under the assumption that the company requires a 12% return from its investments, use net present values to determine which project or projects should be acquired.
2. Compute the internal rate of return for project C2. Use the findings from (1) above; is the internal rate of return greater than or less than 12% for project C2?

Exercise 28-8
Decision to accept additional business

LO^{7,8}

Flynn Company expects to sell 200,000 units of its product during the next period with the following results:

Sales	$3,100,000
Costs and expenses:	
Direct materials	$ 325,000
Direct labour	800,000
Factory overhead	220,000
Selling expenses	300,000
Administrative expenses	514,000
Total costs and expenses	$2,159,000
Net income	$ 941,000

The company has an opportunity to sell 30,000 additional units at a price of $20 per unit. The additional sales would not affect the regular sales. Direct material and direct labour unit costs would be the same for the additional units as they are for the regular units. However, the additional volume would create these incremental effects on costs:
- Total factory overhead would increase by 20%.
- Total administrative expenses would increase by $76,000.

Prepare an appropriate analysis to determine whether the company should accept or reject the offer to sell the additional units at the reduced price.

Community Accountants is thinking of outsourcing its payroll function. It has determined that its in-house payroll function costs $2.91 per transaction, based on a normal volume of 100,000 transactions per year. Its variable costs are $1.76 per transaction, fixed costs directly traceable to the payroll function are $40,000 per year and its common (allocated) fixed costs are $75,000 per year. A local company specializing in payroll processing has quoted a price of $2.50 per transaction.

Should Community Accountants continue with the payroll function in-house or should it outsource that function to the local outsourcer? Support your answer with the relevant analysis.

Exercise 28-9
Payroll outsourcing

$LO^{7,8}$

Felthem Company has 15,000 units of Product A that were manufactured for a total cost of $25 per unit. The 15,000 units can be sold at this stage for $990,000. Alternatively, they can receive further processing at a total additional cost of $180,000 and be converted into 4,400 units of Product B and 10,100 units of Product C. Product B can be sold for $100 per unit and Product C can be sold for $65 per unit.

Exercise 28-10
Sell or process decision

$LO^{7,8}$

Required
Prepare an analysis that shows whether the units of Product A should be processed further.

Davis Company owns a machine that can produce two different products. Product 1 can be produced at the rate of two units per hour and Product 2 can be produced at the rate of three units per hour. The capacity of the machine is 3,800 hours per year. The highly specialized products are sold to a single customer who has agreed to buy all of the company's output up to a maximum of 5,000 units of Product 1 and 7,000 units of Product 2. Selling prices and variable costs per unit to produce the products are:

Exercise 28-11
Analyzing and determining sales mix

LO^7

	Product 1	Product 2
Selling price	$12.75	$9.00
Variable costs	7.50	6.00
Contribution margin	$ 5.25	$3.00

Required
Determine the most profitable sales mix for the company and compute the contribution margin that results from that sales mix.

Exercise 28-12
Analyzing income effects of
eliminating departments

LO[7,8]

Ken Langille, President of Forest Products, has been presented the following information
regarding three of the company's product lines:

| | | | Product Lines | |
	Total	F1	F2	F3
Sales..	$254,000	$104,000	$75,000	$75,000
Variable expenses	118,500	36,500	35,000	47,000
Contribution margin.........................	$135,500	$ 67,500	$40,000	$28,000
Direct fixed expenses*....................	101,500	33,000	38,000	30,500
Common expenses, allocated..........	33,300	17,800	11,000	4,500
Operating income (loss)	$ 700	$ 16,700	$ (9,000)	$ (7,000)

*These costs are traced to the product lines and could be eliminated if the product lines to
which they are traced were discontinued.

Required
Which product lines should be discontinued?

Exercise 28-13
Analyzing income effects of
eliminating departments

LO[7,8]

Sweet Company expects to produce the following income results for next year:

	Dept. M	Dept. N	Dept. O	Dept. P	Dept. T
Sales..........................	$63,000	$ 35,000	$56,000	$42,000	$ 28,000
Expenses:					
Avoidable..................	9,800	36,400	22,400	14,000	37,800
Unavoidable..............	51,800	12,600	4,200	29,400	9,800
Total..........................	$61,600	$ 49,000	$26,600	$43,400	$ 47,600
Net income (loss)	$ 1,400	$(14,000)	$29,400	$(1,400)	$(19,600)

Required
Prepare a combined income statement for the company under each of the following
conditions:
a. Management does not eliminate any department.
b. Management eliminates departments with expected net losses. Explain.
c. Management eliminates departments with less sales dollars than avoidable expenses.

Problems

Problem 28-1A
Computing payback period,
accounting rate of return, and
net present value

LO[2,3,4]

King Company is planning to add a new product to its line. To assemble this product, the
company would have to buy a new machine at a cost of $270,000. The asset is expected to
have a four-year life and a $20,000 salvage value. This additional information is available:

Expected annual sales of new product.........	$1,187,000
Expected costs:	
Direct materials..	312,500
Direct labour	437,500
Factory overhead excluding	
amortization on new machine	202,500
Selling and administrative expenses	100,000
Income taxes	40%

All sales are for cash and all costs are out-of-pocket, except the amortization on the
new machine.

Required

1. Compute the straight-line amortization for each year of the asset's life.
2. Determine expected net income and cash flow for each year of the asset's life.
3. Compute the payback period for this asset, assuming that the cash flows occur evenly throughout each year.
4. Compute the accounting rate of return for this asset, assuming that the net income occurs evenly throughout each year.
5. Compute net present value of the investment with a discount rate of 7%, assuming that all cash flows occur at the end of each year. (Hint: salvage value is a cash inflow at the end of the asset's life.)

Check figure:
Net present value of investment,
$104,301

Hendrix Company has the opportunity to invest in one of two new moulding projects. Project Y requires an investment of $144,000 for new machinery having a four-year life and no salvage value. Project Z requires an investment of $144,000 for new machinery having a three-year life and no salvage value. The two projects would produce the following predicted annual results:

Problem 28-2A
Analyzing and computing payback, return on investment, and net present value

$LO^{2,3,4}$

	Project Y	Project Z
Sales..	$180,000	$150,000
Expenses:		
Direct materials...	24,000	18,000
Direct labour...	37,500	27,000
Factory overhead including amortization................	81,000	78,000
Selling and administrative expenses......................	18,000	18,000
Total expenses	$160,500	$141,000
Operating income..	$ 19,500	$ 9,000
Income taxes (30%)...	5,850	2,700
Net income...	$ 13,650	$ 6,300

Assume that the company uses straight-line amortization and that the cash flows occur evenly throughout the year, and that cash flows occur at the end of each period.

Required

Preparation component:

1. Compute the annual expected cash flows for each project.
2. Compute the payback period for the two projects.
3. Compute the accounting rate of return for each project.
4. Find the net present value of each project, using 8% as the discount rate.

Analysis component:

5. Select the project that you would recommend to management, and explain your choice.

Check figure:
Return on average investment
in Project Y, 18.96%

Problem 28-3A
Computing cash flows and net present values with alternative tax amortization methods

LO[4]

Farr Corporation is considering a new wing development project that would require a $30,000 investment in special test equipment with no salvage value. The project would produce $12,000 of income before amortization at the end of each year for six years. The company's income tax rate is 40%. In compiling its tax return and computing its income tax payments, assume the company can choose between these two alternative amortization schedules:

	Straight-Line Amortization Schedule	Accelerated Amortization Schedule
Year 1	$ 3,000	$ 4,500
Year 2	6,000	7,650
Year 3	6,000	5,355
Year 4	6,000	3,748
Year 5	6,000	2,624
Year 6	3,000	6,123
Total....................	$30,000	$30,000

Check figure:
Net present value of investment (accelerated), $10,190

Required

Preparation component:
1. Produce a five-column table that shows these items for each of the six years: (a) income before amortization, (b) straight-line amortization expense, (c) taxable income, (d) income taxes, and (e) net cash flow. Net cash flow equals the amount of income before amortization minus the income taxes.
2. Produce a five-column table that shows these items for each of the six years: (a) income before amortization, (b) accelerated amortization expense, (c) taxable income, (d) income taxes, and (e) net cash flow. Net cash flow equals the amount of income before amortization minus the income taxes.
3. Compute the net present value of the investment if straight-line amortization is used. Use 10% as the discount rate.
4. Compute the net present value of the investment if accelerated amortization is used. Use 10% as the discount rate.

Analysis component:
5. Explain why the accelerated amortization method increases the net present value of this project.

Problem 28-4A
Income results of added sales

LO[7,8]

Pargo Products Inc. manufactures an adhesive product that it sells to wholesalers at $6.40 per tube. The company manufactures and sells approximately 50,000 tubes each year, and normal costs for the production and sale of this quantity are as follows:

Direct materials..	$ 60,000
Direct labour	50,000
Factory overhead	75,000
Selling expenses...	30,000
Administrative expenses	25,000
Total	$240,000

A mail-order company has offered to buy 5,000 tubes of the adhesive for $4.40 each. These tubes would be marketed under the wholesaler's trade name and would not affect Pargo's sales through its normal channels.

A study of the costs of the new business reveals the following information:
- Direct material costs are 100% variable.
- The per unit direct labour costs for the additional units would be 50% greater than normal because their production would require overtime pay at one-and-one-half times the usual labour rate.

- Two-thirds of the normal annual overhead costs are fixed at any production level from zero to 65,000 units. The remaining one-third of the annual overhead cost is variable with volume.
- There will be no additional selling costs if the new business is accepted.
- Accepting the new business would increase administrative expenses by a fixed amount of $3,000.

Required
Prepare a three-column comparative income statement that shows:
1. Annual operating income for one year without the special order (column 1).
2. Annual operating income that would be received from the new business (column 2).
3. Combined annual operating income from normal business and the new business (column 3).

Check figure:
Combined operating income, $83,000

Duffy Company is capable of producing two products, X and Y, with the same machine in its factory. These facts are known:

Problem 28-5A
Results of alternative sales mixes

LO[7,8]

	Product X	Product Y
Selling price	$70.00	$140.00
Variable costs	28.00	63.00
Contribution	$42.00	$ 77.00
Machine-hours to produce 1 unit	0.4	1.0
Maximum unit sales per month	500	250

The company presently operates the machine for a single eight-hour shift for 22 working days each month. The management is thinking about operating the machine for two shifts, which will increase the machine's availability by another eight hours per day for 22 days per month. This change would require additional fixed costs of $3,500 per month.

Required
1. Determine the contribution margin per machine hour that each product generates.
2. How many units of X and Y should the company produce if it continues to operate with only one shift? What is the total contribution margin produced each month with this mix?
3. If the company adds another shift, how many units of X and Y should the company produce? What is the total contribution margin that would be produced each month with this mix? Should the company add the new shift?
4. Suppose that the company determines it can also increase the maximum sales of Product X to 750 units per month by spending $6,000 per month in marketing efforts. Should the company pursue this tactic together with the double shift?

Check figure:
Contribution margin current mix, $29,204

Problem 28-6A
Analysis of avoidable and unavoidable expenses

LO7,8

The management of Home Appliance Warehouse is trying to decide whether to eliminate its Large Appliances Department (LAD), which has produced losses or low profits for several years. The company's 2004 departmental income statement shows the following results:

Home Appliance Warehouse Income Statement For Year Ended December 31, 2004			
	SAD*	LAD	Combined
Sales	$436,000	$290,000	$726,000
Cost of goods sold	262,000	207,000	469,000
Gross profit from sales	$174,000	$ 83,000	$257,000
Operating expenses:			
Direct expenses:			
Advertising	$ 17,000	$ 12,000	$ 29,000
Store supplies used	4,000	3,800	7,800
Amortization of store equipment	5,000	3,300	8,300
Total direct expenses	$ 26,000	$ 19,100	$ 45,100
Allocated expenses:			
Sales salaries	$ 65,000	$ 39,000	$104,000
Rent expense	9,440	4,720	14,160
Bad debts expense	9,900	8,100	18,000
Office salary	18,720	12,480	31,200
Insurance expense	2,000	1,100	3,100
Miscellaneous office expenses	2,400	1,600	4,000
Total allocated expenses	$107,460	$ 67,000	$174,460
Total expenses	$133,460	$ 86,100	$219,560
Net income (loss)	$ 40,540	$ (3,100)	$ 37,440

*SAD = Small Appliances Department

In analyzing the decision to eliminate LAD, the management has looked at the following items of information:
a. The company has one office worker who earns $600 per week or $31,200 per year and four sales clerks who each earn $500 per week or $26,000 per year.
b. Currently, the full salaries of two sales clerks are charged to SAD. The full salary of one sales clerk is charged to LAD. Because the fourth clerk works half time in both departments, her salary is divided evenly between the two departments.
c. The sales salaries and the office salary currently assigned to LAD would be avoided if the department were eliminated. However, management prefers another plan. Two sales clerks have indicated that they will be quitting soon. Management thinks that the other two clerks can do their work if the one office worker works in sales half time. The office worker's schedule will allow this shift of duties if LAD is eliminated. If this change is implemented, half the office worker's salary would be reported as sales salaries and half would be reported as office salary.
d. The store building is rented under a long-term lease that cannot be changed. Therefore, the space presently occupied by LAD will have to be used by the current SAD. The equipment used by LAD will be used by the current SAD.
e. Closing LAD will eliminate its expenses for advertising, bad debts, and store supplies. It will also eliminate 70% of the insurance expense allocated to the department for coverage on its merchandise inventory. In addition, 25% of the miscellaneous office expenses presently allocated to LAD will be eliminated.

Check figure:
2. Forecasted net income without Department 200, $31,510

Required

Preparation component:
1. Prepare a three-column schedule that lists (a) the company's total expenses (including cost of goods sold), (b) the expenses that would be eliminated by closing the Large Appliance Department, and (c) the expenses that will continue.
2. Prepare a forecasted income statement for the company reflecting the elimination under the assumption that sales and the gross profit will not be affected. The statement should also reflect the reassignment of the office worker to one-half time as a sales clerk.

Analysis component:
3. Prepare a reconciliation of the company's combined net income with the forecasted net income assuming LAD is eliminated. Analyze the reconciliation and explain why you think the department should or should not be eliminated.

Alternate Problems

Douglas Company is considering adding a new product to its line, of which it estimates sales at 20,000 units annually at $24.50 per unit. To manufacture the product will require a new machine having an estimated five-year life, $35,000 salvage value, and costing $140,000. The new product will have direct materials cost of $210,000 and $70,000 of direct labour cost. Manufacturing overhead chargeable to the new product, other than for amortization on the new machine, will be $140,000 annually. Also, $32,200 of additional selling and administrative expenses will be incurred annually in producing and selling the product, and income taxes will take 20% of the before-tax profit. All sales are for cash and all costs are out-of-pocket, except the amortization on the new machine.

Required
1. Compute the straight-line amortization for each year of the asset's life.
2. Compute expected net income and cash flow in each year of the asset's life.
3. Compute the payback period on the investment in the new machine, assuming that the cash flows occur evenly throughout each year.
4. Compute the rate of return on the average investment in the new machine, assuming that the net income occurs evenly throughout each year.
5. Compute the net present value of the investment with a discount rate of 12%, assuming that all cash flows occur at the end of each year. (Hint: Salvage value is a cash inflow at the end of the asset's life.)

Problem 28-1B
Computing payback period, accounting rate of return, and net present value

$LO^{2,3,4}$

Check figure:
Payback period, 4.06 years

Ramsay Company has the opportunity to invest in one of two projects. Project 1 requires an investment of $78,400 for new machinery having a seven-year life and no salvage value. Project 2 requires an investment of $60,000 for new machinery having a five-year life and no salvage value. The two projects would produce the following predicted annual results:

Problem 28-2B
Analyzing and computing payback period, accounting rate of return, and net present value

$LO^{2,3,4}$

	Project 1	Project 2
Sales..	$130,000	$148,000
Expenses:		
Direct materials..	30,000	36,000
Direct labour..	27,000	35,000
Factory overhead including amortization..............	38,000	44,000
Selling and administrative expenses....................	27,000	25,000
Total expenses	$122,000	$140,000
Operating income...	$ 8,000	$ 8,000
Income taxes (25%).......................................	2,000	2,000
Net income..	$ 6,000	$ 6,000

The company uses straight-line amortization. Assume that the cash flows occur evenly throughout the year. For part 4 only, assume cash flows occur at the end of each period.

Required

Preparation component:
1. Compute the expected annual cash flows for each project.
2. Find the payback period for each project.
3. Compute the accounting rate of return for each project.
4. Find the net present value of the investment for the two projects, using 12% as the discount rate.

Analysis component:
5. Select the project that you would recommend to management, and explain your choice.

Check figure:
Project 1; Return on average investment, 15.3%

Problem 28-3B
Computing cash flows and net present values with alternative tax amortization methods

LO⁴

Boucher Company is considering a project that would require a $324,000 investment in an asset having a six-year life and no salvage value. The project would produce $113,400 of income before amortization at the end of each year. The company's income tax rate is 25%. In compiling its tax return and computing its income tax payments, assume the company can choose between these two alternative amortization schedules:

	Straight-Line Amortization Schedule	Accelerated Amortization Schedule
Year 1	$ 32,400	$ 48,600
Year 2	64,800	82,620
Year 3	64,800	57,834
Year 4	64,800	40,484
Year 5	64,800	28,339
Year 6	32,400	66,123
Total.....................	$324,000	$324,000

Check figure:

Net percent value; accelerated amortization method, $82,107

Required

Preparation component:
1. Produce a five-column table that shows these items for each of the six years: (a) income before amortization, (b) straight-line amortization expense, (c) taxable income, (d) income taxes, and (e) net cash flow. Net cash flow equals the amount of income before amortization minus the income taxes.
2. Produce a five-column table that shows these items for each of the six years: (a) income before amortization, (b) accelerated amortization expense, (c) taxable income, (d) income taxes, and (e) net cash flow. Net cash flow equals the amount of income before amortization minus the income taxes.
3. Compute the net present value of the investment if straight-line amortization is used. Use 12% as the discount rate.
4. Compute the net present value of the investment if accelerated amortization is used. Use 12% as the discount rate.

Analysis component:
5. Explain why the accelerated amortization method increases the net present value of this project.

Problem 28-4B
Analyzing income results of additional business

LO⁷,⁸

Boutlier Company annually sells 30,000 units of its product at a price of $30 per unit. At the 30,000-unit production level the product costs $27 a unit to manufacturer and sell, and at this level the company has the following costs and expenses:

Variable costs:	
Direct materials	$180,000
Direct labour	225,000
Factory overhead	135,000
Selling expenses..	45,000
Administrative expenses	36,000
Total	$621,000
Fixed costs:	
Manufacturing overhead...........................	$ 90,000
Selling expenses..	45,000
Administrative expenses	54,000
Total	$189,000

All the units the company presently sells are sold in this country. However, an exporter recently offered to buy 3,000 units of the product for sale abroad. The exporter will pay only $20 per unit, which is below the company's present $27 per unit manufacturing and selling costs.

Required

Prepare a three-column comparative income statement that shows:
1. The operating income for one year without the special order.
2. The operating income that would be received from the new business.
3. The combined results for one year from the usual business and the new business.
4. What sales price would give Boutlier a $3-per-unit profit?

Check figure:
Combined operating
income, $87,900

Brown Company is capable of producing two products, Product 7X and Product 9X, with the same machine in its factory. These facts are known:

Problem 28-5B
Analyzing sales mix strategies

$LO^{7,8}$

	Product 7X	Product 9X
Selling price	$245.00	$280.00
Variable costs	140.00	210.00
Contribution	$105.00	$ 70.00
Machine-hours to produce 1 unit	0.8	0.4
Maximum unit sales per month	525	700

The company presently operates the machine for a single eight-hour shift for 23 working days each month. The management is thinking about operating the machine for two shifts, which will increase the machine's availability by another eight hours per day for 23 days per month. This change would require additional fixed costs of $5,000 per month.

Required

1. Determine the contribution margin per machine hour that each product generates.
2. How many units of Product 7X and Product 9X should the company produce if it continues to operate with only one shift? What is the total contribution margin produced each month with this mix?
3. If the company adds another shift, how many units of Product 7X and Product 9X should the company produce? What is the contribution margin that would be produced each month with this mix? Should the company add the new shift?
4. Suppose that the company determines it can also increase the maximum sales of Product 9X to 800 units per month by spending $4,000 per month in marketing efforts. Should the company pursue this strategy together with the double shift?

Check figure:
Part 3; Contribution
margin, $54,500

Problem 28-6B
Analyzing elimination of a
department

LO7, 8

The management of TeeTime Company is trying to decide whether to eliminate Department Z, which has produced low profits or losses for several years. The company's 2004 departmental income statement shows the following results:

TeeTime Company Departmental Income Statement For Year Ended December 31, 2004			
	Dept. Y	**Dept. Z**	**Combined**
Sales..	$700,000	$175,000	$875,000
Cost of goods sold	461,300	125,100	586,400
Gross profit from sales....................................	$238,700	$ 49,900	$288,600
Operating expenses:			
Direct expenses:			
Advertising	27,000	3,000	30,000
Store supplies used.................................	5,600	1,400	7,000
Amortization of store equipment.............	14,000	7,000	21,000
Total direct expenses	$ 46,600	$ 11,400	$ 58,000
Allocated expenses:			
Sales salaries...	70,200	23,400	93,600
Rent expense	22,080	5,520	27,600
Bad debts expense	21,000	4,000	25,000
Office salary	20,800	5,200	26,000
Insurance expense	4,200	1,400	5,600
Miscellaneous office expenses..............	1,700	2,500	4,200
Total allocated expenses	$139,980	$ 42,020	$182,000
Total expenses..	$186,580	$ 53,420	$240,000
Net income (loss)	$ 52,120	$ (3,520)	$ 48,600

    In analyzing the decision to eliminate Department Z, the management has looked at the following items of information:

a. The company has one office worker who earns $500 per week or $26,000 per year and four sales clerks who each earn $450 per week or $23,400 per year.

b. Currently, the full salaries of three sales clerks are charged to Department Y. The full salary of one sales clerk is charged to Department Z.

c. The sales salaries and the office salary currently assigned to Department Z would be avoided if the department were to be eliminated. However, management prefers another plan. Two sales clerks have indicated that they will be quitting soon. Management thinks that the two remaining clerks can do their work if the one office worker works in sales half time. The office worker's schedule will allow this shift of duties if Department Z is eliminated. If this change is implemented, half the office worker's salary would be reported as sales salaries and half would be reported as office salary.

d. The store building is rented under a long-term lease that cannot be changed. Therefore, the space presently occupied by Department Z will have to be used by the current Department Y. The current Department Y will use the equipment used by Department Z.

e. Closing Department Z will eliminate its expenses for advertising, bad debts, and store supplies. It will also eliminate 65% of the insurance expense allocated to the department for coverage on its merchandise inventory. In addition, 30% of the miscellaneous office expenses presently allocated to Department Z will be eliminated.

Check figure:
2. Forecasted net income without Department Z, $55,560

Required
Preparation component:
1. Prepare a three column schedule that lists (a) the company's total expenses (including cost of goods sold), (b) the expenses that would be eliminated by closing Department Z, and (c) the expenses that will continue.
2. Prepare a forecasted income statement for the company reflecting the elimination under the assumption that sales and gross profit will not be affected. The statement should also reflect the reassignment of the office worker to one-half time as a sales clerk.
Analysis component:
3. Prepare a reconciliation of the company's combined net income with the forecasted net income assuming Department Z is eliminated. Also compare Department Z's revenues and its avoidable expenses and explain why you think the department should or should not be eliminated.

Analytical and Review Problems

Five investment opportunities of equal cost offer the following cash flow patterns:

A & R 28-1

Year	A	B	C	D	E
1	$ 4,000	$ 2,000	$ 2,500	$ 3,000	$ 1,000
2	4,000	2,000	2,500	3,000	1,000
3	4,000	2,000	2,500	3,000	1,000
4	4,000	2,000	2,500	3,000	1,000
5	4,000	2,000	2,500	3,000	1,000
6	1,000	3,000	2,500	2,000	4,000
7	1,000	3,000	2,500	2,000	4,000
8	1,000	3,000	2,500	2,000	4,000
9	1,000	3,000	2,500	2,000	4,000
10	1,000	3,000	2,500	2,000	4,000
Total	$25,000	$25,000	$25,000	$25,000	$25,000

Required
Rank the five alternatives in terms of desirability and justify your ranking.

George Dumphy has been offered an opportunity to submit a bid for the right to provide a garbage disposal service for the local municipality. The contract would run for five years. Mr. Dumphy estimates that his net cash receipts from the disposal business would amount to $120,000 annually. If this bid were accepted, Mr. Dumphy would have to make an initial investment of $24,000 in specialized equipment.

A & R 28-2

Required
What is the maximum amount that Mr. Dumphy can afford to bid for the disposal service business, assuming that he requires a 15% return on his investment? (Do not consider income taxes.)

Select Company manufactures gadgets by carving them out of solid 100-kilogram blocks of raw material. Each block costs $120, and the one gadget from a block can be sold for $200. For many years, the scrap was simply dumped in a large waste pile and eventually biodegraded harmlessly. This wasted material represents about 20% of the total weight of the block.

A & R 28-3

Several years ago, another company developed a product that could be made from this waste. At that time, Select and the other company negotiated an arrangement. Select would bag the waste in 20-kilogram sacks, and the other company would pick them up at Select's factory and pay $40 per bag for them. At the time of entering into the arrangement, the Select bookkeeper had produced an analysis of the costs and concluded that the price of $2 per kilogram produced a profit of $0.10 per kilogram. Although this seemed like a small amount, it was better than nothing, and nothing was all that the company was receiving before. The analysis assigned material cost to the waste as follows:

Item	Selling Price	Percent of Total	Materials Cost*	Materials Cost per Unit
Gadget	$200	83.3%	$100.00	$100 per gadget
Waste	40	16.7	20.00	$1.00 per kg.
Total	$240	100.0%	$120.00	

*Allocated between gadget and waste

The labour cost of putting the waste into the bags was determined to be $0.40 per kilogram. Then, overhead was assigned at the normal rate of 125% of the labour cost. As a result, the total cost per kilogram was determined to be:

Material	$1.00
Labour	0.40
Overhead...............................	0.50
Total cost...............................	$1.90

The incremental overhead for the packaging activity was $0.08 per kilogram, and the remaining $0.42 happened with or without the packaging activity.

A new offer was recently received from a competitor of the company that had been hauling away the bagged waste. This company offered to simply pay $1.20 per kilogram and pick it up at the plant in bulk. Select Company convened a management committee to consider this offer. Sales of gadgets had been high and a lot of waste was being produced. Any additional profit from selling it was considered important.

The senior accountant prepared for the meeting by checking the files for the prior analysis. He concluded that the new arrangement would increase the profit to $0.20 per kilogram, which is the excess of the $1.20 selling price over the raw material cost of $1.00. The junior accountant prepared another analysis that allocated the cost of the raw material differently because the selling prices would change. Here are the results of the junior accountant's allocation:

Item	Selling Price	Percent of Total	Materials Cost*	Materials Cost per Unit
Gadget......................	$200	89.3%	$107.16	$107.15 per gadget
Waste.......................	24	10.7	12.84	$0.642 per kg.
Total.........................	$224	100.0%	$120.00	

*Allocated between gadget and waste

Thus, this accountant concluded that the new deal would create a profit of nearly $0.56 per kilogram, which greatly exceeds the present $0.10 per kilogram.

The marketing manager found the exercise amusing because the waste product used to be simply thrown away. He figured the profit would have to be at least $1.20 per kilogram anyway it was looked at.

In the meeting, the company's controller and president heard the opinions of the other three. When the president appeared to be leaning toward accepting the new offer, the controller quietly said, "The profit on this new deal doesn't come anywhere near the profit on the old one. We would be making a mistake to change now under these terms." The president quickly regained composure, agreed with the controller, and the meeting adjourned.

Required

Who was right? Was this decision sound? Explain what you think and support your position with an analysis of the numbers.

Moncton Livestock Company operates several feedlots, one of which is located at New Castle. The New Castle feedlot no longer produces a profit because of its distance from sources of feed, relatively high transportation costs, and a lack of modern facilities. As a result, management is considering the possibility of constructing a new feedlot in Fredericton.

The new feedlot would be close to a feed source and near meatpackers. If the Fredericton lot were to be built, the New Castle lot would be closed down. The company president favours making the move for several reasons, but several directors have asked for more detailed information before approving the decision. Their main concern is that abandoning the New Castle lot would create a large loss.

You were asked to analyze the proposal and to provide information to help the directors decide whether to support the president's desire to move to Fredericton. You have developed the data described in the following paragraphs:

Loss from abandoning the New Castle lot. The land and facilities of the New Castle lot have a $1 million book value. Virtually none of the machinery or other assets can be sold, and the land is not suitable for any other use without prohibitive reclamation costs. Based on the price predicted by the company's real estate consultant, only $100,000 cash would be received through the sale of the land and the facilities, after considering income taxes. The $900,000 loss from this sale is standing between the directors and their support for the president.

Investment in the new lot. The new Fredericton feedlot would have an upfront total cost of $5 million. In addition to being closer to feed sources and cattle buyers, this feedlot would double the capacity of the New Castle lot. Management estimates that 100,000 head of cattle could be handled every year.

Comparative costs. At their full capacity volumes of 50,000 and 100,000 head, the costs per head at the old lot and the predicted costs per head at the new lot are:

	New Castle Lot	Fredericton Lot
Variable feed, labour, and operating costs (all are out-of-pocket costs)	$88	$72
Amortization (fixed cost).......................	2	5
Total costs per head..............................	$90	$77

The higher per head amortization cost for the new Fredericton lot arises primarily from the higher total cost, even though it will be able to handle a larger volume.

Required

Analyze the alternatives using net present values and make a recommendation. Present any pertinent schedules needed to produce the data used in your analysis.

To make the problem manageable, assume that both feedlots can operate for 10 years. The revenue per head would be the same at the two feedlots. Despite operating at full capacity, the New Castle lot has only been breaking even, which means that the revenue per head is equal to the cost per head just shown. The corporation is subject to a 30% income tax rate. It will not be possible to operate both the New Castle and Fredericton lots. As a reflection of the high risk that they perceive, the directors want to have at least a 15% return on any investment that the company would make in the new Fredericton feedlot.

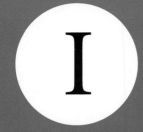

Financial Statement Information

This appendix includes financial statement information from (a) Leon's Furniture Limited and (b) WestJet Airlines Ltd. All of this information is taken from their annual reports. An **annual report** is a summary of the financial results of a company's operations for the year and its future plans. It is directed at external users of financial information, but also affects actions of internal users.

An annual report is also used by a company to showcase itself and its products. Many include attractive pictures, diagrams, and illustrations related to the company, but the *financial section* is its primary objective. This section communicates much information about a company, with most data drawn from the accounting information system.

The layout of each annual report's financial section that is included in this appendix is:

- Auditor's Report
- Financial Statements
- Notes to Financial Statements

This appendix is organized as follows:

- Leon's: I-1 to I-9
- WestJet: I-10 to I-27

There are questions at the end of each chapter that refer to information in this appendix. We encourage readers to spend extra time with these questions as they are especially useful in reinforcing and showing the relevance and diversity of financial reporting.

More current financial information about these and other Canadian corporations can be found online at www.sedar.com.

This is exciting business

2002 Annual Report / Leon's Furniture Limited

Leon's

Management's Responsibility for the Financial Statements

The accompanying consolidated financial statements and all information in this annual report are the responsibility of management and have been approved by the Board of Directors.

The accompanying consolidated financial statements have been prepared by management in accordance with Canadian generally accepted accounting principles. Financial statements are not precise since they include certain amounts based upon estimates and judgements. When alternative methods exist, management has chosen those it deems to be the most appropriate in the circumstances. The financial information presented elsewhere in this Annual Report is consistent with that in the financial statements.

Leon's Furniture Limited (Leon's) maintains systems of internal accounting and administrative controls of high quality, consistent with reasonable costs. Such systems are designed to provide reasonable assurance that the financial information is relevant and reliable and that Leon's assets are appropriately accounted for and adequately safeguarded.

The Board of Directors is responsible for ensuring that management fulfils its responsibilities for financial reporting and is ultimately responsible for reviewing and approving the financial statements. The Board carries out this responsibility principally through its Audit Committee.

The Audit Committee is appointed by the Board and reviews the financial statements and annual report; considers the report of the external auditors; assesses the adequacy of the internal controls of the company; examines the fees and expenses for audit services; and recommends to the Board the independent auditors for appointment by the shareholders. The Committee reports its findings to the Board of Directors for consideration when approving the financial statements for issuance to the shareholders.

These consolidated financial statements have been audited by Ernst & Young LLP, the external auditors, in accordance with Canadian generally accepted auditing standards on behalf of the shareholders. Ernst & Young has full and free access to the Audit Committee.

Mark J. Leon
Vice Chairman and C.E.O.

February 21, 2003

Dominic Scarangella
Vice President and C.F.O.

13

Auditors' Report

To the Shareholders of **Leon's Furniture Limited - Meubles Leon Ltée**

We have audited the consolidated balance sheets of Leon's Furniture Limited - Meubles Leon Ltée as at December 31, 2002 and 2001 and the consolidated statements of income and retained earnings and cash flows for the years then ended. These financial statements are the responsibility of the Company's management. Our responsibility is to express an opinion on these financial statements based on our audits.

We conducted our audits in accordance with Canadian generally accepted auditing standards. Those standards require that we plan and perform an audit to obtain reasonable assurance whether the financial statements are free of material misstatement. An audit includes examining, on a test basis, evidence supporting the amounts and disclosures in the financial statements. An audit also includes assessing the accounting principles used and significant estimates made by management, as well as evaluating the overall financial statement presentation.

In our opinion, these consolidated financial statements present fairly, in all material respects, the financial position of the Company as at December 31, 2002 and 2001 and the results of its operations and its cash flows for the years then ended in accordance with Canadian generally accepted accounting principles.

Ernst & Young LLP

Toronto, Canada,
February 14, 2003

Chartered Accountants

Consolidated Balance Sheets

As at December 31 (in thousands)		2002		2001
ASSETS				
Current				
Cash and cash equivalents	$	29,329	$	19,054
Marketable securities		56,685		80,228
Accounts receivable		31,221		20,724
Inventory		55,047		51,079
Income taxes recoverable		7,563		821
Total current assets		179,845		171,906
Future income tax assets [note 3]		4,010		4,490
Capital assets, net [note 2]		136,584		119,279
	$	320,439	$	295,675
LIABILITIES AND SHAREHOLDERS' EQUITY				
Current				
Accounts payable and accrued liabilities	$	73,151	$	67,953
Customers' deposits		6,664		7,426
Dividends payable		2,520		2,035
Future income tax liabilities [note 3]		5,270		–
Total current liabilities		87,605		77,414
Redeemable share liability [note 7]		199		139
Total liabilities		87,804		77,553
Shareholders' equity				
Common shares [note 8]		9,535		9,325
Retained earnings		223,100		208,797
Total shareholders' equity		232,635		218,122
	$	320,439	$	295,675

See accompanying notes

On behalf of the Board:

Director   Director

Consolidated Statements of Income and Retained Earnings

Years ended December 31 (in thousands, except shares outstanding and earnings per share)	2002	2001
Sales	$ 449,693	$ 425,687
Cost of sales	261,265	248,445
Gross profit	188,428	177,242
Operating expenses (income)		
Salaries and commissions	66,610	62,092
Advertising	27,306	27,263
Rent and property taxes	7,316	7,362
Amortization	8,552	7,742
Employee profit-sharing plan	2,483	2,361
Other operating expenses	25,807	24,790
Interest income	(2,650)	(4,178)
Other income	(10,727)	(13,035)
	124,697	114,397
Income before income taxes	63,731	62,845
Provision for income taxes [note 3]	25,211	26,522
Net income for the year	38,520	36,323
Retained earnings, beginning of year	208,797	192,827
Dividends declared	(19,392)	(7,986)
Excess of cost of share repurchase over carrying value of related shares [note 8]	(4,825)	(12,367)
Retained earnings, end of year	$ 223,100	$ 208,797
Weighted average number of common shares outstanding		
Basic	19,589,298	19,925,675
Diluted	19,956,335	20,265,678
Earnings per share		
Basic	$ 1.96	$ 1.82
Diluted	$ 1.93	$ 1.79

See accompanying notes

15

Leon's

Consolidated Statements of Cash Flows

Years ended December 31 (in thousands)	2002	2001
OPERATING ACTIVITIES		
Net income for the year	$ 38,520	$ 36,323
Add (deduct) items not involving a current cash payment		
Amortization	8,552	7,742
Loss (gain) on sale of capital assets	(6)	12
Future tax expense	5,750	440
Loss (gain) on sale of marketable securities	1,278	(1,072)
	54,094	43,445
Net change in non-cash working capital balances related to operations [note 6]	(17,952)	(10,063)
Cash provided by operating activities	36,142	33,382
INVESTING ACTIVITIES		
Purchase of capital assets	(24,681)	(18,027)
Proceeds on sale of capital assets	11	35
Purchase of marketable securities	(1,180,171)	(1,164,497)
Proceeds on sale of marketable securities	1,202,436	1,163,908
Issuance of series 2002 shares [note 7]	12,104	–
Decrease (increase) in employee share purchase loans [note 7]	(11,825)	83
Cash used in investing activities	(2,126)	(18,498)
FINANCING ACTIVITIES		
Dividends paid	(18,839)	(7,980)
Repurchase of capital stock [note 8]	(4,902)	(12,652)
Cash used in financing activities	(23,741)	(20,632)
Net increase (decrease) in cash and cash equivalents during the year	10,275	(5,748)
Cash and cash equivalents, beginning of year	19,054	24,802
Cash and cash equivalents, end of year	$ 29,329	$ 19,054

See accompanying notes

1. SUMMARY OF SIGNIFICANT ACCOUNTING POLICIES

These consolidated financial statements of Leon's Furniture Limited - Meubles Leon Ltée [the "Company"] have been prepared by management in accordance with Canadian generally accepted accounting principles. The more significant of these accounting policies are summarized as follows:

Principles of consolidation

The consolidated financial statements include the accounts of the Company and its subsidiaries, all of which are wholly owned.

Revenue recognition

Sales are recognized as revenue for accounting purposes upon the customer either picking up the merchandise ordered or when merchandise is delivered to the customer's home.

Foreign exchange translation

Merchandise imported from the United States is recorded at its equivalent Canadian dollar value upon receipt. United States dollar accounts payable are translated at the year-end exchange rate. Gains and losses resulting from translation of United States dollar accounts payable are included in income.

Cash and cash equivalents

Cash equivalents comprise only highly liquid investments with original maturities of less than ninety days.

Marketable securities

Marketable securities, which consist primarily of bonds with maturities not exceeding eight years and an interest rate range of 2.0% to 6.0%, are stated at the lower of cost and market value. Marketable securities and equity instruments are valued at the lower of cost and market value on an aggregate basis.

Inventory

Inventory is valued at the lower of cost, determined on a first-in, first-out basis, and net realizable value.

Capital assets

Capital assets are initially recorded at cost. Normal maintenance and repair expenditures are expensed as incurred. Amortization is provided over the estimated useful lives of the assets using the following annual rates and bases:

Buildings . . . . 5% straight-line
Equipment . . . . 20% to 30% declining balance
Vehicles . . . . 30% declining balance
Computer hardware and software . . . . 14% straight-line
Leasehold improvements . . . . Over the terms of the leases to a maximum of 15 years

No amortization is provided for assets under construction.

Store pre-opening costs

Store pre-opening costs are expensed as incurred.

Income taxes

The Company follows the liability method for accounting for income taxes. Under the liability method, future tax assets and liabilities are determined based on differences between the financial reporting and tax bases of assets and liabilities and are measured using the substantively enacted tax rates and laws that will be in effect when the differences are expected to reverse.

Earnings per share

Basic earnings per share have been calculated using the weighted average number of common shares outstanding during the year. Diluted earnings per share are calculated using the treasury stock method.

17

Fair value of financial instruments

The fair value of financial instruments held by the Company, comprising cash and cash equivalents, marketable securities, accounts receivable, accounts payable and accrued liabilities, customers' deposits and redeemable share liability approximate their carrying values in these consolidated financial statements.

Stock-based compensation

The Canadian Institute of Chartered Accountants ["CICA"] issued new guidance for accounting for stock-based compensation and other stock-based payments that is effective for fiscal years beginning on or after January 1, 2002 and generally applies to awards granted on or after the date of adoption.

The Management Share Purchase Plan [the "Plan"] represents a compensatory plan under the new CICA guidance. The Company has elected not to recognize compensation costs relating to the Plan [note 7].

2. CAPITAL ASSETS

Capital assets consist of the following:

[in thousands]	2002			2001		
	Cost	Accumulated amortization	Net book value	Cost	Accumulated amortization	Net book value
Land	$ 41,378	$ –	$ 41,378	$ 35,073	$ –	$ 35,073
Buildings	116,832	51,566	65,266	105,325	46,981	58,344
Equipment	17,940	11,712	6,228	16,575	10,678	5,897
Vehicles	13,994	11,533	2,461	13,513	10,680	2,833
Computer hardware and software	6,869	4,335	2,534	5,885	3,614	2,271
Leasehold improvements	26,178	7,461	18,717	21,081	6,220	14,861
	$ 223,191	$ 86,607	$ 136,584	$ 197,452	$ 78,173	$ 119,279

Included in the above balances are assets not being amortized with book values of approximately $5,707,000 [2001 - $1,895,000] due to construction in progress.

3. INCOME TAXES

Significant components of the Company's future tax assets are as follows:

[in thousands]	2002	2001
Future tax assets		
Capital assets	$ 4,010	$ 4,490
Total future tax assets	$ 4,010	$ 4,490

Significant components of the Company's current future tax liabilities are as follows:

[in thousands]	2002	2001
Current future tax liabilities		
Marketable securities	$ (326)	$ –
Accounts receivable	4,940	–
Inventory	656	–
Total current future tax liabilities	$ 5,270	$ –

Significant components of the provision for income taxes are as follows:

[in thousands]	2002	2001
Current tax expense	$ 19,461	$ 26,082
Future income tax expense (benefit) relating to origination and reversal of temporary differences	5,775	(1,111)
Future income tax expense (benefit) relating to tax rate reductions	(25)	1,551
Provision for income taxes	$ 25,211	$ 26,522

The total provision for income taxes in the consolidated financial statements is at a rate different than the combined federal and provincial statutory income tax rate of the current year for the following reasons:

	2002		2001	
Tax at combined federal and provincial tax rate	$ 24,511	38.5%	$ 26,018	41.4%
Tax effect of expenses that are not deductible for income tax purposes	23	–	20	–
Tax effect of non-taxable portion of loss (gain) on disposal	159	0.3	(202)	(0.3)
Future tax effect of rate reductions	(25)	–	1,551	2.5
Future tax effect of arising timing differences	(281)	(0.4)	(131)	(0.2)
Federal large corporations tax	21	–	89	0.1
Other, net	803	1.2	(823)	(1.3)
Provision for income taxes	**$ 25,211**	**39.6%**	**$ 26,522**	**42.2%**

4. COMMITMENTS

[a] The estimated cost to complete construction in progress at three locations [one location in 2001] amounted to approximately $4,143,000 as at December 31, 2002 [2001 - $2,100,000].

[b] The Company is obligated under operating leases to future minimum annual rental payments for certain land and buildings as follows:

[in thousands]

2003	$ 389
2004	251
2005	90
2006	90
2007	90
Thereafter	255
	$ 1,165

[c] The Company has issued approximately $1,900,000 in letters of credit with respect to buildings under construction.

5. FRANCHISE OPERATIONS

As at December 31, 2002, a total of twenty-one franchises [2001 - twenty-one] were in operation representing twenty-two [2001 - twenty-two] stores. Sales by franchise stores during the year ended December 31, 2002, on which the Company earns royalty income, amounted to approximately $129,192,000 [2001 - $119,719,000].

6. CONSOLIDATED STATEMENTS OF CASH FLOWS

[a] The net change in non-cash working capital balances related to operations consists of the following:

[in thousands]	2002	2001
Accounts receivable	$ (10,497)	$ (6,119)
Inventory	(3,968)	(1,908)
Income taxes recoverable	(6,742)	(1,706)
Accounts payable and accrued liabilities	4,017	(1,249)
Customers' deposits	(762)	919
	$ (17,952)	$ (10,063)

[b] Income taxes and interest paid:

[in thousands]	2002	2001
Income taxes paid	$ 26,904	$ 28,583
Interest paid	$ 4	$ 1

[c] During the year, capital assets were acquired at an aggregate cost of $25,862,796 [2001 - $18,487,527], of which $3,908,990 [2001 - $2,726,770] is included in accounts payable and accrued liabilities as at December 31, 2002.

19

7. REDEEMABLE SHARE LIABILITY

[in thousands]		2002		2001
Authorized				
89,400 convertible, non-voting, series 1994 shares				
350,000 convertible, non-voting, series 1998 shares				
571,000 convertible, non-voting, series 2002 shares				
Issued				
17,874 series 1994 shares [2001 - 40,437] [note 8]	$	228	$	515
299,566 series 1998 shares [2001 - 299,566]		5,272		5,272
421,000 series 2002 shares [2001 - nil]		12,104		–
Less employee share purchase loans		(17,405)		(5,648)
	$	199	$	139

Under the terms of its Management Share Purchase Plan, the Company advanced non-interest bearing loans to certain of its employees in 1994, 1998 and 2002 to allow them to acquire convertible, non-voting, series 1994 shares, series 1998 shares, and series 2002 shares, respectively, of the Company. These loans are repayable through the application against the loans of any dividends on the shares, with any remaining balance repayable on the date the shares are converted to common shares. Each issued and fully paid for series 1994, 1998 and 2002 share may be converted into one common share at any time after the fifth anniversary date of the issue of these shares and prior to the tenth anniversary of such issue. Each share may also be redeemed at the option of the holder or by the Company at any time after the fifth anniversary date of the issue of these shares and prior to the tenth anniversary of such issue. The redemption price is equal to the original issue price of the shares adjusted for subsequent subdivisions of shares plus accrued and unpaid dividends. The purchase prices of the shares are $12.73 per series 1994 share, $17.60 per series 1998 share and $28.75 per series 2002 share.

Dividends paid to series 1994 to 2002 shareholders of approximately $68,000 [2001 - $69,000] have been used to reduce the respective shareholder loans.

During the year ended December 31, 2002, the Company issued 421,000 series 2002 shares for proceeds of approximately $12,104,000. No shares were cancelled during the year ended December 31, 2002. During the year ended December 31, 2001, the Company did not issue or cancel any shares.

Employee share purchase loans have been netted against the redeemable share liability based upon their terms.

This Management Share Purchase Plan represents a compensatory plan. The terms of the series 2002 shares issued under the Plan and related employee share purchase loans collectively give the employees the ability, but not the obligation, to acquire common shares of the Company. The pro forma impact on net income and earnings per share using the fair value method is not material.

8. COMMON SHARES

The Company's common shares consist of the following:

[in thousands]		2002		2001
Authorized				
Unlimited common shares				
Issued				
19,490,144 common shares [2001 - 19,631,081]	$	9,535	$	9,325

During the year ended December 31, 2002, 22,563 convertible, non-voting series 1994 shares [2001 - 7,139] were converted into common shares with a stated value of approximately $287,000 [2001 - $91,000].

During the year ended December 31, 2002, the Company repurchased 163,500 [2001 - 604,600] of its common shares on the open market pursuant to the terms and conditions of Normal Course Issuer Bids at a net cost of approximately $4,902,000 [2001 - $12,652,000]. All shares repurchased by the Company pursuant to its Normal Course Issuer Bids have been cancelled. The repurchase of common shares resulted in a reduction of share capital in the amount of approximately $77,000 [2001 - $285,000]. The excess net cost over the average book value of the shares of approximately $4,825,000 [2001 - $12,367,000] has been shown as a reduction in retained earnings.

Leon's

WestJet

COAST TO COAST   NEW AIRCRAFT   BETTER AND BIGGER   PLANE TALK   BEST FIGURES OF 2002

Annual Report
The Magazine

The
BEST
of 2002
The Year in Review

FREE
737-700 SERIES
2002 ANNUAL REPORT
WESTJETøS SUCCESS (itøthe people!)

AUDITORS' REPORT TO THE SHAREHOLDERS

We have audited the consolidated balance sheets of WestJet Airlines Ltd. as at December 31, 2002 and 2001 and the consolidated statements of earnings and retained earnings and cash flows for the years then ended. These financial statements are the responsibility of the Corporation's management. Our responsibility is to express an opinion on these financial statements based on our audits.

We conducted our audits in accordance with Canadian generally accepted auditing standards. Those standards require that we plan and perform an audit to obtain reasonable assurance whether the financial statements are free of material misstatement. An audit includes examining, on a test basis, evidence supporting the amounts and disclosures in the financial statements. An audit also includes assessing the accounting principles used and significant estimates made by management, as well as evaluating the overall financial statement presentation.

In our opinion, these consolidated financial statements present fairly, in all material respects, the financial position of the Corporation as at December 31, 2002 and 2001 and the results of its operations and its cash flows for the years then ended in accordance with Canadian generally accepted accounting principles.

[SIGNED] KPMG LLP

Chartered Accountants

Calgary, Canada
February 11, 2003

WESTJET AIRLINES LTD.

Consolidated Balance Sheets

December 31, 2002 and 2001
(Stated in Thousands of Dollars)

	2002	2001
Assets		
Current assets:		
Cash and cash equivalents	$ 100,410	58,942
Accounts receivable	20,532	12,211
Income taxes recoverable	-	779
Prepaid expenses and deposits	19,759	11,643
Inventory	2,314	2,155
	143,015	85,730
Capital assets (note 2)	605,124	300,685
Other long-term assets (note 3)	36,066	6,998
	$ 784,205	$ 393,413
Liabilities and Shareholders' Equity		
Current liabilities:		
Accounts payable and accrued liabilities	$ 67,008	$ 42,019
Income taxes payable	7,982	-
Advance ticket sales	44,195	28,609
Non-refundable guest credits	15,915	12,599
Current portion of long-term debt (note 4)	32,674	8,470
Current portion of obligations under capital lease (note 5)	7,290	3,398
	175,064	95,095
Long-term debt (note 4)	198,996	41,305
Obligations under capital lease (note 5)	16,352	14,400
Future income tax (note 7)	38,037	20,933
	428,449	171,733
Shareholders' equity:		
Share capital (note 6)	211,564	129,268
Retained earnings	144,192	92,412
	355,756	221,680
Commitments and contingencies (notes 5 and 8)		
	$ 784,205	$ 393,413

See accompanying notes to consolidated financial statements.

On behalf of the Board:

[SIGNED] Clive Beddoe, Director
[SIGNED] Wilmot Matthews, Director

WestJet Airlines Ltd.

Consolidated Statements of Earnings and Retained Earnings

Years ended December 31, 2002 and 2001
(Stated in Thousands of Dollars, Except Per Share Data)

	2002	2001
Revenues:		
Guest revenues	$ 643,174	$ 452,910
Charter and other	36,822	25,483
	679,996	478,393
Expenses:		
Aircraft fuel	111,737	84,629
Airport operations	88,586	63,881
Maintenance	81,973	72,317
Flight operations and navigational charges	75,759	52,648
Amortization	52,637	34,332
Sales and marketing	44,707	30,862
General and administration	39,791	20,893
Aircraft leasing	35,822	15,284
Inflight	27,284	16,104
Reservations	20,106	17,777
Employee profit share (note 8(b))	15,233	10,311
	593,635	419,038
Earnings from operations	86,361	59,355
Non-operating income (expense):		
Interest income	3,078	2,837
Interest expense	(7,038)	(5,086)
Gain on foreign exchange	346	496
Gain on disposal of capital assets	97	187
	(3,517)	(1,566)
Earnings before income taxes	82,844	57,789
Income taxes (note 7):		
Current	12,626	15,974
Future	18,438	5,105
	31,064	21,079
Net earnings	51,780	36,710
Retained earnings, beginning of year	92,412	55,702
Retained earnings, end of year	$ 144,192	$ 92,412
Earnings per share:		
Basic	$ 0.70	$ 0.53
Diluted	$ 0.69	$ 0.52

See accompanying notes to consolidated financial statements.

WestJet Airlines Ltd.
Consolidated Statements of Cash Flows

Years ended December 31, 2002 and 2001
(Stated in Thousands of Dollars)

	2002	2001
Cash provided by (used in):		
Operations:		
Net earnings	$ 51,780	$ 36,710
Items not involving cash:		
Amortization	52,637	34,332
Gain on disposal of capital assets	(97)	(187)
Future income tax	18,438	5,105
	122,758	75,960
(Increase) decrease in non-cash working capital	38,866	(8,599)
	161,624	67,361
Financing:		
Increase in long-term debt	190,366	8,947
Repayment of long-term debt	(8,471)	(9,461)
Issuance of common shares	84,634	3,878
Share issuance costs	(3,672)	-
Increase in other long-term assets	(32,257)	(2,230)
Decrease in obligations under capital lease	(6,088)	(2,483)
	224,512	(1,349)
Investments:		
Aircraft additions	(320,871)	(60,518)
Other capital asset additions	(24,031)	(26,271)
Other capital asset disposals	234	694
	(344,668)	(86,095)
Increase (decrease) in cash	41,468	(20,083)
Cash, beginning of year	58,942	79,025
Cash, end of year	$ 100,410	$ 58,942

Cash is defined as cash and cash equivalents.

See accompanying notes to consolidated financial statements.

WestJet Airlines Ltd.
Notes to Consolidated Financial Statements

Years ended December 31, 2002 and 2001
(Tabular Amounts are Stated in Thousands of Dollars, Except Per Share Data)

1. **Significant accounting policies:**

   (a) Basis of presentation:

   These consolidated financial statements include the accounts of the Corporation and its wholly owned subsidiaries, as well as the accounts of HFLP Finance Limited ("HFLP"). The Corporation has no equity ownership in HFLP, however, the Corporation is the primary beneficiary of HFLP's operations (see note 4). All intercompany balances and transactions have been eliminated.

   The preparation of financial statements in conformity with accounting principles generally accepted in Canada requires management to make estimates and assumptions that affect the amounts reported in the financial statements and accompanying notes. Actual results could differ from these estimates.

   (b) Cash and cash equivalents:

   Cash and cash equivalents are comprised of cash and all investments that are highly liquid in nature and generally have a maturity date of three months or less.

   (c) Revenue recognition:

   Guest revenue is recognized when air transportation is provided. Tickets sold but not yet used are included in the balance sheet as advance ticket sales under current liabilities.

   (d) Non-refundable guest credits:

   The Corporation, under certain circumstances, may issue future travel credits which are non-refundable and which expire one year from the date of issue. The utilization of guest credits is recorded as revenue when the guest has flown or upon expiry.

   (e) Foreign currency:

   Monetary assets and liabilities, denominated in foreign currencies, are translated into Canadian dollars at rates of exchange in effect at the balance sheet date. Other assets and revenue and expense items are translated at rates prevailing when they were acquired or incurred. Foreign exchange gains and losses are included in income.

   Effective January 1, 2002, the Corporation has adopted the new standard for exchange gains and losses arising on the translation of long-term monetary items that are denominated in foreign currencies as set forth by the Canadian Institute of Chartered Accountants. Under the new standard these gains and losses are recognized on the income statement as they are incurred. The change in accounting policy was applied retroactively with restatement of prior periods. The application of this standard reduced opening retained earnings at January 1, 2002 by $490,000 and reduced basic and diluted earnings per share ("EPS") by $0.01 for the year ended December 31, 2001.

WestJet Airlines Ltd.

Notes to Consolidated Financial Statements, Page 2

Years ended December 31, 2002 and 2001
(Tabular Amounts are Stated in Thousands of Dollars, Except Per Share Data)

1. Significant accounting policies (continued):

(f) Inventory:

Materials and supplies are valued at the lower of cost and replacement value. Aircraft expendables and consumables are expensed as incurred.

(g) Deferred costs:

Sales and marketing and reservation expenses attributed to advance ticket sales are deferred and expensed in the period the related revenue is recognized. Included in prepaid expenses are $4,161,000 (2001 - $3,643,000) of deferred costs.

(h) Capital assets:

Capital assets are recorded at cost and depreciated to their estimated residual values. Assets under capital leases and leasehold improvements are amortized on a straight-line basis over the term of the lease.

Asset	Basis	Rate
Aircraft net of estimated residual value – 700 series	Cycles	Cycles flown
Aircraft net of estimated residual value – 200 series	Flight hours	Hours flown
Ground property and equipment	Straight-line	5 to 25 years
Spare engines and parts net of estimated residual value – 200 series	Flight hours	Hours flown
Buildings	Straight-line	40 years
Parts – 700 series	Straight-line	20 years

(i) Maintenance costs:

Costs related to the acquisition of an aircraft and preparation for service are capitalized and included in aircraft costs. Heavy maintenance ("D" check) costs incurred on aircraft are capitalized and amortized over the remaining useful service life of the "D" check.

All other maintenance costs are expensed as incurred.

(j) Capitalized costs:

Costs associated with assets under construction are capitalized from inception through to commencement of commercial operations. Interest attributable to funds used to finance the construction of major ground facilities is capitalized to the related asset. Legal and financing costs for the loan facilities are capitalized and amortized over the term of the related loan.

WESTJET AIRLINES LTD.
Notes to Consolidated Financial Statements, Page 3

Years ended December 31, 2002 and 2001
(Tabular Amounts are Stated in Thousands of Dollars, Except Per Share Data)

---

1. **Significant accounting policies (continued):**

   (k) Future income tax:

   The Corporation uses the liability method of accounting for future income taxes. Under this method, current income taxes are recognized for the estimated income taxes payable for the current year. Future income tax assets and liabilities are recognized for temporary differences between the tax and accounting bases of assets and liabilities.

   (l) Stock-based compensation plans:

   Currently all outstanding stock options of the Corporation have been granted to employees of the Corporation and no compensation cost has been recorded for these awards. Consideration paid by employees on the exercise of stock options is recorded as share capital. The Corporation has disclosed the pro forma effect of accounting for these rewards under the fair value based method (see note 6(f)).

   (m) Financial instruments:

   The Corporation utilizes derivatives and other financial instruments to manage its exposure to changes in foreign currency exchange rates, interest rates and jet fuel price volatility. Gains or losses relating to derivatives that are hedges are deferred and recognized in the same period and in the same financial category as the corresponding hedged transactions.

   (n) Per share amounts:

   Basic per share amounts are calculated using the weighted average number of shares outstanding during the year. Diluted per share amounts are calculated based on the treasury stock method, which assumes that any proceeds obtained on exercise of options would be used to purchase common shares at the average price during the period. The weighted average number of shares outstanding is then adjusted by the net change. In computing diluted net earnings per share, 1,339,511 (2001 - 1,319,183) shares were added to the weighted average number of common shares outstanding of 73,942,259 (2001 – 68,889,768) for the year ended December 31, 2002 in determining the dilutive effect of employee stock options.

   (o) Comparative figures:

   Certain prior period balances have been reclassified to conform with current period's presentation and to comply with a change in accounting policy (see note 1(e)).

WESTJET AIRLINES LTD.
Notes to Consolidated Financial Statements, Page 4

Years ended December 31, 2002 and 2001
(Tabular Amounts are Stated in Thousands of Dollars, Except Per Share Data)

2. Capital assets:

2002	Cost		Accumulated depreciation		Net book value	
Aircraft – 700 series	$	212,353	$	786	$	211,567
Aircraft – 200 series		185,765		72,853		112,912
Ground property and equipment		68,791		13,253		55,538
Aircraft under capital lease		30,966		10,035		20,931
Spare engines and parts – 200 series		28,915		8,850		20,065
Buildings		24,576		1,025		23,551
Parts – 700 series		19,593		1,071		18,522
Leasehold improvements		4,514		1,650		2,864
		575,473		109,523		465,950
Deposits on aircraft		131,464		-		131,464
Assets under construction		7,710		-		7,710
	$	714,647	$	109,523	$	605,124

2001	Cost		Accumulated depreciation		Net book value	
Aircraft – 200 series	$	188,000	$	49,912	$	138,088
Ground property and equipment		39,476		7,510		31,966
Spare engines and parts – 200 series		30,166		5,257		24,909
Buildings		23,051		446		22,605
Aircraft under capital lease		18,617		2,980		15,637
Parts – 700 series		12,462		294		12,168
Leasehold improvements		3,539		1,421		2,118
		315,311		67,820		247,491
Deposits on aircraft		53,194		-		53,194
	$	368,505	$	67,820	$	300,685

During the year capital assets were acquired at an aggregate cost of $12,188,000 (2001 - $9,415,000) by means of capital leases and interest costs of nil (2001 - $467,000) were capitalized to assets under construction.

3. Other long-term assets:

Included in other long-term assets is $19,034,000 (2001 - $1,087,000) of unamortized hedge settlements related to the ten leased Boeing Next-Generation aircraft, financing fees of $8,802,000 (2001 – nil), net of accumulated amortization of $123,000 (2001 – nil), related to the facility for the purchase of fifteen Boeing Next-Generation aircraft, security deposits on aircraft and other leaseholds of $7,701,000 (2001 - $4,748,000) and other amounts totaling $529,000 (2001 – $1,163,000).

WestJet Airlines Ltd.

Notes to Consolidated Financial Statements, Page 5

Years ended December 31, 2002 and 2001
(Tabular Amounts are Stated in Thousands of Dollars, Except Per Share Data)

4. Long-term debt:

	2002	2001
$178,777,000 in four individual term loans, amortized on a straight-line basis over a 12 year term, repayable in quarterly principle installments ranging from $913,000 to $955,000, including weighted average interest at 5.28%, guaranteed by the Ex-Im Bank and secured by four aircraft. The first quarterly payments commence February 2003	$ 178,777	$ -
$16,000,000 term loan, repayable in monthly installments of $145,000 including interest at 7.125% (interest rate will be renewed in July 2003 at a fixed rate for up to 5 years), maturing August 2016, secured by the Next-Generation flight simulator and six cross-collateralized aircraft	15,058	15,700
$36,073,000 in eight individual term loans, repayable in monthly installments ranging from $25,000 to $153,000 including weighted average interest at 8.36% with varying maturities ranging between April 2003 through October 2005, secured by seven aircraft	14,626	22,217
$12,000,000 term loan, repayable in monthly installments of $108,000 including interest at 9.03%, maturing April 2011, secured by the hangar facility	11,620	11,858
$11,589,000 term loan, repayable in monthly installments of $1,311,000, including interest of 4.40%, maturing on September 2003	11,589	-
	231,670	49,775
Less current portion	32,674	8,470
	$ 198,996	$ 41,305

The net book value of the assets pledged as collateral for the Corporation's secured borrowings was $292,352,000 as at December 31, 2002 (2001 - $94,485,000).

WestJet Airlines Ltd.

Notes to Consolidated Financial Statements, Page 6

Years ended December 31, 2002 and 2001
(Tabular Amounts are Stated in Thousands of Dollars, Except Per Share Data)

---

4. Long-term debt (continued):

Future scheduled repayments of long-term debt are as follows:

2003	$ 32,674
2004	20,009
2005	21,305
2006	16,092
2007	16,187
2008 and thereafter	125,403
	$ 231,670

The Corporation has a U.S. $478 million facility with the ING Group which is supported by loan guarantees from the Export-Import Bank of the United States (Ex-Im) for U.S. $478 million for the purchase of fifteen Boeing Next-Generation 737-700 series aircraft. Of these aircraft four were delivered in 2002, with the remaining eleven to be delivered over the course of 2003. HFLP is used as the financial intermediary to facilitate the financing agreement to purchase the aircraft.

This facility will be drawn in Canadian dollars in separate installments with 12 year terms for each new aircraft. Each loan will be amortized on a straight-line basis over the 12 year term in quarterly principal installments, with interest calculated on the outstanding principal balance.

The Corporation is charged a commitment fee of 0.125% per annum on the unutilized and uncancelled balance of the loan guarantee, payable at specified dates and upon delivery of an aircraft. As at December 31, 2002 the unutilized balance was U.S. $364 million.

The Corporation has entered into Forward Starting Interest Rate Agreements at rates between 5.36% and 5.85% on the remaining eleven aircraft to be delivered under this facility.

The Corporation has available a facility with a Canadian chartered bank of $6,000,000 for letters of guarantee. At December 31, 2002, letters of guarantee totaling $4,410,000 have been issued under these facilities. The credit facilities are secured by a fixed first charge on one aircraft, a general security agreement and an assignment of insurance proceeds.

Cash interest paid during the year was $5,836,000 (2001 - $5,570,000).

WestJet Airlines Ltd.

Notes to Consolidated Financial Statements, Page 7

Years ended December 31, 2002 and 2001
(Tabular Amounts are Stated in Thousands of Dollars, Except Per Share Data)

5. Leases:

The Corporation has entered into operating leases for aircraft, buildings, computer hardware and software licenses and capital leases relating to computer hardware and aircraft. The obligations, on a calendar-year basis, are as follows (see note 8 for additional lease commitments):

	Capital Leases	Operating Leases
2003	$ 8,880	$ 52,715
2004	8,753	51,071
2005	6,256	49,857
2006	2,913	47,341
2007	-	47,206
2008 and thereafter	-	384,276
Total lease payments	26,802	$ 632,466
Less imputed interest at 7.79%	(3,160)	
Net minimum lease payments	23,642	
Less current portion of obligations under capital lease	(7,290)	
Obligations under capital lease	$ 16,352	

6. Share capital:

The non-voting common shares and the non-voting preferred shares are subject to limitations to be fixed by the directors of the Corporation.

(a) Authorized:

Unlimited number of voting common shares

700,000 non-voting performance shares

Unlimited number of non-voting shares

Unlimited number of non-voting first, second and third preferred shares

WESTJET AIRLINES LTD.
Notes to Consolidated Financial Statements, Page 8

Years ended December 31, 2002 and 2001
(Tabular Amounts are Stated in Thousands of Dollars, Except Per Share Data)

6. **Share capital (continued):**

(b) Issued:

	2002		2001	
	Number	Amount	Number	Amount
Common shares:				
Balance, beginning of year	69,516,897	$ 129,268	67,497,875	$ 125,390
Common share issue	4,500,000	82,500	-	-
Exercise of options	879,019	2,134	2,019,022	3,878
Issued on rounding of stock split	3,693	-	-	-
Share issuance costs	-	(3,672)	-	-
Tax benefit of issue costs	-	1,334	-	-
Balance, end of year	74,899,609	$ 211,564	69,516,897	$ 129,268

(c) Stock split:

On May 3, 2002, the common shares of the Corporation were split on a three for two basis. All number of shares and per share amounts have been restated to reflect the stock split.

(d) Stock Option Plan:

The Corporation has a Stock Option Plan, whereby up to a maximum of 7,476,330 common shares may be issued to officers and employees of the Corporation subject to the following limitations:

(i) the number of common shares reserved for issuance to any one optionee will not exceed 5% of the issued and outstanding common shares at any time;

(ii) the number of common shares reserved for issuance to insiders shall not exceed 10% of the issued and outstanding common shares; and

(iii) the number of common shares issuable under the Plan, which may be issued within a one year period, shall not exceed 10% of the issued and outstanding common shares at any time.

Stock options are granted at a price that equals the market value, have a term of four years and vest over a period of two to three years.

WestJet Airlines Ltd.

Notes to Consolidated Financial Statements, Page 9

Years ended December 31, 2002 and 2001
(Tabular Amounts are Stated in Thousands of Dollars, Except Per Share Data)

---

6. **Share capital (continued):**

(d) Stock Option Plan (continued):

Changes in the number of options, with their weighted average exercise prices, are summarized below:

	2002		2001	
	Number of options	Weighted average exercise price	Number of options	Weighted average exercise price
Stock options outstanding, beginning of year	5,579,517	$ 11.85	5,037,182	$ 6.43
Granted	1,140,292	20.70	2,681,601	14.64
Exercised	(879,019)	2.43	(2,019,022)	1.92
Cancelled	(31,602)	15.67	(120,244)	13.73
Stock options outstanding, end of year	5,809,188	$ 14.99	5,579,517	$ 11.85
Exercisable, end of year	276,159	$ 3.48	829,329	$ 2.41

The following table summarizes the options outstanding and exercisable at December 31, 2002:

	Outstanding			Exercisable Options	
Range of Exercise Prices	Number Outstanding	Weighted Average Remaining Life (years)	Weighted Average Exercise Price	Number Exercisable	Weighted Average Exercise Price
$2.67 - $4.45	276,159	0.33	$ 3.48	276,159	$ 3.48
$10.99 - $12.67	44,381	2.41	12.15	-	-
$13.65 - $14.68	4,355,706	2.02	14.26	-	-
$15.81 - $20.75	1,132,942	3.31	20.70	-	-
	5,809,188	2.19	$ 14.99	276,159	$ 3.48

Upon filing the Corporation's initial public offering on July 13, 1999, 237,533 options were re-priced from $2.67 per share to $4.45 per share and of this amount 125,033 (2001 – 192,533) were remaining at December 31, 2002. The Corporation committed to the holders of the options that it would pay the differential of $1.78 per share upon exercise of those options.

WestJet Airlines Ltd.

Notes to Consolidated Financial Statements, Page 10

Years ended December 31, 2002 and 2001
(Tabular Amounts are Stated in Thousands of Dollars, Except Per Share Data)

6. Share capital (continued):

(e) Employee Share Purchase Plan:

Under the terms of the Employee Share Purchase Plan, employees may contribute up to a maximum of 20% of their gross pay and acquire common shares of the Corporation at the current fair market value of such shares. The Corporation matches the employee contributions and shares may be withdrawn from the Plan after being held in trust for one year. Employees may offer to sell common shares, which have not been held for at least one year, on January 1 and July 1 of each year, to the Corporation for 50% of the then current market price. The Corporation's share of the contributions is recorded as compensation expense and amounted to $10,178,000 (2001 - $6,081,000).

(f) Pro forma disclosure:

The fair value of each option grant is estimated on the date of grant using the Black-Scholes option pricing model with the following weighted average assumptions used for grants in 2002: zero dividend yield; expected volatility of 38%; risk-free rate of 4.5%; and expected life of four years. The weighted average fair value of stock options granted during the year was $8.06 per option.

Had the Corporation accounted for employee stock options issued using the fair value based method, the Corporation's pro forma net earnings and EPS would be as follows:

	As reported 2002	Pro forma 2002
Net earnings	$ 51,780	$ 48,963
Earnings per share:		
Basic	$ 0.70	$ 0.66
Diluted	0.69	0.65

These pro forma earnings reflect compensation cost amortized over the options' vesting period, which varies from two to three years.

WESTJET AIRLINES LTD.

Notes to Consolidated Financial Statements, Page 11

Years ended December 31, 2002 and 2001
(Tabular Amounts are Stated in Thousands of Dollars, Except Per Share Data)

7. **Income taxes:**

Income taxes vary upon the amount that would be computed by applying the basic Federal and Provincial tax rate of 38.1% (2001 – 43.7%) to earnings before income taxes as follows:

	2002	2001
Expected income tax provision	$ 31,544	$ 25,445
Add (deduct):		
Non-deductible expenses	518	459
Other	(358)	(729)
Capital taxes	31	251
Large corporations tax	177	-
Future tax rate reductions	(848)	(4,347)
	$ 31,064	$ 21,079

Cash taxes paid during the year were $3,878,000 (2001 – $25,700,000).

The components of the net future income tax liability are as follows:

	2002	2001
Future income tax asset:		
Share issue costs	$ 1,767	$ 1,127
Future income tax liability:		
Capital assets	39,804	22,060
Net future income tax liability	$ 38,037	$ 20,933

8. **Commitments and contingencies:**

(a) Aircraft:

The Corporation has entered into agreements to lease ten Boeing Next-Generation aircraft, four of which were delivered over the course of 2001, with the remaining six delivered in 2002. Under the terms of these lease agreements, the Corporation received a 737-700 engine for use throughout the period of the leases. Subject to the Corporation's compliance with the terms of the lease agreements, title to the engine will pass to the Corporation at the end of the final lease. The Corporation has also obtained options to lease an additional ten Boeing Next-Generation aircraft to be delivered prior to the end of 2006.

WESTJET AIRLINES LTD.

Notes to Consolidated Financial Statements, Page 12

Years ended December 31, 2002 and 2001
(Tabular Amounts are Stated in Thousands of Dollars, Except Per Share Data)

8. **Commitments and contingencies (continued):**

(a) Aircraft (continued):

The Corporation has also entered into agreements to purchase thirty Boeing Next-Generation aircraft, four of which were delivered over the course of 2002, with the remaining twenty-six to be delivered over the course of 2003 to 2006. This agreement provides the Corporation with the option to purchase an additional forty-four aircraft for delivery prior to the end of 2008.

The remaining estimated amounts to be paid in deposits and purchase prices in U.S. dollars relating to the purchases of the remaining twenty-six aircraft are as follows:

2003	$ 352,244
2004	276,062
2005	151,261
2006	30,603
	$ 810,170

In addition to the existing U.S. $478 million loan guarantee from the Ex-Im Bank (see note 4), the Corporation has received a Preliminary Commitment from the Ex-Im Bank for loan guarantees to support the acquisition of the remaining fifteen Boeing Next-Generation aircraft the Corporation has committed to purchase prior to February 2006.

(b) Employee profit share:

The Corporation has an employee profit sharing plan whereby eligible employees will participate in the pre-tax operating income of the Corporation. The profit share ranges from a minimum of 10% to a maximum of 20% of earnings before employee profit share and income taxes. The amounts paid under the plan are subject to prior approval by the Board of Directors.

(c) Contingencies:

The Corporation is party to legal proceedings and claims that arise during the ordinary course of business. It is the opinion of management that the ultimate outcome of these matters will not have a material effect upon the Corporation's financial position, results of operations or cash flows.

WestJet Airlines Ltd.
Notes to Consolidated Financial Statements, Page 13

Years ended December 31, 2002 and 2001
(Tabular Amounts are Stated in Thousands of Dollars, Except Per Share Data)

---

9. **Risk management:**

(a) Fuel risk management:

The Corporation has mitigated its exposure to jet fuel price volatility through the use of long-term fixed price contracts and contracts with a fixed ceiling price which it has entered into with a fuel supplier. Any premiums paid to enter into these long-term fuel arrangements are recorded as other long-term assets and amortized to fuel expense over the term of the contracts. As at December 31, 2002, the Corporation had a fixed ceiling price fuel contract that is in effect through to June 2003, at an indicative price of U.S. $18.60 per barrel of crude oil. In 2002, this contract represented 32% (2001 – 42%) of the Corporation's fuel requirements.

(b) Foreign currency exchange risk:

The Corporation is exposed to foreign currency fluctuations as certain ongoing expenses are referenced to U.S. dollar denominated prices. The Corporation periodically uses financial instruments, including forward exchange contracts and options, to manage its exposure. At December 31, 2002 the Corporation did not have any foreign currency financial instruments outstanding.

(c) Interest rate risk:

The Corporation has managed its exposure to interest rate fluctuations on debt financing for the next eleven Boeing Next-Generation aircraft scheduled to be delivered over the course of 2003. The Corporation has managed this exposure by entering into Forward Starting Interest Rate Agreements at rates between 5.36% and 5.85%.

The Corporation has entered into fixed rate debt instruments in order to manage its interest rate exposure on existing debt agreements. These agreements are described in note 4.

(d) Credit risk:

The Corporation does not believe it is subject to any significant concentration of credit risk. Most of the Corporation's receivables result from tickets sold to individual guests through the use of major credit cards and travel agents. These receivables are short-term, generally being settled shortly after the sale. The Corporation manages the credit exposure related to financial instruments by selecting counter parties based on credit ratings, limiting its exposure to any single counter party and monitoring the market position of the program and its relative market position with each counter party.

(e) Fair value of financial instruments:

The carrying amounts of financial instruments included in the balance sheet, other than long-term debt, approximate their fair value due to their short term to maturity.

At December 31, 2002, the fair value of long-term debt was approximately $236 million. The fair value of long-term debt is determined by discounting the future contractual cash flows under current financing arrangements at discount rates which represent borrowing rates presently available to the Corporation for loans with similar terms and maturity.

Chart of Accounts

Assets

Current Assets

101 Cash
102 Petty Cash
103 Cash equivalents
104 Temporary investments
105 Allowance to reduce temporary investments to market
106 Accounts receivable
107 Allowance for doubtful accounts
108 GST receivable
109 Interest receivable
110 Rent receivable
111 Notes receivable
119 Merchandise inventory
120 _____ inventory
124 Office supplies
125 Store supplies
126 _____ supplies
128 Prepaid insurance
129 Prepaid _____
131 Prepaid rent
132 Raw materials inventory
133 Goods in process inventory, _____
135 Finished goods inventory

Long-Term Investments

141 Investment in _____ shares
142 Investment in _____ bonds
144 Investment in _____

Property, Plant, and Equipment

151 Automobiles
152 Accumulated amortization, automobiles
153 Trucks
154 Accumulated amortization, trucks
155 Boats
156 Accumulated amortization, boats
157 Professional library
158 Accumulated amortization, professional library
159 Law library

160 Accumulated amortization, law library
161 Furniture
162 Accumulated amortization, Furniture
163 Office equipment
164 Accumulated amortization, office equipment
165 Store equipment
166 Accumulated amortization, store equipment
167 _____ equipment
168 Accumulated amortization, _____ equipment
169 Machinery
170 Accumulated amortization, machinery
173 Building _____
174 Accumulated amortization, building _____
175 Land
176 Leasehold improvements
179 Land improvements, _____
180 Accumulated amortization, land improvements _____

Natural Resources

185 Mineral deposit
186 Accumulated amortization, mineral deposit

Intangible Assets

191 Patents
192 Leasehold
193 Franchise
194 Copyright
196 Organization costs
198 Goodwill

Liabilities

Current Liabilities

201 Accounts payable
202 Insurance payable
203 Interest payable
204 Legal fees payable
205 Short-term notes payable
206 Discount on short-term notes payable

208 Rent payable
209 Salaries payable
210 Wages payable
214 Estimated warranty liability
215 Income taxes payable
216 Common dividends payable
217 Preferred dividends payable
218 EI payable
219 CPP payable
221 Employees' medical insurance payable
222 Employees' retirement program payable
223 Employees' union dues payable
224 PST payable
225 GST payable
226 Estimated vacation pay liability

Unearned Revenues

230 Unearned consulting fees
231 Unearned legal fees
232 Unearned property management fees
233 Unearned _____

Long-Term Liabilities

251 Long-term notes payable
252 Discount on notes payable
253 Long-term lease liability
255 Bonds payable
256 Discount on bonds payable
257 Premium on bonds payable

Equity

Owners' Equity

301 _____ , capital
302 _____ , withdrawals
303 _____ , capital
304 _____ , withdrawals

Corporate Contributed Capital

307 Common shares

310 Common share dividends distributable
313 Contributed capital from the retirement of common shares
315 Preferred shares

Retained Earnings

318 Retained earnings
319 Cash dividends
320 Share dividends

Revenues

401 _____ fees earned
403 _____ services revenue
405 Commission earned
406 Rent earned
407 Dividends earned
408 Earnings from investment in _____
409 Interest earned
413 Sales
414 Sales returns and allowances
415 Sales discounts

Cost of Sales

502 Cost of goods sold
503 Amortization of mine deposit
505 Purchases
506 Purchases returns and allowances
507 Purchases discounts
508 Transportation-in

Manufacturing Accounts

520 Raw materials purchases
521 Freight-in on raw materials
530 Factory payroll
531 Direct labour
540 Factory overhead
541 Indirect materials
542 Indirect labour
543 Factory insurance expired
544 Factory supervision
545 Factory supplies used
546 Factory utilities
547 Miscellaneous production costs
548 Property taxes on factory building
550 Rent on factory building
551 Repairs, factory equipment
552 Small tools written off
560 Amortization of factory equipment
561 Amortization of factory building

Standard Cost Variance Accounts

580 Direct material quantity variance
581 Direct material price variance
582 Direct labour quantity variance
583 Direct labour price variance
584 Factory overhead volume variance
585 Factory overhead controllable variance

Expenses

Amortization

602 Amortization expense, copyrights
603 Amortization expense, _____
604 Amortization expense, boats
605 Amortization expense, automobiles
606 Amortization expense, building _____
608 Amortization expense, land improvements _____
610 Amortization expense, law library
611 Amortization expense, trucks
612 Amortization expense, _____ equipment
614 Amortization expense, _____

Employee Related Expense

620 Office salaries expense
621 Sales salaries expense
622 Salaries expense
623 _____ wages expense
624 Employees' benefits expense

Financial Expenses

630 Cash over and short
633 Interest expense

Insurance Expenses

635 Insurance expense, delivery equipment
636 Insurance expense, building
637 Insurance expense, _____

Rental Expenses

640 Rent expense
641 Rent expense, office space
642 Rent expense, selling space
645 _____ rental expense

Supplies Expense

650 Office supplies expense
651 Store supplies expense
652 _____ supplies expense

Other Expenses

655 Advertising expense
656 Bad debts expense
659 Collection expense
662 Credit card expense
663 Delivery expense
667 Equipment expense
668 Food and drinks expense
671 Gas and oil expense
673 Janitorial expense
674 Legal fees expense
676 Mileage expense
681 Permits expense
682 Postage expense
683 Property taxes expense
684 Repairs expense, _____
688 Telephone expense
689 Travel and entertaining expense
690 Utilities expense
691 Warranty expense
695 Income taxes expense
696 _____ expense

Gains and Losses

701 Gain on retirement of bonds
702 Gain on sale of machinery
703 Gain on sale of investments
705 Gain on _____
804 Loss on market decline of temporary investments
805 Loss on retirement of bonds
806 Loss on sale of investments
807 Loss on sale of machinery
809 Loss on _____

Clearing Accounts

901 Income summary
902 Manufacturing summary

III

Codes of Ethics and Professional Conduct

Selection from the Certified General Accountants of Alberta's Code of Ethical Principles and Rules of Conduct[1]

Code of Ethical Principles

(a) Responsibilities to Society

Members have a fundamental responsibility to safeguard and advance the interests of society. This implies acting with trustworthiness, integrity and objectivity. This responsibility extends beyond a member's own behaviour to the behaviour of colleagues and to the standards of the Association and the profession.

(b) Trust and Duties

Members shall act in the interest of their clients, employers, and interested third parties, and shall be prepared to sacrifice their self-interest to do so. Members shall honour the trust bestowed on them by others, and shall not use their privileged position without their principal's knowledge and consent. Members shall avoid conflicts of interest.

(c) Due Care and Professional Judgement

Members shall strive to continually upgrade and develop their technical knowledge and skills in the areas in which they practice as professionals. This technical expertise shall be employed with due professional care and judgement.

(d) Deceptive Information

Members shall not be associated with any information which the member knows, or ought to know, to be false or misleading, whether by statement or omission.

---

[1] The Certified General Accountants of Alberta, *Code of Ethical Principles and Rules of Conduct.* The complete code can be found at: www.cga-alberta.org.

(e) Professional Practice

Members shall act openly and fairly towards others in the practice of their profession.

(f) Responsibilities to the Profession

Members shall always act in accordance with the duties and responsibilities associated with being members of the profession, and shall carry on work in a manner which will enhance the image of the profession and the Association.

Selection From the Code of Ethics for Certified Management Accountants[2]

A profession is distinguished by certain characteristics including:

- (a) mastery of a particular intellectual skill, acquired by training and education;
- (b) acceptance of duties to society as a whole in addition to duties to the Employer or Client;
- (c) an outlook which is essentially objective; and
- (d) a high standard in the conduct and performance of personal service.

People who use professional services usually find it difficult to assess the specialized knowledge and skills of professionals. That is why professional organizations lay down technical and ethical standards for their members. By enforcing these standards, professional organizations protect the public interest, and users can confidently rely on professionals.

Two important principles underlie this Code, as well as the rules and guidelines, and form a common thread throughout its provisions.

First, a Member must establish and maintain a reputation for integrity, the most basic attribute of a member of the accounting profession. Integrity includes trustworthiness, loyalty, fairness, honour and honesty.

Second, a Member must reject inappropriate conduct, both on a professional and personal level. A Member also has a duty to refrain from behaviour which, while legal, is inconsistent with the high standards of the profession, or calls into question the Member's fitness as a professional. A Member who violates either of these principles will lose the respect and confidence of the public and other accountants.

Through legislation, the accounting profession is self-governing. The privilege of self-governance carries with it special responsibilities. The rationale for the Code of Ethics ("the Code") must be to codify ethics respecting practice as a certified management accountant, to maintain the dignity and honour of the profession, and to protect the public interest. Members must strive for their observance of the Code both individually and collectively. The Code, rules and guidelines are not, however, capable of stating every circumstance a Member may face. Members must therefore consider other ethical and moral considerations, as well as legislation relating to Members and laws of a more general nature, in deciding to pursue a course of action in a given situation.

---

[2] The Society of Management Accountants of Alberta, *Code of Ethics*. The complete code can be found at: www.cga-alberta.org.

All Members should follow both the spirit and the letter of the Code, rules and guidelines.

The willingness and determination of the profession to achieve widespread compliance with the Code, rules and guidelines is a more powerful and basic enforcement mechanism than the imposition of sanctions. A Member must therefore be vigilant respecting his or her own behaviour as well as that of colleagues. However, it is improper to use any provision of the Code, rules and guidelines as an instrument of harassment or as a procedural weapon without a genuine concern respecting the interests of an employer, client, the profession or the public.

Selection from the ICAO Rules of Professional Conduct[3]

To grasp the breadth of the rules of professional conduct, we will review the table of contents for the Institute of Chartered Accountants of Ontario, which includes the following:

FIRST BYLAW OF 1973
FOREWORD
     Application of the rules of professional conduct
     Interpretation of the rules of professional conduct

100 -   GENERAL

     101   Compliance with bylaws, regulations and rules
     102.1   Conviction of criminal or similar offences
     102.2   Reporting disciplinary suspension, expulsion or restriction of right to practise
     103   False or misleading applications
     104   Requirement to reply in writing

200 -   STANDARDS OF CONDUCT AFFECTING THE PUBLIC INTEREST

     201.1,
     .2 & .3   Maintenance of reputation of profession
     201.4   Advocacy services
     202   Integrity and due care
     203.1   Professional competence
     203.2   Co-operation with practice inspections and conduct investigations
     204.1   Objectivity: assurance and specified auditing procedures engagements
     204.2   Objectivity: insolvency engagements
     204.3   Objectivity: disclosure of impairment of objectivity
     205   False or misleading documents and oral representations
     206   Member's compliance with professional standards
     207   Unauthorized benefits

---

[3] ICAO, *Rules of Professional Conduct* (Toronto Institute of Chartered Accountants of Ontario). Other provincial institutes have similar provisions. The complete set of rules can be found at: www.icao.on.ca.

APPENDIX

IV

Present and Future Values

Learning Objectives

LO¹ Describe the earning of interest and the concepts of present and future values.

LO² Apply present value concepts to a single amount by using interest tables.

LO³ Apply future value concepts to a single amount by using interest tables.

LO⁴ Apply present value concepts to an annuity by using interest tables.

LO⁵ Apply future value concepts to an annuity by using interest tables.

Appendix Preview

The concepts of present value are described and applied in Chapter 17. This appendix helps to supplement that discussion with added explanations, illustrations, computations, present value tables, and additional assignments. We also give attention to illustrations, definitions, and computations of future values.

Present and Future Value Concepts

LO¹ Describe the earning of interest and the concepts of present and future values.

There's an old saying, *time is money*. This saying reflects the notion that as time passes, the assets and liabilities we hold are changing. This change is due to interest. *Interest* is the payment to the owner of an asset for its use by a borrower. The most common example of this type of asset is a savings account. As we keep a balance of cash in our accounts, it earns interest that is paid to us by the financial institution. An example of a liability is a car loan. As we carry the balance of the loan, we accumulate interest costs on this debt. We must ultimately repay this loan with interest.

Present and future value computations are a way for us to estimate the interest component of holding assets or liabilities over time. The present value of an amount applies when we either lend or borrow an asset that must be repaid in full at some future date, and we want to know its worth today. The future value of an amount applies when we either lend or borrow an asset that must be repaid in full at some future date, and we want to know its worth at a future date.

The first section focuses on the present value of a single amount. Later sections focus on the future value of a single amount, and then both present and future values of a series of amounts (or annuity).

Present Value of a Single Amount

We graphically express the present value (p) of a single future amount (f) received or paid at a future date in Exhibit IV.1.

Exhibit IV.1

Present Value of
a Single Amount

The formula to compute the present value of this single amount is shown in Exhibit IV.2 where: p = present value; f = future value; i = rate of interest per period; and n = number of periods.

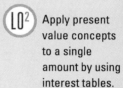

LO² Apply present
value concepts
to a single
amount by using
interest tables.

$$p = \frac{f}{(1 + i)^n}$$

Exhibit IV.2

Present Value of a
Single Amount
Formula

To illustrate the application of this formula, let's assume we need $220 one period from today. We want to know how much must be invested now, for one period, at an interest rate of 10% to provide for this $220.[1] For this illustration the p, or present value, is the unknown amount. In particular, the present and future values, along with the interest rate, are shown graphically as:

$(i = 0.10)$ $f = \$220$

$p = ?$

Conceptually, we know p must be less than $220. This is obvious from the answer to the question: Would we rather have $220 today or $220 at some future date? If we had $220 today, we could invest it and see it grow to something more than $220 in the future. Therefore, if we were promised $220 in the future, we would take less than $220 today. But how much less?

To answer that question we can compute an estimate of the present value of the $220 to be received one period from now using the formula in Exhibit IV.2 as:

$$p = \frac{f}{(1 + i)^n} = \frac{\$220}{(1 + .10)^1} = \$200$$

---

[1] Interest is also called a *discount*, and an interest rate is also called a *discount rate*.

This means we are indifferent between $200 today or $220 at the end of one period.

We can also use this formula to compute the present value for *any number of periods*. To illustrate this computation, we consider a payment of $242 at the end of two periods at 10% interest. The present value of this $242 to be received two periods from now is computed as:

$$p = \frac{f}{(1 + i)^n} = \frac{\$242}{(1 + .10)^2} = \$200$$

These results tells us we are indifferent between $200 today, or $220 one period from today, or $242 two periods from today.

The number of periods (n) in the present value formula does not have to be expressed in years. Any period of time such as a day, a month, a quarter, or a year can be used. But, whatever period is used, the interest rate (i) must be compounded for the same period. This means if a situation expresses n in months, and i equals 12% per year, then we can assume 1% of an amount invested at the beginning of each month is earned in interest per month and added to the investment. In this case, interest is said to be compounded monthly.

A present value table helps us with present value computations. It gives us present values for a variety of interest rates (i) and a variety of periods (n). Each present value in a present value table assumes the future value (f) is 1. When the future value (f) is different than 1, we can simply multiply present value (p) by that future amount to give us our estimate.

The formula used to construct a table of present values of a single future amount of 1 is shown in Exhibit IV.3.

Exhibit IV.3

Present Value
of 1 Formula

$$p = \frac{1}{(1 + i)^n}$$

This formula is identical to that in Exhibit IV.2 except that f equals 1. Table IV.1 at the end of this appendix is a present value table for a single future amount. It is often called a **present value of 1 table**. A present value table involves three factors[2]: p, i, and n. Knowing two of these three factors allows us to compute the third. To illustrate, consider the three possible cases.

Case 1 (solve for p when knowing i and n). Our example above is a case in which we need to solve for p when knowing i and n. To illustrate how we use a present value table, let's again look at how we estimate the present value of $220 ($f$) at the end of one period (n) where the interest rate (i) is 10%. To answer this we go to the present value table (Table IV.1) and look in the row for 1 period and in the column for 10% interest. Here we find a present value (p) of 0.9091 based on a future value of 1. This means, for instance, that $1 to be received 1 period from today at 10% interest is worth $0.9091 today. Since the future value is not $1, but is $220, we multiply the 0.9091 by $220 to get an answer of $200.

Case 2 (solve for n when knowing p and i). This is a case in which we have, say, a $100,000 future value ($f$) valued at $13,000 today ($p$) with an interest rate

---

[2] A fourth is f, but as we already explained, we need only multiple the "1" used in the formula by f.

of 12% (i). In this case we want to know how many periods (n) there are between the present value and the future value. A case example is when we want to retire with $100,000, but have only $13,000 earning a 12% return. How long will it be before we can retire? To answer this we go to Table IV.1 and look in the 12% interest column. Here we find a column of present values (p) based on a future value of 1. To use the present value table for this solution, we must divide $13,000 ($p$) by $100,000 ($f$), which equals 0.1300. This is necessary because a present value table defines f equal to 1, and p as a fraction of 1. We look for a value nearest to 0.1300 (p), which we find in the row for 18 periods (n). This means the present value of $100,000 at the end of 18 periods at 12% interest is $13,000 or, alternatively stated, we must work 18 more years.

Case 3 (solve for i when knowing p and n). This is a case where we have, say, a $120,000 future value ($f$) valued at $60,000 ($p$) today when there are nine periods (n) between the present and future values. Here we want to know what rate of interest is being used. As an example, suppose we want to retire with $120,000, but we only have $60,000 and hope to retire in nine years. What interest rate must we earn to retire with $120,000 in nine years? To answer this we go to the present value table (Table IV.1) and look in the row for nine periods. To again use the present value table we must divide $60,000 ($p$) by $120,000 ($f$), which equals 0.5000. Recall this is necessary because a present value table defines f equal to 1, and p as a fraction of 1. We look for a value in the row for nine periods that is nearest to 0.5000 (p), which we find in the column for 8% interest (i). This means the present value of $120,000 at the end of nine periods at 8% interest is $60,000 or, in our example, we must earn 8% annual interest to retire in nine years.

1. A company is considering an investment expected to yield $70,000 after six years. If this company demands an 8% return, how much is it willing to pay for this investment?

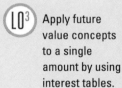

Flashback

Answers—p. IV-9

Future Value of a Single Amount

We use the formula for the present value of a single amount and modify it to obtain the formula for the future value of a single amount. To illustrate, we multiply both sides of the equation in Exhibit IV.2 by $(1 + i)^n$. The result is shown in Exhibit IV.4.

LO^3 Apply future value concepts to a single amount by using interest tables.

$$f = p \times (1 + i)^n$$

Exhibit IV.4

Future Value of a Single Amount Formula

Future value (f) is defined in terms of p, i, and n. We can use this formula to determine that $200 invested for 1 period at an interest rate of 10% increases to a future value of $220 as follows:

$$f = p \times (1 + i)^n$$
$$= \$200 \times (1 + .10)^1$$
$$= \$220$$

This formula can also be used to compute the future value of an amount for *any number of periods* into the future. As an example, assume $200 is invested for three periods at 10%. The future value of this $200 is $266.20 and is computed as:

$$f = p \times (1 + i)^n$$
$$= \$200 \times (1 + .10)^3$$
$$= \$266.20$$

It is also possible to use a future value table to compute future values (f) for many combinations of interest rates (i) and time periods (n). Each future value in a future value table assumes the present value (p) is 1. As with a present value table, if the future amount is something other than 1, we simply multiply our answer by that amount. The formula used to construct a table of future values of a single amount of 1 is shown in Exhibit IV.5.

Exhibit IV.5

Future Value
of 1 Formula

$$f = (1 + i)^n$$

Table IV.2 at the end of this appendix shows a table of future values of a single amount of 1. This type of table is called a **future value of 1 table**.

It is interesting to point out some items in Tables IV.1 and IV.2. Note in Table IV.2, for the row where $n = 0$, that the future value is 1 for every interest rate. This is because no interest is earned when time does not pass. Also notice that Tables IV.1 and IV.2 report the same information in a different manner. In particular, one table is simply the inverse of the other.

To illustrate this inverse relation let's say we invest $100 for a period of five years at 12% per year. How much do we expect to have after five years? We can answer this question using Table IV.2 by finding the future value (f) of 1, for five periods from now, compounded at 12%. From the table we find $f = 1.7623$. If we start with $100, the amount it accumulates to after five years is $176.23 ($100 × 1.7623).

We can alternatively use Table IV.1. Here we find the present value (p) of 1, discounted five periods at 12%, is 0.5674. Recall the inverse relation between present value and future value.[3] This means $p = 1/f$ (or equivalently $f = 1/p$). Knowing this we can compute the future value of $100 invested for five periods at 12% as:

$$f = \$100 \times (1 / 0.5674) = \$176.24$$

A future value table involves three factors: f, i, and n. Knowing two of these three factors allows us to compute the third. To illustrate, consider the three possible cases.

Case 1 (solve for f when knowing i and n). Our example above is a case in which we need to solve for f when knowing i and n. We found that $100 invested for five periods at 12% interest accumulates to $176.24.

Case 2 (solve for n when knowing f and i). This is a case where we have, say, $2,000 ($p$) and we want to know how many periods (n) it will take to accumulate to $3,000 ($f$) at 7% ($i$) interest. To answer this, we go to the future value table

---

[3] Proof of this relation is left for advanced courses.

(Table IV.2) and look in the 7% interest column. Here we find a column of future values (f) based on a present value of 1. To use a future value table, we must divide $3,000 ($f$) by $2,000 ($p$), which equals 1.500. This is necessary because a future value table defines p equal to 1, and f as a multiple of 1. We look for a value nearest to 1.50 (f), which we find in the row for six periods (n). This means $2,000 invested for six periods at 7% interest accumulates to $3,000.

Case 3 (solve for i when knowing f and n). This is a case where we have, say, $2,001 ($p$) and in nine years ($n$) we want to have $4,000 ($f$). What rate of interest must we earn to accomplish this? To answer this, we go to Table IV.2 and search in the row for nine periods. To use a future value table, we must divide $4,000 ($f$) by $2,001 ($p$), which equals 1.9990. Recall this is necessary because a future value table defines p equal to 1, and f as a multiple of 1. We look for a value nearest to 1.9990 (f), which we find in the column for 8% interest (i). This means $2,001 invested for nine periods at 8% interest accumulates to $4,000.

2. Assume you are a winner in a $150,000 cash sweepstakes. You decide to deposit this cash in an account earning 8% annual interest and you plan to quit your job when the account equals $555,000. How many years will it be before you can quit working?

Answers—p. IV-9

Present Value of an Annuity

An annuity is a series of equal payments occurring at equal intervals. One example is a series of three annual payments of $100 each. The present value of an ordinary annuity is defined as the present value of equal payments at equal intervals as of one period before the first payment. An ordinary annuity of $100 and its present value (p) is illustrated in Exhibit IV.6.

LO⁴ Apply present value concepts to an annuity by using interest tables.

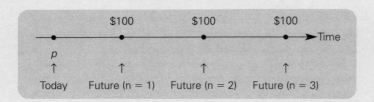

Exhibit IV.6

Present Value of an Ordinary Annuity

One way for us to compute the present value of an ordinary annuity is to find the present value of each payment using our present value formula from Exhibit IV.3. We then would add up each of the three present values. To illustrate, let's look at three, $100 payments at the end of each of the next three periods with an interest rate of 15%. Our present value computations are:

$$p = \frac{\$100}{(1 + .15)^1} + \frac{\$100}{(1 + .15)^2} + \frac{\$100}{(1 + .15)^3} = \$228.32$$

This computation also is identical to computing the present value of each payment (from Table IV.1) and taking their sum or, alternatively, adding the values from Table IV.1 for each of the three payments and multiplying their sum by the $100 annuity payment.

A more direct way is to use a **present value of annuity table**. Table IV.3 at the end of this appendix is one such table. If we look at Table IV.3 where $n = 3$ and $i = 15\%$, we see the present value is 2.2832. This means the present value of an annuity of 1 for 3 periods, with a 15% interest rate, is 2.2832.

A present value of annuity formula is used to construct Table IV.3. It can also be constructed by adding the amounts in a present value of 1 table.[4] To illustrate, we use Tables IV.1 and IV.3 to confirm this relation for the prior example.

From Table IV.1		From Table IV.3	
$i = 15\%, n = 1$	0.8696		
$i = 15\%, n = 2$	0.7561		
$i = 15\%, n = 3$	0.6575		
Total	2.2832	$i = 15\%, n = 3$	2.2832

We can also use business calculators or spreadsheet computer programs to find the present value of an annuity.

3. A company is considering an investment paying $10,000 every six months for three years. The first payment would be received in six months. If this company requires an annual return of 8%, what is the maximum amount they are willing to invest?

Flashback

Answers—p. IV-9

Future Value of an Annuity

LO⁵ Apply future value concepts to an annuity by using interest tables.

We can also compute the future value of an annuity. The future value of an *ordinary annuity* is the accumulated value of each annuity payment with interest as of the date of the final payment. To illustrate, let's consider the earlier annuity of three annual payments of $100. Exhibit IV.7 shows the point in time for the future value (f). The first payment is made two periods prior to the point where future value is determined, and the final payment occurs on the future value date.

Exhibit IV.7

Future Value of an Ordinary Annuity

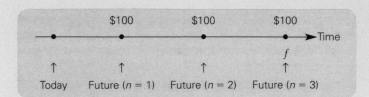

One way to compute the future value of an annuity is to use the formula to find the future value of *each* payment and add them together. If we assume an interest rate of 15%, our calculation is:

$$f = \$100 \times (1 + .15)^2 + \$100 \times (1 + .15)^1 + \$100 \times (1 + .15)^0 = \$347.25$$

---

[4] The formula for the present value of an annuity of 1 is: $p = \dfrac{1 - \dfrac{1}{(1 + i)^n}}{I}$

This is identical to using Table IV.2 and finding the sum of the future values of each payment, or adding the future values of the three payments of 1 and multiplying the sum by $100.

A more direct way is to use a table showing future values of annuities. Such a table is called a **future value of an annuity of 1 table**. Table IV.4 at the end of this appendix is one such table. We should note in Table IV.4 that when $n = 1$, the future values are equal to 1 ($f = 1$) for all rates of interest. That is because the annuity consists of only one payment and the future value is determined on the date of that payment — no time passes between the payment and its future value.

A formula is used to construct Table IV.4.[5] We can also construct it by adding the amounts from a future value of 1 table. To illustrate, we use Tables IV.2 and IV.4 to confirm this relation for the prior example:

From Table IV.2		From Table IV.4	
$i = 15\%$, $n = 0$	1.0000		
$i = 15\%$, $n = 1$	1.1500		
$i = 15\%$, $n = 2$	1.3225		
Total	3.4725	$i = 15\%$, $n = 3$	3.4725

Note the future value in Table IV.2 is 1.0000 when $n = 0$, but the future value in Table IV.4 is 1.0000 when $n = 1$. Is this a contradiction? No. When $n = 0$ in Table IV.2, the future value is determined on the date where a single payment occurs. This means no interest is earned, since no time has passed, and the future value equals the payment. Table IV.4 describes annuities with equal payments occurring at the ***end*** of each period. When $n = 1$, the annuity has one payment, and its future value equals 1 on the date of its final and only payment. Again, no time passes from the payment and its future value date.

4. A company invests $45,000 per year for five years at 12% annual interest. Compute the value of this annuity investment at the end of five years.

Answers—p. IV-9

---

[5] The formula for the future value of an annuity of 1 is: $f = \dfrac{(1 + i)^n - 1}{i}$

Summary of Appendix IV

LO¹ **Describe the earning of interest and the concepts of present and future values.** Interest is payment to the owner of an asset for its use by a borrower. Present and future value computations are a way for us to estimate the interest component of holding assets or liabilities over a period of time.

LO² **Apply present value concepts to a single amount by using interest tables.** The present value of a single amount to be received at a future date is the amount that can be invested now at the specified interest rate to yield that future value.

LO³ **Apply future value concepts to a single amount by using interest tables.** The future value of a single amount invested at a specified rate of interest is the amount that would accumulate by a future date.

LO⁴ **Apply present value concepts to an annuity by using interest tables.** The present value of an annuity is the amount that can be invested now at the specified interest rate to yield that series of equal periodic payments.

LO⁵ **Apply future value concepts to an annuity by using interest tables.** The future value of an annuity to be invested at a specific rate of interest is the amount that would accumulate by the date of the final equal periodic payment.

GUIDANCE ANSWERS TO  **Flashback**

1. $70,000 × 0.6302 = $44,114 (using Table IV.1, $i = 8\%$, $n = 6$).

2. $555,000/$150,000 = 3.7000; Table IV.2 shows this value is not achieved until after 17 years at 8% interest.

3. $10,000 × 5.2421 = $52,421 (using Table IV.3, $i = 4\%$, $n = 6$).

4. $45,000 × 6.3528 = $285,876 (using Table IV.4, $i = 12\%$, $n = 5$).

Quick Study

QS IV-1 Identifying interest rates in tables **LO¹**	You are asked to make future value estimates using the future value of 1 table (Table IV.2). Which interest rate column do you use when working with the following rates? **a.** 8% compounded quarterly **b.** 12% compounded annually **c.** 6% compounded semiannually **d.** 12% compounded monthly
QS IV-2 Present value of an amount **LO²**	Flaherty is considering an investment that, if paid for immediately, is expected to return $140,000 five years hence. If Flaherty demands a 9% return, how much is she willing to pay for this investment?
QS IV-3 Future value of an amount **LO³**	CII, Inc., invested $630,000 in a project expected to earn a 12% annual rate of return. The earnings will be reinvested in the project each year until the entire investment is liquidated 10 years hence. What will the cash proceeds be when the project is liquidated?
QS IV-4 Present value of an annuity **LO⁴**	Beene Distributing is considering a contract that will return $150,000 annually at the end of each year for six years. If Beene demands an annual return of 7% and pays for the investment immediately, how much should it be willing to pay?

Claire Fitch is planning to begin an individual retirement program in which she will invest $1,500 annually at the end of each year. Fitch plans to retire after making 30 annual investments in a program that earns a return of 10%. What will be the value of the program on the date of the last investment?

QS IV-5
Future value of
an annuity

LO^5

Ken Francis has been offered the possibility of investing $2,745 for 15 years, after which he will be paid $10,000. What annual rate of interest will Francis earn? (Use Table IV.1.)

QS IV-6
Interest rate
on an investment

LO^2

Megan Brink has been offered the possibility of investing $6,651. The investment will earn 6% per year and will return Brink $10,000 at the end of the investment. How many years must Brink wait to receive the $10,000? (Use Table IV.1.)

QS IV-7
Number of periods
of an investment

LO^2

Exercises

For each of the following situations identify (1) it as either (a) present or future value and (b) single amount or annuity case, (2) the table you would use in your computations (but do not solve the problem), and (3) the interest rate and time periods you would use.
a. You need to accumulate $10,000 for a trip you wish to take in four years. You are able to earn 8% compounded semiannually on your savings. You only plan on making one deposit and letting the money accumulate for four years. How would you determine the amount of the one-time deposit?
b. Assume the same facts as in (a), except you will make semiannual deposits to your savings account.
c. You hope to retire after working 40 years with savings in excess of $1,000,000. You expect to save $4,000 a year for 40 years and earn an annual rate of interest of 8%. Will you be able to retire with more than $1,000,000 in 40 years?
d. A sweepstakes agency names you a grand prize winner. You can take $225,000 immediately or elect to receive annual installments of $30,000 for 20 years. You can earn 10% annually on investments you make. Which prize do you choose to receive?

Exercise IV-1
Using present and
future value tables

LO^1

Bill Thompson expects to invest $10,000 at 12% and, at the end of the investment, receive $96,463. How many years will elapse before Thompson receives the payment? (Use Table IV.2.)

Exercise IV-2
Number of periods
of an investment

LO^2

Ed Summers expects to invest $10,000 for 25 years, after which he will receive $108,347. What rate of interest will Summers earn? (Use Table IV.2.)

Exercise IV-3
Interest rate on
an investment

LO^2

Betsey Jones expects an immediate investment of $57,466 to return $10,000 annually for eight years, with the first payment to be received in one year. What rate of interest will Jones earn? (Use Table IV.3.)

Exercise IV-4
Interest rate on
an investment

LO^4

Exercise IV-5
Number of periods
of an investment

LO⁴

Keith Riggins expects an investment of $82,014 to return $10,000 annually for several years. If Riggins is to earn a return of 10%, how many annual payments must he receive? (Use Table IV.3.)

Exercise IV-6
Interest rate
on an investment

LO⁵

Steve Algoe expects to invest $1,000 annually for 40 years and have an accumulated value of $154,762 on the date of the last investment. If this occurs, what rate of interest will Algoe earn? (Use Table IV.4.)

Exercise IV-7
Number of periods
of an investment

LO⁵

Katherine Beckwith expects to invest $10,000 annually that will earn 8%. How many annual investments must Beckwith make to accumulate $303,243 on the date of the last investment? (Use Table IV.4.)

Exercise IV-8
Present value
of an annuity

LO⁴

Sam Weber financed a new automobile by paying $6,500 cash and agreeing to make 40 monthly payments of $500 each, the first payment to be made one month after the purchase. The loan bears interest at an annual rate of 12%. What was the cost of the automobile?

Exercise IV-9
Future value
of an amount

LO³

Mark Welsch deposited $7,200 in a savings account that earns interest at an annual rate of 8%, compounded quarterly. The $7,200 plus earned interest must remain in the account 10 years before it can be withdrawn. How much money will be in the account at the end of the 10 years?

Exercise IV-10
Future value of
an annuity

LO⁴

Kelly Malone plans to have $50 withheld from her monthly paycheque and deposited in a savings account that earns 12% annually, compounded monthly. If Malone continues with her plan for 2 1/2 years, how much will be accumulated in the account on the date of the last deposit?

Exercise IV-11
Present value of
bonds

LO²,³

Spiller Corp. plans to issue 10%, 15-year, $500,000 par value bonds payable that pay interest semiannually on June 30 and December 31. The bonds are dated December 31, 2001, and are to be issued on that date. If the market rate of interest for the bonds is 8% on the date of issue, what will be the cash proceeds from the bond issue?

Exercise IV-12
Future value of an
amount plus an
annuity

LO³,⁵

Starr Company has decided to establish a fund that will be used 10 years hence to replace an aging productive facility. The company will make an initial contribution of $100,000 to the fund and plans to make quarterly contributions of $50,000 beginning in three months. The fund is expected to earn 12%, compounded quarterly. What will be the value of the fund 10 years hence?

McAdams Company expects to earn 10% per year on an investment that will pay $606,773 six years hence. Use Table IV.1 to compute the present value of the investment.

Exercise IV-13
Present value
of an amount

LO^3

Catten, Inc., invests $163,170 at 7% per year for nine years. Use Table IV.2 to compute the future value of the investment nine years hence.

Exercise IV-14
Future value
of an amount

LO^3

Compute the amount that can be borrowed under each of the following circumstances:
a. A promise to pay $90,000 in seven years at an interest rate of 6%.
b. An agreement made on February 1, 2002, to make three payments of $20,000 on February 1 of 2003, 2004, and 2005. The annual interest rate is 10%.

Exercise IV-15
Present value of an
amount and annuity

$LO^{2,4}$

On January 1, 2002, a company agrees to pay $20,000 in three years. If the annual interest rate is 10%, determine how much cash the company can borrow with this promise.

Exercise IV-16
Present value
of an amount

LO^2

Find the amount of money that can be borrowed with each of the following promises:

Exercise IV-17
Present value
of an amount

LO^2

Case	Single Future Payment	Number of Years	Interest Rate
a.	$40,000	3	4%
b.	75,000	7	8%
c.	52,000	9	10%
d.	18.000	2	4%
e.	63,000	8	6%
f.	89,000	5	2%

C&H Ski Club recently borrowed money and agreed to pay it back with a series of six annual payments of $5,000 each. C&H subsequently borrowed more money and agreed to pay it back with a series of four annual payments of $7,500 each. The annual interest rate for both loans is 6%.
a. Use Table IV.1 to find the present value of these two annuities. (Round amounts to the nearest dollar.)
b. Use Table IV.3 to find the present value of these two annuities.

Exercise IV-18
Present values
of annuities

LO^4

Otto Co. borrowed cash on April 30, 2002, by promising to make four payments of $13,000 each on November 1, 2002, May 1, 2003, November 1, 2003, and May 1, 2004.
a. How much cash is Otto able to borrow if the interest rate is 8%, compounded semi-annually?
b. How much cash is Otto able to borrow if the interest rate is 12%, compounded semi-annually?
c. How much cash is Otto able to borrow if the interest rate is 16%, compounded semi-annually?

Exercise IV-19
Present value with
semiannual
compounding

$LO^{1,4}$

Table IV.1

Present Value of 1 Due in *n* Periods

Periods												
	1%	2%	3%	4%	5%	6%	7%	8%	9%	10%	12%	15%
1	0.9901	0.9804	0.9709	0.9615	0.9524	0.9434	0.9346	0.9259	0.9174	0.9091	0.8929	0.8696
2	0.9803	0.9612	0.9426	0.9246	0.9070	0.8900	0.8734	0.8573	0.8417	0.8264	0.7972	0.7561
3	0.9706	0.9423	0.9151	0.8890	0.8638	0.8396	0.8163	0.7938	0.7722	0.7513	0.7118	0.6575
4	0.9610	0.9238	0.8885	0.8548	0.8227	0.7921	0.7629	0.7350	0.7084	0.6830	0.6355	0.5718
5	0.9515	0.9057	0.8626	0.8219	0.7835	0.7473	0.7130	0.6806	0.6499	0.6209	0.5674	0.4972
6	0.9420	0.8880	0.8375	0.7903	0.7462	0.7050	0.6663	0.6302	0.5963	0.5645	0.5066	0.4323
7	0.9327	0.8706	0.8131	0.7599	0.7107	0.6651	0.6227	0.5835	0.5470	0.5132	0.4523	0.3759
8	0.9235	0.8535	0.7894	0.7307	0.6768	0.6274	0.5820	0.5403	0.5019	0.4665	0.4039	0.3269
9	0.9143	0.8368	0.7664	0.7026	0.6446	0.5919	0.5439	0.5002	0.4604	0.4241	0.3606	0.2843
10	0.9053	0.8203	0.7441	0.6756	0.6139	0.5584	0.5083	0.4632	0.4224	0.3855	0.3220	0.2472
11	0.8963	0.8043	0.7224	0.6496	0.5847	0.5268	0.4751	0.4289	0.3875	0.3505	0.2875	0.2149
12	0.8874	0.7885	0.7014	0.6246	0.5568	0.4970	0.4440	0.3971	0.3555	0.3186	0.2567	0.1869
13	0.8787	0.7730	0.6810	0.6006	0.5303	0.4688	0.4150	0.3677	0.3262	0.2897	0.2292	0.1625
14	0.8700	0.7579	0.6611	0.5775	0.5051	0.4423	0.3878	0.3405	0.2992	0.2633	0.2046	0.1413
15	0.8613	0.7430	0.6419	0.5553	0.4810	0.4173	0.3624	0.3152	0.2745	0.2394	0.1827	0.1229
16	0.8528	0.7284	0.6232	0.5339	0.4581	0.3936	0.3387	0.2919	0.2519	0.2176	0.1631	0.1069
17	0.8444	0.7142	0.6050	0.5134	0.4363	0.3714	0.3166	0.2703	0.2311	0.1978	0.1456	0.0929
18	0.8360	0.7002	0.5874	0.4936	0.4155	0.3503	0.2959	0.2502	0.2120	0.1799	0.1300	0.0808
19	0.8277	0.6864	0.5703	0.4746	0.3957	0.3305	0.2765	0.2317	0.1945	0.1635	0.1161	0.0703
20	0.8195	0.6730	0.5537	0.4564	0.3769	0.3118	0.2584	0.2145	0.1784	0.1486	0.1037	0.0611
25	0.7798	0.6095	0.4776	0.3751	0.2953	0.2330	0.1842	0.1460	0.1160	0.0923	0.0588	0.0304
30	0.7419	0.5521	0.4120	0.3083	0.2314	0.1741	0.1314	0.0994	0.0754	0.0573	0.0334	0.0151
35	0.7059	0.5000	0.3554	0.2534	0.1813	0.1301	0.0937	0.0676	0.0490	0.0356	0.0189	0.0075
40	0.6717	0.4529	0.3066	0.2083	0.1420	0.0972	0.0668	0.0460	0.0318	0.0221	0.0107	0.0037

Table IV.2

Future Value of 1 Due in *n* Periods

Periods	Rate											
	1%	2%	3%	4%	5%	6%	7%	8%	9%	10%	12%	15%
0	1.0000	1.0000	1.0000	1.0000	1.0000	1.0000	1.0000	1.0000	1.0000	1.0000	1.0000	1.0000
1	1.0100	1.0200	1.0300	1.0400	1.0500	1.0600	1.0700	1.0800	1.0900	1.1000	1.1200	1.1500
2	1.0201	1.0404	1.0609	1.0816	1.1025	1.1236	1.1449	1.1664	1.1811	1.2100	1.2544	1.3225
3	1.0303	1.0612	1.0927	1.1249	1.1576	1.1910	1.2250	1.2597	1.2950	1.3310	1.4049	1.5209
4	1.0406	1.0824	1.1255	1.1699	1.2155	1.2625	1.3108	1.3605	1.4116	1.4641	1.5735	1.7490
5	1.0510	1.1041	1.1593	1.2167	1.2763	1.3382	1.4026	1.4693	1.5386	1.6105	1.7623	2.0114
6	1.0615	1.1262	1.1941	1.2653	1.3401	1.4185	1.5007	1.5869	1.6771	1.7716	1.9738	2.3131
7	1.0721	1.1487	1.2299	1.3159	1.4071	1.5036	1.6058	1.7138	1.8280	1.9487	2.2107	2.6600
8	1.0829	1.1717	1.2668	1.3686	1.4775	1.5938	1.7182	1.8509	1.9926	2.1436	2.4760	3.0590
9	1.0937	1.1951	1.3048	1.4233	1.5513	1.6895	1.8385	1.9990	2.1719	2.3579	2.7731	3.5179
10	1.1046	1.2190	1.3439	1.4802	1.6289	1.7908	1.9672	2.1589	2.3674	2.5937	3.1058	4.0456
11	1.1157	1.2434	1.3842	1.5395	1.7103	1.8983	2.1049	2.3316	2.5804	2.8531	3.4785	4.6524
12	1.1268	1.2682	1.4258	1.6010	1.7959	2.0122	2.2522	2.5182	2.8127	3.1384	3.8960	5.3503
13	1.1381	1.2936	1.4685	1.6651	1.8856	2.1329	2.4098	2.7196	3.0658	3.4523	4.3635	6.1528
14	1.1495	1.3195	1.5126	1.7317	1.9799	2.2609	2.5785	2.9372	3.3417	3.7975	4.8871	7.0757
15	1.1610	1.3459	1.5580	1.8009	2.0789	2.3966	2.7590	3.1722	3.6425	4.1772	5.4736	8.1371
16	1.1726	1.3728	1.6047	1.8730	2.1829	2.5404	2.9522	3.4259	3.9703	4.5950	6.1304	9.3576
17	1.1843	1.4002	1.6528	1.9479	2.2920	2.6928	3.1588	3.7000	4.3276	5.0545	6.8660	10.7613
18	1.1961	1.4282	1.7024	2.0258	2.4066	2.8543	3.3799	3.9960	4.7171	5.5599	7.6900	12.3755
19	1.2081	1.4568	1.7535	2.1068	2.5270	3.0256	3.6165	4.3157	5.1417	6.1159	8.6128	14.2318
20	1.2202	1.4859	1.8061	2.1911	2.6533	3.2071	3.8697	4.6610	5.6044	6.7275	9.6463	16.3665
25	1.2824	1.6406	2.0938	2.6658	3.3864	4.2919	5.4274	6.8485	8.6231	10.8347	17.0001	32.9190
30	1.3478	1.8114	2.4273	3.2434	4.3219	5.7435	7.6123	10.0627	13.2677	17.4494	29.9599	66.2118
35	1.4166	1.9999	2.8139	3.9461	5.5160	7.6861	10.6766	14.7853	20.4140	28.1024	52.7996	133.176
40	1.4889	2.2080	3.2620	4.8010	7.0400	10.2857	14.9745	21.7245	31.4094	45.2593	93.0510	267.864

Table IV.3

Present Value of an Annuity of 1 per Period

Periods	1%	2%	3%	4%	5%	6%	7%	8%	9%	10%	12%	15%
1	0.9901	0.9804	0.9709	0.9615	0.9524	0.9434	0.9346	0.9259	0.9174	0.9091	0.8929	0.8696
2	1.9704	1.9416	1.9135	1.8861	1.8594	1.8334	1.8080	1.7833	1.7591	1.7355	1.6901	1.6257
3	2.9410	2.8839	2.8286	2.7751	2.7232	2.6730	2.6243	2.5771	2.5313	2.4869	2.4018	2.2832
4	3.9020	3.8077	3.7171	3.6299	3.5460	3.4651	3.3872	3.3121	3.2397	3.1699	3.0373	2.8550
5	4.8534	4.7135	4.5797	4.4518	4.3295	4.2124	4.1002	3.9927	3.8897	3.7908	3.6048	3.3522
6	5.7955	5.6014	5.4172	5.2421	5.0757	4.9173	4.7665	4.6229	4.4859	4.3553	4.1114	3.7845
7	6.7282	6.4720	6.2303	6.0021	5.7864	5.5824	5.3893	5.2064	5.0330	4.8684	4.5638	4.1604
8	7.6517	7.3255	7.0197	6.7327	6.4632	6.2098	5.9713	5.7466	5.5348	5.3349	4.9676	4.4873
9	8.5660	8.1622	7.7861	7.4353	7.1078	6.8017	6.5152	6.2469	5.9952	5.7950	5.3282	4.7716
10	9.4713	8.9826	8.5302	8.1109	7.7217	7.3601	7.0236	6.7101	6.4177	6.1446	5.6502	5.0188
11	10.3676	9.7868	9.2526	8.7605	8.3064	7.8869	7.4987	7.1390	6.8052	6.4951	5.9377	5.2337
12	11.2551	10.5753	9.9540	9.3851	8.8633	8.3838	7.9427	7.5361	7.1607	6.8137	6.1944	5.4206
13	12.1337	11.3484	10.6350	9.9856	9.3936	8.8527	8.3577	7.9038	7.4869	7.1034	6.4235	5.5831
14	13.0037	12.1062	11.2961	10.5631	9.8986	9.2950	8.7455	8.2442	7.7862	7.3667	6.6282	5.7245
15	13.8651	12.8493	11.9379	11.1184	10.3797	9.7122	9.1079	8.5595	8.0607	7.6061	6.8109	5.8474
16	14.7179	13.5777	12.5611	11.6523	10.8378	10.1059	9.4466	8.8514	8.3126	7.8237	6.9740	5.9542
17	15.5623	14.2919	13.1661	12.1657	11.2741	10.4773	9.7632	9.1216	8.5436	8.0216	7.1196	6.0472
18	16.3983	14.9920	13.7535	12.6593	11.6896	10.8276	10.0591	9.3719	8.7556	8.2014	7.2497	6.1280
19	17.2260	15.6785	14.3238	13.1339	12.0853	11.1581	10.3356	9.6036	8.9501	8.3649	7.3658	6.1982
20	18.0456	16.3514	14.8775	13.5903	12.4622	11.4699	10.5940	9.8181	9.1285	8.5136	7.4694	6.2593
25	22.0232	19.5235	17.4131	15.6221	14.0939	12.7834	11.6536	10.6748	9.8226	9.0770	7.8431	6.4641
30	25.8077	22.3965	19.6004	17.2920	15.3725	13.7648	12.4090	11.2578	10.2737	9.4269	8.0552	6.5660
35	29.4086	24.9986	21.4872	18.6646	16.3742	14.4982	12.9477	11.6546	10.5668	9.6442	8.1755	6.6166
40	32.8347	27.3555	23.1148	19.7928	17.1591	15.0463	13.3317	11.9246	10.7574	9.7791	8.2438	6.6418

Table IV.4

Future Value of an Annuity of 1 per Period

Periods	1%	2%	3%	4%	5%	6%	7%	8%	9%	10%	12%	15%
1	1.0000	1.0000	1.0000	1.0000	1.0000	1.0000	1.0000	1.0000	1.0000	1.0000	1.0000	1.0000
2	2.0100	2.0200	2.0300	2.0400	2.0500	2.0600	2.0700	2.0800	2.0900	2.1000	2.1200	2.1500
3	3.0301	3.0604	3.0909	3.1216	3.1525	3.1836	3.2149	3.2464	3.2781	3.3100	3.3744	3.4725
4	4.0604	4.1216	4.1836	4.2465	4.3101	4.3746	4.4399	4.5061	4.5731	4.6410	4.7793	4.9934
5	5.1010	5.2040	5.3091	5.4163	5.5256	5.6371	5.7507	5.8666	5.9847	6.1051	6.3528	6.7424
6	6.1520	6.3081	6.4684	6.6330	6.8019	6.9753	7.1533	7.3359	7.5233	7.7156	8.1152	8.7537
7	7.2135	7.4343	7.6625	7.8983	8.1420	8.3938	8.6540	8.9228	9.2004	9.4872	10.0890	11.0668
8	8.2857	8.5830	8.8923	9.2142	9.5491	9.8975	10.2598	10.6366	11.0285	11.4359	12.2997	13.7268
9	9.3685	9.7546	10.1591	10.5828	11.0266	11.4913	11.9780	12.4876	13.0210	13.5795	14.7757	16.7858
10	10.4622	10.9497	11.4639	12.0061	12.5779	13.1808	13.8164	14.4866	15.1929	15.9374	17.5487	20.3037
11	11.5668	12.1687	12.8078	13.4864	14.2068	14.9716	15.7835	16.6455	17.5603	18.5312	20.6546	24.3493
12	12.6825	13.4121	14.1920	15.0258	15.9171	16.8699	17.8885	18.9771	20.1407	21.3843	24.1331	29.0017
13	13.8093	14.6803	15.6178	16.6268	17.7130	18.8821	20.1406	21.4953	22.9534	24.5227	28.0291	34.3519
14	14.9474	15.9739	17.0863	18.2919	19.5986	21.0151	22.5505	24.2149	26.0192	27.9750	32.3926	40.5047
15	16.0969	17.2934	18.5989	20.0236	21.5786	23.2760	25.1290	27.1521	29.3609	31.7725	37.2797	47.5804
16	17.2579	18.6393	20.1569	21.8245	23.6575	25.6725	27.8881	30.3243	33.0034	35.9497	42.7533	55.7175
17	18.4304	20.012	21.7616	23.6975	25.8404	28.2129	30.8402	33.7502	36.9737	40.5447	48.8837	65.0751
18	19.6147	21.4123	23.4144	25.6454	28.1324	30.9057	33.9990	37.4502	41.3013	45.5992	55.7497	75.8364
19	20.8109	22.8406	25.1169	27.6712	30.5390	33.7600	37.3790	41.4463	46.0185	41.1591	63.4397	88.2118
20	22.0190	24.2974	26.8704	29.7781	33.0660	36.7856	40.9955	45.7620	51.1601	57.2750	72.0524	102.444
25	28.2432	32.0303	36.4593	41.6459	47.7271	54.8645	63.2490	73.1059	84.7009	98.3471	133.334	212.793
30	34.7849	40.5681	47.5754	56.0849	66.4388	79.0582	94.4608	113.283	136.308	164.494	241.333	434.745
35	41.6603	49.9945	60.4621	73.6522	90.3203	111.435	138.237	172.317	215.711	271.024	431.663	881.170
40	48.8864	60.4020	75.4013	95.0255	120.800	154.762	199.635	259.057	337.882	442.593	767.091	1,779.09

Credits

Chapter 21, page 1090, photo © T. Anderson, The Image Bank

Chapter 22, page 1142, photo © Canapress Photo Service (Jacques Boissinot)

Chapter 23, page 1196, photo © Sylvain Grandadam/Tony Stone Images

Chapter 24, page 1246, photo © Dick Hemingway: Photography

Chapter 25, page 1296, photo © Comstock Photofile Limited

Chapter 26, page 1340, photo © Canapress Photo Service (Allen Boyko)

Chapter 27, page 1390, photo © Canapress Photo Service (Frank Gunn)

Chapter 28, page 1442, photo © Ron Sangha/Tony Stone Images

Because of their demonstrated interest in advancing post-secondary accounting education, we would like to say a special thank-you to the following organizations.

24 Carrot Catering Ltd.
Certified General Accountants
  Association
CMA Canada

Infosys Technologies Ltd.
Institute of Chartered Accountants
Leon's Furniture Ltd.
WestJet Airlines Ltd.

Index